CHILDREN'S WRITER'S & ILLUSTRATOR'S MARKET

Amy Jones, Editor

An imprint of Penguin Random House LLC
penguinrandomhouse.com

Printed in the United States of America
1st Printing

ISBN 9780593332054

Book design by Alexis Estoye

CONTENTS

FROM THE EDITOR

Welcome to the 33rd Edition of the *Children's Writer's and Illustrator's Market*! In this edition, the goal was not just to balance the articles and listings, but within the articles, to include useful information for writers of the wide age spectrum that encompasses children's writing. So you'll find articles that speak to everything from picture books to YA novels.

In the section of craft articles you'll find excerpts from Ann Whitford Paul's brilliant book, *Writing Picture Books Revised and Expanded Edition*, plus articles about creating believable characters who young readers can identify with and how you can make writer's block work in your favor. You'll also find interviews with bestselling authors including Jacqueline Woodson, Cassandra Clare, N. K. Jemisin, and more. Learn more about promoting your work, balancing your writing with other areas of your life, and tips for how to find the right agent for you in the collection of business and promotion articles.

The completely revised and updated listings in this edition run the gamut from book publishers in the United States and abroad; magazines; agents and art reps; clubs and organizations; conferences and workshops; and contests, awards, and grants.

May the resources provided in this guide help you find success as you write for the next generation of readers.

Yours in writing,
Amy Jones
Editor-in-Chief, *Writer's Digest*
http://twitter.com/AmyMJones_5

HOW TO USE *CHILDREN'S WRITER'S & ILLUSTRATOR'S MARKET*

As a writer, illustrator, or photographer first picking up *Children's Writer's & Illustrator's Market*, you may not know quite how to start using the book. Your impulse may be to flip through the book and quickly make a mailing list, then submit to everyone in hopes that someone will take interest in your work. Well, there's more to it. Finding the right market takes research. The more you know about a market that interests you, the better chance you have of getting work accepted. We've made your job a little easier by putting a wealth of information at your fingertips. Besides providing listings, this directory has a number of tools to help you determine which markets are the best ones for your work. By using these tools, as well as researching on your own, you raise your odds of being published.

USING THE INDEXES

This book lists hundreds of potential buyers of material. To learn which companies want the type of material you're interested in submitting, start with the indexes.

Subject Index

But let's narrow the search further. Take your list of young adult magazines, turn to the **Subject Index**, and find the **Fashion** subheading. Then highlight the names that appear on both lists (**Young Adult** and **Fashion**). Now you have a smaller list of all the magazines that would be interested in your teen fashion article. Read through those listings and decide which seem (or look) best for your work.

Illustrators and photographers can use the **Subject Index** as well. If you specialize in painting animals, for instance, consider sending samples to book and magazine publishers listed under **Animals** and, perhaps, **Nature/Environment**. Because illustrators can simply send general examples of their style to art directors to keep on file, the indexes may be more helpful to artists sending manuscript/illustration packages who need to search for a specific subject. Always read the listings for the potential markets to see the type of work art directors prefer and what type of samples they'll keep on file, and obtain art or photo guidelines if they're available online.

Age-Level Index

Age groups are broken down into these categories in the Age-Level Index:

- **PICTURE BOOKS OR PICTURE-ORIENTED MATERIAL** are written and illustrated for preschoolers to eight-year-olds.
- **YOUNG READERS** are for five- to eight-year-olds.
- **MIDDLE READERS** are for nine- to eleven-year-olds.
- **YOUNG ADULT** is for ages twelve and up.

Age breakdowns may vary slightly from publisher to publisher, but using them as general guidelines will help you target appropriate markets. For example, if you've written an article about trends in teen fashion, check the **Magazines Age-Level Index** under the **Young Adult** subheading.

USING THE LISTINGS

Some listings begin with symbols. Many listings indicate whether submission guidelines are indeed available. If a publisher you're interested in offers guidelines, get them and read them. The same is true with catalogs. Sending for and reading catalogs or browsing them online gives you a better idea of whether your work would fit in with the books a publisher produces. (You should also look at a few of the books in the catalog at a library or bookstore to get a feel for the publisher's material.)

A Note for Artists & Photographers

Along with information for writers, listings provide information for illustrators and photographers. Illustrators will find numerous markets that maintain files of samples for possible future assignments. If you're both a writer and an illustrator, look for markets that accept manuscript/illustration packages and read the information offered under the **Illustration** subhead within the listings.

If you're a photographer, read the information under the **Photography** subhead within listings to see what format buyers prefer. For example, some want the highest resolution .jpg available of an image. Note the type of photos a buyer wants to purchase and the procedures for submitting. It's not uncommon for a market to want a résumé and promotional literature, as well as sample URLs linking to previous work. Listings also note whether model releases and/or captions are required.

QUICK TIPS FOR WRITERS & ILLUSTRATORS

If you're new to the world of children's publishing, reviewing this edition of *Children's Writer's & Illustrator's Market* may have been one of the first steps in your journey to publication. What follows is a list of suggestions and resources that can help make that journey a smooth and swift one:

1. MAKE THE MOST OF *CHILDREN'S WRITER'S & ILLUSTRATOR'S MARKET*. Be sure to take advantage of the articles and interviews in the book. The insights of the authors, illustrators, editors, and agents we've interviewed will inform and inspire you.

2. JOIN THE SOCIETY OF CHILDREN'S BOOK WRITERS AND ILLUSTRATORS. SCBWI, more than 22,000 members strong, is an organization for both beginners and professionals interested in writing and illustrating for children, with more than seventy active regional chapters worldwide. It offers members a slew of information and support through publications, a website, and a host of Regional Advisors overseeing chapters in almost every state in the U.S. and a growing number of locations around the globe. SCBWI puts on a number of conferences, workshops, and events on the regional and national levels (many listed in the **Conferences & Workshops** section of this book). For more information, visit www.scbwi.org.

3. READ NEWSLETTERS. Newsletters, such as *Children's Book Insider*, *Children's Writer*, and the *SCBWI Bulletin* offer updates and new information about publishers on a timely basis and are relatively inexpensive. Many local chapters of SCBWI offer regional newsletters as well.

4. READ TRADE AND REVIEW PUBLICATIONS. Magazines such as *Publishers Weekly* (which offers two special issues each year devoted to children's publishing and is available on newsstands as well as through a digital subscription) offer news, articles, reviews of newly published titles, and ads featuring upcoming and current releases. Referring to them will help you get a feel for what's happening in children's publishing.

5. READ GUIDELINES. Most publishers and magazines offer writers' and artists' guidelines that provide detailed information on needs and submission requirements, and some magazines offer theme lists for upcoming issues. Many publishers and magazines state the availability of guidelines within their listings. You'll often find submission information on publishers' and magazines' websites.

6. LOOK AT PUBLISHERS' CATALOGS. Perusing publishers' catalogs can give you a feel for their line of books and help you decide where your work might fit in. If catalogs are available, visit publishers' websites, which often contain their full catalogs. You can also ask librarians to look at catalogs they have on hand. You can even search Amazon.com by publisher and year. (Click on "book search" then "publisher, date" and plug in, for example, "Lee & Low" under *publisher* and "2021" under *year*. You'll get a list of Lee & Low titles published in 2021, which you can peruse.)

7. VISIT BOOKSTORES. It's not only informative to spend time in bookstores—it's fun, too! Frequently visit the children's section of your local bookstore (whether a chain or an independent) to see the latest from a variety of publishers and the most current issues of children's magazines. Look for books in the genre you're writing or with illustrations similar in style to yours, and spend some time studying them. It's also wise to get to know your local booksellers; they can tell you what's new in the store and provide insight into what kids and adults are buying.

8. READ, READ, READ! While you're at that bookstore, pick up a few things, or keep a list of the books that interest you and check them out of your library. Read and study the latest releases, the award-winners and the classics. You'll learn from other writers, get ideas, and get a feel for what's being published. Think about what works and doesn't work in a story. Pay attention to how plots are constructed and how characters are developed, or the rhythm and pacing of picture book text. It's certainly enjoyable research!

9. TAKE ADVANTAGE OF INTERNET RESOURCES. There are innumerable sources of information available online about writing for children (and anything else you could possibly think of). It's also a great resource for getting (and staying) in touch with other writers and illustrators through listservs, blogs, social networking sites, and email, and it can serve as a vehicle for self-promotion.

10. CONSIDER ATTENDING A CONFERENCE. If time and finances allow, attending a writers conference is a great way to meet peers and network with professionals in the field of children's publishing. As mentioned earlier, SCBWI offers conferences in various locations year round. (See scbwi.org and click on "Events" for a full conference calendar.) General writers' conferences often offer specialized sessions just for those interested in children's writing. Many conferences offer optional manuscript and portfolio critiques as well, giving you feedback from seasoned professionals. See the **Conferences** section of this book for information on conferences.

11. NETWORK, NETWORK, NETWORK! Don't work in a vacuum. You can meet other writers and illustrators through a number of the things listed earlier—SCBWI, conferences, online. Attend local meetings for writers and illustrators whenever you can. Befriend other writers in your area (SCBWI offers members a roster broken down by state)—share guidelines, share subscriptions, be conference buddies and roommates, join a critique group or writing group, exchange information, and offer support. Get online—subscribe to listservs, post on message boards and blogs, visit social networking sites and chatrooms. Exchange addresses, phone numbers, and email addresses with writers or illustrators you meet at events. And at conferences, don't be afraid to talk to people, ask strangers to join you for lunch, approach speakers and introduce yourself, or chat in elevators and hallways.

12. PERFECT YOUR CRAFT AND DON'T SUBMIT UNTIL YOUR WORK IS AT ITS BEST. It's often been said that a writer should try to write every day. Great manuscripts don't happen overnight; there's time, research, and revision involved. As you visit bookstores and study what others have written and illustrated, really step back and look at your own work and ask yourself, *How does my work measure up? Is it ready for editors or art directors to see?* If it's not, keep working. Join a critique group or get a professional manuscript or portfolio critique.

13. BE PATIENT, LEARN FROM REJECTION, AND DON'T GIVE UP! Thousands of manuscripts land on editors' desks; thousands of illustration samples line art directors' file drawers. There are so many factors that come into play when evaluating submissions. Keep in mind that you might not hear back from publishers promptly. Persistence and patience are important qualities in writers and illustrators working toward publication. Keep at it—it will come. It can take a while, but when you get that first book contract or first assignment, you'll know it was worth the wait.

BEFORE YOUR FIRST SALE

If you're just beginning to pursue your career as a children's book writer or illustrator, it's important to learn the proper procedures, formats, and protocol for the publishing industry. This article outlines the basics you need to know before you submit your work to a market.

FINDING THE BEST MARKETS FOR YOUR WORK

Researching markets thoroughly is a basic element of submitting your work successfully. Editors and art directors hate to receive inappropriate submissions; handling them wastes a lot of their time, not to mention your time and money, and they are the main reason some publishers have chosen not to accept material over the transom. By randomly sending out material without knowing a company's needs, you're sure to meet with rejection.

If you're interested in submitting to a particular magazine, see if it's available in your local library or bookstore, or read past articles online. For a book publisher, obtain a book catalog and check a library or bookstore for titles produced by that publisher. Most publishers and magazines have websites that include catalogs or sample articles (websites are given within the listings). Studying such materials carefully will better acquaint you with a publisher's or magazine's writing, illustration, and photography styles and formats.

Many of the book publishers and magazines listed in this book offer some sort of writers', artists', or photographers' guidelines on their websites. It's important to read and study guidelines before submitting work. You'll get a better understanding of what a particular publisher wants. You may even decide, after reading the submission guidelines, that your work isn't right for a company you considered.

SUBMITTING YOUR WORK

Throughout the listings, you'll read requests for particular elements to include when contacting markets. Here are explanations of some of these important submission components.

Queries, Cover Letters & Proposals

A query is a no-more-than-one-page, well-written letter meant to arouse an editor's interest in your work. Query letters briefly outline the work you're proposing and include facts, anecdotes, interviews, or other pertinent information that give the editor a feel for the manuscript's premise—enticing her to want to know more. End your letter with a straightforward request to submit the work, and include information on its approximate length, date it could be completed, and whether accompanying photos or artwork are available.

In a query letter, think about presenting your book as a publisher's catalog would present it. Read through a good catalog and examine how the publishers give enticing summaries of their books in a spare amount of words. It's also important that query letters give editors a taste of your writing style. For good advice and samples of queries, cover letters, and other correspondence, consult *Guide to Literary Agents 30th Edition*, as well as *Formatting & Submitting Your Manuscript, 3rd Ed.* and *The Writer's Digest Guide to Query Letters* (all published by Writer's Digest Books).

- **QUERY LETTERS FOR NONFICTION.** Queries are usually required when submitting nonfiction material to a publisher. The goal of a nonfiction query is to convince the editor your idea is perfect for her readership and that you're qualified to do the job. Note any previous writing experience and include published samples to prove your credentials, especially samples related to the subject matter you're querying about.
- **QUERY LETTERS FOR FICTION.** For a fiction query, explain the story's plot, main characters, conflict, and resolution. Just as in nonfiction queries, make the editor eager to see more.
- **COVER LETTERS FOR WRITERS.** Some editors prefer to review complete manuscripts, especially for picture books or fiction. In such cases, the cover letter (which should be no longer than one page) serves as your introduction, establishes your credentials as a writer, and gives the editor an overview of the manuscript. If the editor asked for the manuscript because of a query, note this in your cover letter.
- **COVER LETTERS FOR ILLUSTRATORS AND PHOTOGRAPHERS.** For an illustrator or photographer, the cover letter serves as an introduction to the art director and establishes professional credentials when submitting samples. Explain what services you can provide as well as what type of follow-up contact you plan to make, if any. Be sure to include the URL of your online portfolio if you have one.

- **RÉSUMÉS.** Often writers, illustrators, and photographers submit résumés with cover letters and samples. They can be created in a variety of formats, from a single page listing information to color brochures featuring your work. Keep your résumé brief, and focus on your achievements, including your clients and the work you've done for them, as well as your educational background and any awards you've received. Do not use the same résumé you'd use for a typical job application.
- **BOOK PROPOSALS.** Throughout the listings in the **Book Publishers** section, listings refer to submitting a synopsis, outline, and sample chapters. Depending on an editor's preference, some or all of these components, along with a cover letter, make up a book proposal.

  A *synopsis* summarizes the book, covering the basic plot (including the ending). It should be easy to read and flow well. The gold standard for synopsis length is one page, single-spaced.

  An *outline* covers your book chapter by chapter and provides highlights of each. If you're developing an outline for fiction, include major characters, plots, and subplots, and book length. Requesting an outline is uncommon, and the word is somewhat interchangeable with *synopsis*.

  Sample chapters give a more comprehensive idea of your writing skill. Some editors may request the first two or three chapters to determine if they're interested in seeing the whole book. Some may request a set number of pages.

Manuscript Formats

When submitting a complete manuscript, follow some basic guidelines. In the upper-left corner of your title page, type your legal name (not pseudonym), address, and phone number. In the upper-right corner, type the approximate word count. All material in the upper corners should be single-spaced. Then type the title (centered) almost halfway down that page, the word "by" two lines under that, and your name or pseudonym two lines under "by."

The first page should also include the title (centered) one-third of the way down. Two lines under that, type "by" and your name or pseudonym. To begin the body of your manuscript, drop down two double spaces and indent five spaces for each new paragraph. There should be one-inch margins around all sides of a full page. (Manuscripts with wide margins are more readable and easier to edit.)

Set your computer to double-space the manuscript body. From page two to the end of the manuscript, include your last name followed by a comma and the title (or key words of the title) in the upper-left corner. The page number should go in the top right corner. Drop down two double spaces to begin the body of each page. If you're submitting a novel, type each chapter title one-third of the way down the page. For more information on manuscript formats, read *Formatting & Submitting Your Manuscript, 3rd Ed.* (Writer's Digest Books).

Picture Book Formats

The majority of editors prefer to see complete manuscripts for picture books. When typing the text of a picture book, don't indicate page breaks and don't type each page of text on a new sheet of paper. And unless you are an illustrator, don't worry about supplying art. Editors will find their own illustrators for picture books. Most of the time, a writer and an illustrator who work on the same book never meet or interact. The editor acts as a go-between who works with the writer and illustrator throughout the publishing process. *How to Write and Sell Children's Picture Books* by Jean E. Karl (Writer's Digest Books) offers advice on preparing text and marketing your work.

If you're an illustrator who has written your own book, consider creating a dummy or storyboard containing both art and text, and then submit it along with your complete manuscript and sample pieces of final art (hi-res PDFs or JPGs—never originals). Publishers interested in picture books specify in their listings what should be submitted. For tips on creating a dummy, refer to *How to Write and Illustrate Children's Books and Get Them Published*, edited by Treld Pelkey Bicknell and Felicity Trotman (North Light Books), or *How to Write, Illustrate, and Design Children's Books* by Frieda Gates (Lloyd-Simone Publishing Company).

Writers may also want to learn the art of dummy-making to help them through the writing process with things like pacing, rhythm, and length. For a great explanation and helpful hints, see the article "Cut and Paste" by Ann Whitford Paul in the Craft & Technique section (excerpted from *Writing Picture Books Revised and Expanded*, Writer's Digest Books, 2018).

Mailing Submissions

Your main concern when packaging material is to be sure it arrives undamaged. If your manuscript is fewer than six pages, simply fold it in thirds and send it in a #10 (business-size) envelope. For a SASE, either fold another #10 envelope in thirds or insert a #9 (reply) envelope, which fits in a #10 neatly without folding.

Another option is folding your manuscript in half in a 6" × 9" (15cm × 23cm) envelope, with a #9 or #10 SASE enclosed. For larger manuscripts, use a 9" × 12" (23cm × 30cm) envelope both for mailing the submission and as a SASE (which can be folded in half). Book manuscripts require sturdy packaging for mailing. Include a self-addressed mailing label and return postage. If asked to send artwork and photographs, remember they require a bit more care in packaging to guarantee they arrive in good condition. Sandwich illustrations and photos between heavy cardboard that is slightly larger than the work. The cardboard can be secured by rubber bands or with tape. If you tape the cardboard together, check that the artwork doesn't stick to the tape. Be sure your name and address appear on the back of each piece of art or each photo in case the material becomes separated. For the packaging, use either a manila envelope, a foam-padded envelope, or a mailer lined with plastic air bubbles. Bind nonjoined edges with reinforced mailing tape and affix a typed mailing label or clearly write your address.

Mailing materials first class ensures quick delivery. Also, first-class mail is forwarded for one year if the addressee has moved, and it can be returned if undeliverable. If you're concerned about your original material reaching its destination, consider other mailing options such as UPS. No matter which way you send material, never send it in a way that requires a signature for receipt. Agents and editors are too busy to sign for packages.

Remember, companies outside your own country can't use your country's postage when returning a manuscript to you. When mailing a submission to another country, include a self-addressed envelope and International Reply Coupons, or IRCs. (You'll see this term in many listings in the Canadian & International Book Publishers section.) Your postmaster can tell you, based on a package's weight, the correct number of IRCs to include to ensure its return. If it's not necessary for an editor to return your work (such as with photocopies), don't include return postage.

Unless requested, it's never a good idea to use a company's fax number to send manuscript submissions. This can disrupt a company's internal business. Study the listings for specifics and visit publisher and market websites for more information.

Emailing Submissions

Most correspondence with editors today is handled over email. This type of communication is usually preferred by publishing professionals because it is easier to deal with as well as free. When sending an emailed submission, make sure to follow submission guidelines. Double-check the recipient's email address. Make sure your subject line has the proper wording, if specific wording is requested. Keep your introduction letter short and sweet. Also, editors and agents usually do not like opening unsolicited attachments, which makes for an awkward situation for illustrators who want to attach .jpgs. One easy way around this is to post some sample illustrations on your website. That way, you can simply paste URL hyperlinks to your work. Editors can click through to look over your illustration samples, and there is no way your submission will be deleted because of attachments. That said, if editors are asking for illustration samples, they are most likely used to receiving unsolicited attachments.

Keeping Submission Records

It's important to keep track of the material you submit. When recording each submission, include the date it was sent, the business and contact name, and any enclosures (such as samples of writing, artwork, or photography). You can create a record-keeping system of your own or look for record-keeping software in your area computer store.

Keep copies of articles or manuscripts you send together with related correspondence to make follow-up easier. When you sell rights to a manuscript, artwork, or photos, you can "close" your file on a particular submission by noting the date the material was accepted, what rights were purchased, the publication date, and payment.

Often writers, illustrators, and photographers fail to follow up on overdue responses. If you don't hear from a publisher within their stated response time, wait another month or so and follow up with an email asking about the status of your submission. Include the title or description, date sent, and a SASE (if applicable) for response. Ask the contact person when she anticipates making a decision. You may refresh the memory of a buyer who temporarily forgot about your submission. At the very least, you will receive a definite "no" and free yourself to send the material to another publisher.

Simultaneous Submissions

Writers and illustrators are encouraged to simultaneously submit—sending the same material to several markets at the same time. Almost all markets are open to this type of communication; those that do not take simultaneous submissions will directly say so in their submission guidelines.

It's especially important to keep track of simultaneous submissions, so if you get an offer on a manuscript sent to more than one publisher, you can instruct other publishers to withdraw your work from consideration. (Or, you can always use the initial offer as a way to ignite interest from other agents and editors. It's very possible to procure multiple offers on your book using this technique.)

AGENTS AND ART REPS

Most children's writers, illustrators, and photographers, especially those just beginning, are confused about whether to enlist the services of an agent or representative. The decision is strictly one that each writer, illustrator, or photographer must make for herself. Some are confident with their own negotiation skills and believe acquiring an agent or rep is not in their best interest. Others feel uncomfortable in the business arena or are not willing to sacrifice valuable creative time for marketing.

About half of children's publishers accept unagented work, so it's possible to break into children's publishing without an agent. Writers targeting magazine markets don't need the services of an agent. In fact, it's practically impossible to find an agent interested in marketing articles and short stories—there simply isn't enough financial incentive.

One benefit of having an agent, though, is it may speed up the process of getting your work reviewed, especially by publishers who don't accept unagented submissions. If an agent has a good reputation and submits your manuscript to an editor, that manuscript will likely bypass the first-read stage (which is generally done by editorial assistants and junior editors) and end up on the editor's desk sooner.

When agreeing to have a reputable agent represent you, remember that she should be familiar with the needs of the current market and evaluate your manuscript/artwork/photos accordingly. She should also determine the quality of your piece and whether it is salable. When your manuscript sells, your agent should negotiate a favorable contract and clear up any questions you have about payments.

Keep in mind that no matter how reputable the agent or rep is, she has limitations. Representation does not guarantee sale of your work. It just means an agent or rep sees potential in your writing, art, or photos. Though an agent or rep may offer criticism or advice on how to improve your work, she cannot make you a better writer, artist, or photographer.

Literary agents typically charge a fifteen percent commission from the sale of writing; art and photo representatives usually charge a twenty five or thirty percent commission. Such fees are taken from advances and royalty earnings. If your agent sells foreign rights or film rights to your work, she will deduct a higher percentage because she will most likely be dealing with an overseas agent with whom she must split the fee.

Be advised that not every agent is open to representing a writer, artist, or photographer who lacks an established track record. Just as when approaching a publisher, the manuscript, artwork, or photos, and query or cover letter you submit to a potential agent must be attractive and professional looking. Your first impression must be as an organized, articulate person. For listings of agents and reps, turn to the **Literary Agents & Art Reps** section.

FEMALE, POWERFUL, AND REAL

A teen author shares how to write authentic female characters that middle-grade and young-adult readers can actually connect with.

by Ren Koppel Torres

I've been obsessed with imaginative fiction for as long as I can remember. I was, objectively, already an expert on sorcery by the time I dressed as a magician for Halloween at age six, the year my little sister dressed as a rabbit (albeit not one quite small enough to fit into my hat). I devoured every adventure book I could get my hands on, and although they filled me with immense joy, I was puzzled and frustrated by the representation of female characters (or, often, lack of representation) in the types of books I enjoyed.

Significant female characters are practically nonexistent in older books. Even newer books with female protagonists are generally male-dominated, and most "strong female leads" are so predictable that from an early age I found I could sort female protagonists into two categories: the "perfect warrior" or the "love interest."

"Perfect warriors" are athletically inclined, stubborn, and linear-thinking (think Tris from the Divergent series). While these characteristics aren't inherently problematic, too many of the characters that fit this description have awfully similar personalities. Writers should be wary of tropes and push themselves to make characters unique; there are many ways to write a female character.

The "love interest" type is self-explanatory: She is often the only female character, doesn't have an intrinsic part to play in the plot, and her role in the story is dependent on her relationship to a man. In *The Maze Runner*, Teresa, the only girl to ever arrive in the

Gladers' concrete labyrinth, is unconscious for most of the story, and her role in the plot is tied to Thomas, the protagonist.

I wanted the identities, ideologies, and strengths of real-life women to be represented on the page. I wanted nuance and complexity. And frankly, I was bored. So, at nine, I decided I'd had enough of searching for the female leads I *wanted* to read about and I wrote my own fantasy novel. I'm glad I did, and I will write more, but one author cannot alter a systemic problem by herself.

We contemporary writers find ourselves amid a cultural shift. After centuries of Western culture in which female characters have been portrayed as incapable, unintelligent, or irrelevant, audiences are demanding more in terms of gender representation. Our language has adapted to these trends and landed us with the buzzwords *strong female lead*. And while current literary trends are a step in the right direction, we still have work to do, especially for middle-grade and young-adult books. Since most YA and MG authors are adults, there's a dangerous gap between the creators of these books and their primary audiences. As a 15-year-old author who is both a creator and a consumer of these genres, I have the benefit of an insider view. Here are four strategies to use in writing successful female leads.

1. UNDERSTAND DIFFERENT LENSES OF REPRESENTATION

Young readers want to experience a different life through the eyes of your protagonists, and in order to root for your characters, readers need to have a handle with which to grasp them. For your plot and setting to feel nuanced and dynamic, including multiple perspectives in your story is crucial. Plus, you avoid the risk of alienating readers who don't fit into a specific group. YA and MG literature as a trend tend to exclude certain perspectives from certain types of stories. Break the mold—don't limit the voices you can have in your book.

How, then, should contemporary writers develop characters? There are different ways to approach representation, and no one way is necessarily "right" or "wrong." Particularly in imaginative fiction, you have the opportunity to rework cultural norms around any marginalized group (not just women). You can perpetuate the status quo of the real world, go the escapist route and ignore or eliminate such prejudices, or flip the status quo completely on its head. Each tactic has its place, and each can appeal to readers for different reasons.

Perpetuating the status quo in your book can make your story seem more realistic and serve as a conflict for your protagonists (as in the many fantasy novels set in pseudo-medieval Europe, with sexism to boot). In *Court of Fives*, for example, Jessamy must defy the obstacles of sexism and classism in order to meet her goal of participating in The Fives competition. In contrast, writing an escapist story without addressing the theme of sexism can come off as refreshing and optimistic, as well as allow more room for you to focus on conflicts unique to your plot. Think Madeleine L'Engle's *A Wrinkle in Time*, a fantastical story (and old favorite of mine) that features multiple well-rounded female protagonists who don't face any obstacles on account of their gender.

In my debut fantasy novel, *The Shadow in Her Pocket*, I took the third option and flipped the status quo. My magical island is governed by a matriarchy, and this is ultimately the root of some of the novel's external conflict. I made this choice not because I believe in denying leadership positions to a particular gender, but because as a reader I was hungry for something new.

2. AIM FOR AGENCY, NOT PERFECTION

Very few of us start out in life with six-pack abs and a library's worth of knowledge. Yet there's a prevailing mentality that a "strong female lead" should be brilliant, morally superior, and able to crush an army with her bare hands. But female protagonists don't need to be perfect—in fact, it's better when they aren't.

Too often the Perfect Female Character conveys to girls that they must be flawless in order to be relevant. Besides, perfect-seeming characters are hardly ever a good idea: They're not accessible or relatable, and worst of all, they're boring. If a character knows everything at the start of the story, she can't grow or develop. A character should undergo an emotional journey in addition to her external quest.

I would define a "strong female lead" as a protagonist who has agency, not a character who is perfect. A character with agency has power over herself and her decisions. She has motivations, obstacles, and goals of her own. This is especially true if a female character is the "love interest" in a hetero relationship: She can be in a relationship while having a personality and destiny separate from the man's.

Additionally, strength is not synonymous with violence or physical prowess. This is not to say that only men should fight in action books. However, we need to create characters of *all* genders with a range of strengths (e.g., emotional, interpersonal, intellectual, and creative). If you hired me for the NBA, I might not do so hot, given the fact that I have no experience and clock in at a towering 4 feet and 10 inches; but drop me in a roomful of artists and it's a different story. A great example is *The Mysterious Benedict Society* by Trenton Lee Stewart, in which the four protagonists have varied personalities and expertise (problem solving, photographic memory, courage/physical dexterity, and poetry), making the characters more interesting and relatable. No one is good at everything, and we should represent people with different abilities and skill sets. Characters with different perspectives make for a richer story and enable you to connect with a wider range of readers.

3. "THERE CAN BE ONLY ONE?"

This isn't the movie *Highlander*, where the immortals have to fight one another to the death until only one of them remains. Don't think that just because one of your main characters is female that you've checked the box for equality. When we include multiple female protagonists and female supporting characters, we avoid writing only one type of female character and steer away from clichés. If female supporting characters are few and far between, then your story feels male dominated.

Growing up, I adored Rick Riordan's Heroes of Olympus series for its dynamic cast of characters. Reading those books made me feel like I was embarking on a journey with a good group of friends. About half of the characters he introduces in this series are girls, all of which have completely different personalities, backgrounds, interests, and strengths. All of them have a fleshed-out character arc, are crucial to the plot, and are ultimately valued by one another. Several of them are people of color (POC), which makes the characters more accessible to a wider range of readers.

Including more female characters isn't forced representation, because lots of women exist in real life—believe me, I've encountered them. Plus, creating a diverse cast of characters allows readers to better understand all of your protagonists. Characters behave differently depending on who they're responding to, and this dynamic makes them more authentic to your readers.

If you do find that your story is male-dominated, *please* don't pit the only two female characters against each other unless there's a genuine plot-centered or ideological reason for the conflict, not just a romance triangle. Catty girl tropes grow boring very quickly. Girls can and do support each other.

4. REDEFINE WHAT BEAUTY MEANS

Not every female protagonist needs to be conventionally attractive, nor does every female protagonist need to dislike how she looks. Too many YA books feature a female protagonist who hates her appearance despite almost every other character remarking how gorgeous she is (like America Singer from *The Selection*). This implies that the character genuinely is conventionally attractive but is too insecure to realize that fact—and this self-loathing is often portrayed as a breed of humbleness. This faux-humility is problematic because not only does it perpetuate the mentality that women must be conventionally beautiful in order to be important, but it also normalizes the hatred of one's appearance.

Recently, I read *The Dispossessed* by Ursula K. Le Guin and was pleasantly surprised that the protagonist's romantic partner, Takver, is described as "not pretty" in a factual manner, yet her appearance is neither an issue for herself nor for the protagonist, who falls in love with her at once. Your female protagonists don't have to be gorgeous, and this doesn't have to be an issue for them.

We don't have to stop writing characters who are insecure about their appearance, but we need to address these insecurities with caution—*especially* in regard to forms of body dysmorphia, eating disorders, or other mental health conditions. These should be treated as aspects of character development, *not* glorified or normalized. Additionally, the world needs more female characters of all types—especially POC girls, disabled girls, and all the girls who aren't given the positive representation they deserve. We need characters who don't conform to traditional standards of "beauty" and who are confident in themselves. Girls need to realize their worth.

In every form of media, girls are bombarded with negative messages about their appearance. I didn't feel comfortable in my own skin until I started questioning the systems and underlying mentalities that contribute to the objectification of women's bodies. The most potent way to rebel against a culture of self-deprecation is to love yourself and encourage others to do the same.

As creators of media—especially as writers of media for kids and teens—we play a major role in shaping popular mentality. We have the power to send any message into the world, starting with the youngest and most impressionable groups of readers. Let's make our message a positive one.

REN KOPPEL TORRES, the teen author of fantasy novel *The Shadow in Her Pocket*, was born in New York City in a Jewish-Mexican-American family. Ren writes for publications including *Writer's Digest* and *Pipeline Artists*, and is passionate about art, rock music, and promoting child literacy. Find Ren at KoppelTorres.com and @KoppelTorres on Twitter.

TELLING YOUR STORY

by Ann Whitford Paul

"...the work of art as completely realized is the result of a long and complex process of exploration...." —Joyce Cary

Remember when you were young, how you loved dressing up like Little Red Riding Hood or Superman? Remember how you changed clothes to play? Maybe you put on a firefighter helmet. Maybe you wore a crown. What does playing dress-up have to do with writing picture books? A lot!

In much the same way you changed outfits, you can change your story by telling it in different ways. Most picture-book stories are told by an *outside* narrator who speaks of the characters using third-person pronouns such as *he, she, it,* and *they*. In a completely unscientific study of twenty-five books I've typed up since the first edition of my book *Writing Picture Books*, the majority—seventeen—were written in third person. Five stories were told by a character who was a *participant* in the story—a first-person narrator. That adds up to twenty-three.

And the odd-duck stories? *Smile Pout-Pout Fish* by Deborah Diesen is told in the apostrophe form, where the narrator talks to something that can't talk back. *Suppose You Meet a Dinosaur: A First Book of Manners* by Judy Sierra is told in the second person, where the writer addresses the reader and listener. Test picture books on your shelves or in the library to see for yourself. You, too, will find most books are told by an outside narrator—in the third person.

Novelist Willa Cather said, "... there are only two or three human stories, and they go on repeating themselves as fiercely as if they had never happened before...." If we accept her statement, then the only way to differentiate our writing from other stories on the same topic is to write them uniquely. Today more than ever, you *must* make your story so original it will leap into an editor's hands and shout, "Publish *me*!"

To do that, explore different ways of telling your story. You may discard each experiment and go back to your original, but, trust me; no journey is wasted in pursuit of a story.

Let's play around with a familiar story by Aesop from 600 B.C.

THE ANT AND THE DOVE

> An Ant went to the bank of a river to quench its thirst and being carried away by the rush of the stream, was on the point of drowning. A Dove sitting on a tree overhanging the water plucked a leaf and let it fall into the stream close to her. The Ant climbed onto it and floated in safety to the bank. Shortly afterwards a birdcatcher came and stood under the tree and laid his lime-twigs for the Dove, which sat in the branches. The Ant, perceiving his design, stung him in the foot. In pain the birdcatcher threw down the twigs, and the noise made the Dove take wing.
>
> ONE GOOD TURN DESERVES ANOTHER.

Narrative voice—third-person-limited point of view

This story above is told in the popular, traditional form of an outside observer who relates what happens but doesn't participate in the action. Notice the narrator doesn't go into Dove's head. He starts his story with Ant and stays with her. As you've seen from my informal study, most picture books are told in this manner—by a single outside observer who goes only into the head of the main character.

Jacob's New Dress by Sarah and Ian Hoffman tells the moving story of a boy named Jacob who wants to wear a dress to his preschool. His mother is supportive, his father is slow to accept it, and one boy at school declares that boys don't wear dresses.

Jacob, though, knows what he wants and has the guts to do what feels right for him. The narrator doesn't allow us into any head but Jacob's. We know the other characters' feelings only by what Jacob hears them say. Read this book, not only for voice but for the way Jacob is an active character insisting on what he wants and solving his problems without much adult interference.

Change the point-of-view character

What happens if I tell this story with Dove as the main character?

> One early morning Dove was munching seeds while sitting on the branch of a tree that overhung a river. "Help! Help!" he heard a thin voice squealing. Ant, struggling against the current, was thrashing about.

> Dove couldn't let her drown. Thinking quickly, he tossed down a leaf. "Climb aboard," he sang. Ant did as directed and rode safely to shore.
>
> That very afternoon, Dove was enjoying his nap when he was jarred awake by a loud scream and the sight of a birdcatcher hobbling off. Ant, the very same one he had rescued earlier, explained, "The birdcatcher was preparing a trap for you. I bit his foot, and off he ran." Dove was so grateful he sang to Ant.
>
> "I'm not your mother;
> I'm not your brother,
> but I believe one good turn
> deserves another."

This example is still told from only one point of view—Dove's. Switching main characters allowed me to expand on his role and put it in a song (a cheesy one), highlighting his singing ability.

Third-person-omniscient (or multiple) point of view

Let's see how this story might read if the narrator jumps between the heads of each character.

> Ant went to the bank of a river to quench her thirst but lost her footing and tumbled into the water. The rush of the stream was carrying her away. She was sure she was a goner.
>
> Luckily Dove was sitting on a tree branch overhanging the water and understood she was in danger. He didn't want Ant to drown, so he plucked a leaf and dropped it close to her. Ant couldn't believe her good fortune. She climbed onto it and floated safely to the bank.
>
> Shortly afterwards a birdcatcher came and stood under Dove's tree. The birdcatcher, dreaming of dove supper, laid his lime-twig trap. But he didn't see Ant.
>
> A good thing too, for Ant, grateful to Dove for saving her life, wanted to return the favor. Hidden by the grass, she crept, crept, crept closer . . . closer and BIT that birdcatcher.
>
> "Yeow!" he howled. Dove awakened with a jerk just in time to see the birdcatcher hobble away.

In this telling, I'm initially in Ant's head, but then I move to Dove's. I even spend time in the birdcatcher's head.

While older readers can easily move from one character's viewpoint to another's, picture-book listeners, who are new to books, story, and plot, may have more trouble. It's best to make the action easy for them to follow. Staying in one character's head allows the listener to know whom to focus on and identify with.

However, *Extra Yarn* by Mac Barnett is an example of a successful book told in third-person-omniscient point of view. The story starts out with Annabelle, the main character, knitting sweaters from a box of never-ending yarn. She knits sweaters for everyone and then for animals. At that point, the author peers into the minds of the townspeople, who are sure she'll run out of yarn. But she doesn't.

Annabelle knits sweaters for houses, churches, barns, and birdhouses. The author also enters the mind of a jealous archduke who tries to buy her box of yarn. When she turns him down, he hires thieves to steal it. You'll have to read the book to find out what happens next. Being a knitter myself, this book appealed to me, but non-knitters will enjoy it, too. It has the feel of an old tale, and the illustrations won Jon Klassen a Caldecott Honor.

First-person, or the lyrical voice

In this point of view, the narrator is one of the story's participants. *I* and *we* are the key words that let you know you're in a first-person story. What happens when our story is told by Ant?

> Danger was the farthest thing from my mind. I was at the bank of a river and thirsty, so I leaned down for a drink. *Splash!* Into the water I fell, and the rushing current carried me away from shore. "Help! Help!" I cried, but we ants are small in body and in voice. No one could hear me. I was a goner for sure.
>
> Lucky for me, Dove was sitting on a branch overhanging the water and tossed me a leaf. I grabbed it, climbed aboard, and floated to shore. Was I grateful?
>
> You bet, and soon I had a chance to show it. A birdcatcher came to Dove's tree and started making a trap for him out of lime-twigs. Time for action!
>
> I stung him badly on the foot. "OWWWWWWWWWWWW!" he howled. The noise warned Dove, who took flight and was saved. Just goes to show that one good turn deserves another.

With this first-person perspective, listeners experience the action and emotion along with Ant. They get into her head and feel her gratitude for her narrow escape. The story's tone changes.

If I'm having trouble getting into my character's head, I write a version in this voice to get to know her better. Perhaps I'll like it and leave it in the lyrical voice, but I may rewrite it again in third person. Either way, my experimentation wasn't wasted because I gained a deeper understanding of my character's feelings.

However, first person has drawbacks. Telling your story this way doesn't allow you an opportunity to write about offstage actions. The main character—the *I*-writer—must be on every page. Also, telling it in this manner lets the reader know that the narrator survives. We might not know in what state, but we're certain he lived to tell the tale.

Check out *Ralph Tells a Story* by Abby Hanlon. Ralph's teacher tells him that stories are everywhere. His classmates always find them, and although Ralph tries and tries, he fails to come up with a story. Since the book is narrated by Ralph, we feel his pain and suffer with him. More importantly, we rejoice in his success when he finally does tell a story.

Now I'm going to tell the story again in first person, but with the birdcatcher as the narrator. Here's the opening:

> I woke this morning with a longing for dove stew. Delicious, delightful, delectable dove stew. I'm not one for inaction. Not me. I gathered string and lime-twigs and set off to make my dream a reality.

You can see how if you wrote this to the end, it wouldn't be the story we started with. That change is what we're after, something to liven up a tired and much-told tale. First-person voices may take several different forms, including letters and journal/diary entries.

One long letter

> Dear Mother,
>
> So much has happened since I left your nest, I had to write. Thank you for teaching me to not ignore those in need. Yesterday, I was sitting on a branch in the loveliest of trees, minding my business, enjoying the breeze. The peace was broken by squeals from the stream below. A poor ant was struggling to swim to shore, but the current was too strong. I couldn't swoop down and pluck her from the water. My beak might have broken her in two, so I came up with an alternate plan. I plucked a leaf from the tree and tossed it down. The ant had just enough energy to pull herself aboard and float to safety.
>
> That might have been the end of the story, but after she'd dried off, caught her breath, and calmed down, along came a birdcatcher. I remember your lesson about flying away from those nasty people, and I would have, but I was dozing and didn't realize he was setting a trap for me. Luckily that birdcatcher was wearing sandals. Even luckier for me that ant was nearby and knew exactly what was up! She bit that birdcatcher's foot! I'd be surprised if you couldn't hear his scream from where you live. You can bet it startled me. Off I flew, and off the birdcatcher hopped, clutching his foot, moaning in pain.
>
> I'm so thankful you taught me that we eat seeds, not insects. If that ant hadn't been around to save me, I shudder to think what would have happened. For one thing, you certainly wouldn't be reading this letter.
>
> Your Loving Son,
> Featherly

My favorite example of a published book told in a single letter is *Nettie's Trip South* by Ann Turner. In this compelling story, Nettie writes to her friend Addie about her experiences visiting the South just before the Civil War. Among other incidents, she describes attending a slave auction and the horror of watching two young children being separated. She returns home forever changed. Although this book was published in 1987, it remains in print. I urge you to read this beautiful and poignant story.

A more contemporary book that takes the form of one letter is *Love, Mouserella* by David Ezra Stein, where a little mouse writes her grandmother a letter about all she's done since her grandmother returned to her home in the country.

Journal or diary

Monday

Dear Diary,

What an exciting day! If it hadn't been for me, there would have been one less ant in this world. I was minding my own business on a low tree branch overhanging a river when I heard the tiniest of screams from an ant splashing in the water, struggling to reach shore. It was easy to see if no one helped her, she would drown. But no one rushed to the rescue. Where were her mom and dad? Her cries grew more frantic, so I tugged a fat maple leaf off of the tree and tossed it down. That ant had just enough strength to pull herself up onto the leaf and float to shore. She was one grateful ant and thanked me profusely.

Friday

Dear Diary,

Remember that ant I wrote about? Now I'm the one who's grateful and thanking her profusely. Here's why:

I was dozing on my tree branch when a horrific howling awakened me just in time to see that birdcatcher, the bane of my existence, clutching his foot and hopping away. I had no idea what to make of this crazy behavior until the ant I'd dropped the leaf to scampered up the tree trunk and explained how she'd stopped that mean man from laying a trap for me: She bit his foot! Good thing the birdcatcher was wearing sandals and good thing the ant knew this was my tree. I'd saved her, so she saved me.

Diary of a Spider by Doreen Cronin is written in diary form and is a great follow-up to her earlier success, *Diary of a Worm*. Now let's be a bit more daring with the story.

Second person

The word *you* is a clue here. Using *you*, the author invites the reader into the story. This is how Aesop's fable might read if written in second person:

If you saw your neighbor's dog tangled up in its leash, what would you do?

I hope you'd rush to its rescue.

Why?

Because someday maybe that dog could help you. And that day might come as soon as the very next day.

You'll hear that dog bark, bark, barking and after you get over your annoyance at the noise, you'll go outside and see smoke coming out of your trash can. You'll grab a hose and spray out the fire. And you'll know it really is true that one good turn deserves another.

Notice here, I took the story in a completely different direction, getting rid of the dove and the ant and inserting a dog. That's the fun of experimenting. Your story can fly off to places you'd never imagined even though the new version was always where it was supposed to be.

Suppose You Meet a Dinosaur makes use of this point of view, but you don't need to look further than the If You Give a … series written by Laura Numeroff: *If You Give a Mouse a Brownie, If You Give a Cat a Cupcake, If You Give a Dog a Donut, If You Give a Moose a Muffin*, and on and on. In each of these, the author talks to the reader. Check out at least one of them to see how involving this form of inviting the listener to participate in the action can be.

In all the retellings, notice I didn't switch the voice midstory. This would confuse our young audience. They wouldn't know who the main character was or with whom to identify. Once you start a picture book in one point of view, stick to it.

A FEW FINAL WORDS

Isn't it interesting to see how changing the point of view can affect a story so markedly? I hope you'll experiment with this in your story and in any future stories you write.

ANN WHITFORD PAUL has published more than twenty picture books (including board books, early-readers, a poetry collection, plus a variety of fiction and nonfiction, rhymed and prose picture book, including the popular series that began with *If Animals Kissed Goodnight*). Many of her poems have appeared in anthologies and her essays have been published by several newspapers. She lives with her husband in Los Angeles and hopes you'll visit her website www.annwhitfordpaul.com. This essay is excerpted from *Writing Picture Books Revised and Expanded Edition* (Writer's Digest, 2018).

THROUGH THE LOOKING GLASS

As publishing endeavors to address diversity and inclusion in fiction, an inevitable question arises: Can authors write characters whose experiences are outside of their own?

by Diana M. Pho

Questions of representation in literature are a tale as old as time, coupled with that other great conundrum: How can we write about experiences outside of our own? The best fiction has the ability to transport readers into another's shoes and make readers consider a new perspective. And while the question of writing the Other is evergreen, the assessment of how to do so successfully is an ever-evolving story.

When I think about why writing across difference is so important, I remember my childhood and how books changed my perception of the world and of myself. Two specific books were a huge influence—Laurence Yep's 1982 novel *Dragon of the Lost Sea* and George Selden's 1960 book *The Cricket in Times Square*—but between them, their treatment of Chinese characters and culture couldn't be more different. Yep spent much time doing research into Chinese myths and legends before even taking up the project, and I was completely swept away by the adventures of the dragon princess Shimmer and the human orphan Thorn on their quest to restore the Inland Sea. *The Cricket in Times Square*, on the other hand, featured racist stereotypes: Sai Fong, who teaches the newspaper boy Mario about the importance of crickets in Chinese culture, speaks with a broad transliterated accent and works out of a derelict laundromat. Mario and his family benefit from talented Chester the cricket, while Sai Fong remains a mystical minor character.

While both books were praised during their time, *The Cricket in Times Square* sent a certain message about Asian characters: We all talked in broken English, held ignoble jobs, and acted only in service to the white characters. Yep's story, however, showed how characters who looked like me could be heroes, and demonstrated that not all fantasies must take place in medieval Europe.

A few lessons for today's authors can be drawn here. One is that writers are capable of composing stories that uplift the marginalized (or, alternatively, ones that push them down). The second is that while Selden might not have realized how racist his portrayal was, and certainly the mostly white literary community of the time didn't either, it doesn't excuse the fact that the book has biased content. And a third lesson is the understanding that writing effective diverse stories is a skill that *can* be learned. Later on in high school, I picked up Robert Olen Butler's 1992 short story collection, "A Good Scent From a Strange Mountain." I was astounded by the way Butler captured life in the Vietnamese immigrant community, which resonated with my own family experiences. Writing the Other *is* possible. It's simply a matter of doing so respectfully, and responsibly.

WRITING IS HARD, BUT WRITING #OWNVOICES IS HARDER

In conversations about the challenge of getting published and the current movements around diversity and inclusion, one misconception I've heard from many aspiring authors is that marginalized writers are getting an "advantage." Historically, culturally dominant voices have had a leg up in publishing (typified by straight, white, able-bodied men). In recognition of that imbalance, it's true that publishers are working hard to right the ship by supporting more books by diverse writers. This is not to hit any sort of "quota," but to bring enriching stories and voices to the marketplace that have long been missing. For example, Angie Thomas's 2017 novel, *The Hate U Give,* has a powerful take on police brutality, made more so from being written by a Black woman affected by this violence. The hashtag #ownvoices has been used online to elevate stories about underrepresented communities as told by writers in those communities.

Despite recent efforts, statistics still show that #ownvoices stories are being left behind in the industry. It's a misunderstanding to think that marginalized authors have a sudden advantage because "diversity is trendy." To take some recent numbers from children's literature: According to the Cooperative Children's Book Center annual survey, multicultural content increased from 28 percent in 2017 to 31 percent in 2018, but the number of Black, Native, and Latinx *writers* only increased from 6 percent to 7 percent. This means that publishers are choosing to publish more white authors who write multicultural content than writers of color. More evidence can be found in the genres I edit, science fiction and fantasy. *Fireside Magazine* has done extensive work in recording the lack of Black writers published in short fiction in their 2016 #BlackSpecFic report, which has been corroborated by *FIYAH* magazine's Presence of Blackness (POB) Score Report of 2018. Such cases illustrate how power dynamics impact who gets published, how they get published, and who gets ignored.

On top of institutional challenges, underrepresented writers face cultural challenges as well. Because of the historic lack of marginalized stories in pop culture, minority writers must deal with the added pressure that their individual story comes to inherently represent the whole of their community. Even the blockbuster success *Crazy Rich Asians* was hit with backlash that it did not represent the entire Asian diaspora. Policing identities has also become an issue: That is, whether a marginalized person can prove they have the "credentials" to write about their own experiences. This has been especially harmful to queer writers who've felt forced to out themselves in order to write about the LGBTQ community.

As long as the majority of industry decision-makers remain white, straight, able-bodied and affluent, anyone who falls outside of those categories will have additional obstacles to overcome in order to be published.

INVADER, TOURIST, OR GUEST: A WRITER'S GUIDE TO CULTURAL DIFFERENCE

Bearing all that in mind, what kind of responsibility does a writer then shoulder when writing characters whose experience extends outside of their own identity? One ethical approach has been described in Nisi Shawl's essay "Appropriate Cultural Appropriation." (Shawl also cowrote *Writing the Other*, the classic volume on this subject, with coauthor Cynthia Ward.) Shawl asks creators what mindset they have when looking to add other cultures or experiences in their work: Are they an "invader," a "tourist," or a "guest"?

An "invader," as the term implies, is the most harmful approach, in which writers act without any regard for the feelings of the community or the responsibilities in representing them. "Invaders arrive without warning, take whatever they want for use in whatever way they see fit," Shawl explains. "Theirs is a position of entitlement without allegiance."

Examples of an invader mindset include:

- cursory research focusing on what seems "exotic" to your world-building;
- projection of stereotypes, desires, or fantasies about a different gender when writing characters instead of making them dynamic people;
- assuming that not including queer people or people of color in a story is being "historically accurate."

Writers who act as "tourists" are a step-up. Tourists acknowledge they are outsiders deeply interested and invested in learning more about the Other. As this term also implies, however, tourists can act positively or negatively—think immersive traveler Anthony Bourdain in *Parts Unknown* versus an undergraduate on spring break in Cancun. A respectful tourist mindset embodies these qualities:

- an honest curiosity and willingness to learn, and ability to ask questions from experts when help is needed;
- awareness that a writer should respect cultural boundaries and not impose their own biases;
- ability to compensate the community for their experiences, whether through financial means or meaningful, equal knowledge-sharing;
- realization that a story offers a visit to a new experience, but also making conscious efforts to boost the originators.

A negative example of a tourist mindset would be "going native": the assumption that one can instantly gain expertise through limited time or experience, and showing such superficial knowledge off in a self-important way.

According to Shawl, acting as a "guest"—being someone with insider knowledge, familiar connections and trust—is a level of authenticity and craft a writer can strive for, but is a status that must be given to them by the community they wish to represent. No one can assume to be a guest, but must instead be welcomed as one.

FURTHER READING

- *Fireside Magazine*. "#BlackSpecFic special report." medium.com/fireside-fiction-company/blackspecfic-571c00033717
- *FIYAH Magazine*. "POB Score: A FIYAH Project." fiyahlitmag.com/blackspecfic/the-pob-score-project
- Lee and Low Books. "The Diversity Gap in Children's Book Publishing." blog.leeandlow.com/2018/05/10/the-diversity-gap-in-childrens-book-publishing-2018
- Nisi Shawl. "Appropriate Cultural Appropriation." writingtheother.com/appropriate-cultural-appropriation
- Nisi Shawl and Cynthia Ward. *Writing the Other: A Practical Approach*. Aqueduct Press: 2005.aqueductpress.com/books/978-1-933500-00-3.php
- Daniel José Older. "12 Fundamentals Of Writing 'The Other' (And The Self)." buzzfeed.com/danieljoseolder/fundamentals-of-writing-the-other
- Uma Krishnaswami. "Interview Wednesday: Stacy Whitman of Tu Books." umakrishnaswami.blogspot.com/2011/07/interview-wednesday-stacy-whitman-of-tu.html

THE NEXT STEPS IN WRITING DIVERSITY

After examining the different approaches as described by Shawl, here are some follow-up actions I'd recommend based on my own editorial experience:

1) Know yourself—and your limitations.

Being able to effectively write from the experience of others requires not just strong ability, but also a level of awareness about yourself and your role as a storyteller. As Daniel José Older acknowledges in his essay "12 Fundamentals of Writing 'The Other' (And the Self)," it's a writer's job to enter into someone else's head. But can writers take ownership of the stories and experiences of another in the process? Would doing so help enrich the reading experience, or would it be considered a type of theft? Older suggests that writers ask themselves: *Why do you feel it falls to you to write someone else's story? Why do you have the right to take on another's voice? And should you do this?*

Especially considering the statistics mentioned earlier, it's important to consider what socio-political advantages you may possess, and how your story might overshadow or limit opportunities for a marginalized community.

2) Do your research—then do research on your research.

Research is key, but *how* you research even more so. Look at your sources and consider whether they hold any possible bias. For example, the popular 19th century photographer Edward Curtis tended to romanticize and mislabel his Native American subjects, thus turning their experience into art that didn't accurately or respectfully depict the community he was portraying. Make sure to use museums, libraries, documentaries, academic sources, community cultural centers, and trusted experts to inform your portrayal.

3) Get some sensitivity readers.

Sensitivity readers (also known as cultural consultants) act like a critique group, except their specialty is evaluating authenticity and flagging any possible incorrect or damaging elements. Always use more than one such reader, as one person should not be treated as if their advice represents an entire people. Change readers with each major revision to maintain a fresh perspective. Be prepared to get some great insights, but also be ready to act accordingly if a sensitivity reader says a story aspect is offensive or inappropriate and must be scrapped. Sensitivity readers should not be treated like stamps of approval, but as advisors whose opinion must be taken seriously. Also, be sure to fairly compensate sensitivity readers—their work is equivalent to a developmental edit and should be treated as such.

4) Realize your story is still your responsibility, not anyone else's.

When your work is published, its criticism will span broadly: Some story aspects may be praised for their authenticity, while others may be seen as inaccurate. Inevitably, you will make mistakes. *That's okay.* No piece of art can be perfect. It's also not the critic's fault for pointing out flaws. While there are many ways to handle reviews, criticism regarding cultural appropriation, racism, sexism, or another form of oppression should not be ignored or cast aside, no matter how much work you've done to avoid harm. You, and only you, are responsible for addressing these criticisms. At the very least, sincerely apologize and make amends to do better, as evidenced with concrete actions.

Reflecting on what you've now learned, does writing across difference sound complicated? Well, it should be! Understanding that alone is the tip of the iceberg. That said, with time, craft and true ethical dedication to your work, it *is* possible to portray diversity effectively. In doing so, you'll also master a good chunk of what it means to be a quality writer. It is an act of courage to put your book out into the world, no matter your background. It is also an act of deep understanding and respect to write the Other well. Poet Nikki Giovanni may have summed up the matter best: "Writers don't write from experience. Writers write from empathy."

DIANA M. PHO is a Hugo Award–nominated editor who currently works as a story producer at Realm. Previously she was an editor at Tor Books and Tor.com Publishing. She is also a published academic, playwright, and activist. This essay was previously published in the February 2019 issue of *Writer's Digest*.

SINISTER, YET SYMPATHETIC

The key to a great story is a villain that readers can relate to. These tips from several international bestselling authors show how to enchant readers with the sinister.

by Sam Boush

Imagine Little Red Riding Hood: ruddy cheeks, basket full of goodies, off to Grandma's house with not a care in the world. She's taking in the sights, smelling flowers, throwing that towel over her meat pies to keep them warm and fresh. The very picture of innocence: unaware that these woods hold danger.

Then, BAM! You know what happens next.

Except this time, it doesn't.

No wolf emerges from the forest, salivating over the savory treats. No heroic woodcutter, no gobbled granny. No threat. No danger. No salvation.

Where's the story in that? Without tension or drama, there's no story at all. And none of it can happen without the most important character: the villain.

Without an antagonist, *Little Red Riding Hood* is a nature walk, *Jaws* is a day at the beach, and *First Blood* is just Rambo sleeping rough. Without a villain, Harry Potter's parents are never murdered, Gotham City's worst crime is jaywalking, and Luke and Leia grow up in a stable, non-planet-destroying household.

Bad guys, please save us from these boring outcomes!

You already know that a story needs a villain. Where we all struggle, however, is making our antagonist convincing, memorable, and frightening all at the same time. It's one of the most fundamental problems every storyteller faces: how to bring an antagonist to life, making them believable in the eyes of readers and letting them reveal their sinister true selves.

Seven international bestselling fiction writers have offered their advice on how to create a compelling villain. They've shared their best practices to help you build the best villain possible—a character every bit as important as your protagonist.

MAKE YOUR VILLAIN RELATABLE

People don't do things just because they're bad. Sure, there are rotten people out there, but most of us behave out of a place of self-rationalization. Villains are the same.

"Villains are tricky," says Robert Dugoni, *Wall Street Journal* bestselling author of the Tracy Crosswhite series. "If you make them too over the top, they're not believable, and if they're not believable they're not frightening. I think most villains are born of circumstance, not genetics. So for an author, I think the question to ask is, 'How far would you go in the same circumstance?' Because what is truly frightening is when the villain is relatable."

Antagonists, like protagonists, think what they're doing is right. Your villain doesn't think they're bad. From their perspective, they're doing what they think is—if not exactly good—at least justifiable. And the more they're driven by a justified purpose, the more relatable they'll be.

None of us would go as far as the murderers that Dugoni's protagonist, homicide detective Tracy Crosswhite, encounters. Though we're not killers ourselves, we can certainly understand the blur in the line between good and evil, which these villains choose to step over. Maybe we've even stepped over lesser lines at one time or another. But what makes a villain relatable is, despite their worst actions, understanding how that journey to the gray area happens.

Maybe it's an obsession with the dark side that goes too far. A white lie that snowballs. A slope that gets a little too slippery, a little too fast. Whatever brings your villain to cross the line, it's more memorable and enthralling if the reader can relate to their decisions, even while disagreeing with them.

KNOW YOUR VILLAIN'S MOTIVATION

In the Harry Potter series, Severus Snape's heart was broken by Lily. In Shakespeare's *Othello*, Iago was unfairly passed over for promotion. In the Lord of the Rings series, Sméagol found one of those rings of power, beginning his transformation into Gollum.

And in the Song of Ice and Fire series, Cersei Lannister was pawned off as a child bride to a king.

What do all these characters have in common? They broke bad as an outcome of circumstance, not because they were just built that way. Like the rest of us, villains are made by their experiences.

Readers want the same from your antagonist. They want to know what brought them to this place of wickedness and what motivates them to go beyond the norms of behavior, toward evil deeds. Readers want to know what continues to drive the villain, despite pressures to give up, admit mistakes and pay for their crimes.

"The most convincing villains are the ones who appear to be completely normal on the surface," says Karin Slaughter, whose books (including the Grant County series) have sold more than 35 million copies worldwide. "They seem just like you or me or your best friend from college or favorite cousin. But once you start to pay attention to their actions, you see that they are very self-oriented and incredibly motivated by something, whatever their own brand of something is, to satisfy themselves at any expense."

So, what motivates your antagonist?

There are many possible reasons for doing evil. Your villain might be activated by greed, raising one favored group over another or revenge. Almost anything will do, as long as it fits with the character and explains why they behave the way they do.

By explaining your villain's motivation, you allow your reader to understand them, even empathize with them.

MAKE YOUR VILLAIN A WORTHY RIVAL

The nature of the protagonist and antagonist are of two opposing forces. The protagonist works to push forward a goal. The antagonist works against that same goal. At the heart of it, this is what makes a story.

But it's not much of a story when the villain doesn't stack up. To be a counterbalance, the villain needs to be a power in her own right. Formidable. Frightening. Moreover, to create real tension, the antagonist should be of an even greater power than the protagonist, so that the reader genuinely worries that the hero won't prevail.

"The villain has to be very skilled at what they do," says Andy Weir, *The New York Times* bestselling author of *The Martian*. "They have to be a good threat or rival to the protagonist."

Granted, Weir recognizes that his antagonists aren't often people and good stories sometimes have nature as the villain. This works just as well. What's a more terrifying villain than a cold red planet 34 million miles from home?

In fact, using place as a villain is common. In *Jurassic Park*, the park is the principle menace, not the bumbling computer programmer, Dennis Nedry. The same applies in many stories. Alice's wonderland is the real villain in *Through the Looking Glass*, just as is Wonka's factory in *Charlie and the Chocolate Factory*.

ALLOW YOUR VILLAIN SOME HUMANITY

Your villain isn't all evil. No one is. In fact, a good villain has hopes and dreams, a past, longings and desires. They're just like the rest of us: human, imperfect.

"Give him a deeply complex, yet relatable reason for doing the evil that he does," says David Baldacci, international bestselling author of *Wish You Well* and *The Christmas Train*. "Allow him a smidgen of redeemable backstory to keep the reader honest and engaged."

Even if you choose to make your villains something other than human, you can still give them personality. Weir's protagonist in *The Martian* has a love/hate relationship with Mars, so not surprisingly, Weir recommends showing the humanity of villains. "The villain is best if they are also likeable," he says. According to Weir, you've succeeded in creating a great villain "if the audience actually roots for them to succeed in the short term. Though, of course, the audience should be rooting against them in the climax."

When your reader really gets to know a villain and sees they aren't all bad, that's when the fun begins. As much as readers love to hate a bad guy, the thing that really gets them hooked is when they also start to see themselves in the villain.

AVOID CLICHÉD VILLAIN DIALOGUE

"Bwa-ha-ha," the villain said, dry-washing her hands in her underground lair. "I'll get you, protagonist, if it's the last thing I do! Say goodbye to your trusty sidekick!"

That may have been painful to read (it was painful to write), but I hope it serves as an example of—and fair warning against—clichéd villain dialogue. We've all seen these kinds of lines in books, movies and TV. It's lazy. It's forgettable. And most of all—the cardinal sin—it's boring.

So how do you write better dialogue for your villain?

Lois Lowry, author of the Newbery Medal–winning books *Number the Stars* and *The Giver*, has written some of the most compelling villains for young readers, including Nazis and politicians. She suggests looking to contemporary examples of humans you might find maleficent and listening to what they say. She also notes that "verbs are always good for villains: *leered, hissed, muttered, lied*."

Caroline Kepnes, author of *You* (which also became a hit Netflix series), recommends getting inside your villain's head. "Explore the difference between the said and the unsaid," she says. "Write the inner monologue that's happening as the scene plays out. Highlighting the mental gymnastics that happen behind the scenes, in the mind, will help ground your characters. You might cut all of it, but you'll learn so much about your characters by analyzing the dimensions of motive and the hidden wounds within each line of dialogue."

When it comes to writing dialogue between your protagonist and antagonist, it comes back to motivation. Kepnes, whose most famous villain is an unrelenting stalker, has some great advice here, too. "The more you know your villain, the more you will create opponents who are specifically threatening," she says. "At the end of the day, we all have certain personality types that bring out the best in us, the worst. I always want to relate to the universal tension, the idea that we all, at times, feel as if people were sent to unnerve us."

DISPLAY YOUR VILLAIN'S BEST SIDE

While a villain's evil deeds are their most notable, it's often their unique (and sometimes even positive) qualities that set them apart. After all, who would Hannibal Lecter be if all he did was dine on human flesh, without the charm and charisma that made him memorable? Or Sherlock Holmes's archenemy, Professor Moriarty, without his cunning? Or Dolores Umbridge without her perfectionism?

"I think creating a compelling villain is no different from creating a compelling protagonist," says Emily St. John Mandel, author of the National Book Award–finalist novel *Station Eleven*. "I'm not sure anyone is completely evil or completely good; so I think a compelling hero or heroine needs to have flaws, and I think a compelling villain needs to have virtues. Your villain will be no less frightening for taking an interest in animal rescue or donating to humanitarian causes or being an excellent parent, but he or she will be a more interesting person for the reader to think about."

Characters often resonate when negative characteristics are offset with positive. Michael Corleone from *The Godfather* wouldn't be the classic bad guy he is in later books if not for his love of family and willingness to sacrifice for them. Similarly, the pirate Long John Silver is dastardly across the board in *Treasure Island*, except in his protective nature toward the young protagonist, Jim. For both Corleone and Silver, we can't bring ourselves to hate them, even though we know they're awful people.

In the end, this insight into character is what makes a universal story. Maybe the hero prevails. Maybe the antagonist comes away victorious. Maybe no one wins, and the conflict lives on. But through the journey, the reader is able to connect with all the characters, believe them, understand them and relate to them.

Even the villain.

SAM BOUSH is the author of *All Systems Down* (Lakewater Press, 2018). His second book, *All Threats Within*, was published in September 2019. This article was previously published in the July/August 2019 issue of *Writer's Digest*.

CUT AND PASTE

Making a Mock-Up Book

by Ann Whitford Paul

Putting together the…book dummy is a necessary process—it is the foundation for your book and lies at the heart of good bookmaking.
—Uri Shulevitz

You've written your story. You've revised the opening until it's tight and engaging. You've experimented with different ways to tell your story and chosen the best one. Your characters are strong, unique, and believable; your plot is a page-turner, and the ending resolves the main conflict. You've tied things together so that your audience will be satisfied and will want to read or hear the book again. Your manuscript, whether written in poetry or prose, is poetic. You've worked to use the right words, and you've cut out unnecessary ones. You should be finished, but …

You're not done yet! You need to make a dummy. A dummy is a layout of your text onto thirty-two pages. It's helpful in determining if the structure of your story fits the picture-book format.

"But I'm not an illustrator," you plead. "I write the words. Illustrators may find making a dummy a positive exercise, but it's a waste of time for me."

Trust me on the helpfulness of dummies. For years I tried to get away with not doing them. Making check marks or stars on the hard copy of my manuscript was surely enough to show me where the page turns came and if I had enough illustration possibilities. *Wrong*! I am one of the converted—a born-again dummy maker. I never send out a manuscript without first doing a dummy—a visual and tactile way of evaluating my story.

Most of us who write for children are kids at heart. Creating a dummy takes you away from your computer and gives your back and neck a break. Cutting and pasting allows you to use different hand and arm muscles, so it can be a nice change of pace.

We think of a dummy as the last stage of the revision process, but it may expose less obvious problems and lead to more revisions and more dummies. None of my dummies are for my editor to see. Some writers sketch out a simple, rough dummy early in the writing process, sometimes even before a word is written. They do this storyboard on a single sheet of paper, dividing it into separate pages and spreads as I have done below:

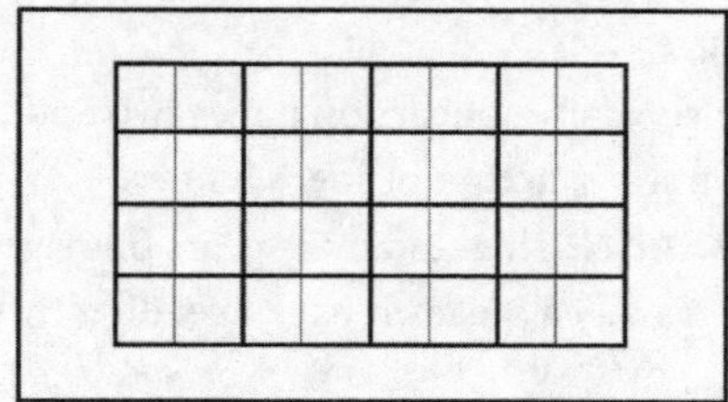

A spread is two facing pages that end up with an illustration that fills and spans both of those pages. You can purchase these forms in most art stores. The writer then uses single words or brief phrases to indicate action, page turns, etc. This initial dummy/storyboard does not include the story text. Its purpose is to give a general overview of the story's spacing.

The dummy we're going to make next is closer to a finished book with numbered pages you can turn. Print a hard copy of your story, and then grab some blank paper, lift-off tape, and scissors.

THE DUMMY FORM

Staple sixteen pieces of 8½" × 11" (22cm × 28cm) paper together along the left side. Picture-book manuscripts rarely have enough text to fill full pieces of paper, so save a tree and use only eight sheets of 8½" × 11" (22cm × 28cm) paper. Cut them in half, either vertically (portrait) or horizontally (landscape). You will then have pieces measuring either 5½" × 8½" (14cm × 22cm) or 11" × 4¼" (28cm × 11cm). Depending on what side you staple it, your dummy may be long or tall. Choose what shape you want your dummy to be, depending on the amount of text and the line lengths. If your text lines are short, you can have a taller dummy. If they are long, you should make a longer dummy.

If you have a particularly brief text, use just four pages of paper; cut them into quarters, and staple them together.

Number your pages from one to thirty-two. The first is page one. Turn the page, and put a two on the back of page one. Number three will go on the right-hand page. Continue in this manner until you reach the back page, which should be thirty-two.

CUTTING AND PASTING

Now you're ready to cut and paste sections of your manuscript onto the pages. To do that, you need to consider how many pages will be taken up by front matter. This can include four different items.

1. **HALF-TITLE PAGE:** This usually appears on page one and traditionally is the title with only a small illustration.
2. **FULL-TITLE PAGE:** This usually appears on pages two and three and includes the title and the writer's, illustrator's, and publisher's names.
3. **COPYRIGHT INFORMATION:** This usually appears on page four.
4. **DEDICATIONS:** They usually appear on page five, directly preceding your story's opening page.

Notice, the repetition of the phrase *usually appears*. These days publishers display a wide range of creativity in laying out front matter. You should browse through picture books to see the variety of ways front-matter information may be presented, but for right now you can familiarize yourself with the approaches listed below.

- Page one of *Me and Momma and Big John* by Mara Rockliff has a half title on page one, and the story opens with a double-spread on pages two and three. The copyright and dedications appear at the end of the book.
- *School's First Day of School* by Adam Rex is a forty-page picture book. Because the endpapers are part of those forty pages, the front matter begins on page four with the dedication and copyright info, and then the half title is on page five. The story begins on pages six and seven.
- *Old Robert and the Sea-Silly Cats* by Barbara Joosse is another forty-page book and begins completely differently. The first sentence is on page one. Pages two and three are a full-title page, and the dedication and copyright info appear on page forty.
- *Bike On, Bear!* by Cynthea Liu has a half title with no illustration on page one. Page two is dedication and copyright info, and page three is another half title, this time with an illustration. The story begins on page four.

- *Mousequerade Ball: A Counting Tale* by Lori Mortensen has a half title on page one, copyright info on page two, and dedications on page three. The story begins on page four.
- *Dot.* by Randi Zuckerberg begins with a half title on page one, copyright info on page two, and dedications on page three, but page four is blank—no picture, no text. The story begins on page five.

When you cut and paste your manuscript, plan where that information will go. Usually I start pasting my story on page six. If I find I need more story pages, I tighten my front matter. Don't use ordinary tape. You need a lift-off tape—Scotch brand calls it "removable tape"—so you can shift text from one page to another without creating tears. I'm a creature of habit and prefer tape, but non-permanent glue sticks and sprays work as well.

BREAKING UP THE TEXT

Always cut whenever one of the following story elements changes.

1. **LOCATION:** Your character leaves the house, enters a store, or goes to a friend's house. The different setting calls for a different picture, which means it's time to move on to the next page.
2. **CHARACTERS:** A new character is introduced, or a character disappears. Mother comes home from work, the tooth fairy sneaks into the bedroom, or the cat hides, but the result is the same: The picture must change.
3. **ACTIONS:** Two characters are fighting. Someone breaks up the fight, and then the characters start working together. Each of these would signal the need for a different illustration.

Note that on odd pages it is not enough to have simple changes in the story. There should be developments dramatic enough to compel your reader to turn the page. Try to leave your character in peril on the odd-numbered pages.

Using your lift-off tape, paste your text onto the pages of your dummy. An important benefit of making a dummy is that it shows whether you have those necessary page turns we discussed in the previous chapter. You'll need to do some experimentation and realigning to decide where your text works best.

Once your dummy is as complete as you can make it, read it aloud with pen or pencil in hand. The act of reading and turning the pages, as your reader will, allows you to see the story in a new way. Then make the necessary changes to your dummy.

I'm always surprised to find changes need to be made because I wait to dummy my manuscript until I think my story is ready to send off. Invariably, though, I discover places for revision I hadn't noticed before. Pay special attention to the following questions when evaluating your dummied manuscript.

Can Your Story Fit into Thirty-Two Pages?

Perhaps your story is quite short and would work better as a board book. But maybe your story needs forty pages. Beware if you are a first-time writer with a manuscript that needs more than the traditional thirty-two pages. Publishing a new writer's book is an expensive gamble for the publishing house. Any additional pages might cause an editor to think twice about buying your story.

Does Your Story Have Enough Illustrations?

The minimum number of pictures is thirteen double-spreads and one single-spread. Thoughts cannot be easily illustrated. The days of characters with thought bubbles over their heads have passed. Nevertheless, dialogue is often printed comic-book style in those kinds of bubbles. Some dialogue can be illustrated. "I'm leaving right now" indicates action and could be illustrated with Rabbit leaving her den. "I'm not sure what to do" would be more difficult. Negative statements, such as "He didn't jump" or "She didn't read her book," would require great creativity on the illustrator's part. Look at *My Favorite Pets: by Gus W. for Ms. Smolinski's Class* to see how Harry Bliss deals with the negative statements Jeanne Birdsall wrote.

Does Your Text Suggest a Variety of Illustrations?

Does your story take place entirely in one room? While Margaret Wise Brown got away with that in *Goodnight Moon,* give your illustrator a break and vary the illustration possibilities. Give your listener a break, too, so she won't be looking at the same pictures over and over again.

Does the Reader Know Your Book's Premise Within the First Three Pages?

After the front matter, no more than three pages should be required to give your reader a good idea of your story's subject matter. Really, though, allowing three pages is being generous. All that opening material should be on the first page.

Does Your Story Have Page Turns?

Not every page needs a cliff-hanger, but something should be left unanswered or unfinished so the reader wants to proceed.

Is the Action Spread Over Thirty-Two Pages?

Or is it clumped together at the beginning or the end? Are big chunks of text on some pages and little slivers on others? Ask yourself whether all that text is important and if some can be deleted.

Are There Spots with Unnecessary Words?

Scrutinize any clumps of dialogue and description. Can they be condensed? Can they be eliminated? Seeing one's text on the page reveals new possibilities for edits.

Does Your Climax Happen in the Story's Final Pages?

Ideally, your climax will occur near page thirty or thirty-one. If it happens on pages sixteen and seventeen, you have a problem and need to cut much of what comes afterwards. On the other hand, you might consider adding more action to your story's middle section.

Do You Tie Up Loose Ends Nicely?

You have until the last page to accomplish this. We discussed this in detail in chapter twelve, which focused on endings. With your dummy, you'll see how well you've handled this element of your story.

Is Your Storytelling Concise, Poetic, and Dramatic?

To answer this question, read your dummy one last time for an overview of how your plot and language work together.

COLOR-TESTING THE DUMMY

After you've made your dummy, get out your highlighters. Use the green highlighter for the *wow* moment, that initial intriguing development that compels the reader to proceed. Turning the pages can sometimes show you the *wow* moment isn't that much of a *wow*.

Next use a blue highlighter to show where the problem of the story is revealed. If this wasn't within the first three pages of text, text juggling and cutting are in order. Using that same blue highlighter, mark the place where the problem is solved. If it comes before pages twenty-eight and twenty-nine, revise to bring it closer to the end of your text. Circle dramatic moments in red. Are there enough? Where did they occur? If they're all close together or too far apart, can they be moved, expanded, or shortened? Then with an ordinary pen or pencil, go through your dummy story again and star places where some question or drama creates a page turn. Remember: These should come on every odd-numbered page. And last of all, the dummy will show if there's a satisfying wrap-up moment on page thirty-two. If you have that, draw yourself a smiley face.

Here's a sample page of one of my dummies, with corrections and changes for you to see.

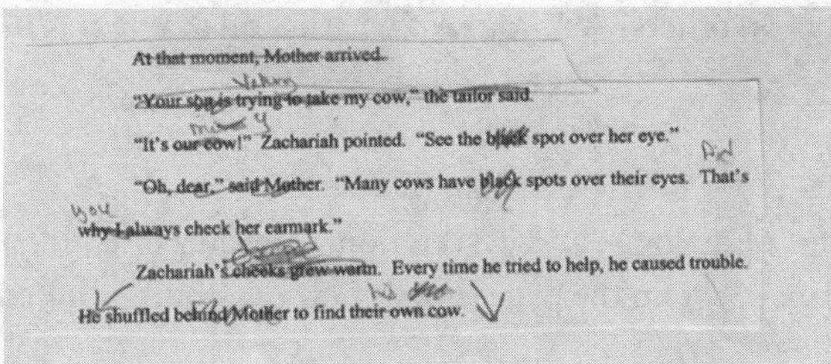

At that moment, Mother arrived.

"Your son is trying to take my cow," the tailor said.

"It's our cow!" Zachariah pointed. "See the black spot over her eye."

"Oh, dear," said Mother. "Many cows have black spots over their eyes. That's why I always check her earmark."

Zachariah's cheeks grew warm. Every time he tried to help, he caused trouble.

He shuffled behind Mother to find their own cow.

Pretty sloppy, isn't it?

A FEW FINAL WORDS

Your dummy doesn't have to be neat and pretty. It's only for you. Don't send it to an editor, but don't trash it. Save each dummy. Later, you can compare it to the published book. The layout may be the same or wildly different. That doesn't matter. Just make sure your story fits the picture-book format. Don't be a dummy—make a dummy!

ANN WHITFORD PAUL has published more than twenty picture books (including board books, early-readers, a poetry collection, plus a variety of fiction and nonfiction, rhymed and prose picture book, including the popular series that began with *If Animals Kissed Goodnight*). Many of her poems have appeared in anthologies and her essays have been published by several newspapers. She lives with her husband in Los Angeles and hopes you'll visit her website www.annwhitfordpaul.com. This essay is excerpted from *Writing Picture Books Revised and Expanded Edition* (Writer's Digest, 2018).

THE CURIOUSLY EFFECTIVE WAY TO BEAT PROCRASTINATION

An author of more than 60 books reveals how he follows his curiosity to beat writer's block.

by Michael La Ronn

"I know I need to be writing this novel, but…"

How many times have you found yourself thinking that? You know you should be writing, but you find yourself surfing the internet, watching cat videos, or worse—staring at the wall, thinking about your story.

Procrastination strikes even the most disciplined writers. Every colleague I know has at least one battle story about their war against procrastination. But is slacking off every now and again a bad thing?

In most cases, procrastination is not productive, but you can turn it into a force for good by adopting a curiosity mindset and practicing a hidden superpower I call "drifting."

HOW WRITER'S BLOCK LED TO A BREAKTHROUGH IN MY NOVEL

I discovered the curiously effective and surprising power of procrastination by accident. I was deep into a novel, and the words wouldn't come. No matter how long I sat in the chair or how hard I stared at the blinking cursor, I couldn't figure out what to write next.

I did the opposite of common wisdom: I stopped writing. I abandoned my manuscript for three days and promised myself that I would start writing again after the three days expired. I let myself "drift" until I found a way forward in the story.

What happened next was a lifelong lesson: Procrastination can be useful if you let it.

On the second night of no writing, my wife and I visited an upscale bakery that we had never been to before. The place captivated me the moment I walked in the door. I recall the scene vividly: mason jar lights with exposed filaments hanging from the ceiling, hipsters enjoying each other's company at reclaimed wood tables, the burnt aromatics of an exotic coffee, people eating croissants and bear claws, spoons clinking against mugs, a rainbow assortment of macarons neatly arranged in a display case on the counter, and so much more. I've only experienced sensory overload like this a handful of times in my life.

When I returned home, I knew that I had to write this bakery into my novel. More importantly, it turned out that this bakery was the very place I needed my heroine to visit. Bye-bye, writer's block!

Thirty minutes in a new place was all I needed to power through the rest of the novel. After publication, readers told me that they loved the bakery scene. In fact, they went out of their way to mention the bakery in their fan mail. The scene that readers loved most in the story was the direct result of procrastination.

What might have happened if I decided instead to force my will on my story instead of setting it aside for a few days? Sure, I would have finished the novel, but it would have taken a trajectory that might not have been as engaging to readers.

After that, I stopped being hard on myself for not being so focused during my writing sessions. I became a believer in the power of drifting.

WHAT IS DRIFTING?

Drifting is when you give in to your mind's curiosity urges. We are trained to believe that our writing sessions can't have any waste. No procrastination. No lost time. We believe we must remain disciplined at all costs.

That doesn't stop our minds from wandering. It's like driving a car down an icy road and skidding out of control; our instinct is to steer in the opposite direction to regain control, but the right thing to do is to steer into the skid. It's counterintuitive, but it works every time.

When you drift, you give your mind permission to do whatever it wants to fuel your creativity. Simply put, you let it be curious. When it starts skidding, you lean into it and see where you end up. You let yourself wander with no real purpose. You experience the world, live life to the fullest, and when you least expect it, inspiration strikes. What's unusual about drifting is that, unlike "waiting for the muse," you can train yourself to produce inspiration on demand.

Sometimes, your mind might wander to another writing project. Other times, it may lead you to places you never thought of, such as getting around to building your author website, which might inspire an idea for marketing your book, which might give you renewed excitement to pick up the story again. Follow your mind where it leads you, be faithful, keep observing the world with a writer's eye, and you might be surprised at what happens. Drifting is about trusting yourself and the process.

Drifting also takes courage. After all, I'm telling you to procrastinate, which is downright dangerous for some. It's easy to drift away constantly and never write, but proper use of this skill requires the discipline to return to your manuscript.

Just like I let myself drift into that bakery, you too can drift your way out of writer's block.

WORDS OF CAUTION!

Just because you set your manuscript aside when drifting, you still must keep your writer's brain active. Keep asking yourself: "What can I learn from this?"

Keeping a writer's journal or a digital notebook on a website like Evernote is helpful in capturing your thoughts and emotions in the moment.

Always ask how you can convert your drifting experiences into your work-in-progress (or future works). If you keep a lookout for inspiration, you're more likely to find it.

REFRAME WRITER'S BLOCK AS AN OPPORTUNITY TO DRIFT, NOT A THREAT

No one enjoys writer's block. When it arrives, we feel as if we've been inflicted with a terrible disease. I've heard many sayings in my writing career, but "I'm so glad I got writer's block today!" isn't one of them.

What if writer's block wasn't a scourge, but a clue? What if it was your inner writer sending you a loud signal that it needs help? Instead of saying, "Now I have to figure out how to break this writer's block," what if you asked, "How can I discover what my inner writer needs so we can move forward with the story and make it stronger?"

Then, drift. The great thing about drifting is that I always learn something that makes me a better writer. While I don't wish for writer's block, I never let it beat me. It always makes me stronger.

Writer's block is just an emotion. When you don't know how to process it, you procrastinate. Professional public speaker and author Mel Robbins calls procrastination a form of stress relief. We know we shouldn't be doing it, but we don't know how else to process the clues our mind is sending us, so we engage in unproductive behavior.

If you approach writer's block as an exciting puzzle to solve, you'll have an easier time processing it. If you can convert the initial feelings of frustration and channel them into feelings of curiosity as you drift, you may find that the writer's block disappears. If you're lucky, you might have better, more intense writing to show for it.

Recently, I was writing a novel set in Chicago. I wanted to make the city a character but felt that the Chicago parts needed more spice. My wife happened to be watching a reality television show where the season finale was set in Chicago. The contestants visited obscure landmarks, which was exactly the inspiration I needed. Thirty minutes and a page full of notes later, my story was stronger because I mixed serendipity with a curiosity mindset. And I had fun watching the show and spending time with my family, too.

That's why I believe writer's block is an opportunity to become a better writer. It's an invitation for you to embrace a curiosity mindset. Drifting is how you do that.

The longer I write, the more I am amazed by how much the writing life is about knowing yourself: your habits, your emotions, your quirks, your triggers. Until you learn them, you'll find yourself repeating patterns you can't see.

DO YOU KNOW THE THREE ROOT CAUSES OF WRITER'S BLOCK?

1. **LACK OF INSPIRATION:** Your creative well is dry and you need an infusion of inspiration.
2. **FEAR:** The inner critic is stomping on your dreams and manipulating you.
3. **LIFE CIRCUMSTANCES:** Sometimes life happens, and it can take us away from writing for a time, and that's okay.

When you understand the cause of the writer's block, you can select the proper strategy to defeat it. Drifting is a good strategy when you suffer from lack of inspiration.

When you learn the patterns, however, you can break them and build more productive habits. For example, I noticed that writer's block always strikes around the first 25 percent of the novel once the euphoria of starting a new book passes. Early in my career, I let that derail me, costing me weeks of productivity. Now I plan for it, which helps me beat potential slowdowns much faster.

PROCRASTINATION IS LIKE CHOLESTEROL

There is good procrastination and bad procrastination. We spend most of our time combating bad procrastination (as we should), but it's helpful to understand what good procrastination looks like.

Good procrastination is anything that leads to progress in your book. In my case, my two-day drift resulted in a breakthrough. Sure, I sacrificed two writing days, but they led to progress. And as my mother says, progress is progress!

Bad procrastination is anything that leads to or intensifies the influence of the "inner critic." You'll know bad procrastination by the internal thoughts that accompany it.

"I can't do this ..."

"Readers will never like this story ..."

"Another writer already published a book with my story idea! Maybe I should scratch this draft and start over ..."

"Other writers on social media are more productive and successful than me ..."

If your procrastination is accompanied by a healthy dose of self-doubt and fear, then you should probably sit in the chair and grind. Better yet, work on yourself emotionally so that you can minimize those feelings. The hardest challenges in the writing life are emotional, not physical. Master the emotional rollercoaster of writing and the entire universe is yours to explore.

Also beware of time. In my case, I only allowed myself a two-day drift. And those two days weren't a true break. I still kept my writer's hat on; I remained on the lookout for anything that would inspire me. You could say that I was actively procrastinating, ready to start writing again at a moment's notice if needed. At the end of the two days, I was prepared to resume writing, whether I found inspiration or not. That's the difference.

If I drifted for six months to find inspiration, then I wouldn't have written this article. Any progress I made in my novel would have been offset with an unfavorable passage of time, forgetting what happened in my story, and rusty writing skills. When you don't write for that long, writer's block is the least of your troubles.

This is why I believe drifting is best done in short bursts. Shorter drifting gives you the inspiration uplift without the negative downsides.

Also, it's worth noting that if you drift every time you write, you won't get anything done. I practice drifting on a regular basis yet have managed to write more than 60 books, so remember that discipline matters.

Think of drifting as a tool in your toolbox. It's not always useful, but it can be effective under the right circumstances.

HEEDING THE CALL: HOW TO DRIFT LIKE A PRO

Here are some ideas to invoke curiosity and drift your way out of writer's block.

Read a Book About Something New

Books are, in their purest form, ideas. Reading in your genre is a smart idea, but sometimes a worldview or philosophy unrelated to your story can inform your writing. For example, Hindu philosophy has inspired my writing in countless ways. I stumbled upon the works of the Hindu philosopher Swami Vivekananda during a drifting session, and his essays completely changed the way I see writing and fiction. That drifting session inspired many themes in future books.

Go to the library, visit a section you've never been to before, spin around until you get dizzy, hold up your finger, and check out the first book you touch. Read the book with an open mind and heart.

Consume Other Content

I can't tell you how many times a television show, movie, or video game inspired a scene in one of my novels. If you're feeling like the words won't come, spend an evening watching Netflix (with your writer's hat on!) and see what happens. Consuming content is one of the most reliable ways to get inspired.

Meet New People

Few things inspire like the rush of meeting someone new. For this reason, I tend to strike up conversations with random strangers, but I do it more when I have writer's block.

Everyone has a unique story, and they're willing to share it. Exposing ourselves to people with different backgrounds helps us become more empathetic as writers and create more engaging characters.

New Experiences

There are probably places you pass every day without thinking about it. It could be a park, a new grocery store, or a street you've never been down before. Maybe you notice a flyer at your local grocery store about a free cooking class they're offering this weekend, or you see an ad on TV about a music festival downtown. Even if you have some hesitation, step outside your comfort zone.

Travel

Traveling is a great way to drift because it combines the above categories. Vacations are notoriously difficult to plan, especially if you've never been to the place you're visiting. Even if you make strict plans, it seems like the best experiences almost always happen because of chance encounters and last-minute decisions.

The next time you're ready to drift, pick one of these categories and get ready for the inspiration to flow!

ENJOY THE RIDE

The distance between you and the end of your manuscript is never a straight line. A book is a journey, and no book is the same. Every story makes different demands of the writer. It's up to you to determine how to navigate the obstacles.

No writer I know can sit in a chair and be a writing machine every minute of every day. We're only human. Treat writer's block as a recurring part of the writing process. Teach yourself to drift and enjoy the journey.

I have a friend who loves to go on road trips. Once, she turned a six-hour trip into a nine-hour trip because she insisted on stopping at every tourist attraction between St. Louis and Des Moines, Iowa. She'd stop for pictures at every windmill, historical landmark, and birthplace of a famous person. The passing time never bothered her because she was living in the moment and making memories. That's how writing can be, too, if you adopt a curiosity mindset. It can be forever fun.

Stay curious and drift like a pro. The writing life is never easy, but it's a lot more manageable if you're having fun. If anything, when you're at a book signing and your adoring fans ask how you beat writer's block, you can smile, give them a sly wink, and tell them it was because you procrastinated.

MICHAEL LA RONN (MichaelLaRonn.com) is the Amazon bestselling author of more than 60 science-fiction and fantasy novels and self-help books for writers. He hosts the popular weekly YouTube channel "Author Level Up" (AuthorLevelUp.com), where he publishes writing advice videos and writing app tutorials. This article first appeared in the May/June 2021 issue of *Writer's Digest*.

JACQUELINE WOODSON

The bestselling National Ambassador for Young People's Literature talks character building, confronting controversial subjects, and the real-world importance of books for kids and teens.

by Jera Brown

Jacqueline Woodson writes about issues that make her feel powerless.

Most recently, that means police brutality as well as mass deportation and its impact on American families. The author of more than 30 books for children, middle-grade, and adult readers, Woodson writes to better understand difficult subjects, but also with the high-minded goal of provoking tangible change—something she has believed literature capable of since she herself was a young reader.

To Woodson, the power of literature comes from creating what Dr. Rudine Sims Bishop—pioneering Ohio State University emeritus professor of children's literature—refers to as "mirrors" and "windows." Says Woodson: Readers "need mirrors to see reflections of themselves in literature, which is reaffirming, but they also need a window to see how the 'Other' lives."

Woodson has used her own background as a black queer woman and her ability to write rich, diverse char-acters to expand the "mirrors and windows" available for children and adults, with an extensive body of work comprising poetry, memoir, fiction, picture books, and cultural criticism.

Among her many accolades, 2014's *Brown Girl Dreaming*, a memoir in verse (using poetic forms instead of traditional paragraphs), was named a Newbery Honor Book and earned Woodson her second Coretta Scott King Award, along with a National Book Award for Young People's Literature. She's the author of four additional Newbery Honor Books: *The Evolution of Calpurnia Tate*, *After Tupac and D Foster*, *Feathers* and *Show Way*. The memoir *Another Brooklyn*, released in 2016, scored Woodson her fourth National Book Award nomination.

In 2018, Woodson began a two-year term for the Library of Congress as National Ambassador for Young People's Literature—an honor previously held by such accomplished authors as Katherine Paterson, Kate DiCamillo, and, most recently, Gene Luen Yang. Established in 2008, the role is designed to raise awareness about the impact of literature on lifelong literacy, starting with the development of young readers.

This August (2018), Woodson is releasing two more books: *Harbor Me* is a middle-grade novel about a group of fifth- and sixth-graders whose families struggle with poverty, deportation and incarceration. *The Day You Begin* is a picture book illustrated by Mexican artist Rafael López that narrates the first-person account of Woodson's great-grandfather—the only black boy in his classroom.

Woodson took a brief respite from her busy schedule to talk with WD about her body of work and the importance of books for kids and teens.

You've said when you feel powerless toward something, you write about it. What exactly do you mean by that?

My writing is always [prompted by] this whole series of questions that I'm asking myself: *Why does this happen? Why does that person behave that way? What is the impact of that behavior? How is that person going to change? What's going to be the catalyst to their change?*

This new book, *Harbor Me*, is about kids dealing with a number of things, including police brutality and someone's father getting deported. And for me, the question is: *What happens when this happens? How do we keep moving forward and what are the tools we have?* [In] figuring that out in the narrative, I'm also figuring it out in my real life, and that's what makes it healing and bearable.

Harbor Me has many protagonists. How do you effectively portray such a diverse set of characters?

Oh my goodness, they surprise me sometimes. The main part of the process was [just] writing. There were holes in their lives, and there were holes in their characters, and the rewriting and the filling in—I think of it the way artists might think of their art process. You're adding layers and layers and layers until your character makes sense, and then you're adding more layers until your character has their metamorphosis. So with each of these characters, it's that same question that is part of the hero's journey, which is: *What is their original world? What is it saying?*

The first character we meet is Esteban. His ordinary world was the world with his mother, father, and sister—and then one day his father doesn't come home. Then he's no longer in that ordinary world because his father has been taken by Immigration and Customs Enforcement. What's going to happen to him? Who are going to be his allies? I just start kind of flushing it out with those questions and see where they take me.

As a YA writer, you often write about "controversial" topics, such as addiction and interracial relationships. Early in your career, you learned from none other than Judy Blume that your books were being banned or challenged by parents in some school systems as a consequence. Is that still the case? How did that make you feel?

I'm sure my books are being challenged all over the place, but it's not like I would know that, right? It's not like someone's calling me up and saying, "Yo, we challenged your book in Waco, Texas." I know that it's a place I never get invited to do a school visit. I've never been invited to Brigham Young University, which has this huge children's literature component. I'm sure that's about race or sexuality or gender—who knows? You don't know how and when you're being challenged until someone like Judy Blume says, "Oh yeah, you're being challenged."

I get asked a lot about my literature in terms of the controversy of it, which, it's not controversial to me. I'm writing about everyday life and real issues and real people—I mean real characters who are trying to find their footing. And I think the thing that is called "controversial" is the thing that makes other people uncomfortable. I'm not uncomfortable writing about this stuff. I write because I think it's so necessary. I would be uncomfortable *not* writing about it.

Do you think writers with marginalized identities or marginalized stories need a unique sense of bravery and boldness in order to make it [in publishing]?

I think every writer needs some bravery and some boldness, and a little bit of a unicorn in them to make it. Eighty percent of writing is about persevering, and when your book bombs, not saying, "I quit," but saying, "Okay, that book bombed, but I have plenty of other stories locked and loaded for my career." You can't go into this fearfully and you can't go into this with a chip on your shoulder saying, "I have a right to have my book make *The New York Times* bestseller list in its first week of publishing." It's not going to happen for 99 percent of writers. You have to go in with integrity, and with faith, and you have to go into this willing to work really hard to get your book out there.

And it's a balance! I mean, I look on Twitter and I see people [where] every single post is about their new book. I'm like, *Stop it already; you're going to drown your book*! Because writing isn't just about writing, it's about the social context in which you're writing. It's about paying attention to the world, and if you publish a book and it's just about your book, you're already failing the rest of the world.

What advice do you have for YA writers tackling topics that might make others uncomfortable?

I think the most dangerous thing a writer can do is think about how a reader is going to react to their writing, because you never know. You don't know the reader, and if you're going to self-censor, if you're so busy thinking about the audience, who are you writing for? The first person you should be writing for is yourself. If you start out thinking, "What does the reader need?" you're going to fail. You're going to be wrong.

That's often the advice I hear for adult writers, but assumed it'd be different for those writing for kids.

Well, the thing about writing for young people is ... you have to know your audience. And I think that's something that might be a little bit different.

If you don't know that when you're writing a middle-grade novel, your protagonists can't be 17 going on 40, then you don't know this genre. You have to know if you're writing about kids in fifth grade, your protagonist needs to be 10 or 11. But does that mean knowing your reader *specifically*? Not so much.

Do you read differently when you're writing middle-grade versus YA or adult novels?

Yes and no. When I'm writing for adults and picture books, I read a lot more poetry. When I'm writing for young adults, that's when I catch up on all my friends' books, and then when I'm writing for middle-grades, I'm usually not reading at all. I want to get into [my own] world, and when reading other people's middle-grade books, it's going to take me into *their* world. Or [if] I'm reading adult stuff, it's going to make my [middle-grade] characters sound too old.

Do you have any advice for writers interested in publishing both YA and adult books?

I think people should just write what they want to write. A lot of times [we] think that we have [to have] the golden elixir that's going to be the answer. The only answer I can give is to *write the dang book*. Write two books at once if that's what's coming to you; write four books. But this is a process, and I'm sure writers have heard this a lot of times, and I think sometimes it's hard to hear, but it is a process. And I've seen so many people who want to know about publishing before they even put pen to paper.

I used to send out short stories and poetry back in the '90s, and we had to send it out by regular mail. But the minute the rejection came back, I always had the next envelope waiting. *Paris Review* rejected it? Let me try *The New Yorker.* Because I just wanted to keep it off my desk, and while it was out there, I wasn't sitting there not writing. I was working on the next thing.

As National Ambassador of Young People's Literature, one of your goals is to spend time with kids in underserved communities. What communities are you focusing on?

I'm hoping to visit a lot of young people in juvenile detention centers and underserved schools. Next week I'm going to Alabama, and I've done some Skyping with women in prison. ... I've been to one school that was primarily autistic kids. I was just in Philadelphia and went to a number of Title I schools and community centers, including one that was [for] adults and children. I've been home like three days, so I feel like I should be able to list more places. It's been such a blur: a lot of young people. I mean, it's been fabulous, and it's [also] been some work.

What do those interactions look like, and what have you learned from these visits?

I just love [the kids] so much! They're still very passionate about reading. Part of my [National Ambassador] platform is [the idea that] Reading = Hope × Change. The gist of it was to get people in rooms together to talk. And I've relearned how interested young people are in engaging and being heard. That gets reconfirmed every time I step into a room with them. A lot of times people think young people are just so into their devices and kind of checked out. One place I went to had a large population of Muslim kids, and so a lot of girls wore hijabs. Just listening to them talk about their spiritual lives and their academic lives was amazing, and [they asked] me about my own spiritual life as a writer and what that means.

What role do you believe literature should play in the lives of young readers?

I think the role that it plays in the lives of young readers, and the role that it can play in the lives of *all* readers, is to create conversation: to be able to engage across lines of socioeconomics, race, gender, and sexuality, and to be the jumping-off point for that conversation. A lot of times people are scared to have very hard conversations, or what they *perceive* to be very hard conversations, and what literature can do is introduce those conversations through characters and make it a safer entry into talking about stuff. When people feel passionate about good books, they want to share them. They want to engage in discussions around them. It also changes people. It stops the routines.

You have two kids. How has your writing changed since becoming a parent? For instance, do you find yourself writing with them in mind, or do you see characters differently?

My kids make me laugh, so I think my writing has gotten funnier at points. I took myself very seriously B.C. (Before Children), and now I definitely feel like having a 16-year-old daughter … a lot of *Another Brooklyn* was inspired by me watching her negotiate the world. I remember my own self at 16, but my kids definitely gave me feedback whether I asked for it or not. And they make me laugh in a way that shows me that young people are finding their way and laughter comes to them. It's not all just brooding.

Is there any parting wisdom you'd like to give aspiring writers?

I know every writer says this, but you can't be a writer if you don't read. It's really important to read the same book again and again and study how other writers do stuff. And of course, read in your genre. You don't know how many people who aspire to write for young people have come to me and said, "Well, I can't be bothered with reading those books."

JERA BROWN is a freelance writer and columnist for *Rebellious Magazine*. Selections from their memoir have been published in *The Rumpus* and *Big Muddy*. This interview was previously published in the September 2018 issue of *Writer's Digest*.

CASSANDRA CLARE

The YA sensation unveils the practical magic behind her bestselling Shadowhunter series and demystifies the secrets of writing for different age groups and fostering representation in fiction.

by Jess Zafarris

Cassandra Clare wrote her first published novel in a closet. That is, in one of those "cozy" New York City spaces, wherein the bed doubles as an office chair and the desk looks suspiciously like a windowsill. At the time, she worked the night shift as a copy editor for the *National Enquirer*, spending daylight hours in her cramped apartment, cranking out chapters, researching agents, writing queries, reworking her manuscript and, eventually, signing a contract for publication of the soon-to-be *New York Times* bestselling YA novel *City of Bones*.

That book would prove to be the first of several bestsellers in a multi-series collection of 12 novels (and counting)—plus several short story anthologies—known as the Shadowhunter Chronicles: tales from an urban fantasy world brimming with angels, demons, warlocks, vampires, and faeries, plus the enemies and allies thereof. Of those, perhaps the best-known series within the broader universe is The Mortal Instruments sextet. Clare's follow up, the Infernal Devices prequel trilogy, harks back to the Victorian Era, and the December 2018 release of *Queen of Air and Darkness* completes The Dark Artifices, a sequel trilogy to Mortal Instruments. Fans of Clare can expect to further explore the Shadowhunter universe in a new trilogy, The Eldest Curses, the first of which was released in Spring 2019.

Despite her early successes, it wasn't until the stellar release of her *third* book that the YA superstar was finally able to ditch her tabloid gig and embrace novel-writing full time. Today, the 45-year-old's books have sold over 50 million copies worldwide in more than 35 languages and have been adapted into film, television, and two manga series.

Clare, whose real name is Judith Lewis, pens her books like clockwork: She's published at least one Shadowhunter book per year since 2007, with additional short stories and collaborative works interspersed among them. Often, she says, the processes overlap such that she's plotting out one book while copy editing its predecessor.

Many of her coauthored works, like The Bane Chronicles novellas with Sarah Rees Brennan and Maureen Johnson, belong to the Shadowhunter universe, while the five-book middle-grade Magisterium series with Holly Black, author of The Spiderwick Chronicles, ventures into an entirely new world.

In conversation with WD, Clare shares her thoughts on plotting a multi-part series, venturing out into middle-grade, collaborating with other writers, and more.

Your world is so intricate. Tell me about your plotting process. How do you lay out your narratives?

I'm an outliner. I know there are people who are plotters and people who are more pantsers, but I am definitely a plotter. I need to know what is going to happen in a story. So I generally start with what I call a "macro-plot," in which I sort of take the story from Point A, where it begins, to the end, and try to lay out the significant moments. And I think pacing is a good way of looking at it, because I'm looking at the moments where the story turns.

For me, there are basically five points where the story turns: You've got the beginning of the story. Then you've got the inciting incident, something that changes things for the character so that the story [takes off]. And that'll be a realization or an event: a birth, a death, something that causes you to answer the question of, *Why now?—Why are you telling this story now, from this point?* And then you have your midpoint, where the story often reverses itself or changes and you learn new information. You usually have the low point of the story where things seem lost for your characters. And then you have your denouement.

I try to plot those out, and that forms a spine on which everything else is built. Then I'll do what I call a "micro-plot," in which I actually plot out each chapter and what is happening in terms of the characters and the arcs and the events that are occurring in order to create a full story.

Obviously those things will change. They're not going to stay completely the same as I move through the story; some things will work, some things won't work. But for me, it helps to have that as a guide. And I think that does help me keep these books, which are quite sprawling and involve a lot of characters, as tightly plotted as possible.

Most of your books take place in the same universe, but you didn't write the series in chronological order. How do you ensure consistency and continuity when you're writing these novels that jump around in time?

I know. I keep thinking, *Why did I do that?* But that's me. I try to be disciplined in my outlining and whatnot, but sometimes it's a case of "follow your bliss"—I do the stories that I'm the most excited about at the time. And it just happened that, when I was finishing up Mortal Instruments, the thing I was most excited about was doing a historical. I had this idea and I loved it, and I wanted to do it. So I jumped back in time and did The Infernal Devices, which is set in 1878. Then I jumped *forward* in time and did The Dark Artifices. And now I'm jumping back to 1903 and doing [a new series called] The Last Hours.

It's imperative for me that I have a bible. I think they often call it that in TV writing as well, where everything is noted down. You know, the genealogy of all the families, what things and how they work, the rules of magic. The location of all the major known places in the books. I refer back to that. If somebody ever stole it, I would be so doomed.

The dialogue in your books feels so natural. Do you have any advice for crafting strong conversations?

Listen to the way people actually talk. To an extent, all written dialogue is stylized where we take out the *ums* and the *ifs* and the *sort ofs* and the minimizing language. And remember that there is a rhythm. That the back-and-forth of talking is rhythmic: Somebody gives information, somebody else reacts. You have to get that pattern down. I love writing dialogue. It's one of my favorite things.

When I was writing Infernal Devices, one thing that was helpful to me was sitting down and listening to audiobooks and plays written in the Victorian Era, so I could get the cadence of Victorian dialogue and the way that they talked. I did it as a sort of immersion thing. For about six months, I only read books, watched movies, and listened to plays that were written in the specific time period my characters were operating in, so that I was sort of walking around thinking in that kind of language.

You have a very dedicated fan base. Have you used their feedback to shape what you've written?

Definitely—when they give me feedback on certain characters or things that they love. I'm very interactive with my fans, and they're very interactive with me. For instance, they absolutely love the character Magnus Bane in The Mortal Instruments series.

He's an immortal warlock, and I thought, *There's no reason he couldn't be in The Infernal Devices*, so I put him in. People love him so much and it was great to see him at a different stage of his life. It was in large part fan feedback that caused me to include him as a significant character in that other series.

That character—Magnus—is gay, correct? And beyond him, diversity is core to your books. Why is having a diverse cast of characters important to you, and how do you avoid falling victim to stereotypes when you're writing these characters?

[Magnus's boyfriend] Alec is based on a friend of mine I knew when I was younger who committed suicide because he was gay and his family did not accept that. Alec was a way of giving him—though he wasn't around—a story that he would have loved. He, like me, was a big fan of science fiction and fantasy, a big fan of stories and adventurers and kickass fighters. To see a character who was like him, who was this badass demon fighter and got to have all these adventures, would have meant the world to him. What I thought when I created Alec was, *This will hopefully be something that can mean a lot to people who want to see themselves reflected.* There's not enough representation across all the boards.

And in the same vein, I've tried to create many other characters that people can see themselves in. There are autistic Shadowhunter characters. There are trans characters. There are characters with different body types. There are characters of different ability, and all these characters of different races and ethnicities. Being a Shadowhunter—being this cool sort of hero—isn't restricted to any one kind of person.

In terms of avoiding stereotypes, it's something that you have to keep an eye out for. When I create characters that are not like me, I always use sensitivity readers. When I was writing, for instance, the trans character Diana, who is in The Dark Artifices, I met with many trans women who live in my area and talked to them extensively about how to build her character, how to know exactly what to avoid. That was my first question. I sat down [and asked], "What do you not want to see in this character? What do you not want me to express?" And then when the book was done, I had trans readers give me their feedback and changed it accordingly.

Mortal Instruments is often referred to as a YA "urban fantasy" series, but you've said in the past that it has also been categorized as YA romance. How do you feel about those genre designations?

They're marketing designations. When I first sold my book, it was sold as urban fantasy. And that's what we looked at it as. And then *Twilight* came out and suddenly all of these publishers were pushing books toward being marketed as romance. There is romance in The Mortal Instruments, absolutely. I love romance and I love writing it, so that's not a problem. There were definitely books that I saw out there that were not romance that were sort of shoehorned into this category. Then we got *The Hunger Games*, and everything was marketed as a dystopia.

One thing about having a career that's now spanned about a decade is that no longer happens to me. In the early days of my books, my publisher did a lot of designing kind of romantic-looking marketing for them—part of that paranormal romance marketing boom. I'm glad that has faded away. Now the books are marketed as their own thing.

One of the things I love about YA, actually, is that it's not broken down into those categories [as much as adult fiction]. It's all together in the bookstore. So you write a mystery and then a romance and then a science-fiction book, they're all going to be shelved together. But if you're an adult author, all of those books would be shelved separately in the bookstore. YA encourages intersectional fiction. It doesn't matter if your book is difficult to shelve. If you've written a science-fiction romance, you don't have to worry about where it's going to end up.

How does your process change when you're writing with co-authors?

I've written with a bunch of coauthors who are friends of mine—Robin Wasserman, Sarah Rees Brennan, Maureen Thompson—on the anthology series we've done, which are short stories set in my [Shadowhunter] world. I was influenced to do this by classic urban fantasy, books like the Thieves' World [anthologies] I grew up reading where groups of writers would get together and write different stories all set in the same world. This was something that I grew up thinking of as completely normal, and then I realized it wasn't something that people were still doing. I was like, "Let's bring it back."

That was interesting because these are all people who are very familiar with my world and my characters. We have workshops on my books together. They definitely know what they're doing. So we would sit there and kind of back-and-forth these ideas. It was almost like working in a writer's room on a television show, where you all know the characters and you all know the world and you're sort of tossing ideas back and forth—that could happen or this other thing could happen.

And then when I wrote with Holly Black, and we created Magisterium, which is a five-book series for middle-grade, it was totally different. We had to build the world from the ground up, *together*. It wasn't my world; it was *our* world. We were both equally responsible for building all the pieces of the magic system. And I didn't have any veto power. With the anthologies, I'm kind of like the showrunner because it's my world. But with this, Holly and I had equal say. It's a different balance. They're both fun in different ways.

Did you find writing for middle-grade more difficult?

I was worried that I wouldn't have a middle-grade voice. That was how the whole discussion with Holly started—I was reading Percy Jackson in an airport. I said [to Holly], "I have this idea that I think would be a great middle-grade book but I don't know if I have a middle-grade voice." She wrote The Spiderwick Chronicles, which are classics, and she sort of sat up and said, "I have a middle-grade voice."

We decided then [that] we could write this together. When we sat down to write the beginning—because we were going to use it to sell the publishers—she plopped it down in front of me and said, "Let's see your middle-grade voice." I was like, "You know, this is like teaching someone to swim by throwing them into the pool." But I started writing and she was like, "This is great. This is exactly what middle-grade is like." I was like, "Oh, thank god."

I think I got there not because I have an inherent ability to do this, but because I'd read a ton of middle-grade before I had sat down to start. If you want to write in a genre you're not used to, the best thing you can do is sit down and spend a couple of weeks reading in that genre.

JESS ZAFARRIS was the content director for Writer's Digest. She is now an audience engagement editor at Adweek. This article was previously published in the February 2019 issue of *Writer's Digest*.

N. K. JEMISIN

The master fantasy world-builder reveals her secrets to success on Patreon and speculates on how the imagination might test-drive our future.

by Jera Brown

N. K. Jemisin wants to be a "storyteller of a writer." It's an ambition she claims not to have mastered, but many who have lost themselves in Jemisin's tales of captive gods and stone eaters are sure to disagree.

Through her three epic fantasy series (the Inheritance trilogy, the Dreamblood duology and the Broken Earth trilogy) as well as dozens of short stories and a novella, Jemisin has become known as a master world creator, each world brought to life through their detailed histories and unique mythology. And even though Jemisin's stories are set in universes where magic is commonplace, Jemisin's writing feels pressingly relevant to our own world. Her stories are based on flawed power structures and deeply held prejudices with devastating consequences. There's also hope—a constant theme through Jemisin's latest book, *How Long 'til Black Future Month*. The short story collection, published in November 2018, imagines futures for people of color like herself.

Storytelling is not just about the tales themselves, but also the connection between the storyteller and their audience. Outside of her work, Jemisin cultivates a bond with her readers through means such as her writing groups and outspoken activism in the fantasy and science fiction communities. This bond has paid off. In 2016, Jemisin quit her day job to focus on writing full-time with the generous support of her fans through the Patreon platform.

Among Jemisin's accolades, her debut novel, *The Hundred Thousand Kingdoms,* was short-listed for the James Tiptree Jr. Award, earned the Sense of Gender Award from the Japanese Association for Gender, Fantasy, and Science Fiction, and a Locus Award for Best

First Novel. In 2018, when *The Stone Sky* (the final book in Jemisin's Broken Earth trilogy) won the Best Novel Hugo award, Jemisin became the first author to win three Hugo Best Novel awards in a row. The novel also earned a Nebula Award for Best Novel and a Locus award for Best Fantasy Novel.

Jemisin spoke to *Writer's Digest* about her relationship to her readers and how she creates other worlds.

You were able to move into writing full time thanks to the support of your fans via Patreon. Can you tell us about making that decision?

It was not my decision 100 percent. I liked my day job [as a career counselor and academic advisor], and I really didn't want to give the job up. But at the time, my mother was ill and deteriorating. And my writing career had become more than full time. *The Fifth Season* came out and sold like gangbusters, which is great. But it meant that I immediately started getting a deluge of interview requests, and when you have a nine-to-five job, you can only do interviews between 5:30 and seven, and you've got to eat somewhere in there, and write on top of that.

Some things had started to give, and the things that had started to give were my health and my sanity. It was to the point where the only reason I hadn't quit already was because I was afraid of the finances of the writer's life, because I had done that before. Back at the beginning of my career, I had taken about a year-and-a-half off after I got the contract for the Inheritance trilogy. I discovered that I did not function well not having structure, not having people to interact with other than family, not having a purpose or sense of fulfillment. Because the thing about my day job was helping real people in real time and working with marginalized kids.

So given the stress that I was under, either I was going to break or I had to do something. That was when I decided to try Patreon.

What was that experience like?

Honestly, I didn't think it was going to work. There were some popular authors and artists who were making a great deal of money through Patreon, but I was just a midlist author. At the time, the Dreamblood series was the only thing that I had the royalty statement for, and I knew the sales of the last book of the series were not fantastic. So I was like, *If I do this, am I going to end up on the street?* That was the fear. I launched it on a Friday afternoon around 5:00 thinking nobody's going to pay any attention and by the end of the weekend, it was fully funded, and I was quitting my job.

Terror was the feeling that I had beforehand going into it and shock afterward. I still am making more than my initial goal of $3,000 a month, which was just enough to cover my rent and health insurance (at least before Trump, that was enough to cover my health insurance).

What advice do you have for other writers considering pursuing fan-based funding?

First and foremost, you do have to be a known person. I've seen friends who were writers that didn't have any books out attempting it, and it doesn't usually go well. The sense that I get from the people who contribute to my Patreon is that they do so out of a sense of personal relationship. They've read my books, and they feel like they know me on some level. And, to a degree, they do, because I put a lot of myself into my books.

They want to contribute to the writer that they've seen already and make sure that that writer produces more work. It's not just an altruistic thing on their part; it's a desire for more of the same.

So if you are a writer who's got some stuff out there and feel like you've built even a small audience, then it can be useful for you. You're not necessarily going to get rent and insurance money, but you are very likely going to get enough to cover a few utility bills. Even just $200 a month can make difference because everybody's living paycheck to paycheck. People should just manage their expectations going into it.

Make sure your story doesn't get too detailed. When you're explaining to people what you need, you don't want them to start, like, trying to work out your budget for you. I've seen mostly women feeling uncomfortable asking about money and so they literally delineate every single line of what they would spend XYZ on, and because they are working in a patriarchal environment, men jump in and start nitpicking how they're spending the money. When you go and look at men's Patreon [profiles], they're not offering you their life story. They're literally saying, "I need X for Y," and that's all you need to say.

What do your supporters expect in return?

You owe your readers whatever you've promised them. Once a month, I post an original vignette or a short story based on the world of the books that I've written so far. But you do have to deliver on that.

Now the readers can be reasonable about it; when I tell my readers I am deep in deadline hell and can't produce the thing that I told them I was going to try and produce for a while, for example.

The people I've seen have trouble with it are the ones that are not able to deliver on anything, and people will vote with their dollars for that.

In the introduction to your newest book, *How Long 'til Black Future Month,* you explained that you write "proof of concept" stories to "test drive potential novel worlds." Once the concept seems viable, where do you go from there?

If you read "Stone Hunger," [from *How Long 'til Black Future Month*] and then read the Broken Earth series, you would see where I did not like the way that "Stone Hunger" depicted the magical form orogeny. In that short story, it was very "sense specific." The character thought of everything in terms of the taste of food, and that wasn't going to work, because I wanted it to be effectively a science that had gone wrong.

Once I finish the proof-of-concept story and have sent it to people and have seen how they react to it, then I decide from there what I need to change or refine in order to make the world building work for a novel. What that usually means is that I simply start writing. I start doing test chapters to see what voices work best. I tried many voices with the Broken Earth until the second person thing just kind of clicked and seemed like the right voice, and that's a purely instinctual thing.

And, as I went forward, I realized that the concept of the magic from the short story wasn't going to work, but the rest of the world was fine.

You took a year off of novel writing to focus on short stories. The process improved your longer fiction by teaching you about the "quick hook and the deep character" and by giving you "space to experiment with unusual plots and story forms." How did you learn to trust whether your experimental forms were working?

Nearly all of the short stories [in *How Long 'til Black Future Month*] were run through one writing group or another. I didn't do a lot of experimental stuff to begin with, because I didn't know what the hell I was doing, and because I didn't even really know how to read experimental stuff at first. That was partly what that year was about. One of the magazines that I read during that year was *Strange Horizons*, for example, which does a lot of wide-ranging styles, everything from the very didactic to slipstream or interstitial, and a lot of new weird stuff. So that helped me learn how to read it, and then I finally felt more willing to try and write it.

In your blog and when you speak publicly, you frequently mention your readers.

Well, we're storytellers. Storytellers work with an audience. That's normal, isn't it?

I'd hope so. I do think that many writers seem to go off into their own world and are less interested in that dialogue and more interested in just presenting something.

Well, that's their personal choice, and not everybody feels comfortable with it. I get it. To me though, I've always wanted to be a storyteller. When I was a teenager, I used to babysit kids, and I would tell them stories to entertain them. I've traveled to lots of different places in the world. I've seen storytellers, and I've always admired the hell out of them. It's a different art form from writing. It is an art form that I have nowhere near mastered, but I try to be a storyteller of a writer and to me that's what it's supposed to be. But everyone's mileage varies, I guess.

In your acceptance speech for your latest Hugo Award, you explain, "As this genre finally, however grudgingly, acknowledges that the dreams of the marginalized matter, and that all of us have a future, so will the world." Do you believe that speculative fiction has the power to change society?

I didn't used to think so, and then I started to realize, first off that I was underestimating it, and then second of all that other people had already done that calculation and were using it for evil. It sounds kind of corny, but I started to realize it when right-wingers tried to take over fandom. When you started trying to take over every bit of media, and you suddenly see Nazis in video games and comic books trying their damnedest to squish out people who are different from young, straight, white boys, and harassing and trying to dox them, there's a reason for that.

I don't necessarily think it's a one-for-one relationship. I don't think that I'll write a book and it'll change the world. But I do tend to think that the things we are capable of imagining and believing are our future are influenced by all of the media that we consume.

Growing up, I had a really hard time imagining a future for myself and for other Black people because when you looked at science fiction, you did not see Black people in the future. There had been some kind of unspoken apocalypse that wiped us all out, and Asians, and everybody else too. Certainly that's not what the creators of those works intended to convey, but that was what their work did convey by their exclusion.

People often point out—and I don't know how true this is—but one of the reasons that America became comfortable enough with the idea of a Black man and the presidency to elect Obama was because, in TV and film, presidents had been Black for quite some time. So we pursue in reality the things that we're capable of imagining and those of us who are in industries or fields that play with imagination have a responsibility to depict futures that are for everyone. And I think that if we can manage to start doing that, then it makes it easier for people in the present day who are trying to influence policy to say, "Look, this is just like in *Star Trek*, we can do blah, blah, blah."

Is there anything else you'd like to convey to other writers?

The industry is changing in some good ways. It's still got a lot of the old blind spots, and it's still struggling to fully embrace futures and mythologies other than what it's familiar with, and that's not entirely surprising. Business has always been reactive rather than proactive. Artists may sometimes have to go outside of traditional channels in order to get our vision realized, but I do like the fact that more people now have the ability to get their work out there.

People encouraged you to self-publish after the *Killing Moon*—your first novel that landed you an agent—didn't find a publisher, but you wanted the book to be in libraries ... Is the only channel other than traditional press self-publishing?

There's small press publishing, but small press publishing also doesn't get you in the library. But you decide on the publishing method that satisfies what it is that you want. A lot of people simply want to make the maximum amount of money possible. For them, self-publishing is perfect because they can control how much they spend on production and marketing. And there's no nobody else kind of like taking chunks out of that profit. They're willing to pay in time for that flexibility. I am not willing to pay in time. Time is my most precious resource, not money.

JERA BROWN is a freelance writer and columnist for *Rebellious Magazine*. Selections from their memoir-in-progress have been published in *The Rumpus* and *Big Muddy*. This interview appeared in the May/June 2019 issue of *Writer's Digest*.

LEIGH BARDUGO

The bestselling author talks finding YA fantasy stardom and why, if pursuing a dream, you're always on the right track.

by Baihley Gentry

Leigh Bardugo has always written the stories she wanted to write.

When querying her debut, *Shadow and Bone*—in which she introduced readers to a Czarist Russia-inspired world where individuals called Grisha have the mystical ability to manipulate matter—Bardugo was faced with a publishing-industry reality. Although young adult novels were popular at the time, and her premise was unique and compelling, no literary agents seemed interested in epic or high fantasy books for young readers.

She forged ahead anyway.

"I knew very little about the market. I learned that many [agents] would not even entertain the idea of that kind of book," she says. "It's wise to know what's out there, [but don't] let that hinder you. If you have an idea, pursue it. [Think] about things that make your story a story that only you could tell—those are the things that will stand out."

The strength of that story did eventually resonate with a rep, and the series was sold in a three-book deal in 2010. Within a week of its release in 2012, *Shadow and Bone* sky-rocketed to the top of *The New York Times* bestseller list—as did her six books after that: 2013's *Siege and Storm* and 2014's *Ruin and Rising*, which rounded out the Grisha trilogy; 2015's *Six of Crows* and 2016's *Crooked Kingdom*, a "heist-con" duology Bardugo likens to "*Ocean's 11* meets *Game of Thrones*"; and her two latest stand-alones in 2017: *The Language of Thorns*, her first short story collection, and *Wonder Woman: Warbringer*, about the superhero's teen years.

In sum, her books have sold more than 1 million copies combined internationally, and have earned such accolades as RT Reviewers Choice Awards in 2012 and 2015, and multiple starred reviews from *Publishers Weekly*, *Kirkus Reviews* and *School Library Journal*. Bardugo regularly writes short stories for Tor.com, and she has appeared in various anthologies, including *Last Night a Superhero Saved My Life* with notable names like Jodi Picoult and Neil Gaiman, and *Slasher Girls & Monster Boys* alongside Jonathan Maberry and Kendare Blake.

Despite the impressive trajectory of her career, the path from aspiring author to bestseller was a circuitous one.

Born in Jerusalem and raised in Southern California, Bardugo's lifelong aspiration to be a writer led her to earn a degree in journalism from Yale. While struggling for years to finish a first draft of a novel ("I didn't know yet that I was an outliner, and how badly I needed structure in order to work"), she took jobs in copywriting, advertising, and as a Hollywood makeup and special effects artist.

It wasn't until she brushed off "some pretty wonky ideas" espoused by media, TV, and film about what it meant to produce creative work that Bardugo was able to embrace a "terrible, messy, ugly first draft." That experience taught her some thing valuable: "Let go of the idea that somehow you can outsmart a first draft," she says. "Because I have never met anybody who can."

The YA fantasy maestro took a break from promoting *The Language of Thorns* and *Wonder Woman: Warbringer* to talk world-building, personal perseverance and more.

The runaway success of a debut can put a lot of pressure on subsequent follow-ups. How did you manage to cope with that so gracefully?

When a book lists, there's the illusion of runaway success. My [first book] listed, but it's not as if you hit *The New York Times* bestseller list and all of a sudden they give you the keys to a magical clubhouse and you've suddenly arrived. That's one book, and a book does not make a career. Certainly, I had a wonderful push from my publisher and got very lucky. I'm very aware of what it means to have a publisher back you. But your job as a writer, no matter what else is happening, is to continue to produce work—whether you're succeeding or failing. [You have to put] aside ideas about sales or success or ambition, and just work.

You know, I think I have a journey that looks smooth from the outside. And I'm always a little hesitant to talk about it because I don't want people to get a false impression about what it takes to get published. But [up until the point of publishing *Shadow and Bone*], I did face plenty of rejection, and even after I signed with [my agent], every single one of those rejections stung. Because the marvel of the information age is that you're still getting email rejections months and months after you sent them. [Laughs]. And so, until *Shadow and Bone* came out, I would read those rejections—because, of course, I had to read every single one of them—and I would think, *Well, maybe they're right and everybody else is wrong*. Part of the journey is that horrific balance of, you know, delusions of grandeur and abject humility that I think writers walk the line of all the time.

You've talked about losing faith in your ability to become a professional writer. What would you tell others who are struggling with that same feeling?

I want to be really clear about something: I think we kind of fetishize the creative life. We have the vision of what it means to be an author, where you sit in your garret or looking out at your view and you give everything to your art and you commit fully to it. But the reality is that most of us have bills to pay. We have loans to pay off. We have educations to pay for. Some of us have children to take care of or other relatives or dependents or responsibilities.

And the idea that somehow you're not a real writer if you are pursuing taking care of yourself and your life, as you pursue your art, is an incredibly damaging one. Very few people have the wherewithal or the safety net to be able to pursue writing full time from moment one. And I want people to understand that you can absolutely work a job, sometimes two jobs, and have those responsibilities—and still write. I didn't fail to become a writer, and therefore had to take a job. I had to take a job to keep a roof over my head because I had student loans to pay off. And that's the way it works.

For writers trying to balance life and art, how would you encourage them to stay motivated in pursuing their passion?

Set realistic goals. Sometimes that means doing something like NaNoWriMo, or it means saying, "I'm just going to write 500 words a day, but I'm going to write 500 words a day." Or "I'm going to do writing sprints for 30 minutes before work." Or in the 45 minutes when my kid is napping, or whatever it is. Carve out a time, find a process that works for you and don't compare yourself to anybody else.

[And] get offline. Stop reading about what other authors are doing. Stop reading reviews. Let yourself be immersed in the story that you're writing.

Remember: There is no expiration date on your talent. I did not publish my first book until I was 35 years old. If you have a story to tell, it doesn't matter when you tell it. Just get it onto the page and let go of any of the ideas that somehow it's less worthwhile because it took you a little longer to get there than it took others.

Man, you're inspiring me!

[Laughs.] Oh, good. Do it. Do it.

You've said before that there is no right way to write a book. You've been publishing at least one book per year since 2012, which is an impressive output. Describe your process.

I'm an outliner. I write through a three-act structure. I build all of my books in pretty much the exact same way: I have the idea, I write it out onto a single page so that I essentially have a book that is one-page long, and then I begin to fill in all of the things that I know. I build this kind of ramshackle zero-draft, that operates as an extended outline, and that is what becomes the musculature of the book. Now, when I get into the work of actually writing the scenes and revising the book into something that it can be, that process changes a little depending on the project.

A big part of writing is the discomfort of the work not being what you want it to be and the feelings of doubt or failure that come with not being able to make the idea instantly into what you want it to be.

Everybody processes differently, but [the exact method] is something you can keep coming back to when you feel psychologically embattled. A big part of writing is the discomfort of the work not being what you want it to be and the feelings of doubt or failure that come with not being able to make the idea instantly into what you want it to be.

Your books have very elaborate, well-rounded worlds. I haven't read a book in a long time where I felt so there. When world-building, where do you typically begin?

I start with my characters and with the story, the plot. When a reader enters the first chapter of your book, they're trying to get their bearings. It's our job as authors to give them the signals they need in order to be able to navigate that world. The great challenge of world-building is not building the world. You could build a world with maps and languages and all these things [and still be missing something]. It's releasing that information to the reader. The world-building that really falls into place first is what I always describe as the sense of power—helping readers understand how power flows in the book. That could mean governmental power, personal power, magical power, whatever. But [determining how power flows] is going to determine how your characters behave on the page, and what they're able or not able to do.

You had help creating the Grisha Trilogy's Ravkan language from David Peterson, who assisted with developing the Dothraki language in HBO's *Game of Thrones*. What was that like?

David and I met at Worldcon several years ago. I went to a presentation of his on Dothraki. He has been kind enough to be a resource for me as we've worked through the [Grisha] books, although we do occasionally butt heads because he wants me to be much more ambitious in my language in the book, and he's very probably right.

You write a lot of diverse characters without falling victim to stereotypes. Do you think attitudes about diversity in publishing have shifted, or does the industry still have a ways to go?

I think both of those things are true. I think that there's a new dedication to making sure that not only is representation better, but that marginalized authors and voices that maybe didn't have voices before are increasingly given platforms in publishing. And that is not only as writers, but as editors and in everything from publicity to sales. That said, I don't think there's any question that there's a long way to go because that is a long process and because until the fundamental power structures change, until the gatekeepers are different, I don't think we're going to see the kind of change that we really need to see—in the way not only that stories are told, but in the way they reach readers.

I'm sure many authors ask you what's trending in YA. What do you think is the ideal balance of writing what you're passionate about and understanding what's drawing readers in the industry?

You have to know the market. So you have to know what's selling, what isn't selling anymore, what people are fatigued by. But that doesn't mean you can say, "Oh, well, I [can't write that ever]." There was a period of time where people would say, "Oh, no more vampire books," or "no more dystopians," or no more this or that. But that is really false because what that actually meant was no more of that particular kind of story. We need a different take on vampires or we need to see a dystopian that is simply described as science fiction. YA shifts and moves faster than most other categories because so much work is being generated and consumed so quickly. And to be frank, I think if I brought *Shadow and Bone* out now, it would not have the same reception it had in 2012. Be aware of the market, but really, being aware of the market is just one part of being a storyteller and thinking about craft.

What's next for you?

Well, *King of Scars* is the first book in my upcoming duology that continues the story of the Grishaverse, and will pick up the story of Nikolai Lantsov, the young king of Ravka. And I'm [also working on] *Ninth House,* my first novel for adults. It is the start of a series set at Yale, a dark fantasy that focuses on the secret societies among East Coast elites. I've got a couple of other things cooking, but nothing I can discuss just yet.

I heard you have a band, which is probably the coolest side hustle ever. What type of music do you play?

Our lead guitarist would probably punch me for this, but I've always described it as "geek rock." It's sort of like if you put the Pixies and the New Pornographers and a little bit of They Might Be Giants in a blender. I mostly sing. Unfortunately, all of our lives got taken over by adulthood: Our guitarist had a baby. Our bassist had a baby. Our drummer bought a house. I landed my dream job. But we do occasionally meet up for band brunch and one of these days we'll have a reunion show.

I think that when you're writing, being creative in other ways is really useful and therapeutic. And whether that's creating visual art or making music—or hell, even baking—as long as you're doing something that's keeping you engaged and keeping you from chewing over reviews on Goodreads, I think you're better off.

BAIHLEY GENTRY is the former associate editor of *Writer's Digest*, in which this interview originally appeared in March/April 2018.

JANE YOLEN

Children's author Jane Yolen discusses writing more than 400 books.

by Ryan G. Van Cleave

For decades, Jane Yolen has been an iconic force in children's literature—from board books like *Merbaby's Lullaby* to middle-grade novels like *Trash Mountain*, and from picture books like *Owl Moon* to YA novels like *Mapping the Bones*, she's done it all. And she's done it well.

In March 2021, Jane's 400th published book—the picture book *Bear Outside*—reached the hands of readers. Along the way, Jane has embraced the role of mentor, role model, and friend to writers, teachers, librarians, parents, and children everywhere.

Writer's Digest talked to her about her writing process, staying prolific, and the social responsibility of writers.

How often does someone ask an astonishingly specific question about a book from long, long ago?

Not as much as you'd think! But when that happens, I'm truthful. I say, "I don't remember the book because it's so old."

Plus, I'm very involved in about two dozen picture books and poems, and a novel right now. That's where all my brainpower is. Honestly, I'm always moving forward. I'm like the great white shark—you have to keep moving or you die.

Let's talk about getting to 400 books. What were some of the highlights along the way?

Obviously, 1963—the year my first two books were published. And there was the book I secretly wrote for my father. Because he was the international high-flying champion, he'd been invited to write *The Young Sportsman's Guide to Kite Flying*. One day, he told me, "I've signed the contracts. I've signed the check. Now will you write the book?"

I was 19 at the time and had written magazine pieces, poetry, and a bit of nonfiction, but I'd never actually written a book. It was a great exercise for me, though he didn't put my name on the book.

When did you realize book 400 was going to happen?

My 365th and 366th books were coming out on the same day, so my daughter Heidi said, "Let's have a party!" which we held at the Eric Carle Museum. We even made calendars because you could read a different book of mine every day for a year—even if it was a leap year. And that was a big deal.

As I headed out to the party, I checked to see what else I'd sold. I realized another 30 books of mine would be coming out in the next three or four years. I started thinking, *If I live long enough, maybe I'll get to see 400.*

Which you did within three years of that realization.

And I've got 30 more new books under contract beyond my 400th, so now I'm thinking that maybe I'll get to 500!

You don't reach lofty career numbers like that without a good process. How do you stay so prolific?

I have a very low threshold of boredom. If I get bored or lost or stymied by a manuscript, I just turn to something else—usually another manuscript. Sometimes it's something new, and sometimes it's a manuscript that's been sitting on its rear end long enough that I now know what to do with it.

Do picture books come easier to you than other books?

With a picture book, sometimes you just get an entire idea and you sit down and, almost in one breath, exhale it. That doesn't happen often, but it happens occasionally. It's like writing a poem.

Got an example of that?

Owl Moon. I first thought of it when Heidi was young and going owling with her dad, but I couldn't write it until I had the voice for it. That came when Heidi was in college, so 15 years later? It wasn't that I hadn't tried. I tried it with a father's voice. I tried it with a mother's voice. I tried it from an unknown narrator's point of view.

It took me all that time to figure out—try it from the girl's voice. The moment I realized I could do it from the child's point of view, the book practically wrote itself.

What else can you share about your process for writing so many books?

Sometimes a story sings to you. It says, "I'm next. I want you. You want me. I've got the idea. I can do it! Give me a chance!"

And sometimes an editor sends a contract and a check, then says, "We want this book, but it's not right. We want you to fix it."

What about the manuscripts that don't sell?

Recently, I'd taken some manuscripts that went unsold, and I turned them into easy readers. And now I have more easy readers coming out than practically anybody. Why? Because that was the voice I just didn't know those stories needed.

I've written things that started out as a poem and became a graphic novel—there's no reason, it just happens.

And sometimes you have to leave something alone for a while, until it tells you what it is. It's like your child growing up. You always thought the child was going to be the next generation of writers, and she becomes a lawyer instead. That happens all the time. So why shouldn't it happen with manuscripts?

Great point! Let's talk about critics. How do you deal with them?

The first critic is yourself. And you have to put that critic aside in order to finish something. My second critic is the critique partners who are in my writing group. And occasionally, my daughter Heidi, or if I'm writing with another writer. But at some point, you have to say, OK, whoa, I'm in charge here. And then you let that internal editor come out. And that editor has to be very honest with you.

You know, we start with a muse who says, "You can do it, here's the idea, go for it!" And you do! But at some point, you have to step back and look at it with an editor's eye, with the parent's eye, with a child's eye.

The next problem is getting it past my agent—the terrific Elizabeth Harding—who is very, very honest with me. She might say, "This is not working." Or "I think you missed the market." Or "No one's buying this kind of book now." Or "Let's try it everywhere!"

And sometimes the books she loves most don't go anywhere, because we all love books for different reasons, and that means editors might not agree that something is saleable, or maybe it's just not for them.

What about external critics?

I've had some brutal critiques, and I've had some put-her-on-the-pedestal-and-worship critiques. Ultimately, it's their judgment, not yours, not your critique partners', not your editor's, not your agent's, not the kid who's sitting on the sofa with their mother. It's just theirs. And, honestly, of all the critiques, the child reader's is the one I care most about.

After the book is out, nothing a critic or reviewer says is going to change the story. But the child curates the story over and over again, finding something new and interesting at every reading. It becomes a lodestone.

Exactly. Now, you're a vocal person on social media, and you're a constant champion of both writers and the world of kidlit. What is the social responsibility of a writer?

First, you owe it to yourself—as well as the manuscript, and the public who wants it—to do your very best. No half measures. Butt in chair, and heart on the page. That's how you work. But you also have to be willing to listen to the people you trust who are telling you when it needs something more because children are being taught by children's book writers to either love or hate books. Sometimes it works and you hook them for life. Sometimes they never get it. That doesn't mean you do less.

I work harder on children's books because I know they change lives. If any children's book writer isn't aware of that fact, they better learn it quickly.

I think what we're seeing now is wonderful for kids who have never seen themselves in books before and are finding themselves there. And that ranges from kids of color, kids from different ethnicities, kids who are physically challenged, kids who identify with different genders. They're seeing themselves in the pages of books where they hadn't before. That's something important that the children's book world has been working on for the past few years. The industry is beginning to be successful at it.

Is it fair to say you prefer writing for kids?

I think that writing for young readers is more important than writing for adults. By the time people are adults, we are pretty much set in stone. But children's books encourage growth and change, and the books they love reside in their hearts forever in a way that adult books rarely do.

You've written pretty much every type of book there is. But what's your true writing self?

I have a sweet spot for short works—poetry, short stories, and children's books. One needn't write *Moby Dick* to tell a whale story. (Though I enjoy reading *Moby Dick* enough to reread it every 10 years.)

I could write short works like these all day long. The problem is that I occasionally have ideas for bigger nonfiction books or big poetry collections or novels. Those characters just start nagging at me. And I want to do those books. So, then I go and I write *Finding Baba Yaga*, which is a novel in verse, or I write *Sister Light, Sister Dark*, which is a fantasy trilogy for adults, though it has quite a few kid readers, too.

If something really shouts at me, I listen. But mostly, I'm in the sweet spot.

Picture book writers often talk about the thematic or structural through lines of a story. What are some through lines of your life?

I was a New Yorker who married a West Virginian who taught me about long walks, looking at birds, and really paying attention. He's the father in *Owl Moon*, and he appears in a lot of my books. He died 15 years ago, and now I'm with Peter, who's also a birder and a teacher, as David was. Peter's also a published writer—poetry and nonfiction.

So, the through line of my life seems to be looking at nature, reading a lot of books, writing a lot of books. And falling in love with the same man twice. Just as I often do with books.

RYAN G. VAN CLEAVE directs the creative writing program at Ringling College of Art and Design. He's also the author *The Weekend Book Proposal* and *Memoir Writing for Dummies*, as well as 20+ other books. His latest project is a children's book blog, OnlyPictureBooks.com. This interview was first published in the September/October 2021 issue of *Writer's Digest*.

ELIZABETH ACEVEDO

The National Book Award winner talks writing novels in verse, tips for NaNoWriMo success, and developing characters for YA.

by Amy Jones

A poet, an aspiring chef, a healer, and a chess player: Elizabeth Acevedo writes about creative teen girls making their own way in a world that isn't always kind. It didn't come as too much of a surprise that Acevedo herself took up a creative hobby during the pandemic lockdown. But the way she brought it back to writing, however, was the revelation.

While discussing having patience during the revision process, Acevedo noted that she had started making candles, and she learned that each candle has a curing time during which it sits untouched before it can be burned. This allows the fragrance to fully reveal itself. "That thinking has helped with writing for me," she said. "Sometimes things just need time to come slowly into their own, to almost get concrete, and then you can start messing with it. So, for me, at least that language feels like it's just part of the process. It's curing. It's not that I'm wasting time or losing time. It's doing something."

The process works. Her debut novel, *The Poet X*, won the National Book Award, a Michael L. Printz Award, and the Pura Belpré Award, among others. Written in verse, it tells the story of Xiomara Batista learning to find her voice, both poetic and otherwise, in the face of challenges at school, church, and home. Acevedo's sophomore prose novel, *With the Fire on High*, follows Emoni Santiago's senior year in high school as she juggles being a teen mother, schoolwork, and the culinary arts class that could potentially change her post-graduation prospects. Her 2020 novel, *Clap When You Land*, also written in verse, alternates between two sisters, Yahaira in NYC and Camino in Sosúa, Dominican Republic, as they deal with the death of their father in a plane crash—and learn of the other sister's existence.

In all three novels, Acevedo channels the students she taught as an 8th grade teacher, the stories they wanted to see on their classroom bookshelves, and what Acevedo herself wanted to read as a young adult. She balances the true-to-life struggles teenagers face—making life-altering choices, learning who to trust, and discovering that parental figures have lives outside of being caregivers—with a foreshadowing that each of them has a bright future ahead. As satisfying as that balance is for readers, it becomes even more impressive when you consider the beautiful language and stunning execution of the novels.

Like most writers, getting to that level wasn't always an easy or clear path. Acevedo made use of her MFA, her time as a slam poet, and the National Novel Writing Month (NaNoWriMo) challenge to help get the initial words on the page. With preparations for the upcoming November writing challenge in full swing, that's where we began our conversation.

I wanted to talk a little bit about NaNoWriMo. How did the challenge help you with your writing?

The first time I did it was in 2013, and at that point, I had written maybe a third of what ended up being my first novel, *The Poet X*. But I was really afraid of prose. I had dabbled with prose and had short stories and a manuscript I'd been working on. But I think that NaNoWriMo really was a challenge to get out of my own head.

I was in grad school at the time getting my MFA in poetry, and so I was working on a thesis. So, it really was the one opportunity I gave myself to attempt something that no one is checking for. The speed of it and the inability I had to second guess myself, the fun of what wound up being *With the Fire on High*, the second novel I published, of finding this character that was a chef—my NaNoWriMo version had her doing all kinds of things—I think I just gave myself so much permission to play. I really appreciate that process. I've never written a novel quite like that one in terms of how quickly and how much I allowed myself, to get my 1,700 words a day and keep it moving.

This issue comes out right as writers will be prepping for the challenge. What kind of advice do you have for them, for during the challenge or for the post-challenge when it comes time for revision?

For the challenge, having prompts for yourself would be helpful, particularly on those days that maybe you're stuck. There were moments that I very much knew the next thing that had to happen was this and so I knew what I was writing next. But then there were times when I just didn't know, and I had to give myself prompts or assignments to get myself thinking about the character. I think that in terms of the pre-work before starting NaNoWriMo, have 30 days' worth of prompts that you can respond to. You won't need them for every day, but on a day you're stuck and you only have an hour to write like, well, I know what I'm doing. And even if it's just work that now you know more about the character and the story, even if it doesn't end up in the actual manuscript, you're in the world every single day. And I think [that's] critical.

Plan for Thanksgiving. I did. I remember, I lived in D.C. and my whole family's in New York and I traveled up to New York that year. I was hiding in my mom's bedroom trying to get my last few words out. So just plan for the fact that those two or three days are mayhem and maybe get a couple of extra hundred words here and there. I very much gave myself permission to write anywhere and everywhere. If I was on the train, if I was at the gym on the bike—every word was closer to my word count. Those bits and spurts add up.

And the only thing I would say for after is, give yourself a full four to six weeks to not look at the thing. I think everyone wants to jump in and see what they made, [but] those fresh eyes do so much for your ability to discern what's really sharp and the days you hit it out of the park, and what you're just going to have to let go of because it wasn't your best thinking. Sometimes that's hard to see right after. Everyone says this, but like truly, truly, I can only double down on giving the revision the time.

You mentioned that NaNoWriMo allowed you to discover who one of the characters was in one of your books. In general, when you draft, what comes first: the character or the story?

It's odd because I would say that neither comes fully fleshed for me and it depends on every story. With this one, *With the Fire on High*, I would say I began thinking about it a week before NaNoWriMo and the character came first. I wasn't planning on doing NaNoWriMo. I wasn't planning on working on that book. I was watching "Chopped" and this very voice-y, particular character came forth, and I realized that there was something there.

With *The Poet X*, I had the premise, this idea of a young woman who has issues with her body and begins taking up space on the stage as a way to kind of own and have full agency. I knew what would happen before I knew who she was, what are the issues, what are the conflicts.

So, every book is a little bit different, but I will say I'm most definitely character-driven. I don't think I'm as interested in the turns of a book as I am in a character study or what I'm supposed to get from this particular person that is being drawn on the page.

With *The Poet X* and *With the Fire on High*, they're both told through the one character's perspective, and then with *Clap When You Land*, you moved on to two characters, which made sense for the plot. Was it a challenge to write from the perspective of two characters? What did it allow you to do creatively in terms of the character development and interiority that writing from one did not?

It was definitely a challenge, particularly because I did not figure out until I'd already finished the draft that I needed both characters. My first draft of the novel was written entirely from Yahaira's perspective, the sister in New York. I fully planned for that to be the story. When I finished, I kept feeling like there's something missing. It doesn't have the urgency, or the heart of it is missing. I had a conversation with Ibi Zoboi, who wrote *American Street* and *Pride* and was the editor for *Black Enough*. I was telling her about the story, and Ibi is Haitian, so we talk about the islands often, and our experiences of the islands that our people share, and she's like, "Girl, you need the other sister! How do you have this whole book about the secret sister we never hear from? Like, that's the narrative in real life—you have someone secret in a way—I don't think the book can do that." And it just completely blew open the book for me.

That character that came forth, Camino, she hijacked the book. She was just so witty and sharp. Her conflict feels so compelling and so true. It was really hard to then figure out the two voices, how to weave them together, how to make sure that no one was just the reporter just telling us the facts while the other person had the actual growth in the story. Having this one character that felt so true made me have to lift the whole portion that I had written already and make it just as interesting and sharp. I had to give that character her own secrets and wants and needs in a way that they hadn't been fully developed up until I had someone to juxtapose her to.

At the level of the verse, with *The Poet X*, I could do full-on free verse. And with this, I wanted a little bit more structure, and I thought readers would need it. They would need more cues, both visually and in terms of rhythm, to make sure that they knew they were in a different perspective. So, it was a different requirement for me.

The Poet X came out several years ago, so I don't feel like I'm going to give too much away—but Xiomara's journal of her poems is deliberately set on fire by someone in her family, and I feel like that is the ultimate betrayal for a writer, to have your work destroyed. Was that always part of the story or did that come out of revision and needing to push your characters further?

That came out of revision. I wasn't sure. I kept arriving at junctures where I knew the stakes had to be raised and it was more just a feeling like, now something else has to happen. I remember arriving at the first one where she had had this wonderful day with Aman, and they had a date, and I knew it can't all be peaches and roses. What's going to happen? It's the only autobiographical piece in the novel, where she gets caught kissing on the train, that had happened to me. My father was on the train next door. I didn't know. He was pressed up against the windows and had to get off a stop early. So, I remember arriving at that and being like, what would be something that would get Xiomara's mom really upset? Oh, *life* comes in! That's perfect.

But I thought that was going to be the scene that set everything off. When I wrote it, there was still so much that needed to be unpacked and so much growing the character had to do to really shift the dynamic of that mother-daughter relationship. It didn't feel like that was enough yet. I didn't know that that's what was going to happen. I had to just keep revising and keep working toward, what could be worse than being made to kneel on rice for getting caught kissing on a train? What is something that still feels within the means of unjustifiable, but not necessarily physical violence, which I wanted to maybe allude to, or let it be loosely veiled, not something that we saw on the page? I wanted other ways to demonstrate how control was being deployed. Or how disdain was being deployed.

So, it came from revision. It came from really knowing the characters and thinking through what feels possible. And it was delightful to land on that answer, to be very true. I know a lot of people get really upset at this part of the book, but for me, I remember getting there and being like, *Yes! I figured it out!* This is the thing that shifts everything. It felt inevitable, but also took me such a long time to get there that, when I tell you the triumph I felt writing those scenes—I don't think people would imagine is what I'm feeling when I'm writing it.

You started with slam poetry, and I wondered if you think about the line breaks differently in the poems that you're going to be speaking out loud vs. the ones that are more visual in the novels?

I think because I started rapping and started with hip hop and then moved to performance poetry, my lines were always initially governed by the four-count. Most hip hop is going to be on the four-count and trying to fit everything into the four-count. Moving from that to poetry slams and competitive or poems for competition or for oral poetry, it was entirely the breath. I'm going to stop the line where I'm going to need to take a breath, or I'm going to stop the line where naturally I feel the rhythm has come to an end. And that was its own kind of cadence, often just iambic pentameter. So, the line didn't necessarily end on the most important word. I didn't know necessarily about radical enjambment, or any enjambment, it was just, I'm going to follow my breath. Typically, if you look at a poem that hasn't been written to be read, that's been written to be heard, they're really long lines because it's how many words can you get in a breath before you have to move on. And so, my poems were across the entire page.

I think that with the novels and in general, post- going to workshops and seeing the power of what enjambment could do, what line breaks could do, how they could either imitate the body or do something that the body cannot do, create a juxtaposition that's powerful. That when words rhyme, you can have an enjambment, that they should be either opposing words or words that bring different images to mind. The first word of a line, the last word of the line before, how are they in relationship? What are the sounds that they have? Is there a way that they're naturally linked so that the reader's almost hinged into the next line? I think once I'd been calculating all of those things, it just felt like I had so many tools for the page and to reach readers on a page.

But yeah, I think I approached line breaks very much about gut impact. About how do I create multiple meanings and space for multiple meanings? What's a word that feels strong? I very often don't end on an article. I try not to end on a pronoun. I'm going to end on a noun. I'm not even going to end on a verb, I'm going to end on an image, on something that the reader can hold. I have my own internal rules on how I want the page to look and how I want it to feel, and I break those rules.

Depending on where we are in the story and particularly a novel in verse, you have to be so thoughtful about the actual margins. I wrote the entire manuscript, and then I get it back [from the editor] and they're like, none of these margins work. So then I have to rewrite 50, 60 poems so that they fit differently in the margins that we need for printing. I have to make exceptions to my own hard, fast rules, but it felt critical to treat the books in the same way that I would treat a poetry collection, with the same thoughtfulness of all of the things that are at play. Perhaps because I had a chapbook and was working on my MFA in poetry before I began writing in verse, I was aware of what I had seen in verse novels prior to, and the ways in which I felt like writers didn't use the full toolkit. Or they didn't have the full toolkit or weren't even attempting to expand their toolkit. Often what you're told is that a novel in verse just broken prose, and I went in very much trying to reject that notion.

Using those tools of poetry in a novel and then going back and writing a prose novel, it feels like not having them at my disposal would feel almost restrictive in some way, because they're so powerful in the verse novels. Do you find it harder to go back to prose and just write in paragraphs and sentences?

Yeah, I think *With the Fire on High* I did and the rhythm of the novel, you kind of see that. I was still figuring it out. So, there are moments where whatever action is happening, she was going to school, and then there'll be a whole section that's reflective. I think the interiority I still brought in, and I almost brought it in as these asides. Here's a moment where you're just in her head while she contemplates something, almost the same way the essays function in *The Poet X*. But I also got new tools: My verse novels don't have a lot of dialogue because I believe a verse novel can't carry a lot of dialogue. It's too easy to lose track of what's being said. And also, how is it supposed to sound in voice without it just sounding too poetic? I just don't think you can make it work quite as well.

You also can't have a large cast in a verse novel. I think there are only so many characters that a reader can pay attention to unless you're reading *The Odyssey* or *The Iliad*. You lose focus. There are not enough markers that you are meeting someone new. I think verse is trying to elide a lot of that, but what I get in prose is, I get a lot of dialogue and

I get more characters and I get the ability to create description for two pages in a way that might not work with verse. There's a trade-off.

But no, I find prose a lot harder. I think my adult novel [forthcoming, Ecco, 2023] is going to show some of the ways that I'm now seeing verse affect my prose and playing with blanks and playing with spacing and borrowing techniques from poetry to kind of remix the way I've learned that I had to write prose.

Do you have any last advice for our readers?

I get so many questions about mentors and for me, it's: Look sideways. My mentors have been homies. The people I learn writing from is, *Oh, Safia [Elhillo] who uses ampersands? Wait, let me figure out what this is doing.* I think so often we want to look at the people who have done something already to teach us, but I found that the people who are doing alongside us are—they're studying and also trying to learn. And so, it's an incredible opportunity and an easier opportunity than to try to get a mentor or writing advisor. It's almost always easier to get a critique partner. I'll look at your works if you look at mine. And finding that trust early on, I think is critical.

AMY JONES is editor-in-chief of WD. Follow her on twitter @AmyMJones_5. This interview was first published in the September/October 2021 issue of *Writer's Digest*.

BLOGGING BASICS

by Robert Lee Brewer

In these days of publishing and media change, writers have to build platforms and learn how to connect to audiences if they want to improve their chances of publication and overall success. There are many methods of audience connection available to writers, but one of the most important is through blogging.

Since I've spent several years successfully blogging—both personally and professionally—I figure I've got a few nuggets of wisdom to pass on to writers who are curious about blogging or who already are.

Here's my quick list of tips:

1. **START BLOGGING TODAY.** If you don't have a blog, use Blogger, WordPress, or some other blogging software to start your blog today. It's free, and you can start off with your very personal "Here I am, world" post.
2. **START SMALL.** Blogs are essentially simple, but they can get complicated (for people who like complications). However, I advise bloggers start small and evolve over time.
3. **USE YOUR NAME IN YOUR URL.** This will make it easier for search engines to find you when your audience eventually starts seeking you out by name. For instance, my url is http://robertleebrewer.blogspot.com. If you try Googling "Robert Lee Brewer," you'll notice that My Name Is Not Bob is one of the top five search results (behind my other blog: Poetic Asides).
4. **UNLESS YOU HAVE A REASON, USE YOUR NAME AS THE TITLE OF YOUR BLOG.** Again, this helps with search engine results. My Poetic Asides blog includes my name in the title, and it ranks higher than My Name Is Not Bob. However, I felt the play on my name was worth the trade off.
5. **FIGURE OUT YOUR BLOGGING GOALS.** You should return to this step every couple months, because it's natural for your blogging goals to evolve over time. Initially,

your blogging goals may be to make a post a week about what you have written, submitted, etc. Over time, you may incorporate guests posts, contests, tips, etc.

6. **BE YOURSELF.** I'm a big supporter of the idea that your image should match your identity. It gets too confusing trying to maintain a million personas. Know who you are and be that on your blog, whether that means you're sincere, funny, sarcastic, etc.
7. **POST AT LEAST ONCE A WEEK.** This is for starters. Eventually, you may find it better to post once a day or multiple times per day. But remember: Start small and evolve over time.
8. **POST RELEVANT CONTENT.** This means that you post things that your readers might actually care to know.
9. **USEFUL AND HELPFUL POSTS WILL ATTRACT MORE VISITORS.** Talking about yourself is all fine and great. I do it myself. But if you share truly helpful advice, your readers will share it with others, and visitors will find you on search engines.
10. **TITLE YOUR POSTS IN A WAY THAT GETS YOU FOUND IN SEARCH ENGINES.** The more specific you can get the better. For instance, the title "Blogging Tips" will most likely get lost in search results. However, the title "Blogging Tips for Writers" specifies which audience I'm targeting and increases the chances of being found on the first page of search results.
11. **LINK TO POSTS IN OTHER MEDIA.** If you have an email newsletter, link to your blog posts in your newsletter. If you have social media accounts, link to your blog posts there. If you have a helpful post, link to it in relevant forums and on message boards.
12. **WRITE WELL, BUT BE CONCISE.** At the end of the day, you're writing blog posts, not literary manifestos. Don't spend a week writing each post. Try to keep it to an hour or two tops and then post. Make sure your spelling and grammar are good, but don't stress yourself out too much.
13. **FIND LIKE-MINDED BLOGGERS.** Comment on their blogs regularly and link to them from yours. Eventually, they may do the same. Keep in mind that blogging is a form of social media, so the more you communicate with your peers the more you'll get out of the process.
14. **RESPOND TO COMMENTS ON YOUR BLOG.** Even if it's just a simple "Thanks," respond to your readers if they comment on your blog. After all, you want your readers to be engaged with your blog, and you want them to know that you care they took time to comment.
15. **EXPERIMENT.** Start small, but don't get complacent. Every so often, try something new. For instance, the biggest draw to my Poetic Asides blog are the poetry prompts and challenges I issue to poets. Initially, that was an experiment—one that worked very well. I've tried other experiments that haven't panned out, and that's fine. It's all part of a process.

SEO TIPS FOR WRITERS

Most writers may already know what SEO is. If not, SEO stands for *search engine optimization*. Basically, a site or blog that practices good SEO habits should improve its rankings in search engines, such as Google and Bing. Most huge corporations have realized the importance of SEO and spend enormous sums of time, energy, and money on perfecting their SEO practices. However, writers can improve their SEO without going to those same extremes.

In this section, I will use the terms of *site pages* and *blog posts* interchangeably. In both cases, you should be practicing the same SEO strategies (when it makes sense).

Here are my top tips on ways to improve your SEO starting today:

1. **USE APPROPRIATE KEYWORDS.** Make sure that your page displays your main keyword(s) in the page title, content, URL, title tags, page header, image names, and tags (if you're including images). All of this is easy to do, but if you feel overwhelmed, just remember to use your keyword(s) in your page title and content (especially in the first and last 50 words of your page).
2. **USE KEYWORDS NATURALLY.** Don't kill your content and make yourself look like a spammer to search engines by overloading your page with your keyword(s). You don't get SEO points for quantity but for quality. Plus, one of the main ways to improve your page rankings is when you…
3. **DELIVER QUALITY CONTENT.** The best way to improve your SEO is by providing content that readers want to share with others by linking to your pages. Some of the top results in search engines can be years old, because the content is so good that people keep coming back. So, incorporate your keywords in a smart way, but make sure it works organically with your content.
4. **UPDATE CONTENT REGULARLY.** If your site looks dead to visitors, then it'll appear that way to search engines too. So update your content regularly. This should be very easy for writers who have blogs. For writers who have sites, incorporate your blog into your site. This will make it easier for visitors to find your blog to discover more about you on your site (through your site navigation tools).
5. **LINK BACK TO YOUR OWN CONTENT.** If I have a post on Blogging Tips for Writers, for instance, I'll link back to it if I have a Platform Building post, because the two complement each other. This also helps clicks on my blog, which helps SEO. The one caveat is that you don't go crazy with your linking and that you make sure your links are relevant. Otherwise, you'll kill your traffic, which is not good for your page rankings.
6. **LINK TO OTHERS YOU CONSIDER HELPFUL.** Back in 2000, I remember being ordered by my boss at the time (who didn't last too much longer afterward) to ignore any competitive or complementary websites—no matter how helpful their content—because they were our competitors. You can try basing your online

strategy on these principles, but I'm nearly 100 percent confident you'll fail. It's helpful for other sites and your own to link to other great resources. I shine a light on others to help them out (if I find their content truly helpful) in the hopes that they'll do the same if ever they find my content truly helpful for their audience.

7. **GET SPECIFIC WITH YOUR HEADLINES.** If you interview someone on your blog, don't title your post with an interesting quotation. While that strategy may help get readers in the print world, it doesn't help with SEO at all. Instead, title your post as "Interview With (insert name here)." If you have a way to identify the person further, include that in the title too. For instance, when I interview poets on my Poetic Asides blog, I'll title those posts like this: Interview With Poet Erika Meitner. Erika's name is a keyword, but so are the terms *poet* and *interview*.
8. **USE IMAGES.** Many expert sources state that the use of images can improve SEO, because it shows search engines that the person creating the page is spending a little extra time and effort on the page than a common spammer. However, I'd caution anyone using images to make sure those images are somehow complementary to the content. Don't just throw up a lot of images that have no relevance to anything. At the same time…
9. **OPTIMIZE IMAGES THROUGH STRATEGIC LABELING.** Writers can do this by making sure the image file is labeled using your keyword(s) for the post. Using the Erika Meitner example above (which does include images), I would label the file "Erika Meitner headshot.jpg"—or whatever the image file type happens to be. Writers can also improve image SEO through the use of captions and ALT tagging. Of course, at the same time, writers should always ask themselves if it's worth going through all that trouble for each image or not. Each writer has to answer that question for him (or her) self.
10. **USE YOUR SOCIAL MEDIA PLATFORM TO SPREAD THE WORD.** Whenever you do something new on your site or blog, you should share that information on your other social media sites, such as Twitter, Facebook, LinkedIn, online forums, etc. This lets your social media connections know that something new is on your site/blog. If it's relevant and/or valuable, they'll let others know. And that's a great way to build your SEO.

Programmers and marketers could get even more involved in the dynamics of SEO optimization, but I think these tips will help most writers out immediately and effectively while still allowing plenty of time and energy for the actual work of writing.

BLOG DESIGN TIPS FOR WRITERS

Design is an important element to any blog's success. But how can you improve your blog's design if you're not a designer? I'm just an editor with an English Lit degree and no formal training in design. However, I've worked in media for more than two decades now and can share some very fundamental and easy tricks to improve the design of your blog.

Here are my seven blog design tips for writers:

1. **USE LISTS.** Whether they're numbered or bullet points, use lists when possible. Lists break up the text and make it easy for readers to follow what you're blogging.
2. **BOLD MAIN POINTS IN LISTS.** Again, this helps break up the text while also highlighting the important points of your post.
3. **USE HEADINGS.** If your posts are longer than 300 words and you don't use lists, then please break up the text by using basic headings.
4. **USE A READABLE FONT.** Avoid using fonts that are too large or too small. Avoid using cursive or weird fonts. Times New Roman or Arial works, but if you want to get "creative," use something similar to those.
5. **LEFT ALIGN.** English-speaking readers are trained to read left to right. If you want to make your blog easier to read, avoid centering or right aligning your text (unless you're purposefully calling out the text).
6. **USE SMALL PARAGRAPHS.** A good rule of thumb is to try and avoid paragraphs that drone on longer than five sentences. I usually try to keep paragraphs to around three sentences myself.
7. **ADD RELEVANT IMAGES.** Personally, I shy away from using too many images. My reason is that I only like to use them if they're relevant. However, images are very powerful on blogs, so please use them—just make sure they're relevant to your blog post.

If you're already doing everything on my list, keep it up! If you're not, then you might want to rethink your design strategy on your blog. Simply adding a header here and a list there can easily improve the design of a blog post.

GUEST POSTING TIPS FOR WRITERS

Recently, I've broken into guest posting as both a guest poster and as a host of guest posts (over at my Poetic Asides blog). So far, I'm pretty pleased with both sides of the guest posting process. As a writer, it gives me access to an engaged audience I may not usually reach. As a blogger, it provides me with fresh and valuable content I don't have to create. Guest blogging is a rare win-win scenario.

That said, writers could benefit from a few tips on the process of guest posting:

1. **PITCH GUEST POSTS LIKE ONE WOULD PITCH ARTICLES TO A MAGAZINE.** Include what your hook is for the post, what you plan to cover, and a little about who you are. Remember: Your post should somehow benefit the audience of the blog you'd like to guest post.

2. **OFFER PROMOTIONAL COPY OF YOUR BOOK (OR OTHER GIVEAWAYS) AS PART OF YOUR GUEST POST.** Having a random giveaway for people who comment on a blog post can help spur conversation and interest in your guest post, which is a great way to get the most mileage out of your guest appearance.
3. **CATER POSTS TO AUDIENCE.** As the editor of *Writer's Market* and *Poet's Market*, I have great range in the topics I can cover. However, if I'm writing a guest post for a fiction blog, I'll write about things of interest to a novelist—not a poet.
4. **MAKE IT PERSONAL, BUT PROVIDE NUGGET.** Guest posts are a great opportunity for you to really show your stuff to a new audience. You could write a very helpful and impersonal post, but that won't connect with readers the same way as if you write a very helpful and personal post that makes them want to learn more about you (and your blog, your book, your Twitter account, etc.). Speaking of which…
5. **SHARE LINKS TO YOUR WEBSITE, BLOG, SOCIAL NETWORKS, ETC.** After all, you need to make it easy for readers who enjoyed your guest post to learn more about you and your projects. Start the conversation in your guest post and keep it going on your own sites, profiles, etc. And related to that…
6. **PROMOTE YOUR GUEST POST THROUGH YOUR NORMAL CHANNELS ONCE THE POST GOES LIVE.** Your normal audience will want to know where you've been and what you've been doing. Plus, guest posts lend a little extra "street cred" to your projects. But don't stop there…
7. **CHECK FOR COMMENTS ON YOUR GUEST POST AND RESPOND IN A TIMELY MANNER.** Sometimes the comments are the most interesting part of a guest post (no offense). This is where readers can ask more in-depth or related questions, and it's also where you can show your expertise on the subject by being as helpful as possible. And guiding all seven of these tips is this one:
8. **PUT SOME EFFORT INTO YOUR GUEST POST.** Part of the benefit to guest posting is the opportunity to connect with a new audience. Make sure you bring your A-game, because you need to make a good impression if you want this exposure to actually help grow your audience. Don't stress yourself out, but put a little thought into what you submit.

ONE ADDITIONAL TIP: Have fun with it. Passion is what really drives the popularity of blogs. Share your passion and enthusiasm, and readers are sure to be impressed.

ROBERT LEE BREWER is a senior editor with the Writer's Digest Writing Community and author of *Smash Poetry Journal*. Follow him on Twitter @robertleebrewer.

THE AGENT QUERY TRACKER

Submit smarter and follow up faster with these simple spreadsheets to revolutionize your record-keeping.

by Tyler Moss

Everyone knows the real magic of writing comes from time spent in the chair, those sessions in which your fingertips flitting across the keyboard can barely keep pace with the electric current sparking through your brain.

Those in-between periods, full of administrative tasks—the querying, the tracking of payments, the day-to-day doldrums that occupy the interstitial moments of a writer's life—become an afterthought. But when such responsibilities are given short shrift, the inevitable result is disorganization—which at best can impede creativity and at worst can have dire consequences. Missed payments, embarrassing gaffes (querying the same agent twice, or realizing you have no record of where your previous agent submitted your last novel), and incomplete records come tax time are entirely avoidable headaches.

Still, organized record-keeping takes work. Which is why we decided to do it for you.

This does not have to mean you're about to start spending more time on these tasks—in fact, quite the opposite. Once you invest in a standard process up front, each future action will require little more than filling out a few cells in a spreadsheet. (Learn to love them as I have for their clean, quadrilateral beauty.)

You can use the simple guides on the following pages to customize forms of your own, whether you're querying an agent, tracking the places your agent is submitting, or working on your freelancing career between projects.

AGENT QUERY TRACKER

AGENT	**Example:** Booker M. Sellington		
AGENCY	The Booker M. Sellington Agency		
EMAIL	BMS@bmsagency.com		
DATE QUERIED	8/1/16		
MATERIALS SENT	Query, Synopsis, first 10 pages		
DATE FOLLOWED UP	9/1/16		
RESPONSE	Request for additional materials		
ADDITIONAL MATERIALS REQUESTED	Full manuscript		
DATE FOLLOWED UP	10/15/16		
RESPONSE	Offer of representation		
NOTES	Specializes in thrillers		

Few writers hit the jackpot and manage to land a literary agent on their first query. As this process can take weeks or months, and as agency guidelines vary widely, it can be helpful to keep a detailed record of whom you have contacted, what agency they work for, what materials you've sent in, and the specifics of their responses. Customize your own tracker starting from these column headings:

- **AGENT, AGENCY, & EMAIL:** Where you are sending your query
- **POLICY AGAINST QUERYING MULTIPLE AGENTS AT AGENCY:** [Optional Field] Some agencies have a no-from-one-agent-means-no-from-the-whole-agency policy; noting this saves you time and embarrassment, particularly at larger firms where multiple reps might seem like a potential fit
- **DATE QUERIED & MATERIALS SENT:** When and what you submitted, always following guidelines (query letter, first ten pages, synopsis, proposal, etc.)
- **"NO RESPONSE MEANS NO" POLICY:** [Optional Field] Agents who specify in their guidelines that no response equates to a rejection, meaning you shouldn't follow up
- **DATE FOLLOWED UP:** In the event of no response and excluding those with the policy noted above
- **RESPONSE:** A rejection, a request to see more, or any constructive feedback
- **ADDITIONAL MATERIALS REQUESTED & DATE SENT:** Typically a full or partial manuscript is requested if your query garners interest

- **DATE FOLLOWED UP:** For a full or partial, follow up after at least four weeks if there's no response (unless you have an offer for representation elsewhere, in which case you'll follow up immediately to request a decision or withdraw your manuscript from consideration)
- **RESPONSE:** The agent's final feedback or response
- **NOTES:** Any helpful info on your interaction with the agent or agency, or feedback that could be addressed before additional querying (e.g., "The protagonist often behaves erratically and inconsistently," or "The manuscript could use a proofread")

If you opt to forgo seeking representation and instead are submitting directly to publishers that accept unagented submissions, then I suggest you make a separate spreadsheet to track that information, swapping the headings **AGENT** and **AGENCY** for **ACQUIRING EDITOR** and **IMPRINT/PUBLISHER**, respectively.

ORGANIZE YOUR QUERIES

Both versions of the tracker are available for download at writersdigest.com/GLA-18.

AGENT SUBMISSIONS TO PUBLISHER TRACKER

IMPRINT/PUBLISHER	**Example:** Pendant Publishing		
ACQUIRING EDITOR	Elaine Benes		
DATE SENT	8/1/16		
DATE FOLLOWED UP	9/1/16		
RESPONSE	Pass		
EDITOR'S COMMENTS	Says a "book about nothing" is not right for their Spring 2018 lineup		
ADDITIONAL NOTES	Suggests changes to plot in which the judge sentences protagonist to be the antagonist's butler		

After signing with an agent, it's critical to stay in close communication as she sends your manuscript to publishers. Such records allow you to stay involved in the direction of your career, gather essential data about the imprints your agent believes you'd be best suited for, and pinpoint commonalities or contradictions in feedback. And if you must someday sever ties with your agent, you'll have what you need to help your new representation pick up right where your old representation left off. Keep record of the following details.

- **IMPRINT/PUBLISHER, ACQUIRING EDITOR, & DATE SENT:** The details of exactly where and when your agent submitted your manuscript
- **DATE FOLLOWED UP:** Date on which your agent followed up with the acquiring editor if you did not receive an initial response
- **RESPONSE:** Accepted, rejected, revise-and-resubmit request
- **EDITOR'S COMMENTS:** A one-line description highlighting any relevant feedback received
- **ADDITIONAL NOTES:** Miscellaneous information about the publisher, editor or the overall interaction between agent and publishing house

PRO TIP: SAVE SPREADSHEETS TO GOOGLE DRIVE

Recently I read a news story in which a writer in New Orleans ran into his burning home to save the manuscripts of two completed novels stored on his computer—the only place he had them saved. Luckily, he weathered the blaze and escaped with laptop in hand. Though we can admire his dedication to his work, there are any number of digital-age options that could've prevented this horrible scenario—among them, Google Drive.

The system is ideal for uploading a fresh document of your manuscript every time you make changes, storing files online in addition to on your computer (Google Drive has an online storage function similar to services such as Dropbox and Microsoft OneDrive).

Google Drive allows you to create documents, spreadsheets, slide shows, and more, all of which can be accessed from anywhere—laptop, tablet, smartphone—by logging into a free Google account. Such items are easily shared with your co-author, agent, or publicist for more efficient record keeping or file sharing. It's also a great place to create and modify the trackers from this article.

Simply log in to your account at google.com/drive (or create one for free), hit the New button in the top left corner of the interface and click on Google Sheets. This will open a new window with a clean spreadsheet, where you can then begin entering the appropriate column headings. Title the spreadsheet by clicking "Untitled spreadsheet" at the top of the page. Once complete, you'll be able to open up your Freelance Payment Tracker or Agent Query Tracker on any device with an Internet connection—far from flames or flood.

FREELANCE PITCH TRACKER

SUBJECT	**Example:** Essay about meeting Stephen King in the waiting room at the dentist		
PUBLICATION	*Writer's Digest*		
EDITOR	Tyler Moss		
EMAIL	wdsubmissions@aimmedia.com		
PITCH SUBMITTED	8/1/16		
FOLLOW UP	8/15/16		
RESULT	Accepted		
DEADLINE	10/15/16		
NOTES	$0.50 cents/word for 600 words		

For freelance writers, ideas are currency—but they don't exist in a vacuum. Once you've brainstormed a solid premise and started to pitch potential markets, the resulting interactions can quickly clutter your in-box. Avoid losing track by recording your pitches in a spreadsheet with the following column headings:

- **SUBJECT:** One-line description of your story idea
- **PUBLICATION:** Name of magazine, website, or newspaper you pitched to
- **EDITOR & EMAIL:** Where you sent your pitch
- **PITCH SUBMITTED:** When the query was sent
- **FOLLOW UP:** The date on which you plan to follow up if you haven't received a response (typically two weeks later, unless the submission guidelines specify otherwise)
- **RESULT:** Accepted, rejected, asked to rework
- **DEADLINE:** If accepted, date story is due
- **NOTES:** Additional info, based on your interactions with the editor (e.g., "Publication pays too little," or "Editor rejected pitch, but encouraged pitching again soon")

In addition to keeping track of irons currently in the fire, this spreadsheet is invaluable for later looking up contact info of editors you haven't emailed in a while.

If you want to track submissions to literary journals, simply switch out the column headings **SUBJECT** and **PUBLICATION** with **STORY TITLE** and **JOURNAL**, respectively, ax the **FOLLOW UP** column (journals tend to operate on slower, more sporadic schedules, sometimes without full-time staff), and replace the **DEADLINE** column with **READING FEE** (so you can evaluate and track any submission expenses where applicable).

ORGANIZE YOUR FREELANCE LIFE

Find both the freelance pitch and journal versions of this pitch tracker available for download at writersdigest.com/GLA-18.

FREELANCE PAYMENT TRACKER

ARTICLE HEADLINE	**Example:** Tongue Tied		
PUBLICATION/URL	*Ball & String Magazine*		
PAYMENT	$500		
DATE PUBLISHED	July 2016		
TOTAL WORDS	1,000		
$/WORD	$0.40 cents/word		
INVOICE #	#2014-1		
INVOICE SUBMITTED	8/12/16		
PAID	8/30/16		

When you've been commissioned to write a piece, it's vital to document the status of your payment. Not only will it keep you from missing a check, but it's incredibly useful for noting what a publication has paid you in the past and comparing the rates of different publications for which you freelance—which can help you prioritize your time by targeting the most lucrative outlets. It's also a lifesaver come April 15.

As depicted in the example spreadsheet above, you can use the following column headings to trace the path of your payments:

- **HEADLINE:** Title of the finished, published piece
- **PUBLICATION/URL:** Outlet that published the article and, if applicable, the URL where the article can be found online
- **PAYMENT:** Total payment received for work
- **DATE PUBLISHED:** Date article went live online, or issue month if for a print magazine or journal
- **TOTAL WORDS & $/WORD:** Length of the piece and amount you were paid per word, found by dividing the total payment by the total number of words (a common standardization for freelance payment rates)
- **INVOICE # & SUBMITTED:** Unique number of the invoice you submitted for this particular article (if applicable), and date on which it was submitted

- **PAID:** Date on which you received the payment, most commonly via check or direct deposit

Of course, you can also use this same basic format to develop a spreadsheet that covers advances, royalties, speaking honoraria, etc. Use the basic format outlined here to construct your own customized version.

TYLER MOSS is the former editor-in-chief of *Writer's Digest*. He is currently a content strategist and freelance writer. Follow him on Twitter @tjmoss11.

GETTING AN AGENT 101

by Jennifer D. Foster

Considered the "gatekeepers" to (large) publishing houses, literary agents are often your best bet to getting your foot in the door and making a name for yourself in the book (and even the motion picture, but that's another story!) world. But do you really need an agent? And exactly how do you find one? What are the tell-tale signs of a reputable (and not-so-reputable) literary agent? And how do you make the author-agent relationship work? Key insights, helpful tips, and sound advice from authors, editors, publishing consultants, editorial directors, literary agents, writing instructors, and heads of professional writing organizations give you the inside track.

WHAT LITERARY AGENTS DO

While the Writers' Union of Canada website states that "about 70 percent of the books published in Canada do not have an agent-assisted contract," it's a radically different story in the United States. In her book *Publishing 101: A First-Time Author's Guide to Getting Published, Marketing and Promoting Your Book, and Building a Successful Career* (Jane Friedman, 2015), Jane Friedman reveals that "in today's market, probably about 80 percent of books that the New York publishers acquire are sold to them by agents." But before taking the often-challenging plunge of getting a literary agent, do your homework to determine it you actually need one to get your manuscript published. And in order to figure that out, it's necessary to understand what, exactly, literary agents are and what they do. Jennifer Croll, editorial director of Greystone Books in Vancouver, explains it this way: "Agents act as both scouts and filters—they sort through what's out there and actively search to find the authors and proposals that are most likely to be published." Linden MacIntyre, award-winning journalist, internationally bestselling and Scotiabank

Giller Prize–winning author, and former host of *The Fifth Estate*, concurs. "Agents know the world of publishing, who matters, and established agents are known and recognized by editors and publishers. A recommendation from a credible agent will usually assure that someone of influence in publishing will read the manuscript."

Trevor Cole, Toronto, Ontario–based, award-winning author of *The Whisky King*, *Hope Makes Love*, and *Practical Jean*, further clarifies. An agent is beneficial "if you are committed to producing well-crafted book-length prose on a consistent professional basis." And, he says, "if the agent is part of a large house, they will have international contacts and sub-agents who can give your book its best chance at international distribution." Quite simply, "if an agent loves a book you've written, they will go to bat for it hard," he says, adding, "and once an editor agrees to buy the book, the agent's job is to get the best possible financial deal for you." Geoffrey Taylor, director of the International Festival of Authors in Toronto, Ontario, says that "an agent is the conduit for an author's work. This could mean anything from national to world rights. It could include all print forms, electronic, and video/film platforms." He says that agents have a lot of "experience with contracts and can usually negotiate better terms and a higher cash advance against future sales." Terence Green explains further. "A book contract can easily be twenty pages or more. An agent familiar with the publishing business understands which clauses are negotiable, and to what degree, and can customize the boilerplate contracts often tendered as a matter of rote to ones that are more palatable and fair-minded to all parties." Martha Kanya-Forstner, editor-in-chief of Doubleday Canada, and McClelland & Stewart, and vice president of Penguin Random House Canada, reveals that "it is exceptionally difficult for authors to negotiate the value of their own work, [and it is] much better to have an agent secure the best deal possible and ensure that all terms of that deal are then met."

Martha Webb, proprietor and literary agent with CookeMcDermid in Toronto, Ontario, sees the agent's role as that of career guide and activist. "We are an author's advocate throughout the life of their work, and the liaison between the author and publisher. Our goal is to find the best possible publishing arrangements for the author's work ... to support and advocate for their interests throughout the process and to advise them throughout their writing career." Carolyn Forde, literary agent and international rights director for Westwood Creative Artists in Toronto, Ontario, sums up the advocate role this way: "The agent supports and advises their clients. We do many, many contracts a year, and most authors won't do more than one a year (and even that would be considered a lot), so we do know what's industry standard, what's author friendly and what isn't."

In an online interview with Authornomics, agent Katherine Sands, with the Sarah Jane Freymann Literary Agency in New York, takes it even further, explaining that "literary agent now means content manager ... the work is hands-on with a role in developing and marketing an author's name and material for print, digital, and other media—

not just centered around a book deal." She believes "the digital age is revolutionizing everything and reinvented agents are now far more involved in creating opportunities for writing clients' content in emerging markets: for books, to be used online, with partners, in podcasts, in products, and in digital media to accrue sales. The new agent focus is on how writers can market and maximize their works across a wide slate." Lori Hahnel, Calgary-based author of *After You've Gone, Love Minus Zero,* and *Nothing Sacred* and creative writing teacher at Mount Royal University and the Alexandra Writers' Centre Society, notes another role of the agent—that of editor. "Today more than ever, agents are taking on an editorial role. As publishers employ fewer and fewer editors, they need the manuscripts they get from agents to be in nearly publishable form when they're submitted."

Agents also handle other types of administrative and editorial-type tasks, such as checking royalty statements and hunting down overdue royalty checks; submitting books to reviewers and literary contests; and submitting future manuscripts to editors/publishers.

DETERMINING NEED

"Academic writing, and those working in less commercially successful genres likely don't need an agent," says Webb. Friedman, in her blog post "How to Find a Literary Agent for Your Book," adds that "if you're writing for a niche market (e.g., vintage automobiles) or wrote an academic or literary work, then you might not need an agent." Why? "Agents are motivated to take on clients based on the size of the advance they think they can get. If your project doesn't command a decent advance, then you may not be worth an agent's time, and you'll have to sell the project on your own." Kelsey Attard, managing editor of Freehand Books in Calgary, Alberta, says that "it depends on your goals … and also it depends on your genre. There are virtually no agents who represent poets, for example." Anita Purcell, executive director of the Canadian Authors Association, expounds further. "If you write poetry, short stories, or novellas, agents are not likely to take you on, and you have a better chance pitching directly to smaller presses that specialize in your particular genre." And, she adds, "authors who have been offered a contract with a publisher may want to get an agent to represent their interests before actually signing the contract. It is far easier to land an agent when you've got a firm offer from a publisher in hand."

Croll notes that those who want to work with an independent (indie) publisher can most likely get by without an agent. But, literary representation is essential for any writer wanting to make money by accessing most major publishing houses and editors, especially since the merging of many publishing companies has resulted in huge conglomerates with multiple imprints. "Editors often review agented submission first—and give them more consideration—because those submissions have already gone through a sort of vetting process," says Croll. And, shares Attard, "those biggest publishers typically don't accept unsolicited submissions from unagented authors." In the same online interview with Authornomics, Sands paints this picture: "Try this test at home: Call a leading publisher tomorrow and try to get anyone to discuss your work. An agent has the greenlight to do this, but a civilian is unlikely to penetrate the publisher's robotic turnaround, shielding editors from unrepresented writers." And, she poses, "betcha you can't find out which newly-hired editor would really love your literotic chiller about a sexy ichthyologist who must solve eco-system crime in Namibia."

Dawn Green, British Columbia–based author of *In the Swish and How Samantha Became a Revolutionary*, has this perspective. "I think any author who wants to just be an author, just be writing novels full time, requires an agent who will allow them time to focus on their craft." Stephanie Sinclair, senior literary agent with Transatlantic Agency in Toronto, Ontario, shares Dawn Green's sentiment: "The contracts are often very tricky, and without an agent, the process can end up taking up so much time, the author has no time/energy left to write! My job is to help my authors, so they can just focus on the writing." Like Sands, Dawn Green also holds that "an agent needs to help a writer market and brand themselves. It's that classic difference between art and business." And, she adds, "today, it seems that more time needs to be put into the social media and networking side of things, and that is not easy for most introverted writers to do."

Taylor Brown, Wilmington, North Carolina–based bestselling author of the novels *Fallen Land, The River of Kings, and Gods of Howl Mountain*, views the author-agent relationship from this lens. "Once your work has been published in book form, your agent's help only becomes that much more important. I think of an agent as a 'corner man' or woman of sorts." As well, he says, "they can do everything from giving feedback on manuscripts to helping interpret communications from your publisher to acting as a sounding board for important career changes. I could hardly imagine this career without an agent."

BEFORE THE QUERY

Most (good) literary agents receive hundreds of submissions a week from prospective clients, so time is precious, and second chances are rare. Part of doing your homework in finding an agent, before even entering the literary agent querying process, is ensuring your manuscript is the absolute best it can be. You want to be ready to hit "Send" as soon as an agent requests pages. In a guest blog post about finding a literary agent for The Writers' Workshop, novelist Harry Bingham says that means having a rock-solid product. "Write a good book. A stunning one. A dazzling one. One that echoes in the consciousness. One that makes a professional reader (i.e. agent/editor) sit up late with tears in their eyes." Sands agrees. In her book *Making the Perfect Pitch: How to Catch a Literary Agent's Eye* (The Writer Books, 2004), she says, "Literary agents must be enchanted, seduced, and won over to take you on as a client."

But how do you ensure this? Have your manuscript professionally evaluated; give it to trusted beta readers for invaluable constructive feedback. "They will find idiosyncrasies in your manuscript that will surprise you and also offer suggestions. Then after you make the edits, send the manuscript to a copy editor. Agents can spot professionalism a mile away," says Lynne Wiese Sneyd, owner of LWS Literary Services in Tucson, Arizona, and literary consultant for the Tucson Festival of Books. Hiring a professional editor will ensure the manuscript is error-free and at-the-ready for agent consideration. Brown shares Wiese Sneyd's philosophy. "A professional editor who has a record of helping shepherd books to publication is simply invaluable. You cannot depend on the agent seeing the potential in your work. They are not looking for potential. They are looking for a book they can sell right now."

THE QUERY: SOME DOS AND DON'TS

Also, make sure your pitch to an agent is bang-on in every aspect. If you can't write an enticing query letter, you may not convince a literary agent that you can write a compelling book. Jan Kardys, a literary agent at Black Hawk Literary Agency LLC in Redding, Connecticut, and chairman of the Unicorn Writers' Conference, offers these tips for honing your query and book summary: "It is helpful for writers to study book publishers' websites and study catalog copy. Once you study author's bio(s) and read the descriptions of their books, you get great ideas." Sinclair explains the pitch process this way: "Know who you are submitting to. When people send letters referencing some of my other clients and my taste, I know they have done their homework, which makes me immediately pay close attention." According to Sands, "it's the pitch and nothing but the pitch that gets a writer selected from the leaning tower of queries in a literary agent's office ... The writing you do about your writing is as important as the writing itself." It is "part 'hello,' part cover letter, part interview for the coveted job of book author," she says. Agents, she stresses, "are looking first for a reason to keep reading, then for a reason to represent you ... you want your pitch to give crystal clear answers—fast."

Some of those answers, says Croll, include being able to clearly describe the market for your book—who is going to buy it. "Selling your manuscript to a publisher is how an agent makes a living—that is their source of income. They are motivated to take on authors who will create work they can actually sell." And remember that your query letter is a form of communication, "so try to come across as a real person and not a pitching robot following a formula," advises Webb. Purcell couldn't agree more. "Always personalize your letter: make sure you use the agent's name and spell it correctly. If possible, find something you share in common, whether it's having the same birthplace, a mutual love of horror, or having met at a writers' conference." Like Webb, Purcell says "the query letter should not read like a form letter that is sent to every agent and publisher."

Hahnel, like Wiese Sneyd, suggests soliciting feedback from respected beta readers. The input will help "polish your query and your sample chapters until they shine." Purcell suggests taking it a step further. Writers "should ask experienced authors to review their query letter before submitting it." Why go to all this effort? "The bar is very, very high now, and so anything you can do to put your best foot forward is in your best interest," stresses Forde.

Hahnel also recommends having "a synopsis ready. Not all agents ask for them, but some will." As for a query letter, she says "don't clutter it with unnecessary information, such as courses you've taken or retreats you've gone on." Be polite and professional, says Hahnel, and ensure a confident and positive tone. "Don't say negative things like, 'I'm not sure if you'll like this.' or 'You probably won't want to read all of this.'" Attard recommends this: "Be brief, engaging, and also (at least for literary writing) let your manuscript be the star." Forde offers similar sound advice for a query. "Keep it short and concise—tell me about the book and about you. Don't try to be cute or memorable. Don't compare your book to the best book in the genre. If you say it's the next Harry Potter, what I hear is that you have unrealistic expectations." Purcell has this sage query-writing advice. "Agents often say that what catches their interest most is when writers manage to avoid some of the pitfalls of new writers, such as telling the agent that they're good writers (show, don't tell), or that all their family and friends loved the manuscript (of course they did, they love you), or that they've been wanting to be published authors since they were six years old (few writers haven't)." She says what also catches agents' interest is "when writers seem to have a strong understanding of their genre, as well as the distinction between commercial, upmarket, and literary writing."

A FEW WISE WORDS ON PLATFORM

Purcell says that it's all about branding right now "And writers should look at their social media platforms and their website, if they have one, with a critical eye that asks: 'What is my current brand and how appealing is that brand to a potential agent or publisher? Are there any posts or images that might turn an agent or publisher off?'" And, she adds, "if they're unpublished, writers need to think about what makes them stand out as good candidates for representation by the agent. Have they won any writing competitions? Are they authorities on the subject matter?"

WHERE TO FIND AGENTS

Once your manuscript is ultra-polished and ready for publication, and you've decided to take the leap and find an agent, one way is to conduct online research. "I think a writer should be a good sleuth," says Dawn Green. "And most agents/agencies are clear on their websites about what they are looking for." She also suggests researching to see if agents have given (online) interviews and made additional comments about what they're looking for in a manuscript.

Publishers Marketplace is a helpful online research tool. For a $25 monthly membership, writers/authors can get snapshots of top literary agencies, seeing which books agents have sold and editors' buying patterns. A membership also offers industry news updates and deal reports. The "Dealmaker" lists a contact database and a rights and proposals board posting—all helpful for determining which agent to pitch and also for knowing how to entice each one. "It's one of the most extensive databases of agents," says Wiese Sneyd. "It's an amazing resource."

Word of mouth is also helpful. Ask authors (especially in your genre) you know and trust, and whose work you respect who their agent is and request a candid assessment of their professional and personal style. "Referrals from existing clients are also an excellent way to get an agent's attention, so if you are able to ask an established writer, do so," recommends Forde. With Brown, he's the one making the connection for the writer. "In several cases, I have come across an unrepresented writer whose work I admire and recommended them to my agent."

Another method is to read the acknowledgment section of books with a similar audience or vibe to yours, as well as those of your favorite authors, who often list their agent with a huge "thank you." In a *Forbes'* blog post by contributor Nick Morgan, he succinctly explains the process: "Find books that are similar to what you hope yours will be, and that you like, and read the acknowledgments. Every writer thanks her agent fulsomely in the acknowledgments, or she'll never publish again."

Writers' conferences are also another viable route to find agents who are actively seeking new titles/authors. These agents are often speakers/panelists there, offering writers the chance to meet with them one-on-one to pitch their manuscript. "Face-to-face meetings with agents can help you get a foot in the door—as long as you keep it professional and respectful," notes Purcell. Hahnel knows "two people who were able to sign with agents at 'speed-dating' sessions at conferences," but, she stresses, "I understand it's not a super-common occurrence." Taylor says to attend myriad industry events, including in-store appearances, book launches and festivals. "Talk to people. Often those in attendance are part of the book industry. Always tell people you are an author. You never know who you may be talking to."

QueryTracker.net has helped more than 2,400 authors find a literary agent. Among its many online freebies are a detailed database of more than 1,500 agent profiles, including author comments from their experience with said agent; an agent query-tracking feature; and data that lists agent reply rates, typical response times, etc. WritersDigest.com also offers a handy online feature called "New Agency Alerts" that profiles "new literary agents actively seeking writers, books, and queries now. These agents are building their client lists." AgentQuery.com, which says it's "the internet's largest free database of literary agents," lets you search for agents (around one thousand of them) by category, offers an online social networking community (great for the query process) and provides agent and agency updates. Attard maintains that authors and writers should check out the deal listings on *Publishers Weekly*, and *Quill & Quire*, investigating the agents listed in those deal announcements. And annual print directories, such as the *Literary Market Place: The Directory of the American Book Publishing Industry* (which offers listings to "reach the people who publish, package, review, represent, edit, translate, typeset, illustrate, design, print, bind, promote, publicize, ship, and distribute"), are often available in your local library's reference section, says Purcell.

Brown suggests submitting to literary magazines and contests. "These publications still attract the attention of agents," he assures. He also recommends using social media. Brown "drew the attention of a couple of agents after becoming active on Twitter." Why? "I believe some of the younger literary agents monitor social media for young writers who are making waves with their essays or stories." Attard is in agreement. "Some agents are active on social media, so follow a few and get a sense of what they like and don't like, and what you should avoid doing! It can be really valuable to get a sense of how they work."

And while a seasoned, big-name agent may be able to get you an impressive advance on your book and secure an ironclad contract, don't be afraid to go with a newer literary agent, someone who's "hungry" and will most likely have more time and offer a high level of personal attention to champion not only your book, but also your literary career. Attard suggests that "if an agent is new without many prior sales, consider their history in the industry. Do they have the connections necessary to be successful?" And, cautions Webb, "a junior agent—and everyone needs to start somewhere—should be a junior agent within a reputable agency, who has the support of more senior agents behind her." In the same vein is the size of the literary agency. "This doesn't necessarily correlate with the quality of the agent or the size of the deal you can expect," verifies Friedman in her blog post "How to Find a Literary Agent for Your Book."

THE "GOOD" AGENT

What are the signs of a good literary agent? According to the website of the Canadian Authors Association, "reputable agents will be up to date on current publishing trends … and serve as experts in market sales, so they will help ensure your book gets a good cover design, and more attention from the publisher's publicity department." Purcell affirms that agents "represent you [the author], not the publisher, and will negotiate for more money, subsidiary rights, and protection clauses. Good agents are also in it for the long haul: they are as interested in building the author's career as they are in selling the first book."

MacIntyre shares the same mindset. He says that many writers aren't interested in the "bureaucracy and the fine points of the book business," so a good agent, "in addition to possessing literary instincts and professional connections, has a mercenary skill set. An agent should be a partner and a friend, but strong enough to speak truth to vanity. An agent will offer an essential service but is not a servant." He also says good agents attend myriad international book fairs; have strong professional relationships with influential editors; "play bad-cop where money matters matter; play mom/dad when the creative muse becomes petulant and sulky; pick up the tab (now and then); offer tactful commentary and advice (but not instruction) on creative issues; and know the difference between momentary insecurity and reality-based despair." MacIntyre also believes good agents have "the sensibilities and judgment of an editor; the skills of an accountant; the temerity of a union boss; a sense of humor, irony; good taste in food, drink and literature; and patience."

Kanya-Forstner stresses that "the best agents search widely and actively for new, diverse and challenging voices; for writers who bring something essential to the conversations in which they participate." She says that "the best agents are the most discerning, taking on only those clients whose work they know they can champion with the utmost integrity and confidence. The work they then submit comes with the weight of their endorsement and credibility." To Kanya-Forstner, "the best agents make it their business to be familiar with the sensibilities and interests of individual editors and with the publishing identity and strengths of individual imprints. The best agents pride themselves on being successful matchmakers."

Kardys says a "talented agent" will suggest to a writer several tactics, such as building a platform before the book deal—social media, contact lists, and doing events or writing articles/stories; provide ideas on how to market the book; and edit the writer's book summary." For her, "ideally, the best literary agents have a background as a former book editor, subsidiary rights experience at a book publisher, or the agent has started their publishing career by working for another literary agency before leaving to start their own agency."

Cole sees a good agent as "someone who seems to 'get' your work, who understands what you're writing now, and what you want to write in the future." And, adds Kanya-Forstner, since "publishing is a constantly changing business, the best agents stay on top of market trends, shifts in buying habits and retail practices." Terence Green describes the good agent in these terms: "A good agent knows editors and what they are looking for. They can provide shortcuts to editors. Many editors won't even look at unsolicited manuscripts, trusting the judgment of respected agents." So, the good agent, he says, is "in essence, the editor's first reader, winnowing the field appropriately for the editor." Friedman believes a good agent is not only an author's business manager, but also an author's "mentor and cheerleader." She shares these wise sentiments in her blog post: Literary agents are "also there to hold your hand when things go wrong with the editor or publisher. They prop you up when you're down, they celebrate your successes publicly, they look for opportunities you might not see, and they attend to your financial best interests as well as your big-picture career growth." Purcell stresses that "because the bulk of their work involves sales and negotiation, [editors] should be confident and assertive in their dealings, but always professional and respectful in their treatment of people, including you." She also believes agents should be "strategic thinkers" with strong social media skills. And "being well-organized is also a useful quality in a literary agent, since they need to juggle a variety of authors, editors, and projects."

THE "BAD" AGENT

While the list of qualities and skills of a good agent is long, the list for a "bad" one is comparable. Since there is no worldwide professional organization responsible for vetting agents and maintaining agent standards, virtually anyone can hang out their "Agent" shingle. Beware of sweet-talking scammers, secretive behavior, those who don't treat you as a business partner, those who don't communicate respectfully and clearly, and those who don't reply in a timely manner. They aren't legit agents. Never, ever give a literary agent money upfront—not as a retainer, not for administrative expenses, and not for a reading fee/feedback. An agent only gets paid—somewhere between 10 and 15 percent of an author's earnings—when an author gets paid and the publisher's advance is received. And 20 to 25 percent is standard for foreign sales (when translation rights are licensed to foreign book publishers), since the commission is often split between foreign and domestic agents. Cole says that "if you send a manuscript to an agent and she doesn't respond after a few months, that's an agent I wouldn't bother approaching further." And, he stresses, "if you're working with an agent, and she can't give you a list of the publishers she's sent your manuscript to, that's an agent who probably isn't working hard for you." Similarly, Taylor says that "if your agent is not directing you towards a deal, perhaps it is not the best fit."

Kardys feels the following are red flags: "A writer should not work with an agent who has no experience in the book field or hasn't offered suggested changes in the manuscript." However, she says, "if the book requires major work, an agent shouldn't sign up a writer as a client." And "if the agent doesn't know the basic points of a contract, the payment structures for an advance and the latest changes in the book marketplace, you should be cautious," she warns. Friedman, in her blog post, stresses that "if an agent passes you a publisher's boilerplate contact to sign with no changes, you may be in big trouble." Hahnel says to avoid agents with "non-existent client lists or sales history." And, she alerts, "beware of agents who only work with a few publishers."

According to a Science Fiction & Fantasy Writers of America blog post by A.C. Crispin, "real agents don't advertise. They don't have to. If you see an agency name in a sponsored Google ad or in the back of a writer's magazine, odds are they're a scam." And, says

Crispin in that same post, "any agent that claims their client list is 'confidential' should be regarded with wariness, and their credentials should be investigated with extra care." Also, avoid agents who don't help with improving your query and/or proposal package. In her blog post, Friedman says only a few authors can put together a "crackerjack proposal." She stresses that "an agent should be ensuring the pitch or proposal is primed for success, and this almost always requires at least one round of feedback and revision."

Membership in the newly founded Professional Association of Canadian Literary Agents (PACLA), which only permits established literary agents to join and has a strict Code of Practice, or in the Association of Authors' Representatives, Inc. (AAR), for which its some 400 member must meet the highest standards and subscribe to its bylaws and Canon of Ethics, is a positive sign, but not necessarily a guarantee. Friedman states that "people in the industry should recognize the name of your agent." She also warns that if no online mention or reference to your agent can be found and if the agent isn't a member of the AAR, "that's a red flag. Check his track record carefully. See who he's sold to and how recently." And, forewarns Purcell, "generally speaking, if an agent is pursuing you rather than the other way around, think twice—most agents already have a stable of promising authors and rarely need to be the wooer." These are all reasons why, says, Terence Green, "one must do one's 'due diligence' in the matter, just as one would before venturing into any business investment."

HOW TO KEEP THE GOOD ONES

If you do secure a literary agent, be mindful that, like in any good relationship, the author-agent "marriage" can only thrive on mutual trust and respect, shared enthusiasm and open communication. Says Purcell: "I think it's important to have a connection with your literary agent. If there isn't a genuine and mutual feeling of respect and liking for one another, the relationship may sour over time." Sinclair thinks "it's important that you can enjoy a meal together. It's an intimate relationship in a way, so you want to be sure you like each other!" Cole advises to "be reliable, meet your deadlines and appreciate [your agent's] hard work." And Webb says to "be open to feedback and trust that your agent wants to make a success of your book and your career." But, don't expect to sit back and let your agent do all of the legwork. "Be proactive about your career, boosting your platform whenever you can, and be someone who editors want to work with," she advises. Wiese Sneyd concurs. "Learn the business ahead of time. Respect an agent's time. Avoid excessive emails. Don't expect an agent to teach you the ins and outs of publishing. You'll have questions, of course, but enter the relationship as a savvy author."

Kardys advises to "always put in writing the obligations and duties of the writer and the agent" and to "encourage open communication and timelines." She also stresses to "listen carefully when your agent tells you to build your social media platform and make a list of email contacts, as later you will not have time to do this intense work when your book is published." Brown's suggestions are also a list of dos. Only a small percentage of writers get to have an agent represent their work, he says, and "there will be ups and downs and stressors of all kinds." But, he notes, "it's important to keep in mind that many writers only dream of having such problems! So try to enjoy the whole experience, even the worries and frustrations. They are all part of the story."

MAKING THE FINAL DECISION

Kanya-Forstner advises that "agents are only as good as the authors they represent, or for new agents, as good as the writers whose work they champion on social platforms and in public discourse about books." Refer to an agent's client list, which rights they've sold, when and in which countries, view their photograph, their (literary) likes and dislikes (Goodreads is a good resource to check), their Twitter feed, their website or their company's website, and weigh it all with any kind of gut feeling you may have to help you make your final choice. It all boils down to feelings and sensibilities—a kind of personal chemistry. MacIntyre concurs: "Basically, it will come down to a gut-level response, based on impressions and the compatibility of personalities." Author Chuck Sambuchino takes a similar stance. In his online WritersDigest.com article entitled "11 Steps to Finding the Agent Who'll Love your Book," he says that, after making your list of agents to contact, "rank agents in the likelihood of a love match."

THE SUBMISSION PROCESS IN A NUTSHELL

After doing your research into finding suitable agents, it's absolutely essential to find out what each agent wants in a submission. "Be professional, read about the formatting details the agency wants and let your story do the selling," says Dawn Green. Purcell shares in her tips, adding, "it's important to find out what their preferences are and to follow their guidelines faithfully. If they want the manuscript double-spaced in the courier font with one-inch margins, that's what you should give them. You're sending them a message if you don't." Sambuchino concurs in his online piece. "Getting through the front door is often about playing by the rules. Don't send anything less—or more—than each agent has asked for." If the agent specifies that they don't want attachments, "that means they want the query letter and up to ten pages of the manuscript imbedded in the body of the email, even if that looks ugly," says Purcell. Also, says Sambuchino, be sure you're submitting to four to eight agents only at a time, giving each agent their own separate email or mailed package. "Keep things professional. No gimmicks." And don't argue if/when you get a "no thank you" reply. "An agent is not attacking you. They know the business, they know what sells, and they are honestly trying to help your words get noticed," says Dawn Green, adding not to take agent criticism personally. Taylor suggests that if you receive a "no," be sure to "follow up with a thank you and ask if they might suggest who might be interested. Sometimes advice comes your way, or even your work gets a second look. Often publishing is luck and timing."

BEYOND THE QUERY

Be sure to keep track of your submissions and their results. Sambuchino says that "if you aren't getting any page requests, your query needs work. If you're getting partial requests but then nothing, your first draft pages aren't snagging the reader. If you're getting full requests but no nibbles, it's time to take a look at the full manuscript again." Use each rejection and any feedback you may get from an agent to fine-tune your next set of submissions. "This is not an easy business, and rejection is the norm, not the exception. I like to think of rejections as marks of honor," says Brown. "It's not how many times you get knocked down; it's how many times you get back up. Each rejection is one step closer to publication. Keep the faith. Keep going. It's worth it." And be prepared to wait for as long as it takes to find your perfect match. "My experience," clarifies Terence Green, "has always been that this is not a business for the impatient."

Perhaps the best advice to keep in mind during this journey comes from Cole: "Too many beginning writers with a half-finished manuscript think the first thing they need to do is get an agent, as if that will solve everything and ensure a flourishing writing career. It doesn't work that way," he warns. "The first thing you need to do is master your craft and produce a damn good book. An agent can't make you a good writer. An agent can't make you a success. That's up to you."

JENNIFER D. FOSTER is a Toronto, Canada-based freelance writer and editor, and her company is Planet Word. Her clients are from the book and custom publishing, magazine, and marketing and communications fields and include House of Anansi Press, Art Gallery of Ontario, TC Media Inc., *Quill & Quire*, PwC Management Services, *The Globe and Mail*, and *Canadian Children's Book News*. When Jennifer's not busy spilling ink for her first novel, she enjoys mentoring novice editors and writers, theater, traveling, gardening, camping, women's roller derby, urban hiking, baking, and yoga. Jennifer is administrative director of Rowers Reading Series and vice president of Canadian Authors Association, Toronto branch. Find her online at lifeonplanetword.wordpress.com.

30-DAY PLATFORM CHALLENGE

Build Your Writing Platform in a Month

by Robert Lee Brewer

Whether writers are looking to find success through traditional publication or the self-publishing route, they'll find a strong writer platform will help them in their efforts. A platform is not marketing; it's the actual and quantifiable reach writers have to their target audience.

Here is a 30-day platform challenge I've developed to help writers get started in their own platform-building activities without getting overwhelmed. By accomplishing one task for one day, writers can feel a sense of accomplishment and still handle their normal daily activities. By the end of the month, writers should have a handle on what they need to do to keep growing their platform into the future.

DAY 1: DEFINE YOURSELF

For Day 1, define yourself. Don't worry about where you'd like to be in the future. Instead, take a look at who you are today, what you've already accomplished, what you're currently doing, etc.

EXAMPLE DEFINE YOURSELF WORKSHEET

Here is a chart I'm using (with my own answers). Your worksheet can ask even more questions. The more specific you can be the better for this exercise.

NAME (AS USED IN BYLINE): Robert Lee Brewer

POSITION(S): Senior Content Editor - Writer's Digest Writing Community; Author; Freelance Writer; Blogger; Event Speaker; Den Leader - Cub Scouts; Curator of Insta-poetry Series

SKILL(S): Editing, creative writing (poetry and fiction), technical writing, copywriting, database management, SEO, blogging, newsletter writing, problem solving, idea generation, public speaking, willingness to try new things, community building.

SOCIAL MEDIA PLATFORMS: Facebook, LinkedIn, Google+, Twitter, Tumblr, Blogger.

URLs: www.writersdigest.com/editor-blogs/poetic-asides; http://robertleebrewer.blogspot.com/; www.robertleebrewer.com

ACCOMPLISHMENTS: Named 2010 Poet Laureate of Blogosphere; spoken at several events, including Writer's Digest Conference, AWP, Austin International Poetry Festival, Houston Poetry Fest, and more; author of Solving the World's Problems (Press 53); published and sold out of two limited edition poetry chapbooks, *Enter* and *Escape*; edited several editions of *Writer's Market* and *Poet's Market*; former GMVC conference champion in the 800-meter run and MVP of WCHS cross country and track teams; undergraduate award-winner in several writing disciplines at University of Cincinnati, including Journalism, Fiction, and Technical Writing; BA in English Literature from University of Cincinnati with certificates in writing for Creative Writing-Fiction and Professional and Technical Writing.

INTERESTS: Writing (all genres), family (being a good husband and father), faith, fitness (especially running and disc golf), fantasy football, reading.

IN ONE SENTENCE, WHO AM I? Robert Lee Brewer is a married Methodist father of five children (four sons and one daughter) who works as an editor but plays as a writer, specializing in poetry and blogging.

As long as you're being specific and honest, there are no wrong answers when it comes to defining yourself. However, you may realize that you have more to offer than you think. Or you may see an opportunity that you didn't realize even existed.

DAY 2: SET YOUR GOALS

For today's platform-building task, set your goals. Include short-term goals and long-term goals. In fact, make a list of goals you can accomplish by the end of this year; then, make a list of goals you'd like to accomplish before you die.

EXAMPLE GOALS

Here are some of examples from my short-term and long-term goal lists:

SHORT-TERM GOALS:

- Promote new book, *Solving the World's Problems*.
- In April, complete April PAD Challenge on Poetic Asides blog.
- Get *Writer's Market 2016* to printer ahead of schedule.
- Get *Poet's Market 2016* to printer ahead of schedule.
- Lead workshop at Poetry Hickory event in April.
- Etc.

LONG-TERM GOALS:

- Publish book on platform development for small businesses.
- Raise 5 happy and healthy children into 5 happy, healthy, caring, and self-sufficient adults.
- Continue to learn how to be a better husband and human being.
- Become a bestselling novelist.
- Win Poet Laureate of the Universe honors.
- Etc.

Some writers may ask what defining yourself and creating goals has to do with platform development. I maintain that these are two of the most basic and important steps in the platform-building process, because they define who you are and where you want to be.

A successful platform strategy should communicate who you are and help you get where you'd like to be (or provide you with a completely new opportunity). If you can't communicate who you are to strangers, then they won't realize how you might be able to help them or why you're important to them. If you don't have any goals, then you don't have any direction or purpose for your platform.

By defining who you are and what you want to accomplish, you're taking a huge step in establishing a successful writing and publishing career.

DAY 3: JOIN FACEBOOK

For today's task, create a profile on Facebook. Simple as that. If you don't have one, it's as easy as going to www.facebook.com and signing up. It takes maybe 5 or 10 minutes. If that.

10 FACEBOOK TIPS FOR WRITERS

Many readers probably already have a Facebook profile, and that's fine. If you have already created a profile (or are doing so today), here are some tips for handling your profile:

- Complete your profile. The most checked page on most profiles is the About page. The more you share the better.
- Make everything public. Like it or not, writers are public figures. If you try to hide, it will limit the potential platform.
- Think about your audience in everything you do. When your social media profiles are public, anyone can view what you post. Keep this in mind at all times.
- Include a profile pic of yourself. Avoid setting your avatar as anything but a headshot of yourself. Many people don't like befriending a family pet or cartoon image.
- Update your status regularly. If you can update your status once per day, that's perfect. At the very least, update your status weekly. If your profile is a ghost town, people will treat it like one.
- Communicate with friends on Facebook. Facebook is a social networking site, but networking happens when you communicate. So communicate.
- Be selective about friends. Find people who share your interests. Accept friends who share your interests. Other folks may be fake or inappropriate connections trying to build their "friend" totals.
- Be selective about adding apps. If you're not sure, it's probably best to avoid. Many users have wasted days, weeks, and even months playing silly games on Facebook.
- Join relevant groups. The emphasis should be placed on relevancy. For instance, I'm a poet, so I join poetry groups.
- Follow relevant fan pages. As with groups, the emphasis is placed on relevancy. In my case, I'm a fan of several poetry publications.

In addition to the tips above, be sure to always use your name as it appears in your byline. If you're not consistent in how you list your name in your byline, it's time to pick a name and stick with it. For instance, my byline name is Robert Lee Brewer—not Robbie Brewer, Bob Brewer, or even just Robert Brewer.

There are times when I absolutely can't throw the "Lee" in there, but the rest of the time it is Robert Lee Brewer. And the reasoning behind this is that it makes it easier for people who know me elsewhere to find and follow me on Facebook (or whichever social media site). Name recognition is super important when you're building your writer platform.

DAY 4: JOIN TWITTER

For today's task, create a Twitter account. That's right. Go to www.twitter.com and sign up—if you're not already. This task will definitely take less than 5 minutes.

As with Facebook, I would not be surprised to learn that most readers already have a Twitter account. Here are three important things to keep in mind:

- **MAKE YOUR PROFILE BIO RELEVANT.** You might want to use a version of the sentence you wrote for Day 1's task. Look at my profile (twitter.com/robertleebrewer) if you need an example.
- **USE AN IMAGE OF YOURSELF.** One thing about social media (and online networking) is that people love to connect with other people. So use an image of yourself—not of your pet, a cute comic strip, a new age image, flowers, robots, etc.
- **MAKE YOUR TWITTER HANDLE YOUR BYLINE—IF POSSIBLE.** For instance, I am known as @RobertLeeBrewer on Twitter, because I use Robert Lee Brewer as my byline on articles, in interviews, at speaking events, on books, etc. Be as consistent with your byline as humanly possible.

Once you're in Twitter, try finding some worthwhile tweeps to follow. Also, be sure to make a tweet or two. As with Facebook, people will only interact with your profile if it looks like you're actually there and using your account.

SOME BASIC TWITTER TERMINOLOGY

Twitter has a language all its own. Here are some of the basics:

- **TWEET.** This is what folks call the 280-character messages that can be sent on the site. Anyone who follows you can access your tweets.
- **RT.** RT stands for retweet. This is what happens when someone shares your tweet, usually character for character. It's usually good form to show attribution for the author of the original tweet.
- **DM.** DM stands for direct message. This is a good way to communicate with someone on Twitter privately. I've actually had a few opportunities come my way through DMs on Twitter.
- **#.** The #-sign stands for hashtag. Hashtags are used to organize group conversations. For instance, Writer's Digest uses the #wdc to coordinate messages for their Writer's Digest Conferences. Anyone can start a hashtag, and they're sometimes used to add humor or emphasis to a tweet.
- **FF.** FF stands for follow Friday—a day typically set asides to highlight follow-worthy tweeps (or folks who use Twitter). There's also a WW that stands for writer Wednesday.

DAY 5: START A BLOG

For today's task, create a blog. You can use Blogger (www.blogger.com), WordPress (www.wordpress.com), or Tumblr (www.tumblr.com). In fact, you can use another blogging platform if you wish. To complete today's challenge, do the following:

- **CREATE A BLOG.** That is, sign up (if you don't already have a blog), pick a design (these can usually be altered later if needed), and complete your profile.
- **WRITE A POST FOR TODAY.** If you're not sure what to cover, you can just introduce yourself and share a brief explanation of how your blog got started. Don't make it too complicated.

If you already have a blog, excellent! You don't need to create a new one, but you might want to check out some ways to optimize what you have.

OPTIMIZE YOUR BLOG

Here are some tips for making your blog rock:

- **USE IMAGES IN YOUR POSTS.** Images are eye candy for readers, help with search engine optimization, and can even improve clicks when shared on social media sites, such as Facebook and Twitter.
- **USE HEADERS IN POSTS.** Creating and bolding little headlines in your posts will go a long way toward making your posts easier to read and scan. Plus, they'll just look more professional.
- **WRITE SHORT.** Short sentences (fewer than 10 words). Short paragraphs (fewer than five sentences). Concision is precision in online composition.
- **ALLOW COMMENTS.** Most bloggers receive very few (or absolutely zero) comments in the beginning, but it pays to allow comments, because this gives your audience a way to interact with you. For my personal blog, I allow anyone to comment on new posts, but those that are more than a week old require my approval.

DAY 6: READ AND COMMENT ON A POST

For today's task, read at least one blog post and comment on it (linking back to your blog). And the comment should not be something along the lines of, "Hey, cool post. Come check out my blog." Instead, you need to find a blog post that really speaks to you and then make a thoughtful comment.

Here are a few possible ways to respond.

- **SHARE YOUR OWN EXPERIENCE.** If you've experienced something similar to what's covered in the post, share your own story. You don't have to write a book or anything, but maybe a paragraph or two.
- **ADD ANOTHER PERSPECTIVE.** Maybe the post was great, but there's another angle that should be considered. Don't be afraid to point that angle out.
- **ASK A QUESTION.** A great post usually will prompt new thoughts and ideas—and questions. Ask them.

As far as linking back to your blog, you could include your blog's URL in the comment, but also, most blogs have a field in their comments that allow you to share your URL. Usually, your name will link to that URL, which should either be your blog or your author website (if it offers regularly updated content).

It might seem like a lot of work to check out other blogs and comment on them, but this is an incredible way to make real connections with super users. These connections can lead to guest post and interview opportunities. In fact, they could even lead to speaking opportunities too.

DAY 7: ADD SHARE BUTTONS TO YOUR BLOG

For today's challenge, add share buttons to your blog and/or website.

The easiest way to do this is to go to www.addthis.com and click on the Get AddThis button. It's big, bright, and orange. You can't miss it.

Basically, the site will give you button options, and you select the one you like best. The AddThis site will then provide you with HTML code that you can place into your site and/or blog posts. Plus, it provides analytics for bloggers who like to see how much the buttons are boosting traffic.

If you want customized buttons, you could enlist the help of a programmer friend or try playing with the code yourself. I recently learned that some really cool buttons on one friend's blog were created by her husband (yes, she married a programmer, though I don't think she had her blog in mind when she did so).

Plus, most blogging platforms are constantly adding new tools. By the time you read this article, there are sure to be plenty of fun new buttons, apps, and widgets available.

Here's the thing about social sharing buttons: They make it very easy for people visiting your site to share your content with their social networks via Facebook, Twitter, LinkedIn, Instagram, Pinterest, and other sites. The more your content is shared the wider your writer platform.

DAY 8: JOIN LINKEDIN

For today's challenge, create a LinkedIn profile. Go to www.linkedin.com and set it up in a matter of minutes. After creating profiles for Facebook and Twitter, this task should be easy.

LINKEDIN TIPS FOR WRITERS

In many ways, LinkedIn looks the same as the other social networks, but it does have its own quirks. Here are a few tips for writers:

- **USE YOUR OWN HEAD SHOT.** You've heard this advice before. People want to connect with people, not family pets and/or inanimate objects.
- **COMPLETE YOUR PROFILE.** The more complete your profile the better. It makes you look more human.
- **GIVE THOUGHTFUL RECOMMENDATIONS TO RECEIVE THEM.** Find people likely to give you recommendations and recommend them first. This will prompt them to return the favor.
- **SEARCH FOR CONNECTIONS YOU ALREADY HAVE.** This is applicable to all social networks. Find people you know to help you connect with those you don't.
- **MAKE MEANINGFUL CONNECTIONS WITH OTHERS.** Remember: It's not about how many connections you make; it's about how many meaningful connections you make.
- **MAKE YOUR PROFILE EASY TO FIND.** You can do this by using your byline name. (For instance, I use linkedin.com/in/robertleebrewer.)
- **TAILOR YOUR PROFILE TO YOUR VISITOR.** Don't fill out your profile thinking only about yourself; instead, think about what your target audience might want to learn about you.

LinkedIn is often considered a more "professional" site than the other social networks like Facebook, Instagram, and Twitter. For one thing, users are prompted to share their work experience and request recommendations from past employers and current coworkers.

However, this site still offers plenty of social networking opportunities for people who can hook up with the right people and groups.

DAY 9: RESPOND TO AT LEAST THREE TWEETS

For today's task, respond to at least three tweets from other tweeps on Twitter.

Since Day 4's assignment was to sign up for Twitter, you should have a Twitter account—and you're hopefully following some other Twitter users. Just respond to at least three tweets today.

As far as your responses, it's not rocket science. You can respond with a "great article" or "cool quote." A great way to spread the wealth on Twitter is to RT (retweet) the original tweet with a little note. This accomplishes two things:

- One, it lets the tweep know that you appreciated their tweet (and helps build a bond with that person); and
- Two, it brings attention to that person for their cool tweet.

Plus, it helps show that you know how to pick great resources on Twitter, which automatically improves your credibility as a resource on Twitter.

DAY 10: DO A GOOGLE SEARCH ON YOURSELF

For today's task, do a search on your name.

First, see what results appear when you search your name on Google (google.com). Then, try searching on Bing (bing.com). Finally, give Yahoo (yahoo.com) a try.

By searching your name, you'll receive insights into what others will find (and are already finding) when they do a search specifically for you. Of course, you'll want to make sure your blog and/or website is number one in the search results. If it isn't, we'll be covering SEO (or search engine optimization) topics later in this challenge.

OTHER SEARCH ENGINES

For those who want extra credit, here are some other search engines to try searching (for yourself):

- DuckDuckGo.com
- Ask.com
- Dogpile.com
- Yippy.com
- YouTube.com

(Note: It's worth checking out which images are related to your name as well. You may be surprised to find which images are connected to you.)

DAY 11: FIND A HELPFUL ARTICLE AND LINK TO IT

For today's task, find a helpful article (or blog post) and share it with your social network—and by social network, I mean that you should share it on Facebook, Twitter, and LinkedIn at a minimum. If you participate on message boards or on other social networks, share in those places as well.

Before linking to an article on fantasy baseball or celebrity news, however, make sure your article (or blog post) aligns with your author platform goals. You should have an idea of who you are and who you want to be as a writer, and your helpful article (or blog post) should line up with those values.

Of course, you may not want to share articles for writers if your platform is based on parenting tips or vampires or whatever. In such cases, you'll want to check out other resources online. Don't be afraid to use a search engine.

For Twitter, you may wish to use a URL shortener to help you keep under the 280-character limit. Here are five popular URL shorteners:

- bit.ly. This is my favorite.
- goo.gl. Google's URL shortener.
- owl.ly. Hootsuite's URL shortener.
- deck.ly. TweetDeck's URL shortener.
- su.pr. StumbleUpon's URL shortener.

By the way, here's an extra Twitter tip. Leave enough room in your tweets to allow space for people to attribute your Twitter handle if they decide to RT you. For instance, I always leave at least 20 characters to allow people space to tweet "RT @robertleebrewer" when retweeting me.

DAY 12: WRITE A BLOG POST AND INCLUDE CALL TO ACTION

For today's task, write a new blog post for your blog. In the blog post, include a call to action at the end of the post.

What's a call to action?

I include calls to action at the end of all my posts. Sometimes, they are links to products and services offered by my employer (Active Interest Media) or some other entity. Often, I include links to other posts and ways to follow me on other sites. Even the share buttons are a call to action of sorts.

Why include a call to action?

A call to action is good for giving readers direction and a way to engage more with you. Links to previous posts provide readers with more helpful or interesting information. Links to your social media profiles give readers a way to connect with you on those sites. These calls to action are beneficial to you and your readers when they are relevant.

What if I'm just getting started?

Even if you are completely new to everything, you should have an earlier blog post from last week, a Twitter account, a Facebook account, and a LinkedIn account. Link to these at the end of your blog post today. It's a proper starting place.

And that's all you need to do today. Write a new blog post with a call to action at the end. (By the way, if you're at a loss and need something to blog about, you can always comment on that article you shared yesterday.)

DAY 13: LINK TO POST ON SOCIAL MEDIA PROFILES

For today's challenge, link your blog post from yesterday to your social networks.

At a minimum, these social networks should include Facebook, Twitter, and LinkedIn. However, if you frequent message boards related to your blog post or other social networks (like Instagram, Pinterest, etc.), then link your blog post there as well.

I understand many of you may have already completed today's challenge. If so, hooray! It's important to link your blog to your social media accounts and vice versa. When they work together, they grow together.

Is it appropriate to link to my blog post multiple times?

All writers develop their own strategies for linking to their articles and blog posts, but here's my rule. I will usually link to each blog post on every one of my social networks at least once. Since I have a regular profile and a fan page on Facebook, I link to each of those profiles once—and I only link to posts once on LinkedIn. But Twitter is a special case.

The way Twitter works, tweets usually only have a few minutes of visibility for tweeps with an active stream. Even tweeps with at least 100 follows may only have a 30-minute to hour window of opportunity to see your tweet. So for really popular and timely blog posts, I will tweet them more often than once on Twitter.

That said, I'm always aware of how I'm linking and don't want to become that annoying spammer that I typically avoid following in my own social networking efforts.

LINKING TIPS

Some tips on linking to your post:

- Use a URL shortener. These are discussed above.

- Apply title + link formula. For instance, I might Tweet this post as: Platform Challenge: Day 13: (link). It's simple and to the point. Plus, it's really effective if you have a great blog post title.
- Frame the link with context. Using this post as an example, I might Tweet: Take advantage of social media by linking to your blog posts: (link). Pretty simple, and it's an easy way to link to the same post without making your Twitter feed look loaded with the same content.
- Quote from post + link formula. Another tactic is to take a funny or thought-provoking quote from the post and combine that with a link. Example Tweet: "I will usually link to each blog post on every one of my social networks at least once." (link). Again, easy stuff.

DAY 14: JOIN INSTAGRAM

For today's task, create an Instagram (Instagram.com) profile.

Many of you may already have Instagram profiles, but this social networking site and app is a little different than Facebook and Twitter. While all three offer opportunities for sharing video and photos, Instagram really emphasizes visual elements.

That might not seem like a good fit for writers, who are often more about text than visual cues. But there are opportunities for writers on this platform. And it's one more venue where the people (or your potential audience) are.

Here are a few getting started tips for Instagram:

- Complete your profile completely. Use your name, concisely describe who you are and what you're about, and make your profile public.
- Use an image of yourself. Not a cartoon. Not an animal. Not a piece of art. Remember that people like to connect with other people.
- Post new content regularly. Let people know you are using your account. A new post every day or three is a good way to achieve this.
- Use unique and relevant hashtags. These provide a way for people with similar interests who aren't already connected to you to find you.

DAY 15: MAKE THREE NEW CONNECTIONS

For today's task, make an attempt to connect with at least three new people on one of your social networks.

Doesn't matter if it's Facebook, Twitter, LinkedIn, or Instagram. The important thing is that you find three new people who appear to share your interests and that you try to friend, follow, or connect to them.

As a person who has limited wiggle room for approving new friends on Facebook, I'd like to share what approach tends to work the best with me for approving new friend requests. Basically, send your request and include a brief message introducing yourself and why you want to connect with me.

That's right. The best way to win me over is to basically introduce yourself. Something along the lines of, "Hello. My name is Robert Lee Brewer, and I write poetry. I read a poem of yours in *XYZ Literary Journal* that I totally loved and have sent you a friend request. I hope you'll accept it." Easy as that.

Notice that I did not mention anything about checking out my blog or reading my poems. How would you like it if someone introduced themselves and then told you to buy their stuff? It sounds a bit telemarketer-ish to me.

While it's important to cultivate the relationships you already have, avoid getting stuck in a rut when it comes to making connections. Always be on the lookout for new connections who can offer new opportunities and spark new ideas. Your writing and your career will benefit.

DAY 16: ADD EMAIL FEED TO BLOG

For today's challenge, add an email feed to your blog.

There are many ways to increase traffic to your blog, but one that has paid huge dividends for me is adding Feedblitz to my blog. As the subscribers to my email feed have increased, my blog traffic has increased as well. In fact, after great content, I'd say that adding share buttons (mentioned above) and an email feed are the top two ways to build traffic.

Though I have an account on Tumblr, I'm just not sure if it offers some kind of email/RSS feed service.

The reason I think email feeds are so useful is that they pop into my inbox whenever a new post is up, which means I can check it very easily on my phone when I'm waiting somewhere. In fact, this is how I keep up with several of my favorite blogs. It's just one more way to make your blog content accessible to readers in a variety of formats.

If I remember, this task didn't take me long to add, but I've been grateful for finally getting around to adding it ever since.

DAY 17: TAKE PART IN A TWITTER CONVERSATION

For today's task, take part in a Twitter conversation.

Depending upon the time of month or day of week, there are bound to be any number of conversations happening around a hashtag (mentioned above). For instance, various conferences and expos have hashtag conversations that build around their panels and presentations.

Poets will often meet using the #poetparty hashtag. Other writers use #amwriting to communicate about their writing goals. Click on the hashtag to see what others are saying, and then, jump in to join the conversation and make new connection on Twitter.

DAY 18: THINK ABOUT SEO

For today's task, I want you to slow down and think a little about SEO (which is tech-speak for search engine optimization, which is itself an intelligent way of saying "what gets your website to display at or near the top of a search on Google, Bing, Yahoo, etc.").

So this task is actually multi-pronged:

- Make a list of keywords that you want your website or blog to be known for. For instance, I want my blog to be known for terms like "Robert Lee Brewer," "Writing Tips," "Parenting Tips," "Platform Tips," "Living Tips," etc. Think big here and don't limit yourself to what you think you can actually achieve in the short term.
- Compare your website or blog's current content to your keywords. Are you lining up your actual content with how you want your audience to view you and your online presence? If not, it's time to think about how you can start offering content that lines up with your goals. If so, then move on to the next step, which is…
- Evaluate your current approach to making your content super SEO-friendly. If you need some guidance, check out my SEO Tips for Writers below. There are very simple things you can do with your titles, subheads, and images to really improve SEO. Heck, I get a certain bit of traffic every single day just from my own SEO approach to content—sometimes on surprising posts.
- Research keywords for your next post. When deciding on a title for your post and subheads within the content, try researching keywords. You can do this using Google's free keyword tool (googlekeywordtool.com). When possible, you want to use keywords that are searched a lot but that have low competition. These are the low-hanging fruit that can help you build strong SEO for your website or blog.

A note on SEO: It's easy to fall in love with finding keywords and changing your content to be keyword-loaded and blah-blah-blah. But resist making your website or blog a place that is keyword-loaded and blah-blah-blah. Because readers don't stick around for too much keyword-loaded blah-blah-blah. It's kind of blah. And bleck. Instead, use SEO and keyword research as a way to optimize great content and to take advantage of opportunities as they arise.

SEO TIPS FOR WRITERS

Here are a few SEO tips for writers:

- Use keywords naturally. That is, make sure your keywords match the content of the post. If they don't match up, people will abandon your page fast, which will hurt your search rankings.
- Use keywords appropriately. Include your keywords in the blog post title, opening paragraph, file name for images, headers, etc. Anywhere early and relevant should include your keyword to help place emphasis on that search term, especially if it's relevant to the content.
- Deliver quality content. Of course, search rankings are helped when people click on your content and spend time reading your content. So provide quality content, and people will visit your site frequently and help search engines list you higher in their rankings.
- Update content regularly. Sites that are updated more with relevant content rank higher in search engines. Simple as that.
- Link often to relevant content. Link to your own posts; link to content on other sites. Just make sure the links are relevant and of high interest to your audience.
- Use images. Images help from a design perspective, but they also help with SEO, especially when you use your main keywords in the image file name.
- Link to your content on social media sites. These outside links will help increase your ranking on search engines.
- Guest post on other sites/blogs. Guest posts on other blogs are a great way to provide traffic from other relevant sites that increase the search engine rankings on your site.

DAY 19: WRITE A BLOG POST

For today's task, write a new blog post.

Include a call to action (for instance, encourage readers to sign up for your email feed and to share the post with others using your share buttons) and link to it on your social networks. Also, don't forget to incorporate SEO.

One of the top rules of finding success with online tools is applying consistency. While it's definitely a great thing if you share a blog post more than once a week, I think it's imperative that you post at least once a week.

The main reason? It builds trust with your readers that you'll have something to share regularly and gives them a reason to visit regularly.

So today's task is not about making things complicated; it's just about keeping it real.

DAY 20: CREATE EDITORIAL CALENDAR

For today's task, I want you to create an editorial calendar for your blog (or website). Before you start to panic, read on.

First, here's how I define an editorial calendar: A list of content with dates attached to when the content goes live. For instance, I created an editorial calendar specifically for my Platform Challenge and "Platform Challenge: Day 20" was scheduled to go live on day 20.

It's really simple. In fact, I keep track of my editorial calendar with a paper notebook, which gives me plenty of space for crossing things out, jotting down ideas, and attaching Post-It notes.

EDITORIAL CALENDAR IDEAS

Here are tips for different blogging frequencies:

- Post once per week. If you post once a week, pick a day of the week for that post to happen each week. Then, write down the date for each post. Beside each date, write down ideas for that post ahead of time. There will be times when the ideas are humming and you get ahead on your schedule, but there may also be times when the ideas are slow. So don't wait, write down ideas as they come.
- Post more than once per week. Try identifying which days you'll usually post (for some, that may be daily). Then, for each of those days, think of a theme for that day. For instance, my 2012 schedule offered Life Changing Moments on Wednesdays and Poetic Saturdays on Saturdays.

You can always change plans and move posts to different days, but the editorial calendar is an effective way to set very clear goals with deadlines for accomplishing them. Having that kind of structure will improve your content—even if your blog is personal, fictional, poetic, etc. Believe me, I used to be a skeptic before diving in, and the results on my personal blog speak for themselves.

One more benefit of editorial calendars

There are times when I feel less than inspired. There are times when life throws me several elbows as if trying to prevent me from blogging. That's when I am the most thankful for maintaining an editorial calendar, because I don't have to think of a new idea on the spot; it's already there in my editorial calendar.

Plus, as I said earlier, you can always change plans. I can alter the plan to accommodate changes in my schedule. So I don't want to hear that an editorial calendar limits spontaneity or inspiration; if anything, having an editorial calendar enhances it.

One last thing on today's assignment

Don't stress yourself out that you have to create a complete editorial calendar for the year or even the month. I just want you to take some time out today to think about it, sketch some ideas, and get the ball rolling. I'm 100 percent confident that you'll be glad you did.

DAY 21: SIGN UP FOR SOCIAL MEDIA TOOL

For today's task, try joining one of the social media management tools, such as Tweetdeck, Hootsuite, or Seesmic.

Social media management tools are popular among social media users for one reason: They help save time and effort in managing multiple social media platforms. For instance, they make following specific threads in Twitter a snap.

I know many social media super users who swear by these tools, but I actually have tried them and decided to put in the extra effort to log in to my separate social media accounts manually each day.

Here's my reasoning: I like to feel connected to my profile and understand how it looks and feels on a day-to-day basis. Often, the design and feel of social media sites will change without notice, and I like to know what it feels like at ground zero.

DAY 22: PITCH GUEST BLOG POST

For today's task, pitch a guest blog post to another blogger.

Writing guest posts is an incredible way to improve your exposure and expertise on a subject, while also making a deeper connection with the blogger who is hosting your guest post. It's a win for everyone involved.

In a recent interview with super blogger Jeff Goins, he revealed that most of his blog traffic came as a result of his guest posting on other blogs. Some of these blogs were directly related to his content, but he said many were in completely different fields.

GUEST POST PITCHING TIPS

After you know where you want to guest blog, here are some tips for pitching your guest blog post:

- Let the blogger know you're familiar with the blog. You should do this in one sentence (two sentences max) and be specific. For instance, a MNINB reader could say, "I've been reading your Not Bob blog for months, but I really love this Platform Challenge." Simple as that. It lets me know you're not a spammer, but it doesn't take me a long time to figure out what you're trying to say.

- Propose an idea or two. Each idea should have its own paragraph. This makes it easy for the blogger to know where one idea ends and the next one begins. In a pitch, you don't have to lay out all the details, but you do want to be specific. Try to limit the pitch to 2-4 sentences.
- Share a little about yourself. Emphasis on "a little." If you have previous publications or accomplishments that line up with the blog, share those. If you have expertise that lines up with the post you're pitching, share those. Plus, include any details about your online platform that might show you can help bring traffic to the post. But include all this information in 1-4 sentences.
- Include your information. When you close the pitch, include your name, email, blog (or website) URL, and other contact information you feel comfortable sharing. There's nothing more awkward for me than to have a great pitch that doesn't include the person's name. Or a way to learn more about the person.

What do I do after the pitch is accepted?

First off, congratulations! This is a great opportunity to show off your writing skills. Here's how to take advantage of your guest post assignment:

- **WRITE AN EXCEPTIONAL POST.** Don't hold back your best stuff for your blog. Write a post that will make people want to find more of your writing.
- **TURN IN YOUR POST ON DEADLINE.** If there's a deadline, hit it. If there's not a deadline, try to turn around the well-written post in a timely manner.
- **PROMOTE THE GUEST POST.** Once your guest post has gone live, promote it like crazy by linking to your post on your blog, social networks, message boards, and wherever else makes sense for you. By sending your own connections to this guest post, you're establishing your own expertise—not only through your post but also your connections.

DAY 23: CREATE A TIME MANAGEMENT PLAN

For today's task, create a time management plan.

You may be wondering why I didn't start out the challenge with a time management plan, and here's the reason: I don't think some people would've had any idea how long it takes them to write a blog post, share a link on Twitter and Facebook, respond to social media messages, etc. Now, many of you probably have a basic idea—even if you're still getting the hang of your new-fangled social media tools.

Soooo…the next step is to create a time management plan that enables you to be "active" socially and connect with other writers and potential readers while also spending a majority of your time writing and publishing.

As with any plan, you can make this as simple or complicated as you wish. For instance, my plan is to do 15 minutes or less of social media after completing each decent-sized task on my daily task list. I use social media time as a break, which I consider more productive than watching TV or playing Angry Birds.

I put my writing first and carve out time in the mornings and evenings to work on poetry and fiction. Plus, I consider my blogging efforts part of my writing too. So there you go.

My plan is simple and flexible, but if you want to get hardcore, break down your time into 15-minute increments. Then, test out your time management plan to see if it works for you. If not, then make minor changes to the plan until it has you feeling somewhat comfortable with the ratio of time you spend writing and time you spend building your platform.

Remember: A platform is a life-long investment in your career. It's not a sprint, so you have to pace yourself. Also, it's not something that happens overnight, so you can't wait until you need a platform to start building one. Begin today and build over time—so that it's there when you need it.

DAY 24: TAKE PART IN A FACEBOOK CONVERSATION

For today's task, take part in a conversation on Facebook.

You should've already participated in a Twitter conversation, so this should be somewhat similar—except you don't have to play with hashtags and 280-character restrictions. In fact, you just need to find a group conversation or status update that speaks to you and chime in with your thoughts.

Don't try to sell or push anything when you join a conversation. If you say interesting things, people will check out your profile, which if filled out will lead them to more information about you (including your website, blog, any books, etc.).

Goal one of social media is making connections. If you have everything else optimized, sales and opportunities will take care of themselves.

DAY 25: CONTACT AN EXPERT FOR AN INTERVIEW POST

For today's task, find an expert in your field and ask if that expert would like to be interviewed.

If you can secure the interview, this will make for a great blog post. Or it may help you secure a freelance assignment with a publication in your field. Or both, and possibly more.

How to Ask for an Interview

Believe it or not, asking for an interview with an expert is easy. I do it all the time, and these are the steps I take.

- **FIND AN EXPERT ON A TOPIC.** This is sometimes the hardest part: figuring out who I want to interview. But I never kill myself trying to think of the perfect person, and here's why: I can always ask for more interviews. Sometimes, it's just more productive to get the ball rolling than come up with excuses to not get started.
- **LOCATE AN EMAIL FOR THE EXPERT.** This can often be difficult, but a lot of experts have websites that share either email addresses or have online contact forms. Many experts can also be reached via social media sites, such as Facebook, Twitter, LinkedIn, Instagram, etc. Or they can be contacted through company websites. And so on.
- **SEND AN EMAIL ASKING FOR AN EMAIL INTERVIEW.** Of course, you can do this via an online contact form too. If the expert says no, that's fine. Respond with a "Thank you for considering and maybe we can make it work sometime in the future." If the expert says yes, then it's time to send along the questions.

How to Handle an Email Interview

Once you've secured your expert, it's time to compose and send the questions. Here are some of my tips.

- **ALWAYS START OFF BY ASKING QUESTIONS ABOUT THE EXPERT.** This might seem obvious to some, but you'd be surprised how many people start off asking "big questions" right out of the gate. Always start off by giving the expert a chance to talk about what he or she is doing, has recently done, etc.
- **LIMIT QUESTIONS TO 10 OR FEWER.** The reason for this is that you don't want to overwhelm your expert. In fact, I usually ask around eight questions in my email interviews. If I need to, I'll send along some follow-up questions, though I try to limit those as well. I want the expert to have an enjoyable experience, not a horrible experience. After all, I want the expert to be a connection going forward.
- **TRY NOT TO GET TOO PERSONAL.** If experts want to get personal in their answers, that's great. But try to avoid getting too personal in the questions you ask, because you may offend your expert or make them feel uncomfortable. Remember: You're interviewing the expert, not leading an interrogation.
- **REQUEST ADDITIONAL INFORMATION.** By additional information, I mean that you should request a headshot and a preferred bio—along with any links. To make the interview worth the expert's time, you should afford them an opportunity to promote themselves and their projects in their bios.

Once the Interview Goes Live…

Link to it on your social networks and let your expert know it is up (and include the specific link to the interview). If you're not already searching for your next expert to interview, be sure to get on it.

DAY 26: WRITE A BLOG POST AND LINK TO SOCIAL PROFILES

For today's task, write a new blog post.

In your blog post, include a call to action and link it on your social networks. Also, don't forget SEO.

Remember: One of the top rules of finding success with online tools is applying consistency. While it's definitely a great thing if you share a blog post more than once a week, I think it's imperative that you post at least once a week.

The main reason? It builds trust with your readers that you'll have something to share regularly and gives them a reason to visit regularly.

If this sounds repetitive, good; it means my message on consistency is starting to take root.

DAY 27: JOIN ANOTHER SOCIAL MEDIA SITE

For today's task, join one new social media site. I will leave it up to you to decide which new social media site it will be.

Maybe you'll join Pinterest. Maybe you'll choose Goodreads. Heck, you might go with RedRoom or some social media site that's not even on my radar at the time of this article. Everything is constantly evolving, which is why it's good to always try new things.

To everyone who doesn't want another site to join…

I understand your frustration and exhaustion. During a normal month, I'd never suggest someone sign up for so many social media sites in such a short period of time, but this isn't a normal month. We're in the midst of a challenge!

And no, I don't expect you to spend a lot of time on every social media site you join. That's not always the point when you first sign up. No, you sign up to poke around and see if the site interests you at all. See if you have any natural connections. Try mingling a little bit.

If the site doesn't appeal to you, feel free to let it be for a while. Let me share a story with you.

How I Came to Rock Facebook and Twitter

My Facebook and Twitter accounts both boast more than 5,000 followers (or friends/subscribers) today. But both accounts were originally created and abandoned, because they just weren't right for me at the time that I signed up.

For Facebook, I just didn't understand why I would abandon a perfectly good MySpace account to play around on a site that didn't feature the same level of music and personal blogging that MySpace did. But then, MySpace turned into Spam-opolis, and the rest is history.

For Twitter, I just didn't get the whole tweet concept, because Facebook already had status updates. Why tweet when I could update my status on Facebook?

But I've gained a lot professionally and personally from Facebook and Twitter—even though they weren't the right sites for me initially. It's not like Facebook is going to be around forever.

The Importance of Experimentation

Or as I prefer to think of it: The importance of play. You should constantly try new things, whether in your writing, your social media networks, or the places you eat food. Not only does it make life more exciting and provide you with new experiences and perspective, but it also helps make you a more well-rounded human being.

So don't complain about joining a new social media site. Instead, embrace the excuse to try something new, especially when there are only three more tasks left this month (and I promise no more new sites after today).

DAY 28: READ POST AND COMMENT ON IT

For today's task, read and comment on a blog post, making sure that your comment links back to your blog or website.

If you remember, this was the same task required way back on Day 6. How far we've come, though it's still a good idea to stay connected and engaged with other bloggers. I know I find that sometimes I start to insulate myself in my own little blogging communities and worlds—when it's good to get out and read what others are doing. In fact, that's what helped inspire my Monday Advice for Writers posts—it gives me motivation to read what others are writing (on writing, of course).

DAY 29: MAKE A TASK LIST

For today's task, make a task list of things you are going to do on each day next month. That's right, I want you to break down 31 days with 31 tasks for each day—similar to what we've done this month.

You see, I don't want you to quit challenging yourself once this challenge is over. Of course, you get to decide what the tasks will be. So if you aren't into new social media sites, don't put them on your list. Instead, focus on blog posts, commenting on other sites, linking to articles, contacting experts, or whatever it is that you are going to do next month to keep momentum building toward an incredible author platform.

Somewhere near the end of the month, you should have a day set aside with one task: Make a task list of things to do on each day of the next month. And so on and so forth. Keep it going, keep it rolling, and your efforts will continue to gain momentum and speed. I promise.

DAY 30: ENGAGE THE WORLD

For today's task, engage the world.

By this, I mean that you should comment on status updates, ask questions, share answers, start debates, continue debates, and listen—that's right, don't be that person who dominates a conversation and makes it completely one-sided.

Engage the world by entering the conversation. Engage the world by having the courage to take risks and share things of consequence. Engage the world by having the courage to make mistakes and fail and learn from those mistakes and failures.

The only people who never fail are those who never try, and those people never succeed at anything except avoiding failure and success. Don't be that person. Engage the world and let the world engage you.

ROBERT LEE BREWER is a senior editor with the Writer's Digest Writing Community and author of *Smash Poetry Journal*. Follow him on Twitter @robertleebrewer.

DIVERSE BOOKS MATTER

The push to publish a broader range of voices is no fad—it's an industry course correction long overdue. Here, a literary agent unpacks the movement taking books by storm.

by Ammi-Joan Paquette

One of the most common questions I'm asked as a literary agent at writers' conferences these days—and one that I'm always happy to hear—is some variation on: "How do you feel about the increased focus on diversity in publishing? What changes are you seeing in this area?"

Why am I happy to hear it? Because it's a question that didn't really come up five years ago, or at least not to this extent. It *should* be coming up, and the fact that it does so with increasing frequency is in itself a sign of the industry's change and forward progress.

But first, a caveat: This won't be an article detailing the history, statistics, or specific trajectory of diversity in publishing. I'm neither a scholar nor an analyst, and while I do love a good spreadsheet, I am not qualified to deliver any type of comprehensive treatise. What I hope to do here is share my broader perspective as an active member of the publishing community—both as a consumer of books and someone who helps funnel them along toward your bookshelves. Thus here's a primer, if you will, for those who may be less familiar with the subject and could use an overview on diversity in publishing today.

WHAT READERS WANT

To begin, someone who may not be up on the movement might be wondering: *What's this all about?* Well, historically, published books have largely focused their lens on white, straight, able-bodied characters. *What's wrong with that*, you ask? It's not what's there that's the problem; it's what's *not* there. Seeing ourselves reflected in the books—and media—we consume can be a way of legitimizing our own journey, struggles and questions. Seeing the reflection of someone else's journey, a journey that may be entirely unlike our own, provides an essential portal into the experiences of others, fostering empathy, understanding and growth. Simply put, readers want, *need*, to see themselves in the books they read. In recent years, that need has begun to be addressed with a growing range of books reflecting a broader, truer lens. A more diverse selection of books means more mirrors to reflect our experiences, and more windows to offer glimpses into lives unlike our own. Win-win, right?

"As someone obsessed with and who writes small-town America, if you don't see diversity in your town, you're not looking hard enough."
—Julie Murphy, author of *Dumplin'*

WHAT AGENTS & EDITORS WANT

Certainly I cannot speak for all of the publishing community, but from what I've seen as a literary agent working largely in publishing for young readers, I can safely say: There is a great and a growing hunger for diverse books—in terms of culture, race, sexuality, gender, ability, class, and beyond. When I meet with editors and talk about what they're looking to acquire, almost invariably the conversation will come around to: "I want to see more diverse books, and books by diverse authors."

"We talk about representation every single day. When I started in publishing two decades ago at a different company, we weren't allowed to use the word *gay* in describing a character unless it was specifically tagged a 'gay book' and was geared toward that community only. Now it feels like there

is a real push toward diversity, a focus on and celebration of that."
—John Morgan, executive editor at Imprint, a part of Macmillan Children's Publishing Group

This appetite is also seen in the formation of social media campaigns to enhance visibility for underrepresented voices, such as the popular #DVpit event on Twitter (created by literary agent Beth Phelan), where authors can pitch their diverse projects in real-time. Interested agents and editors can—and do—request these manuscripts, and the event already has an impressive rate of authors signing with agents and getting book deals. And initiatives like We Need Diverse Books have provided resources and a rallying point for writers of marginalized communities and beyond.

Bear in mind: This is a process. The skewed balance of worldview in literature didn't happen overnight, and the shift to a more accurate and complete representation will not happen overnight either. But readers are hungry for it. Agents are hungry for it. Editors are hungry for it. What comes next?

WHAT WRITERS CAN DO

Some people have called diversity in publishing a "trend." Let me be clear, it's nothing of the sort. It is, and will continue to be, a gradual shifting—*a correction in the market*, so to speak—an increased awareness for those writing and publishing from a place of privilege that there are important stories out there that were formerly overlooked. It's an initiative that I believe will only grow more as marginalized authors continue to gain confidence and experience and wherewithal to make their stories known, and as publishers continue not only to diversify their acquisitions, but also their staff at every step of the publishing process.

"'Diversity' should just be called 'reality.' Your books, your TV shows, your movies, your articles, your curricula, need to reflect *reality*."
—Tananarive Due, author of *The Living Blood*

One contentious issue right now is the debate over whether authors can—or should—write from a perspective that is outside their own race or culture. Those arguing against point to the glut of inauthentic voices crowding the shelves and taking space and attention from those writing from their "own voice" viewpoints. On the other side, some argue that authors writing only their own distinct gender, race, culture and specific background would make for dull books indeed.

On one thing all sides agree, however: Any author writing outside their culture should do so thoughtfully, respectfully, and deliberately. If you're considering doing so, ask: *Why am I the one telling this particular story? What is my touch-point or connection that makes me an authentic narrator for this character?* Next, be willing to put in the work. Research is good, but that alone isn't enough. Talk, interview, experience. Bring in readers of the race or culture in question to critique your work—and then *listen* to what they're saying, and make the necessary changes.

WHAT THE FUTURE HOLDS

One has only to look at *The New York Times* bestsellers list or the National Book Awards list to see how whole-heartedly readers and critics alike are taking to this shift toward greater and more accurate representation. In the last year, books by authors of color have repeatedly sold in high-stakes auctions, with foreign and film deals flocking in their wake. This is especially the case in YA and children's publishing, but adult fiction is catching on as well. It turns out that people like to see themselves in the books—and media—they consume. It makes logical, and financial, sense.

What does this all mean for you? If you're a marginalized writer: There's never been a better time to tell your story. If you're writing from a place of privilege: Be willing to educate yourself, and in the works you do create, strive for honesty, authenticity, inclusivity.

Publishing is experiencing a period of growth. Things are changing, yet more change is still needed. Diversity is not a fad, trend, or marketing gimmick. It is a lifestyle; a requirement. The new normal.

AMMI-JOAN PAQUETTE is a senior literary agent with Erin Murphy Literary Agency and the author of many books for young readers. This article previously appeared in the March/April 2018 issue of *Writer's Digest*.

THE FUTURE IS YOURS TO CREATE

Where do you want your writing career to take you? Follow these guided prompts to identify the goals you want to accomplish and how to get there.

by Nina Amir

Significant life events tend to focus your attention on where you want to go and what you want to accomplish as a writer. These milestones provide an opportunity to decide how to create your writing life and career anew in the future.

I celebrated my 60th birthday this year. Not surprisingly, this milestone caused me to re-evaluate my writing goals for the foreseeable future. I pulled out a list of all my nonfiction book ideas and thought long and hard about which ones I still want to pursue. Additionally, I considered my early career goals and if I want to focus time and energy on them in the next few years. A good look at where my writing career has taken me also helped me determine where I want to go.

I realized that I needed to make some big decisions and take action to create the future I want as a writer and ensure my body of work has an impact on the world. The global pandemic, which was raging as I marked my birthday, provided a reminder that I might not have as long as I'd like to accomplish my goals. If I wanted to create the writing career of my dreams, I had to start immediately.

START CREATING YOUR FUTURE NOW

Each of us creates the future in every moment. It's in the present—the now—that we determine what types of experiences and opportunities we will have tomorrow, next week, next month, or next year. However, as author and personal development expert Tony Robbins says, "It's in our moments of decision that our destiny is shaped."

You don't have to wait for obvious time markers or global pandemics to determine how you want to show up as a writer and what type of impact your work has in the world. In fact, you have numerous opportunities to make those decisions and take action on them.

For instance, this month—September 2020—offers a powerful time for self and career evaluation as well as for deciding to pivot your writing career, revamp your writing plan, or create new writing goals. To begin, answer one question: *What would you like your writing life and career to look like in the future?* In your answer lies the foundation for your creation plan.

1. EXERCISE

Journaling provides a great way to think about how to create your future writing life. In your journal, answer the following questions intended to help you decide what you want your writing life to look like and how to create it. Be sure to answer them in detail and use descriptive—even emotional—language. Let your mind go wild. Allow yourself to dream big.

1. What writing opportunities could you take advantage of right now?
2. What would you change right now about your current works-in-progress?
3. What three things do you need to do to achieve your goals before year end?

4 REASONS TO CREATE NEW WRITING GOALS NOW

You might be wondering why you should rethink and revamp your writing career this month. I can think of three significant reasons. Consider that you are headed into the last quarter of the year. You have only four months left to accomplish your 2020 writing goals. Also, the world has changed significantly since we entered the new decade. That fact alone necessitates realigning your writing with current trends and the new needs of your readers.

Of course, you can create your writing future anew for no other reason than you feel inspired to do so. There is no need to wait for the new year or some other milestone.

2. EXERCISE

In a journal, answer the following questions. Compose your answers with as much detail, description, and emotion as possible.

1. Where have you gotten off track with your writing journey, and how can you get on track?
2. What have you always wished you could do as a writer ... if only things were different?
3. What topics or projects will you commit to making a priority going forward?
4. What would you like your writing life to look like in three, six, 12, 24, or 48 months?

WHAT ARE YOUR ASPIRATIONS?

The aspirations you had three years or three months ago may no longer be the ones you have today. That's why it's important to do a career review and get clear on your current writing goals.

When I reviewed my writing career, I realized I'd gotten off track. I've not written about the topics nearest and dearest to my heart, but I would still like to do so.

What about you? Have you gotten off track or let your most significant passion projects lie forgotten in a computer file? Now is a great time to choose your path and make your life's work a priority.

Perhaps your interests and goals have changed over the years. What inspires you today that you'd like to write about?

Possibly, life derailed your writing career. Your career review may make it apparent that your job, health, or family responsibilities have left little time to write. How can you make writing a priority and fit it into your schedule?

As you develop clarity around your aspirations, passions, and goals, you can effectively create a new plan for realizing your dreams.

3. EXERCISE

Brainstorm how you can make a positive difference with your words. Answering the following questions in your journal will generate new ideas:

1. What is your purpose as a writer? How do you want to be of service?
2. How can your writing contribute to the betterment of your readers or the world?
3. If you were going to make your most significant difference as a writer, what would you have to start—or stop—doing right now to create that future?
4. What issues are most important to you, and how can you write about them to ignite discussion?

HOW WILL YOU MAKE A DIFFERENCE?

As I conducted my career review, I realized that I place an enormous amount of importance on contribution. I want my work to make a positive and meaningful difference in the world. When I receive an email telling me one of my books or blog posts inspired or motivated a reader—or even changed a life—I know I am being of service and that my work is impacting readers.

Writers are leaders, role models, and influencers. You have the chance now to focus on how your published work will make a difference.

The most memorable writers often dovetail their writing ability and interests with a desire to challenge how people think, behave, and see the world. As a result, their work—fiction and nonfiction—contributes to the betterment of their readers or society at large. Consider William Faulkner (*The Sound and the Fury*, *As I Lay Dying*, *Light in August*, and *Absalom, Absalom!*), who shed light on moral issues through his stories about Mississippi. Harriet Beecher Stowe's *Uncle Tom's Cabin* describes the real lives of enslaved persons, and Toni Morrison's *Beloved* offers a look at the destructive legacy of slavery. In *Man's Search for Meaning*, Viktor E. Frankl uncovers the human drive for meaning and explains how it helped him survive a Nazi concentration camp. More recently, *Storming the Wall* by Todd Miller opens readers' eyes to the economic and political implications of climate change, and *Know My Name* by Chanel Miller allows readers to better understand the inherent problems in sexual assault cases.

Many people write because they feel called to do so. They believe they must write, not because it's their nature, but because it's their purpose. Whether you write fiction or nonfiction, you can focus your writing on contribution—on making a difference. Not only will your work be more memorable if you do so, but you will feel more fulfilled in the process. Your body of work will also become a powerful and meaningful legacy.

HOW WILL YOU TAKE ACTION?

It's worth taking to heart the quote, "A goal without a plan is just a wish," which has been attributed to Antoine de Saint-Exupéry, author of *The Little Prince*. Indeed, if you don't develop a strategy that helps you create your future, the days, weeks, and months to come will turn out just like the previous ones.

To create a different future, you need a plan. Now that you have clarity on the future you desire, turn your aspirations into action steps.

In my case, I need to prioritize the books I want to write in the next five or 10 years and then decide what steps are necessary to complete them. If I want to publish my novel, for example, I could hire an editor to work with me on the manuscript. If I want to tackle one of my nonfiction book ideas, I need to plan the content and develop a book proposal. And if I want to write for publications, I need to choose and study appropriate magazines and send query letters to editors.

Every one of your writing projects or goals needs its own plan. Each plan is comprised of a variety of action steps that could make your wish come true.

Napoleon Hill said, "A goal is a dream with a deadline." Move your dream of the future one step closer to reality by putting the completion date on your calendar. Then, work backward from that date and set mini-deadlines for the tasks necessary to meet your original deadline.

4. EXERCISE

Look over your answers to the questions posed in this article. Prioritize the actions you need to take to create the future you've envisioned. The following questions will help you do so.

1. When you consider the next decade, what is your overarching goal as a writer?
2. To realize that aspiration, what three things must you start doing right now? What three things must you stop doing?
3. What writing projects do you want to complete in the next year? (Choose no more than three.)
4. What five steps do you need to take to complete each priority project?

TURN TOWARD YOUR FUTURE

Birth, deaths, commemorative occasions, and holidays provide reminders to consider where you have been and still want to go, what you have done, and what you still want to accomplish. However, every moment represents a new milestone and opportunity to create your future as a writer. Allow your purpose, aspirations, and vision of the writer you want to be and the contribution you want to make guide you toward that future.

NINA AMIR (NinaAmir.com) is known as the Inspiration to Creation Coach. As an author coach, she supports writers on every step of the journey to successful authorship. Additionally, she is one of 800 elite Certified High Performance Coaches working worldwide but the only one specifically supporting writers with personal development. Nina has written three traditionally published books for aspiring authors, *How to Blog a Book*, *The Author Training Manual*, and *Creative Visualization for Writers*, as well as a host of self-published books and ebooks, including the Write Nonfiction NOW! series of guides. She has had 19 books on the Amazon Top 100 List and as many as six books on the Authorship bestseller list at the same time. She also is an award-winning blogger and journalist. To further support writers, Nina founded WriteNonfictionNow.com, the Nonfiction Writers' University, and Author of Change Transformational Programs. She also established the Inspired Creator Community, which provides personal and spiritual growth coaching with the bonus of group author coaching and nonfiction writing and publishing resources. This article originally appeared in the September/October 2020 issue of *Writer's Digest*.

FUNDING YOUR WRITING WITH PATREON

by Lucy A. Snyder

Many writers dream of quitting their day jobs and becoming full-time freelancers. And while that *is* achievable, it's a difficult prospect for poets, playwrights, and midlist-fiction writers. Writing organizations such as the Science Fiction & Fantasy Writers of America consider a minimum professional rate for fiction to be six cents a word. Many novels only receive advances of $5,000–$10,000. Think about your basic living costs. A book that took years to write may only cover rent for a few months. Making up the difference as a freelancer is challenging, to say the least!

The good news: Crowdfunding can fill that uncomfortable financial gap. Kickstarter and Indiegogo are great for funding specific projects such as novels, plays, anthologies, and poetry collections. But if you're seeking ongoing, monthly support for your creative endeavors, take a closer look at Patreon (patreon.com).

THE BIG IDEA

Launched in 2013, Patreon is conceptually the modern version of the old system whereby artists and writers sought out wealthy patrons for support—but the key difference is that popular Patreon creators are supported by dozens or hundreds of people rather than a single rich benefactor. In practice, Patreon gives creators tools for publishing a wide variety of subscription content. Editors use it to publish monthly online magazines, and fiction writers use it to serialize their novels-in-progress. Artists post sketches-in-progress or commissions for individual patrons. Others post videos or audio tracks of music or narration. Educators can use the built-in integration with Discord (a voice/text-chat system) to host discussions or workshops.

And while you post as much content as your imagination can summon, the site handles all the billing. Creators can charge by the post or by the month. Opting for monthly charges lets you set up tiered rewards as you would with Kickstarter. Rewards can be anything you can legally fulfill: For instance, for $2 a month, my supporters get a weekly poem; for $3 a month they receive weekly writing prompts plus my poetry. For $30 a month, they receive all my writing plus detailed feedback on 2,000 words of their own work. Patreon takes 5 percent of processed payments, plus additional processing fees to move funds to PayPal or Stripe. Some creators resent the fees, but most see them as a fair trade for a suite of extremely versatile tools.

GETTING STARTED WITH PATREON

1. Research Patreons like yours at graphtreon.com, and emulate successes.
2. Craft a compelling personal narrative about why you're seeking patrons.
3. Offer a variety of appealing patron rewards. Avoid rewards that require shipping.
4. Focus on rewards that you are *certain* you can consistently provide.
5. Plan to spend time promoting your campaign on social media every month.
6. Recruit friends and colleagues to help with promotion. Word of mouth is critical.
7. Make a content creation/posting calendar and stick to it.
8. Poll your patrons periodically to gauge their satisfaction.
9. Reassess your promotional tactics and ability to meet reward goals after a couple of months; change your strategies as needed.

THE BENEFITS

Income is the first thing people wonder about when they start exploring Patreon. Graphtreon is an extremely useful tool for tracking and analyzing various campaigns. Go to graphtreon.com/patreon-creators/writing to view the writers who have the most total patrons or who earn the most money per month. The site collects a great deal of insightful data, and before you set up your own Patreon you should take a look at the top creators' pages to figure out what you can learn from their successes.

Authors Seanan McGuire and N. K. Jemisin bring in thousands of dollars per month through their Patreons. McGuire rewards her patrons with stories, writing tutorials, and more. Jemisin is able to write fiction full time because of her campaign. Her rewards range from cute cat videos to ARCs of her forthcoming books.

True, most don't earn as much as McGuire or Jemisin—each had an established readership *before* they launched their campaigns—but their success shows what's possible.

My Patreon covers a significant chunk of my mortgage each month. I treat it like a serious part-time job, and the work I've put into it has definitely paid off.

Authors who take a casual approach typically earn $50–$150 per month. That's enough to cover a utility bill, which can make a huge difference for some households. And if your Patreon isn't performing well? Seek feedback and try new tactics; you're free to change your campaign whenever and however you like.

Some writers use the money they bring in to fund others' Patreons. This is a way to create goodwill and to network with other writers. If your campaign's earnings are too small to matter to you personally, use them to boost others and get access to great content in the process. Community and connections matter, and Patreon gives you the tools to build both.

But Patreon isn't just about the money. It's also a vehicle for creative inspiration. I love writing poetry, but it doesn't pay very well. Over time I'd abandoned it for fiction; I wanted to change that. So, I set my poem-a-week reward level. The result? I've been writing a whole lot of new poetry, and my subscribers enjoy it. Use Patreon to set (and meet!) new goals for yourself.

THE LONG HAUL

Unlike other crowdfunding, Patreon campaigns don't have a pre-set ending. You'll post your promised content monthly, weekly, maybe even daily. Compared to the sprint of Kickstarter, the marathon of Patreon can be exhausting. You risk turning something fun into a chore.

You have to keep promoting if you want to build followers. Even if you're posting solid content, count on losing a patron (or several) every month as people's finances and interests change. Many of us find self-promotion to be tedious and somewhat shameful, and having to constantly go out with your hat in your hand can be demoralizing. Focus on providing a good value to your subscribers and emphasize that in your promotional efforts.

Avoiding burnout is crucial for ensuring that you can maintain a solid campaign. By all means, set some reward levels that will challenge you creatively, but for the rest? Play to your strengths and interests. For instance, if you have several finished novels that you've trunked, dust those off, revise them and serialize them. Sit down and figure out what you can comfortably accomplish in a month, and then focus on doing what you do best. Chances are, if it's something you love, your patrons will love it, too.

LUCY A. SNYDER (lucysnyder.com) is the Bram Stoker Award-winning author of a dozen books and more than 100 short stories. This essay was originally published in the October 2018 issue of *Writer's Digest*.

THE TIME AND ENERGY GAME

Finding that you're spending too much time on everything except writing? Here are some ideas for a solution.

by Elizabeth Sims

Most of us understand the concept of return on investment (ROI). You deposit money in a bank; they pay you interest while lending out your money to others. You buy shares on the stock exchange hoping those shares will rise in value or pay dividends. You buy a bungalow so you have a place to live, a Chevrolet so you can go places, a week on Maui so you can relax.

As writers, we buy computers to write and edit on, and all the other goods and services we need to do our thing. Those too are investments, and it's fairly easy to calculate whether the return on your investment is positive, neutral, or negative. A positive ROI is good!

When it comes to our time and energy, though, that's different. How we spend any particular chunk of time can affect our life-force to the positive or to the negative. Call it energy, fortitude, spirit, drive, optimism, zest—we have it, and we spend it wisely or foolishly. Unlike time, our life-force ebbs and flows. We gather ourselves for a challenging task, we do the task, then we feel spent. We must recharge before facing the next challenge. The mental and emotional come together in the life-force.

I note that life-force is different from physical energy, but it augments it. One can be close to physical exhaustion from reaching a mountain peak after a long climb, or from completing a triathlon, and yet feel exhilarated, cheerful, ready to plan what's next.

As writers, how do we care for and maximize our time and life-force? How do we manage the invisibles? It boils down to organization and choices.

WRITING ENVIRONMENT

Order Your Tasks

Get into the habit of writing down all your gotta-dos on one list and all your wanna-dos on another. Put the most important ones at the top, or make a little star next to the most important ones. Go after the stars on both lists. When your lists need refreshing, take two minutes to do it.

When you get a few gotta-dos out of the way, it's easier to grab time for the wanna-dos. Is writing on your gotta-do list or on your wanna-do list?

Cut Distractions

This doesn't mean crawl into an isolation chamber, though I suppose that's tempting sometimes. The indistinct bustle of a café has been shown to be a benevolent environment for writers. But isolation-chamber-like computer apps that limit one's time online have many fans; if the concept attracts you, try one and see how it goes.

CYA: Clear Your Area

Physical order can promote mental and spiritual order. An uncluttered space is an invitation, like a fresh notebook. While it's true some geniuses have worked well in a cluttered environment, I believe they worked well in spite of the clutter, not because of it. Good free advice abounds online on clearing clutter and organizing your space. See how much you can get done in half a day—or half an hour.

Shed the Psychic Burden of Digital Clutter

Digital clutter can sap your life-force and your time. Hardly anybody thought of this 20 or 30 years ago, when the magic of word processing and digital files was young, and email didn't exist except for computer nerds. But now, given today's ease of writing emails and digital documents, it's tempting to get lazy about organizing them. A tiny amount of effort at organization can free your mind.

Documents

Writers generate piles of documents. My files, which include multiple versions of my novels and other books, all my freelance work, supporting information, and my personal files, number just short of 8,000. Yet within seconds, I can find my recipe for walnut brownies, the third draft of the first article I wrote for this magazine, or the names of the cemeteries my grandparents are buried in.

Searching by keywords is great. But I often want to visually scan lists of files of like kind. Therefore, I routinely make new folders and, when it seems good to do, subfolders. The key is to always look for ways to gather micro subjects into macro collections. Let's say you have a file or folder for each short story you've written. If those folders are all jumbled in an alphabetical list that includes a PDF of the specifications of your new golf clubs or every query letter you wrote before agents all used email, that can get bewildering. Just make a new folder called Short Stories and round up all your individual files and folders into it. Make another one called Queries. Put everything else in Miscellaneous until patterns emerge. This is something you know intuitively already, but putting some mindfulness into organization makes such a difference for your inner peace.

I keep one large folder called "Z Archives," into which I dump old low-priority stuff that I still want to keep. The "Z" is so the folder appears at the bottom of the list, so my eye, when looking at my list of folders, doesn't have to waste a millisecond scanning past it at the top.

If you use a note-taking and organizing app like Evernote, do the same with folders and subfolders, or it'll quickly turn cumbersome.

Email

I was flabbergasted recently to lay eyes on a young friend's email inbox: more than 2,000 messages, some read, some unread, with no ancillary files set up for saving messages he might want later. "Dude, seriously?" was all I could say.

- Quickly dispatch your email every day:

  Delete almost everything.

  Answer the few things that need answering.

  File the rest. If creating multiple files feels daunting, just make two: Friends-Family and The Rest (for receipts and shipping confirmations, newsletters you might want to refer to, etc.). The search function on most email apps is so good, you should be able to find stuff that way.
- Unsubscribe fiercely from unwanted mass emails as soon as they show up. If you do this for about a week, you'll be amazed.
- If you follow some blogs by email, skim them as soon as they come in. Get the main point and either file the message just in case you might want to revisit it (yeah, right) or delete.
- Cherish your friends, but don't let them take up your time and life-force with junk emails. That message that cajoles to you add something cute and send it to 10 friends? The pang of deleting it is so very worth the freedom you'll feel.

I just checked how many emails I have saved in several dozen folders: more than 71,000. They're fine where they are; I don't have to look at them, and I can search to find anything if I want it. Every day, I get my inbox to empty or almost empty. And although today I'm working on several projects on deadline and my lawn is a little too high, my soul is at peace.

I could delete some of my old correspondence with no harm done, but my alma mater has dibs on my archives, both physical and digital, so they stay where they are.

WRITING-LIFE TIP:

In case you find your archives wanted by an organization, know that they want to do the sorting and selecting after you leave the planet. So, while you should organize your stuff for best benefit to you, don't delete stuff you've saved for whatever obscure reason.

Set Perma-Reminders for Thursday Afternoons

If you've been a good worker bee during the week, you should feel fairly stress-free by Thursday afternoon. But it's still work time, and it's not Friday, with its temptations for goofing off. I have perma-reminders on my digital calendar's Thursday afternoons for digital file maintenance, checking my calendar for upcoming birthdays for loved ones, and an overall review of my gotta-do and wanna-do lists.

MARKETING EFFICIENCY

Social Media

If you, like me, hate social media, the marketing gurus will soothingly stroke your arm and say, "But all you have to do is automate it with one of these scheduling apps!" Which still ignores the main issue of having to write posts or at least choose content to begin with. You can hire someone to do it for you, if you can afford it and don't mind the dishonesty of paying someone to pretend to be you.

- Choose your bandwagons. Some authors do well on just one or two from the palette of Facebook, Twitter, Instagram, Reddit, YouTube, etc.
- Be okay with limiting your time on social media. If you love doing it, fabulous. If not, budget your time and accept who you are.
- When you do show up on social media, choose to be a listener more than an opinion-spewer.

Paid Advertising

Employ the Pareto principle. It's worth looking up, but in brief, the Pareto principle says that you get 80 percent of your return on 20 percent of your effort. For instance, some authors write books very fast, because they know they can get a book that's 80 percent good by spending 20 percent of the time it would take to write a 100 percent good book. That may or may not be for you, depending on how you feel about quality vs. expedience.

In matters of marketing, Pareto can be helpful. If you find you get best results with one paid-advertising outlet, whether it be Amazon, Facebook, or Twitter ads, or some other, consider concentrating on the one or two with the highest returns, and dumping the rest.

Review your numbers. Make choices. Invest with care, but don't fall prey to "paralysis by analysis." Keep it simple and go forth.

ASSIST YOUR MENTAL ROI

One of my favorite Zen stories is that of the master who pours tea into a student's cup to the rim, and on to overflowing. The student cries out for him to stop. The master says, "How can a full cup accept new tea?" Meaning how can a full mind accept and learn anything new? How can a cluttered mind foster creativity? One must clear out the little monkeys running around in there pulling levers and throwing things.

I'm against extra work, so my favorite mind-clearing activity can be done any time, anywhere, alongside anything else one may be doing: breath awareness. It's the simplest thing in the world, and yields incredible rewards. Look into it, give it a try when you're doing anything at all, and see how it goes. It takes no special effort. We breathe in; we breathe out.

MIND THE BODY

I hope to be an old lady someday, and I don't want to be a crabbed-over one. So I get out for daily walks, and in accordance with Pareto, I spend about six minutes twice a day doing high-intensity training (HIT) using no equipment. Check it out; evidence is building that short spurts of HIT give the benefits of much longer workouts for cellular health and strength. I'm no expert, so check with your health professional before undertaking anything new.

TRASH TOXIC ADVICE

I started to write out a sample list of toxic advice for writers, whether it's check email only once a day, rise before sunup, or hit a certain word count without fail. Then I realized that any hard-and-fast rule can turn toxic. Why? Because if we commit to something, then fall short, we risk standing in front of the bathroom mirror at 2 A.M. boxing our own ears and calling ourselves ugly names. To hell with that! Self-discipline is fabulous. But give yourself some leeway. Nobody gets extra points in heaven because they boxed their own ears.

Choose to be your best self every day and you can't go wrong.

THE BEAUTY OF JUST BUMPING IT

For years, my office storage closet had no door. I liked it that way, but knew it would look tidier if I put up a door, or at least a tasteful curtain. I let the item linger on my to-do list.

When it came time to sell the house, I worried about that door-less closet, but still procrastinated. The house sold to a buyer who liked the door-less closet just fine. I could have saved myself those years of back-of-the-mind static.

Look around and see what jobs you can just bump and forget.

I might add, the belief in "good enough" can be freeing, whether you're painting a room or buying groceries or outlining a novel. Is it perfect? No. It never is. Is it good enough? Yes? Declare victory and move on.

THE WRITING PROCESS

For writers, word count is our report card. Good productivity means more chances for finished products, publishing contracts, and happy fans. It means more raw material to work with and refine into something excellent and saleable.

Good, workable apps abound that involve timing, accountability, and more. Just search around and give one of them a try. The one I've used has gone out of business, so I can't recommend it.

Voice-to-text apps are cool and getting cooler—as in easier to use. I've enjoyed Dragon Naturally Speaking (no compensation here or for any other brand name you see in this piece) to write as fast as I can talk. My results need a lot of editing, which dilutes the experience, especially because I can touch-type extremely fast. However, if you're struggling to get something—anything!—down on paper, so to speak, voice to text can be a godsend. With practice, any voice-to-text app works better and better.

Here are some practical actions for maximizing ROI during the writing process:

- If you're an outliner, fine. If not, make a few notes as to where you want your story to go *today*. That is, set a course for yourself before each writing session. It's easy, and it gives you a measure of purpose, as well as peace of mind.
- Get better at touch-typing. A good free tutorial is TypingClub.com, but there are many more.
- Before starting any fiction project, generate a list of character names, so you can grab one quickly while you're flowing in first-draft mode. Nothing kills momentum so needlessly as having to stop and come up with a character name. I find it awkward to use placeholders such as "Mr. X" or "Kid Y" instead of a real name. Even if you wind up changing a name later, this practice serves to keep up your pace.
- Try a plot generator. Seriously. Look around online and try one just for fun. You might make a surprising breakthrough, or at the very least, have a few laughs!
- Don't stop to edit. Eyes forward.

- Resist the urge to break away and look something up. I use square brackets around something I need to research later. An example might look like this:

  Barbara stopped at a hardware store in [town between Austin and San Antonio] and bought a tool kit and a work jacket.

  Later, you can then search on square brackets to be sure you don't miss anything.

One of the most effective individuals I've ever known was a simple man who never seemed to hurry, yet accomplished tremendous amounts of work and exploration. He once told me he made the most of every minute.

"How?" I asked.

He said he lived by this quotation by Ralph Waldo Emerson:

"Adopt the pace of nature: Her secret is patience."

Isn't that nice?

Writer's Digest contributing editor **ELIZABETH SIMS** (ElizabethSims.com) is the author of 13 books, including *You've Got a Book in You: A Stress-Free Guide to Writing the Book of Your Dreams* (WD Books). She's also a writing coach and freelance editor. This article first appeared in the March/April 2021 issue of *Writer's Digest*.

BOOK PUBLISHERS

There's no magic formula for getting published. It's a matter of getting the right manuscript on the right editor's desk at the right time. Before you submit it's important to learn publishers' needs, see what kind of books they're producing, and decide which publishers your work is best suited for. *Children's Writer's & Illustrator's Market* is but one tool in this process.

To help you narrow down the list of possible publishers for your work, we've included indexes at the back of this book. The **Subject Index** lists book and magazine publishers according to their fiction and nonfiction needs or interests. The **Age-Level Index** indicates which age groups publishers cater to.

If you write contemporary fiction for young adults, for example, and you're trying to place a book manuscript, go first to the Subject Index. Locate the fiction categories under Book Publishers and copy the list under Contemporary. Then go to the Age-Level Index and highlight the publishers on the Contemporary list that are included under the Young Adults heading. Read the listings for the highlighted publishers to see if your work matches their needs.

Remember, *Children's Writer's & Illustrator's Market* should not be your only source for researching publishers. Here are a few other sources of information:

- The Society of Children's Book Writers and Illustrators (SCBWI) offers members an annual market survey of children's book publishers for the cost of postage or free online at www.scbwi.org. (SCBWI membership information can also be found at www.scbwi.org.)
- The Children's Book Council website (www.cbcbooks.org) gives information on member publishers.
- Check publishers' websites. Many include their complete catalogs, which you can browse. Web addresses are included in many publishers' listings.
- Spend time at your local bookstore to see who's publishing what. While you're there, browse through *Publishers Weekly* and *The Horn Book*.

SUBSIDY & SELF-PUBLISHING

Some determined writers who receive rejections from royalty publishers may look to subsidy and co-op publishers as an option for getting their work into print. These publishers ask writers to pay all or part of the costs of producing a book. We strongly advise writers and illustrators to work only with publishers who pay them. For this reason, we've adopted a policy not to include any subsidy or co-op publishers in *Children's Writer's & Illustrator's Market* (or any other Writer's Digest Books market book).

If you're interested in publishing your book just to share it with friends and relatives, self-publishing is a viable option, but it involves time, energy, and money. You oversee all book production details. Check with a local printer for advice and information on cost or check online for print-on-demand publishing options (which are often more affordable).

Whatever path you choose, keep in mind that the market is flooded with submissions, so it's important for you to hone your craft and submit the best work possible. Competition from thousands of other writers and illustrators makes it more important than ever to research publishers before submitting—read their guidelines, look at their catalogs, check out a few of their titles, and visit their websites.

ABDO PUBLISHING CO.

8000 W. 78th St., Suite 310, Edina MN 55439. (800)800-1312. **Fax:** (952)831-1632. **E-mail:** nonfiction@abdopublishing.com. **Website:** www.abdopublishing.com. ABDO publishes nonfiction children's books (pre-kindergarten to 8th grade) for school and public libraries—mainly history, sports, biography, geography, science, and social studies. "Please specify each submission as either nonfiction, fiction, or illustration. Publishes hardcover originals. **Publishes 300 titles/year.**

TERMS Guidelines online.

ABRAMS BOOKS FOR YOUNG READERS

195 Broadway, 9th Floor, New York NY 10007. **Website:** www.abramsyoungreaders.com. **Contact:** Managing Editor. Publishes hardcover and a few paperback originals. **Publishes 250 titles/year.**

Abrams no longer accepts unsolicted mss or queries.

FICTION Publishes hardcover and "a few" paperback originals. Averages 150 total titles/year.

ILLUSTRATION Illustrations only: Do not submit original material; copies only.

TIPS "We are one of the few publishers who publish almost exclusively illustrated books. We consider ourselves the leading publishers of art books and high-quality artwork in the U.S. Once the author has signed a contract to write a book for our firm the author must finish the manuscript to agreed-upon high standards within the schedule agreed upon in the contract."

ALADDIN

Simon & Schuster, 1230 Avenue of the Americas, New York NY 10020. (212)698-7000. **Website:** www.simonandschusterpublishing.com/aladdin. Aladdin also publishes Aladdin M!X, for those readers too old for kids' books, but not quite ready for adult or young adult novels. **Contact:** Acquisitions Editor. Aladdin publishes picture books, beginning readers, chapter books, middle grade and tween fiction and nonfiction, and graphic novels and nonfiction in hardcover and paperback, with an emphasis on commercial, kid-friendly titles. Publishes hardcover/paperback originals and imprints of Simon & Schuster Children's Publishing Children's Division.

HOW TO CONTACT Simon & Schuster does not review, retain or return unsolicited materials or artwork. "We suggest prospective authors and illustrators submit their mss through a professional literary agent."

ALGONQUIN YOUNG READERS

P.O. Box 2225, Chapel Hill NC 27515. **Website:** algonquinyoungreaders.com. Algonquin Young Readers is a new imprint that features books for readers 7-17. "From short illustrated novels for the youngest independent readers to timely and topical crossover young adult fiction, what ties our books together are unforgettable characters, absorbing stories, and superior writing.

FICTION Algonquin Young Readers publishes fiction and a limited number of narrative nonfiction titles for middle grade and young adult readers. "We don't publish poetry, picture books, or genre fiction."

HOW TO CONTACT Query with 15-20 sample pages and SASE.

ILLUSTRATION "At this time, we do not accept unsolicited submissions for illustration."

TERMS Guidelines online.

AMG PUBLISHERS

AMG International, Inc., 6815 Shallowford Rd., Chattanooga TN 37421. (423)894-6060. **E-mail:** sales@amgpublishers.com. **Website:** www.amgpublishers.com. **Contact:** Amanda Jenkins, Sales Manager/Author Liaison. Publishing division of AMG International began in 1985 with release of the *Hebrew-Greek Key Word Study Bible* in the King James Version. This groundbreaking study Bible is now published in four other Bible translations. In-depth study and examination of original biblical languages provide some of our core Bible study and reference tools. In 1998, AMG launched the successful Following God Bible study series (primarily for women) that examine key characters of the Bible along with life application principles. "Profits from sales of our books and Bibles are funneled back into world missions and childcare efforts of parent organization, AMG International." Publishes hardcover and trade paperback originals, electronic originals, and audio Bible originals. **Publishes 5-10 titles/year. 25% of books from first-time authors. 35% from unagented writers.**

FICTION "We are not presently acquiring fiction of any genre, though we continue to publish a number of titles in the young adult inspirational fantasy category."

NONFICTION Bibles, reference works, devotionals, and workbook Bible studies. Does not want self-help, memoir, autobiography, biography, fiction, New Age, prosperity gospel.

HOW TO CONTACT Query with letter first, e-mail preferred. 300 queries/manuscripts per year Responds in 6 months to queries, 6 months to proposals/mss. Publishes book 12-18 months after acceptance of ms.

TERMS Pays 10-16% royalty on net sales. Advance negotiable. Book catalog and guidelines online. Think of the submission proposal as your sales brochure. It should show your idea in the best light. Put extra effort into this piece. It should be between 10-20 pages, plus sample chapters. You are making your first impression.

TIPS "AMG is open to well-written, niche Bible study, reference, and devotional books that meet immediate needs."

Ⓐ AMULET BOOKS

Imprint of Abrams, 195 Broadway, 9th Floor, New York NY 10007. **Website:** www.amuletbooks.com. *Does not accept unsolicited mss or queries.* **10% of books from first-time authors.**

FICTION Middle readers: adventure, contemporary, fantasy, history, science fiction, sports. Young adults/teens: adventure, contemporary, fantasy, history, science fiction, sports, suspense.

ILLUSTRATION Works with 10-12 illustrators/year. Uses both color and b&w. Query with samples. Contact: Chad Beckerman, art director. Samples filed.

PHOTOGRAPHY Buys stock images and assigns work.

ARTE PUBLICO PRESS

University of Houston, 4902 Gulf Fwy, Rm 100, Houston TX 77204-2004. **Fax:** (713)743-2847. **E-mail:** submapp@uh.edu. **Website:** artepublicopress.com. Arte Publico Press is the oldest and largest publisher of Hispanic literature for children and adults in the United States. "We are a showcase for Hispanic literary creativity, arts and culture. Our endeavor is to provide a national forum for U.S.-Hispanic literature." Publishes hardcover originals, trade paperback originals and reprints. **Publishes 25-30 titles/year. 50% of books from first-time authors. 80% from unagented writers.**

FICTION "Written by U.S.-Hispanics."

NONFICTION Hispanic civil rights issues for new series: The Hispanic Civil Rights Series.

HOW TO CONTACT Submissions made through online submission form. Submissions made through online submission form. 1,000 queries; 2,000 mss received/year. Responds in 1 month to queries and proposals; 4 months to mss. Publishes book 2 years after acceptance of ms.

TERMS Pays 10% royalty on wholesale price. Provides 20 author's copies; 40% discount on subsequent copies. Pays $1,000-3,000 advance. Book catalog available free. Guidelines online.

TIPS "Include cover letter in which you 'sell' your book—why should we publish the book, who will want to read it, why does it matter, etc. Use our ms submission online form. Format files accepted are: Word, plain/text, rich/text files. Other formats will not be accepted. Manuscript files cannot be larger than 5MB. Once editors review your ms, you will receive an e-mail with the decision. Revision process could take up to 4 months."

ASCEND BOOKS

7221 W. 79th St., Suite 206, Overland Park KS 66204. (913)948-5500. **E-mail:** bsnodgrass@ascendbooks.com. **Website:** ascendbooks.com. **Contact:** Robert Snodgrass. Ascend Books is a highly specialized publishing company with a burgeoning presence in the sports, entertainment, and children's books. Ascend Books is positioned to acquire and execute publishing projects in a tightly defined market–that of sports celebrities, including athletes, coaches, and teams, and of significant anniversary celebrations of sports institutions, such as football bowl games, franchises, and halls of fame. Ascend Books also works with celebrities and educators in the fields of entertainment and children's books. Ascend Books differentiates itself from traditional publishers by extending the intellectual property of a book and its author into professional speaking and educational avenues. Currently Ascend Books publishes a variety of formats each year—in a variety of subject areas. Our Publishing Initiative can provide a multi-dimensional approach for a select number of titles. The Ascend Books distribution team shepherds thousands of books from press to audience each month. Ascend employs professionals in editorial, sales, production, and distribution roles. Our stringent publishing criteria however, limits the number of books we publish each year. When we accept and initiate a book publishing project we put our full resources of talented editors, collaborators, photographers, artists and sales professionals behind each project. The Ascend Books Team works with setting goals, then establishing defined objectives to maximize the sales opportunities for each title on our list. When the decision is made to proceed on a book, we put the full strength of our sales, editorial, production and distribution resources to work. Ascend Books is positioned to acquire and execute publishing projects written by national and regional sports celebrities and educators. Our authors include athletes, coaches, and the teams themselves. Ascend Books also works with celebrities and educators in the fields of entertainment and children's books. **Publishes 12-15 titles/year. 50% of books from first-time authors. 75% from unagented writers.**

HOW TO CONTACT Responds in 4-6 weeks.

TERMS Pays advance. Catalog online.

Ⓐ ATHENEUM BOOKS FOR YOUNG READERS

Simon & Schuster, 1230 Avenue of the Americas, New York NY 10020. **Website:** simonandschusterpublishing.com/atheneum. Publishes hardcover originals.

FICTION All in juvenile versions. "We have few specific needs except for books that are fresh, interesting and well written. Fad topics are dangerous, as are works you haven't polished to the best of your ability. We also don't need safety pamphlets, ABC books, coloring books and board books. In writing picture book texts, avoid the coy and 'cutesy,' such as stories about characters with alliterative names." Agented submissions only. No paperback romance-type fiction.

NONFICTION Publishes hardcover originals, picture books for young kids, nonfiction for ages 8-12 and novels for middle-grade and young adults. 100% require freelance illustration. Agented submissions only.

TERMS Guidelines for #10 SASE.

TIPS "Study our titles."

AVON ROMANCE

HarperCollins Publishers, 195 Broadway, New York NY 10007. **E-mail:** info@avonromance.com. **Website:** www.avonromance.com. Avon has been publishing award-winning books since 1941. It is recognized for having pioneered the historical romance category and continues to bring the best of commercial literature to the broadest possible audience. Publishes paperback and digital originals and reprints. **Publishes 400 titles/year.**

HOW TO CONTACT Submit a query and ms via the online submission form.

BAEN PUBLISHING ENTERPRISES

(919)570-1640. **E-mail:** info@baen.com; toni@baen.com. **Website:** www.baen.com. Publishes hardcover, trade paperback and mass market paperback originals and reprints.

HOW TO CONTACT Submit synopsis and complete ms. "Electronic submissions are strongly preferred. Attach manuscript as a Rich Text Format (.rtf) file. Any other format will not be considered." Additional submission guidelines online. Include estimated word count, brief bio. Send SASE or IRC. Responds in 9-12 months. No simultaneous submissions. Sometimes comments on rejected mss. Responds in 9-12 months to mss.

TERMS Book catalog available free. Guidelines online.

TIPS "Keep an eye and a firm hand on the overall story you are telling. Style is important but less important than plot. Good style, like good breeding, never calls attention to itself. Read *Writing to the Point*, by Algis Budrys. We like to maintain long-term relationships with authors."

Ⓐ BALZER + BRAY

HarperCollins Children's Books, 195 Broadway, New York NY 10007. **Website:** www.harpercollinschildrens.com. "We publish bold, creative, groundbreaking picture books and novels that appeal directly to kids in a fresh way." **Publishes 10 titles/year.**

FICTION Picture Books, Young Readers: adventure, animal, anthology, concept, contemporary, fantasy, history, humor, multicultural, nature/environment, poetry, science fiction, special needs, sports, suspense. Middle readers, young adults/teens: adventure, animal, anthology, contemporary, fantasy, history, humor, multicultural, nature/environment, poetry, science fiction, special needs, sports, suspense.

NONFICTION "We will publish very few nonfiction titles, maybe 1-2 per year."

HOW TO CONTACT Contact editor. Agented submissions only. Publishes book 18 months after acceptance.

ILLUSTRATION Works with 10 illustrators/year. Uses both color and b&w. Illustrations only: send tearsheets to be kept on file. Responds only if interested. Samples are not returned.

PHOTOGRAPHY Works on assignment only.

TERMS Offers advances. Pays illustrators by the project.

Ⓐ BANCROFT PRESS

P.O. Box 65360, Baltimore MD 21209-9945. (410)358-0658. **Fax:** (410)764-1967. **E-mail:** bruceb@bancroftpress.com. **Website:** www.bancroftpress.com. **Contact:** Bruce Bortz, editor/publisher (memoirs, health, investment, politics, history, humor, literary novels, mystery/thrillers, chick lit, young adult). "Bancroft Press is a general trade publisher. Our only mandate is 'books that enlighten.' Our most recent emphasis, with *The Missing Kennedy* and *Both Sides of the Line*, has been on memoirs." Publishes hardcover and trade paperback originals as well as e-books and audiobooks. **Publishes 4-6 titles/year. 50% of books from first-time authors. 80% from unagented writers.**

NONFICTION "We advise writers to visit the website." All quality books on any subject of interest to the publisher.

HOW TO CONTACT Submit complete ms. Submit proposal package, outline, 5 sample chapters, competition/market survey. Responds in 6-12 months. Publishes book up to 3 years after acceptance of ms.

TERMS Pays 8-15% royalty on retail price. Pays $750-2,500 advances. Guidelines online.

TIPS "We advise writers to visit our website and to be familiar with our previous work. Patience is the number one attribute contributors must have. It takes us a very long time to get through submitted material, because we are such a small company. Also, we only publish 4-6 books per year, so it may take a long time for your optioned book to be published. We like to be able to market our books to be used in schools and in libraries. We prefer fiction that bucks trends and moves in a new direction. We are especially interested in mysteries and humor (especially humorous mysteries)."

Ⓐ BANTAM BOOKS

Imprint of Penguin Random House, Inc., 1745 Broadway, New York NY 10019. (212)782-9000. **Website:** www.randomhousebooks.com. *Not seeking mss at this time.*

BAREFOOT BOOKS

23 Bradford St., 2nd Floor, Concord MA 01742. **Website:** www.barefootbooks.com. **Contact:** Acquisitions Editor. "We are a small, independent publishing company that publishes high-quality picture books for children of all ages and specializes in the work of artists and writers from many cultures. We focus on themes that support independence of spirit, encourage openness to others, and foster a life-long love of learning. Prefers full manuscript." Publishes hardcover and trade paperback originals. **Publishes 30 titles/year. 35% of books from first-time authors. 60% from unagented writers.**

FICTION "Barefoot Books only publishes children's picture books and anthologies of folktales. We do not publish novels."

HOW TO CONTACT Barefoot Books is not currently accepting ms queries or submissions. 2,000 queries received/year. 3,000 mss received/year.

ILLUSTRATION Works with 20 illustrators/year. Uses color artwork only. Reviews ms/illustration packages from artists. Send query and art samples or dummy for picture books. Query with samples or send promo sheet and tearsheets. Responds only if interested. Samples returned with SASE. Pays authors royalty of 5% based on retail price. Offers advances. Sends galleys to authors. Originals returned to artist at job's completion.

TERMS Pays advance. Book catalog for 9x12 SAE stamped with $1.80 postage.

BEHRMAN HOUSE INC.

241B Milburn Ave., Milburn NJ 07041. (973)379-7200. **Fax:** (973)379-7280. **E-mail:** submissions@behrmanhouse.com. **Website:** www.behrmanhouse.com. **Contact:** Editorial Committee. Publishes books on all aspects of Judaism: history, cultural, textbooks, holidays. "Behrman House publishes quality books of Jewish content—history, Bible, philosophy, holidays, ethics—for children and adults." **12% of books from first-time authors.**

NONFICTION All levels: Judaism, Jewish educational textbooks. Average word length: young reader—1,200; middle reader—2,000; young adult—4,000.

HOW TO CONTACT Submit outline/synopsis and sample chapters. Responds in 1 month to queries; 2 months to mss. Publishes book 18 months after acceptance.

ILLUSTRATION Works with 6 children's illustrators/year. Reviews ms/illustration packages from artists. "Query first." Illustrations only: Query with samples; send unsolicited art samples by mail. Responds to queries in 1 month; mss in 2 months.

PHOTOGRAPHY Purchases photos from freelancers. Buys stock and assigns work. Uses photos of families involved in Jewish activities. Uses color and b&w prints. Photographers should query with samples. Send unsolicited photos by mail. Submit portfolio for review.

TERMS Pays authors royalty of 3-10% based on retail price or buys ms outright for $1,000-5,000. Offers advance. Pays illustrators by the project (range: $500-5,000). Book catalog free on request. Guidelines online.

BELLEBOOKS

P.O. Box 300921, Memphis TN 38130. (901)344-9024. **Fax:** (901)344-9068. **E-mail:** bellebooks@bellebooks.com. **Website:** www.bellebooks.com. BelleBooks began by publishing Southern fiction. It has become a "second home" for many established authors, who also continue to publish with major publishing houses. **Publishes 30-40 titles/year.**

FICTION "Yes, we'd love to find the next Harry Potter, but our primary focus for the moment is publishing for the teen market."

HOW TO CONTACT Query e-mail with brief synopsis and credentials/credits with full ms attached (RTF format preferred).

TERMS Guidelines online.

TIPS "Our list aims for the teen reader and the crossover market. If you're a 'Southern Louise Rennison,' that would catch our attention. Humor is always a plus. We'd love to see books featuring teen boys as protagonists. We're happy to see dark edgy books on serious subjects."

Ⓐ BERKLEY

Penguin Random House, 1745 Broadway, New York NY 10019. **Website:** penguin.com. The Berkley Publishing Group publishes a variety of general nonfiction and fiction including the traditional categories of romance, mystery and science fiction. Publishes paperback and mass market originals and reprints. **Publishes 700 titles/year.**

"Due to the high volume of manuscripts received, most Penguin Random House imprints do not normally accept unsolicited mss. The preferred and standard method for having mss considered for publication by a major publisher is to submit them through an established literary agent."

FICTION No occult fiction.

NONFICTION No memoirs or personal stories.

HOW TO CONTACT Prefers agented submissions.

BESS PRESS

3565 Harding Ave., Honolulu HI 96816. (808)734-7159. **Fax:** (808)732-3627. **Website:** www.besspress.com. Bess Press is a family-owned independent book publishing company based in Honolulu. For over 30 years, Bess Press has been producing both educational and popular general interest titles about Hawai'i and the Pacific.

NONFICTION "We are constantly seeking to work with authors, artists, photographers, and organizations that are developing works concentrating on Hawai'i and the Pacific. Our goal is to regularly provide customers with new, creative, informative, educational, and entertaining publications that are directly connected to or flowing from Hawai'i and other islands in the Pacific region." Not interested in material that is unassociated with Hawai'i or the greater Pacific in theme. Please do not submit works if it does not fall into this regional category.

HOW TO CONTACT Submit your name, contact information, working title, genre, target audience, short (4-6 sentences) description of your work, identifies target audience(s), explains how your work differs from other books already publishing on the same subject, includes discussion of any additional material with samples. All submissions via e-mail. Responds in 4 months.

TERMS Catalog online. Guidelines online.

TIPS "As a regional publisher, we are looking for material specific to the region (Hawaii and Micronesia), preferably from writers and illustrators living within (or very familiar with) the region. As a regional publisher, we are looking for material specific to the region (Hawaii and Micronesia), preferably from writers and illustrators living within (or very familiar with) the region."

BETHANY HOUSE PUBLISHERS

Division of Baker Publishing Group, 6030 E. Fulton Rd., Ada MI 49301. (616)676-9185. **Fax:** (616)676-9573. **Website:** bakerpublishinggroup.com/bethanyhouse. Bethany House Publishers specializes in books that communicate Biblical truth and assist people in both spiritual and practical areas of life. Considers unsolicited work only through a professional literary agent or through manuscript submission services, Authonomy or Christian Manuscript Submissions. Guidelines online. *All unsolicited mss returned unopened.* Publishes hardcover and trade paperback originals, mass market paperback reprints. **Publishes 90-100 titles/year. 2% of books from first-time authors. 50% from unagented writers.**

HOW TO CONTACT Responds in 3 months to queries. Publishes a book 1 year after acceptance.

TERMS Pays royalty on net price. Pays advance. Book catalog for 9 x 12 envelope and 5 first-class stamps.

TIPS "Bethany House Publishers' publishing program relates Biblical truth to all areas of life—whether in the framework of a well-told story, of a challenging book for spiritual growth, or of a Bible reference work. We are seeking high-quality fiction and nonfiction that will inspire and challenge our audience."

Ⓐ BEYOND WORDS PUBLISHING, INC.

20827 NW Cornell Rd., Suite 500, Hillsboro OR 97124. (503)531-8700. **Fax:** (503)531-8773. **E-mail:** info@beyondword.com. **Website:** www.beyondword.com. **Contact:** Submissions Department (for agents only). "At this time, we are not accepting any unsolicited queries or proposals, and recommend that all authors work with a literary agent in submitting their work." Publishes hardcover and trade paperback originals and paperback reprints. **Publishes 10-15 titles/year.**

NONFICTION For adult nonfiction, wants whole body health, the evolving human, and transformation. For children and YA, wants health, titles that inspire kids' power to incite change, and titles that allow young readers to explore and/or question traditional wisdom and spiritual practices. Does not want children's picture books, adult fiction, cookbooks, textbooks, reference books, photography books, or illustrated coffee table books.

HOW TO CONTACT Agent should submit query letter with proposal, including author bio, 5 sample chapters, complete synopsis of book, market analysis, SASE. Agent should submit query letter with proposal, including author bio, 5 sample chapters, complete synopsis of book, market analysis, SASE.

Ⓐ BLOOMSBURY CHILDREN'S BOOKS

Imprint of Bloomsbury USA, 1385 Broadway, 5th Floor, New York NY 10018. **Website:** www.bloomsbury.com/us/childrens. No phone calls or e-mails. *Agented submissions only.* **Publishes 60 titles/year. 25% of books from first-time authors.**

HOW TO CONTACT *Agented submissions only.* Responds in 6 months.

TERMS Pays royalty. Pays advance. Book catalog online. Guidelines online.

BOLD STROKES BOOKS, INC.

P.O. Box 249, Valley Falls NY 12094. (518)677-5127. **Fax:** (518)677-5291. **E-mail:** sandy@boldstrokesbooks.com. **Website:** www.boldstrokesbooks.com. **Contact:** Sandy Lowe, senior editor. Publishes trade paperback originals and reprints; electronic originals and reprints. **Publishes 120+ titles/year. 10-20% of books from first-time authors. 95% from unagented writers.**

FICTION "Submissions should have a gay, lesbian, transgendered, or bisexual focus and should be positive and life-affirming." We do not publish any non-lgbtqi focused works.

HOW TO CONTACT Submit completed ms with bio, cover letter, and synopsis—electronically only. Submit completed ms with bio, cover letter, and synopsis electronically only. 300 queries/year; 300 mss/year. Responds in 1 month to queries; 2 months to proposals; 4 months to mss. Publishes ms 6-16 months after acceptance.

TERMS Sliding scale based on sales volume and format. Pays advance. Guidelines online.

TIPS "We are particularly interested in authors who are interested in craft enhancement, technical development, and exploring and expanding traditional genre definitions and boundaries and are looking for a long-term publishing relationship. LGBTQ-focused works only."

BOYDS MILLS & KANE

19 W. 21st St., #1201, New York NY 10010. **E-mail:** info@bmkbooks.com. **Website:** www.boydsmillspress.com. Boyds Mills Press publishes picture books, nonfiction, activity books, and paperback reprints. Their titles have been named notable books by the International Reading Association, the American Library Association, and the National Council of Teachers of English. They've earned numerous

awards, including the National Jewish Book Award, the Christopher Medal, the NCTE Orbis Pictus Honor, and the Golden Kite Honor. Boyds Mills Press welcomes unsolicited submissions from published and unpublished writers and artists. Submit a ms with a cover letter of relevant information, including experience with writing and publishing. Label the package "Manuscript Submission" and include an SASE. For art samples, label the package "Art Sample Submission." All submissions will be evaluated for all imprints.

FICTION Interested in picture books and middle grade fiction. Do not send a query first. Send the entire ms of picture book or the first 3 chapters and a plot summary for middle grade fiction (will request the balance of ms if interested).

NONFICTION Include a detailed bibliography with submission. Highly recommends including an expert's review of your ms and a detailed explanation of the books in the marketplace that are similar to the one you propose. References to the need for this book (by the National Academy of Sciences or by similar subject-specific organizations) will strengthen your proposal. If you intend for the book to be illustrated with photos or other graphic elements (charts, graphs, etc.), it is your responsibility to find or create those elements and to include with the submission a permissions budget, if applicable. Finally, keep in mind that good children's nonfiction has a narrative quality—a story line—that encyclopedias do not; please consider whether both the subject and the language will appeal to children.

HOW TO CONTACT Responds to mss within 3 months.

ILLUSTRATION Illustrators submitting a picture book should include the ms, a dummy, and a sample reproduction of the final artwork that reflects the style and technique you intend to use. Do not send original artwork.

TERMS Catalog online. Guidelines online.

BRONZE MAN BOOKS

Millikin University, 1184 W. Main, Decatur IL 62522. (217)424-6264. **E-mail:** sfrech@millikin.edu. **Website:** www.bronzemanbooks.com. **Contact:** Dr. Randy Brooks, publisher; Stephen Frech, editorial board, Edwin Walker, editorial board. A student-owned and operated press located on Millikin University's campus in Decatur, Ill., Bronze Man Books is dedicated to integrating quality design and meaningful content. The company exposes undergraduate students to the process of publishing by combining the theory of writing, publishing, editing and designing with the practice of running a book publishing company. This emphasis on performance learning is a hallmark of Millikin's brand of education. Publishes hardcover, trade paperback, literary chapbooks and mass market paperback originals. **Publishes 2-3 titles/year. 80% of books from first-time authors. 100% from unagented writers.**

FICTION Subjects include art, graphic design, exhibits, general.

HOW TO CONTACT Submit completed ms. Only e-mail inquiries are welcome. Responds in 1-3 months. Publishes book 6-12 months after acceptance.

TERMS Outright purchase based on wholesale value of 10% of a press run.

TIPS "The art books are intended for serious collectors and scholars of contemporary art, especially of artists from the Midwestern US. These books are published in conjunction with art exhibitions at Millikin University or the Decatur Area Arts Council. The children's books have our broadest audience, and the literary chapbooks are intended for readers of contemporary fiction, drama, and poetry."

C&T PUBLISHING

1651 Challenge Dr., Concord CA 94520-5206. (925)677-0377. **Fax:** (925)677-0373. **E-mail:** roxanec@ctpub.com. **Website:** www.ctpub.com. **Contact:** Roxane Cerda. "C&T publishes well-written, beautifully designed books on quilting, sewing, fiber crafts, embroidery, dollmaking, mixed media and crafting for children." Publishes hardcover and trade paperback originals. **Publishes 50 titles/year. 50% of books from first-time authors. 90% from unagented writers.**

NONFICTION Extensive proposal guidelines are available on the company's website.

HOW TO CONTACT Responds in 2 months to queries.

TERMS Pays royalty. Book catalog free; guidelines online.

TIPS "In our industry, we find that how-to books have the longest selling life. Quiltmakers, sewing enthusiasts, needle artists, fiber artists and young crafters are our audience. We like to see new concepts or techniques. Include some great samples, and you'll get our attention quickly. Dynamic design is hard to resist, and if that's your forte, show us what you've done."

CALKINS CREEK

Boyds Mills Press, 19 W. 21st St., #1201, New York NY 10010. **Website:** www.boydsmillspress.com. "We aim to publish books that are a well-written blend of creative writing and extensive research, which emphasize important events, people, and places in U.S. history."

HOW TO CONTACT Submit outline/synopsis and 3 sample chapters. Submit outline/synopsis and 3 sample chapters.

ILLUSTRATION Accepts material from international illustrators. Works with 25 (for all Boyds Mills Press imprints) illustrators/year. Uses both color and b&w. Reviews ms/illustration packages. For ms/illustration packages: Submit ms with 2 pieces of final art. Submit ms/illustration packages to address above, label package "Manuscript Submission." Reviews work for future assignments. If interested in illustrating future titles, query with samples. Submit samples to address above. Label package "Art Sample Submission."

PHOTOGRAPHY Buys stock images and assigns work. Submit photos to: address above, label package "Art Sample Submission." Uses color or b&w 8×10 prints. For first contact, send promo piece (color or b&w).

TERMS Pays authors royalty or work purchased outright. Guidelines online.

TIPS "Read through our recently published titles and review our catalog. When selecting titles to publish, our emphasis will be on important events, people, and places in U.S. history. Writers are encouraged to submit a detailed bibliography, including secondary and primary sources, and expert reviews with their submissions."

Ⓐ CANDLEWICK PRESS

99 Dover St., Somerville MA 02144. (617) 661-3330. **Fax:** (617) 661-0565. **E-mail:** bigbear@candlewick.com. **Website:** www.candlewick.com. "Candlewick Press publishes high-quality, illustrated children's books for ages infant through young adult. We are a truly child-centered publisher." Publishes hardcover and trade paperback originals, and reprints. **Publishes 200 titles/year. 5% of books from first-time authors.**

Candlewick Press is not accepting queries or unsolicited mss at this time.

FICTION Picture books: animal, concept, contemporary, fantasy, history, humor, multicultural, nature/environment, poetry. Middle readers, young adults: contemporary, fantasy, history, humor, multicultural, poetry, science fiction, sports, suspense/mystery.

NONFICTION Picture books: concept, biography, geography, nature/environment. Young readers: biography, geography, nature/environment.

HOW TO CONTACT "We currently do not accept unsolicited editorial queries or submissions. If you are an author or illustrator and would like us to consider your work, please read our submissions policy (online) to learn more."

ILLUSTRATION "Candlewick prefers to see a range of styles from artists along with samples showing strong characters (human or animals) in various settings with various emotions."

TERMS Pays authors royalty of 2½-10% based on retail price. Offers advance.

TIPS "*We no longer accept unsolicited mss.* See our website for further information about us."

CAPSTONE PRESS

Capstone Young Readers, 1710 Roe Crest Dr., North Mankato MN 56003. **E-mail:** authors@capstonepub.com; il.sub@capstonepub.com. **Website:** www.capstonepub.com. The Capstone Press imprint publishes nonfiction with accessible text on topics kids love to capture interest and build confidence and skill in beginning, struggling, and reluctant readers, grades pre-K-9.

FICTION Send fiction submissions via e-mail (author.sub@capstonepub.com). Include the following, in the body of the e-mail: sample chapters, resume, and a list of previous publishing credits.

NONFICTION Send nonfiction submissions via postal mail. Include the following: resume, cover letter, and up to 3 writing samples.

HOW TO CONTACT Responds only if submissions fit needs. Mss and writing samples will not be returned. "If you receive no reply within 6 months, you should assume the editors are not interested."

ILLUSTRATION Send fiction illustration submissions via e-mail (il.sub@capstonepub.com). Include the following, in the body of the e-mail: sample artwork, resume, and a list of previous publishing credits. For nonfiction illustrations, send via e-mail (nf.il.sub@capstonepub.com) sample artwork (2-4 pieces) and a list of previous publishing credits.

TERMS Catalog available upon request. Guidelines online.

CAROLRHODA BOOKS, INC.

1251 Washington Ave. N., Minneapolis MN 55401. **Website:** www.lernerbooks.com. "We will continue to seek targeted solicitations at specific reading levels and in specific subject areas. The company will list these targeted solicitations on our website and in national newsletters, such as the SCBWI Bulletin." Interested in "boundary-pushing" teen fiction. *Lerner Publishing Group no longer accepts submissions to any of their imprints except for Kar-Ben Publishing.*

Ⓐ CARTWHEEL BOOKS

Imprint of Scholastic Trade Division, 557 Broadway, New York NY 10012. (212)343-6100. **Website:** www.scholastic.com. Cartwheel Books publishes innovative books for children, up to age 8. "We are looking for 'novelties' that are books first, play objects second. Even without its gimmick, a Cartwheel Book should stand alone as a valid piece of children's literature." Publishes novelty books, easy readers, board books, hardcover and trade paperback originals.

FICTION Again, the subject should have mass market appeal for very young children. Humor can be helpful, but not necessary. Mistakes writers make are a reading level that is too difficult, a topic of no interest or too narrow, or mss that are too long.

NONFICTION Cartwheel Books publishes for the very young, therefore nonfiction should be written in a manner that is accessible to preschoolers through 2nd grade. Often writers choose topics that are too narrow or "special" and do not appeal to the mass market. Also, the text and vocabulary are frequently too difficult for our young audience.

HOW TO CONTACT *Accepts mss from agents only.*

TERMS Guidelines available free.

CEDAR FORT, INC.

2373 W. 700 S, Springville UT 84663. (801)489-4084. **Website:** www.cedarfort.com. "Each year we publish well over 100 books, and many of those are by first-time authors. At the same time, we love to see books from established authors. As one of the largest book publishers in Utah, we have the capability and enthusiasm to make your book a success, whether you are a new author or a returning one. We want to publish uplifting and edifying books that help people think about what is important in life, books people enjoy reading to relax and feel better about themselves, and books to help improve lives. Although we do put out several children's books each year, we are extremely selective. Our children's books must have strong religious or moral values, and must contain outstanding writing and an excellent storyline." Publishes hardcover, trade paperback originals and reprints, mass market paperback and electronic reprints. **Publishes 150 titles/year. 60% of books from first-time authors. 95% from unagented writers.**

HOW TO CONTACT Submit completed ms. Query with SASE; submit proposal package, including outline, 2 sample chapters; or submit completed ms. Receives 200 queries/year; 600 mss/year. Responds in 1 month on queries; 2 months on proposals; 4 months on mss. Publishes book 10-14 months after acceptance.

TERMS Pays 10-12% royalty on wholesale price. Pays $2,000-50,000 advance. Catalog and guidelines online.

TIPS "Our audience is rural, conservative, mainstream. The first page of your ms is very important because we start reading every submission, but good-writing and plot keep us reading."

CHARLESBRIDGE PUBLISHING

85 Main St., Watertown MA 02472. (617)926-0329. **Fax:** (617)926-5720. **E-mail:** tradeeditorial@charlesbridge.com. **Website:** www.charlesbridge.com. "Charlesbridge publishes high-quality books for children, with a goal of creating lifelong readers and lifelong learners. Our books encourage reading and discovery in the classroom, library, and home. We believe that books for children should offer accurate information, promote a positive worldview, and embrace a child's innate sense of wonder and fun. To this end, we continually strive to seek new voices, new visions, and new directions in children's literature. We are now accepting young adult novels for consideration." Publishes hardcover and trade paperback nonfiction and fiction, children's books for the trade and library markets. **Publishes 50 titles/year. 10-20% of books from first-time authors. 40% from unagented writers.**

FICTION Strong stories with enduring themes. Charlesbridge publishes both picture books and transitional bridge books (books ranging from early readers to middle-grade chapter books). Our fiction titles include lively, plot-driven stories with strong, engaging characters. No alphabet books, board books, coloring books, activity books, or books with audiotapes or CD-ROMs.

NONFICTION Strong interest in nature, environment, social studies, and other topics for trade and library markets.

HOW TO CONTACT Please submit only 1 ms at a time. For picture books and shorter bridge books, please send a complete ms. For fiction books longer than 30 ms pages, please send a detailed plot synopsis, a chapter outline, and 3 chapters of text. If sending a young adult novel, mark the front of the envelope with "YA novel enclosed." Please note, for YA, e-mail submissions are preferred to the following address; yasubs@charlesbridge.com. Only responds if interested. Full guidelines on site. 4,000 submissions/year. Responds in 3 months. Publishes 2-4 years after acceptance.

TERMS Pays royalty. Pays advance.

TIPS "To become acquainted with our publishing program, we encourage you to review our books and visit our website where you will find our catalog."

CHICAGO REVIEW PRESS

814 N. Franklin St., Chicago IL 60610. (312)337-0747. **Fax:** (312)337-5110. **E-mail:** krota@chicagoreviewpress.com; jpohlen@chicagoreviewpress.com. **Website:** www.chicagoreviewpress.com. **Contact:** Jerome Pohlen. "Chicago Review Press publishes high-quality, nonfiction, educational activity books that extend the learning process through hands-on projects and accurate and interesting text. We look for activity books that are as much fun as they are constructive and informative."

NONFICTION Young readers, middle readers and young adults: activity books, arts/crafts, multicultural, history, nature/environment, science. "We're interested in hands-on, educational books; anything else probably will be rejected." Average length: young readers and young adults—144-160 pages.

HOW TO CONTACT Enclose cover letter and a brief synopsis of book in 1-2 paragraphs, table of contents and first 3 sample chapters; prefers not to receive e-mail queries. For children's activity books include a few sample activities with a list of the others. Full guidelines available on site. Responds in 2 months. Publishes a book 1-2 years after acceptance.

ILLUSTRATION Works with 6 illustrators/year. Uses primarily b&w artwork. Reviews ms/illustration packages from artists. Submit 1-2 chapters of ms with corresponding pieces of final art. Illustrations only: Query with samples, résumé. Responds only if interested. Samples returned with SASE.

PHOTOGRAPHY Buys photos from freelancers ("but not often"). Buys stock and assigns work. Wants "instructive photos. We consult our files when we know what we're looking for on a book-by-book basis." Uses b&w prints.

TERMS Pays authors royalty of 7.5-12.5% based on retail price. Offers advances of $3,000-6,000. Pays illustrators and photographers by the project (range varies considerably). Book catalog available for $3. Ms guidelines available for $3.

TIPS "We're looking for original activity books for small children and the adults caring for them—new themes and enticing projects to occupy kids' imaginations and promote their sense of personal creativity. We like activity books that are as much fun as they are constructive. Please write for guidelines so you'll know what we're looking for."

CHRONICLE BOOKS

680 Second St., San Francisco CA 94107. **E-mail:** submissions@chroniclebooks.com. **Website:** www.chroniclebooks.com. "We publish an exciting range of books, stationery, kits, calendars, and novelty formats. Our list includes children's books and interactive formats; young adult books; cookbooks; fine art, design, and photography; pop culture; craft, fashion, beauty, and home decor; relationships, mind-body-spirit; innovative formats such as interactive journals, kits, decks, and stationery; and much, much more." **Publishes 90 titles/year.**

FICTION Only interested in fiction for children and young adults. No adult fiction.

NONFICTION "We're always looking for the new and unusual. We do accept unsolicited manuscripts and we review all proposals. However, given the volume of proposals we receive, we are not able to personally respond to unsolicited proposals unless we are interested in pursuing the project."

HOW TO CONTACT Submit complete ms (picture books); submit outline/synopsis and 3 sample chapters (for older readers). Will not respond to submissions unless interested. Will not consider submissions by fax, e-mail or disk. Do not include SASE; do not send original materials. No submissions will be returned. Submit via mail or e-mail (prefers e-mail for adult submissions; only by mail for children's submissions). Submit proposal (guidelines online) and allow 3 months for editors to review and for children's submissions, allow 6 months. If submitting by mail, do not include SASE since our staff will not return materials. Responds to queries in 1 month. Publishes a book 1-3 years after acceptance.

ILLUSTRATION Works with 40-50 illustrators/year. Wants "unusual art, graphically strong, something that will stand out on the shelves. Fine art, not mass market." Reviews ms/illustration packages from artists. "Indicate if project *must* be considered jointly, or if editor may consider text and art separately." Illustrations only: Submit samples of artist's work (not necessarily from book, but in the envisioned style). Slides, tearsheets and color photocopies OK. (No original art.) Dummies helpful. Résumé helpful. Samples suited to our needs are filed for future reference. Samples not suited to our needs will be recycled. Queries and project proposals responded to in same time frame as author query/proposals."

PHOTOGRAPHY Purchases photos from freelancers. Works on assignment only.

TERMS Generally pays authors in royalties based on retail price, "though we do occasionally work on a flat fee basis." Advance varies. Illustrators paid royalty based on retail price or flat fee. Book catalog for 9x12 SAE and 8 first-class stamps. Ms guidelines for #10 SASE.

CLARION BOOKS

Houghton Mifflin Co., 215 Park Ave. S., New York NY 10003. **Website:** www.hmhco.com. "Clarion Books publishes picture books, nonfiction, and fiction for infants through grade 12. Avoid telling your stories in verse unless you are a professional poet. *We are no longer responding to your unsolicited submission unless we are interested in publishing it. Please do not include a SASE. Submissions will be recycled, and you will not hear from us regarding the status of your submission unless we are interested. We regret that we cannot respond personally to each submission, but we do consider each and every submission we receive.*" Publishes hardcover originals for children. **Publishes 50 titles/year.**

FICTION "Clarion is highly selective in the areas of historical fiction, fantasy, and science fiction. A novel must be superlatively written in order to find a place on the list. Mss that arrive without an SASE of adequate size will *not* be responded to or returned. Accepts fiction translations."

NONFICTION No unsolicited mss.

HOW TO CONTACT Submit complete ms. No queries, please. Send to only *one* Clarion editor. Query with SASE. Submit proposal package, sample chapters, SASE. Responds in 2 months to queries. Publishes a book 2 years after acceptance.

ILLUSTRATION Pays illustrators royalty; flat fee for jacket illustration.

TERMS Pays 5-10% royalty on retail price. Pays minimum of $4,000 advance. Guidelines online.

TIPS "Looks for freshness, enthusiasm—in short, life."

CRABTREE PUBLISHING COMPANY

347 Fifth Ave., Suite 1402-145, New York NY 10116. (212)496-5040; (800)387-7650. **Fax:** (800)355-7166. **Website:** www.crabtreebooks.com. Crabtree Publishing Company is dedicated to producing high-quality books and educational products for K-8+. Each resource blends accuracy, immediacy, and eye-catching illustration with the goal of inspiring nothing less than a life-long interest in reading and learning in children. The company began building its reputation in 1978 as a quality children's non-fiction book publisher with acclaimed author Bobbie Kalman's first series about the early pioneers. The Early Settler Life Series became a mainstay in schools as well as historic sites and museums across North America.

"Crabtree does not accept unsolicited manuscripts. Crabtree Publishing has an editorial team in-house that creates curriculum-specific book series."

TIPS "Since our books are for younger readers, lively photos of children and animals are always excellent." Portfolio should be diverse and encompass several subjects rather than just 1 or 2; depth of coverage of subject should be intense so that any publishing company could, conceivably, use all or many of a photographer's photos in a book on a particular subject."

THE CREATIVE COMPANY

P.O. Box 227, Mankato MN 56002. (800)445-6209. **Fax:** (507)388-2746. **Website:** www.thecreativecompany.us. "We are currently not accepting fiction submissions." **Publishes 140 titles/year.**

NONFICTION Picture books, young readers, young adults: animal, arts/crafts, biography, careers, geography, health, history, hobbies, multicultural, music/

dance, nature/environment, religion, science, social issues, special needs, sports. Average word length: young readers—500; young adults—6,000.

HOW TO CONTACT Submit outline/synopsis and 2 sample chapters, along with division of titles within the series. Responds in 3-6 months. Publishes a book 2 years after acceptance.

PHOTOGRAPHY Buys stock. Contact: Photo Editor. Model/property releases not required; captions required. Uses b&w prints. Submit cover letter, promo piece. Ms and photographer guidelines available for SAE.

TERMS Guidelines available for SAE.

TIPS "We are accepting nonfiction, series submissions only. Fiction submissions will not be reviewed or returned. Nonfiction submissions should be presented in series (4, 6, or 8) rather than single."

CRESTON BOOKS

P.O. Box 9369, Berkeley CA 94709. **E-mail:** submissions@crestonbooks.co. **Website:** crestonbooks.co. Creston Books is author-illustrator driven, with talented, award-winning creators given more editorial freedom and control than in a typical New York house. **50% of books from first-time authors. 50% from unagented writers.**

HOW TO CONTACT Please paste text of picture books or first chapters of novels in the body of e-mail. Words of Advice for submitting authors listed on the site.

TERMS Pays advance. Catalog online. Guidelines online.

DARBY CREEK PUBLISHING

Lerner Publishing Group, 1251 Washington Ave. N., Minneapolis MN 55401. (612)332-3344. **Fax:** (612)332-7615. **Website:** www.lernerbooks.com. "Darby Creek publishes series fiction titles for emerging, striving and reluctant readers ages 7 to 18 (grades 2-12). From beginning chapter books to intermediate fiction and page-turning YA titles, Darby Creek books engage readers with strong characters and formats they'll want to pursue." Darby Creek does not publish picture books. Publishes children's chapter books, middle readers, young adult. Mostly series. **Publishes 25 titles/year.**

"We are currently not accepting any submissions. If that changes, we will provide all children's writing publications with our new info."

FICTION Middle readers, young adult. Recently published: *The Surviving Southside* series, by various authors; *The Agent Amelia* series, by Michael Broad; *The Mallory McDonald* series, by Laurie B. Friedman; and *The Alien Agent* series, by Pam Service.

NONFICTION Middle readers: biography, history, science, sports. Recently published *Albino Animals*, by Kelly Milner Halls, illustrated by Rick Spears; *Miracle: The True Story of the Wreck of the Sea Venture*, by Gail Karwoski.

ILLUSTRATION Illustrations only: Send photocopies and résumé with publishing history. "Indicate which samples we may keep on file and include SASE and appropriate packing materials for any samples you wish to have returned."

TERMS Offers advance-against-royalty contracts.

DARK HORSE COMICS, INC.

10956 SE Main St., Milwaukie OR 97222. (503)652-8815. **Fax:** (503)654-9440. **Website:** www.darkhorse.com. "In addition to publishing comics from top talent like Frank Miller, Mike Mignola, Stan Sakai and internationally-renowned humorist Sergio Aragonés, Dark Horse is recognized as the world's leading publisher of licensed comics."

FICTION Comic books, graphic novels. Published *Astro Boy Volume 10 TPB*, by Osamu Tezuka and Reid Fleming; *Flaming Carrot Crossover #1* by Bob Burden and David Boswell.

HOW TO CONTACT Submit synopsis to dhcomics@darkhorse.com. See website (www.darkhorse.com) for detailed submission guidelines and submission agreement, which must be signed. Include a full script for any short story or single-issue submission, or the first eight pages of the first issue of any series. Submissions can no longer be mailed back to the sender.

TIPS "If you're looking for constructive criticism, show your work to industry professionals at conventions."

DAWN PUBLICATIONS

12402 Bitney Springs Rd., Nevada City CA 95959. (530)274-7775. **Fax:** (530)274-7778. **Website:** www.dawnpub.com. **Contact:** Carol Malnor, associate editor. "Dawn Publications is dedicated to inspiring in children a sense of appreciation for all life on earth. Dawn looks for nature awareness and appreciation titles that promote a relationship with the natural world and specific habitats, usually through inspiring treatment and nonfiction." Dawn accepts mss submissions by e-mail; follow instructions posted on website. Submissions by mail OK. Publishes hardcover and trade paperback originals. **Publishes 6 titles/year. 15% of books from first-time authors. 90% from unagented writers.**

HOW TO CONTACT 2,500 queries or mss received/year. Automated confirmation of submission sent upon receipt. Followup in 2 months if interested. Publishes book 1-2 years after acceptance.

ILLUSTRATION Works with 5 illustrators/year. Will review ms/illustration packages from artists. Query; send ms with dummy. Illustrations only: Query with samples, résumé.

TERMS Pays advance. Book catalog and guidelines online.

TIPS "Publishes mostly creative nonfiction with lightness and inspiration." Looking for "picture books expressing nature awareness with inspirational quality leading to enhanced self-awareness." Does not publish anthropomorphic works; no animal dialogue.

KATHY DAWSON BOOKS

Penguin Random House, 1745 Broadway, New York NY 10019. (212)366-2000. **Website:** kathydawsonbooks.tumblr.com. Mission statement: Publish stellar novels with unforgettable characters for children and teens that expand their vision of the world, sneakily explore the meaning of life, celebrate the written word, and last for generations. The imprint strives to publish tomorrow's award contenders: quality books with strong hooks in a variety of genres with universal themes and compelling voices—books that break the mold and the heart.

HOW TO CONTACT Accepts fiction queries via snail mail only. Include cover sheet with one-sentence elevator pitch, main themes, author version of catalog copy for book, first 10 pages of ms (double-spaced, Times Roman, 12 point type), and publishing history. No SASE needed. Responds only if interested. Responds only if interested.

TERMS Guidelines online.

Ⓐ DELACORTE PRESS

An imprint of Random House Children's Books, a division of Penguin Random House LLC, New York, 1745 Broadway, New York NY 10019. (212)782-9000. **Website:** randomhousekids.com; randomhouseteens.com. Publishes middle grade and young adult fiction in hard cover, trade paperback, mass market and digest formats.

All query letters and manuscript submissions must be submitted through an agent or at the request of an editor.

DIAL BOOKS FOR YOUNG READERS

Imprint of Penguin Random House, 1745 Broadway, New York NY 10019. (212)366-2000. **Website:** www.penguin.com/children. "Dial Books for Young Readers publishes quality picture books for ages 18 months-6 years; lively, believable novels for middle readers and young adults; and occasional nonfiction for middle readers and young adults." Publishes hardcover originals. **Publishes 50 titles/year. 20% of books from first-time authors.**

FICTION Especially looking for lively and well-written novels for middle grade and young adult children involving a convincing plot and believable characters. The subject matter or theme should not already be overworked in previously published books. The approach must not be demeaning to any minority group, nor should the roles of female characters (or others) be stereotyped, though we don't think books should be didactic, or in any way message-y. No topics inappropriate for the juvenile, young adult, and middle grade audiences. No plays.

HOW TO CONTACT Accepts unsolicited queries and up to 10 pages for longer works and unsolicited mss for picture books. Will only respond if interested. Only responds if interested. "We accept entire picture book manuscripts and a maximum of 10 pages for longer works (novels, easy-to-reads). When submitting a portion of a longer work, please provide an accompanying cover letter that briefly describes your manuscript's plot, genre (i.e. easy-to-read, middle grade or YA novel), the intended age group, and your publishing credits, if any." 5,000 queries received/year. Responds in 4-6 months to queries.

ILLUSTRATION Send nonreturnable samples, no originals. Show children and animals.

TERMS Pays royalty. Pays varies advance. Book catalog and guidelines online.

TIPS "Our readers are anywhere from preschool age to teenage. Picture books must have strong plots, lots of action, unusual premises, or universal themes treated with freshness and originality. Humor works well in these books. A very well-thought-out and intelligently presented book has the best chance of being taken on. Genre isn't as much of a factor as presentation."

DIVERTIR

P.O. Box 232, North Salem NH 03073. **E-mail:** info@divertirpublishing.com. **Website:** www.divertirpublishing.com. **Contact:** Kenneth Tupper, publisher. Divertir Publishing is an independent publisher located in Salem, NH. "Our goal is to provide interesting and entertaining books to our readers, as well as to offer new and exciting voices in the writing community the opportunity to publish their work. We seek to combine an understanding of traditional publishing with a unique understanding of the modern market to best serve both our authors and readers." Publishes trade paperback and electronic originals. **Publishes 6-12 titles/year. 70% of books from first-time authors. 100% from unagented writers.**

FICTION "We are particularly interested in the following: science fiction, fantasy, alternate history, contemporary mythology, mystery and suspense, paranormal, and urban fantasy." Does not consider erotica or mss with excessive violence.

NONFICTION "We are particularly interested in the following: political/social commentary, current events, and humor/satire." "We currently do not publish memoirs."

HOW TO CONTACT Electronically submit proposal package, including synopsis and query letter with author's bio. 1,000 submissions received/year. Responds in 1-3 months on queries; 3-4 months on proposals and mss. Publishes ms 9-12 months after acceptance.

TERMS Pays 10-15% royalty on wholesale price (for novels and nonfiction). Does not pay advance. Catalog online. Guidelines online.

TIPS "Please see our Author Info page (online) for more information."

DUTTON CHILDREN'S BOOKS

Penguin Random House, 1745 Broadway, New York NY 10019. **Website:** www.penguin.com. Dutton Children's Books publishes high-quality fiction and nonfiction for readers ranging from preschoolers to young adults on a variety of subjects. Currently emphasizing middle grade and young adult novels that offer a fresh perspective. De-emphasizing photographic nonfiction and picture books that teach a lesson. Publishes hardcover originals as well as novelty formats. **Publishes 100 titles/year. 15% of books from first-time authors.**

"Cultivating the creative talents of authors and illustrators and publishing books with purpose and heart continue to be the mission and joy at Dutton."

FICTION Dutton Children's Books has a diverse, general interest list that includes picture books; easy-to-read books; and fiction for all ages, from first chapter books to young adult readers.

HOW TO CONTACT Query. Responds only if interested. Query. Responds only if interested. Query. Only responds if interested.

TERMS Pays royalty on retail price. Offers advance. Pays royalty on retail price. Pays advance.

EDUPRESS, INC.

Teacher Created Resources, 12621 Western Ave., Garden Grove CA 92841. (800)662-4321. **Fax:** (800)525-1254. **Website:** www.edupress.com. **Contact:** Editor-in-Chief. Edupress, Inc., publishes supplemental curriculum resources for PK-6th grade. Currently emphasizing Common Core reading and math games and materials.

"Our mission is to create products that make kids want to go to school."

HOW TO CONTACT Submit complete ms via mail or e-mail with "Manuscript Submission" as the subject line. Responds in 2-4 months. Publishes ms 1-2 years after acceptance.

ILLUSTRATION Query with samples. Contact: Cathy Baker, product development manager. Responds only if interested. Samples returned with SASE.

PHOTOGRAPHY Buys stock.

TERMS Work purchased outright from authors. Catalog online.

TIPS "We are looking for unique, research-based, quality supplemental materials for Pre-K through 6th grade. We publish mainly reading and math materials in many different formats, including games. Our materials are intended for classroom and home schooling use. We do not publish picture books."

WILLIAM B. EERDMANS PUBLISHING CO.

2140 Oak Industrial Dr. NE, Grand Rapids MI 49505. (616)459-4591. **Fax:** (616)459-6540. **E-mail:** info@eerdmans.com. **Website:** www.eerdmans.com. "The majority of our adult publications are religious and most of these are academic or semi-academic in character (as opposed to inspirational or celebrity books), though we also publish general trade books on the Christian life. Our nonreligious titles, most of them in regional history or on social issues, aim, similarly, at an educated audience." Publishes hardcover and paperback originals and reprints.

NONFICTION "We prefer that writers take the time to notice if we have published anything at all in the same category as their manuscript before sending it to us."

HOW TO CONTACT Query with SASE. Query with TOC, 2-3 sample chapters, and SASE for return of ms. Responds in 4 weeks.

TERMS Book catalog and ms guidelines free.

ELLYSIAN PRESS

E-mail: publisher@ellysianpress.com. **Website:** www.ellysianpress.com. **Contact:** Maer Wilson. "Ellysian Press is a speculative fiction house. We seek to create a sense of home for our authors, a place where they can find fulfillment as artists. Just as exceptional mortals once sought a place in the Elysian Fields, now exceptional authors can find a place here at Ellysian Press. We are accepting submissions in the following genres only: Fantasy, Science Fiction, Paranormal, Paranormal Romance, Horror, along with Young/New Adult in these genres. Please submit polished manuscripts. It's best to have work read by critique groups or beta readers prior to submission. Please note: We do not publish children's books, picture books, or Middle Grade books. We do not publish books outside the genres listed above." Publishes fantasy, science fiction, paranormal, paranormal romance, horror, and young/new adult in these genres. **25% of books from first-time authors. 90% from unagented writers.**

HOW TO CONTACT "We accept online submissions only. Please submit a query letter, a synopsis and the first ten pages of your manuscript in the body of your e-mail. The subject line should be as follows: QUERY – Your Last Name, TITLE, Genre." If we choose to request more, we will request the full manuscript in standard format. This means your manuscript should be formatted as per the guidelines on our website. Please do not submit queries for any genres not listed above. Please do not submit children's books, picture books or Middle Grade books. You may email queries to submissions(at)ellysianpress(dot)com. Responds in 1 week for queries; 4-6 weeks for partials and fulls. Publishes ms 18+ months after acceptance.

TERMS Pays quarterly. Does not pay advance. Catalog online. Guidelines online.

ELM BOOKS

1175 Hwy. 130, Laramie WY 82070. (610)529-0460. **E-mail:** leila.elmbooks@gmail.com. **Website:** www.elm-books.com. **Contact:** Leila Monaghan, publisher. "Follow us on Facebook to learn about our latest calls for science fiction, mystery and romance stories. We also welcome submissions of middle grade fiction featuring diverse children. No picture book submissions."

FICTION "Follow us on Facebook to learn about our latest calls for science fiction, mystery and romance stories. We also welcome submissions of middle grade fiction featuring diverse children. No picture book submissions."

HOW TO CONTACT Send inquiries for middle grade fiction featuring diverse children via e-mail to leila.elmbooks@gmail.com. No mail inquiries.

TERMS Pays royalties.

ENSLOW PUBLISHERS, INC.

101 W. 23rd St., Suite 240, New York NY 10011. (973)771-9400. **Fax:** (877)980-4454. **E-mail:** customerservice@enslow.com. **Website:** www.enslow.com. Enslow publishes nonfiction and fiction series books for young adults and school-age children. Publishes hardcover originals. 10% require freelance illustration. **Publishes 250 titles/year.**

NONFICTION "Interested in new ideas for series of books for young people." No fiction, fictionalized history, or dialogue.

HOW TO CONTACT Responds in 1 month to queries. Publishes ms 1 year after acceptance.

TERMS Pays royalty on net price with advance or flat fee. Pays advance. Guidelines via e-mail.

TIPS "We love to receive resumes from experienced writers with good research skills who can think like young people."

FACTS ON FILE, INC.

Infobase, 132 W. 31st St., 16th Floor, New York NY 10001. (800)322-8755. **Fax:** (800)678-3633. **E-mail:** llikoff@infobase.com; custserv@infobaselearning.com. **Website:** www.infobase.com. **Contact:** Laurie Likoff. Facts On File produces high-quality reference materials in print and digital format on a broad range of subjects for the school and public library market and the general nonfiction trade. Publishes hardcover originals and reprints and e-books as well as reference databases, streaming video and instructional courses. **Publishes 150-200 titles/year. 10% of books from first-time authors. 45% from unagented writers.**

NONFICTION "We publish serious, informational e-books for a targeted audience. All our books must have strong library interest, but we also distribute books effectively to the trade. Our library books fit the junior and senior high school curriculum." No computer books, technical books, cookbooks, biographies (except YA), pop psychology, humor, fiction or poetry.

HOW TO CONTACT Query or submit outline and sample chapter with SASE. No submissions returned without SASE. Responds in 2 months to queries. Responds in 6 months to 1 year.

ILLUSTRATION Commissions line art only.

TERMS Pays 10% royalty on retail price. Pays $3-5,000 advance. Reference catalog available online. Guidelines online.

TIPS "Our audience is school and public libraries for our more reference-oriented books and libraries, schools and bookstores for our less reference-oriented informational titles."

FAMILIUS

E-mail: bookideas@familius.com. **Website:** familius.com. **Contact:** Acquisitions. Familius publishes beautiful books for children and adults that include boardbooks, picturebooks, interactive books, reference, cook, gift,and regional. Familius publishes based on our ten habits of happy families and to fulfill our mission to help families be happy. Familius believes every family deserves to be happy. Publishes hardcover, trade paperback, and electronic originals and reprints. **Publishes 60 titles/year. 30% of books from first-time authors. 70% from unagented writers.**

FICTION All picture books must align with Familius values statement listed on the website footer.

NONFICTION All mss must align with Familius mission statement to help families be happy as well as the Familius 10 habits of happy families.

HOW TO CONTACT Submit a proposal package, including a synopsis, 3 sample chapters, and your author platform. Submit a proposal package, including an outline, 1 sample chapter, competition evaluation, and your author platform. 1000 queries; 1000 mss received/year. Familius is unable to respond to all submissions and only responds to submissions the company decides to explore for possible acquisition. Publishes book 12-24 months after acceptance.

TERMS Royalties are 10-20% royalty on wholesale (net) price, 30% for digital, and 50% for rights. All illustrated books have royalties split between author and illustrator. Nominal advances are paid. Catalog online and print. Proposals should be sent to bookideas@familius.com and should include a cover letter with pitch, competitive analysis, compete story if children's and table of contents as well as sample chapter if adult, and author platform.

FAMILYLIFE PUBLISHING

FamilyLife, a division of Campus Crusade for Christ, P.O. Box 7111, Little Rock AR 72223. (800)358-6329. **Website:** www.familylife.com. FamilyLife is dedicated to effectively developing godly families. We publish connecting resources—books, videos, audio resources, and interactive multi-piece packs—that help husbands and wives communicate better, and parents and children build stronger relationships. Publishes hardcover and trade paperback originals. **Publishes 3-12 titles/year. 1% of books from first-time authors. 90% from unagented writers.**

NONFICTION FamilyLife Publishing exists to create resources to connect your family. "We publish very few books. Become familiar with what we offer. Our resources are unique in the marketplace. Discover what makes us unique, match your work to our style, and then submit."

HOW TO CONTACT Query with SASE. Submit proposal package, outline, 2 sample chapters. 250 queries received/year. 50 mss received/year. Responds in 3 months to queries; 6 months to proposals and mss. Publishes ms 2 years after acceptance.

TERMS Pays 2-18% royalty on wholesale price. Makes outright purchase of 250. Book catalog online.

FARRAR, STRAUS & GIROUX

18 W. 18th St., New York NY 10011. (646)307-5151. **Website:** us.macmillan.com/fsg. **Contact:** Editorial Department. "We publish original and well-written material for all ages." Publishes hardcover originals and trade paperback reprints. **Publishes 75 titles/year. 5% of books from first-time authors. 50% from unagented writers.**

FICTION Do not query picture books; just send ms. Do not fax or e-mail queries or mss.

NONFICTION All levels.

HOW TO CONTACT Send cover letter describing submission with first 50 pages. Send cover letter describing submission with first 50 pages. 6,000 queries and mss received/year. Responds in 2-3 months. Publishes ms 18 months after acceptance.

TERMS Pays 2-6% royalty on retail price for paperbacks, 3-10% for hardcovers. Pays $3,000-25,000 advance. Catalog available by request. Guidelines online.

Ⓐ FEIWEL AND FRIENDS

Macmillan Children's Publishing Group, 175 Fifth Ave., New York NY 10010. (646)307-5151. **Website:** us.macmillan.com. Feiwel and Friends is a publisher of innovative children's fiction and nonfiction literature, including hardcover, paperback series, and individual titles. The list is eclectic and combines quality and commercial appeal for readers ages 0-16. The imprint is dedicated to "book by book" publishing, bringing the work of distinctive and oustanding authors, illustrators, and ideas to the marketplace. This market does not accept unsolicited mss due to the volume of submissions; they also do not accept unsolicited queries for interior art. The best way to submit a ms is through an agent.

TERMS Catalog online.

FERGUSON PUBLISHING CO.

Infobase Publishing, 132 W. 31st St., 17th Floor, New York NY 10001. (800)322-8755. **E-mail:** editorial@factsonfile.com. **Website:** www.infobasepublishing.com. "We are primarily a career education publisher that publishes for schools and libraries. We need writers who have expertise in a particular career or career field (for possible full-length books on a specific career or field)." Publishes hardcover and trade paperback originals. **Publishes 50 titles/year.**

NONFICTION "We publish work specifically for the elementary/junior high/high school/college library reference market. Works are generally encyclopedic in nature. Our current focus is career encyclopedias and young adult career sets and series. We consider manuscripts that cross over into the trade market." No mass market, poetry, scholarly, or juvenile books, please.

HOW TO CONTACT Query or submit an outline and 1 sample chapter. Responds in 6 months to queries.

TERMS Pays by project. Guidelines online.

TIPS "We like writers who know the market—former or current librarians or teachers or guidance counselors."

Ⓐ FIRST SECOND

Macmillan Children's Publishing Group, 175 5th Ave., New York NY 10010. **E-mail:** mail@firstsecondbooks.com. **Website:** www.firstsecondbooks.com. First Second is a publisher of graphic novels and an imprint of Macmillan Children's Publishing Group. First Second does not accept unsolicited submissions.

HOW TO CONTACT Responds in about 6 weeks.

TERMS Catalog online.

FLASHLIGHT PRESS

527 Empire Blvd., Brooklyn NY 11225. (718)288-8300. **Fax:** (718)972-6307. **Website:** www.flashlightpress.com. **Contact:** Shari Dash Greenspan, editor. Publishes hardcover original children's picture books for 4-8 year olds. **Publishes 2-3 titles/year. 50% of books from first-time authors. 50% from unagented writers.**

FICTION Average word length: 1,000 words. Picture books: contemporary, humor, multicultural.

HOW TO CONTACT "Query by e-mail only, after carefully reading our submission guidelines online. Do not send anything by snail mail." 2,000 queries received/year. "Only accepts e-mail queries according to submission guidelines." Publishes ms up to 3 years after acceptance.

TERMS Pays 8-10% royalty on net. Pays advance. Book catalog online. Guidelines online.

FORWARD MOVEMENT

412 Sycamore St., Cincinnati OH 45202. (513)721-6659; (800)543-1813. **Fax:** (513)721-0729. **E-mail:** editorialstaff@forwardmovement.org. **Website:** www.forwardmovement.org. "Forward Movement was established to help reinvigorate the life of the church. Many titles focus on the life of prayer, where our relationship with God is centered, death, marriage, baptism, recovery, joy, the Episcopal Church and more. Currently emphasizing prayer/spirituality." **Publishes 30 titles/year.**

NONFICTION "We are an agency of the Episcopal Church. There is a special need for tracts of under 8 pages. (A page usually runs about 200 words.) On rare occasions, we publish a full-length book."

HOW TO CONTACT Query with SASE or by e-mail with complete ms attached. Responds in 1 month.

TERMS Book catalog free. Guidelines online.

TIPS "Audience is primarily Episcopalians and other Christians."

FREE SPIRIT PUBLISHING, INC.

6325 Sandburg Rd., Suite 100, Minneapolis MN 55427-3674. (612)338-2068. **Fax:** (612)337-5050. **E-mail:** acquisitions@freespirit.com. **Website:** www.freespirit.com. "Free Spirit is the leading publisher of learning tools that support young people's social-emotional health and educational needs. We help children and teens think for themselves, overcome challenges, and make a difference in the world." Free Spirit does not accept general fiction, poetry or storybook submissions. Publishes trade paperback originals and reprints. **Publishes 25-30 titles/year.**

FICTION "Please review catalog and author guidelines (both available online) for details before submitting proposal. If you'd like material returned, enclose a SASE with sufficient postage."

NONFICTION "Many of our authors are educators, mental health professionals, and youth workers involved in helping kids and teens." No general fiction or picture storybooks, poetry, single biographies or autobiographies, books with mythical or animal characters, or books with religious or New Age content. We are not looking for academic or religious materials, or books that analyze problems with the nation's school systems.

HOW TO CONTACT Query with cover letter stating qualifications, intent, and intended audience and market analysis (comprehensive list of similar titles and detailed explanation of how your book stands out from the field), along with your promotional plan, outline, 2 sample chapters (note: for early childhood submissions, the entire text is required for evaluation), resume, SASE. Do not send original copies of work. Responds to proposals within 6 months.

ILLUSTRATION Works with 5 illustrators/year. Submit samples to creative director for consideration. If appropriate, samples will be kept on file and artist will be contacted if a suitable project comes up. Enclose SASE if you'd like materials returned.

PHOTOGRAPHY Uses stock photos. Does not accept photography submissions.

TERMS Book catalog and guidelines online.

TIPS "Our books are issue-oriented, jargon-free, and solution-focused. Our audience is children, teens, teachers, parents and youth counselors. We are especially concerned with kids' social and emotional well-being and look for books with ready-to-use strategies for coping with today's issues at home or in school—written in everyday language. We are not looking for academic or religious materials, or books that analyze problems with the nation's school systems. Instead, we want books that offer practical, positive advice so kids can help themselves, and parents and teachers can help kids succeed."

GIBBS SMITH

P.O. Box 667, Layton UT 84041. (801)544-9800. **Fax:** (801)544-8853. **E-mail:** debbie.uribe@gibbs-smith.com. **Website:** www.gibbs-smith.com. **Publishes 3 titles/year. 50% of books from first-time authors. 50% from unagented writers.**

NONFICTION Middle readers: activity, arts/crafts, cooking, how-to, nature/environment, science. Average word length: picture books—under 1,000 words; activity books—under 15,000 words.

HOW TO CONTACT Submit an outline and writing samples for activity books; query for other types of books. Responds in 2 months. Publishes ms 1-2 years after acceptance.

ILLUSTRATION Works with 2 illustrators/year. Reviews ms/illustration packages from artists. Query. Submit ms with 3-5 pieces of final art. Illustrations only: Query with samples; provide résumé, promo sheet, slides (duplicate slides, not originals). Responds only if interested. Samples returned with SASE; samples filed.

TERMS Pays illustrators by the project or royalty of 2% based on retail price. Sends galleys to authors; color proofs to illustrators. Original artwork returned at job's completion. Pays authors royalty of 2% based on retail price or work purchased outright ($500 minimum). Offers advances (average amount: $2,000). Book catalog available for 9×12 SAE and $2.30 postage. Ms guidelines available by e-mail.

TIPS "We target ages 5-11. We do not publish young adult novels or chapter books."

THE GLENCANNON PRESS

P.O. Box 1428, El Cerrito CA 94530. (510)455-9027. **Website:** www.glencannon.com. **Contact:** Bill Harris (maritime, maritime children's). "We publish quality books about ships and the sea." Average print order: 300. Member PMA, BAIPA. Promotes titles through direct mail, magazine advertising and word of mouth. Accepts unsolicited mss. Often comments on rejected mss. Publishes hardcover and paperback originals and hardcover reprints. **Publishes 3-4 titles/year. 25% of books from first-time authors. 100% from unagented writers.**

NONFICTION "We specialize on books about ships and the sea, with an emphasis on the U.S. merchant marine and navy."

HOW TO CONTACT Submit complete ms. Include brief bio, list of publishing credits. Send SASE for return of ms or send a disposable ms and SASE for reply only. 20 Responds in 1 month to queries; 2 months to mss. Publishes ms 6-24 months after acceptance.

TERMS Pays 10-20% royalty. Does not pay advance. Available on request. Submit complete paper ms with SASE. "We do not look at electronic submissions due to the danger of computer viruses."

TIPS "Write a good story in a compelling style."

Ⓐ DAVID R. GODINE, PUBLISHER

15 Court Square, Suite 320, Boston MA 02108. (617)451-9600. **Fax:** (617)350-0250. **E-mail:** info@godine.com. **Website:** www.godine.com. "We publish books that matter for people who care." This publisher is no longer considering unsolicited mss of any type. Only interested in agented material.

HOW TO CONTACT Only interested in agented material.

ILLUSTRATION Only interested in agented material. Works with 1-3 illustrators/year. "Please do not send original artwork unless solicited. Almost all of the children's books we accept for publication come to us with the author and illustrator already paired up. Therefore, we rarely use freelance illustrators."

Ⓐ GOLDEN BOOKS FOR YOUNG READERS GROUP

1745 Broadway, New York NY 10019. **Website:** www.penguinrandomhouse.com. "Random House Books aims to create books that nurture the hearts and minds of children, providing and promoting quality books and a rich variety of media that entertain and educate readers from 6 months to 12 years." *Random House-Golden Books does not accept unsolicited mss, only agented material.* They reserve the right not to return unsolicited material. **2% of books from first-time authors.**

TERMS Pays authors in royalties; sometimes buys mss outright. Book catalog free on request.

Ⓐ GROSSET & DUNLAP PUBLISHERS

Penguin Random House, 1745 Broadway, New York NY 10019. **Website:** www.penguin.com. Grosset & Dunlap publishes children's books that show children that reading is fun, with books that speak to their interests, and that are affordable so that children can build a home library of their own. Focus on licensed properties, series and readers. "Grosset & Dunlap publishes high-interest, affordable books for children ages 0-10 years. We focus on original series, licensed properties, readers and novelty books." Publishes hardcover (few) and mass market paperback originals. **Publishes 140 titles/year.**

HOW TO CONTACT *Agented submissions only.*

TERMS Pays royalty. Pays advance.

GROUP PUBLISHING, INC.

1515 Cascade Ave., Loveland CO 80539. **E-mail:** info@group.com. **Website:** www.group.com. "Our mission is to equip churches to help children, youth, and adults grow in their relationship with Jesus." Publishes trade paperback originals. **Publishes 65 titles/year. 40% of books from first-time authors. 95% from unagented writers.**

NONFICTION "We're an interdenominational publisher of resource materials for people who work with adults, youth or children in a Christian church setting. We also publish materials for use directly by youth or children (such as devotional books, workbooks or Bibles stories). Everything we do is based on concepts of active and interactive learning as described in *Why Nobody Learns Much of Anything at Church: And How to Fix It*, by Thom and Joani Schultz. We need new, practical, hands-on, innovative, out-of-the-box ideas—things that no one's doing . . . yet."

HOW TO CONTACT Query with SASE. Submit proposal package, outline, 3 sample chapters, cover letter, introduction to book, and sample activities if appropriate. 500 queries; 500 mss received/year. Responds in 1 month to queries; 6 months to proposals and mss. Publishes ms 18 months after acceptance.

TERMS Pays up to 10% royalty on wholesale price or makes outright purchase or work for hire. Pays up to $1,000 advance. Book catalog for 9x12 envelope and 2 first-class stamps.

TIPS "Our audience consists of pastors, Christian education directors, youth leaders, and Sunday school teachers."

GRYPHON HOUSE, INC.

P.O. Box 10, 6848 Leon's Way, Lewisville NC 27023. (800)638-0928. **E-mail:** info@ghbooks.com. **Website:** www.gryphonhouse.com. "At Gryphon House, our goal is to publish books that help teachers and parents enrich the lives of children from birth through age 8. We strive to make our books useful for teachers at all levels of experience, as well as for parents, caregivers, and anyone interested in working with children." Query. Submit outline/synopsis and 2 sample chapters. Responds to queries/mss in 6 months. Publishes a book 18 months after acceptance. Will consider simultaneous submissions, e-mail submissions. Book catalog and ms guidelines available via website or with SASE. Publishes trade paperback originals. **Publishes 12-15 titles/year.**

NONFICTION Currently emphasizing social-emotional intelligence and classroom management; de-emphasizing literacy after-school activities.

HOW TO CONTACT "We prefer to receive a letter of inquiry and/or a proposal, rather than the entire manuscript. Please include: the proposed title, the purpose of the book, table of contents, introductory material, 20-40 sample pages of the actual book. In addition, please describe the book, including the intended audience, why teachers will want to buy it, how it is different from other similar books already published, and what qualifications you possess that make you the appropriate person to write the book. If you have a writing sample that demonstrates that you write clear, compelling prose, please include it with your letter." Responds in 3-6 months to queries.

ILLUSTRATION Works with 4-5 illustrators/year. Uses b&w realistic artwork only. Query with samples, promo sheet. Responds in 2 months. Samples returned with SASE; samples filed. Pays illustrators by the project.

PHOTOGRAPHY Pays photographers by the project or per photo. Sends edited ms copy to authors. Original artwork returned at job's completion.

TERMS Pays royalty on wholesale price. Guidelines available online.

TIPS "We are looking for books of creative, participatory learning experiences that have a common conceptual theme to tie them together. The books should be on subjects that parents or teachers want to do on a daily basis."

HACHAI PUBLISHING

527 Empire Blvd., Brooklyn NY 11225. (718)633-0100. **Fax:** (718)633-0103. **E-mail:** info@hachai.com; dlr@hachai.com. **Website:** www.hachai.com. **Contact:** Devorah Leah Rosenfeld, editor. Hachai is dedicated to producing high quality Jewish children's literature, ages 2-10. Story should promote universal values such as sharing, kindness, etc. Publishes hardcover originals. **Publishes 5 titles/year. 75% of books from first-time authors.**

> "All books have spiritual/religious themes, specifically traditional Jewish content. We're seeking books about morals and values; the Jewish experience in current and Biblical times; and Jewish observance, Sabbath and holidays."

FICTION Picture books and young readers: contemporary, historical fiction, religion. Middle readers: adventure, contemporary, problem novels, religion. Does not want to see fantasy, animal stories, romance, problem novels depicting drug use or violence.

HOW TO CONTACT Submit complete ms. Submit complete ms. Responds in 2 months to mss.

ILLUSTRATION Works with 4 illustrators/year. Uses primary color artwork, some b&w illustration. Reviews ms/illustration packages from authors. Submit ms with 1 piece of final art. Illustrations only: Query with samples; arrange personal portfolio review. Responds in 6 weeks. Samples returned with SASE; samples filed.

TERMS Work purchased outright from authors for $800-1,000. Guidelines online.

TIPS "We are looking for books that convey the traditional Jewish experience in modern times or long ago; traditional Jewish observance such as Sabbath and holidays and mitzvos such as mezuzah, blessings etc.; positive character traits (middos) such as honesty, charity, respect, sharing, etc. We are also interested in historical fiction for young readers (7-10) written with a traditional Jewish perspective and highlighting the relevance of Torah in making important choices. Please, no animal stories, romance, violence, preachy sermonizing. Write a story that incorporates a moral, not a preachy morality tale. Originality is the key. We feel Hachai publications will appeal to a wider readership as parents become more interested in positive values for their children."

Ⓐ HARPERCOLLINS

195 Broadway, New York NY 10007. (212)207-7000. **Website:** www.harpercollins.com. HarperCollins, one of the largest English language publishers in the world, is a broad-based publisher with strengths in academic, business and professional, children's, educational, general interest, and religious and spiritual books, as well as multimedia titles. Publishes hardcover and paperback originals and paperback reprints.

FICTION "We look for a strong story line and exceptional literary talent."

HOW TO CONTACT Agented submissions only. *All unsolicited mss returned.*

TERMS Pays royalty. Pays negotiable advance.

TIPS "We do not accept any unsolicited material."

HEALTH COMMUNICATIONS, INC.

3201 SW 15th St., Deerfield Beach FL 33442. (954)360-0909, ext. 232. **Fax:** (954)360-0034. **Website:** www.hcibooks.com. **Contact:** Editorial Committee. "While HCI is a best known for recovery publishing, today recovery is only one part of a publishing program that includes titles in self-help and psychology, health and wellness, spirituality, inspiration, women's and men's issues, relationships, family, teens and children, memoirs, mind/body/spirit integration, and gift books." Publishes hardcover and trade paperback nonfiction only. **Publishes 60 titles/year.**

HOW TO CONTACT Responds in 3-6 months.

TERMS Guidelines online.

TIPS "Due to the volume of submissions, Health Communications cannot guarantee response times or personalize responses to individual proposals. Under no circumstances do we accept phone calls or e-mails pitching submissions."

HELLGATE PRESS

L&R Publishing, LLC, P.O. Box 3531, Ashland OR 97520. (541)973-5154. **E-mail:** sales@hellgatepress.com. **Website:** www.hellgatepress.com. **Contact:** Harley B. Patrick. "Hellgate Press specializes in military history, veteran memoirs, other military topics, travel adventure, and historical/adventure fiction." **Publishes 15-25 titles/year. 85% of books from first-time authors. 95% from unagented writers.**

HOW TO CONTACT Query/proposal by e-mail only. No phone queries, please. *Do not send mss.* Responds in 1-2 month to queries. Publishes ms 4-6 months after acceptance.

TERMS Pays royalty.

HEYDAY

c/o Acquisitions Editor, Box 9145, Berkeley CA 94709. **E-mail:** editor@heydaybooks.com. **Website:** www.heydaybooks.com. **Contact:** Marthine Satris, acquisitions editor. Heyday is an independent, nonprofit publisher with a focus on California and the American West. We publish nonfiction books that explore history, celebrate Native cultural renewal, fight injustice, and honor nature. Publishes hardcover originals, trade paperback originals, and reprints. **Publishes 15-20 titles/year. 50% of books from first-time authors. 90% from unagented writers.**

NONFICTION Books about California or in which California figures significantly. We are not acquiring children's books at this time.

HOW TO CONTACT Responds in 3 months. Publishes book ~18 months after acceptance.

TERMS Book catalog online. If you think that Heyday would be an appropriate publisher for your manuscript, send us a query or proposal by email to editor (at) heydaybooks (dot) com (please include "Heyday" in your subject line, or your proposal may be discarded), or by post to Heyday, P.O. Box 9145, Berkeley, CA 94709 (please include a self-addressed stamped envelope if you would like your submission materials returned). Please include the following: A cover letter introducing yourself and your qualifications; a brief description of your project; an annotated table of contents and list of illustrations (if any); notes on the audiences you are trying to reach and why your book will appeal to them; a list of comparable titles and a brief description of the ways your book adds to the existing literature; estimates of your book's expected length and your timeline for completing the writing; a sample chapter. We will do our best to respond to your query within twelve weeks of receiving it. No follow-up calls, please.

HOLIDAY HOUSE, INC.

425 Madison Ave., New York NY 10017. (212)688-0085. **Fax:** (212)421-6134. **E-mail:** info@holidayhouse.com. **Website:** holidayhouse.com. "Holiday House publishes children's and young adult books for the school and library markets. We have a commitment to publishing first-time authors and illustrators. We specialize in quality hardcovers from picture books to

young adult, both fiction and nonfiction, primarily for the school and library market." Publishes hardcover originals and paperback reprints. **Publishes 50 titles/year. 5% of books from first-time authors. 50% from unagented writers.**

FICTION Children's books only.

HOW TO CONTACT Query with SASE. No phone calls, please. Please send the entire ms, whether submitting a picture book or novel. "All submissions should be directed to the Editorial Department, Holiday House. We do not accept certified or registered mail. There is no need to include a SASE. We do not consider submissions by e-mail or fax. Please note that you do not have to supply illustrations. However, if you have illustrations you would like to include with your submission, you may send detailed sketches or photocopies of the original art. Do not send original art." Responds in 4 months. Publishes 1-2 years after acceptance.

ILLUSTRATION Accepting art samples, not returned.

TERMS Pays royalty on list price, range varies. Guidelines for #10 SASE.

TIPS "We need manuscripts with strong stories and writing."

HOPEWELL PUBLICATIONS

P.O. Box 11, Titusville NJ 08560. **Website:** www.hopepubs.com. **Contact:** E. Martin, publisher. "Hopewell Publications specializes in classic reprints—books with proven sales records that have gone out of print—and new titles of interest. Our catalog spans from 1 to 60 years of publication history. We print fiction and nonfiction, and we accept agented and unagented materials. Submissions are accepted online only." Format publishes in hardcover, trade paperback, and electronic originals; trade paperback and electronic reprints. **Publishes 20-30 titles/year. 25% of books from first-time authors. 75% from unagented writers.**

HOW TO CONTACT Query online using our online guidelines. Query online using online guidelines. Receives 2,000 queries/year; 500 mss/year. Responds in 3 months to queries; 6 months to proposals; 9 months to mss. Publishes ms 6-12 months after acceptance.

TERMS Pays royalty on retail price. Catalog online. Guidelines online.

HOUGHTON MIFFLIN HARCOURT BOOKS FOR CHILDREN

Imprint of Houghton Mifflin Trade & Reference Division, 222 Berkeley St., Boston MA 02116. (617)351-5000. **Fax:** (617)351-1111. **Website:** www.houghtonmifflinbooks.com. Houghton Mifflin Harcourt gives shape to ideas that educate, inform, and above all, delight. *Does not respond to or return mss unless interested.* Publishes hardcover originals and trade paperback originals and reprints. **Publishes 100 titles/year. 10% of books from first-time authors. 60% from unagented writers.**

NONFICTION Interested in innovative books and subjects about which the author is passionate.

HOW TO CONTACT Submit complete ms. Query with SASE. Submit sample chapters, synopsis. 5,000 queries received/year. 14,000 mss received/year. Responds in 4-6 months to queries. Publishes ms 2 years after acceptance.

TERMS Pays 5-10% royalty on retail price. Pays variable advance. Guidelines online.

IMBRIFEX BOOKS

Flattop Productions, Inc., 8275 S. Eastern Ave., Suite 200, Las Vegas NV 89123. (702)309-0130. **E-mail:** acquisitions@imbrifex.com. **Website:** https://imbrifex.com. **Contact:** Mark Sedenquist. Imbrifex Books publishes both fiction and nonfiction. We have a particular interest in road trip guidebooks and guidebooks for outdoor recreation, especially hiking and fly fishing. Fiction-wise, we are looking for popular and literary novels for adults and young adults. We consider both stand-alone titles and series. **Publishes 6-8 titles/year. 70% of books from first-time authors. 60% from unagented writers.**

HOW TO CONTACT Responds in 2 months.

TERMS Pays advance. Guidelines online.

IMMEDIUM

P.O. Box 31846, San Francisco CA 94131. (415)452-8546. **Fax:** (360)937-6272. **Website:** www.immedium.com. **Contact:** Submissions Editor. "Immedium focuses on publishing eye-catching children's picture books, Asian-American topics, and contemporary arts, popular culture, and multicultural issues." Publishes hardcover and trade paperback originals. **Publishes 4 titles/year. 50% of books from first-time authors. 90% from unagented writers.**

HOW TO CONTACT Submit complete ms. Submit complete ms. 50 queries received/year. 25 mss received/year. Responds in 1-3 months. Publishes book 2 years after acceptance.

TERMS Pays 5% royalty on wholesale price. Pays on publication. Catalog online. Guidelines online.

TIPS "Our audience is children and parents. Please visit our site."

IMPACT PUBLISHERS, INC.

5674 Shattuck Ave., Oakland CA 94609. **E-mail:** proposals@newharbinger.com. **Website:** www.newharbinger.com/imprint/impact-publishers. **Contact:** Acquisitions Department. "Our purpose is to make the best human services expertise available to the widest possible audience. We publish only popular psychology and self-help materials written in everyday language by professionals with advanced degrees and significant experience in the human services." **Publishes 3-5 titles/year. 20% of books from first-time authors.**

NONFICTION Young readers, middle readers, young adults: self-help.

HOW TO CONTACT Query or submit complete ms, cover letter, résumé. Responds in 3 months.

ILLUSTRATION Works with 1 illustrator/year. Not accepting freelance illustrator queries.

TERMS Pays authors royalty of 10-12%. Offers advances. Book catalog for #10 SASE with 2 first-class stamps. Guidelines for SASE.

TIPS "Please do not submit fiction, poetry or narratives."

INCENTIVE PUBLICATIONS, INC.

233 N. Michigan Ave., Suite 2000, Chicago IL 60601. **E-mail:** incentive@worldbook.com. **Website:** www.incentivepublications.com. "Incentive publishes developmentally appropriate teacher/school administrator/parent resource materials and supplementary instructional materials for children in grades K-12. Actively seeking proposals for student workbooks, all grades/all subjects, and professional development resources for pre K-12 classroom teachers and school administrators." Publishes paperback originals. **Publishes 10-15 titles/year. 25% of books from first-time authors. 100, but agent proposals welcome% from unagented writers.**

NONFICTION Instructional, teacher/administrator professional development books in pre-K through 12th grade.

HOW TO CONTACT Query with synopsis and detailed outline. Responds in 1 month to queries. an average of 1 year

TERMS Pays royalty, or makes outright purchase.

INDIANA HISTORICAL SOCIETY PRESS

450 W. Ohio St., Indianapolis IN 46202. (317)233-6073. **Fax:** (317)233-0857. **E-mail:** ihspress@indianahistory.org. **Website:** www.indianahistory.org. **Contact:** Submissions Editor. Publishes hardcover and paperback originals. **Publishes 10 titles/year.**

NONFICTION All topics must relate to Indiana. "We seek book-length manuscripts that are solidly researched and engagingly written on topics related to Indiana: biography, history, literature, music, politics, transportation, sports, agriculture, architecture, and children's books."

HOW TO CONTACT Query with SASE. Responds in 1 month to queries.

JEWISH LIGHTS PUBLISHING

LongHill Partners, Inc., Sunset Farm Offices, Rt. 4, P.O. Box 237, Woodstock VT 05091. (802)457-4000. **Fax:** (802)457-4004. **E-mail:** submissions@turnerpublishing.com. **Website:** www.jewishlights.com. "Jewish Lights publishes books for people of all faiths and all backgrounds who yearn for books that attract, engage, educate and spiritually inspire. Our authors are at the forefront of spiritual thought and deal with the quest for the self and for meaning in life by drawing on the Jewish wisdom tradition. Our books cover topics including history, spirituality, life cycle, children, self-help, recovery, theology and philosophy. At this point we plan to do only two books for children annually, and one will be for younger children (ages 4-10)." Publishes hardcover and trade paperback originals, trade paperback reprints. **Publishes 30 titles/year. 50% of books from first-time authors. 75% from unagented writers.**

FICTION Picture books, young readers, middle readers: spirituality. "We are not interested in anything other than spirituality."

NONFICTION Picture book, young readers, middle readers: activity books, spirituality. "We do *not* publish haggadot, biography, poetry, memoirs, or cookbooks."

HOW TO CONTACT Query with outline/synopsis and 2 sample chapters; submit complete ms for picture books. Query. Responds in 6 months to queries. Publishes ms 1 year after acceptance.

TERMS Pays authors royalty of 10% of revenue received; 15% royalty for subsequent printings. Book catalog and guidelines online.

TIPS "We publish books for all faiths and backgrounds that also reflect the Jewish wisdom tradition. Explain in your cover letter why you're submitting your project to us in particular. Make sure you know what we publish."

JOURNEYFORTH

Imprint of BJU Press, 1430 Wade Hampton Blvd., Greenville SC 29609. **E-mail:** journeyforth@bjupress.com. **Website:** www.journeyforth.com. **Contact:** Nancy Lohr. JourneyForth Books publishes fiction and nonfiction that reflects a worldview based solidly on the Bible and that encourages Christians to live out their faith. JourneyForth is an imprint of BJU Press. Publishes paperback originals. **Publishes 6-8 titles/year. 30% of books from first-time authors. 80% from unagented writers.**

FICTION "Our fiction is for the youth market only and is based on a Christian worldview. Our catalog ranges from first chapter books to YA titles." Does not want picture books, short stories, romance, speculative fiction, poetry, or fiction for the adult market.

NONFICTION Christian living, Bible studies, church and ministry, church history. "We produce books for the adult Christian market that are from a conservative Christian worldview."

HOW TO CONTACT Submit proposal with synopsis, market analysis of competing works, and first 5 chapters. Will look at simultaneous submissions, but not multiple submissions. 300+ Responds in 1 month to queries; 3 months to mss. Publishes book 12-18 months after acceptance.

TERMS Pays authors royalty based on wholesale price. Pays royalty. Pays advance. Book catalog available free in SASE or online. Guidelines online—https://www.bjupress.com/books/freelance.php

TIPS "Study the publisher's guidelines. We are looking for engaging text and a biblical worldview. Will read hard copy submissions, but prefer e-mail queries/proposals/submissions."

JUST US BOOKS, INC.

P.O. Box 5306, East Orange NJ 07019. (973)672-7701. **Fax:** (973)677-7570. **Website:** justusbooks.com. "Just Us Books is the nation's premier independent publisher of Black-interest books for young people. Our books focus primarily on the culture, history, and contemporary experiences of African Americans."

FICTION Just Us Books is currently accepting queries for chapter books and middle reader titles only. "We are not considering any other works at this time."

HOW TO CONTACT Query with synopsis and 3-5 sample pages.

TERMS Guidelines online.

TIPS "We are looking for realistic, contemporary characters; stories and interesting plots that introduce both conflict and resolution. We will consider various themes and story-lines, but before an author submits a query we urge them to become familiar with our books."

KAEDEN BOOKS

P.O. Box 16190, Rocky River OH 44116. **Website:** www.kaeden.com. "Children's book publisher for education K-3 market: reading stories, fiction/nonfiction, chapter books, science, and social studies materials." Publishes paperback originals. **Publishes 12-20 titles/year. 30% of books from first-time authors. 95% from unagented writers.**

FICTION "We are looking for stories with humor, surprise endings, and interesting characters that will appeal to children in kindergarten through third grade." No sentence fragments. Please do not submit: queries, ms summaries, or résumés, mss that stereotype or demean individuals or groups, mss that present violence as acceptable behavior.

NONFICTION Mss should have interesting topics and information presented in language comprehensible to young students. Content should be supported with details and accurate facts.

HOW TO CONTACT Submit complete ms. "Can be as minimal as 25 words for the earliest reader or as much as 2,000 words for the fluent reader. Beginning chapter books are welcome. Our readers are in kindergarten to third grade, so vocabulary and sentence structure must be appropriate for young readers. Make sure that all language used in the story is of an appropriate level for the students to read independently. Sentences should be complete and grammatically correct." Submit complete ms. "Can be as minimal as 25 words for the earliest reader or as much as 2,000 words for the fluent reader. Beginning chapter books are welcome. Our readers are in kindergarten to third grade, so vocabulary and sentence structure must be appropriate for young readers. Make sure that all language used in the story is of an appropriate level for the students to read independently. Sentences should be complete and grammatically correct." 1,000 mss received/year. Responds only if interested. Publishes ms 6-9 months after acceptance.

ILLUSTRATION Work with 8-10 illustrators per year. Looking for samples that are appropriate for children's literature. Submit color samples no larger than 8 1/2×11. Samples kept on file. Responds only if interested. "No originals, disks or slides please." Samples not returned.

TERMS Work purchased outright from authors. Pays royalties to previous authors. Book catalog and guidelines online.

TIPS "Our audience ranges from kindergarten-third grade school children. We are an educational publisher. We are particularly interested in humorous stories with surprise endings and beginning chapter books."

KAR-BEN PUBLISHING

Lerner Publishing Group, 241 North First St., Minneapolis MN 55401. **E-mail:** editorial@karben.com. **Website:** www.karben.com. **Contact:** Joni Sussman. Kar-Ben publishes exclusively Jewish-themed children's books. Publishes hardcover, trade paperback, board books and e-books. **Publishes 25 titles/year. 20% of books from first-time authors. 70% from unagented writers.**

FICTION "We seek picture book mss 800-1,000 words on Jewish-themed topics for children." Picture books: Adventure, concept, folktales, history, humor, multicultural, religion, special needs; must be on a Jewish theme. Average word length: picture books–1,000. Recently published titles: *The Count's Hanukkah Countdown*, *Sammy Spider's First Book of Jewish Holidays*, *The Cats of Ben Yehuda Street*.

NONFICTION "In addition to traditional Jewish-themed stories about Jewish holidays, history, folktales and other subjects, we especially seek stories that reflect the rich diversity of the contemporary Jewish community." Picture books, young readers; Jewish history, Israel, Holocaust, folktales, religion, social issues, special needs; must be of Jewish interest. No textbooks, games, or educational materials.

HOW TO CONTACT Submit full ms. Picture books only. Submit completed ms. 800 mss received/year. Only responds if interested. Most mss published within 2 years.

TERMS Pays 5% royalty on NET sale. Pays $500-2,500 advance. Book catalog online; free upon request. Guidelines online.

TIPS "Authors: Do a literature search to make sure similar title doesn't already exist. Illustrators: Look at our online catalog for a sense of what we like—bright colors and lively composition."

KREGEL PUBLICATIONS

2450 Oak Industrial Dr. NE, Grand Rapids MI 49505. (616)451-4775. **Fax:** (616)451-9330. **E-mail:** kregelbooks@kregel.com. **Website:** www.kregelpublications.com. "Our mission as an evangelical Christian publisher is to provide—with integrity and excellence—trusted, Biblically based resources that challenge and encourage individuals in their Christian lives. Works in theology and Biblical studies should reflect the historic, orthodox Protestant tradition." Publishes hardcover and trade paperback originals and reprints. **Publishes 90 titles/year. 20% of books from first-time authors. 10% from unagented writers.**

FICTION Fiction should be geared toward the evangelical Christian market. Wants books with fast-paced, contemporary storylines presenting a strong Christian message in an engaging, entertaining style.

NONFICTION "We serve evangelical Christian readers and those in career Christian service."

HOW TO CONTACT Finds works through The Writer's Edge and Christian Manuscript Submissions ms screening services. Finds works through The Writer's Edge and Christian Manuscript Submissions ms screening services. Responds in 2-3 months. Publishes ms 12-16 months after acceptance.

TERMS Pays royalty on wholesale price. Pays negotiable advance. Guidelines online.

TIPS "Our audience consists of conservative, evangelical Christians, including pastors and ministry students."

LEAPFROG PRESS

Box 505, Fredonia NY 14063. **E-mail:** leapfrog@leapfrogpress.com. **Website:** www.leapfrogpress.com. **Contact:** Nathan Carter, acquisitions editor; Lisa Graziano, publicity. **Publishes 4-6 titles/year. 50% of books from first-time authors. 75% from unagented writers.**

FICTION "We search for beautifully written literary titles and market them aggressively to national trade and library accounts. We also sell film, translation, foreign, and book club rights." Publishes paperback originals. Books: acid-free paper; sewn binding. Print runs range from about 1,000 to 4,000. Distributes titles through Consortium Book Sales and Distribution, St. Paul, MN. Promotes titles through all national review media, bookstore readings, author tours, website, radio shows, chain store promotions, advertisements, book fairs. "Genres often blur; look for good writing. We are most interested in works that are quirky, that fall outside of any known genre,and of course well written and finely crafted. We are most interested in literary fiction." Genre romance, fantasy, and Western. Religious. Occult. Picture books.

HOW TO CONTACT Query with several chapters or stories through Submittable. 2,000 submissions received/year. Response time varies. One week to several months. Publishes ms approximately 1 year after acceptance.

TERMS Pays 10% royalty on net receipts. Average advance: negotiable. Guidelines online. Submissions through Submittable only.

TIPS "We like anything that is superbly written and genuinely original. We like the idiosyncratic and the peculiar. We rarely publish nonfiction. Send only your best work, and send only completed work that is ready. That means the completed ms has already been through extensive editing and is ready to be judged. We consider submissions from both previously published and unpublished writers, and both agented and unagented submissions. We do not accept submissions through postal mail and cannot return physical letters or manuscripts."

LEE & LOW BOOKS

95 Madison Ave., #1205, New York NY 10016. (212)779-4400. **E-mail:** general@leeandlow.com. **Website:** www.leeandlow.com. "Our goals are to meet a growing need for books that address children of color, and to present literature that all children can identify with. We only consider multicultural children's books. Sponsors a yearly New Voices Award for first-time picture book authors of color. Contest rules online at website or for SASE." Publishes hardcover originals and trade paperback reprints. **Publishes 12-14 titles/year. 20% of books from first-time authors. 50% from unagented writers.**

FICTION Picture books, young readers: anthology, contemporary, history, multicultural, poetry. Picture book, middle reader: contemporary, history, multicultural, nature/environment, poetry, sports. Average word length: picture books—1,000-1,500 words. "We do not publish folklore or animal stories."

NONFICTION Picture books: concept. Picture books, middle readers: biography, history, multicultural, science and sports. Average word length: picture books-1,500-3,000.

HOW TO CONTACT Submit complete ms. Receives 100 queries/year; 1,200 mss/year. Responds in 6 months to mss if interested. Publishes book 2 years after acceptance.

ILLUSTRATION Works with 12-14 illustrators/year. Uses color artwork only. Reviews ms/illustration packages from artists. Contact: Louise May. Illustrations only: Query with samples, résumé, promo sheet and tearsheets. Responds only if interested. Samples returned with SASE; samples filed. Original artwork returned at job's completion.

PHOTOGRAPHY Buys photos from freelancers. Works on assignment only. Model/property releases required. Submit cover letter, résumé, promo piece and book dummy.

TERMS Pays net royalty. Pays authors advances against royalty. Pays illustrators advance against royalty. Photographers paid advance against royalty. Book catalog available online. Guidelines available online or by written request with SASE.

TIPS "Check our website to see the kinds of books we publish. Do not send mss that don't fit our mission."

Ⓐ LITTLE, BROWN BOOKS FOR YOUNG READERS

Hachette Book Group USA, 1290 Avenue of the Americas, New York NY 10104. (212)364-1100. **Fax:** (212)364-0925. **Website:** littlebrown.com. "Little, Brown and Co. Children's Publishing publishes all formats including board books, picture books, middle grade fiction, and nonfiction YA titles. We are looking for strong writing and presentation, but no predetermined topics." *Only interested in solicited agented material.* **Publishes 100-150 titles/year.**

FICTION Average word length: picture books—1,000; young readers—6,000; middle readers—15,000- 50,000; young adults—50,000 and up.

NONFICTION "Writers should avoid looking for the 'issue' they think publishers want to see, choosing instead topics they know best and are most enthusiastic about/inspired by."

HOW TO CONTACT *Agented submissions only.* Responds in 1-2 months. Publishes ms 2 years after acceptance.

ILLUSTRATION Works with 40 illustrators/year. Illustrations only: Query art director with b&w and color samples; provide résumé, promo sheet or tearsheets to be kept on file. Does not respond to art samples. Do not send originals; copies only. Accepts illustration samples by postal mail or e-mail.

PHOTOGRAPHY Works on assignment only. Model/property releases required; captions required. Publishes photo essays and photo concept books. Uses 35mm transparencies. Photographers should provide résumé, promo sheets or tearsheets to be kept on file.

TERMS Pays authors royalties based on retail price. Pays illustrators and photographers by the project or royalty based on retail price. Sends galleys to authors; dummies to illustrators. Pays negotiable advance.

TIPS "In order to break into the field, authors and illustrators should research their competition and try to come up with something outstandingly different."

Ⓐ LITTLE SIMON

Imprint of Simon & Schuster, 1230 Avenue of the Americas, New York NY 10020. (212)698-1295. **Fax:** (212)698-2794. **Website:** www.simonandschuster.com/kids. "Our goal is to provide fresh material in an innovative format for preschool to age 8. Our books are often, if not exclusively, format driven." Publishes novelty and branded books only.

FICTION Novelty books include many things that do not fit in the traditional hardcover or paperback format, such as pop-up, board book, scratch and sniff, glow in the dark, lift the flap, etc. Children's/juvenile. No picture books. Large part of the list is holiday-themed.

NONFICTION "We publish very few nonfiction titles." No picture books.

HOW TO CONTACT *Currently not accepting unsolicited mss.*

TERMS Offers advance and royalties.

MAGINATION PRESS

750 First St. NE, Washington DC 20002. (202)336-5618. **Fax:** (202)336-5624. **E-mail:** magination@apa.org. **Website:** www.apa.org. Magination Press is an imprint of the American Psychological Association. "We publish books dealing with the psycho/therapeutic resolution of children's problems and psychological issues with a strong self-help component." Submit complete ms. Full guidelines available on site. Materials returned only with SASE. **Publishes 12 titles/year. 75% of books from first-time authors.**

FICTION All levels: psychological and social issues, self-help, health, parenting concerns and special needs. Picture books, middle school readers.

NONFICTION All levels: psychological and social issues, self-help, health, multicultural, special needs.

HOW TO CONTACT Responds to queries in 1-2 months; mss in 2-6 months. Publishes a book 18-24 months after acceptance.

ILLUSTRATION Works with 10-15 illustrators/year. Reviews ms/illustration packages. Will review artwork for future assignments. Responds only if interested, or immediately if SASE or response card is included. "We keep samples on file."

MARVEL COMICS

135 W. 50th St., 7th Floor, New York NY 10020. **Website:** www.marvel.com. Publishes hardcover originals and reprints, trade paperback reprints, mass market comic book originals, electronic reprints.

FICTION Our shared universe needs new heroes and villains; books for younger readers and teens needed.

HOW TO CONTACT Submit inquiry letter, idea submission form (download from website), SASE. Responds in 3-5 weeks to queries.

TERMS Pays on a per page work for hire basis or creator-owned which is then contracted. Pays negotiable advance. Guidelines online.

MASTER BOOKS

P.O. Box 726, Green Forest AR 72638. **E-mail:** submissions@newleafpress.net. **Website:** www.masterbooks.com. **Contact:** Craig Froman, acquisitions editor. Publishes 3 middle readers/year; 2 young adult nonfiction titles/year; 10 homeschool curriculum titles; 20 adult trade books/year. **5% of books from first-time authors. 99% from unagented writers.**

NONFICTION Picture books: activity books, animal, nature/environment, creation. Young readers, middle readers, young adults: activity books, animal, biography Christian, nature/environment, science, creation.

HOW TO CONTACT Submission guidelines on website. http://www.nlpg.com/submissions We are no longer able to respond to every query. If you have not heard from us within 90 days, it means we are unable to partner with you on that particular project. Publishes book 1 year after acceptance.

TERMS Pays authors royalty of 3-15% based on wholesale price. Book catalog available upon request. Guidelines online.

TIPS "All of our children's books are creation-based, including topics from the Book of Genesis. We look also for home school educational material as we are expanding our home school curriculum resources."

MARGARET K. MCELDERRY BOOKS

Imprint of Simon & Schuster Children's Publishing Division, 1230 Sixth Ave., New York NY 10020. (212)698-7200. **Website:** imprints.simonandschuster.biz/margaret-k-mcelderry-books. "Margaret K. McElderry Books publishes hardcover and paperback trade books for children from pre-school age through young adult. This list includes picture books, middle grade and teen fiction, poetry, and fantasy. The style and subject matter of the books we publish is almost unlimited. We do not publish textbooks, coloring and activity books, greeting cards, magazines, pamphlets, or religious publications." **Publishes 30 titles/year. 15% of books from first-time authors. 50% from unagented writers.**

FICTION *No unsolicited mss.*

NONFICTION *No unsolicited mss. Agented submissions only.*

HOW TO CONTACT *Agented submissions only.*

TERMS Pays authors royalty based on retail price. Pays illustrator royalty of by the project. Pays photographers by the project. Original artwork returned at job's completion. Offers $5,000-8,000 advance for new authors. Guidelines for #10 SASE.

TIPS "Read! The children's book field is competitive. See what's been done and what's out there before submitting. We look for high quality: an originality of ideas, clarity and felicity of expression, a well organized plot, and strong character-driven stories. We're looking for strong, original fiction, especially mysteries and middle grade humor. We are always interested in picture books for the youngest age reader. Study our titles."

MEDIA LAB BOOKS

Topix Media Lab, 14 Wall St., Suite 4B, New York NY 10005. **Website:** onnewsstandsnow.com. **Contact:** Phil Sexton, vice president and publisher. Media Lab Books partners with high-profile brands and expert authors to publish books designed to inform, educate and entertain readers around the world. "The authors and brands we work with have unique ideas, loyal fans and followers, strong platforms, and amazing stories to tell. We specialize in highly visual, illustrated books that surprise and delight readers of all ages. From *The Official John Wayne Handy Book of Bushcraft* to *Cooking for Wizards, Warriors and Dragons*, we truly have something for everyone. Ultimately, we're looking for creative nonfiction ideas from authors with a voice (and a platform) or unique brands with a passionate following. Though we specialize in creating visually dynamic books built around big brands, we're also interested in original works that focus on popular topics in most nonfiction categories, but ones that are given a unique, one-of-a-kind spin that demands publication. For example, *MI6 Spy Skills for Civilians*, by former British agent Red Riley." Publishes cooking, children's books, games, puzzles, reference, humor, biography, history. **Publishes 20 titles/year. 10% of books from first-time authors. 60% from unagented writers.**

HOW TO CONTACT Responds in 30 days. Publishes ms 12-18 months after acceptance.

TERMS Catalog available. Electronic submissions only. On the first page of the document, please include author's name and contact information. Please send full submission packet, including overview, USP (unique selling proposition), comparable titles, proposed TOC, and 1-3 sample chapters (no more than 50 pages).

TIPS "Be sure to check out the kind of books we've already published. You'll see that most of them are brand-driven. The ones that are author-driven address popular topics with a unique approach. More general books are of no interest unless the topic in question is trending and there's minimal competition in the market."

MILKWEED EDITIONS

1011 Washington Ave. S., Suite 300, Minneapolis MN 55415. (612)332-3192. **Fax:** (612)215-2550. **Website:** www.milkweed.org. Publishes 3-4 middle readers/year. 25% of books by first-time authors. "Milkweed Editions publishes with the intention of making a humane impact on society, in the belief that literature is a transformative art uniquely able to convey the essential experiences of the human heart and spirit. To that end, Milkweed Editions publishes distinctive voices of literary merit in handsomely designed, visually dynamic books, exploring the ethical, cultural, and esthetic issues that free societies need continually to address." Publishes hardcover, trade paperback, and electronic originals; trade paperback and electronic reprints. **Publishes 15-20 titles/year. 25% of books from first-time authors. 75% from unagented writers.**

FICTION Novels for adults and for readers 8-13. High literary quality. For adult readers: literary fiction, nonfiction, poetry, essays. Middle readers: adventure, contemporary, fantasy, multicultural, nature/environment, suspense/mystery. Average length: middle readers—90-200 pages. No romance, mysteries, science fiction.

HOW TO CONTACT "Please submit a query letter with three opening chapters (of a novel) or three representative stories (of a collection). Publishes YR." Responds in 6 months. Publishes book in 18 months.

TERMS Pays authors variable royalty based on retail price. Offers advance against royalties. Pays varied advance from $500-10,000. Book catalog online. Only accepts submissions during open submission periods. See website for guidelines.

TIPS "We are looking for excellent writing with the intent of making a humane impact on society. Please read submission guidelines before submitting and acquaint yourself with our books in terms of style and quality before submitting. Many factors influence our selection process, so don't get discouraged. Nonfiction is focused on literary writing about the natural world, including living well in urban environments."

THE MILLBROOK PRESS

Lerner Publishing Group, 1251 Washington Ave N, Minneapolis MN 55401. **E-mail:** info@lernerbooks.com. **Website:** www.lernerbooks.com. **Contact:** Carol Hinz, editorial director. "Millbrook Press publishes informative picture books, illustrated nonfiction titles, and inspiring photo-driven titles for grades K–5. Our authors approach curricular topics with a fresh point of view. Our fact-filled books engage readers with fun yet accessible writing, high-quality photographs, and a wide variety of illustration styles. We cover subjects ranging from the parts of speech and other language arts skills; to history, science, and math; to art, sports, crafts, and other interests. Millbrook Press is the home of the best-selling Words Are CATegorical® series and Bob Raczka's Art Adventures. We do not accept unsolicited manuscripts from authors. Occasionally, we may put out a call for submissions, which will be announced on our website."

MISSOURI HISTORY MUSEUM PRESS

The Missouri Historical Society, P.O. Box 11940, St. Louis MO 63112. (314)746-4559. **Fax:** (314)746-4548. **E-mail:** lmitchell@mohistory.org. **Website:** www.mohistory.org. **Contact:** Lauren Mitchell. "Our mission is to expose our readers—through the books we publish, our magazine, Gateway, and our online publications, History Happens Here and Voices—to perspectives of St. Louis and Missouri not usually introduced in simple history lessons. Mining both the historical and contemporary cultural, social, and political issues of our region, we strive to publish stories that resonate with our community and highlight the common heritage we all share." Publishes hardcover and trade paperback books on the history of Missouri. **Publishes 2-3 titles/year. 10% of books from first-time authors. 80% from unagented writers.**

HOW TO CONTACT Query with SASE and request author-proposal form. 30 queries; 20 mss received/year. Responds in 3-4 months. Ms published 15 months after acceptance.

TERMS Pays 8-10% royalty. Guidelines available.

TIPS "We're looking for new perspectives, even if the topics are familiar. You'll get our attention with nontraditional voices and views."

Ⓐ MOODY PUBLISHERS

Moody Bible Institute, 820 N. LaSalle Blvd., Chicago IL 60610. (800)678-8812. **Fax:** (312)329-4157. **Website:** www.moodypublishers.org. **Contact:** Acquisitions Coordinator. "The mission of Moody Publishers is to educate and edify the Christian and to evangelize the non-Christian by ethically publishing conservative, evangelical Christian literature and other media for all ages around the world, and to help provide resources for Moody Bible Institute in its training of future Christian leaders." Publishes hardcover, trade, and mass market paperback originals. **Publishes 60 titles/year. 1% of books from first-time authors. 80% from unagented writers.**

NONFICTION "We are no longer reviewing queries or unsolicited manuscripts unless they come to us through an agent, are from an author who has published with us, an associate from a Moody Bible

Institute ministry or a personal contact at a writer's conference. Unsolicited proposals will be returned only if proper postage is included. We are not able to acknowledge the receipt of your unsolicited proposal."

HOW TO CONTACT *Agented submissions only.* Does not accept unsolicited nonfiction submissions. 1,500 queries received/year. 2,000 mss received/year. Responds in 2-3 months to queries. Publishes book 1 year after acceptance.

TERMS Royalty varies. Book catalog for 9×12 envelope and 4 first-class stamps. Guidelines online.

TIPS "In our fiction list, we're looking for Christian storytellers rather than teachers trying to present a message. Your motivation should be to delight the reader. Using your skills to create beautiful works is glorifying to God."

MOUNTAIN PRESS PUBLISHING CO.

P.O. Box 2399, Missoula MT 59806. (406)728-1900 or (800)234-5308. **Fax:** (406)728-1635. **E-mail:** info@mtnpress.com. **Website:** www.mountain-press.com. **Contact:** Jennifer Carey, editor. "We are expanding our Roadside Geology, Geology Underfoot, and Roadside History series (done on a state-by-state basis). We are interested in well-written regional field guides—plants and flowers—and readable history and natural history." Publishes hardcover and trade paperback originals. **Publishes 15 titles/year. 50% of books from first-time authors. 90% from unagented writers.**

Expanding children's/juvenile nonfiction titles.

NONFICTION No personal histories or journals, poetry or fiction.

HOW TO CONTACT Query with SASE. Submit outline, sample chapters. Responds in 3 months to queries. Publishes ms 2 years after acceptance.

TERMS Pays 7-12% royalty on wholesale price. Book catalog online.

TIPS "Find out what kind of books a publisher is interested in and tailor your writing to them; research markets and target your audience. Research other books on the same subjects. Make yours different. Don't present your manuscript to a publisher—sell it. Give the information needed to make a decision on a title. Please learn what we publish before sending your proposal. We are a 'niche' publisher."

MSI PRESS LLC

1760-F Airline Hwy, #203, Hollister CA 95023. **Fax:** (831)886-2486. **E-mail:** editor@msipress.com. **Website:** www.msipress.com. **Contact:** Betty Lou Leaver, Ph.D., managing editor (self-help, spirituality, religion, memoir, mind/body/spirit, some humor, popular psychology, foreign language & culture, parenting). "We are a small press that specializes in award-winning quality publications, refined through strong personal interactions and productive working relationships between our editors and our authors. A small advance may be offered to previously published authors with a strong book, strong platform, and solid sales numbers. We will accept first-time authors with credibility in their fields and a strong platform, but we do not offer advances to first-time authors. We may refer authors with a good book but little experience or lacking a strong platform to San Juan Books, our hybrid publishing venture." Publishes trade paperback originals and corresponding e-books. **Publishes 10-15 titles/year. 50% of books from first-time authors. 100% from unagented writers.**

NONFICTION "We continue to expand our spirituality, psychology, and self-help lines and are interested in adding to our collection of books in Spanish. We do not do or publish translations." Does not want erotica or political theses.

HOW TO CONTACT Submit proposal package, including: annotated outline, 1 sample chapter, professional resume, platform information. Electronic submissions preferred. We are open to foreign writers (non-native speakers of English), but please have an English editor proofread the submission prior to sending; if the query letter or proposal is written in poor English, we will not take a chance on a manuscript. 100-200 Responds in 2 weeks to queries sent by e-mail and to proposals submitted via the template on our website. Proposals sent by USPS may take longer. If response not received in 2 weeks, okay to query. Publishes ms 6-10 months after acceptance.

TERMS Pays 10% royalty on retail price for paperbacks and hard cover books; pays 50% royalty on net for e-books. By exception, pays small advance to previously published authors with good sales history. Catalog online. Guidelines online.

TIPS "Learn the mechanics of writing. Too many submissions are full of grammar and punctuation errors and poorly worded with trite expressions. Read to write; observe and analyze how the great authors of all time use language to good avail. Capture our attention with active verbs, not bland description haunted by linking verbs. Before writing your book, determine its audience, write to that audience, and go about developing your credibility with that audience—and then tell us what you have done and are doing in your proposal."

NATIONAL GEOGRAPHIC CHILDREN'S BOOKS

1145 17th St. NW, Washington DC 20036-8199. (800)647-5463. **Website:** kids.nationalgeographic.com. National Geographic Children's Books provides quality nonfiction for children and young adults by award-winning authors. *This market does not currently accept unsolicited mss.*

NBM PUBLISHING

160 Broadway, Suite 700, East Bldg., New York NY 10038. **E-mail:** nbmgn@nbmpub.com. **Website:** nbmpub.com. **Contact:** Terry Nantier, editor. Publishes graphic novels for an audience of YA/adults. Types of books include fiction, mystery, biographies and social parodies. **Publishes 16 titles/year. 5% of books from first-time authors. 90% from unagented writers.**

HOW TO CONTACT Responds to e-mail 1-2 days; mail 1 week. Publishes ms 1 year after acceptance.

TERMS Advance negotiable. Catalog online.

TOMMY NELSON

Imprint of Thomas Nelson, Inc., P.O. Box 141000, Nashville TN 37214-1000. (615)889-9000. **Fax:** (615)902-2219. **Website:** www.tommynelson.com. "Tommy Nelson publishes children's Christian nonfiction and fiction for boys and girls up to age 14. We honor God and serve people through books, videos, software and Bibles for children that improve the lives of our customers." Publishes hardcover and trade paperback originals. **Publishes 50-75 titles/year.**

FICTION No stereotypical characters.

HOW TO CONTACT *Does not accept unsolicited mss. Does not accept unsolicited mss.*

TERMS Guidelines online.

TIPS "Know the Christian Booksellers Association market. Check out the Christian bookstores to see what sells and what is needed."

NOMAD PRESS

2456 Christain St., White River Junction VT 05001. (802)649-1995. **E-mail:** info@nomadpress.net. **Website:** www.nomadpress.net. **Contact:** Acquisitions Editor. "We produce nonfiction children's activity books that bring a particular science or cultural topic into sharp focus. Nomad Press does not accept unsolicited manuscripts. If authors are interested in contributing to our children's series, please send a writing resume that includes relevant experience/expertise and publishing credits."

Nomad Press does not accept picture books, fiction, or cookbooks.

NONFICTION Middle readers: activity books, history, science. Average word length: middle readers—30,000.

HOW TO CONTACT Responds to queries in 3-4 weeks. Publishes book 1 year after acceptance.

TERMS Pays authors royalty based on retail price or work purchased outright. Offers advance against royalties. Catalog online.

TIPS "We publish a very specific kind of nonfiction children's activity book. Please keep this in mind when querying or submitting."

NORTHSOUTH BOOKS

600 Third Ave., 2nd Floor, New York NY 10016. **E-mail:** submissionsb@gmail.com. **Website:** www.northsouth.com. **Contact:** Beth Terrill.

FICTION Looking for fresh, original fiction with universal themes that could appeal to children ages 3-8. "We typically do not acquire rhyming texts, since our books must also be translated into German."

HOW TO CONTACT Submit picture book mss (1,000 words or less) via e-mail.

TERMS Guidelines online.

OHIO UNIVERSITY PRESS

30 Park Place, Suite 101, Athens OH 45701. **Fax:** (740)593-4536. **Website:** www.ohioswallow.com. **Contact:** Gillian Berchowitz, director. "In addition to scholarly works in African studies, Appalachian studies, US history, and other areas, Ohio University Press publishes a wide range of creative works as part of its Hollis Summers Poetry Prize (yearly deadline in December), its Modern African Writing series, and under its trade imprint, Swallow Press." Publishes hardcover and trade paperback originals and reprints. **Publishes 45-50 titles/year. 20% of books from first-time authors. 95% from unagented writers.**

NONFICTION "We prefer queries or detailed proposals, rather than manuscripts. Editors will request the complete manuscript if it is of interest."

HOW TO CONTACT Query via e-mail or with SASE; or online. Responds in 1-3 months. Publishes ms 1 year after acceptance.

TERMS Sometimes pays advance. Catalog online. Guidelines online.

TIPS "Rather than trying to hook the editor on your work, let the material be compelling enough and well-presented enough to do it for you."

OOLIGAN PRESS

369 Neuberger Hall, 724 SW Harrison St., Portland OR 97201. (503)725-9410. **Website:** ooligan.pdx.edu. **Contact:** Acquisitions Co-Managers. "We seek to publish regionally significant works of literary, historical, and social value. We define the Pacific Northwest as Northern California, Oregon, Idaho, Washington, British Columbia, and Alaska. We recognize the importance of diversity, particularly within the publishing industry, and are committed to building a literary community that includes traditionally underrepresented voices; therefore, we are interested in works originating from, or focusing on, marginalized communities of the Pacific Northwest." Publishes trade paperbacks, electronic originals, and reprints. **Publishes 3-4 titles/year. 90% of books from first-time authors. 90% from unagented writers.**

FICTION "We seek to publish regionally significant works of literary, historical, and social value. We define the Pacific Northwest as Northern California, Oregon, Idaho, Washington, British Columbia, and Alaska. We recognize the importance of diversity, particularly within the publishing industry, and are committed to building a literary community that includes traditionally underrepresented voices; therefore, we are interested in works originating from, or focusing on, marginalized communities of the Pacific Northwest." Does not want romance, horror, westerns, incomplete mss.

NONFICTION Cookbooks, self-help books, how-to manuals.

HOW TO CONTACT Query with SASE. *"At this time we cannot accept science fiction or fantasy submissions."* Submit a query through Submittable. If accepted, then submit proposal package, outline, 4 sample chapters, projected page count, audience, marketing ideas, and a list of similar titles. 250-500 queries; 50-75 mss received/year. Responds in 3 weeks for queries; 3 months for proposals. Publishes ms 12-18 months after acceptance.

TERMS Pays negotiable royalty on retail price. Catalog online. Guidelines online.

TIPS "Search the blog for tips."

Ⓐ ORCHARD BOOKS (US)

557 Broadway, New York NY 10012. **Website:** www.scholastic.com. *Orchard is not accepting unsolicited mss.* **Publishes 20 titles/year. 10% of books from first-time authors.**

FICTION Picture books, early readers, and novelty: animal, contemporary, history, humor, multicultural, poetry.

TERMS Most commonly offers an advance against list royalties.

OUR SUNDAY VISITOR, INC.

200 Noll Plaza, Huntington IN 46750. **E-mail:** jlindsey@osv.com. **Website:** www.osv.com. "We are a Catholic publishing company seeking to educate and deepen our readers in their faith. Currently emphasizing devotional, inspirational, Catholic identity, apologetics, and catechetics." Publishes paperback and hardbound originals. **Publishes 40-50 titles/year.**

Our Sunday Visitor, Inc. is publishing only those children's books that are specifically Catholic. See website for submission guidelines.

NONFICTION Prefers to see well-developed proposals as first submission with annotated outline and definition of intended market; Catholic viewpoints on family, prayer, and devotional books, and Catholic heritage books. Picture books, middle readers, young readers, young adults.

HOW TO CONTACT Query, submit complete ms, or submit outline/synopsis and 2-3 sample chapters. Responds in 2 months. Publishes ms 1-2 years after acceptance.

TERMS Pays authors royalty of 10-12% net. Pays illustrators by the project (range: $25-1,500). Book catalog for 9×12 envelope and first-class stamps; ms guidelines available online.

TIPS "Stay in accordance with our guidelines."

RICHARD C. OWEN PUBLISHERS, INC.

P.O. Box 585, Katonah NY 10536. (914)232-3903; (800)262-0787. **E-mail:** richardowen@rcowen.com. **Website:** www.rcowen.com. **Contact:** Richard Owen, publisher. "We publish child-focused books, with inherent instructional value, about characters and situations with which 5, 6, and 7-year-old children can identify—books that can be read for meaning, entertainment, enjoyment and information. We include multicultural stories that present minorities in a positive and natural way. Our stories show the diversity in America." Not interested in lesson plans, or books of activities for literature studies or other content areas. Submit complete ms and cover letter.

"Due to high volume and long production time, we are currently limiting to nonfiction submissions only."

NONFICTION "Our books are for kindergarten, first- and second-grade children to read on their own. The stories are very brief—up to 2,000 words—yet well structured and crafted with memorable characters, language, and plots. Picture books, young readers: animals, careers, history, how-to, music/dance, geography, multicultural, nature/environment, science, sports. Multicultural needs include: Good stories respectful of all heritages, races, cultural—African American, Hispanic, American Indian, Asian, European, Middle Eastern." Wants lively stories. No "encyclopedic" type of information stories. Average word length: under 500 words.

HOW TO CONTACT Responds to mss in 1 year. Publishes book 2-3 years after acceptance.

ILLUSTRATION Works with 20 illustrators/year. Uses color artwork only. Illustration only: Send color copies/reproductions or photos of art or provide tearsheets; do not send slides or originals. Include SASE and cover letter. Responds only if interested; samples filed.

TERMS Pays authors royalty of 5% based on net price or outright purchase (range: $25-500). Offers no advances. Pays illustrators by the project (range: $100-2,000) or per photo (range: $50-150). Book catalog available with SASE. Ms guidelines with SASE or online.

OZARK MOUNTAIN PUBLISHING, INC.

Big Sandy Press, Cannon Holdings, LLC, P.O. Box 754, Huntsville AR 72740. (479)738-2348 ext. 1. **Fax:** (479)738-2448. **E-mail:** info@ozarkmt.com. **Website:** www.ozarkmt.com. **Contact:** Nancy Vernon, general manager. New Age/Metaphysical or Spiritual material (Please do not send Poetry, Daily Inspirational Books or Cards, as we do not publish this style.) Publishes trade paperback originals. **Publishes 8-10 titles/year. 50% of books from first-time authors. 95% from unagented writers.**

FICTION New Age/Metaphysical or Spiritual, Historical, Paranormal, Youth and Teen material (Please do not send Poetry, Daily Inspirational Books or Cards, as we do not publish this style.) No phone calls please

NONFICTION New Age/Metaphysical or Spiritual, Historical, Paranormal, Youth and Teen material (Please do not send Poetry, Daily Inspirational Books or Cards, as we do not publish this style.) No phone calls please.

HOW TO CONTACT Query with SASE. Submit completed manuscripts. Guidelines online. No phone calls please. 50-75 queries; 150-200 mss received/year. Responds in 6 months to mss. Publishes ms within 18 months after acceptance.

TERMS Pays 10% royalty on retail or wholesale price. Pays $250-500 advance. Book catalog online. Guidelines online. Include postcard for notification of receipt. No phone call please. Payment required for unaccepted mss to be returned—all other unaccepted mss will be destroyed.

TIPS "We envision our audience to be open minded, spiritually expanding. Please do not call to check on submissions. Do not submit electronically. Send hard copy only."

PAGESPRING PUBLISHING

PageSpring Publishing, P.O. Box 21133, Columbus OH 43221. **Website:** www.pagespringpublishing.com. PageSpring Publishing is a small independent publisher with two imprints: Cup of Tea Books and Lucky Marble Books. Cup of Tea Books publishes women's fiction, with particular emphasis on mystery and humor. Lucky Marble Books publishes young adult and middle grade fiction. "We are looking for engaging characters and well-crafted plots that keep our readers turning the page. We accept e-mail queries only; see our website for details." Publishes trade paperback and electronic originals. **Publishes 4-5 titles/year. 75% of books from first-time authors. 100% from unagented writers.**

FICTION Lucky Marble Books publishes middle grade and young adult novels. Cup of Tea Books publishes women's fiction. Lucky Marble Books publishes middle grade and young adult novels. No children's picture books.

HOW TO CONTACT Submit proposal package via e-mail only. Include synopsis and 30 sample pages. Responds in 3 months. Publishes ms 12 months after acceptance.

TERMS Pays royalty. Guidelines online.

TIPS "Cup of Tea Books is particularly interested in cozy mystery novels. Lucky Marble Books is looking for funny, age-appropriate tales for middle grade and young adult readers."

PAPERCUTZ

160 Broadway, Suite 700E, New York NY 10038. (646)559-4681. **Fax:** (212)643-1545. **Website:** www.papercutz.com. Publisher of graphic novels for kids and teens. Publishes major licenses and author created comics. **Publishes 40 titles/year. 5% of books from first-time authors. 90% from unagented writers.**

FICTION "Independent publisher of graphic novels including popular existing properties aimed at the teen and tween market."

HOW TO CONTACT Responds in 2-4 weeks. Publishes ms 1 year after acceptance.

TERMS Pays advance.

TIPS "Be familiar with our titles—that's the best way to know what we're interested in publishing. If you are somehow attached to a successful tween or teen property and would like to adapt it into a graphic novel, we may be interested. We also take submissions for new series preferably that have already a following online."

PAUL DRY BOOKS

1700 Sansom St., Suite 700, Philadelphia PA 19103. (215)231-9939. **Fax:** (215)231-9942. **E-mail:** editor@pauldrybooks.com. **Website:** pauldrybooks.com. "We publish fiction, both novels and short stories, and nonfiction, biography, memoirs, history, and essays, covering subjects from Homer to Chekhov, bird watching to jazz music, New York City to shogunate Japan." Hardcover and trade paperback originals, trade paperback reprints.

HOW TO CONTACT "We do not accept unsolicited manuscripts."

TERMS Book catalog online.

TIPS "Our aim is to publish lively books 'to awaken, delight, and educate'—to spark conversation. We publish fiction and nonfiction, and essays covering subjects from Homer to Chekhov, bird watching to jazz music, New York City to shogunate Japan."

PAULINE BOOKS & MEDIA

50 St. Paul's Ave., Boston MA 02130. (617)522-8911. **Fax:** (617)541-9805. **E-mail:** design@paulinemedia.com; editorial@paulinemedia.com. **Website:** www.pauline.org. "Submissions are evaluated on adherence to Gospel values, harmony with the Catholic faith tradition, relevance of topic, and quality of writing." For board books and picture books, the entire manuscript should be submitted. For easy-to-read, young readers, and middle reader books and teen books, please send a cover letter accompanied by a synopsis and two sample chapters. "Electronic submissions are encouraged. We make every effort to respond to unsolicited submissions within 2 months." Publishes trade paperback originals and reprints. **Publishes 40 titles/year. 5% from unagented writers.**

FICTION Children's and teen fiction only. "We are now accepting submissions for easy-to-read and middle reader chapter, and teen well documented historical fiction. We would also consider well-written fantasy, fairy tales, myths, science fiction, mysteries, or romance if approached from a Catholic perspective and consistent with church teaching. Please see our writer's guidelines."

NONFICTION Picture books, young readers, middle readers, teen: religion and fiction. Average word length: picture books—500-1,000; young readers—8,000-10,000; middle readers—15,000-25,000; teen—30,000-50,000. Recently published children's titles: *Bible Stores for Little Ones* by Genny Monchapm; *I Forgive You: Love We Can Hear, Ask for and Give* by Nicole Lataif; *Shepherds to the Rescue* (first place Catholic Book Award Winner) by Maria Grace Dateno; *FSP*; *Jorge from Argentina*; *Prayers for Young Catholics*. Teen Titles: *Teens Share the Mission* by Teens; *Martyred: The Story of Saint Lorenzo Ruiz*; *Ten Commandmenst for Kissing Gloria Jean* by Britt Leigh; *A.K.A. Genius* (2nd Place Catholic Book Award Winner) by Marilee Haynes; *Tackling Tough Topics* with Faith and Fiction by Diana Jenkins. No memoir/autobiography, poetry, or strictly nonreligious works currently considered.

HOW TO CONTACT Submit proposal package, including outline, 1-2 sample chapters, cover letter, synopsis, intended audience and proposed length. Responds in 2 months. Publishes a book approximately 11-18 months after acceptance.

ILLUSTRATION Works with 10-15 illustrators/year. Uses color and black-and-white artwork. Samples and résumés will be kept on file unless return is requested and SASE provided.

TERMS Varies by project, but generally are royalties with advance. Flat fees sometimes considered for smaller works. Book catalog online. Guidelines online.

TIPS "Manuscripts may or may not be explicitly catechetical, but we seek those that reflect a positive worldview, good moral values, awareness and appreciation of diversity, and respect for all people. All material must be relevant to the lives of readers and must conform to Catholic teaching and practice."

PAULIST PRESS

997 Macarthur Blvd., Mahwah NJ 07430. (201)825-7300. **Fax:** (201)825-8345. **E-mail:** submissions@paulistpress.com. **Website:** www.paulistpress.com. **Contact:** Trace Murphy, Editorial Director. Paulist Press publishes ecumenical theology, Roman Catholic studies, and books on scripture, liturgy, spirituality, church history, and philosophy, as well as works on faith and culture. Also publishes 2-3 children's titles a year. **10% of books from first-time authors. 95% from unagented writers.**

HOW TO CONTACT Accepts submissions via e-mail. Receives 400 submissions/year. Responds in 3 months to queries and proposals; 3-4 months on mss. Publishes a book 12-18 months after receipt of final, edited ms.

TERMS Royalties and advances are negotiable. Pays negotiable advance. Book catalog online. Guidelines online.

PEACHTREE PUBLISHING COMPANY INC.

Peachtree Publishing Company Inc., 1700 Chattahoochee Ave., Atlanta GA 30318. (404)876-8761. **Fax:** (404)875-2578. **E-mail:** hello@peachtree-online.com. **Website:** www.peachtree-online.com. "We publish a broad range of subjects and perspectives, with emphasis on innovative plots and strong writing." Publishes hardcover and trade paperback originals. **Publishes 30 titles/year. 25% of books from first-time authors. 25% from unagented writers.**

FICTION Picture books, young readers: adventure, animal, concept, history, nature/environment. Middle readers: adventure, animal, history, nature/environment, sports. Young adults: fiction, mystery, adventure. Does not want to see science fiction, romance.

NONFICTION Picture books: animal, history, nature/environment. Young readers, middle readers, young adults: animal, biography, nature/environment. Does not want to see religion.

HOW TO CONTACT Submit complete ms with SASE, or summary and 3 sample chapters with SASE. Responds in 6 months and mss. Publishes ms 1 year after acceptance.

ILLUSTRATION Works with 8-10 illustrators/year. Illustrations only: Query production manager or art director with samples, résumé, slides, color copies to keep on file. Responds only if interested. Samples returned with SASE; samples filed.

TERMS Pays royalty on retail price. Book catalog for 6 first-class stamps. Guidelines online.

PELICAN PUBLISHING COMPANY

1000 Burmaster St., Gretna LA 70053. (504)368-1175. **Fax:** (504)368-1195. **E-mail:** editorial@pelicanpub.com. **Website:** www.pelicanpub.com. "We believe ideas have consequences. One of the consequences is that they lead to a best-selling book. We publish books to improve and uplift the reader. Currently emphasizing business and history titles." Publishes 20 young readers/year; 1 middle reader/year. "Our children's books (illustrated and otherwise) include history, biography, holiday, and regional. Pelican's mission is to publish books of quality and permanence that enrich the lives of those who read them." Publishes hardcover, trade paperback and mass market paperback originals and reprints.

FICTION We publish no adult fiction. Young readers: history, holiday, science, multicultural and regional. Middle readers: Louisiana History. Multicultural needs include stories about African Americans, Irish-Americans, Jews, Asian Americans, and Hispanics. Does not want animal stories, general Christmas stories, "day at school" or "accept yourself" stories. Maximum word length: young readers—1,100; middle readers—40,000. No young adult, romance, science fiction, fantasy, gothic, mystery, erotica, confession, horror, sex, or violence. Also no psychological novels.

NONFICTION "We look for authors who can promote successfully. We require that a query be made first. This greatly expedites the review process and can save the writer additional postage expenses." Young readers: biography, history, holiday, multicultural.

Middle readers: Louisiana history, holiday, regional. No multiple queries or submissions.

HOW TO CONTACT Submit outline, clips, 2 sample chapters, SASE. Full guidelines on website. Responds in 1 month to queries; 3 months to mss. Requires exclusive submission. Publishes 9-18 months after acceptance.

ILLUSTRATION Works with 20 illustrators/year. Reviews ms/illustration packages from artists. Query first. Illustrations only: Query with samples (no originals). Responds only if interested. Samples returned with SASE; samples kept on file.

TERMS Pays authors in royalties; buys ms outright "rarely." Illustrators paid by "various arrangements." Advance considered. Book catalog and ms guidelines online.

TIPS "We do extremely well with cookbooks, popular histories, and business. We will continue to build in these areas. The writer must have a clear sense of the market and knowledge of the competition. A query letter should describe the project briefly, give the author's writing and professional credentials, and promotional ideas."

Ⓐ PENGUIN RANDOM HOUSE, LLC

Division of Bertelsmann Book Group, 1745 Broadway, New York NY 10019. (212)782-9000. **Website:** www.penguinrandomhouse.com. Penguin Random House LLC is the world's largest English-language general trade book publisher. *Agented submissions only. No unsolicited mss.*

PERSEA BOOKS

277 Broadway, Suite 708, New York NY 10007. (212)260-9256. **Fax:** (212)267-3165. **E-mail:** info@perseabooks.com. **Website:** www.perseabooks.com. The aim of Persea is to publish works that endure by meeting high standards of literary merit and relevance. "We have often taken on important books other publishers have overlooked, or have made significant discoveries and rediscoveries, whether of a single work or writer's entire oeuvre. Our books cover a wide range of themes, styles, and genres. We have published poetry, fiction, essays, memoir, biography, titles of Jewish and Middle Eastern interest, women's studies, American Indian folklore, and revived classics, as well as a notable selection of works in translation."

HOW TO CONTACT Queries should include a cover letter, author background and publication history, a detailed synopsis of the proposed work, and a sample chapter. Please indicate if the work is simultaneously submitted. Responds in 8 weeks to proposals; 10 weeks to mss.

TERMS Guidelines online.

PFLAUM PUBLISHING GROUP

3055 Kettering Blvd., Suite 100, Dayton OH 45439. (800)543-4383. **Website:** www.pflaum.com. "Pflaum Publishing Group, a division of Peter Li, Inc., serves the specialized market of religious education, primarily Roman Catholic. We provide high quality, theologically sound, practical, and affordable resources that assist religious educators of and ministers to children from preschool through senior high school." **Publishes 20 titles/year.**

HOW TO CONTACT Query with SASE.

TERMS Payment by outright purchase. Book catalog and ms guidelines free.

PHAIDON PRESS

65 Bleecker St., 8th Floor, New York NY 10012. (212)652-5400. **Fax:** (212)652-5410. **E-mail:** submissions@phaidon.com. **Website:** www.phaidon.com. Phaidon Press is the world's leading publisher of books on the visual arts, with offices in London, Paris, Berlin, Barcelona, Milan, New York and Tokyo. Their books are recognized worldwide for the highest quality of content, design, and production. They cover everything from art, architecture, photography, design, performing arts, decorative arts, contemporary culture, fashion, film, travel, cookery and children's books. Publishes hardcover and trade paperback originals and reprints. **Publishes 100 titles/year. 40% of books from first-time authors. 90% from unagented writers.**

HOW TO CONTACT Submit proposal package and outline, or submit complete ms. Submissions by e-mail or fax will not be accepted. 500 mss received/year. Responds in 3 months to proposals. Publishes ms 1 year after acceptance.

TERMS Pays royalty on wholesale price, if appropriate. Offers advance, if appropriate. Book catalog available free. Guidelines online.

TIPS "Please do not contact us to obtain an update on the status of your submission until we have had your submission for at least three months, as we will not provide updates before this period of time has elapsed. Phaidon does not assume any responsibility for any unsolicited submissions, or any materials included with a submission."

Ⓐ PHILOMEL BOOKS

Imprint of Penguin Random House, 1745 Broadway, New York NY 10019. (212)414-3610. **Website:** www.penguin.com. "We look for beautifully written, engaging manuscripts for children and young adults." Publishes hardcover originals. **Publishes 8-10 titles/year. 5% of books from first-time authors. 20% from unagented writers.**

NONFICTION Picture books.

HOW TO CONTACT *No unsolicited mss. Agented submissions only.*

ILLUSTRATION Works with 8-10 illustrators/year. Reviews ms/illustration packages from artists. Query with art sample first. Illustrations only: Query with samples. Send résumé and tearsheets. Responds to art samples in 1 month. Original artwork returned at job's completion. Samples returned with SASE or kept on file.

TERMS Pays authors in royalties. Average advance payment "varies." Illustrators paid by advance and in royalties. Pays negotiable advance.

PIANO PRESS

P.O. Box 85, Del Mar CA 92014. (619)884-1401. **Fax:** (858)755-1104. **E-mail:** pianopress@pianopress.com. **Website:** www.pianopress.com. **Contact:** Elizabeth C. Axford, editor. "We publish music-related books, either fiction or nonfiction, music-related coloring books, songbooks, sheet music, CDs, and music-related poetry."

FICTION Picture books, young readers, middle readers, young adults: folktales, multicultural, poetry, music. Average word length: picture books—1,500-2,000.

NONFICTION Picture books, young readers, middle readers, young adults: multicultural, music/dance. Average word length: picture books—1,500-2,000.

HOW TO CONTACT Responds if interested. Publishes book 1 year after acceptance.

ILLUSTRATION Works with 1 or 2 illustrators/year. Reviews ms/illustration packages from artists. Query. Illustrations only: Query with samples. Responds in 3 months. Samples returned with SASE; samples filed.

PHOTOGRAPHY Buys stock and assigns work. Looking for music-related, multicultural. Model/property releases required. Uses glossy or flat, color or b&w prints. Submit cover letter, résumé, client list, published samples, stock photo list.

TERMS Pays authors, illustrators, and photographers royalties based on the retail price. Book catalog online.

TIPS "We are looking for music-related material only for the juvenile market. Please do not send non-music-related materials. Query by e-mail first before submitting anything."

PIÑATA BOOKS

Imprint of Arte Publico Press, University of Houston, 4902 Gulf Fwy., Bldg. 19, Room 100, Houston TX 77204-2004. (713)743-2845. **Fax:** (713)743-3080. **E-mail:** submapp@uh.edu. **Website:** www.artepublicopress.com. "Piñata Books is dedicated to the publication of children's and young adult literature focusing on U.S. Hispanic culture by U.S. Hispanic authors. Arte Publico's mission is the publication, promotion and dissemination of Latino literature for a variety of national and regional audiences, from early childhood to adult, through the complete gamut of delivery systems, including personal performance as well as print and electronic media." Publishes hardcover and trade paperback originals. **Publishes 10-15 titles/year. 80% of books from first-time authors.**

NONFICTION Piñata Books specializes in publication of children's and young adult literature that authentically portrays themes, characters and customs unique to U.S. Hispanic culture.

HOW TO CONTACT Submissions made through online submission form. Responds in 2-3 months to queries; 4-6 months to mss. Publishes book 2 years after acceptance.

ILLUSTRATION Works with 6 illustrators/year. Uses color artwork only. Reviews ms/illustration packages from artists. Query or send portfolio (slides, color copies). Illustrations only: Query with samples or send résumé, promo sheet, portfolio, slides, client list and tearsheets. Responds only if interested. Samples not returned; samples filed.

TERMS Pays 10% royalty on wholesale price. Pays $1,000-3,000 advance. Book catalog and guidelines online.

TIPS "Include cover letter with submission explaining why your manuscript is unique and important, why we should publish it, who will buy it, etc."

PINEAPPLE PRESS, INC.

P.O. Box 3889, Sarasota FL 34230. (941)706-2507. **Fax:** (800)746-3275. **Website:** www.pineapplepress.com. **Contact:** June Cussen, executive editor. "We are seeking quality nonfiction on diverse topics for the library and book trade markets. Our mission is to publish good books about Florida." Publishes hardcover and trade paperback originals. **Publishes 21 titles/year. 50% of books from first-time authors. 95% from unagented writers.**

FICTION Picture books, young readers, middle readers, young adults: animal, folktales, history, nature/environment.

NONFICTION Picture books: animal, history, nature/environmental, science. Young readers, middle readers, young adults: animal, biography, geography, history, nature/environment, science.

HOW TO CONTACT Query or submit outline/synopsis and 3 sample chapters. 1,000 queries; 500 mss received/year. Responds in 2 months. Publishes a book 1 year after acceptance.

ILLUSTRATION Works with 2 illustrators/year. Reviews ms/illustration packages from artists. Query with nonreturnable samples. Contact: June Cussen, executive editor. Illustrations only: Query with brochure, nonreturnable samples, photocopies, résumé. Responds only if interested. Samples returned with SASE, but prefers nonreturnable; samples filed.

TERMS Pays authors royalty of 10-15%. Book catalog for 9×12 SAE with $1.32 postage. Guidelines online.

TIPS "Quality first novels will be published, though we usually only do one or two novels per year and they must be set in Florida. We regard the author/editor relationship as a trusting relationship with communication open both ways. Learn all you can about the publishing process and about how to promote your book once it is published. A query on a novel without a brief sample seems useless."

POLIS BOOKS

E-mail: info@polisbooks.com. **Website:** www.polisbooks.com. "Polis Books is an independent publishing company actively seeking new and established authors for our growing list. We are actively acquiring titles in mystery, thriller, suspense, procedural, traditional crime, science fiction, fantasy, horror, supernatural, urban fantasy, romance, erotica, commercial women's fiction, commercial literary fiction, young adult and middle grade books." **Publishes 40 titles/year. 33% of books from first-time authors. 10% from unagented writers.**

HOW TO CONTACT Query with 3 sample chapters and bio via e-mail. 500+ Only responds to submissions if interested For e-book originals, ms published 6-9 months after acceptance. For frontlist print titles, 9-15 months.

TERMS Offers advance against royalties. Guidelines online.

PRINCETON ARCHITECTURAL PRESS

202 Warren St., Hudson NY 12534. (518)671-6100. **E-mail:** submissions@papress.com. **Website:** www.papress.com. Publishes hardcover and trade paperback originals. **Publishes 50 titles/year. 65% of books from first-time authors. 95% from unagented writers.**

Princeton Architectural Press is a leading publisher in architecture, landscape architecture, design, and visual culture, as well as illustrated children's books.

NONFICTION Does not publish highly technical or purely academic titles.

HOW TO CONTACT 300 queries; 150 mss received/year. Responds in 2 months. Publishes book 1 year after acceptance.

TERMS Pays royalty on wholesale price. Catalog available in print and online. Princeton Architectural Press accepts proposals concerning architecture, landscape architecture, graphic design, and visual culture. Submissions of illustrated children's books are also welcome. Electronic submissions only. See website for detailed submission guidelines.

Ⓐ PUFFIN BOOKS

Imprint of Penguin Random House, 1745 Broadway, New York NY 10019. (212)366-2000. **Website:** www.penguin.com. "Puffin Books publishes high-end trade paperbacks and paperback reprints for preschool children, beginning and middle readers, and young adults." Publishes trade paperback originals and reprints. **Publishes 175-200 titles/year.**

NONFICTION "Women in history books interest us."

HOW TO CONTACT *No unsolicited mss. Agented submissions only.* Publishes book 1 year after acceptance.

ILLUSTRATION Reviews artwork. Send color copies.

PHOTOGRAPHY Reviews photos. Send color copies.

TIPS "Our audience ranges from little children 'first books' to young adult (ages 14-16). An original idea has the best luck."

Ⓐ RANDOM HOUSE CHILDREN'S BOOKS

1745 Broadway, New York NY 10019. (212)782-9000. **Website:** www.penguinrandomhouse.com. "Producing books for preschool children through young adult readers, in all formats from board to activity books to picture books and novels, Random House Children's Books brings together world-famous franchise characters, multimillion-copy series and top-flight, award-winning authors, and illustrators." Submit mss through a literary agent.

FICTION "Random House publishes a select list of first chapter books and novels, with an emphasis on fantasy and historical fiction." Chapter books, middle-grade readers, young adult.

HOW TO CONTACT *Does not accept unsolicited mss.*

ILLUSTRATION The Random House publishing divisions hire their freelancers directly. To contact the appropriate person, send a cover letter and résumé to the department head at the publisher as follows: "Department Head" (e.g., Art Director, Production Director), "Publisher/Imprint" (e.g., Knopf, Doubleday, etc.), 1745 Broadway New York, NY 10019. Works with 100-150 freelancers/year. Works on assignment only. Send query letter with résumé, tearsheets and printed samples; no originals. Samples are filed. Negotiates rights purchased. Assigns 5 freelance design jobs/year. Pays by the project.

TIPS "We look for original, unique stories. Do something that hasn't been done before."

RAZORBILL

Penguin Young Readers Group, 1745 Broadway, New York NY 10019. (212)414-3427. **Website:** www.razorbillbooks.com. "This division of Penguin Young Readers is looking for the best and the most original of commercial contemporary fiction titles for middle grade and YA readers. A select quantity of nonfiction titles will also be considered." **Publishes 30 titles/year.**

FICTION Middle Readers: adventure, contemporary, graphic novels, fantasy, humor, problem novels. Young adults/teens: adventure, contemporary, fantasy, graphic novels, humor, multicultural, suspense, paranormal, science fiction, dystopian, literary, romance. Average word length: middle readers—40,000; young adult—60,000.

NONFICTION Middle readers and young adults/teens: concept.

HOW TO CONTACT Submit cover letter with up to 30 sample pages. Submit cover letter with up to 30 sample pages. Responds in 1-3 months. Publishes book 1-2 after acceptance.

TERMS Offers advance against royalties.

TIPS "New writers will have the best chance of acceptance and publication with original, contemporary material that boasts a distinctive voice and well-articulated world. Check out website to get a better idea of what we're looking for."

REDLEAF LANE

Redleaf Press, 10 Yorkton Ct., St. Paul MN 55117. (800)423-8309. **E-mail:** info@redleafpress.org. **Website:** www.redleafpress.org. **Contact:** David Heath, director. Redleaf Lane publishes engaging, high-quality picture books for children. "Our books are unique because they take place in group-care settings and reflect developmentally appropriate practices and research-based standards."

TERMS Guidelines online.

RIPPLE GROVE PRESS

P.O. Box 910, Shelburne VT 05482. **Website:** www.ripplegrovepress.com. **Contact:** Robert Broder. Ripple Grove Press is an independent, family-run children's book publisher. "We started Ripple Grove Press because we have a passion for well-told and beautifully illustrated stories for children. Our mission is to bring together great writers and talented illustrators to make the most wonderful books possible. We hope our books find their way to the cozy spot in your home." Publishes hardcover originals. **Publishes 3-6 titles/year.**

FICTION We are looking for something unique, that has not been done before; an interesting story that captures a moment with a timeless feel. We are looking for picture driven stories for children ages 2-6. Please do not send early readers, middle grade, or YA mss. No religious stories. Please do not submit your story with page breaks or illustration notes. Do not submit a story with doodles or personal photographs.

Do not send your "idea" for a story, send your story in manuscript form.

HOW TO CONTACT Submit completed mss. Accepts submissions by mail and e-mail. E-mail preferred. Please submit a cover letter including a summary of your story, the age range of the story, a brief biography of yourself, and contact information. 3,000 submissions/year. "Given the volume of submissions we receive we are no longer able to individually respond to each. Please allow 5 months for us to review your submission. If we are interested in your story, you can expect to hear from us within that time. If you do not hear from us after that time, we are not interested in publishing your story. It's not you, it's us! We receive thousands of submissions and only publish a few books each year. Don't give up!" Average length of time between acceptance of a book-length ms and publication is 12-18 months.

TERMS Authors and illustrators receive royalties on net receipts. Pays negotiable advance. Catalog online. Guidelines online.

TIPS "Please read children's picture books. Please read our books to see what we look for in a story and in art. We create books that capture a moment, so that a child can create their own."

Ⓐ ROARING BROOK PRESS

Macmillan Children's Publishing Group, 175 Fifth Ave., New York NY 10010. (646)307-5151. **Website:** us.macmillan.com. Roaring Brook Press is an imprint of MacMillan, a group of companies that includes Henry Holt and Farrar, Straus & Giroux. *Roaring Brook is not accepting unsolicited mss.*

FICTION Picture books, young readers, middle readers, young adults: adventure, animal, contemporary, fantasy, history, humor, multicultural, nature/environment, poetry, religion, science fiction, sports, suspense/mystery.

NONFICTION Picture books, young readers, middle readers, young adults: adventure, animal, contemporary, fantasy, history, humor, multicultural, nature/environment, poetry, religion, science fiction, sports, suspense/mystery.

HOW TO CONTACT *Not accepting unsolicited mss or queries. Not accepting unsolicited mss or queries.*

ILLUSTRATION Works with 25 illustrators/year. Illustrations only: Query with samples. Do not send original art; copies only through the mail. Samples returned with SASE.

TERMS Pays authors royalty based on retail price.

TIPS "You should find a reputable agent and have him/her submit your work."

ROSEN PUBLISHING

29 E. 21st St., New York NY 10010. (800)237-9932. **Fax:** (888)436-4643. **Website:** www.rosenpublishing.com. Artists and writers should contact customer service team through online form for information about contributing to Rosen Publishing. Rosen Publishing is an independent educational publishing house, established to serve the needs of students in grades Pre-K-12 with high interest, curriculum-correlated materials. Rosen publishes more than 700 new books each year and has a backlist of more than 7,000.

ROWMAN & LITTLEFIELD PUBLISHING GROUP

4501 Forbes Blvd., Suite 200, Lanham MD 20706. (301)459-3366. **Fax:** (301)429-5748. **Website:** www.rowmanlittlefield.com. **Contact:** Linda Ganster. "We are an independent press devoted to publishing social science and humanities titles that engage, inform and educate: innovative, thought-provoking texts for college courses; research-based titles for professionals eager to remain abreast of developments within their domains; and general interest books intended to convey important trends to an educated readership. Our approach emphasizes thought leadership balanced with a deep understanding of the areas in which we publish. We offer a forum for responsible voices representing the diversity of opinion on college campuses, and take special pride in our commitment to covering critical societal issues." Textbooks, nonfiction general interest titles, professional development works,references, and select trade in hardcover and paperback.

NONFICTION "Rowman & Littlefield is seeking proposals in the serious nonfiction areas of history, politics, current events, religion, sociology, criminal justice, social work, philosophy, communication and education. All proposal inquiries can be e-mailed or mailed to the respective acquisitions editor listed on the contacts page on our website."

TERMS Pays advance. Book catalog online. Guidelines online. Please submit to only one R&L editor at a time. Multiple submissions slows down the process, and editors are very good about sharing proposals.

SADDLEBACK EDUCATIONAL PUBLISHING

3120-A Pullman St., Costa Mesa CA 92626. (888)735-2225. **E-mail:** contact@sdlback.com. **Website:** www.sdlback.com. Saddleback is always looking for fresh, new talent. "Please note that we primarily publish books for kids ages 12-18."

FICTION "We look for diversity for our characters and content."

HOW TO CONTACT Mail typed submission along with a query letter describing the work simply and where it fits in with other titles.

SAGUARO BOOKS, LLC

16845 E. Ave. of the Fountains, Ste. 325, Fountain Hills AZ 85268. **E-mail:** mjnickum@saguarobooks.com. **Website:** www.saguarobooks.com. **Contact:** Mary Nickum, CEO. Saguaro Books, LLC is a publishing company specializing in middle grade and young adult ficiton by first-time authors. Publishes trade paperback and electronic originals. **Publishes 4-6 titles/year. 100% of books from first-time authors. 100% from unagented writers.**

Only first-time authors (previously unpublished) authors will be considered. No Agents, please.

FICTION Ms should be well-written; signed letter by a professional editor is required. Does not want agented work.

HOW TO CONTACT Query via e-mail before submitting work. Any material sent before requested will be ignored. Receives 60-80 queries/year, 8-10 mss/year. Responds within 3 months only if we're interested. Publishes ms 18-24 months after acceptance.

TERMS Pays 20% royalties after taxes and publication costs. Does not offer advance. Catalog online. Guidelines by e-mail.

TIPS "Visit our website before sending us a query. Pay special attention to the For Authors Only page."

SALINA BOOKSHELF

1120 W. University Ave., Suite 102, Flagstaff AZ 86001. (877)527-0070. **Fax:** (928)526-0386. **Website:** www.salinabookshelf.com. Publishes trade paperback originals and reprints. **Publishes 4-5 titles/year. 50% of books from first-time authors. 100% from unagented writers.**

FICTION Submissions should be in English or Navajo. "All our books relate to the Navajo language and culture."

NONFICTION "We publish children's bilingual readers." Nonfiction should be appropriate to science and social studies curriculum grades 3-8.

HOW TO CONTACT Query with SASE. Responds in 3 months to queries. Publishes ms 1 year after acceptance.

TERMS Pays varying royalty. Pays advance.

SANTA MONICA PRESS

P.O. Box 850, Solana Beach CA 92075. (858)832-7906. **E-mail:** books@santamonicapress.com. **Website:** www.santamonicapress.com. Santa Monica Press has been publishing an eclectic line of non-fiction books for over 25 years. "Our critically acclaimed titles are sold in chain, independent, on-line, and university bookstores around the world, as well as in some of the most popular retail, gift, and museum outlets in North America. Our authors are recognized experts who are sought after by the media and receive newspaper, magazine, internet, social media, radio, and television coverage both nationally and internationally. At Santa Monica Press, we're not afraid to cast a wide editorial net. Our list of lively and modern nonfiction titles includes books in such categories as pop culture, film, music, humor, biography, travel, and sports, as well as regional titles focused on California. Please note that we have recently added Young Adult Historical Fiction and Young Adult Narrative Non-Fiction to our list. We look forward to receiving your submission!" Publishes hardcover, trade paperback, and ebook originals. **Publishes 15 titles/year. 50% of books from first-time authors. 75% from unagented writers.**

FICTION Historical young adult fiction and young adult narrative nonfiction only.

HOW TO CONTACT Submit proposal package, including outline, 2-3 sample chapters, biography, marketing and publicity plans, analysis of competitive titles. Please see the Author Guidelines page on our website. Responds in 1-2 months to proposals. Publishes book 1 year after acceptance.

TERMS Pays 6-10% royalty on net price. Pays $500–$5,000+ advance.

TIPS "Visit our website before submitting to view our author guidelines and to get a clear idea of the types of books we publish. Carefully analyze your book's competition and tell us what makes your book different—and what makes it better. Also let us know what promotional and marketing opportunities you, as the author, bring to the project."

SASQUATCH BOOKS

1904 Third Ave., Suite 710, Seattle WA 98101. (206)467-4300. **Fax:** (206)467-4301. **E-mail:** custserv@sasquatchbooks.com. **Website:** www.sasquatchbooks.com. "Sasquatch Books publishes books for and from the Pacific Northwest, Alaska, and California is the nation's premier regional press. Sasquatch Books' publishing program is a veritable celebration of regionally written words. Undeterred by political or geographical borders, Sasquatch defines its region as the magnificent area that stretches from the Brooks Range to the Gulf of California and from the Rocky Mountains to the Pacific Ocean. Our top-selling Best Places® travel guides serve the most popular destinations and locations of the West. We also publish widely in the areas of food and wine, gardening, nature, photography, children's books, and regional history, all facets of the literature of place. With more than 200 books brimming with insider information on the West, we offer an energetic eye on the lifestyle, landscape, and worldview of our region. Considers queries and proposals from authors and agents for new projects that fit into our West Coast regional publishing program. We can evaluate query letters, proposals, and complete mss." Publishes regional hardcover and trade paperback originals. **Publishes 30 titles/year. 20% of books from first-time authors. 75% from unagented writers.**

FICTION Young readers: adventure, animal, concept, contemporary, humor, nature/environment.

NONFICTION "We are seeking quality nonfiction works about the Pacific Northwest and West Coast regions (including Alaska to California). The literature of place includes how-to and where-to as well as history and narrative nonfiction." Picture books: activity books, animal, concept, nature/environment. "We publish a variety of nonfiction books, as well as children's books under our Little Bigfoot imprint."

HOW TO CONTACT Query first, then submit outline and sample chapters with SASE. Send submissions to The Editors. E-mailed submissions and queries are not recommended. Please include return postage if you want your materials back. Responds to queries in 3 months. Publishes book 6-9 months after acceptance.

ILLUSTRATION Accepts material from international illustrators. Works with 5 illustrators/year. Uses both color and b&w. Reviews ms/illustration packages. For ms/illustration packages: Query. Submit ms/illustration packages to The Editors. Reviews work for future assignments. If interested in illustrating future titles, query with samples. Samples returned with SASE. Samples filed.

TERMS Pays royalty on cover price. Pays wide range advance. Guidelines online.

TIPS "We sell books through a range of channels in addition to the book trade. Our primary audience consists of active, literate residents of the West Coast."

Ⓐ SCHOLASTIC LIBRARY PUBLISHING

90 Old Sherman Turnpike, Danbury CT 6816. (203)797-3500. **Fax:** (203)797-3197. **E-mail:** slpservice@scholastic.com. **Website:** www.scholastic.com/librarypublishing. "Scholastic Library is a leading publisher of reference, educational, and children's books. We provide parents, teachers, and librarians with the tools they need to enlighten children to the pleasure of learning and prepare them for the road ahead. Publishes informational (nonfiction) for K-12; picture books for young readers, grades 1-3." Publishes hardcover and trade paperback originals.

Accepts agented submissions only.

FICTION Publishes 1 picture book series, Rookie Readers, for grades 1-2. Does not accept unsolicited mss.

NONFICTION Photo-illustrated books for all levels: animal, arts/crafts, biography, careers, concept, geography, health, history, hobbies, how-to, multicultural, nature/environment, science, social issues, special needs, sports. Average word length: young readers—2,000; middle readers—8,000; young adult—15,000.

HOW TO CONTACT *Does not accept fiction proposals.* Query; submit outline/synopsis, resume, and/or list of publications, and writing sample. SASE required for response.

ILLUSTRATION Works with 15-20 illustrators/year. Uses color artwork and line drawings. Illustrations only: Query with samples or arrange personal portfolio review. Responds only if interested. Samples returned with SASE. Samples filed. Do not send originals. No phone or e-mail inquiries; contact only by mail.

TERMS Pays authors royalty based on net or work purchased outright. Pays illustrators at competitive rates.

Ⓐ SCHOLASTIC PRESS

Imprint of Scholastic, Inc., 557 Broadway, New York NY 10012. (212)343-6100. **Fax:** (212)343-4713. **Website:** www.scholastic.com. Scholastic Press publishes fresh, literary picture book fiction and nonfiction; fresh, literary nonseries or nongenre-oriented middle grade and young adult fiction. Currently emphasizing subtly handled treatments of key relationships in children's lives; unusual approaches to commonly dry subjects, such as biography, math, history, or science. Deemphasizing fairy tales (or retellings), board books, genre, or series fiction (mystery, fantasy, etc.). Publishes hardcover originals. **Publishes 60 titles/year. 1% of books from first-time authors.**

FICTION Looking for strong picture books, young chapter books, appealing middle grade novels (ages 8-11) and interesting and well-written young adult novels. Wants fresh, exciting picture books and novels—inspiring, new talent.

HOW TO CONTACT *Agented submissions only.* 2,500 queries received/year. Responds in 3 months to queries; 6-8 months to mss. Publishes book 2 years after acceptance.

ILLUSTRATION Works with 30 illustrators/year. Uses both b&w and color artwork. Illustrations only: Query with samples; send tearsheets. Responds only if interested. Samples returned with SASE. Original artwork returned at job's completion.

TERMS Pays royalty on retail price. Pays variable advance.

TIPS "Read *currently* published children's books. Revise, rewrite, rework and find your own voice, style and subject. We are looking for authors with a strong and unique voice who can tell a great story and have the ability to evoke genuine emotion. Children's publishers are becoming more selective, looking for irresistible talent and fairly broad appeal, yet still very willing to take risks, just to keep the game interesting."

SEEDLING CONTINENTAL PRESS

520 E. Bainbridge St., Elizabethtown PA 17022. (800)233-0759. **Website:** www.continentalpress.com. "Continental publishes educational materials for grades K-12, specializing in reading, mathematics, and test preparation materials. We are not currently accepting submissions for Seedling leveled readers or instructional materials."

FICTION Young readers: adventure, animal, folktales, humor, multicultural, nature/environment. Does not accept texts longer than 12 pages or over 300 words. Average word length: young readers—100.

NONFICTION Young readers: animal, arts/crafts, biography, careers, concept, multicultural, nature/environment, science. Does not accept texts longer than 12 pages or over 300 words. Average word length: young readers—100.

HOW TO CONTACT Submit complete ms. Responds to mss in 6 months. Publishes book 1-2 years after acceptance.

ILLUSTRATION Works with 8-10 illustrators/year. Uses color artwork only. Reviews ms/illustration packages from artists. Submit ms with dummy. Illustrations only: Color copies or line art. Responds only if interested. Samples returned with SASE only; samples filed if interested.

PHOTOGRAPHY Buys photos from freelancers. Works on assignment only. Model/property releases required. Uses color prints and 35mm transparencies. Submit cover letter and color promo piece.

TERMS Work purchased outright from authors.

TIPS "See our website. Follow writers' guidelines carefully and test your story with children and educators."

SHIPWRECKT BOOKS PUBLISHING COMPANY LLC

309 W. Stevens Ave., Rushford MN 55971. **E-mail:** contact@shipwrecktbooks.com. **Website:** www.shipwrecktbooks.press. **Contact:** Tom Driscoll, managing editor. Publishes trade paperback originals, mass market paperback originals, and electronic originals. **Publishes 6-10 titles/year. 60% of books from first-time authors. 80% from unagented writers.**

NONFICTION Does not want religious.

HOW TO CONTACT Use submissions portal at www.shipwrecktbooks.press; follow guidelines. Paper submissions are no longer accepted. Use submissions portal at www.shipwrecktbooks.press; follow guidelines. Paper submissions are no longer accepted. Receives 1,000 submissions/year. Responds to queries within 6 months. Average length of time between acceptance of a book-length ms and publication is 6-18 months.

TERMS Authors receive 35% royalties unless otherwise negotiated. Catalog and guidelines online. No longer accepts paper submissions. Use the electronic submissions portal found on our website. www.shipwrecktbooks.press.

TIPS Quality writing. Please follow our guidelines. Creative development and manuscript editorial services available. Please use electronic submissions portal found on our website: www.shipwrecktbooks.press.

SILVER DOLPHIN BOOKS

(858)457-2500. **E-mail:** infosilverdolphin@readerlink.com. **Website:** www.silverdolphinbooks.com. Silver Dolphin Books publishes activity, novelty, and educational nonfiction books for preschoolers to 12-year-olds. Highly interactive formats such as the Field Guides and Uncover series both educate and entertain older children. "We will consider submissions only from authors with previously published works."

HOW TO CONTACT Submit cover letter with full proposal and SASE.

Ⓐ SIMON & SCHUSTER BOOKS FOR YOUNG READERS

Imprint of Simon & Schuster Children's Publishing, 1230 Avenue of the Americas, New York NY 10020. (212)698-7000. **Fax:** (212)698-2796. **Website:** www.simonsayskids.com. "Simon and Schuster Books For Young Readers is the Flagship imprint of the S&S Children's Division. We are committed to publishing a wide range of contemporary, commercial, award-winning fiction and nonfiction that spans every age of children's publishing. BFYR is constantly looking to the future, supporting our foundation authors and franchises, but always with an eye for breaking new ground with every publication. We publish high-quality fiction and nonfiction for a variety of age groups and a variety of markets. Above all, we strive to publish books that we are passionate about." *No unsolicited mss.* All unsolicited mss returned unopened. Publishes hardcover originals. **Publishes 75 titles/year.**

NONFICTION Picture books: concept. All levels: narrative, current events, biography, history. "We're looking for picture books or middle grade nonfiction that have a retail potential. No photo essays."

HOW TO CONTACT *Agented submissions only.* Publishes ms 2-4 years after acceptance.

ILLUSTRATION Works with 70 illustrators/year. Do not submit original artwork. Does not accept unsolicited or unagented illustration submissions.

TERMS Pays variable royalty on retail price. Guidelines online.

TIPS "We're looking for picture books centered on a strong, fully-developed protagonist who grows or changes during the course of the story; YA novels that are challenging and psychologically complex; also imaginative and humorous middle-grade fiction. And we want nonfiction that is as engaging as fiction. Our imprint's slogan is 'Reading You'll Remember.' We aim to publish books that are fresh, accessible and family-oriented; we want them to have an impact on the reader."

SKINNER HOUSE BOOKS

The Unitarian Universalist Association, 24 Farnsworth St., Boston MA 02210. (617)742-2100, ext. 603. **Fax:** (617)948-6466. **E-mail:** bookproposals@uua.org. **Website:** www.uua.org/publications/skinnerhouse. **Contact:** Betsy Martin. "We publish titles in Unitarian Universalist faith, liberal religion, history, biography, worship, and issues of social justice. Most of our children's titles are intended for religious education or worship use. They reflect Unitarian Universalist values. We also publish inspirational titles of poetic prose and meditations. Writers should know that Unitarian Universalism is a liberal religious denomination committed to progressive ideals. Currently emphasizing social justice concerns." Publishes trade paperback originals and reprints. **Publishes 10-20 titles/year. 30% of books from first-time authors. 100% from unagented writers.**

FICTION Only publishes fiction for children's titles for religious instruction.

NONFICTION All levels: activity books, multicultural, music/dance, nature/environment, religion.

HOW TO CONTACT Query or submit proposal with cover letter, TOC, 2 sample chapters. Responds to queries in 1 month. Publishes 1 year after acceptance.

ILLUSTRATION Works with 2 illustrators/year. Uses both color and b&w. Reviews ms/illustration packages from artists. Query. Contact: Suzanne Morgan, design director. Responds only if interested. Samples returned with SASE.

PHOTOGRAPHY Buys stock images and assigns work. Contact: Suzanne Morgan, design director.

Uses inspirational types of photo's. Model/property releases required; captions required. Uses color, b&w. Submit cover letter, resume.

TERMS Book catalog for 6×9 SAE with 3 first-class stamps. Guidelines online.

TIPS "From outside our denomination, we are interested in manuscripts that will be of help or interest to liberal churches, Sunday School classes, parents, ministers, and volunteers. Inspirational/spiritual and children's titles must reflect liberal Unitarian Universalist values."

Ⓐ LIZZIE SKURNICK BOOKS

(718)797-0676. **Website:** lizzieskurnickbooks.com. Lizzie Skurnick Books, an imprint of Ig Publishing, is devoted to reissuing the very best in young adult literature, from the classics of the 1930s and 1940s to the social novels of the 1970s and 1980s. Ig does not accept unsolicited mss, either by e-mail or regular mail. If you have a ms that you would like Ig to take a look at, send a query through online contact form. If interested, they will contact. All unsolicited mss will be discarded.

SKY PONY PRESS

307 W. 36th St., 11th Floor, New York NY 10018. (212)643-6816. **Fax:** (212)643-6819. **Website:** skyponypress.com. Sky Pony Press is the children's book imprint of Skyhorse Publishing. "Following in the footsteps of our parent company, our goal is to provide books for readers with a wide variety of interests."

FICTION "We will consider picture books, early readers, midgrade novels, novelties, and informational books for all ages."

NONFICTION "Our parent company publishes many excellent books in the fields of ecology, independent living, farm living, wilderness living, recycling, and other green topics, and this will be a theme in our children's books. We are also searching for books that have strong educational themes and that help inform children of the world in which they live."

HOW TO CONTACT Submit ms or proposal. Submit proposal via e-mail.

TERMS Guidelines online.

SLEEPING BEAR PRESS

2395 South Huron Parkway #200, Ann Arbor MI 48104. (800)487-2323. **Fax:** (734)794-0004. **E-mail:** submissions@sleepingbearpress.com. **Website:** www.sleepingbearpress.com. **Contact:** Manuscript Submissions.

FICTION Picture books: adventure, animal, concept, folktales, history, multicultural, nature/environment, religion, sports. Young readers: adventure, animal, concept, folktales, history, humor, multicultural, nature/environment, religion, sports. Average word length: picture books—1,800.

HOW TO CONTACT Accepts unsolicited queries 3 times per year. See website for details. Query with sample of work (up to 15 pages) and SASE. Please address packages to Manuscript Submissions.

TERMS Book catalog available via e-mail.

SOURCEBOOKS FIRE

1935 Brookdale Rd., Suite 139, Naperville IL 60563. (630)961-3900. **Fax:** (630)961-2168. **E-mail:** submissions@sourcebooks.com. **Website:** www.sourcebooks.com. "We're actively acquiring knockout books for our YA imprint. We are particularly looking for strong writers who are excited about promoting and building their community of readers, and whose books have something fresh to offer the ever-growing young adult audience. We are not accepting any unsolicited or unagented manuscripts at this time. Unfortunately, our staff can no longer handle the large volume of manuscripts that we receive on a daily basis. We will continue to consider agented manuscripts." See website for details.

HOW TO CONTACT Query with the full ms attached in Word doc.

SPENCER HILL PRESS

27 W. 20th St., Suite 1102, New York NY 10011. **Website:** www.spencerhillpress.com. Spencer Hill Press is an independent publishing house specializing in sci-fi, urban fantasy, and paranormal romance for young adult readers. "Our books have that 'I couldn't put it down!' quality."

FICTION "We are interested in young adult, new adult, and middle grade sci-fi, psych-fi, paranormal, or urban fantasy, particularly those with a strong and interesting voice."

HOW TO CONTACT Check website for open submission periods.

TERMS Guidelines online.

STAR BRIGHT BOOKS

13 Landsdowne St., Cambridge MA 02139. (617)354-1300. **Fax:** (617)354-1399. **E-mail:** lolabush@star-

brightbooks.com. **Website:** www.starbrightbooks.com. **Contact:** Lola Bush. Star Bright Books accepts unsolicited mss and art submissions. "We welcome submissions for picture books and longer works, both fiction and particularly nonfiction." Also beginner readers and chapter books. Currently seeking bios, math infused books. **Publishes 12 titles/year. 75% of books from first-time authors. 99% from unagented writers.**

NONFICTION Very keen on biographies and anything of interest to children.

HOW TO CONTACT How things work, how things are made, nature. history, multi-ethnic. Responds in several months. Publishes ms 1-3 years after acceptance.

TERMS Pays advance as well as flat fee Catalog online.

STERLING PUBLISHING CO., INC.

1166 Avenue of the Americas, 17th Floor, New York NY 10036. (212)532-7160. **Website:** www.sterlingpublishing.com. "Sterling publishes highly illustrated, accessible, hands-on, practical books for adults and children. Our mission is to publish high-quality books that educate, entertain, and enrich the lives of our readers." Publishes hardcover and paperback originals and reprints. **15% of books from first-time authors.**

FICTION Publishes fiction for children.

NONFICTION Proposals on subjects such as crafting, decorating, outdoor living, and photography should be sent directly to Lark Books at their Asheville, North Carolina offices. Complete guidelines can be found on the Lark site: www.larkbooks.com/submissions. Publishes nonfiction only.

HOW TO CONTACT Submit to attention of "Children's Book Editor." Submit outline, publishing history, 1 sample chapter (typed and double-spaced), SASE. "Explain your idea. Send sample illustrations where applicable. For children's books, please submit full mss. We do not accept electronic (e-mail) submissions. Be sure to include information about yourself with particular regard to your skills and qualifications in the subject area of your submission. It is helpful for us to know your publishing history—whether or not you've written other books and, if so, the name of the publisher and whether those books are currently in print."

ILLUSTRATION Works with 50 illustrators/year. Reviews ms/illustration packages from artists. Illustrations only: Send promo sheet. Contact: Karen Nelson, creative director. Responds in 6 weeks. Samples returned with SASE; samples filed.

PHOTOGRAPHY Buys stock and assigns work. Contact: Karen Nelson.

TERMS Pays royalty or work purchased outright. Offers advances (average amount: $2,000). Catalog online. Guidelines online.

TIPS "We are primarily a nonfiction activities-based publisher. We have a picture book list, but we do not publish chapter books or novels. Our list is not trend-driven. We focus on titles that will backlist well. "

STONE ARCH BOOKS

1710 Roe Crest Rd., North Mankato MN 56003. **Website:** www.stonearchbooks.com.

FICTION Imprint of Capstone Publishers.Young readers, middle readers, young adults: adventure, contemporary, fantasy, humor, light humor, mystery, science fiction, sports, suspense. Average word length: young readers—1,000-3,000; middle readers and early young adults—5,000-10,000.

HOW TO CONTACT Submit outline/synopsis and 3 sample chapters. Electronic submissions preferred. Full guidelines available on website.

ILLUSTRATION Works with 35 illustrators/year. Uses both color and b&w.

TERMS Work purchased outright from authors. Catalog online.

TIPS "A high-interest topic or activity is one that a young person would spend their free time on without adult direction or suggestion."

SUNBURY PRESS, INC.

PO Box 548, Boiling Springs PA 17007. **E-mail:** info@sunburypress.com. **Website:** www.sunburypress.com. Sunbury Press, Inc., headquartered in Mechanicsburg, PA, is a publisher of trade paperback, hardcover and digital books featuring established and emerging authors in many fiction and non-fiction categories. Sunbury's books are printed in the USA and sold through leading booksellers worldwide. "Please use our online submission form." Publishes trade paperback and hardcover originals and reprints; electronic originals and reprints. **Publishes 60 titles/year. 40% of books from first-time authors. 95% from unagented writers.**

FICTION "We are seeking manuscripts for our three fiction imprints: Milford House Press, Brown Posey Press, and Hellbender Books." Does not want vampires, zombies, erotica.

NONFICTION "We are currently seeking war memoirs of all kinds and local / regional histories and biographies. We are also looking for American Revolution manuscripts."

HOW TO CONTACT Please use our online submission service. Please use our online submission service. Receives 1,000 queries/year; 500 mss/year. Responds in 3 months. Publishes ms 6 months after acceptance.

TERMS Pays 10% royalty on wholesale price. Catalog and guidelines online. Online submission form.

TIPS "We are a rapidly growing small press with six diverse imprints. We currently have over 250 authors and 500 works under management."

SUNSTONE PRESS

Box 2321, Santa Fe NM 87504. (800)243-5644. **Website:** www.sunstonepress.com. **Contact:** Submissions Editor. Sunstone's original focus was on nonfiction subjects that preserved and highlighted the richness of the American Southwest but it has expanded its view over the years to include mainstream themes and categories—both nonfiction and fiction—that have a more general appeal.

HOW TO CONTACT Query with 1 sample chapter. Query with 1 sample chapter.

TERMS Guidelines online.

TANTOR MEDIA

Recorded Books, 6 Business Park Rd., Old Saybrook CT 06475. (860)395-1155. **Fax:** (860)395-1154. **E-mail:** rightsemail@tantor.com. **Website:** www.tantor.com. **Contact:** Ron Formica, director of acquisitions. Tantor Media, a division of Recorded Books, is a leading audiobook publisher, producing more than 100 new titles every month. We do not publish print or e-books. Publishes audiobooks only. **Publishes 1,500 titles/year.**

We are not publishing print/e-book titles.

HOW TO CONTACT Not accepting print submissions. Responds in 2 months.

TERMS Catalog online. Not accepting print or e-book queries. We only publish audiobooks.

TEACHERS COLLEGE PRESS

1234 Amsterdam Ave., New York NY 10027. (212)678-3929. **Fax:** (212)678-4149. **E-mail:** tcp.cs@aidcvt.com. **Website:** www.teacherscollegepress.com. "Teachers College Press publishes a wide range of educational titles for all levels of students: early childhood to higher education. Publishing books that respond to, examine, and confront issues pertaining to education, teacher training, and school reform." Publishes hardcover and paperback originals and reprints. **Publishes 60 titles/year.**

NONFICTION This university press concentrates on books in the field of education in the broadest sense, from early childhood to higher education: good classroom practices, teacher training, special education, innovative trends and issues, administration and supervision, film, continuing and adult education, all areas of the curriculum, computers, guidance and counseling, and the politics, economics, philosophy, sociology, and history of education. We have recently added women's studies to our list. The Press also issues classroom materials for students at all levels, with a strong emphasis on reading and writing and social studies.

HOW TO CONTACT Submit outline, sample chapters. Responds in 2 months to queries. Publishes ms 1 year after acceptance.

TERMS Pays industry standard royalty. Pays advance. Book catalog available free. Guidelines online.

KATHERINE TEGEN BOOKS

HarperCollins, 195 Broadway, New York NY 10007. **Website:** www.harpercollins.com. Katherine Tegen Books publishes high-quality, commercial literature for children of all ages, including teens. Talented authors and illustrators who offer powerful narratives that are thought-provoking, well-written, and entertaining are the core of the Katherine Tegen Books imprint. *Katherine Tegen Books accepts agented work only.*

TILBURY HOUSE PUBLISHERS

WordSplice Studio, Inc., 12 Starr St., Thomaston ME 04861. (207)582-1899. **Fax:** (207)582-8772. **E-mail:** info@tilburyhouse.com. **Website:** www.tilburyhouse.com. **Publishes 24 titles/year.**

FICTION Picture books: multicultural, nature/environment. Special needs include books that teach children about and honoring diversity.

NONFICTION Regional history/maritime/nature, and children's picture books that deal with issues, such as bullying, multiculturalism, etc. science/nature.

HOW TO CONTACT Send art/photography samples and/or complete ms to info@tilburyhouse.com. Submit complete ms for picture books or outline/synopsis for longer works. Now uses online submission form. Responds to mss in 6 months. Publishes ms 1.5 years after acceptance.

PHOTOGRAPHY Buys photos from freelancers. Works on assignment only.

TERMS Pays royalty based on wholesale price. Guidelines and catalog online.

TIPS "We are always interested in stories that will encourage children to understand the natural world and the environment, as well as stories with social justice themes. We really like stories that engage children to become problem solvers as well as those that promote respect, tolerance and compassion."

TOR BOOKS

Tom Doherty Associates, 175 Fifth Ave., New York NY 10010. **Website:** www.tor-forge.com. Tor Books is the "world's largest publisher of science fiction and fantasy, with strong category publishing in historical fiction, mystery, western/Americana, thriller, YA." **Publishes 10-20 titles/year.**

HOW TO CONTACT Submit first 3 chapters, 3-10 page synopsis, dated cover letter, SASE.

TERMS Pays author royalty. Pays illustrators by the project. Book catalog available. Guidelines online.

TRIANGLE SQUARE

Seven Stories Press, 140 Watts St., New York NY 10013. (212)226-8760. **Fax:** (212)226-1411. **E-mail:** info@sevenstories.com. **Website:** https://www.sevenstories.com/imprints/triangle-square. Triangle Square is a children's and young adult imprint of Seven Story Press.

HOW TO CONTACT Send a cover letter with 2 sample chapters and SASE. Send c/o Acquisitions.

TWILIGHT TIMES BOOKS

P.O. Box 3340, Kingsport TN 37664. **E-mail:** publisher@twilighttimesbooks.com. **Website:** www.twilighttimesbooks.com. **Contact:** Andy M. Scott, managing editor. "We publish compelling literary fiction by authors with a distinctive voice." Published 5 debut authors within the last year. Averages 120 total titles; 15 fiction titles/year. Member: AAP, IBPA, PAS, SPAN, SLF. **85% from unagented writers.**

HOW TO CONTACT Accepts unsolicited mss. Do not send complete mss. Queries via e-mail only. Include estimated word count, brief bio, list of publishing credits, marketing plan. Responds in 4 weeks to queries; 2 months to mss.

TERMS Pays 8-15% royalty. Guidelines online.

TIPS "The only requirement for consideration at Twilight Times Books is that your novel must be entertaining and professionally written."

Ⓐ TYNDALE HOUSE PUBLISHERS, INC.

351 Executive Dr., Carol Stream IL 60188. (800)323-9400. **Fax:** (800)684-0247. **Website:** www.tyndale.com. "Tyndale House publishes practical, user-friendly Christian books for the home and family." Publishes hardcover and trade paperback originals and mass paperback reprints. **Publishes 15 titles/year.**

FICTION "Christian truths must be woven into the story organically. No short story collections. Youth books: character building stories with Christian perspective. Especially interested in ages 10-14. We primarily publish Christian historical romances, with occasional contemporary, suspense, or standalones."

HOW TO CONTACT *Agented submissions only. No unsolicited mss.*

ILLUSTRATION Uses full-color for book covers, b&w or color spot illustrations for some nonfiction. Illustrations only: Query with photocopies (color or b&w) of samples, résumé.

PHOTOGRAPHY Buys photos from freelancers. Works on assignment only.

TERMS Pays negotiable royalty. Pays negotiable advance. Guidelines online.

TIPS "All accepted manuscripts will appeal to Evangelical Christian children and parents."

Ⓐ VIKING CHILDREN'S BOOKS

1745 Broadway, New York NY 10019. **Website:** www.penguin.com. "Viking Children's Books is known for humorous, quirky picture books, in addition to more traditional fiction. We publish the highest quality fiction, nonfiction, and picture books for pre-schoolers through young adults." *Does not accept unsolicited submissions.* Publishes hardcover originals. **Publishes 70 titles/year.**

FICTION All levels: adventure, animal, contemporary, fantasy, history, humor, multicultural, nature/environment, poetry, problem novels, romance, science fiction, sports, suspense/mystery.

NONFICTION All levels: biography, concept, history, multicultural, music/dance, nature/environment, science, and sports.

HOW TO CONTACT *Agented submissions only.* Responds in 6 months. Publishes book 1-2 years after acceptance.

ILLUSTRATION Works with 30 illustrators/year. Responds to artist's queries/submissions only if interested. Samples returned with SASE only or samples filed. Originals returned at job's completion.

TERMS Pays 2-10% royalty on retail price or flat fee. Pays negotiable advance.

TIPS "No 'cartoony' or mass-market submissions for picture books."

WESTERN PSYCHOLOGICAL SERVICES

625 Alaska Ave., Torrance CA 90503. (424)201-8800 or (800)648-8857. **Fax:** (424)201-6950. **Website:** www.wpspublish.com. "Western Psychological Services publishes psychological and educational assessments that practitioners trust. Our products allow helping professionals to accurately screen, diagnose, and treat people in need. WPS publishes practical books and games used by therapists, counselors, social workers, and others in the helping professionals who work with children and adults." Publishes psychological and educational assessments and some trade paperback originals. **Publishes 2 titles/year. 90% of books from first-time authors. 95% from unagented writers.**

NONFICTION "We publish children's books dealing with feelings, anger, social skills, autism, family problems."

HOW TO CONTACT Submit complete ms. 60 queries received/year. 30 mss received/year. Responds in 2 months to queries. Publishes ms 1 year after acceptance.

TERMS Pays 5-10% royalty on wholesale price. Book catalog available free. Guidelines online.

WESTMINSTER JOHN KNOX PRESS

Flyaway Books, Division of Presbyterian Publishing Corp., 100 Witherspoon St., Louisville KY 40202. **Fax:** (502)569-5113. **E-mail:** submissions@wjkbooks.com. **Website:** www.wjkbooks.com. Flyaway Books is a new imprint for children's picture books that intentionally publishes diverse content, authors, and illustrators. See our website www.flyawaybooks.com for more details and submission instructions. "All WJK books have a religious/spiritual angle, but are written for various markets-scholarly, professional, and the general reader. Flyaway Books is a new children's picture book imprint that is intentionally diverse in content and authorship. E-mail submissions only. No submissions by mail. No phone queries. We do not publish fiction, poetry, or dissertations. We do not return or respond to submissions received by mail and do not respond to unsolicited phone messages. Westminster John Knox is affiliated with the Presbyterian Church (U.S.A.). " Publishes hardcover and paperback originals. **Publishes 60 titles/year. 10% of books from first-time authors. 75% from unagented writers.**

Looking for fresh and challenging voices writing about social justice issues (race, LGBTQI, immigration, women's rights, economic justice, etc.) from a religious, spiritual, or humanitarian perspective. Looking for biblical studies and theology texts for graduate and seminary students and core textbooks in Bible for undergraduates. See more at www.wjkbooks.com. Flyaway Books is looking for picture books for a trade, school, and progressive church audience. See more at www.flyawaybooks.com.

NONFICTION No dissertations.

HOW TO CONTACT submissions@flyawaybooks.com Submit proposal package according to the WJK book proposal guidelines found online. 1,000 submissions received/year. Responds in 2-3 months.

ILLUSTRATION Contact submissions@flyawaybooks.com.

TERMS Pays royalty on net price. Pays advance. Catalog online. Proposal guidelines online.

WHITE MANE KIDS

73 W. Burd St., Shippensburg PA 17257. (717)532-2237. **Fax:** (717)532-6110. **E-mail:** marketing@whitemane.com. **Website:** www.whitemane.com. **Contact:** Harold Collier, acquisitions editor.

FICTION Middle readers, young adults: history (primarily American Civil War). Average word length: middle readers—30,000. Does not publish picture books.

NONFICTION Middle readers, young adults: history. Average word length: middle readers—30,000. Does not publish picture books.

HOW TO CONTACT Query. Submit outline/synopsis and 2-3 sample chapters. Book proposal form on website. Responds to queries in 1 month, mss in 6-9 months. Publishes book 18 months after acceptance.

ILLUSTRATION Works with 4 illustrators/year. Illustrations used for cover art only. Responds only if interested. Samples returned with SASE.

PHOTOGRAPHY Buys stock and assigns work. Submit cover letter and portfolio.

TERMS Pays authors royalty of 7-10%. Pays illustrators and photographers by the project. Book catalog and writer's guidelines available for SASE.

TIPS "Make your work historically accurate. We are interested in historically accurate fiction for middle and young adult readers. We do *not* publish picture books. Our primary focus is the American Civil War and some America Revolution topics."

ALBERT WHITMAN & COMPANY

250 S. Northwest Hwy., Suite 320, Park Ridge IL 60068. (800)255-7675. **Fax:** (847)581-0039. **E-mail:** submissions@albertwhitman.com. **Website:** www.albertwhitman.com. Albert Whitman & Company publishes books for the trade, library, and school library market. Interested in reviewing the following types of projects: Picture book manuscripts for ages 2-8; novels and chapter books for ages 8-12; young adult novels; nonfiction for ages 3-12 and YA; art samples showing pictures of children. Best known for the classic series The Boxcar Children® Mysteries. "We are no longer reading unsolicited queries and manuscripts sent through the US mail. We now require these submissions to be sent by e-mail. You must visit our website for our guidelines, which include instructions for formatting your e-mail. E-mails that do not follow this format may not be read. We read every submission within 4 months of receipt, but we can no longer respond to every one. If you do not receive a response from us after four months, we have declined to publish your submission." Publishes in original hardcover, paperback, boardbooks. **Publishes 60 titles/year. 10% of books from first-time authors. 50% from unagented writers.**

FICTION Picture books (up to 1,000 words); middle grade (up to 35,000 words); young adult (up to 70,000 words).

NONFICTION Picture books up to 1,000 words.

HOW TO CONTACT For picture books, submit cover letter and brief description. For middle grade and young adult, send query, synopsis, and first 3 chapters. Submit cover letter, brief description.

TERMS Guidelines online.

THE WILD ROSE PRESS

P.O. Box 708, Adams Basin NY 14410-0708. (585)752-8770. **E-mail:** queryus@thewildrosepress.com. **Website:** www.thewildrosepress.com. **Contact:** Rhonda Penders, editor-in-chief. Publishes paperback originals, reprints, and e-books in a POD format. **Publishes approx. 60 fiction titles/year.**

HOW TO CONTACT *Does not accept unsolicited mss.* Send query letter with outline and synopsis of up to 5 pages. Accepts all queries by e-mail. Include estimated word count, brief bio, and list of publishing credits. Agented fiction less than 1%. Always comments on rejected mss. Responds to queries in 4 weeks; mss in 12 weeks. Publishes ms 1 year after acceptance.

TERMS Pays royalty of 7% minimum; 40% maximum. Sends prepublication galleys to author. Guidelines online.

TIPS "Polish your manuscript, make it as error free as possible, and follow our submission guidelines."

Ⓐ PAULA WISEMAN BOOKS

1230 Sixth Ave., New York NY 10020. (212)698-7000. **Fax:** (212)698-2796. **Website:** kids.simonandschuster.com. Paula Wiseman Books is an imprint of Simon & Schuster Children's Publishing that launched in 2003. It has since gone on to publish over 70 award-winning and bestselling books, including picture books, novelty books, and novels. The imprint focuses on stories and art that are childlike, timeless, innovative, and centered in emotion. "We strive to publish books that entertain while expanding the experience of the children who read them, as well as stories that will endure, including those based in other cultures. We are committed to publishing new talent in both picture books and novels. We are actively seeking submissions from new and published authors and artists through agents and from SCBWI conferences." **Publishes 30 titles/year. 15% of books from first-time authors.**

FICTION Considers all categories. Average word length: picture books—500; others standard length.

NONFICTION Picture books: animal, biography, concept, history, nature/environment. Young readers: animal, biography, history, multicultural, nature/environment, sports. Average word length: picture books—500; others standard length.

HOW TO CONTACT Does not accept unsolicited or unagented mss.

ILLUSTRATION Works with 15 illustrators/year. Does not accept unsolicited or unagented illustrations or submissions.

WOODBINE HOUSE

6510 Bells Mill Rd., Bethesda MD 20817. (301)897-3570. **Fax:** (301)897-5838. **E-mail:** info@woodbinehouse.com. **Website:** www.woodbinehouse.com. **Contact:** Acquisitions Editor. Woodbine House publishes books for or about individuals with disabilities to help those individuals and their families live fulfilling and satisfying lives in their homes, schools, and communities. Publishes trade paperback originals. **Publishes 10 titles/year. 15% of books from first-time authors. 90% from unagented writers.**

FICTION Receptive to stories re: developmental and intellectual disabilities, e.g., autism and cerebral palsy.

NONFICTION Publishes books for and about children with disabilities. No personal accounts or general parenting guides.

HOW TO CONTACT Submit complete ms with SASE. Submit outline, and at least 3 sample chapters. Responds in 3 months to queries. Publishes ms 18 months after acceptance.

TERMS Pays 10-12% royalty. Guidelines online.

TIPS "Do not send us a proposal on the basis of this description. Examine our catalog or website and a couple of our books to make sure you are on the right track. Put some thought into how your book could be marketed (aside from in bookstores). Keep cover letters concise and to the point; if it's a subject that interests us, we'll ask to see more."

Ⓐ WORDSONG

19 W. 21st St., #1201, New York NY 10010. **Fax:** (570)253-0179. **Website:** www.wordsongpoetry.com. "We publish fresh voices in contemporary poetry."

HOW TO CONTACT Responds to mss in 3 months.

ILLUSTRATION Works with 7 illustrators/year. Reviews ms/illustration packages from artists. Submit complete ms with 1 or 2 pieces of art. Illustrations only: Query with samples best suited to the art (postcard, 8½ × 11, etc.). Label package "Art Sample Submission." Responds only if interested. Samples returned with SASE.

PHOTOGRAPHY Assigns work.

TERMS Pays authors royalty or work purchased outright.

TIPS "Collections of original poetry, not anthologies, are our biggest need at this time. Keep in mind that the strongest collections demonstrate a facility with multiple poetic forms and offer fresh images and insights. Check to see what's already on the market and on our website before submitting."

WORLD BOOK, INC.

180 N. LaSalle St., Suite 900, Chicago IL 60601. (312)729-5800. **Fax:** (312)729-5600. **E-mail:** service@worldbook.com. **Website:** www.worldbook.com. World Book, Inc. (publisher of The World Book Encyclopedia), publishes reference sources and nonfiction series for children and young adults in the areas of science, mathematics, English-language skills, basic academic and social skills, social studies, history, and health and fitness. "We publish print and non-print material appropriate for children ages 3-14. WB does not publish fiction, poetry, or wordless picture books."

NONFICTION Young readers: animal, arts/crafts, careers, concept, geography, health, reference. Middle readers: animal, arts/crafts, careers, geography, health, history, hobbies, how-to, nature/environment, reference, science. Young adult: arts/crafts, careers, geography, health, history, hobbies, how-to, nature/environment, reference, science.

HOW TO CONTACT Query. Responds to queries in 2 months. Publishes book 18 months after acceptance.

ILLUSTRATION Works with 10-30 illustrators/year. Illustrations only: Query with samples. Responds only if interested. Samples returned with SASE; samples filed "if extra copies and if interested."

PHOTOGRAPHY Buys stock and assigns work. Needs broad spectrum; editorial concept, specific natural, physical and social science spectrum. Model/property releases required; captions required. Submit cover letter, résumé, promo piece (color and b&w).

TERMS Payment negotiated on project-by-project basis.

WORLD WEAVER PRESS

Website: www.worldweaverpress.com. **Contact:** WWP Editors. World Weaver Press publishes digital and print editions of speculative fiction at various lengths for adult, young adult, and new adult audiences. "We believe in great storytelling." **Publishes 6-9 titles/year. 95% from unagented writers.**

FICTION "We believe that publishing speculative fiction isn't just printing words on the page — it's the act of weaving brand new worlds. Seeking speculative fiction in many varieties: protagonists who have strength, not fainting spells; intriguing worlds with well-developed settings; characters that are to die for (we'd rather find ourselves in love than just in lust)." Full list of interests on website. Not currently open to full-length fiction. Check anthology submission guidelines for short fiction calls.

HOW TO CONTACT Not currently open for queries. Full guidelines will be updated approximately one month before queries reopen. Frequently open for submissions for themed short story anthologies. Check website for details. Responds to query letters within 3 weeks. Responses to mss requests take longer. Publishes ms 6-24 months after acceptance.

TERMS Average royalty rate of 39% net on all editions. No advance. Catalog online. Guidelines on website.

WORTHYKIDS

Hachette Book Group, 6100 Tower Circle, Suite 210, Franklin TN 37067. (615) 221-0996. **E-mail:** idealsinfo@hbgusa.com. **Website:** https://www.worthykids.com/. "WorthyKids is an imprint of Hachette Book Group and publishes 20-30 new children's titles a year, primarily for 2-8 year-olds. Our backlist includes more than 400 titles, including The Berenstain Bears, VeggieTales, and Frosty the Snowman. We publish picture books, activity books, board books, and novelty/sound books covering a wide array of topics, such as Bible stories, holidays, early learning, history, family relationships, and values. Our bestselling titles include *The Story of Christmas, The Story of Easter, The Sparkle Box, Seaman's Journal, How Do I Love You?, God Made You Special, The Berenstain Bears' Please and Thank You Book*, and *My Daddy and I*. Through our dedication to publishing high-quality and engaging books, we never forget our obligation to our littlest readers to help create those special moments with books."

FICTION WorthyKids publishes fiction and nonfiction picture books for children ages 2 to 8. Subjects include holiday, faith/inspirational, family values, and patriotic themes; relationships and values; and general fiction. Picture book mss should be no longer than 800 words. Board book mss should be no longer than 250 words.

HOW TO CONTACT Editors will review complete mss only; please do not send query letters or proposals. Previous publications, relevant qualifications or background, and a brief synopsis of your manuscript may be included in a cover letter. Please send copies only—we cannot be responsible for an original ms. Include your name, address, and phone number or e-mail address on every page. Do not include original art or photographs. We do not accept digital submissions via e-mail or other electronic means. Send complete mss to: WorthyKids, Attn: SUBMISSIONS, 6100 Tower Circle, Suite 210, Franklin TN 37067. Due to the high volume of submissions, we are only able to respond to unsolicited manuscripts of interest to our publishing program. We cannot discuss submissions by telephone or in person and we cannot provide detailed editorial feedback.

ZUMAYA PUBLICATIONS, LLC

3209 S. Interstate 35, Austin TX 78741. (512)333-4055. **Fax:** (512)276-6745. **E-mail:** business@zumayapublishing.com. **Website:** www.zumayapublications.com. **Contact:** Elizabeth K. Burton. Zumaya Publications is a digitally-based micro-press publishing mainly in on-demand trade paperback and e-book formats in an effort to reduce environmental impact. "We currently offer approximately 190 fiction titles in the mystery, SF/F, historical, romance, LGBTQ, horror, and occult genres in adult, young adult, and middle reader categories. In 2016, we launched our graphic and illustrated novel imprint, Zumaya Fabled Ink. We publish approximately 10-15 new titles annually, at least five of which are from new authors. We do *not* publish erotica or graphic erotic romance at this time. We accept only electronic queries; all others will be discarded unread. A working knowledge of computers and relevant software is a necessity, as our production process is completely digital." Publishes trade paperback and electronic originals. **Publishes 10-15 titles/year. 5% of books from first-time authors. 100% from unagented writers.**

Zumaya was publishing diversity before it became a thing, and is always looking for fiction that presents the wonderful multiplicity of cultures in the world in ways that can lower the divisions that are too often keeping us from understanding one another. We also love books about people who are often either overlooked altogether or presented in clichéd ways. A romance between two 80-year-olds? Bring it on. A police procedural where the officers have happy home lives? Yes, please. We like the idea of having fiction that reflects the manifold realities of people everywhere, even if the world they inhabit resides only in the author's imagination.

FICTION "We are open to all genres, particularly GLBT and YA/middle grade, historical and western, New Age/inspirational (no overtly Christian materials, please), non-category romance, thrillers. We encourage people to review what we've already published so as to avoid sending us more of the same, at least, insofar as the plot is concerned. While we're always looking for good mysteries, especially cozies, mysteries with historical settings, and police procedurals, we want original concepts rather than slightly altered versions of what we've already published. We do not publish erotica or graphically erotic romance at this time." Does not want erotica, graphically erotic romance, experimental, literary (unless it fits into one of our established imprints).

NONFICTION "The easiest way to figure out what we're looking for is to look at what we've already done. Our main nonfiction interests are in collections of true ghost stories, ones that have been investigated or thoroughly documented, memoirs that address specific regions and eras from a 'normal person' viewpoint and books on the craft of writing. That doesn't mean we won't consider something else."

HOW TO CONTACT A copy of our rules of submission is posted on our website and can be downloaded. They are rules rather than guidelines and should be read carefully before submitting. It will save everyone time and frustration. Electronic query only. 1,000 queries; 50 mss requested/year. Responds in 3 months to queries and proposals; 6 months to mss. Publishes book 2 years after acceptance.

TERMS Pay 20% of net on paperbacks, net defined as cover price less printing and other associated costs; 50% of net on all e-books. Does not pay advance. Catalog online. Guidelines online. "We do not accept hard-copy queries or submissions."

TIPS "We're catering to readers who may have loved last year's best seller but not enough to want to read 10 more just like it. Have something different. If it does not fit standard pigeonholes, that's a plus. On the other hand, it has to have an audience. And if you're not prepared to work with us on promotion and marketing, particularly via social media, it would be better to look elsewhere."

CANADIAN & INTERNATIONAL BOOK PUBLISHERS

While the United States is considered the largest market in children's publishing, the children's publishing world is by no means strictly dominated by the United States. After all, the most prestigious children's book extravaganza in the world occurs each year in Bologna, Italy, at the Bologna Children's Book Fair and some of the world's most beloved characters were born in the United Kingdom (i.e., Winnie-the-Pooh and Mr. Potter).

In this section you'll find book publishers from English-speaking countries around the world from Canada, Australia, New Zealand, and the United Kingdom. The listings in this section look just like the United States Book Publishers section; and the publishers listed are dedicated to the same goal—publishing great books for children.

Like always, be sure to study each listing and research each publisher carefully before submitting material. Determine whether a publisher is open to United States or international submissions, as many publishers accept submissions only from residents of their own country. Some publishers accept illustration samples from foreign artists, but do not accept manuscripts from foreign writers. Illustrators do have a slight edge in this category as many illustrators generate commissions from all around the globe. Visit publishers' websites to be certain they publish the sort of work you do. Visit online bookstores to see if publishers' books are available there. Write or email to request catalogs and submission guidelines.

When mailing requests or submissions out of the United States, remember that United States postal stamps are useless on your SASE. Always include International Reply Coupons (IRCs) with your SAE. Each IRC is good for postage for one letter. So if you want the publisher to return your manuscript or send a catalog, be sure to enclose enough IRCs to pay the postage..

As in the rest of *Children's Writer's & Illustrator's Market*, the maple leaf ✪ symbol identifies Canadian markets. Look for International ➲ symbol throughout *Children's Writer's &*

Illustrator's Market as well. Several of the Society of Children's Book Writers and Illustrator's (SCBWI) international conferences are listed in the Conferences & Workshops section along with other events in locations around the globe. Look for more information about SCBWI's international chapters on the organization's website, www.scbwi.org.

ALLEN & UNWIN

406 Albert St., East Melbourne VIC 3002, Australia. (61)(3)9665-5000. **E-mail:** fridaypitch@allenandunwin.com. **Website:** www.allenandunwin.com. Allen & Unwin publish over 80 new books for children and young adults each year, many of these from established authors and illustrators. "However, we know how difficult it can be for new writers to get their work in front of publishers, which is why we've decided to extend our innovative and pioneering Friday Pitch service to emerging writers for children and young adults."

TERMS Guidelines online.

ANDERSEN PRESS

20 Vauxhall Bridge Rd., London SW1V 2SA, United Kingdom. **E-mail:** anderseneditorial@penguinrandomhouse.co.uk. **Website:** www.andersenpress.co.uk. Andersen Press is a specialist children's publisher. "We publish picture books, for which the required text would be approximately 500 words (maximum 1,000), juvenile fiction for which the text would be approximately 3,000-5,000 words and older fiction up to 75,000 words. We do not publish adult fiction, nonfiction, poetry, or short story anthologies."

HOW TO CONTACT Send all submissions by post: Query and full ms for picture books; synopsis and 3 chapters for longer fiction.

TERMS Guidelines online.

ANNICK PRESS, LTD.

15 Patricia Ave., Toronto ON M2M 1H9, Canada. (416)221-4802. **Fax:** (416)221-8400. **Website:** www.annickpress.com. **Contact:** The Editors. Annick Press maintains a commitment to high quality books that entertain and challenge. Our publications share fantasy and stimulate imagination, while encouraging children to trust their judgment and abilities. *Does not accept unsolicited mss.* Publishes picture books, juvenile and YA fiction and nonfiction; specializes in trade books. **Publishes 25 titles/year. 20% of books from first-time authors. 80-85% from unagented writers.**

FICTION Publisher of children's books. Not accepting picture books at this time.

HOW TO CONTACT 5,000 queries received/year. 3,000 mss received/year. Publishes a book 2 years after acceptance.

TERMS Pays authors royalty of 5-12% based on retail price. Offers advances (average amount: $3,000). Pays illustrators royalty of 5% minimum. Book catalog and guidelines online.

THE BRUCEDALE PRESS

P.O. Box 2259, Port Elgin ON N0H 2C0, Canada. (519)832-6025. **E-mail:** info@brucedalepress.ca. **Website:** brucedalepress.ca. The Brucedale Press publishes books and other materials of regional interest and merit, as well as literary, historical, and/or pictorial works. Accepts works by Canadian authors only. Book submissions reviewed November to January. Submissions to *The Leaf Journal* accepted in September and March only. Manuscripts must be in English and thoroughly proofread before being sent. Use Canadian spellings and style. Publishes hardcover and trade paperback originals. **Publishes 3 titles/year. 75% of books from first-time authors. 100% from unagented writers.**

HOW TO CONTACT Publishes book 1 year after acceptance.

TERMS Pays royalty. Book catalog online. "Unless responding to an invitation to submit, query first by Canada Post with outline and sample chapter to book-length manuscripts. Send full manuscripts for work intended for children." Guidelines online.

TIPS "Our focus is very regional. In reading submissions, I look for quality writing with a strong connection to the Queen's Bush area of Ontario. All authors should visit our website, get a catalog, and read our books before submitting. Except for contest entries, we do not review manuscripts sent from outside Canada."

CHILD'S PLAY (INTERNATIONAL) LTD.

Child's Play, Ashworth Rd. Bridgemead, Swindon, Wiltshire SN5 7YD, United Kingdom. 01793 616286. **E-mail:** neil@childs-play.com; office@childs-play.com. **Website:** www.childs-play.com. **Contact:** Sue Baker, Neil Burden, manuscript acquisitions. Specializes in nonfiction, fiction, educational material, multicultural material. Produces 30 picture books/year; 10 young readers/year. "A child's early years are more important than any other. This is when children learn most about the world around them and the language they need to survive and grow. Child's Play aims to create exactly the right material for this all-important time." **Publishes 40 titles/year.**

"Due to a backlog of submissions, Child's Play is currently no longer able to accept anymore manuscripts."

FICTION Picture books: adventure, animal, concept, contemporary, folktales, multicultural, nature/environment. Young readers: adventure, animal, anthology, concept, contemporary, folktales, humor, multicultural, nature/environment, poetry. Average word length: picture books—1,500; young readers—2,000.

NONFICTION Picture books: activity books, animal, concept, multicultural, music/dance, nature/environment, science. Young readers: activity books, animal, concept, multicultural, music/dance, nature/environment, science. Average word length: picture books—2,000; young readers—3,000.

HOW TO CONTACT Publishes book 2 years after acceptance.

ILLUSTRATION Accepts material from international illustrators. Works with 10 illustrators/year. Uses color artwork only. Reviews ms/illustration packages. For ms/illustration packages: Query or submit ms/illustration packages to Sue Baker, editor. Reviews work for future assignments. If interested in illustrating future titles, query with samples, CD, website address. Submit samples to Annie Kubler, art director. Responds in 10 weeks. Samples not returned. Samples filed.

TIPS "Look at our website to see the kind of work we do before sending. Do not send cartoons. We do not publish novels. We do publish lots of books with pictures of babies/toddlers."

CHRISTIAN FOCUS PUBLICATIONS

Geanies House, Fearn, Tain Ross-shire Scotland IV20 1TW, United Kingdom. (44)1862-871-011. **Fax:** (44)1862-871-699. **E-mail:** submissions@christianfocus.com. **Website:** www.christianfocus.com. **Contact:** Director of Publishing. Specializes in Christian material, nonfiction, fiction, educational material. **Publishes 22-32 titles/year. 2% of books from first-time authors.**

FICTION Picture books, young readers, adventure, history, religion. Middle readers: adventure, problem novels, religion. Young adult/teens: adventure, history, problem novels, religion. Average word length: young readers—5,000; middle readers—max 10,000; young adult/teen—max 20,000.

NONFICTION All levels: activity books, biography, history, religion, science. Average word length: picture books—5,000; young readers—5,000; middle readers—5,000-10,000; young adult/teens—10,000-20,000.

HOW TO CONTACT Query or submit outline/synopsis and 3 sample chapters. Include Author Information Form from site with submission. Will consider electronic submissions and previously published work. Responds to queries in 2 weeks; mss in 3-6 months. Publishes book 1 year after acceptance.

ILLUSTRATION Works on 15-20 potential projects. "Some artists are chosen to do more than one. Some projects just require a cover illustration, some require full color spreads, others black and white line art." **Contact:** Catherine Mackenzie, children's editor. Responds in 2 weeks only if interested. Samples are not returned.

PHOTOGRAPHY "We only purchase royalty free photos from particular photographic associations. However portfolios can be presented to our designer." **Contact:** Daniel van Straaten. Photographers should send cover letter, résumé, published samples, client list, portfolio.

TIPS "Be aware of the international market as regards writing style/topics as well as illustration styles. Our company sells rights to European as well as Asian countries. Fiction sales are not as good as they were. Christian fiction for youngsters is not a product that is performing well in comparison to nonfiction such as Christian biography/Bible stories/church history, etc."

CURIOUS FOX

Brunel Rd., Houndmills, Basingstoke Hants RG21 6XS, United Kingdom. **E-mail:** submissions@curious-fox.com. **Website:** www.curious-fox.com. "Do you love telling good stories? If so, we'd like to hear from you. Curious Fox is on the lookout for UK-based authors, whether new talent or established authors with exciting ideas. We take submissions for books aimed at ages 3-young adult. If you have story ideas that are bold, fun, and imaginative, then please do get in touch!"

HOW TO CONTACT "Send your submission via e-mail to submissions@curious-fox.com. Include the following in the body of the email, not as attachments: Sample chapters, résumé, list of previous publishing credits, if applicable. We will respond only if your writing samples fit our needs."

ILLUSTRATION Please submit any illustrations/artwork by e-mail.

TERMS Guidelines online.

FERNWOOD PUBLISHING, LTD.

32 Ocenavista Ln., Black Point NS B0J 1B0, Canada. (902)857-1388. **Fax:** (902)857-1328. **E-mail:** info@fernpub.ca. **Website:** www.fernwoodpublishing.ca. **Contact:** Errol Sharpe, publisher. "Fernwood's objective is to publish critical works which challenge existing scholarship. We are a political and academic publisher. We publish critical books in the social sciences and humanities and for the trade market." Publishes trade paperback originals. **Publishes 35-40 titles/year. 40% of books from first-time authors. 100% from unagented writers.**

FICTION Roseway publishes fiction, young adult fiction, children's fiction and autobiography that deals with social justice issues.

NONFICTION "Our main focus is in the social sciences and humanities, emphasizing Indigenous resistance and resurgence, politics, capitalism, political economy, women, gender, sexuality, crime and law, international development and social work-for use in college and university courses."

HOW TO CONTACT Guidelines online. Submit proposal package, outline, sample chapters. 120 queries received/year. 50 mss received/year. Responds in 6 weeks to proposals. Publishes ms 12-18 months after acceptance.

TERMS Pays 7-10% royalty on wholesale price. Pays advance. Guidelines online.

FITZHENRY & WHITESIDE LTD.

195 Allstate Pkwy., Markham ON L3R 4T8, Canada. (905)477-9700. **Fax:** (905)477-2834. **E-mail:** godwit@fitzhenry.ca. **Website:** www.fitzhenry.ca/. Emphasis on Canadian authors and illustrators, subject or perspective. "Until further notice, we will not be accepting unsolicited submissions." **Publishes 15 titles/year. 10% of books from first-time authors.**

HOW TO CONTACT Publishes book 1-2 years after acceptance.

ILLUSTRATION Works with approximately 10 illustrators/year. Reviews ms/illustration packages from artists. Submit outline and sample illustration (copy). Illustrations only: Query with samples and promo sheet. Samples not returned unless requested.

PHOTOGRAPHY Buys photos from freelancers. Buys stock and assigns work. Captions required. Uses b&w 8×10 prints; 35mm and 4×5 transparencies, 300+ dpi digital images. Submit stock photo list and promo piece.

TERMS Pays authors 8-10% royalty with escalations. Offers "respectable" advances for picture books, split 50/50 between author and illustrator. Pays illustrators by project and royalty. Pays photographers per photo.

TIPS "We respond to quality."

FLYING EYE BOOKS

62 Great Eastern St., London EC2A 3QR, United Kingdom. (44)(0)207-033-4430. **E-mail:** picturbksubs@nobrow.net. **Website:** www.flyingeyebooks.com. Flying Eye Books is the children's imprint of award-winning visual publishing house Nobrow. FEB seeks to retain the same attention to detail and excellence in illustrated content as its parent publisher, but with a focus on the craft of children's storytelling and nonfiction.

TERMS Guidelines online.

FRANCES LINCOLN CHILDREN'S BOOKS

Frances Lincoln, 74-77 White Lion St., London N1 9PF, United Kingdom. (44)(20)7284-4009. **Website:** www.franceslincoln.com. "Our company was founded by Frances Lincoln in 1977. We published our first books two years later, and we have been creating illustrated books of the highest quality ever since, with special emphasis on gardening, walking and the outdoors, art, architecture, design and landscape. In 1983, we started to publish illustrated books for children. Since then we have won many awards and prizes with both fiction and nonfiction children's books." **Publishes 100 titles/year. 6% of books from first-time authors.**

FICTION Average word length: picture books—1,000; young readers—9,788; middle readers—20,653; young adults—35,407.

NONFICTION Average word length: picture books—1,000; middle readers—29,768.

HOW TO CONTACT Query by e-mail. Responds in 6 weeks to mss. Publishes book 18 months after acceptance.

ILLUSTRATION Works with approx 56 illustrators/year. Uses both color and b&w. Reviews ms/illustration packages from artist. Sample illustrations. Illustrations only: Query with samples. Responds only if interested. Samples are returned with SASE. Samples are kept on file only if interested.

PHOTOGRAPHY Buys stock images and assign work. Uses children, multicultural photos. Submit cover letter, published samples, or portfolio.

FRANKLIN WATTS

Hachette Children's Books, Carmelite House, 50 Victoria Embankment, London EC4Y 0DZ, United Kingdom. (44)(20)7873-6000. **Fax:** (44)(20)7873-6024. **Website:** www.franklinwatts.co.uk. Franklin Watts is well known for its high quality and attractive information books, which support the National Curriculum and stimulate children's enquiring minds. *Generally does not accept unsolicited mss.*

GROUNDWOOD BOOKS

128 Sterling Rd., Lower Level, Attention: Submissions, Toronto ON M6R 2B7, Canada. (416)363-4343. **Fax:** (416)363-1017. **E-mail:** submissions@groundwoodbooks.com. **Website:** groundwoodbooks.com. "We are always looking for new authors of novel-length fiction for children of all ages. Our mandate is to publish high-quality, character-driven literary fiction. We do not generally publish stories with an obvious moral or message, or genre fiction such as thrillers or fantasy." Publishes 19 picture books/year; 2 young readers/year; 3 middle readers/year; 3 young adult titles/year, approximately 2 nonfiction titles/year.

HOW TO CONTACT Submit a cover letter, synopsis and sample chapters via e-mail. "Due to the large number of submissions we receive, Groundwood regrets that we cannot accept unsolicited manuscripts for picture books." Responds to mss in 6-8 months.

TERMS Offers advances. Visit website for guidelines.

GUERNICA EDITIONS

287 Templemead Drive, Hamilton ON L8W 2W4, Canada. (905)599-5304. **E-mail:** michaelmirolla@guernicaeditions.com. **Website:** www.guernicaeditions.com. **Contact:** Michael Mirolla, editor/publisher (poetry, nonfiction, short stories, novels). Guernica Editions is a literary press that produces works of poetry, fiction and nonfiction often by writers who are ignored by the mainstream. "We feature an imprint (MiroLand) which accepts memoirs, how-to books, graphic novels, and genre fiction." A new imprint, Guernica World Editions, features writers who are non-Canadian. *Please note: special conditions apply in agreements made with authors who are non-Canadian. Please query first.* Publishes trade paperback originals and reprints. **Publishes 40-50 titles/year. 20% of books from first-time authors. 99% from unagented writers.**

FICTION "We wish to open up into the literary fiction world and focus less on poetry."

HOW TO CONTACT E-mail queries only. Query by e-mail only. Several hundred mss received/year. Responds in 1 week to queries/proposals; 6-8 months to mss. Publishes 24-36 months after acceptance.

TERMS Canadian authors: Pays 10% royalty on either cover or retail price. Non-Canadian authors: to be negotiated. Canadian authors: Pays $450-750 advance. Non-Canadian authors: to be negotiated. Book catalog online. Queries and submissions accepted via e-mail January 1-April 30.

HERITAGE HOUSE PUBLISHING CO., LTD.

103-1075 Pendergast St., Victoria BC V8V 0A1, Canada. (250)360-0829. **E-mail:** heritage@heritagehouse.ca. **Website:** www.heritagehouse.ca. **Contact:** Lara Kordic, senior editor. "Heritage House publishes books that celebrate the historical and cultural heritage of Canada, particularly Western Canada and the Pacific Northwest. We also publish some children's titles, titles of national interest and a series of books aimed at young and casual readers, called *Amazing Stories*. We accept simultaneous submissions, but indicate on your query that it is a simultaneous submission." Publishes mostly trade paperback and some hardcovers. **Publishes 25-30 titles/year. 50% of books from first-time authors. 90% from unagented writers.**

HOW TO CONTACT Query by e-mail. Include synopsis, outline, 2-3 sample chapters with indication of illustrative material available, and marketing strategy. 200 queries; 100 mss received/year. Responds in 6 months to queries. Publishes book within 1-2 years of acceptance.

TERMS Pays 12-15% royalty on net proceeds. Advances are rarely paid. Catalog and guidelines online.

TIPS "Our books appeal to residents of and visitors to the northwest quadrant of the continent. We're looking for good stories and good storytellers. We focus on work by Canadian authors."

KIDS CAN PRESS

25 Dockside Dr., Toronto ON M5A 0B5, Canada. (416)479-7000. **Fax:** (416)960-5437. **Website:** www.kidscanpress.com. **Contact:** Corus Quay, acquisitions.

Kids Can Press is currently accepting unsolicited mss from Canadian adult authors only.

FICTION Picture books, young readers: concepts. "We do not accept young adult fiction or fantasy novels for any age." Adventure, animal, contemporary, folktales, history, humor, multicultural, nature/environment, special needs, sports, suspense/mystery. Average word length: picture books 1,000-2,000; young readers 750-1,500; middle readers 10,000-15,000; young adults over 15,000.

NONFICTION Picture books: activity books, animal, arts/crafts, biography, careers, concept, health, history, hobbies, how-to, multicultural, nature/environment, science, social issues, special needs, sports. Young readers: activity books, animal, arts/crafts, biography, careers, concept, history, hobbies, how-to, multicultural. Middle readers: cooking, music/dance. Average word length: picture books 500-1,250; young readers 750-2,000; middle readers 5,000-15,000.

HOW TO CONTACT Submit outline/synopsis and 2-3 sample chapters. For picture books submit complete ms. Responds in 6 months only if interested. Publishes book 18-24 months after acceptance.

ILLUSTRATION Works with 40 illustrators/year. Reviews ms/illustration packages from artists. Send color copies of illustration portfolio, cover letter outlining other experience. Contact: Art Director. Illustrations only: Send tearsheets, color photocopies. Responds only if interested.

LANTANA PUBLISHING

London, United Kingdom. **E-mail:** info@lantanapublishing.com. **Website:** www.lantanapublishing.com. Lantana Publishing is a young, independent publishing house producing inclusive picture books for children. "Our mission is to publish outstanding writing for young readers by giving new and aspiring BAME authors and illustrators a platform to publish in the UK and by working with much-loved authors and illustrators from around the world. Lantana's award-winning titles have so far received high praise, described as 'dazzling', 'delectable', 'enchanting' and 'exquisite' by bloggers and reviewers. They have been nominated for a Kate Greenaway Medal (three times), received starred Kirkus reviews (three times), been shortlisted for the Teach Early Years Awards, the North Somerset Teachers' Book Awards, and the Sheffield Children's Books Awards, and won the Children's Africana Best Book Award. Lantana's founder, Alice Curry, is the recipient of the 2017 Kim Scott Walwyn Prize for women in publishing."

FICTION "We primarily publish picture books for 4-8 year-olds with text no longer than 500 words (and we prefer 200-400 words). We love writing that is contemporary and fun. We particularly like stories with modern-day settings in the UK or around the world, especially if they feature BAME families, and stories that lend themselves to great illustration."

NONFICTION "We accept some nonfiction content for the 7-11 range if it is international in scope."

HOW TO CONTACT Responds in 6 weeks.

TERMS Pays royalty. Pays advance. Guidelines online.

MANOR HOUSE PUBLISHING, INC.

452 Cottingham Crescent, Ancaster ON L9G 3V6, Canada. (905)648-2193. **E-mail:** mbdavie@manor-house.biz. **Website:** www.manor-house-publishing.com. **Contact:** Mike Davie, president (novels and nonfiction). Manor House is currently looking for new fully edited, ready-to-run titles to complete our spring-fall release lineup. This is a rare opportunity for authors, including self-published, to have existing or ready titles picked up by Manor House and made available to retailers throughout the world, while our network of rights agents provide more potential revenue streams via foreign language rights sales. We are currently looking for titles that are ready or nearly ready for publishing to be released this season. Such titles should be written by Canadian citizens residing in Canada and should be profitable or with strong market sales potential to allow full cost recovery and profit for publisher and author. Of primary interest are business and self-help titles along with other nonfiction, including new age. We will also consider non-Canadian writers provided the manuscript meets literary standards and profitability is a certainty. Publishes hardcover, trade paperback, and mass market paperback originals (and reprints if they meet specific criteria—best to inquire with publisher). **Publishes 5-6 titles/year. 90% of books from first-time authors. 90% from unagented writers.**

FICTION Stories should mainly be by Canadian authors residing in Canada, have Canadian settings and characters should be Canadian, but content should have universal appeal to wide audience. In some cases, we will consider publishing non-Canadian fiction authors—provided they demonstrate publishing their book will be profitable for author and publisher. We will also consider non-Canadian writers provided the manuscript meets literary standards and profitability is a certainty.

NONFICTION "We are currently looking for titles that are ready or nearly ready for publishing. Such titles should be written by Canadian citizens residing in Canada and should be profitable or with strong market sales potential to allow full cost recovery and profit for publisher and author. Of primary interest are Business and self-help titles along with other nonfiction, including new age. We are also open to publishing non-Canadian authors (nonfiction works only)—provided non-Canadian authors can further provide us with a very good indication of demand for their book (Eg: actual or expected advance book orders from speaker venues, corporations, agencies or authors on a non-returnable basis) so we are assured the title will likely be a profitable venture for both author and publisher."

HOW TO CONTACT Query via e-mail. Submit proposal package, clips, bio, 3 sample chapters. Submit complete ms. 30 queries; 20 mss received/year. Queries and mss to be sent by e-mail only. "We will respond in 30 days if interested—if not, there is no response. Please do not follow up unless asked to do so." Publishes book 6 mos to 1 year after acceptance.

TERMS Pays 10% royalty on retail price. Book catalog online. Guidelines available.

TIPS "Our audience includes everyone-the general public/mass audience. Self-edit your work first, make sure it is well written and well edited with strong Canadian content and/or content of universal appeal (preferably with a Canadian connection of some kind). We will also consider non-Canadian writers provided the manuscript meets literary standards and profitability is a certainty."

ON THE MARK PRESS

15 Dairy Ave., Napanee ON K7R 1M4, Canada. (800)463-6367. **Fax:** (800)290-3631. **Website:** www.onthemarkpress.com. Publishes books for the Canadian curriculum. **15% of books from first-time authors.**

PHOTOGRAPHY Buys stock images.

ORCA BOOK PUBLISHERS

1016 Balmoral Rd., Victoria BC V8T 1A8, Canada. (800)210-5277. **Fax:** (877)408-1551. **E-mail:** orca@orcabook.com. **Website:** www.orcabook.com. **Contact:** Amy Collins, editor (picture books); Sarah Harvey, editor (young readers); Andrew Wooldridge, editor (juvenile and teen fiction); Bob Tyrrell, publisher (YA, teen); Ruth Linka, associate editor (rapid reads). Only publishes Canadian authors. Publishes hardcover and trade paperback originals, and mass market paperback originals and reprints. **Publishes 30-50 titles/year. 20% of books from first-time authors. 75% from unagented writers.**

FICTION Picture books: animals, contemporary, history, nature/environment. Middle readers: contemporary, history, fantasy, nature/environment, problem novels, graphic novels. Young adults: adventure, contemporary, hi-lo (Orca Soundings), history, multicultural, nature/environment, problem novels, suspense/mystery, graphic novels. Average word length: picture books—500-1,500; middle readers—20,000-35,000; young adult—25,000-45,000; Orca Soundings—13,000-15,000; Orca Currents—13,000-15,000. No romance, science fiction.

NONFICTION Only publishes Canadian authors.

HOW TO CONTACT Query with SASE. Submit proposal package, outline, clips, 2-5 sample chapters, SASE. 2,500 queries; 1,000 mss received/year. Responds in 1 month to queries; 2 months to proposals and mss. Publishes book 12-18 months after acceptance.

ILLUSTRATION Works with 8-10 illustrators/year. Reviews ms/illustration packages from artists. Submit ms with 3-4 pieces of final art. "Reproductions only, no original art please." Illustrations only: Query with samples; provide résumé, online portfolio. Responds in 2 months. Samples returned with SASE; samples filed. 4 to 8 copies, digital proofs, tear sheets, press sheets.

TERMS Pays 10% royalty. Book catalog for 8½x11 SASE. Guidelines online.

TIPS "Our audience is students in grades K-12. Know our books, and know the market."

PAJAMA PRESS

181 Carlaw Ave., Suite 207, Toronto ON M4M 2S1, Canada. 4164662222. **E-mail:** annfeatherstone@pajamapress.ca. **Website:** pajamapress.ca. **Contact:** Ann Featherstone, senior editor. "We publish picture

books—both for the very young and for school-aged readers, as well as novels for middle grade readers and contemporary or historical fiction for young adults aged 12+. Our nonfiction titles typically contain a strong narrative element. Pajama Press is also looking for mss from authors of diverse backgrounds. Stories about immigrants are of special interest." **Publishes 15-20 titles/year. 20% of books from first-time authors. 80% from unagented writers.**

FICTION Vampire novels; romance (except as part of a literary novel); fiction with overt political or religious messages

NONFICTION "Our nonfiction titles typically contain a strong narrative element; for example, juvenile biographies and narratives about wildlife rescue." Does not want how-to books, activity books, books for adults, psychology books, educational resources.

HOW TO CONTACT Pajama Press considers digital queries accompanied by picture books texts or the first 3 chapters of novel length projects. Your query should include an overview of your submission and some information about your writing background. Pajama Press prefers not to look at simultaneous submissions. Please notify us if you are submitting your project to another publisher. Please e-mail your queries and submissions to annfeatherstone@pajamapress.ca. In the interest of saving trees, Pajama Press does not accept physical mss. Any mss mailed to our office will be recycled unopened. 1,000 Responds in 6 weeks. Publishes ms 1-3 years after acceptance.

TERMS Pays advance. Guidelines online.

RANDOM HOUSE CHILDREN'S PUBLISHERS UK

20 Vauxhall Bridge Rd., London SW1V 2SA, United Kingdom. **Website:** www.randomhousechildrens.co.uk. *Only interested in agented material.* **Publishes 250 titles/year.**

FICTION Picture books: adventure, animal, anthology, contemporary, fantasy, folktales, humor, multicultural, nature/environment, poetry, suspense/mystery. Young readers: adventure, animal, anthology, contemporary, fantasy, folktales, humor, multicultural, nature/environment, poetry, sports, suspense/mystery. Middle readers: adventure, animal, anthology, contemporary, fantasy, folktales, humor, multicultural, nature/environment, problem novels, romance, sports, suspense/mystery. Young adults: adventure, contemporary, fantasy, humor, multicultural, nature/environment, problem novels, romance, science fiction, suspense/mystery. Average word length: picture books—800; young readers—1,500-6,000; middle readers—10,000-15,000; young adults—20,000-45,000.

ILLUSTRATION Works with 50 illustrators/year. Reviews ms/illustration packages from artists. Query with samples. Contact: Margaret Hope. Samples are returned with SASE (IRC).

PHOTOGRAPHY Buys photos from freelancers. Contact: Margaret Hope. Photo captions required. Uses color or b&w prints. Submit cover letter, published samples.

TERMS Pays authors royalty. Offers advances.

TIPS "Although Random House is a big publisher, each imprint only publishes a small number of books each year. Our lists for the next few years are already full. Any book we take on from a previously unpublished author has to be truly exceptional. Manuscripts should be sent to us via literary agents."

RONSDALE PRESS

3350 W. 21st Ave., Vancouver BC V6S 1G7, Canada. (604)738-4688. **Fax:** (604)731-4548. **Website:** ronsdalepress.com. **Contact:** Ronald B. Hatch (fiction, poetry, nonfiction, social commentary); Veronica Hatch (YA novels and short stories). "Ronsdale Press is a Canadian literary publishing house that publishes 12 books each year, four of which are young adult titles. Of particular interest are books involving children exploring and discovering new aspects of Canadian history or Canadian social issues." Publishes trade paperback originals. **Publishes 12 titles/year. 40% of books from first-time authors. 95% from unagented writers.**

FICTION Young adults: Canadian novels. Average word length: middle readers and young adults—50,000 to 70,000. fantasy, science fiction.

NONFICTION Middle readers, young adults: animal, biography, history, multicultural, social issues. Average word length: young readers—90; middle readers—90. "We publish a number of books for children and young adults in the age 10 to 15 range. We are especially interested in YA historical novels. We regret that we can no longer publish picture books."

HOW TO CONTACT Submit complete MS if you are certain it is right for Ronsdale Press. Submit complete ms if you feel it is perfect for Ronsdale Press. If not perfect, submit the first 60 pages. An e-mail query of one page with a bio and writing credits will be answered quickly 40 queries; 800 mss received/year. Responds to queries in 2 weeks; mss in 2 months. Publishes book 1 year after acceptance.

ILLUSTRATION Works with 2 illustrators/year. Reviews ms/illustration packages from artists. Requires only cover art. Responds in 2 weeks. Samples returned with SASE. Originals returned to artist at job's completion.

TERMS Pays 10% royalty on retail price. Book catalog for #10 SASE. Guidelines online. Please, no first drafts or uneditited drafts.

TIPS "Ronsdale Press is a literary publishing house, based in Vancouver, and dedicated to publishing books from across Canada, books that give Canadians new insights into themselves and their country. We aim to publish the best Canadian writers."

SCHOLASTIC CHILDREN'S BOOKS UK

Euston House, 24 Eversholt St., London VI NW1 1DB, United Kingdom. **E-mail:** contactus@scholastic.co.uk. **Website:** www.scholastic.co.uk.

Scholastic UK does not accept unsolicited submissions. Unsolicited illustrations are accepted, but please do not send any original artwork as it will not be returned.

TIPS "Getting work published can be a frustrating process, and it's often best to be prepared for disappointment, but don't give up."

SCRIBE PUBLICATIONS

18-20 Edward St., Brunswick VIC 3056, Australia. (61) (3)9388-8780. **E-mail:** info@scribepub.com.au. **Website:** www.scribepublications.com.au. **Contact:** Anna Thwaites. Scribe has been operating as a wholly independent trade-publishing house for almost 40 years. What started off in 1976 as a desire on publisher Henry Rosenbloom's part to publish 'serious non-fiction' as a one-man band has turned into a multi-award-winning company with 20 staff members in two locations—Melbourne, Australia and London, England —and a scout in New York. Scribe publishes over 65 nonfiction and fiction titles annually in Australia and about 40 in the United Kingdom. "We currently have acquiring editors working in both our Melbourne and London offices. We spend each day sifting through submissions and manuscripts from around the world, and commissioning and editing local titles, in an uncompromising pursuit of the best books we can find, help create, and deliver to readers. We love what we do, and we hope you will, too." **Publishes 70 titles/year. 10-20% from unagented writers.**

HOW TO CONTACT Submit synopsis, sample chapters, CV. "Please refer first to our website before contacting us or submitting anything, because we explain there who we will accept proposals from."

TERMS Guidelines online.

TIPS "We are only able to consider unsolicited submissions if you have a demonstrated background of writing and publishing for general readers."

SECOND STORY PRESS

20 Maud St., Suite 401, Toronto ON M5V 2M5, Canada. (416)537-7850. **Fax:** (416)537-0588. **E-mail:** info@secondstorypress.ca. **Website:** www.secondstorypress.ca. "Please keep in mind that as a feminist press, we are looking for non-sexist, non-racist and non-violent stories, as well as historical fiction, chapter books, novels and biography."

FICTION Considers non-sexist, non-racist, and non-violent stories, as well as historical fiction, chapter books, picture books.

NONFICTION Picture books: biography.

HOW TO CONTACT Accepts appropriate material from residents of Canada only. "Send a synopsis and up to 3 sample chapters. If you are submitting a picture book you can send the entire manuscript. Illustrations are not necessary." No electronic submissions or queries. Guidelines on site.

SWEET CHERRY PUBLISHING

Unit 36, Vulcan Business Complex, Vulcan Rd., Leicestershire LE5 3EF, United Kingdom. **E-mail:** info@sweetcherrypublishing.com. **Website:** www.sweetcherrypublishing.com. Sweet Cherry Publishing is an independent publishing company based in Leicester. "We specialize in middle-grade series. Our aim is to provide children with compelling worlds and engaging characters that they will want to revisit again and again."

FICTION We are looking for inclusive and topical children's books.

ILLUSTRATION Freelance illustrators are welcome to submit via our website.

TERMS Offers one-time fee for work that is accepted. Send the first 3 chapters or 3,000 words along with a synopsis, author biography, and cover letter detailing your target audience and your plans for further books in the series.

TIPS "Submit a cover letter and a synopsis with 3 sample chapters via email. Please note that we do not accept submissions by post."

TAFELBERG PUBLISHERS

Imprint of NB Publishers, P.O. Box 879, Cape Town 8000, South Africa. (27)(21)406-3033. **Fax:** (27)(21)406-3812. **E-mail:** engela.reinke@nb.co.za. **Website:** www.tafelberg.com. **Contact:** Engela Reinke. General publisher best known for Afrikaans fiction, authoritative political works, children's/youth literature, and a variety of illustrated and nonillustrated nonfiction. **Publishes 10 titles/year.**

FICTION Picture books, young readers: animal, anthology, contemporary, fantasy, folktales, hi-lo, humor, multicultural, nature/environment, scient fiction, special needs. Middle readers, young adults: animal (middle reader only), contemporary, fantasy, hi-lo, humor, multicultural, nature/environment, problem novels, science fiction, special needs, sports, suspense/mystery. Average word length: picture books—1,500-7,500; young readers—25,000; middle readers—15,000; young adults—40,000.

HOW TO CONTACT Submit complete ms. Submit outline, information on intended market, bio, and 1-2 sample chapters. Responds to queries in 2 weeks; mss in 6 months. Publishes book 1 year after acceptance.

ILLUSTRATION Works with 2-3 illustrators/year. Reviews ms/illustration packages from artists. Send ms with dummy or e-mail and jpegs. Contact: Louise Steyn, publisher. Illustrations only: Query with brochure, photocopies, résumé, URL, JPEGs. Responds only if interested. Samples not returned.

TERMS Pays authors royalty of 15-18% based on wholesale price.

TIPS "Writers: Story needs to have a South African or African style. Illustrators: I'd like to look, but the chances of getting commissioned are slim. The market is small and difficult. Do not expect huge advances. Editorial staff attended or plans to attend the following conferences: IBBY, Frankfurt, SCBWI Bologna."

THISTLEDOWN PRESS LTD.

410 2nd Ave., Saskatoon SK S7K 2C3, Canada. (306)244-1722. **Fax:** (306)244-1762. **E-mail:** editorial@thistledownpress.com. **Website:** www.thistledownpress.com. **Contact:** Allan Forrie, publisher. "Thistledown originates books by Canadian authors only, although we have co-published titles by authors outside Canada. We do not publish children's picture books." **40% of books from first-time authors. 40% from unagented writers.**

FICTION Young adults: adventure, anthology, contemporary, fantasy, humor, poetry, romance, science fiction, suspense/mystery, short stories. Average word length: young adults—40,000.

HOW TO CONTACT Submit outline/synopsis and sample chapters. *Does not accept mss.* Do not query by e-mail. "Please note: we are not accepting middle years (ages 8-12) nor children's manuscripts at this time." See Submission Guidelines on Website. Responds to queries in 6 months. Publishes book 1 year after acceptance.

ILLUSTRATION Prefers agented illustrators but "not mandatory." Works with few illustrators. Illustrations only: Query with samples, promo sheet, slides, tearsheets. Responds only if interested. Samples returned with SASE; samples filed.

TERMS Pays authors royalty of 10-12% based on net dollar sales. Pays illustrators and photographers by the project (range: $250-750). Rarely pays advance. Book catalog on website. Guidelines online.

TIPS "Send cover letter including publishing history and SASE."

TRADEWIND BOOKS

202-1807 Maritime Mews, Granville Island, Vancouver BC V6H 3W7, Canada. (604)662-4405. **Website:** www.tradewindbooks.com. "Tradewind Books publishes juvenile picture books and young adult novels. Requires that submissions include evidence that author has read at least 3 titles published by Tradewind Books." Publishes hardcover and trade paperback originals. **Publishes 5 titles/year. 15% of books from first-time authors. 50% from unagented writers.**

FICTION Average word length: 900 words.

HOW TO CONTACT Send complete ms for picture books. *YA novels by Canadian authors only. Chapter books by US authors considered.* For chapter books/Middle Grade Fiction, submit the first three chapters, a chapter outline and plot summary. Responds to mss in 2 months. Publishes book 3 years after acceptance.

ILLUSTRATION Works with 3-4 illustrators/year. Reviews ms/illustration packages from artists. Send illustrated ms as dummy. Illustrations only: Query with samples. Responds only if interested. Samples returned with SASE; samples filed.

TERMS Pays 7% royalty on retail price. Pays variable advance. Book catalog and ms guidelines online.

USBORNE PUBLISHING

83-85 Saffron Hill, London EC1N 8RT, United Kingdom. (44)207430-2800. **Fax:** (44)207430-1562. **E-mail:** mail@usborne.co.uk. **Website:** www.usborne.com. "Usborne Publishing is a multiple-award-winning, worldwide children's publishing company publishing almost every type of children's book for every age from baby to young adult."

FICTION Young readers, middle readers: adventure, contemporary, fantasy, history, humor, multicultural, nature/environment, science fiction, suspense/mystery, strong concept-based or character-led series. Average word length: young readers—5,000-10,000; middle readers—25,000-50,000; young adult—50,000-100,000.

HOW TO CONTACT *Agented submissions only.*

ILLUSTRATION Works with 100 illustrators per year. Illustrations only: Query with samples. Samples not returned; samples filed.

PHOTOGRAPHY Contact: Usborne Art Department. Submit samples.

TERMS Pays authors royalty.

TIPS "Do not send any original work and, sorry, but we cannot guarantee a reply."

WHITECAP BOOKS, LTD.

210 - 314 W. Cordova St., Vancouver BC V6B 1 E8, Canada. (604)681-6181. **Fax:** (905)477-9179. **Website:** www.whitecap.ca. "Whitecap Books is a general trade publisher with a focus on food and wine titles. Although we are interested in reviewing unsolicited ms submissions, please note that we only accept submissions that meet the needs of our current publishing program. Please see some of most recent releases to get an idea of the kinds of titles we are interested in." Publishes hardcover and trade paperback originals. **Publishes 30 titles/year. 20% of books from first-time authors. 90% from unagented writers.**

NONFICTION Young children's and middle reader's nonfiction focusing mainly on nature, wildlife and animals. "Writers should take the time to research our list and read the submission guidelines on our website. This is especially important for children's writers and cookbook authors. We will only consider submissions that fall into these categories: cookbooks, wine and spirits, regional travel, home and garden, Canadian history, North American natural history, juvenile series-based fiction. At this time, we are not accepting the following categories: self-help or inspirational books, political, social commentary, or issue books, general how-to books, biographies or memoirs, business and finance, art and architecture, religion and spirituality."

HOW TO CONTACT Submit cover letter, synopsis, SASE via ground mail. See guidelines online. 500 queries received/year; 1,000 mss received/year. Responds in 2-3 months to proposals. Publishes book 1 year after acceptance.

ILLUSTRATION Works with 1-2 illustrators/year. Uses color artwork only. Reviews ms/illustration packages from artists. Query. Contact: Rights and Acquisitions. Illustrations only: Send postcard sample with tearsheets. Contact: Michelle Furbacher, art director. Responds only if interested.

PHOTOGRAPHY Only accepts digital photography. Submit stock photo list. Buys stock and assigns work. Model/property releases required.

TERMS Pays royalty. Pays negotiated advance. Catalog and guidelines online.

TIPS "We want well-written, well-researched material that presents a fresh approach to a particular topic."

MAGAZINES

Children's magazines are a great place for unpublished writers and illustrators to break into the market. Writers, illustrators, and photographers alike may find it easier to get book assignments if they have tearsheets from magazines. Having magazine work under your belt shows you're professional and have experience working with editors and art directors and meeting deadlines.

But magazines aren't merely a breaking-in point. Writing, illustration, and photo assignments for magazines let you see your work in print quickly, and the magazine market can offer steady work and regular paychecks (a number of them pay on acceptance). Book authors and illustrators may have to wait a year or two before receiving royalties from a project. The magazine market is also a good place to use research material that didn't make it into a book project you're working on. You may even work on a magazine idea that blossoms into a book project.

TARGETING YOUR SUBMISSIONS

It's important to know the topics typically covered by different children's magazines. To help you match your work with the right publications, we've included several indexes in the back of this book. The **Subject Index** lists both book and magazine publishers by the fiction and nonfiction subjects they're seeking.

If you're a writer, use the Subject Index in conjunction with the **Age-Level Index** to narrow your list of markets. Targeting the correct age group with your submission is an important consideration. Many rejection slips are sent because a writer has not targeted a manuscript to the correct age. Few magazines are aimed at children of all ages, so you must be certain your manuscript is written for the audience level of the particular magazine you're submitting to. Magazines for children (just as magazines for adults) may also target a specific gender.

Each magazine has a different editorial philosophy. Language usage also varies between periodicals, as does the length of feature articles and the use of artwork and photographs. Reading magazines *before* submitting is the best way to determine if your material is appropriate. Also, because magazines targeted to specific age groups have a natural turnover in readership every few years, old topics (with a new slant) can be recycled.

Because many kids' magazines sell subscriptions through direct mail or schools, you may not be able to find a particular publication at bookstores or newsstands. Check your local library, or send for copies of the magazines you're interested in. Most magazines in this section have sample copies available and will send them for a SASE or small fee.

Also, many magazines have submission guidelines and theme lists available for a SASE. Check magazines' websites, too. Many offer excerpts of articles, submission guidelines, and theme lists and will give you a feel for the editorial focus of the publication.

Watch for the Canadian ✪ and International ➲ symbols. These publications' needs and requirements may differ from their United States counterparts.

AQUILA

Studio 2 Willowfield Studios, 67a Willowfield Rd., Eastbourne BN22 8AP, England. (44)(132)343-1313. **E-mail:** editor@aquila.co.uk. **Website:** www.aquila.co.uk. "*Aquila* is an educational magazine for readers ages 8-13 including factual articles (no pop/celebrity material), arts/crafts, and puzzles." Entire publication aimed at juvenile market. Estab. 1993. Circ. 40,000.

FICTION Young Readers: animal, contemporary, fantasy, folktales, health, history, humorous, multicultural, nature/environment, problem solving, religious, science fiction, sports, suspense/mystery. Middle Readers: animal, contemporary, fantasy, folktales, health, history, humorous, multicultural, nature/environment, problem solving, religious, romance, science fiction, sports, suspense/mystery. Length: 1,000-1,150 words. Pays £90.

NONFICTION Young Readers: animal, arts/crafts, concept, cooking, games/puzzles, health, history, how-to, interview/profile, math, nature/environment, science, sports. Middle Readers: animal, arts/crafts, concept, cooking, games/puzzles, health, history, interview/profile, math, nature/environment, science, sports. Query. Length: 600-800 words. Pays £90.

HOW TO CONTACT Accepts queries by mail, e-mail.

TERMS Pays on publication. Sample copy: £5. Guidelines online.

TIPS "We only accept a high level of educational material for children ages 8-13 with a good standard of literacy and ability."

ASK

E-mail: ask@cricketmedia.com. **Website:** www.cricketmedia.com. "*Ask* is a magazine of arts and sciences for curious kids ages 7-10 who like to find out how the world works." Estab. 2002.

NONFICTION Needs humor, photo feature, profile. "*ASK* commissions most articles but welcomes queries from authors on all nonfiction subjects. Particularly looking for odd, unusual, and interesting stories likely to interest science-oriented kids. Writers interested in working for *ASK* should send a résumé and writing sample (including at least 1 page unedited) for consideration." Length: 200-1,600.

HOW TO CONTACT Send submissions to: Art Submissions Coordinator, Cricket Media, 70 E. Lake St., Suite 800, Chicago IL 60601. Accepts queries by e-mail, online submission form.

ILLUSTRATION Illustrations are by assignment only. Please do not send original artwork. Send postcards, promotional brochures, or color photocopies. Be sure that each sample is marked with your name, address, phone number, and website or blog. Art submissions will not be returned.

TERMS Rights vary. Byline given. Guidelines online.

BABYBUG

Cricket Media, Inc., 7926 Jones Branch Dr., Suite 870, McLean VA 22102. (703)885-3400. **Website:** www.cricketmedia.com. "*Babybug*, a look-and-listen magazine, presents simple poems, stories, nonfiction, and activities that reflect the natural playfulness and curiosity of babies and toddlers." Estab. 1994. Circ. 45,000.

FICTION Wants very short, clear fiction, rhythmic, rhyming. Submit complete ms via online submissions manager. Length: up to 6 sentences. Pays up to 25¢/word.

NONFICTION "First Concepts," a playful take on a simple idea, expressed through very short nonfiction. See recent issues for examples. Submit through online submissions manager: cricketmag.submittable.com/submit. Length: up to 6 sentences. Pays up to 25¢/word.

POETRY "We are especially interested in rhythmic and rhyming poetry. Poems may explore a baby's day, or they may be more whimsical." Submit via online submissions manager. Pays up to $3/line; $25 minimum.

HOW TO CONTACT Send submissions to: Art Submissions Coordinator, Cricket Media, 70 E. Lake St., Suite 800, Chicago IL 60601. Responds in 3-6 months to mss. Accepts queries by online submission form.

ILLUSTRATION "Please **do not** send original artwork. Send postcards, promotional brochures, or color photocopies. Be sure that each sample is marked with your name, address, phone number and website or blog. Art submissions will not be returned."

TERMS Rights vary. Byline given. Pays on publication. 50% freelance written. Guidelines online.

TIPS "We are particularly interested in mss that explore simple concepts, encourage very young children's imaginative play, and provide opportunities for adult readers and babies to interact. We welcome work that reflects diverse family cultures and traditions."

BREAD FOR GOD'S CHILDREN

Bread Ministries, INC., P.O. Box 1017, Arcadia FL 34265. (863)494-6214. **E-mail:** bread@breadministries.org. **Website:** www.breadministries.org. **Contact:** Judith M. Gibbs, editor. An interdenominational Christian teaching publication published 4-6 times/year written to aid children and youth in leading a Christian life. Estab. 1972. Circ. 10,000 (U.S. and Canada).

FICTION "We are looking for writers who have a solid knowledge of Biblical principles and are concerned for the youth of today living by those principles. Stories must be well written, with the story itself getting the message across—no preaching, moralizing, or tag endings." Needs historical, religious. Young readers, middle readers, young adult/teen: adventure, religious, problem-solving, sports. Looks for "teaching stories that portray Christian lifestyles without preaching." Send complete ms. Length: 600-800 words for young children; 900-1,500 words for older children. Pays $40-50.

NONFICTION Needs inspirational. All levels: how-to. "We do not want anything detrimental to solid family values. Most topics will fit if they are slanted to our basic needs." Send complete ms. Length: 500-800 words.

HOW TO CONTACT Responds in 6 months to mss. Publishes ms an average of 6 months after acceptance. Accepts queries by mail.

ILLUSTRATION "The only illustrations we purchase are those occasional good ones accompanying an accepted story."

TERMS Pays on publication. Pays $30-50 for stories; $30 for articles. Sample copies free for 9x12 SAE and 5 first-class stamps (for 2 copies). Buys first rights. Byline given. Publication No kill fee. 10% freelance written. Sample copy for 9x12 SAE and 5 first-class stamps. Guidelines for #10 SASE.

TIPS "We want stories or articles that illustrate overcoming obstacles by faith and living solid, Christian lives. Know our publication and what we have used in the past. Know the readership and publisher's guidelines. Stories should teach the value of morality and honesty without preaching. Edit carefully for content and grammar."

BRILLIANT STAR

1233 Central St., Evanston IL 60201. (847)853-2354. **E-mail:** brilliant@usbnc.org; hparsons@usbnc.org. **Website:** www.brilliantstarmagazine.org. **Contact:** Heidi Parsons, associate editor. "*Brilliant Star* empowers kids to explore their roles as world citizens. Inspired by the principles of peace and unity in the Baha'i Faith, the magazine and website encourage readers to use their virtues to make the world a better place. Universal values of good character, such as kindness, courage, creativity, and helpfulness, are presented through fiction, nonfiction, activities, interviews, puzzles, cartoons, games, music, and art." Estab. 1969.

FICTION "We print fiction with kids ages 10-12 as the protagonists who resolve their problems themselves." Submit complete ms. Length: 700-1,400 words. Pays 3 contributor's copies.

NONFICTION Middle readers: arts/crafts, games/puzzles, geography, how-to, humorous, multicultural, nature/environment, religion, social issues. Query. Length: 300-700 words. Pays 3 contributor's copies.

POETRY "We only publish poetry written by children at the moment."

HOW TO CONTACT Accepts queries by e-mail.

ILLUSTRATION Reviews ms/illustration packages from artists. Illustrations only; query with samples. Contact: Aaron Kreader, graphic designer, at brilliant@usbnc.org. Responds only if interested. Samples kept on file. Credit line given.

PHOTOS Buys photos with accompanying ms only. Model/property release required; captions required. Responds only if interested.

TERMS Buys first rights and reprint rights for mss, artwork, and photos. Byline given. Guidelines available for SASE or via e-mail.

TIPS "*Brilliant Star*'s content is developed with a focus on children in their 'tween' years, ages 8-12. This is a period of intense emotional, physical, and psychological development. Familiarize yourself with the interests and challenges of children in this age range. Protagonists in our fiction are usually in the upper part of our age range: 10-12 years old. They solve their problems without adult intervention. We appreciate seeing a sense of humor but not related to bodily functions or put-downs. Keep your language and concepts age-appropriate. Use short words, sentences, and paragraphs. Activities and games may be submitted in rough or final form. Send us a description of your activity along with short, simple instructions. We avoid long, complicated activities that require adult supervision. If you think they will be helpful, please provide step-by-step rough sketches of the instructions. You may also submit photographs to illustrate the activity."

CADET QUEST MAGAZINE

Calvinist Cadet Corps, 1333 Alger St. SE, Grand Rapids MI 49507. (616)241-5616. **Fax:** (616)241-5558. **E-mail:** submissions@calvinistcadets.org. **Website:** www.calvinistcadets.org. **Contact:** Steve Bootsma, editor. Magazine published 7 times/year. *Cadet Quest Magazine* shows boys 9-14 how God is at work in their lives and in the world around them. Estab. 1958. Circ. 6,000.

FICTION "Fast-moving, entertaining stories that appeal to a boy's sense of adventure or to his sense of humor are welcomed. Stories must present Christian life realistically and help boys relate Christian values to their own lives. Stories must have action without long dialogues. Favorite topics for boys include sports and athletes, humor, adventure, mystery, friends, etc. They must also fit the theme of that issue of *Cadet Quest.* Stories with preachiness and/or clichés are not of interest to us." No fantasy, science fiction, fashion, horror, or erotica. Send complete ms by mail or e-mail (in body of e-mail; no attachments). Length: 1,000-1,300 words. Pays 5¢/word and 1 contributor's copy.

NONFICTION Needs informational. Send complete ms via postal mail or e-mail (in body of e-mail; no attachments). Length: up to 1,500 words. Pays 5¢/word and 1 contributor's copy.

HOW TO CONTACT Responds in 2 months to mss. Publishes ms 4-11 months after acceptance. Accepts queries by mail, e-mail.

ILLUSTRATION Works on assignment only. Reviews ms/illustration packages from artists.

PHOTOS Pays $5 each for photos purchased with ms.

TERMS Buys all rights, first rights, and second rights. Rights purchased vary with author and material. Byline given. Pays on acceptance. No kill fee. 90 Sample copy for 9x12 SASE and $1.45 postage. Guidelines online.

TIPS "The best time to submit stories/articles is early in the year (January-April). Also remember readers are boys ages 9-14. Stories must reflect or add to the theme of the issue and be from a Christian perspective."

CHEMMATTERS

American Chemical Society, Education Division, 1155 16th St., NW, Washington DC 20036. (202)872-6164. **Fax:** (202)872-8068. **E-mail:** chemmatters@acs.org. **Website:** www.acs.org/chemmatters. **Contact:** Patrice Pages, editor; Cornithia Harris, art director. Covers topics of interest to teenagers and that can be explained with chemistry. *ChemMatters*, published 4 times/year, is a magazine that helps high school students find connections between chemistry and the world around them. Estab. 1983. Circ. 30,000.

NONFICTION Query with published clips. Pays $700-$1,000 for article.

HOW TO CONTACT Responds in 4 weeks to queries and mss. Publishes ms 6 months after acceptance. Accepts queries by mail, e-mail.

ILLUSTRATION Buys 3 illustrations/issue; 12 illustrations/year. Uses color artwork only. Works on assignment only. Reviews ms/illustration packages from artists. Query. Illustrations only: Query with promo sheet, résumé. Samples returned with self-addressed stamped envelope; samples not filed. Credit line given.

PHOTOS Looking for photos of high school students engaged in science-related activities. Model/property release required; captions required. Uses color prints, but prefers high-resolution PDFs. Query with samples. Responds in 2 weeks.

TERMS Minimally buys first North American serial rights but prefers to buy all rights, reprint rights, electronic rights for ms. Buys all rights for artwork; nonexclusive first rights for photos. Byline given. Pays on acceptance. 100% freelance written. Sample copies and writer's guidelines free (available as e-mail attachment upon request).

TIPS "Be aware of the content covered in a standard high school chemistry textbook. Choose themes and topics that are timely, interesting, fun, *and* that relate to the content and concepts of the first-year chemistry course. Articles should describe real people involved with real science. Best articles feature young people making a difference or solving a problem."

CLICK

E-mail: click@cricketmedia.com. **Website:** www.cricketmag.com. Magazine covering areas of interest for children ages 3-7. "*Click* is a science and exploration magazine for children ages 3-7. Designed and written with the idea that it's never too early to encourage a child's natural curiosity about the world,

Click's 40 full-color pages are filled with amazing photographs, beautiful illustrations, and stories and articles that are both entertaining and thought-provoking."

Does not accept unsolicited mss.

NONFICTION Query by e-mail with résumé and published clips. Length: 200-500 words.

HOW TO CONTACT Send submissions to: Art Submissions Coordinator, Cricket Media, 70 E. Lake St., Suite 800, Chicago IL 60601. Buys print, digital, promotional rights. Accepts queries by e-mail.

ILLUSTRATION Illustrations are by assignment only. Please do not send original artwork. Send postcards, promotional brochures, or color photocopies. Be sure that each sample is marked with your name, address, phone number, and website or blog. Art submissions will not be returned.

TERMS Rights vary. Sample copy available online. Guidelines available online.

TIPS "The best way for writers to understand what *Click* is looking for is to read the magazine. Writers are encouraged to examine several past copies before submitting a query."

COBBLESTONE

E-mail: cobblestone@cricketmedia.com. **Website:** www.cricketmedia.com. "*Cobblestone* is interested in articles of historical accuracy and lively, original approaches to the subject at hand." American history magazine for ages 8-14. Circ. 15,000.

"*Cobblestone* stands apart from other children's magazines by offering a solid look at 1 subject and stressing strong editorial content, color photographs throughout, and original illustrations." *Cobblestone* themes and deadline are available on website or with SASE.

FICTION Needs adventure. Query by e-mail with published clips. Length: up to 800 words. Pays 20-25¢/word.

NONFICTION Needs historical, humor, interview, personal experience, photo feature. Query by e-mail with published clips. Length: 700-800 words for feature articles; 300-600 words for supplemental nonfiction. Pays 20-25¢/word.

POETRY Serious and light verse considered. Must have clear, objective imagery. Length: up to 100 lines/poem. Pays on an individual basis.

HOW TO CONTACT Send submissions to: Art Submissions Coordinator, Cricket Media, 70 E. Lake St., Suite 800, Chicago IL 60601. Accepts queries by e-mail.

ILLUSTRATION Illustrations are by assignment only. Please do not send original artwork. Send postcards, promotional brochures, or color photocopies. Be sure that each sample is marked with your name, address, phone number, and website or blog. Art submissions will not be returned.

TERMS Buys all rights. Byline given. Pays on publication. Offers 50% kill fee. 50% freelance written. Sample copy available online. Guidelines available online.

TIPS "Review theme lists and past issues to see what we're looking for."

COLLEGEXPRESS MAGAZINE

Carnegie Communications, LLC, 2 LAN Dr., Suite 100, Westford MA 1886. **E-mail:** info@carnegiecomm.com. **Website:** www.collegexpress.com. *CollegeXpress Magazine*, formerly *Careers and Colleges*, provides juniors and seniors in high school with editorial, tips, trends, and websites to assist them in the transition to college, career, young adulthood, and independence.

Distributed to 10,000 high schools and reaches 1.5 million students.

TIPS "Articles with great quotes, good reporting, good writing. Rich with examples and anecdotes. Must tie in with the objective to help teenaged readers plan for their futures. Current trends, policy changes and information regarding college admissions, financial aid, and career opportunities."

CRICKET

Cricket Media, Inc., 7926 Jones Branch Dr., Suite 870, McLean VA 22102. (703)885-3400. **Website:** www.cricketmag.com. *Cricket* is a monthly literary magazine for ages 9-14. Publishes 9 issues/year. Estab. 1973. Circ. 73,000.

FICTION Needs realistic, contemporary, historic, humor, mysteries, fantasy, science fiction, folk/fairy tales, legend, myth. No didactic, sex, religious, or horror stories. Submit via online submissions manager (cricketmag.submittable.com). Length: 1,200-1,800 words. Pays up to 25¢/word.

NONFICTION *Cricket* publishes thought-provoking nonfiction articles on a wide range of subjects: history, biography, true adventure, science and technology, sports, inventors and explorers, architecture and engineering, archaeology, dance, music, theater, and art. Articles should be carefully researched and include a solid bibliography that shows that research has gone beyond reviewing websites. Submit via online submissions manager (cricketmag.submittable.com). Length: 1,200-1,800 words. Pays up to 25¢/word.

POETRY *Cricket* publishes both serious and humorous poetry. Poems should be well-crafted, with precise and vivid language and images. Poems can explore a variety of themes, from nature, to family and friendships, to whatever you can imagine that will delight our readers and invite their wonder and emotional response. Length: up to 35 lines/poem. Most poems run 8-15 lines. Pays up to $3/line.

HOW TO CONTACT Send submissions to: Art Submissions Coordinator, Cricket Media, 70 E. Lake St., Suite 800, Chicago IL 60601. Responds in 3-6 months to mss. Accepts queries by online submission form.

ILLUSTRATION "Please do not send original artwork. Send postcards, promotional brochures, or color photocopies. Be sure that each sample is marked with your name, address, phone number and website or blog. Art submissions will not be returned."

TERMS Byline given. Pays on publication. Sample copy available online. Guidelines available online.

TIPS Writers: "Read copies of back issues and current issues. Adhere to specified word limits. *Please* do not query." Would currently like to see more fantasy and science fiction. Illustrators: "Send only your best work and be able to reproduce that quality in assignments. Put name and address on *all* samples. Know a publication before you submit."

DRAMATICS MAGAZINE

Educational Theatre Association, 2343 Auburn Ave., Cincinnati OH 45219. (513)421-3900. **E-mail:** gbossler@schooltheatre.org. **Website:** schooltheatre.org. **Contact:** Gregory Bossler, editor-in-chief. *Dramatics* is for students (mainly high school age) and teachers of theater. The magazine wants student readers to grow as theater artists and become a more discerning and appreciative audience. Material is directed to both theater students and their teachers, with strong student slant. Tries to portray the theater community in all its diversity. Estab. 1929. Circ. 45,000.

FICTION Young adults: drama (one-act and full-length plays). "We prefer unpublished scripts that have been produced at least once." Does not want to see plays that show no understanding of the conventions of the theater. No plays for children, no Christmas or didactic "message" plays. Submit complete ms. Buys 5-9 plays/year. Emerging playwrights have better chances with résumé of credits. Length: 10 minutes to full length. Pays $100-500 for plays.

NONFICTION Needs how-to, profile, practical articles on acting, directing, design, production, and other facets of theater; career-oriented profiles of working theater professionals. Submit complete ms. Length: 750-3,000 words. Pays $50-500 for articles.

HOW TO CONTACT Publishes ms 3 months after acceptance. Accepts queries by mail, e-mail.

ILLUSTRATION Buys 3-8 illustrations/year. Works on assignment only. Arrange portfolio review; send résumé, promo sheets, and tearsheets. Responds only if interested. Samples returned with SASE; sample not filed. Credit line given. Pays up to $300 for illustrations.

PHOTOS Buys photos with accompanying ms only. Looking for "good-quality production or candid photography to accompany article. We very occasionally publish photo essays." Model/property release and captions required. Prefers hi-res JPG files. Will consider prints or transparencies. Query with résumé of credits. Responds only if interested.

TERMS Byline given. Pays on acceptance. Sample copy available for 9x12 SAE with 4-ounce first-class postage. Guidelines available for SASE.

TIPS "Obtain our writer's guidelines and look at recent back issues. The best way to break in is to know our audience—drama students, teachers, and others interested in theater—and write for them. Writers who have some practical experience in theater, especially in technical areas, have an advantage, but we'll work with anybody who has a good idea. Some freelancers have become regular contributors."

FACES

E-mail: faces@cricketmedia.com. **Website:** www.cricketmedia.com. "Published 9 times/year, *Faces* covers world culture for ages 9-14. It stands apart from other children's magazines by offering a solid look at 1 subject and stressing strong editorial content, color photographs throughout, and original illustrations. *Faces* offers an equal balance of feature articles and activities, as well as folktales and legends." Estab. 1984. Circ. 15,000.

FICTION Fiction accepted: retold legends, folktales, stories, and original plays from around the world, etc., relating to the theme. Needs ethnic. Query with cover letter, one-page outline, bibliography. Pays 20-25¢/word.

NONFICTION Needs historical, interview, personal experience, photo feature, feature articles (in-depth nonfiction highlighting an aspect of the featured culture, interviews, and personal accounts), 700-800 words; supplemental nonfiction (subjects directly and indirectly related to the theme), 300-600 words. Query by e-mail with cover letter, one-page outline, bibliography. Pays 20-25¢/word.

HOW TO CONTACT Send submissions to: Art Submissions Coordinator, Cricket Media, 70 E. Lake St., Suite 800, Chicago IL 60601.

ILLUSTRATION Illustrations are by assignment only. Please do not send original artwork. Send postcards, promotional brochures, or color photocopies. Be sure that each sample is marked with your name, address, phone number, and website or blog. Art submissions will not be returned.

TERMS Buys print, digital, promotional rights. Buys all rights. Byline given. Pays on publication. Offers 50% kill fee. 90-100% freelance written. Sample copy available online. Guidelines available online.

TIPS "Writers are encouraged to study past issues of the magazine to become familiar with our style and content. Writers with anthropological and/or travel experience are particularly encouraged; *Faces* is about world cultures. All feature articles, recipes, and activities are freelance contributions."

FUN FOR KIDZ

P.O. Box 227, Bluffton OH 45817. (419)358-4610. **Website:** funforkidz.com. **Contact:** Marilyn Edwards, articles editor. "*Fun for Kidz* is an activity magazine that maintains the same wholesome values as the other publications. Each issue is also created around a theme. There is nothing in the magazine to make it out dated. *Fun for Kidz* offers creative activities for children with extra time on their hands." Estab. 2002.

NONFICTION Needs picture-oriented material, young readers, middle readers: animal, arts/crafts, cooking, games/puzzles, history, hobbies, how-to, humorous, problem-solving, sports, carpentry projects. Submit complete ms with SASE, contact info, and notation of which upcoming theme your content should be considered for. Length: 300-750 words. Pays minimum 5¢/word for articles; variable rate for games and projects, etc.

HOW TO CONTACT Accepts queries by mail.

ILLUSTRATION Works on assignment mostly. "We are anxious to find artists capable of illustrating stories and features. Our inside art is pen and ink." Query with samples. Samples kept on file. Pays $35 for full page and $25 for partial page.

PHOTOS "We use a number of b&w photos inside the magazine; most support the articles used." Photos should be in color. Pays $5 per photo.

TERMS Buys first North American serial rights. Byline given. Pays on acceptance. Sample copy: $6 in U.S., $9 in Canada, and $12.25 internationally. Guidelines online.

TIPS "Our point of view is that every child deserves the right to be a child for a number of years before he or she becomes a young adult. As a result, *Fun for Kidz* looks for activities that deal with timeless topics, such as pets, nature, hobbies, science, games, sports, careers, simple cooking, and anything else likely to interest a child."

GIRLS' LIFE

3 S. Frederick St., Suite 806, Baltimore MD 21202. (410)426-9600. **Fax:** (866)793-1531. **Website:** www.girlslife.com. **Contact:** Karen Bokram, founding editor and publisher; Kelsey Haywood, senior editor; Chun Kim, art director. Bimonthly magazine covering girls ages 9-15. Estab. 1994. Circ. 2.16 million.

FICTION "We accept short fiction. They should be stand-alone stories and are generally 2,500-3,500 words." Needs short stories.

NONFICTION Needs book excerpts, essays, general interest, how-to, humor, inspirational, interview, new product, travel. Query by mail with published clips. Submit complete ms on spec only. "Features and articles should speak to young women ages 10-15 looking for new ideas about relationships, family, friends, school, etc. with fresh, savvy advice. Front-of-the-book columns and quizzes are a good place to start." Length: 700-2,000 words. Pays $350/regular column; $500/feature.

HOW TO CONTACT Editorial lead time 4 months. Responds in 1 month to queries. Publishes an average of 3 months after acceptance. Accepts queries by mail, e-mail.

PHOTOS State availability with submission if applicable. Reviews contact sheets, negatives, transparencies. Negotiates payment individually. Captions, identification of subjects, model releases required. State availability. Captions, identification of subjects, model releases required. Reviews contact sheets, negatives, transparencies. Negotiates payment individually.

TERMS Buys all rights. Byline given. Pays on publication. Sample copy for $5 or online. Guidelines online.

TIPS "Send thought-out queries with published writing samples and detailed résumé. Have fresh ideas and a voice that speaks to our audience—not down to them. And check out a copy of the magazine or visit girlslife.com before submitting."

GREEN TEACHER

Green Teacher, 95 Robert St., Toronto ON M5S 2K5, Canada. (416)960-1244. **Fax:** (416)925-3474. **E-mail:** tim@greenteacher.com; info@greenteacher.com. **Website:** www.greenteacher.com. **Contact:** Tim Grant, co-editor; Amy Stubbs, editorial assistant. "We're a nonprofit organization dedicated to helping educators, both inside and outside of schools, promote environmental awareness among young people aged 6-19." Estab. 1991. Circ. 15,000.

NONFICTION Needs multicultural, nature, environment. Query. Submit one-page summary or outline. Length: 1,500-3,500 words.

HOW TO CONTACT Responds to queries in 1 week. Publishes ms 8 months after acceptance. Accepts queries by mail, e-mail.

ILLUSTRATION Buys 3 illustrations/issue from freelancers; 10 illustrations/year from freelancers. B&w artwork only. Works on assignment only. Reviews ms/illustration packages from artists. Query with samples; tearsheets. Responds only if interested. Samples not returned. Samples filed. Credit line given.

PHOTOS Purchases photos both separately and with accompanying mss. "Activity photos, environmental photos." Query with samples. Responds only of interested.

GUIDE

Pacific Press Publishing Association, P.O. Box 5353, Nampa ID 83653. (208)465-2579. **E-mail:** guide@pacificpress.com. **Website:** www.guidemagazine.org. **Contact:** Randy Fishell, editor; Brandon Reese, designer. *Guide* is a Christian story magazine for young people ages 10-14. The 32-page, 4-color publication is published weekly by the Pacific Press. Their mission is to show readers, through stories that illustrate Bible truth, how to walk with God now and forever. Estab. 1953.

NONFICTION Needs humor, personal experience, religious. Send complete ms. "Each issue includes 3-4 true stories. *Guide* does not publish fiction, poetry, or articles (devotionals, how-to, profiles, etc.). However, we sometimes accept quizzes and other unique nonstory formats. Each piece should include a clear spiritual element." Looking for pieces on adventure, personal growth, Christian humor, inspiration, biography, story series, and nature. Length: 1,000-1,200 words. Pays 7-10¢/word.

HOW TO CONTACT Responds in 6 weeks to mss. Accepts queries by mail, e-mail.

TERMS Buys first serial rights. Byline given. Pays on acceptance. Sample copy free with 6x9 SAE and 2 first-class stamps. Guidelines available on website.

TIPS "Children's magazines want mystery, action, discovery, suspense, and humor—no matter what the topic. For us, truth is stronger than fiction."

HIGHLIGHTS FOR CHILDREN

803 Church St., Honesdale PA 18431. (570)253-1080. **Fax:** (570)251-7847. **E-mail:** eds@highlights.com (Do not send submissions to this address.). **Website:** www.highlights.com. **Contact:** Christine French Cully, editor-in-chief. Monthly magazine for children ages 6-12. "This book of wholesome fun is dedicated to helping children grow in basic skills and knowledge, in creativeness, in ability to think and reason, in sensitivity to others, in high ideals, and worthy ways of living—for children are the world's most important people." We publish stories and articles for beginning and advanced readers. Up to 400 words for beginning readers, up to 750 words for advanced readers. Guidelines updated regularly at Highlights.submittable.com. Estab. 1946. Circ. Approximately 1 million.

FICTION Stories appealing to girls and boys ages 6-12. Vivid, full of action. Engaging plot, strong characterization, lively language. Prefers stories in which a child protagonist solves a dilemma through his or her own resources. No stories glorifying war, crime or violence. See Highlights.submittable.com. Up to 475 words for beginning readers. Up to 750 words for advanced readers. Pays $175 and up.

NONFICTION See guidelines online. Up to 400 words for beginning readers. Up to 750 words for advanced readers. Pays $175 and up for articles; pays $40 and up for crafts, activities, and puzzles.

POETRY See Highlights.submittable.com. No previously published poetry. Buys all rights. 16 lines maximum. Pays $50 and up.

HOW TO CONTACT Responds in 2 months. Accepts queries by online submission form.

TERMS Buys all rights. Byline given. Pays on acceptance. 70% freelance written. Guidelines online.

TIPS "We update our guidelines and current needs regularly at Highlights.submittable.com. Read several recent issues of the magazine before submitting. In addition to fiction, nonfiction, and poetry, we purchase crafts, puzzles, and activities that will stimulate children mentally and creatively. We judge each submission on its own merits. Expert reviews and complete bibliography are required for nonfiction. Include special qualifications, if any, of author. Speak to today's kids. Avoid didactic, overt messages. Even though our general principles haven't changed over the years, we are contemporary in our approach to issues."

HUNGER MOUNTAIN

Vermont College of Fine Arts, 36 College St., Montpelier VT 5602. (802)828-8517. **E-mail:** hungermtn@vcfa.edu. **Website:** www.hungermtn.org. "We accept picture book, middle grade, YA, and YA crossover work (text only—for now). We're looking for polished pieces that entertain, that show the range of adolescent experience, and that are compelling, creative, and will appeal to the devoted followers of the kid-lit craft, as well as the child inside us all." Editor: Erin Stalcup. **Contact:** Cameron Finch, managing editor. Annual perfect-bound journal covering high-quality fiction, poetry, creative nonfiction, craft essays, writing for children, and artwork. Four contests held annually, one in each genre. Accepts high-quality work from unknown, emerging, or successful writers. Publishing fiction, creative nonfiction, poetry, and young adult & children's writing. Four writing contests annually. *Hunger Mountain* is a print and online journal of the arts. The print journal is about 200 pages, 7x9, professionally printed, perfect-bound, with full-bleed color artwork on cover. Press run is 1,000. Over 10,000 visits online monthly. Uses online submissions manager (Submittable). Member: CLMP. Estab. 2002. Circ. 1,000.

FICTION "We look for work that is beautifully crafted and tells a good story, with characters that are alive and kicking, storylines that stay with us long after we've finished reading, and sentences that slay us with their precision." Needs experimental, humorous, novel excerpts, short stories, slice-of-life vignettes. No genre fiction, meaning science fiction, fantasy, horror, detective, erotic, etc. Submit ms using online submissions manager: https://hungermtn.submittable.com/submit. Length: up to 10,000 words. Pays $50 for general fiction.

NONFICTION "We welcome an array of traditional and experimental work, including, but not limited to, personal, lyrical, and meditative essays, memoirs, collages, rants, and humor. The only requirements are recognition of truth, a unique voice with a firm command of language, and an engaging story with multiple pressure points." Submit complete ms using online submissions manager at Submittable. Length: up to 10,000 words. Pays $50 for general fiction or creative nonfiction, for both children's lit and general adult lit.

POETRY Submit 1-5 poems at a time. "We are looking for truly original poems that run the aesthetic gamut: lively engagement with language in the act of pursuit. Some poems remind us in a fresh way of our own best thoughts; some poems bring us to a place beyond language for which there aren't quite words; some poems take us on a complicated language ride that is, itself, its own aim. Complex poem-architectures thrill us and still-points in the turning world do, too. Send us the best of what you have." Submit using online submissions manager. No light verse, humor/quirky/catchy verse, greeting card verse. Pays $25 for poetry up to 2 poems (plus $5/poem for additional poems).

HOW TO CONTACT Responds in 4-6 months to mss. Publishes ms an average of 1 year after acceptance. Accepts queries by online submission form.

PHOTOS Send photos.

TERMS Buys first worldwide serial rights. Byline given. Pays on publication. No kill fee. Single issue: $12; subscription: $18 for 2 issues/2 years; back issue: $8. Checks payable to Vermont College of Fine Arts, or purchase online. Guidelines online.

TIPS "Mss must be typed, prose double-spaced. Poets submit poems as one document. No multiple genre submissions. Fresh viewpoints and human interest are very important, as is originality and diversity. We are committed to publishing an outstanding journal of the arts. Do not send entire novels, mss, or short story collections. Do not send previously published work."

JACK AND JILL

U.S. Kids, P.O. Box 88928, Indianapolis IN 46208. (317)634-1100. **E-mail:** jackandjill@uskidsmags.com.

Website: www.uskidsmags.com. Bimonthly magazine published for children ages 6-12. *Jack and Jill* is an award-winning magazine for children ages 6-12. It promotes the healthy educational and creative growth of children through interactive activities and articles. The pages are designed to spark a child's curiosity in a wide range of topics through articles, games, and activities. Inside you will find: current real-world topics in articles in stories; challenging puzzles and games; and interactive entertainment through experimental crafts and recipes. Please do not send artwork. "We prefer to work with professional illustrators of our own choosing. Write entertaining and imaginative stories for kids, not just about them. Writers should understand what is funny to kids, what's important to them, what excites them. Don't write from an adult 'kids are so cute' perspective. We're also looking for health and healthful lifestyle stories and articles, but don't be preachy." Estab. 1938. Circ. 40,000.

FICTION Submit complete ms via postal mail; no e-mail submissions. "The tone of the stories should be fun and engaging. Stories should hook readers right from the get-go and pull them through the story. Humor is very important! Dialogue should be witty instead of just furthering the plot. The story should convey some kind of positive message. Possible themes could include self-reliance, being kind to others, appreciating other cultures, and so on. There are a million positive messages, so get creative! Kids can see preachy coming from a mile away, though, so please focus on telling a good story over teaching a lesson. The message—if there is one—should come organically from the story and not feel tacked on." Length: 600-800 words. Pays $25 minimum.

NONFICTION Submit complete ms via postal mail; no e-mail submissions. Queries not accepted. We are especially interested in features or Q&As with regular kids (or groups of kids) in the *Jack and Jill* age group who are engaged in unusual, challenging, or interesting activities. No celebrity pieces, please. Length: up to 700 words. Pays $25 minimum.

POETRY Submit via postal mail; no e-mail submissions. Wants light-hearted poetry appropriate for the age group. Mss must be typewritten with poet's contact information in upper-right corner of each poem's page. SASE required. Length: up to 30 lines/poem. Pays $25-50.

HOW TO CONTACT Responds to mss in 3 months. Publishes ms an average of 8 months after acceptance. Accepts queries by mail.

TERMS Buys all rights. Byline given. Pays on publication. 50% freelance written. Guidelines online.

TIPS "We are constantly looking for new writers who can tell good stories with interesting slants—stories that are not full of outdated and time-worn expressions. We like to see stories about kids who are smart and capable but not sarcastic or smug. Problem-solving skills, personal responsibility, and integrity are good topics for us. Obtain current issues of the magazine and study them to determine our present needs and editorial style."

KEYS FOR KIDS DEVOTIONAL

Keys for Kids Ministries, 2060 43rd St., Grand Rapids MI 49508. **E-mail:** editorial@keysforkids.org. **Website:** www.keysforkids.org. **Contact:** Courtney Lasater, Editor. Quarterly devotional featuring stories and Scripture verses for children ages 6-12 that help kids dig into God's Word and apply it to their lives. Please put your name and contact information on the first page of your submission. We prefer to receive submissions via our website. Story length is typically 340-375 words. To see full guidelines or submit a story, please go to www.keysforkids.org/writersguidelines. Estab. 1982. Circ. 55,000 print (not including digital circulation).

FICTION Needs short contemporary stories with spiritual applications for kids. Please suggest a key verse and an appropriate Scripture passage, generally 3-10 verses, to reinforce the theme of your story. (See guidelines for more details on devotional format.) Length: Up to 375 words. Pays $30.

HOW TO CONTACT Editorial lead time 6-8 months. Responds in 2-4 months. Typically publishes stories 9-12 months after acceptance. Accepts queries by e-mail, online submission form.

TERMS Buys all rights. Byline given. Pays on acceptance. 95% freelance. Sample copy online or contact editorial@keysforkids.org. Guidelines online at www.keysforkids.org/writersguidelines.

TIPS We love devotional stories that use an everyday object/situation to illustrate a spiritual truth (especially in a fresh, unique way) with characters that pull the reader into the story. The length and format of our stories is very specific, so please review our guidelines and read several sample stories before submitting.

LADYBUG

Website: www.cricketmag.com. *Ladybug* magazine is an imaginative magazine with art and literature for young children ages 3-6. Publishes 9 issues/year. Estab. 1990. Circ. 125,000.

FICTION Needs imaginative contemporary stories, original retellings of fairy and folk tales, multicultural stories. Submit via online submissions manager: cricket.submittable.com. Length: up to 800 words. Pays up to 25¢/word.

NONFICTION Seeks "simple explorations of interesting places in a young child's world (such as the library and the post office), different cultures, nature, and science. These articles can be straight nonfiction, or they may include story elements, such as a fictional child narrator." Submit via online submissions manager: cricketmag.submittable.com. Length: up to 400 words. Pays up to 25¢/word.

POETRY Wants poetry that is "rhythmic, rhyming; serious, humorous." Submit via online submissions manager: cricket.submittable.com. Length: up to 20 lines/poem. Pays up to $3/line ($25 minimum).

HOW TO CONTACT Send submissions to: Art Submissions Coordinator, Cricket Media, 70 E. Lake St., Suite 800, Chicago IL 60601. Responds in 6 months to mss. Accepts queries by online submission form.

ILLUSTRATION Prefers "bright colors; all media, but uses watercolor and acrylics most often; same size as magazine is preferred but not required." To be considered for future assignments: "Please do not send original artwork. Send postcards, promotional brochures, or color photocopies. Be sure that each sample is marked with your name, address, phone number and website or blog. Art submissions will not be returned."

TERMS Acquires print and digital rights, plus promotional rights. Byline given. Pays on publication. Guidelines available online.

LEADING EDGE MAGAZINE

Brigham Young University, 4087 JKB, Provo UT 84602. **E-mail:** editor@leadingedgemagazine.com; fiction@leadingedgemagazine.com; art@leadingedgemagazine.com; poetry@leadingedgemagazine.com; nonfiction@leadingedgemagazine.com. **Website:** www.leadingedgemagazine.com. **Contact:** Abigail Miner, editor-in-chief. Semiannual magazine covering science fiction and fantasy. "*Leading Edge* is a magazine dedicated to new and upcoming talent in the fields of science fiction, fantasy, and horror. We strive to encourage developing and established talent and provide high-quality speculative fiction to our readers." Does not accept mss with sex, excessive violence, or profanity. Accepts unsolicited submissions. Estab. 1981. Circ. 200.

FICTION Needs fantasy, horror, science fiction. Send complete ms with cover letter and SASE. Include estimated word count. Length: up to 15,000 words. Pays 1¢/word; $50 maximum.

NONFICTION Needs essays, expose, interview, personal experience, reviews. Send complete ms with cover letter and SASE. Include estimated word count. Send to nonfiction@leadingedgemagazine.com. Length: up to 15,000 words. Pays 1¢/word; $50 maximum.

POETRY Publishes 2-4 poems per issue. Poetry should reflect both literary value and popular appeal and should deal with science fiction- or fantasy-related themes. Cover letter is preferred. Include name, address, phone number, length of poem, title, and type of poem at the top of each page. Please include SASE with every submission. Pays $10 for first 4 pages; $1.50/each subsequent page.

HOW TO CONTACT Responds within 12 months to mss. Publishes ms an average of 2-4 months after acceptance. Accepts queries by mail, e-mail.

ILLUSTRATION Buys 24 illustrations/issue; 48 illustrations/year. Uses b&w artwork only. Works on assignment only. Contact: Art Director. Illustrations only: Send postcard sample with portfolio, samples, URL. Responds only if interested. Samples filed. Credit line given.

TERMS Buys first North American serial rights. Byline given. Pays on publication. No kill fee. 90% freelance written. Single copy: $6.99. "We no longer provide subscriptions, but *Leading Edge* is now available on Amazon Kindle, as well as print-on-demand." Guidelines online.

TIPS "Buy a sample issue to know what is currently selling in our magazine. Also, make sure to follow the writer's guidelines when submitting."

THE LOUISVILLE REVIEW

Spalding University, 851 S. Fourth St., Louisville KY 40203. (502)873-4398. **E-mail:** louisvillereview@spalding.edu. **Website:** www.louisvillereview.org. **Contact:** Ellyn Lichvar, managing editor. *The Louisville Review*, published twice/year, prints poetry, fiction, nonfiction, and drama. Has a section devoted to poetry by writers under age 18 (grades K-12) called "The Children's Corner." *The Louisville Review* is 150 pages, digest-sized, flat-spined. Receives about 700 submissions/year, accepts about 10%. Estab. 1976.

FICTION Needs novel excerpts, short stories. Submit complete ms by mail or online submissions manager. Also publishes plays. No word limit, but prefers shorter pieces. Pays contributor's copies.

NONFICTION Needs essays. Submit via online submissions manager. No word limit, but prefers shorter pieces. Pays contributor's copies.

POETRY Accepts submissions via online manager; please see website for more information. "Poetry by children must include permission of parent to publish if accepted. Address those submissions to 'The Children's Corner.'" Reads submissions year round. Has published poetry by Wendy Bishop, Gary Fincke, Michael Burkard, and Sandra Kohler. Pays contributor's copies.

HOW TO CONTACT Responds in 3-6 months to mss. Accepts queries by e-mail.

TERMS Sample copy: $5. Single copy: $8. Subscription: $14/year, $27/2 years, $40/3 years (foreign subscribers add $6/year for s&h). Guidelines online.

MUSE

E-mail: muse@cricketmedia.com. **Website:** www.cricketmag.com. "The goal of *Muse* is to give as many children as possible access to the most important ideas and concepts underlying the principal areas of human knowledge. Articles should meet the highest possible standards of clarity and transparency, aided, wherever possible, by a tone of skepticism, humor, and irreverence." Estab. 1996. Circ. 40,000.

FICTION Needs science fiction. Query with published clips. Length: 1,000-1,600 words.

NONFICTION Needs interview, photo feature, profile, entertaining stories from the fields of science, technology, engineering, art, and math. Query by e-mail with published clips. Length: 1,200-1,800 words for features; 500-800 words for profiles and interviews; 100-300 words for photo essays.

HOW TO CONTACT Send submissions to: Art Submissions Coordinator, Cricket Media, 70 E. Lake St., Suite 800, Chicago IL 60601. Accepts queries by e-mail.

ILLUSTRATION Illustrations are by assignment only. Please do not send original artwork. Send postcards, promotional brochures, or color photocopies. Be sure that each sample is marked with your name, address, phone number, and website or blog. Art submissions will not be returned.

NATIONAL GEOGRAPHIC KIDS

National Geographic Society, 1145 17th St. NW, Washington DC 20036. **E-mail:** ashaw@ngs.org. **Website:** www.kids.nationalgeographic.com. **Contact:** Michelle Tyler, editorial assistant. Magazine published 10 times/year. "It's our mission to find fresh ways to entertain children while educating and exciting them about their world." Estab. 1975. Circ. 1.3 million.

"We do not want poetry, sports, fiction, or story ideas that are too young—our audience is between ages 6-14."

NONFICTION Needs general interest, humor, interview, technical. Query with published clips and résumé. Length: 100-1,000 words. Pays $1/word for assigned articles.

HOW TO CONTACT Editorial lead time 6+ months. Publishes ms an average of 6 months after acceptance. Accepts queries by mail.

PHOTOS State availability. Captions, identification of subjects, model releases required. Reviews contact sheets, negatives, transparencies, prints. Negotiates payment individually.

TERMS Buys all rights. Makes work-for-hire assignments. Byline given. Pays on acceptance. Offers 10% kill fee. 70% freelance written. Sample copy for #10 SASE. Guidelines online.

TIPS "Submit relevant clips. Writers must have demonstrated experience writing for kids. Read the magazine before submitting."

NATURE FRIEND MAGAZINE

4253 Woodcock Lane, Dayton VA 22821. (540)867-0764. **E-mail:** info@naturefriendmagazine.com; editor@naturefriendmagazine.com; photos@naturefriendmagazine.com. **Website:** www.naturefriendmagazine.com. **Contact:** Kevin Shank, editor. Monthly children's magazine covering creation-based nature. *Nature Friend* includes stories, puzzles, science experiments, and nature experiments. All submissions need to honor God as creator. Estab. 1983. Circ. 8,000.

Picture-oriented material and conversational material needed.

NONFICTION Needs how-to. Send complete ms. Length: 250-900 words. Pays 5¢/word.

HOW TO CONTACT Editorial lead time 4 months. Responds in 6 months to mss.

PHOTOS Send photos. Captions, identification of subjects required. Reviews prints. Offers $20-75/photo.

TERMS Buys first rights, buys one-time rights. Byline given. Pays on publication. No kill fee. 80% freelance written. Sample copy: $5, postage paid. Guidelines available on website.

TIPS "We want to bring joy and knowledge to children by opening the world of God's creation to them. We endeavor to create a sense of awe about nature's Creator and a respect for His creation. We'd like to see more submissions on hands-on things to do with a nature theme (not collecting rocks or leaves—real stuff). Also looking for good stories that are accompanied by good photography."

SHINE BRIGHTLY

GEMS Girls' Clubs, 1333 Alger St., SE, Grand Rapids MI 49507. (616)241-5616. **Fax:** (616)241-5558. **E-mail:** shinebrightly@gemsgc.org. **Website:** www.gemsgc.org. **Contact:** Kelli Gilmore, managing editor. Monthly magazine from September to May with a double issue for September/October. "Our purpose is to lead girls into a living relationship with Jesus Christ and to help them see how God is at work in their lives and the world around them. Puzzles, crafts, stories, and articles for girls ages 9-14." Estab. 1970. Circ. 13,000.

FICTION Does not want "unrealistic stories and those with trite, easy endings. We are interested in manuscripts that show how real girls can change the world." Needs ethnic, historical, humorous, mystery, religious, slice-of-life vignettes. Believable only. Nothing too preachy. Submit complete ms in body of e-mail. No attachments. Length: 700-900 words. Pays up to $35, plus 2 copies.

NONFICTION Needs humor, inspirational, interview, personal experience, photo feature, religious, travel. Submit complete ms in body of e-mail. No attachments. Length: 100-800 words. Pays up to $35, plus 2 copies.

POETRY Limited need for poetry. Pays $5-15.

HOW TO CONTACT Responds in 2 months to mss. Publishes ms an average of 4 months after acceptance.

ILLUSTRATION Samples returned with SASE. Credit line given.

PHOTOS Purchased with or without ms. Appreciate multicultural subjects. Reviews 5x7 or 8x10 clear color glossy prints. Pays $25-50 on publication.

TERMS Buys first North American serial rights, buys second serial (reprint) rights, buys simultaneous rights. Byline given. Pays on publication. No kill fee. 60% freelance written. Works with new and published/established writers. Sample copy with 9x12 SASE with 3 first class stamps and $1. Guidelines online.

TIPS Writers: "Please check our website before submitting. We have a specific style and theme that deals with how girls can impact the world. The stories should be current, deal with pre-adolescent problems and joys, and help girls see God at work in their lives through humor as well as problem-solving." Prefers not to see anything on the adult level, secular material, or violence. Writers frequently oversimplify the articles and often write with a Pollyanna attitude. An author should be able to see his/her writing style as exciting and appealing to girls ages 9-14. The style can be fun, but also teach a truth. Subjects should be current and important to *SHINE brightly* readers. Use our theme update as a guide. We would like to receive material with a multicultural slant."

SKIPPING STONES

A Multicultural Literary Magazine, Skipping Stones. Inc., P. O. Box 3939, Eugene OR 97403-0939. (541)342-4956. **E-mail:** editor@skippingstones.org. **Website:** www.skippingstones.org. **Contact:** Arun Toké, editor. "*Skipping Stones* is an award-winning multicultural, nonprofit magazine that promotes cooperation, creativity and celebration of cultural and ecological richness. We encourage submissions by children of color, minorities and underrepresented populations. We want material meant for children and young adults/teenagers with multicultural or ecological awareness themes. Think, live and write as if you were a child, tween or teen. We want material that gives insight to cultural celebrations, lifestyle, customs and traditions, glimpse of daily life in other countries and cultures. Photos, songs, artwork are most welcome if they illustrate/highlight the points. Translations are invited if your submission is in a language other than English." Themes may include cultural celebrations, living abroad, challenging disability, hospitality customs of various cultures, cross-cultural understanding, African, Asian and Latin American cultures, humor, international understanding, turning points and magical moments in life, caring for the earth, spirituality, and multicultural awareness. *Skipping Stones* is magazine-sized, saddle-stapled, printed on recycled paper. We have published quarterly during the school year (4 issues) until January 2021, but now we are publishing online as a result of current global pandemic conditions. Estab. 1988. Circ. 1,200 print, plus online and Web.

FICTION Middle readers, young adult/teens: contemporary, meaningful, humorous. All levels: folktales, multicultural, nature/environment. Multicultural needs include: bilingual or multilingual pieces; use of words from other languages; settings in other countries, cultures or multi-ethnic communities. Needs adventure, ethnic, historical, humorous, multicultural, international, social issues. No suspense or romance stories. Send complete ms. Length: 1,000 words maximum. Pays 6 contributor's copies.

NONFICTION Needs essays, general interest, humor, inspirational, interview, opinion, personal experience, photo feature, travel. All levels: animal, biography, cooking, games/puzzles, history, humorous, interview/profile, multicultural, nature/environment, creative problem-solving, religion and cultural celebrations, sports, travel, social and international awareness. Does not want to see preaching, violence or abusive language. Send complete ms. Length: 1,000 words maximum. Pays 4 contributor's copies.

POETRY Submit up to 5 poems at a time. Considers simultaneous submissions; no previously published poems. Accepts e-mail submissions. Cover letter is preferred. "Include your cultural background, experiences, and the inspiration behind your creation." Time between acceptance and publication is 6-9 months. "A piece is chosen for publication when most of the editorial staff feel good about it." Seldom comments on rejected poems. Publishes multi-theme issues. Responds in up to 4 months. Poems by youth under the age of 19 only. Length: 30 lines maximum. Pays 2 contributor's copies, offers 40% discount for more copies and subscription, if desired.

HOW TO CONTACT Editorial lead time 3-4 months. Responds only if interested. Send nonreturnable samples. Publishes ms an average of 4-8 months after acceptance. Accepts queries by mail, e-mail.

ILLUSTRATION Prefers illustrations by teenagers and young adults. Will consider all illustration packages. Manuscript/illustration packages: Query; submit complete ms with final art; submit tearsheets. Responds in 4 months. Credit line given.

PHOTOS Black & white as well as color photos are welcome. Needs: youth 7-17, international, nature, celebrations. Send photos. Captions required. Reviews 4X6 prints, low-res JPEG files. Offers no additional payment for photos.

TERMS Buys first North American serial rights, nonexclusive reprint, and electronic rights. Byline given. No kill fee. 80% freelance written. Sample: $7. Guidelines available online or for SASE.

TIPS "Be original and innovative. Use multicultural, nature, or cross-cultural themes. Multilingual submissions are welcome."

SPARKLE

GEMS Girls' Clubs, 1333 Alger St. SE, Grand Rapids MI 49507. (616)241-5616. **Fax:** (616)241-5558. **E-mail:** sparkle@gemsgc.org. **Website:** www.gemsgc.org. **Contact:** Kelli Gilmore, managing editor; Lisa Hunter, art director/photo editor. Monthly magazine for girls ages 6-9 from October to March. Mission is to prepare young girls to live out their faith and become world-changers. Strives to help girls make a difference in the world. Looks at the application of scripture to everyday life. Also strives to delight the reader and cause the reader to evalute her own life in light of the truth presented. Finally, attempts to teach practical life skills. Estab. 2002. Circ. 9,000.

FICTION Young readers: adventure, animal, contemporary, ethnic/multicultural, fantasy, folktale, health, history, humorous, music and musicians, mystery, nature/environment, problem-solving, religious, recipes, service projects, slice-of-life, sports, suspense/mystery, vignettes, interacting with family and friends. Send complete ms. Length: 100-400 words. Pays $35 maximum.

NONFICTION Young readers: animal, arts/crafts, biography, careers, cooking, concept, games/puzzles, geography, health, history, hobbies, how-to, humor, inspirational, interview/profile, math, multicultural, music/drama/art, nature/environment, personal experience, photo feature, problem-solving, quizzes, recipes, religious, science, social issues, sports, travel. Looking for inspirational biographies, stories from Zambia, and ideas on how to live a green lifestyle. Send complete ms. Length: 100-400 words. Pays $35 maximum.

POETRY Prefers rhyming. "We do not wish to see anything that is too difficult for a first grader to read. We wish it to remain light. The style can be fun but should also teach a truth." No violence or secular material.

HOW TO CONTACT Editorial lead time 3 months. Responds 3 months to mss. Accepts queries by e-mail.

ILLUSTRATION Buys 1-2 illustrations/issue; 8-10 illustrations/year. Uses color artwork only. Works on assignment only. Reviews ms/illustration packages from artists. Send ms with dummy. Illustrations only: send promo sheet. Contact: Sara DeRidder. Responds in 3 weeks only if interested. Samples returned with SASE; samples filed. Credit line given.

PHOTOS Send photos. Identification of subjects required. Reviews at least 5X7 clear color glossy prints, GIF/JPEG files on CD. Offers $25-50/photo.

TERMS Buys first North American serial rights, first rights, one-time rights, second serial (reprint), first rights, second rights. Byline given. Pays on publication. 40% freelance written. Sample copy for 9x13 SAE, 3 first-class stamps, and $1 for coverage/publication cost. Guidelines available for #10 SASE or online.

TIPS "Keep it simple. We are writing to first to third graders. It must be simple yet interesting. Mss should build girls up in Christian character but not be preachy. They are just learning about God and how He wants them to live. Mss should be delightful as well as educational and inspirational. Writers should keep stories simple but not write with a 'Pollyanna' attitude. Authors should see their writing style as exciting and appealing to girls ages 6-9. Subjects should be current and important to *Sparkle* readers. Use our theme as a guide. We would like to receive material with a multicultural slant."

SPIDER

Website: www.cricketmag.com. Monthly reading and activity magazine for children ages 6-9. "*Spider* introduces children to the highest-quality stories, poems, illustrations, articles, and activities. It was created to foster in beginning readers a love of reading and discovery that will last a lifetime. We're looking for writers who respect children's intelligence." Estab. 1994. Circ. 70,000.

FICTION Wants "complex and believable" stories. Needs fantasy, humorous. No romance, horror, religious. Submit complete ms via online submissions manager (cricketmag.submittable.com). Length: 300-1,000 words. Pays up to 25¢/word.

NONFICTION Submit complete ms via online submissions manager (cricketmag.submittable.com). Length: 300-800 words. Pays up to 25¢/word.

POETRY Submit up to 5 poems via online submissions manager (cricketmag.submittable.com). "Poems should be succinct, imaginative, and accessible; we tend to avoid long narrative poems." Length: up to 20 lines/poem. Pays up to $3/line.

HOW TO CONTACT Send submissions to: Art Submissions Coordinator, Cricket Media, 70 E. Lake St., Suite 800, Chicago IL 60601. Responds in 6 months to mss. Accepts queries by online submission form.

ILLUSTRATION "Please do not send original artwork. Send postcards, promotional brochures, or color photocopies. Be sure that each sample is marked with your name, address, phone number and website or blog. Art submissions will not be returned."

TERMS Rights purchased vary. Byline given. Pays on publication. 85% freelance written. Sample copy available online. Guidelines available online.

TIPS "We'd like to see more of the following: engaging nonfiction, fillers, and 'takeout page' activities; folktales, fairy tales, science fiction, and humorous stories. Most importantly, do not write down to children."

YOUNG RIDER

2030 Main Street, Irvine CA 92614. (949) 855-8822. **Fax:** (949) 855-3045. **E-mail:** yreditor@i5publishing.com. **Website:** www.youngrider.com. "*Young Rider* magazine teaches young people, in an easy-to-read and entertaining way, how to look after their horses properly, and how to improve their riding skills safely."

FICTION Needs young adults: adventure, animal, horses. "We would prefer funny stories, with a bit of conflict, which will appeal to the 13-year-old age group. They should be written in the third person, and about kids." Query. Length: 800-1,000 words. Pays $150.

NONFICTION Needs young adults: animal, careers, famous equestrians, health (horse), horse celebrities, riding. Query with published clips. Length: 800-1,000 words. Pays $200/story.

PHOTOS Buys photos with accompanying ms only. Uses high-res digital images only—in focus, good light. Model/property release required; captions required.

TERMS Byline given. Guidelines available online.

TIPS "Fiction must be in third person. Read magazine before sending in a query. No 'true story from when I was a youngster.' No moralistic stories. Fiction must be up-to-date and humorous, teen-oriented. No practical or how-to articles—all done in-house."

AGENTS & ART REPS

This section features listings of literary agents and art reps who either specialize in, or represent a good percentage of, children's writers and/or illustrators. While there are a number of children's publishers who are open to nonagented material, using the services of an agent or rep can be beneficial to a writer or artist. Agents and reps can get your work seen by editors and art directors more quickly. They are familiar with the market and have insights into which editors and art directors would be most interested in your work. Also, they negotiate contracts and will likely be able to get you a better deal than you could get on your own.

Agents and reps make their income by taking a percentage of what writers and illustrators receive from publishers. The standard percentage for agents is 10 to 15 percent; art reps generally take 25 to 30 percent. We have not included any agencies in this section that charge reading fees.

WHAT TO SEND

When putting together a package for an agent or rep, follow the guidelines given in their listings. Most agents open to submissions prefer initially to receive a query letter describing your work. For novels and longer works, some agents ask for an outline and a number of sample chapters, but you should send these only if you're asked to do so. Never fax or email query letters or sample chapters to agents without their permission. Just as with publishers, agents receive a large volume of submissions. It may take them a long time to reply, so you may want to query several agents at one time. It's best, however, to have a complete manuscript considered by only one agent at a time. Always include a self-addressed, stamped envelope (SASE).

For initial contact with art reps, send a brief query letter and self-promo pieces, following the guidelines given in the listings. If you don't have a flier or brochure, send photocopies. Always include a SASE.

For those who both write and illustrate, some agents listed will consider the work of author/illustrators. Read through the listings for details.

As you consider approaching agents and reps with your work, keep in mind that they are very choosy about whom represent. Your work must be high quality and presented professionally to make an impression on them. For more information on approaching agents and additional listings, see *Guide to Literary Agents* (Writer's Digest Books).

AN ORGANIZATION FOR AGENTS

In some listings of agents you'll see references to AAR (The Association of Authors' Representatives). This organization requires its members to meet an established list of professional standards and code of ethics.

The objectives of AAR include keeping agents informed about conditions in publishing and related fields; encouraging cooperation among literary organizations; and assisting agents in representing their author-clients' interests. Officially, members are prohibited from directly or indirectly charging reading fees. They offer writers a list of member agents on their website. They also offer a list of recommended questions an author should ask an agent and other FAQs, all found on their website.

A+B WORKS

Website: http://aplusbworks.com. **Contact:** Amy Jameson, Brandon Jameson. A+B Works is a creative services agency, offering literary representation, editorial coaching, and graphic design. Amy represents writers as an agent for YA, MG, graphic novels and picture books (both fiction and nonfiction). Brandon is a graphic designer who works with clients from all disciplines, including authors, to create brands, websites, and other visual materials.

MEMBER AGENTS Amy Jameson (picture books, middle grade and young adult).

HANDLES Does not want women's fiction, or any other books for adults.

HOW TO CONTACT Query via online submission form. "Due to the high volume of queries we receive, we can't guarantee a response." Accepts simultaneous submissions.

ADAMS LITERARY

7845 Colony Rd., C4 #215, Charlotte NC 28226. (704)542-1440. **Fax:** (704)542-1450. **E-mail:** info@adamsliterary.com. **Website:** www.adamsliterary.com. **Contact:** Tracey Adams, Josh Adams. Adams Literary is a full-service literary agency exclusively representing children's and young adult authors and artists.

Temporarily closed to submissions.

MEMBER AGENTS Tracey Adams, Josh Adams.

HANDLES Represents "the finest children's book and young adult authors and artists."

RECENT SALES *I'm Not Dying with You Tonight*, by Gilly Segal and Kimberly Jones (Sourcebooks); *None Shall Sleep*, by Ellie Marney (Little, Brown); Aurora's End, by Amie Kaufman and Jay Kristoff (Knopf Books for Young Readers); *The Blackbird Girls*, by Anne Blankman (Viking); *The Rice in the Pot Goes Round and Round*, by Wendy Shang (Orchard Books); *The Court of Miracles*, by Kester Grant (Knopf Random House); *Dark Rise*, by C. S. Pacat (Quill Tree Books); *Empire of the Vampire*, by Jay Kristoff (St. Martin's Press).

TERMS Agent receives 15% commission on domestic sales; 20% on foreign sales. Offers written contract.

HOW TO CONTACT **Submit through online form on website only.** Send e-mail if that is not operating correctly. All submissions and queries should first be made through the online form on website. Will not review—and will promptly recycle—any unsolicited submissions or queries received by mail. Before submitting work for consideration, review complete guidelines online, as the agency sometimes shuts off to new submissions. Accepts simultaneous submissions. "While we have an established client list, we do seek new talent—and we accept submissions from both published and aspiring authors and artists."

TIPS "Guidelines are posted (and frequently updated) on our website."

AEVITAS CREATIVE MANAGEMENT

19 W. 21st St., Suite 501, New York NY 10010. (212)765-6900. **Website:** aevitascreative.com.

MEMBER AGENTS Esmond Harmsworth, managing partner; David Kuhn, managing partner; Todd Shuster, managing partner; Jennifer Gates, senior partner; Laura Nolan, senior partner; Janet Silver, senior partner; Bridget Wagner Matzie, partner; Rick Richter, partner; Jane von Mehren, partner; Lauren Sharp, senior agent; Rob Arnold, agent; Sarah Bowlin, agent; Michelle Brower, agent; Lori Galvin, agent; David Granger, agent; Sarah Lazin, agent; Sarah Levitt, agent; Will Lippincott, agent; Jen Marshall, agent; Penny Moore, agent; Jon Michael Darga, agent; Maggie Cooper, agent; Chelsey Heller, agent; Georgia Francis King, agent; Karen Brailsford, agent; Chris Bacci, agent; Danya Kukafka, agent; Micahel Signorelli, agent; Lauren Sharp, agent; Becky Sweren, agent; Erica Bauman, agent; Justin Brouckaert, agent; Catharine Strong, associate agent; Daniella Cohen, associate agent; Nate Muscato, agent.

HOW TO CONTACT Find specific agents on the Aevitas website to see their specific interests and guidelines. Accepts simultaneous submissions.

AITKEN ALEXANDER ASSOCIATES

291 Gray's Inn Rd., Kings Cross, London WC1X 8QJ, United Kingdom. (020)7373-8672. **Fax:** (020)7373-6002. **E-mail:** reception@aitkenalexander.co.uk. **Website:** www.aitkenalexander.co.uk.

MEMBER AGENTS Clare Alexander (literary, commercial, memoir, narrative nonfiction, history); Lesley Thorne; Lisa Baker; Chris Wellbelove; Emma Patterson; Steph Adams; Amy St. Johnston; Monica MacSwain.

HANDLES "We specialize in literary fiction and nonfiction." Does not represent illustrated children's books, poetry, or screenplays.

RECENT SALES *A Country Row, A Tree*, by Jo Baker (Knopf); *Noonday*, by Pat Barker (Doubleday); *Beatle-*

bone, by Kevin Barry (Doubleday); *Spill Simmer Falter Wither*, by Sara Baume (Houghton Mifflin).

HOW TO CONTACT "If you would like to submit your work to us, please e-mail your covering letter with a short synopsis and the first 30 pages (as a Word document) to submissions@aitkenalexander.co.uk indicating if there is a specific agent who you would like to consider your work. Although every effort is made to respond to submissions, if we have not responded within three months please assume that your work is not right for the agency's list. Please note that the Indian Office does not accept unsolicited submissions." Accepts simultaneous submissions. Obtains most new clients through recommendations from others, solicitations.

ALIVE LITERARY AGENCY

5001 Centennial Blvd. #50742, Colorado Springs CO 80908. **Website:** www.aliveliterary.com. Alive is the largest, most influential literary agency for inspirational content and authors.

MEMBER AGENTS Bryan Norman (popular nonfiction, biography/memoir/autobiography, spiritual growth, inspirational, literary); Lisa Jackson (popular nonfiction, biography/memoir/autobiography, spiritual growth, inspirational, literary, women's nonfiction); Rachel Jacobson.

HANDLES This agency specializes in inspirational fiction, Christian living, how-to, and commercial nonfiction. Actively seeking inspirational, literary and mainstream fiction, inspirational nonfiction, and work from authors with established track records and platforms. Does not want to receive poetry, scripts, or dark themes.

TERMS Agent receives 15% commission on domestic sales. Offers written contract; two-month notice must be given to terminate contract.

HOW TO CONTACT "Because all our agents have full client loads, they are only considering queries from authors referred by clients and close contacts. Please refer to our guidelines at http://aliveliterary.com/submissions. Authors referred by an Alive client or close contact are invited to send proposals to submissions@aliveliterary.com." Your submission should include a referral (name of referring Alive client or close contact in the e-mail subject line. In the e-mail, please describe your personal or professional connection to the referring individual), a brief author biography (including recent speaking engagements, media appearances, social media platform statistics, and sales histories of your books), a synopsis of the work for which you are seeking agency representation (including the target audience, sales and marketing hooks, and comparable titles on the market), and the first 3 chapters of your manuscript. Alive will respond to queries meeting the above guidelines within 8-10 weeks.

TIPS "Rewrite and polish until the words on the page shine. Endorsements, a solid platform, and great connections may help, provided you can write with power and passion. Hone your craft by networking with publishing professionals, joining critique groups, and attending writers' conferences."

BETSY AMSTER LITERARY ENTERPRISES

607 Foothill Blvd. #1061, La Cañada Flintridge CA 91012. **Website:** www.amsterlit.com; www.cummingskidlit.com. **Contact:** Betsy Amster (adult); Mary Cummings (children's and young adult). Betsy Amster Literary Enterprises is a full-service literary agency located in Los Angeles, California. We handle publishing rights and all ancillary rights (such as film, TV, audio, and foreign) for the authors we represent. We work with both first-time and established writers and are known for our expert attention to every aspect of the publishing process.

HANDLES "Betsy Amster is actively seeking strong narrative nonfiction, particularly by journalists; outstanding literary fiction; witty, intelligent commercial women's fiction; character-driven mysteries and thrillers that open new worlds to us; high-profile self-help, psychology, and health, preferably research-based; and cookbooks and food narratives by West Coast–based chefs and food writers with an original viewpoint and national exposure. Does not want to receive poetry, romances, western, science fiction, action/adventure, screenplays, fantasy, techno-thrillers, spy capers, apocalyptic scenarios, or political or religious arguments. Mary Cummings is actively seeking great read-aloud picture books and middle-grade novels with strong story arcs, a spunky central character, and warmth, humor, or quirky charm as well as picture-book biographies and lyrically written children's nonfiction on science, nature, mindfulness, and social awareness."

RECENT SALES **Betsy Amster**: *L.A. Weather*, by María Amparo Escandón (Flatiron); *The Taste of Sugar*, by Marisel Vera (Liveright); *How to Write a Nov-*

el in 20 Pies: Sweet and Savory Secrets for Surviving the Writing Life, by Amy Wallen, illustrated by Emil Wilson (Andrews McMeel); *Sugarproof: The Hidden Dangers of Sugar That Are Putting Your Child's Health at Risk and What You Can Do*, by Michael I. Goran, Ph.D. and Emily Ventura, Ph.D., M.P.H. (Avery); *The Highly Sensitive Parent: Be Brilliant in Your Role, Even When the World Overwhelms You*, by Elaine N. Aron, Ph.D. (Citadel); *Nora Ephron: A Life*, by Kristin Marguerite Doidge (Chicago Review Press); *The Lost Gutenberg: The Astounding Story of One Book's Five-Hundred-Year Odyssey*, by Margaret Leslie Davis (TarcherPerigee). **Mary Cummings**: *Show the World*, by Angela Dalton (Philomel); *I Was*, by Katherine Hocker (Candlewick); *Valenslime*, by Joy Keller (Feiwel & Friends); *Be Black Girl Be*, by T.B. Darks (Balzer & Bray);*The Art of Magic*, by Hannah Voskuil (Carolrhoda); *To Boldly Go*, by Angela Dalton (HarperCollins).

TERMS Agent receives 15% commission on domestic sales; 20% commission on foreign sales. Offers written contract, binding for 1 year; three-month notice must be given to terminate contract. Charges for photocopying, postage, messengers, galleys/books used in submissions to foreign and film agents and to magazines for first serial rights. (Please note that it is rare to incur much in the way of expenses now that most submissions are made by e-mail.)

HOW TO CONTACT "For children's picture books, please embed the entire text in the body of your e-mail. For longer middle-grade and YA fiction and nonfiction, please embed the first 3 pages." Accepts simultaneous submissions. Obtains most new clients through recommendations from others, solicitations, and conferences.

AZANTIAN LITERARY AGENCY

Website: www.azantianlitagency.com. **Contact:** Jennifer Azantian.

MEMBER AGENTS Jennifer Azantian; Renae Moore; T.S. Ferguson; Alexandra Weiss; Andrea Walker; Amanda Rutter; Masha Gunic.

HANDLES Stories that explore meaningful human interactions against fantastic backdrops, underrepresented voices, obscure retold fairy tales, quirky middle grade, modernized mythologies, psychological horror, literary science fiction, historical fantasy, magical realism, internally consistent epic fantasy, and spooky stories for younger readers.

HOW TO CONTACT During open submission windows only: send your query letter, 1-2 page synopsis, and first 10 pages through the form on ALA's website. Accepts simultaneous submissions.

BARONE LITERARY AGENCY

385 North St., Batavia OH 45103. (513)293-7864. **Fax:** (513)586-0795. **E-mail:** baronelit@outlook.com. **Website:** www.baroneliteraryagency.com. **Contact:** Denise Barone. Represents Yvette Geer, Katemarie Collins, Curt Rude, Molly Zenk, Sarah Biglow, Suzanne Hay, Cathy Bennett, Rebekah Purdy, Michele Barrow-Belisle, Angharad Jones, Denise Gwen, Laurie Albano, Robert E. Hoxie, Rhonda Vincent, Anna Snow, and Jennifer Petersen Fraser.

"As a licensed attorney and a published writer, I know a lot about the publishing industry, and will bring additional expertise to contract negotiations."

HANDLES Actively seeking adult contemporary romance. Does not want textbooks.

RECENT SALES *The List*, by Yvette Geer (Cayelle Publishing), *Her Hot Alaskan Doc*, by Denise Gwen (Cayelle Publishing), *Hunted, Allied*, and *Fated*, by Molly Zenk and Sarah Biglow (Cayelle Publishing), *Haunting You*, by Molly Zenk (Intrigue Publishing); *The Beekeeper*, by Robert E. Hoxie (Six Gun Pictures); *All The Glittering Bones*, by Anna Snow (Entangled Publishing); *Devon's Choice*, by Cathy Bennett (Clean Reads); *Molly's Folly*, by Denise Gwen (Clean Reads); *In Deep*, by Laurie Albano (Solstice Publishing); *The Trouble with Charlie*, by Cathy Bennett (Clean Reads); *The Fairy Godmother Files: Cinderella Complex*, by Rebekah L. Purdy (Clean Reads).

TERMS Agency receives 15% commission on domestic sales; 20% on foreign sales. Offers written contract.

HOW TO CONTACT "Due to the massive number of submissions that I receive, I can no longer respond to queries. You will not hear back from me unless I am interested in your work. Please do not send anything through the mail. I accept only email queries. If I like your query letter, I will ask for the first 3 chapters and a synopsis as attachments." Accepts simultaneous submissions. Obtains new clients by queries/submissions via e-mail only.

TIPS "The best writing advice I ever got came from a fellow writer, who wrote, 'Learn how to edit yourself,' when signing her book to me."

THE BENT AGENCY

145 Lyme Road Suite 206, Hanover NH 03755. **E-mail:** info@thebentagency.com. **Website:** www.thebentagency.com. **Contact:** Jenny Bent.

MEMBER AGENTS Jenny Bent (adult fiction, including women's fiction, romance, and crime/suspense; she particularly likes novels with magical or fantasy elements that fall outside of genre fiction; young adult and middle-grade fiction; memoir; humor); Molly Ker Hawn (young adult and middle-grade fiction and nonfiction); Nicola Barr (literary and commercial fiction for adults and children, and nonfiction in the areas of sports, popular science, popular culture, and social and cultural history); Victoria Cappello (commercial and literary adult fiction as well as narrative nonfiction); Gemma Cooper (all ages of children's and young adult books, including picture books); Claire Draper (graphic novels for all ages, middle-grade and young adult fiction, feminist memoir and essay collections); Louise Fury (picture books, literary middle-grade, and all young adult; adult fiction: speculative fiction, suspense/thriller, commercial fiction, and all subgenres of romance; nonfiction: cookbooks and pop culture); Sarah Hornsley (commercial and accessible literary adult fiction and nonfiction in the area of memoir, lifestyle, and narrative nonfiction); James Mustelier (literary and commercial adult, young adult, and middle-grade fiction); Zoë Plant (adult fiction (sci-fi/fantasy, horror) as well as middle-grade and young adult fiction); John Silbersack (adult fiction (mystery/thriller, literary fiction, sci-fi/fantasy), adult nonfiction (history, current events, politics, biography, memoir, science and pop culture) as well as some young adult and middle-grade); Laurel Symonds (children's fiction and nonfiction, from picture books to young adult); Desiree Wilson (commercial and literary fiction for middle grade, young adult, and adults, graphic novels for all ages, and memoir).

HOW TO CONTACT "Tell us briefly who you are, what your book is, and why you're the one to write it. Then include the first 10 pages of your material in the body of your e-mail. We respond to all queries; please resend your query if you haven't had a response within 4 weeks." Please check agency website to see which agents are accepting submissions. Accepts simultaneous submissions.

VICKY BIJUR LITERARY AGENCY

27 W. 20th St., Suite 1003, New York NY 10011. **Website:** www.vickybijuragency.com.

MEMBER AGENTS Vicky Bijur; Alexandra Franklin.

HANDLES "We are not the right agency for screenplays, picture books, poetry, self-help, science fiction, fantasy, horror, or romance."

RECENT SALES *That Darkness*, by Lisa Black; *Long Upon the Land*, by Margaret Maron; *Daughter of Ashes*, by Marcia Talley.

HOW TO CONTACT "Please send a query letter of no more than 3 paragraphs on what makes your book special and unique, a very brief synopsis, its length and genre, and your biographical information, along with the first 10 pages of your manuscript. Please let us know in your query letter if it is a multiple submission, and kindly keep us informed of other agents' interest and offers of representation. If sending electronically, paste the pages in an e-mail as we don't open attachments from unfamiliar senders. If sending by hard copy, please include an SASE for our response. If you want your material returned, include an SASE large enough to contain pages and enough postage to send back to you." Accepts simultaneous submissions.

DAVID BLACK LITERARY AGENCY

335 Adams St., Suite 2707, Brooklyn NY 11201. (718)852-5500. **Fax:** (718)852-5539. **Website:** www.davidblackagency.com. **Contact:** David Black, owner.

MEMBER AGENTS David Black; Jenny Herrera; Gary Morris; Joy E. Tutela (narrative nonfiction, memoir, history, politics, self-help, investment, business, science, women's issues, GLBT issues, parenting, health and fitness, humor, craft, cooking and wine, lifestyle and entertainment, commercial fiction, literary fiction, MG, YA); Susan Raihofer (commercial fiction and nonfiction, memoir, pop culture, music, inspirational, thrillers, literary fiction); Sarah Smith (memoir, biography, food, music, narrative history, social studies, literary fiction); Rica Allanic; Ayla Zuraw-Friedland.

RECENT SALES Some of the agency's best-selling authors include: Erik Larson, Stuart Scott, Jeff Hobbs, Mitch Albom, Gregg Olsen, Jim Abbott, and John Bacon.

HOW TO CONTACT "To query an individual agent, please follow the specific query guidelines outlined in the agent's profile on our website. Not all agents are currently accepting unsolicited queries. To query the agency, please send a 1-2 page query letter describing your book, and include information about any previously published works, your audience, and your platform." Do not e-mail your query unless an agent specifically asks for an e-mail. Accepts simultaneous submissions.

BOND LITERARY AGENCY

201 Milwaukee St., Suite 200, Denver CO 80206. (303)781-9305. **E-mail:** sandra@bondliteraryagency.com; becky@bondliteraryagency.com; patrick@bondliteraryagency.com. **Website:** www.bondliteraryagency.com. **Contact:** Sandra Bond. The agency is small, with a select list of writers. Represents adult and young adult fiction, both literary and commercial, including mysteries and women's fiction. Nonfiction interests include narrative, history, science and business.

MEMBER AGENTS Sandra Bond, agent (fiction: adult commercial and literary, mystery/thriller/suspense, women's, historical, young adult; nonfiction: narrative, history, science, business); Becky LeJeune, associate agent (fiction: horror, mystery/thriller/suspense, science fiction/fantasy, historical, general fiction, young adult); Patrick Munnelly (horror, fantasy, political science, current affairs, health & wellness, fitness, and graphic novels).

HANDLES Agency does not represent romance, poetry, young reader chapter books, children's picture books, or screenplays.

RECENT SALES *The Past Is Never*, by Tiffany Quay Tyson; *Cold Case: Billy the Kid*, by W.C. Jameson; *Women in Film: The Truth and the Timeline*, by Jill S. Tietjen and Barbara Bridges; Books 7 & 8 in the Hiro Hattori Mystery Series, by Susan Spann.

HOW TO CONTACT Please submit query by e-mail (absolutely no attachments unless requested). No unsolicited mss. "They will let you know if they are interested in seeing more material. No phone calls, please." Accepts simultaneous submissions.

BOOK CENTS LITERARY AGENCY, LLC

Website: www.bookcentsliteraryagency.com. **Contact:** Christine Witthohn. "It is our goal not only to assist our clients in selling their creative work(s), but to also assist them with growing their writing careers and helping them reach their targeted audiences. We will make it our mission to work hard and be diligent, and to keep the lines of communication open with the authors we represent. We are not an agency whose main interest is in acquiring large numbers of clients. Rather, we are looking to find quality authors with fresh and creative voices who are not afraid to write what they love. We aggressively sell and license our clients' titles in all formats in both domestic and foreign markets. We concentrate on print, digital, audio, dramatic, large print, serial, multimedia, and graphic, as well as other rights and licenses. We also collaborate with our authors on marketing and promotional ideas, assist in implementing branding strategies, and help our authors reach their targeted audience(s)."

HANDLES Actively seeking upmarket fiction, commercial fiction (particularly if it has crossover appeal), women's fiction (emotional and layered), romance (single title or category), mainstream mystery/suspense, thrillers (particularly psychological), and young adult. For a detailed list of what this agency is currently searching for, visit the website. Does not want to receive third party submissions, previously published titles, short stories/novellas, erotica, inspirational, historical, science fiction/fantasy, horror/pulp/slasher thrillers, middle-grade, children's picture books, poetry, or screenplays. Does not want stories with priests/nuns, religion, abuse of children/animals/elderly, rape, or serial killers.

HOW TO CONTACT Submit via agency website. Does not accept mail or e-mail submissions.

TIPS Sponsors the International Women's Fiction Festival in Matera, Italy. See www.womensfictionfestival.com for more information. Ms. Witthohn is also the U.S. rights and licensing agent for leading French publisher Bragelonne, German publisher Egmont, and Spanish publisher Edebe.

BOOKENDS LITERARY AGENCY

Website: www.bookendsliterary.com. **Contact:** Jessica Faust, Kim Lionetti, Jessica Alvarez, Moe Ferrara, Tracy Marchini, Rachel Brooks, Naomi Davis, Amanda Jain, James McGowan, Emily Forney. "Since opening its doors in 1999, BookEnds Literary Agency has never strayed from our original goal: achieving dreams and doing what we love. Representing fiction and nonfiction for adults and children alike, BookEnds agents continue to live their dreams while helping authors achieve theirs. First opened as a book packaging company, we were originally looking to take our own fresh and fun ideas and find just the right people to create the books publishers and readers were looking for. Over time, we missed working on fiction and seeing what could come from an author's imagination as well as an author's platform. So not 2 years after opening its doors, BookEnds changed its literary status to agency."

"While the industry has changed, and BookEnds has grown, the one thing we've never lost is our passion and love for books and the authors who create them."

MEMBER AGENTS Jessica Faust (women's fiction, upmarket, literary, mysteries, thrillers, suspense); Kim Lionetti (romance, women's fiction, young adult, cozy mystery, suspense); Jessica Alvarez (romance, women's fiction, mystery, nonfiction); Moe Ferrara (picture book, middle-grade, young adult, adult: graphic novels, LGBT-centric, contemporary, romance/romantic comedy, light horror, magical realism, re-tellings, light science fiction, fantasy, humorous (picture book)); Tracy Marchini (picture book, middle-grade, children's illustration, and young adult: fiction and nonfiction); Rachel Brooks (adult romance, young adult, upmarket and commercial women's fiction, mysteries); Naomi Davis (science fiction, fantasy, young adult, romance, middle grade, picture book); Amanda Jain (nonfiction and adult: mystery, romance, women's fiction, upmarket, historical fiction); James McGowan (picture book fiction and nonfiction, upmarket, mystery, suspense, thriller, crime, illustrators); Emily Forney (picture book, middle-grade, young adult, historical fiction, adult romance).

HANDLES "BookEnds is currently accepting queries from published and unpublished writers in the areas of romance, mystery, suspense, science fiction and fantasy, horror, women's fiction, picture books, middle-grade, and young adult. In nonfiction we represent titles in the following areas: current affairs, reference, business and career, parenting, pop culture, coloring books, general nonfiction, and nonfiction for children and teens." BookEnds does not represent short fiction, poetry, screenplays, or techno-thrillers.

HOW TO CONTACT Visit website for the most up-to-date guidelines and current preferences. BookEnds agents accept all submissions through their personal Query Manager forms. These forms are accessible on the agency website under Submissions. Accepts simultaneous submissions.

THE BOOK GROUP

20 W. 20th St., Suite 601, New York NY 10011. (212)803-3360. **Website:** www.thebookgroup.com. The Book Group is a full service literary agency located in the heart of Manhattan. Launched in 2015 by publishing industry veterans. The Book Group shares a singular passion: to seek out and cultivate writers, and to serve as their champions throughout their careers. "We represent a wide range of distinguished authors, including critically acclaimed and bestselling novelists, celebrated writers of children's literature, and award-winning historians, food writers, memoirists and journalists."

MEMBER AGENTS Julie Barer; Faye Bender; Brettne Bloom (fiction: literary and commercial fiction, select young adult; nonfiction, including cookbooks, lifestyle, investigative journalism, history, biography, memoir, and psychology); Elisabeth Weed (upmarket fiction, especially plot-driven novels with a sense of place); Dana Murphy (story-driven fiction with a strong sense of place, narrative nonfiction/essays with a pop-culture lean, and YA with an honest voice); Brenda Bowen; Jamie Carr; Nicole Cunningham; DJ Kim.

HANDLES Please do not send poetry or screenplays.

RECENT SALES *This Is Not Over*, by Holly Brown; *Perfect Little World*, by Kevin Wilson; *City of Saints & Thieves*, by Natalie C. Anderson; *The Runaway Midwife*, by Patricia Harman; *Always*, by Sarah Jio; *The Young Widower's Handbook*, by Tom McAllister.

HOW TO CONTACT Send a query letter and 10 sample pages to submissions@thebookgroup.com, with the first and last name of the agent you are querying in the subject line. All material must be in the body of the e-mail, as the agents do not open attachments. "If we are interested in reading more, we will get in touch with you as soon as possible." Accepts simultaneous submissions.

BOOKS & SUCH LITERARY MANAGEMENT

52 Mission Circle, Suite 122, PMB 170, Santa Rosa CA 95409. **E-mail:** representation@booksandsuch.com. **Website:** www.booksandsuch.com. **Contact:** Janet Kobobel Grant, Wendy Lawton, Rachel Kent, Cynthia Ruchti, Barb Roose, Mary DeMuth.

HANDLES This agency specializes in general and inspirational fiction and nonfiction, and in the Christian booksellers market. Actively seeking well-crafted material that presents Judeo-Christian values, even if only subtly. Sci-fi, fantasy, erotica

RECENT SALES A full list of this agency's clients (and the awards they have won) is on the agency website.

TERMS Agent receives 15% commission on domestic sales; 20% commission on foreign sales. Offers written contract; two-month notice must be given to terminate contract. No additional charges.

HOW TO CONTACT Query via e-mail only; no attachments. Accepts simultaneous submissions. Obtains most new clients through recommendations from others, conferences.

TIPS "Our agency highlights personal attention to individual clients that includes coaching on how to thrive in a rapidly changing publishing climate, grow a career, and get the best publishing offers possible."

BOOKSTOP LITERARY AGENCY

(925)254-2664. **E-mail:** info@bookstopliterary.com. **Website:** www.bookstopliterary.com. BookStop Literary has been representing authors and illustrators of books for children and young adults since 1984. BookStop does not represent books for the general adult audience. Please visit our website and look at agent bios for more information.

MEMBER AGENTS Kendra Marcus; Minju Chang; Karyn Fischer.

HANDLES Please see agent bios on our website for more information about our individual areas of interest. Please see agent bios on our website for more information about our individual areas of interest. We do not accept books for the general adult audience or screenplays.

TERMS Agent receives 15% commission on domestic sales. Offers written contract, binding for 1 year.

HOW TO CONTACT Please look at the agent bios on our website and address your submission to the appropriate agent via Query Manager. Accepts simultaneous submissions.

BRADFORD LITERARY AGENCY

5694 Mission Center Rd., #347, San Diego CA 92108. (619)521-1201. **E-mail:** queries@bradfordlit.com. **Website:** www.bradfordlit.com. **Contact:** Laura Bradford, Natalie Lakosil, Sarah LaPolla, Kari Sutherland, Jennifer Chen Tran. "The Bradford Literary Agency is a boutique agency which offers a full range of representation services to authors who are both published and pre-published. Our mission at the Bradford Literary Agency is to form true partnerships with our clients and build long-term relationships that extend from writing the first draft through the length of the author's career."

Picture book writers should contact Natalie only at this agency.

MEMBER AGENTS Laura Bradford (romance [historical, romantic suspense, paranormal, category, contemporary, erotic], mystery, women's fiction, thrillers/suspense, middle grade & YA); Kari Sutherland (children's literature, middle grade, YA, upmarket women's fiction, magical realism, historical dramas, light-hearted contemporary fiction, biography, humor, and parenting); Jennifer Chen Tran (women's fiction, YA, middle grade, graphic novels, narrative nonfiction, parenting, culinary, lifestyle, business, memoir, parenting, psychology); Katherine Wessbecher.

HANDLES Laura Bradford does not want to receive poetry, screenplays, short stories, westerns, horror, new age, religion, crafts, cookbooks, gift books. Natalie Lakosil does not want to receive inspirational novels, memoir, romantic suspense, adult thrillers, poetry, screenplays. Sarah LaPolla does not want to receive nonfiction, picture books, inspirational/spiritual novels, romance, or erotica. Kari Sutherland does not want to receive horror, romance, erotica, memoir, adult sci-fi/fantasy, thrillers, cookbooks, business, spiritual/religious, poetry, or screenplays. Jennifer Chen Tran does not want to receive picture books, sci-fi/fantasy, urban fantasy, westerns, erotica, poetry, or screenplays.

RECENT SALES Sold 80 titles in the last year, including Vox by Christina Dalcher (Berkley); *The Last 8*, by Laura Pohl (Sourcebooks Fire); *You'll Miss Me When I'm Gone*, by Rachel Solomon (Simon Pulse); *Monday's Not Coming*, by Tiffany Jackson (Harper Collins); *Where She Fell*, by Kaitlin Ward (Adaptive); *Into the Nightfell Wood*, by Kristin Bailey (Katherine Tegen Books); *Yasmin the Explorer*, by Saadia Faruqi (Capstone); *Fix Her Up*, by Tessa Bailey (Entangled); *The Protector*, by HelenKay Dimon (Avon); *The Spitfire Girls*, by Soraya Lane (St. Martins); *Highland Wrath*, by Madeline Martin (Diversion); *Everybody's Favorite Book*, by Mike Allegra (Macmillan); *The Hook Up*, by Erin McCarthy (PRH); *Next Girl to Die*, by Dea Poirier (Thomas & Mercer); *The Fearless King*, by Katee Robert (Entangled); *Noble Hops*, by Layla Reyne (Carina Press); *The Rogue on Fifth Avenue*, by Joanna Shupe (Kensington).

TERMS Agent receives 15% commission on domestic sales; 25% commission on foreign sales. Offers written contract. Charges for extra copies of books for foreign submissions.

HOW TO CONTACT Accepts e-mail queries only; For submissions to Laura Bradford, send to queries@bradfordlit.com. For submissions to Natalie Lakosil, use the form listed on the website under the "How to Submit" page. For submissions to Sarah LaPolla, send to sarah@bradfordlit.com. For submissions to Kari Sutherland, send to kari@bradfordlit.com. For submissions to Jennifer Chen Tran, send to jen@bradfordlit.com. The entire submission must appear in the body of the e-mail and not as an attachment. The subject line should begin as follows: "QUERY: (the title of the ms or any short message that is important should follow)." For fiction: e-mail a query letter along with the first chapter of ms and a synopsis. Include the genre and word count in your query letter. Nonfiction: e-mail full nonfiction proposal including a query letter and a sample chapter. Accepts simultaneous submissions. Obtains most new clients through queries.

BRANDT & HOCHMAN LITERARY AGENTS, INC.

1501 Broadway, Suite 2605, New York NY 10036. (212)840-5760. **Fax:** (212)840-5776. **Website:** brandthochman.com. **Contact:** Gail Hochman or individual agent best suited for the submission.

MEMBER AGENTS Gail Hochman (works of literary fiction, idea-driven nonfiction, literary memoir and children's books); Marianne Merola (fiction, nonfiction and children's books with strong and unique narrative voices); Bill Contardi (voice-driven young adult and middle grade fiction, commercial thrillers, psychological suspense, quirky mysteries, high fantasy, commercial fiction and memoir); Emily Forland (voice-driven literary fiction and nonfiction, memoir, narrative nonfiction, history, biography, food writing, cultural criticism, graphic novels, and young adult fiction); Emma Patterson (fiction from dark, literary novels to upmarket women's and historical fiction; narrative nonfiction that includes memoir, investigative journalism, and popular history; young adult fiction); Jody Kahn (literary and upmarket fiction; narrative nonfiction, particularly books related to sports, food, history, science and pop culture—including cookbooks, and literary memoir and journalism); Henry Thayer (nonfiction on a wide variety of subjects and fiction that inclines toward the literary). The e-mail addresses and specific likes of each of these agents is listed on the agency website.

HANDLES No screenplays or textbooks.

RECENT SALES This agency sells 40-60 new titles each year. A full list of their hundreds of clients is on the agency website.

TERMS Agent receives 15% commission on domestic sales; 20% commission on foreign sales.

HOW TO CONTACT "We accept queries by e-mail and regular mail; however, we cannot guarantee a response to e-mailed queries. For queries via regular mail, be sure to include a SASE for our reply. Query letters should be no more than 2 pages and should include a convincing overview of the book project and information about the author and his or her writing credits. Address queries to the specific Brandt & Hochman agent whom you would like to consider your work. Agent e-mail addresses and query preferences may be found at the end of each agent profile on the 'Agents' page of our website." Accepts simultaneous submissions. Obtains most new clients through recommendations from others.

TIPS "Write a letter which will give the agent a sense of you as a professional writer—your long-term interests as well as a short description of the work at hand."

M. COURTNEY BRIGGS

Derrick & Briggs, LLP, BancFirst Fower, Suite 2700, 100 N. Broadway Ave., Oklahoma City OK 73102. (405)235-1900. **Fax:** (405)235-1995. **Website:** www.derrickandbriggs.com. "M. Courtney Briggs combines her primary work as a literary agent with expertise in intellectual property, entertainment law, and estates and probate. Her clients are published authors (exclusively), theatres, and a variety of small businesses and individuals."

CURTIS BROWN, LTD.

228 East 45th St., New York NY 10017. (212)473-5400. **Website:** www.curtisbrown.com. Represents authors and illustrators of fiction, nonfiction, picture books, middle grade, young adult.

MEMBER AGENTS Ginger Clark (science fiction, fantasy, paranormal romance, literary horror, and young adult and middle grade fiction); Kerry

D'Agostino (literary and commercial fiction, as well as narrative nonfiction and memoir); Katherine Fausset (literary fiction, upmarket commercial fiction, journalism, memoir, popular science, and narrative nonfiction); Sarah Gerton (fiction and nonfiction for middle grade and young adult in all genres); Holly Frederick; Peter Ginsberg, president; Elizabeth Harding, vice president (represents authors and illustrators of juvenile, middle-grade and young adult fiction); Ginger Knowlton, executive vice president (authors and illustrators of children's books in all genres—picture book, middle grade, young adult fiction and nonfiction); Timothy Knowlton, CEO; Jonathan Lyons (biographies, history, science, pop culture, sports, general narrative nonfiction, mysteries, thrillers, science fiction and fantasy, and young adult fiction); Laura Blake Peterson, vice president (memoir and biography, natural history, literary fiction, mystery, suspense, women's fiction, health and fitness, young adult, faith issues and popular culture); Steven Salpeter (literary fiction, fantasy, graphic novels, historical fiction, mysteries, thrillers, young adult, narrative nonfiction, gift books, history, humor, and popular science).

RECENT SALES This agency prefers not to share information on specific sales.

TERMS Agent receives 15% commission on domestic sales; 20% on foreign sales. Offers written contract. 75-day notice must be given to terminate contract. Charges for some postage (overseas, etc.).

HOW TO CONTACT Please refer to the "Agents" page on the website for each agent's submission guidelines. Accepts simultaneous submissions. Obtains most new clients through recommendations from others, solicitations, conferences.

BROWNE & MILLER LITERARY ASSOCIATES

(312)922-3063. **Website:** www.browneandmiller.com. **Contact:** Danielle Egan-Miller, president. Founded in 1971 by Jane Jordan Browne, Browne & Miller Literary Associates is the Chicago area's leading literary agency. Danielle Egan-Miller became president of the agency in 2003 and has since sold hundreds of books with a heavy emphasis on commercial adult fiction. Her roster includes several New York Times best-selling authors and numerous prize- and award-winning writers. She loves a great story well told.

"We are very hands-on and do much editorial work with our clients. We are passionate about the books we represent and work hard to help clients reach their publishing goals."

HANDLES Browne & Miller is most interested in literary and commercial fiction, women's fiction, women's historical fiction, literary-leaning crime fiction, dark suspense/domestic suspense,romance, and Christian/inspirational fiction by established authors, and a wide range of platform-driven nonfiction by nationally-recognized author-experts. "We do not represent children's books of any kind or Young Adult; no adult Memoirs; we do not represent horror, science fiction or fantasy, short stories, poetry, original screenplays,or articles."

HOW TO CONTACT Query via e-mail only; no attachments. Do not send unsolicited mss. Accepts simultaneous submissions.

ANDREA BROWN LITERARY AGENCY, INC.

E-mail: andrea@andreabrownlit.com; caryn@andreabrownlit.com; lauraqueries@gmail.com; jennifer@andreabrownlit.com; kelly@andreabrownlit.com; jennL@andreabrownlit.com; jamie@andreabrownlit.com; jmatt@andreabrownlit.com; kathleen@andreabrownlit.com; lara@andreabrownlit.com; soloway@andreabrownlit.com; jemiscoe@andreabrownlit.com; saritza@andreabrownlit.com; paige@andreabrownlit.com. **Website:** www.andreabrownlit.com. The Andrea Brown Literary Agency was founded in August 1981 and has offices in the San Francisco Bay area, San Diego, Los Angeles, New York, and Chicago. "Our agency specializes in children's literature. We work to bring to light the voices and perspectives of new writers as well as to nurture and develop the careers of experienced authors. Our goal, whether seeking to secure a publishing contract for a first book or a fiftieth book, is to make sure that clients are not only published, but published well. Our philosophy is to remain a 'small' agency at heart. We invest a great deal of personal care and attention in each project, and we are hands-on in all aspects of our interactions with clients. We work closely with clients in an editorial capacity and we devise a strategy at every stage of the writing process that will enable us to find the best publisher for each book. In doing so, we think about both short-term and long-term goals for our clients, always keeping the trajectory of a successful career in mind. Our agents have backgrounds in New

York publishing, editing, academia, business, teaching, writing and film, and one of our strengths as an agency is that we work collaboratively. Our clients have the benefit not only of their individual agent's expertise but of the combined experience and vision of the group. As a West Coast based agency, we follow a tradition of West Coast innovation in our passion for discovering new voices, in our efforts to make New York publishing more inclusive of voices from other parts of the country, and in our attempt to see publishing trends that result from this broader perspective. We combine this approach with access, standing, and visibility in the publishing community at large. Our agents make regular trips to New York, attend industry conventions, and participate as faculty at writers' conferences all over the country. We ensure a high profile for our clients and actively keep our fingers on the pulse of publishing."

Writers should review the large agent bios on the agency website to determine which agent to contact. Please choose only one agent to query. The agents share queries, so a no from one agent at Andrea Brown Literary Agency is a no from all. *E-queries only.*

MEMBER AGENTS Andrea Brown (president); Laura Rennert (executive agent); Caryn Wiseman (senior agent); Jennifer Laughran (senior agent); Jennifer Rofé (senior agent); Kelly Sonnack (senior agent); Jamie Weiss Chilton (senior agent); Jennifer Mattson (agent); Kathleen Rushall (agent); Lara Perkins (agent); Saritza Hernandez (agent); Jennifer March Soloway (associate agent); Jemiscoe Chambers-Black (associate agent); Paige Terlip (associate agent).

HANDLES Specializes in all kinds of children's books—illustrators and authors. 98% juvenile books. Considers: nonfiction, fiction, picture books, young adult.

RECENT SALES Supriya Kelkar's middle grade novel *American As Paneer Pie* to Jennifer Ung at Aladdin, at auction, by Kathleen Rushall. Mitali Perkins's *You Bring the Distant Near*, sold at auction, in a two-book deal, to Grace Kendall at Farrar, Straus Children's, by Laura Rennert. Cynthia Salaysay's YA novel *Private Lessons* to Kate Fletcher at Candlewick, by Jennifer March Soloway. Dev Petty's picture book text, *The Bear Must Go On* to Talia Benamy at Philomel, by Jennifer Rofe. Carrie Pearson's nonfiction picture book text *A Girl Who Leaped, A Woman Who Soared* to Simon Boughton at Norton Children's by Kelly Sonnack. K. C. Johnson's YA novel, *This is My America* to Chelsea Eberly at Random House Children's in a two-book deal by Jennifer March Soloway. Nancy Castaldo's nonfiction YA, *Water* to Elise Howard at Algonquin Young Readers, by Jennifer Laughran. Kate Messner's picture book text, *The Next President* to Melissa Manlove at Chronicle Children's, in a two book deal, by Jennifer Laughran. Amber Lough's YA novel, *Summer of War* to Amy Fitzgerald at Carolrhoda Lab by Laura Rennert and Jennifer March Soloway. Andrea Zimmerman and David Clemesha's picture book *All Buckled Up!* to Jeffrey Salane at Little Simon, in a two-book deal by Jamie Weiss Chilton. Jennifer Berne's picture book *Dinosaur Doomsday* to Melissa Manlove at Chronicle Children's by Caryn Wiseman. Tami Charles's *Serena Williams—G.O.A.T.: Making the Case for the Greatest of All Time*, a sports biography of Serena Williams to Ada Zhang at Sterling Children's by Lara Perkins. Katy Loutzenhiser's YA *If You're Out There* to Donna Bray at Balzer & Bray in a two-book deal by Jennifer Mattson. Barry Eisler's *The Killer Collective*, as well as a John Rain prequel, and two more in the Livia Lone series, to Gracie Doyle at Thomas & Mercer, in a major deal by Laura Rennert. Maggie Stiefvater's The Raven Cycle series to Universal Cable Productions by Laura Rennert.

TERMS Agent receives 15% commission on domestic sales; 25% commission on foreign sales. Offers written contract. No fees.

HOW TO CONTACT Writers should review the large agent bios on the agency website to determine which agent to contact. Please choose only one agent to query. The agents share queries, so a no from one agent at Andrea Brown Literary Agency is a no from all. (Note that Jennifer Laughran and Kelly Sonnack only receive queries by querymanager - please visit the agency's website for information.) For picture books, submit a query letter and complete ms in the body of the e-mail. For fiction, submit a query letter and the first 10 pages in the body of the e-mail. For nonfiction, submit proposal, first 10 pages in the body of the e-mail. Illustrators: submit a query letter and 2-3 illustration samples (in jpeg format), link to online portfolio, and text of picture book, if applicable. "We only accept queries via e-mail. No attachments, with the exception of jpeg illustrations from illustrators." Visit the agents' bios on our website and choose only one agent to whom you will submit your e-query. Send a short e-mail query letter to that agent with "QUE-

RY" in the subject field. Accepts simultaneous submissions. Obtains most new clients through queries and referrals from editors, clients and agents. Check website for guidelines and information.

KIMBERLEY CAMERON & ASSOCIATES

1550 Tiburon Blvd., #704, Tiburon CA 94920. (415)789-9191. **Website:** www.kimberleycameron.com. **Contact:** Kimberley Cameron.

MEMBER AGENTS Kimberley Cameron; Elizabeth Kracht (nonfiction: memoir, self-help, spiritual, investigative, creative / fiction: women's, literary, historical, mysteries, thrillers); Amy Cloughley (literary and upmarket fiction, women's, historical, narrative nonfiction, travel or adventure memoir); Mary C. Moore (fantasy, science fiction, upmarket "book club," genre romance, thrillers with female protagonists, and stories from marginalized voices); Lisa Abellera (currently closed to unsolicited submissions); Dorian Maffei (only open to submissions requested through Twitter pitch parties, conferences, or #MSWL).

HANDLES "We are looking for a unique and heartfelt voice that conveys a universal truth."

HOW TO CONTACT Prefers queries via site. Only query one agent at a time. For fiction, fill out the correct submissions form for the individual agent and attach the first 50 pages and a synopsis (if requested) as a Word doc or PDF. For nonfiction, fill out the correct submission form of the individual agent and attach a full book proposal and sample chapters (includes the first chapter and no more than 50 pages) as a Word doc or PDF. Accepts simultaneous submissions. Obtains new clients through recommendations from others, solicitations.

CHALBERG & SUSSMAN

115 W. 29th St., Third Floor, New York NY 10001. (917)261-7550. **Website:** www.chalbergsussman.com.

MEMBER AGENTS Terra Chalberg; Rachel Sussman (narrative journalism, memoir, psychology, history, humor, pop culture, literary fiction).

RECENT SALES The agents' sales and clients are listed on their website.

HOW TO CONTACT To query by e-mail, please contact one of the following: terra@chalbergsussman.com, rachel@chalbergsussman.com, nicole@chalbergsussman.com, lana@chalbergsussman.com. To query by regular mail, please address your letter to one agent and include SASE. Accepts simultaneous submissions.

CHASE LITERARY AGENCY

11 Broadway, Suite 1010, New York NY 10004. (212)477-5100. **E-mail:** farley@chaseliterary.com. **Website:** www.chaseliterary.com. **Contact:** Farley Chase. "After starting out at *The New Yorker,* I moved to The New Press and later became an editor at Talk Miramax Books. I spent 8 years as a literary agent at the Waxman Literary Agency, and I founded Chase Literary Agency in 2012. I live in NYC with my wife and dog and am a graduate of Macalester College. Over my more than 13 years as a literary agent and 19 years in publishing, I've been fortunate to work with distinguished authors of fiction and nonfiction. They include winners of the Pulitzer Prize, MacArthur Fellows, Members of Congress, Olympic Gold Medalists, and members of the Baseball Hall of Fame."

HANDLES No romance, science fiction, or young adult.

RECENT SALES *Devil in the Grove: Thurgood Marshall, the Groveland Boys, and the Dawn of a New America* , by Gilbert King (Harper); *Heads in Beds: A Reckless Memoir of Hotels, Hustles, and So-Called Hospitality,* by Jacob Tomsky (Doubleday); *And Every Day Was Overcast,* by Paul Kwiatowski (Black Balloon); *The Badlands Saloon,* by Jonathan Twingley (Scribner).

HOW TO CONTACT E-query farley@chaseliterary.com. If submitting fiction, please include the first few pages of the ms with the query. "I do not response to queries not addressed to me by name. I'm keenly interested in both fiction and nonfiction. In fiction, I'm looking for both literary or commercial projects in either contemporary or historical settings. I'm open to anything with a strong sense of place, voice, and, especially plot. I don't handle science fiction, romance, supernatural or young adult. In nonfiction, I'm especially interested in narratives in history, memoir, journalism, natural science, military history, sports, pop culture, and humor. Whether by first-time writers or long time journalists, I'm excited by original ideas, strong points of view, detailed research, and access to subjects which give readers fresh perspectives on things they think they know. I'm also interested in visually-driven and illustrated books. Whether they involve photography, comics, illustrations, or art I'm taken by creative storytelling with visual elements, four color or black and white." Accepts simultaneous submissions.

THE CHUDNEY AGENCY

72 N. State Rd., Suite 501, Briarcliff Manor NY 10510. (914)465-5560. **E-mail:** steven@thechudneyagency.com. **Website:** www.thechudneyagency.com. **Contact:** Steven Chudney.

Please always check our website before you contact us for the latest information about our agnecy and what we're looking for.

HANDLES "At this time, the agency is only looking for author/illustrators (one individual), who can both write and illustrate wonderful picture books. The author/illustrator must really know and understand the prime audience's needs and wants of the child reader! Storylines should be engaging, fun, with a hint of a life lessons and cannot be longer than 700 words. With chapter books, middle grade and teen novels, I'm primarily looking for quality, contemporary literary fiction: novels that are exceedingly well-written, with wonderful settings and developed, unforgettable characters. I'm looking for historical fiction that will excite me, young readers, editors, and reviewers, and will introduce us to unique characters in settings and situations, countries, and eras we haven't encountered too often yet in children's and teen literature." Does not want most fantasy and no science fiction.

HOW TO CONTACT No snail mail submissions for fiction/novels. Queries only. Please do not send any text for novels. Submission package info from us to follow should we be interested in your project. For children's picture books, we only want author/illustrator projects. Submit a pdf with full text and at least 5-7 full-color illustrations. Accepts simultaneous submissions.

FRANCES COLLIN, LITERARY AGENT

E-mail: queries@francescollin.com. **Website:** www.francescollin.com. The agency represents the Estates of John Williams (*Stoner, Butcher's Crossing, Augustus*) and Esther Forbes (*Johnny Tremain*), among others. Fran Collin is the Trustee for the Estate of Rachel Carson (*Silent Spring*). Clients include Sarah Blake, Nadine Darling, Kirsten Kaschock, Wendy Sparrow/Wendy Laine, Christopher Merkner, Barbara Hambly, Vonda N. McIntyre, Marilyn Hacker, Caroline Stevermer, Ana Veciana-Suarez, the Estate of Robert Bright and the Estate of Hal Borland. Formerly the Marie Rodell-Frances Collin Literary Agency. Celebrating 71 years as an agency!

HANDLES Actively seeking authors who are invested in their unique visions and who want to set trends not chase them. "I'd like to think that my authors are unplagiarizable by virtue of their distinct voices and styles." Does not want previously self-published work. Query with new mss only, please.

HOW TO CONTACT "We periodically close to queries, so please check our Publishers Marketplace account or other social media accounts before querying. When we are open to queries, we ask that writers send a traditional query e-mail describing the project and copy and paste the first 5 pages of the manuscript into the body of the e-mail. We look forward to hearing from you at queries@francescollin.com. Please send queries to that e-mail address. Any queries sent to another e-mail address within the agency will be deleted unread." Accepts simultaneous submissions.

DON CONGDON ASSOCIATES INC.

110 William St., Suite 2202, New York NY 10038. (212)645-1229. **Fax:** (212)727-2688. **E-mail:** dca@doncongdon.com. **Website:** doncongdon.com.

MEMBER AGENTS Cristina Concepcion (crime fiction, narrative nonfiction, political science, journalism, history, books on cities, classical music, biography, science for a popular audience, philosophy, food and wine, iconoclastic books on health and human relationships, essays, and arts criticism); Michael Congdon (commercial and literary fiction, suspense, mystery, thriller, history, military history, biography, memoir, current affairs, and narrative nonfiction [adventure, medicine, science, and nature]); Katie Grimm (literary fiction, historical, women's fiction, short story collections, graphic novels, mysteries, young adult, middle-grade, memoir, science, academic); Katie Kotchman (business [all areas], narrative nonfiction [particularly popular science and social/cultural issues], self-help, success, motivation, psychology, pop culture, women's fiction, realistic young adult, literary fiction, and psychological thrillers); Maura Kye-Casella (narrative nonfiction, cookbooks, women's fiction, young adult, self-help, and parenting); Susan Ramer (literary fiction, upmarket commercial fiction [contemporary and historical], narrative nonfiction, social history, cultural history, smart pop culture [music, film, food, art], women's issues, psychology and mental health, and memoir).

HANDLES Susan Ramer: "Not looking for romance, science fiction, fantasy, espionage, mysteries, politics, health/diet/fitness, self-help, or sports." Katie Kotchman: "Please do not send her screenplays or poetry."

RECENT SALES This agency represents many bestselling clients such as David Sedaris and Kathryn Stockett.

HOW TO CONTACT "We are currently accepting queries from new and established authors via email only. A query letter consists of a one-page description or synopsis of your work and your relevant background information. We ask that you paste the first chapter into the body of your email following your query letter. We do not accept unsolicited manuscripts. Due to the volume of queries we receive, we regret that we are unable to reply to each one. We will only respond if we are requesting additional material. You must include the word "Query" and the agent's full name in your subject heading. Please include your query, sample chapter, your full name, and complete email address in the body of the email, as we do not open unsolicited attachments for security reasons. Please query only one agent within the agency at a time. For a listing of specific agent interests, please see our Agents section." Accepts simultaneous submissions.

COOKE MCDERMID LITERARY MANAGEMENT

320 Front St. W., Suite 1105, Toronto ON M5V 3B6, Canada. (647)788-4010. **E-mail:** info@cookemcdermid.com. **Website:** www.mcdermidagency.com. **Contact:** Anne McDermid.

MEMBER AGENTS Anne McDermid; Martha Webb; Dean Cooke; Sally Harding; Suzanne Brandreth; Ron Eckel; Rachel Letofsky; Stephanie Sinclair; Paige Sisley.

HANDLES The agency represents literary novelists and commercial novelists of high quality, and also writers of nonfiction in the areas of memoir, biography, history, literary travel, narrative science, and investigative journalism. "We also represent a certain number of children's and YA writers and writers in the fields of science fiction and fantasy."

HOW TO CONTACT Query via e-mail or mail with a brief bio, description, and first 5 pages of project only. Accepts simultaneous submissions. *No unsolicited manuscripts.* Obtains most new clients through recommendations from others.

CREATIVE MEDIA AGENCY, INC.

(212)812-1494. **E-mail:** paige@cmalit.com. **Website:** www.cmalit.com. **Contact:** Paige Wheeler. Founded in 1997, Creative Media Agency, Inc. focuses on representing professional writers in a variety of genres and subject matters, and cultivating the evolving agent-author relationship. With over 20 years of experience, we work to discover authors and nurture long-standing careers every step of the way. Our goal is to go beyond simply selling an author's book. From the first contract to the final sales figures, CMA has every detail covered: editorial work, marketing and publicity plans, royalties, and foreign rights. We have tailored our agency to meet an author's every need to get them performing the best in their field. CMA has represented New York Times and USA Today best sellers, as well as winners of the RITA, Edgar, Agatha, Anthony, Shamus, and other major awards. In addition to established authors, we welcome many first-time authors pursuing publication and a career in writing.

HANDLES Fiction: All commercial and upscale (think book club) fiction, as well as women's fiction, romance (all types), mystery, thrillers, inspirational/Christian and psychological suspense. I enjoy both historical fiction as well as contemporary fiction, so do keep that in mind. I seem to be especially drawn to a story if it has a high concept and a fresh, unique voice. Nonfiction: I'm looking for both narrative nonfiction and prescriptive nonfiction. I'm looking for books where the author has a huge platform and something new to say in a particular area. Some of the areas that I like are lifestyle, relationship, parenting, business/entrepreneurship, food-subsistence-homesteading topics, wish fulfillment memoir, popular/trendy reference projects and women's issues. I'd like books that would could be a Hello Sunshine Bookclub pick. Does not want to receive children's picture books, science fiction, fantasy, poetry or academic nonfiction.

HOW TO CONTACT E-query. Write "query" in your e-mail subject line. For fiction, paste in the first 5 pages of the ms after the query. For nonfiction, paste in an extended author bio as well as the marketing section of your book proposal after the query. Accepts simultaneous submissions.

RICHARD CURTIS ASSOCIATES, INC.

200 E. 72nd St., Suite 28J, New York NY 10021. (212)772-7363. **Website:** www.curtisagency.com.

HANDLES Actively seeking nonfiction (but no memoir), women's fiction (especially contemporary), thrillers, science fiction, middle-grade, and young adult. Does not want screenplays.

RECENT SALES Sold 50 titles in the last year, including *Safecracker*, by Dave McOmiey; *Champions Series*, by Janet Dailey; and *Taking Mt. Exxon*, by Philip Jett.

TERMS Agent receives 15% commission on domestic sales; 25% commission on foreign sales. Offers written contract. Charges for photocopying, express mail, international freight, book orders.

HOW TO CONTACT Use submission procedure on website. "We also read one-page query letters accompanied by SASE." Accepts simultaneous submissions.

D4EO LITERARY AGENCY

7 Indian Valley Rd., Weston CT 06883. (203)544-7180. **Fax:** (203)544-7160. **Website:** www.d4eoliteraryagency.com. **Contact:** Bob Diforio.

TERMS Offers written contract, binding for 2 years; automatic renewal unless 60 days notice given prior to renewal date. Charges for photocopying and submission postage.

HOW TO CONTACT Each of these agents has a different submission e-mail and different tastes regarding how they review material. See all on their individual agent pages on the agency website. Obtains most new clients through recommendations from others.

LAURA DAIL LITERARY AGENCY, INC.

121 W. 27th St., Suite 1201, New York NY 10001. (212)239-7477. **Website:** www.ldlainc.com.

MEMBER AGENTS Laura Dail; Carrie Pestritto; Elana Roth Parker.

HANDLES Specializes in women's fiction, literary fiction, young adult fiction, as well as both practical and idea-driven nonfiction. "Due to the volume of queries and mss received, we apologize for not answering every e-mail and letter. None of us handles children's picture books or chapter books. No New Age. We do not handle screenplays or poetry."

HOW TO CONTACT Accepts queries via QueryManager. Accepts simultaneous submissions.

DARHANSOFF & VERRILL LITERARY AGENTS

529 11th Street, Third Floor, Brooklyn NY 11215, US. (917)305-1300. **Website:** www.dvagency.com.

MEMBER AGENTS Liz Darhansoff; Chuck Verrill; Michele Mortimer; Eric Amling.

HANDLES We are readers of literary fiction, narrative nonfiction, memoir, contemporary young adult, graphic novels, and all manner of crime and mystery. Our nonfiction interests range from art and design to food and cooking to yoga and mindfulness to animal welfare and environmental causes to feminism and progressive causes. While we lean into dystopian and speculative fiction, we rarely match up to fantasy, science fiction, or paranormal work.

HOW TO CONTACT We are readers of literary fiction, narrative nonfiction, memoir, contemporary young adult, graphic novels, and sophisticated crime and mystery. Please see our website for submission guidelines. Accepts simultaneous submissions. We are currently pursuing new talent to add to our roster

LIZA DAWSON ASSOCIATES

(212)465-9071. **Website:** www.lizadawsonassociates.com. **Contact:** Caitie Flum.

MEMBER AGENTS Liza Dawson, queryliza@lizadawsonassociates.com (plot-driven literary and popular fiction, historical, thrillers, suspense, history, psychology [both popular and clinical], politics, narrative nonfiction, and memoirs); Caitlin Blasdell, querycaitlin@lizadawsonassociates.com (science fiction, fantasy [both adult and young adult], parenting, business, thrillers, and women's fiction); Hannah Bowman, queryhannah@lizadawsonassociates.com (commercial fiction [especially science fiction and fantasy, young adult] and nonfiction in the areas of mathematics, science, and spirituality); Caitie Flum, querycaitie@lizadawsonassociates.com (commercial fiction, especially historical, women's fiction, mysteries, crossover fantasy, young adult, and middle-grade; nonfiction in the areas of theater, current affairs, and pop culture); Rachel Beck, queryrachel@lizadawson.com; Tom Miller, querytom@lizadawson.com.

HANDLES Multiple agents at this agency represent young adult mss. This agency specializes in readable literary fiction, thrillers, mainstream historicals, women's fiction, young adult, middle-grade, academics, historians, journalists, and psychology.

TERMS Agent receives 15% commission on domestic sales; 20% commission on foreign sales. Offers written contract.

HOW TO CONTACT Query by e-mail only. No phone calls. Each of these agents has their own specific submission requirements, which you can find online at the agency's website. Obtains most new clients through recommendations from others, conferences, and queries.

THE JENNIFER DE CHIARA LITERARY AGENCY

245 Park Ave., 39th Floor, New York NY 10167. (212) 372-8989. **E-mail:** jenndec@aol.com. **Website:** www.jdlit.com. **Contact:** Jennifer De Chiara.

MEMBER AGENTS Jennifer De Chiara, Stephen Fraser, Marie Lamba, Roseanne Wells, Savannah Brooks, Erin Clyburn, Megan Barnard, Marlo Berliner, Zabe Ellor, Tara Gilbert, Amy Giuffrida, Stefanie Molina, Tori Sharp.

TERMS Agent receives 15% commission on domestic sales. Offers written contract.

HOW TO CONTACT Each agent has their own e-mail submission address and submission instructions; check the website for the current updates, as policies do change. Only query one agent at a time. Accepts simultaneous submissions. Obtains most new clients through recommendations from others, conferences, query letters.

DEFIORE & COMPANY

47 E. 19th St., 3rd Floor, New York NY 10003. (212)925-7744. **Fax:** (212)925-9803. **Website:** www.defliterary.com.

MEMBER AGENTS Brian DeFiore (popular nonfiction, business, pop culture, parenting, commercial fiction); Laurie Abkemeier (memoir, parenting, business, how-to/self-help, popular science); Matthew Elblonk (young adult, popular culture, narrative nonfiction); Caryn Karmatz-Rudy (popular fiction, self-help, narrative nonfiction); Adam Schear (commercial fiction, humor, young adult, smart thrillers, historical fiction, quirky debut literary novels, popular science, politics, popular culture, current events); Meredith Kaffel Simonoff (smart upmarket women's fiction, literary fiction [especially debut], literary thrillers, narrative nonfiction, nonfiction about science and tech, sophisticated pop culture/humor books); Rebecca Strauss (literary and commercial fiction, women's fiction, urban fantasy, romance, mystery, young adult, memoir, pop culture, select nonfiction); Lisa Gallagher (fiction and nonfiction); Miriam Altshuler (adult literary and commercial fiction, narrative nonfiction, middle-grade, young adult, memoir, narrative nonfiction, self-help, family sagas, historical novels); Reiko Davis (adult literary and upmarket fiction, narrative nonfiction, young adult, middle-grade, memoir); Linda Kaplan; Chris Park; Tanusri Prasanna; Parik Kostan; Emma Haviland-Blunk.

HANDLES "Please be advised that we are not considering dramatic projects at this time."

TERMS Agent receives 15% commission on domestic sales; 20% commission on foreign sales. Offers written contract; 10-day notice must be given to terminate contract. Charges clients for photocopying and overnight delivery (deducted only after a sale is made).

HOW TO CONTACT Query with SASE or e-mail to submissions@defliterary.com. "Please include the word 'query' in the subject line. All attachments will be deleted; please insert all text in the body of the e-mail. For more information about our agents, their individual interests, and their query guidelines, please visit our 'About Us' page on our website." Accepts simultaneous submissions. Obtains most new clients through recommendations from others.

JOELLE DELBOURGO ASSOCIATES, INC.

101 Park St., Montclair NJ 07042. (973)773-0836. **E-mail:** joelle@delbourgo.com. **Website:** www.delbourgo.com. **Contact:** Joelle Delbourgo. "We are a boutique agency representing a wide range of nonfiction and fiction. Nonfiction: narrative, research-based and prescriptive nonfiction, including history, current affairs, education, psychology and personal development, parenting, science, business and economics, diet and nutrition, and cookbooks. Adult and young adult commercial and literary fiction, some middle grade. We do not represent plays, screenplays, poetry and picture books."

MEMBER AGENTS Joelle Delbourgo; Jacqueline Flynn.

HANDLES "We are former publishers and editors with deep knowledge and an insider perspective. We have a reputation for individualized attention to clients, strategic management of authors' careers, and creating strong partnerships with publishers for our clients." We are looking for strong narrative and prescriptive nonfiction including science, history, health and medicine, business and finance, sociology, parenting, women's issues. We prefer books by credentialed experts and seasoned journalists, especially ones that are research-based. We are taking on very few memoir projects. In fiction, you can send mystery and thriller, commercial women's fiction, book club fiction and literary fiction. Do not send scripts, picture books, poetry.

RECENT SALES *Big Time*, Ben H. Winters (Mulholland); *Enslaved: The Sunken History of the Transatlantic Slave Trade*, Simcha Jacobovici and Sean Kinglsey (Pegasus); *Reclaiming Body Trust*, Hilary Kinavey and Dana Sturtevant (Tarcher Perigee); *Crazy to Leave You*, Marilyn Simon Rothstein (Lake Union); *We Share the Same Sky*, Rachael Cerrotti (Blackstone); *Julian*, Philip Freeman (Yale University Press); *Go Big Now*, Julia Pimsleur (New World Library); *The Rule of St. Benedict*, Philip Freeman (St. Martins Essentials)

TERMS Agent receives 15% commission on domestic sales and 20% commission on foreign sales as well as television/film adaptation when a co-agent is involved. Offers written contract. Standard industry commissions. Charges clients for postage and photocopying.

HOW TO CONTACT E-mail queries only are accepted. Query one agent directly, not multiple agents at our agency. No attachments. Put the word "Query" in the subject line. If you have not received a response in 60 days you may consider that a pass. Do not send us copies of self-published books. For nonfiction, send your query only once you have a completed proposal. For fiction and memoir, embed the first 10 pages of ms into the e-mail after your query letter. Please no attachments. If we like your first pages, we may ask to see your synopsis and more manuscript. Accepts simultaneous submissions. Our clients come via referral, and occasionally over the transom.

TIPS "Do your homework. Do not cold call. Read and follow submission guidelines before contacting us. Do not call to find out if we received your material. No e-mail queries. Treat agents with respect, as you would any other professional, such as a doctor, lawyer or financial advisor."

SANDRA DIJKSTRA LITERARY AGENCY

1155 Camino del Mar, PMB 515, Del Mar CA 92014. **E-mail:** queries@dijkstraagency.com. **Website:** www.dijkstraagency.com. The Dijkstra Agency was established over 35 years ago and is known for guiding the careers of many best-selling fiction and nonfiction authors, including Amy Tan, Lisa See, Maxine Hong Kingston, Chitra Divakaruni, Eric Foner, Marcus Rediker, and many more. "We handle nearly all genres, except for poetry." Please see www.dijkstraagency.com for each agent's interests.

MEMBER AGENTS President: Sandra Dijkstra (adult only). Acquiring Associate agents: Elise Capron (adult only); Jill Marr (adult only); Thao Le (adult and YA); Jessica Watterson (subgenres of adult romance, and women's fiction); Suzy Evans (adult and YA); Jennifer Kim (adult and YA).

TERMS Works in conjunction with foreign and film agents. Agent receives 15% commission on domestic sales and 20% commission on foreign sales. Offers written contract. No reading fee.

HOW TO CONTACT "Please see guidelines on our website, www.dijkstraagency.com. Please note that we only accept e-mail submissions. Due to the large number of unsolicited submissions we receive, we are only able to respond those submissions in which we are interested." Accepts simultaneous submissions.

TIPS "Remember that publishing is a business. Do your research and present your project in as professional a way as possible. Only submit your work when you are confident that it is polished and ready for prime-time. Make yourself a part of the active writing community by getting stories and articles published, networking with other writers, and getting a good sense of where your work fits in the market."

DONAGHY LITERARY GROUP

(647)527-4353. **E-mail:** stacey@donaghyliterary.com. **Website:** www.donaghyliterary.com. **Contact:** Stacey Donaghy. "Donaghy Literary Group provides full-service literary representation to our clients at every stage of their writing career. Specializing in commercial fiction, we seek middle grade, young adult, new adult and adult novels."

MEMBER AGENTS Stacey Donaghy (women's fiction, LGBTQ, Diverse and #Ownvoice, psychological thrillers, domestic suspense, contemporary romance, and YA); Valerie Noble (historical, science fiction and fantasy [think Kristin Cashore and Suzanne Collins] for young adults and adults); Sue Miller (YA, urban fantasy, contemporary romance).

TERMS Agent receives 15% commission on domestic sales; 20% commission on foreign sales. Offers written contract, 30-day notice must be given to terminate contract.

HOW TO CONTACT Visit agency website for "new submission guidelines" Do not e-mail agents directly. This agency only accepts submissions through the QueryManager database system. Accepts simultaneous submissions.

TIPS "Only submit to one DLG agent at a time, we work collaboratively and often share projects that may be better suited to another agent at the agency."

DUNHAM LITERARY, INC.

Website: www.dunhamlit.com. **Contact:** Jennie Dunham.

MEMBER AGENTS Jennie Dunham, Leslie Zampetti.

HANDLES "We are not looking for Westerns, genre romance, poetry, or individual short stories."

RECENT SALES *The Bad Kitty Series*, by Nick Bruel (Macmillan); *Believe*, by Robert Sabuda (Candlewick); *The Gollywhopper Games* and Sequels, by Jody Feldman (HarperCollins); Show Me A Sign by Ann LeZotte (Scholastic); *The Low Desert*, by Tod Goldberg (Counterpoint).

TERMS Agent receives 15% commission on domestic sales; 20% commission on foreign sales.

HOW TO CONTACT We accept queries by email only.

Please include a brief description of the project, brief author bio, and the first 5 pages with the query.

Attachments will not be opened.

Paper queries NOT accepted. Accepts simultaneous submissions. Obtains most new clients through recommendations from others.

DUNOW, CARLSON & LERNER AGENCY

27 W. 20th St., Suite 1107, New York NY 10011. (212)645-7606. **E-mail:** mail@dclagency.com. **Website:** www.dclagency.com.

MEMBER AGENTS Jennifer Carlson (narrative nonfiction writers and journalists covering current events and ideas and cultural history, as well as literary and upmarket commercial novelists); Henry Dunow (quality fiction–literary, historical, strongly written commercial–and with voice-driven nonfiction across a range of areas–narrative history, biography, memoir, current affairs, cultural trends and criticism, science, sports); Betsy Lerner (nonfiction writers in the areas of psychology, history, cultural studies, biography, current events, business; fiction: literary, dark, funny, voice driven); Yishai Seidman (broad range of fiction: literary, postmodern, and thrillers; nonfiction: sports, music, and pop culture); Amy Hughes (nonfiction in the areas of history, cultural studies, memoir, current events, wellness, health, food, pop culture, and biography; also literary fiction); Eleanor Jackson (literary, commercial, memoir, art, food, science and history); Julia Kenny (fiction—adult, middle grade and YA—and is especially interested in dark, literary thrillers and suspense); Edward Necarsulmer IV (strong new voices in teen & middle grade as well as picture books); Stacia Decker; Rachel Vogel (nonfiction, including photography, humor, pop culture, history, memoir, investigative journalism, current events, science, and more); Arielle Datz (fiction—adult, YA, or middle-grade—literary and commercial, nonfiction—essays, unconventional memoir, pop culture, and sociology).

RECENT SALES A full list of agency clients is on the website.

HOW TO CONTACT Query via snail mail with SASE, or by e-mail. E-mail preferred, paste 10 sample pages below query letter. No attachments. Will respond only if interested. Accepts simultaneous submissions.

DYSTEL, GODERICH & BOURRET LLC

1 Union Square W., Suite 904, New York NY 10003. (212)627-9100. **Fax:** (212)627-9313. **Website:** www.dystel.com.

"We have discovered many of our most talented authors in the slush pile. We read everything that is sent to us, whether we decide to represent it or not." Dystel & Goderich Literary Management recently acquired the client list of Bedford Book Works.

MEMBER AGENTS Jane Dystel; Miriam Goderich, miriam@dystel.com (literary and commercial fiction as well as some genre fiction, narrative nonfiction, pop culture, psychology, history, science, art, business books, and biography/memoir); Stacey Glick, sglick@dystel.com (adult narrative nonfiction including memoir, parenting, cooking and food, psychology, science, health and wellness, lifestyle, current events, pop culture, YA, middle grade, children's nonfiction, and select adult contemporary fiction); Michael Bourret, mbourret@dystel.com (middle grade and young adult fiction, commercial adult fiction, and all sorts of nonfiction, from practical to narrative; he's especially interested in food and cocktail related books, memoir, popular history, politics, religion (though not spirituality), popular science, and current events); Jim McCarthy, jmccarthy@dystel.com (literary women's fiction, underrepresented voices, mysteries, romance, paranormal fiction, narrative nonfiction, memoir, and paranormal nonfiction); Jessica Papin, jpapin@dystel.com (plot-driven literary and smart commercial fiction, and narrative nonfiction across a range of subjects, including history, medicine, science, economics and women's issues); Lauren Abramo, labramo@dystel.com (humorous middle grade and contemporary YA on the children's side, and upmarket commercial fiction and well-paced literary fiction on the adult side; adult narrative nonfiction, especially pop culture, psychology, pop science, reportage, media, and contemporary culture; in nonfiction, has a strong preference for interdisciplinary approaches, and in all categories she's especially interested in underrepresented voices); John Rudolph, jrudolph@dystel.com (picture book author/illustrators, middle grade, YA, select commercial fiction, and narrative nonfiction—especially in music, sports, history, popular science, "big think", performing arts, health, business, memoir, military history, and humor); Sharon Pelletier, spelletier@dystel.com (smart commercial fiction, from upmarket women's fiction to domestic suspense to literary thrillers, and strong contemporary romance novels; compelling nonfiction projects, especially feminism and religion); Amy Bishop, abishop@dystel.com (commercial and literary women's fiction, fiction from diverse authors, historical fiction, YA, personal narratives, and biographies); Michaela Whatnall, mwatnall@dystel.com; Cat Hosch, chosch@dystel.com; Andrew Dugan, adugan@dystel.com; Melissa Melo, mmelo@dystel.com.

HANDLES "We are actively seeking fiction for all ages, in all genres." No plays, screenplays, or poetry.

TERMS Agent receives 15% commission on domestic sales; 19% commission on foreign sales. Offers written contract.

HOW TO CONTACT Query via e-mail and put "Query" in the subject line. "Synopses, outlines or sample chapters (say, one chapter or the first 25 pages of your manuscript) should either be included below the cover letter or attached as a separate document. We won't open attachments if they come with a blank e-mail." Accepts simultaneous submissions. Obtains most new clients through recommendations from others, solicitations, conferences.

TIPS "DGLM prides itself on being a full-service agency. We're involved in every stage of the publishing process, from offering substantial editing on mss and proposals, to coming up with book ideas for authors looking for their next project, negotiating contracts and collecting monies for our clients. We follow a book from its inception through its sale to a publisher, its publication, and beyond. Our commitment to our writers does not, by any means, end when we have collected our commission. This is one of the many things that makes us unique in a very competitive business."

EDEN STREET LITERARY

P.O. Box 30, Billings NY 12510. **E-mail:** info@edenstreetlit.com. **Website:** www.edenstreetlit.com. **Contact:** Liza Voges. Eden Street represents over 40 authors and author-illustrators of books for young readers from pre-school through young adult. Their books have won numerous awards over the past 30 years. Eden Street prides themselves on tailoring services to each client's goals, working in tandem with them to achieve literary, critical, and commercial success. Welcomes the opportunity to work with additional authors and illustrators. This agency gives priority to members of SCBWI.

At the moment we are not open to submisssions except to those attending SCBWI conferences where we are attending, if that should change, we will update the information.

RECENT SALES *Dream Dog*, by Lou Berger; *Biscuit Loves the Library*, by Alyssa Capucilli; *The Scraps Book*, by Lois Ehlert; *Two Bunny Buddies*, by Kathryn O. Galbraith; *Between Two Worlds*, by Katherine Kirkpatrick.

HOW TO CONTACT E-mail a picture book ms or dummy; a synopsis and 3 chapters of a MG or YA novel; a proposal and 3 sample chapters for nonfiction. Accepts simultaneous submissions.

JUDITH EHRLICH LITERARY MANAGEMENT, LLC

146 Central Park W., 20E, New York NY 10023. (646)505-1570. **Fax:** (646)505-1570. **E-mail:** jehrlich@judithehrlichliterary.com. **Website:** www.judithehrlichliterary.com. Judith Ehrlich Literary Management LLC, established in 2002 and based in New York City, is a full service agency. "We represent nonfiction and fiction, both literary and commercial for the mainstream trade market. Our approach is very hands on, editorial, and constructive with the primary goal of helping authors build successful writing careers." Special areas of interest include compelling narrative nonfiction, outstanding biographies and mem-

oirs, lifestyle books, works that reflect our changing culture, women's issues, psychology, science, social issues, current events, parenting, health, history, business, and prescriptive books offering fresh information and advice. "We also seek and represent stellar commercial and literary fiction, including romance and other women's fiction, historical fiction, literary mysteries, and select thrillers. Our agency deals closely with all major and independent publishers. When appropriate, we place our properties with foreign agents and co-agents at leading film agencies in New York and Los Angeles."

MEMBER AGENTS Judith Ehrlich, jehrlich@judithehrlichliterary.com (upmarket, literary and quality commercial fiction, nonfiction: narrative, women's, business, prescriptive, medical and health-related topics, history, and current events).

HANDLES Does not want to receive novellas, poetry, textbooks, plays, or screenplays.

RECENT SALES Fiction: *The Bicycle Spy*, by Yona Zeldis McDonough (Scholastic); *The House on Primrose Pond*, by Yona McDonough (NAL/Penguin); *You Were Meant for Me*, by Yona McDonough (NAL/Penguin); *Echoes of Us: The Hybrid Chronicles*, Book 3 by Kat Zhang (HarperCollins); *Once We Were: The Hybrid Chronicles* Book 2, by Kat Zhang (HarperCollins). Nonfiction: *Listen to the Echoes: The Ray Bradbury Interviews (Deluxe Edition)*, by Sam Weller (Hat & Beard Press); *What are The Ten Commandments?*, by Yona McDonough (Grosset & Dunlap); *Little Author in the Big Woods: A Biography of Laura Ingalls Wilder*, by Yona McDonough (Christy Ottaviano Books/Henry Holt); *Ray Bradbury: The Last Interview: And Other Conversations*, by Sam Weller (Melville House); *Who Was Sojourner Truth?*, by Yona McDonough (Grosset & Dunlap); *Power Branding: Leveraging the Success of the World's Best Brands*, by Steve McKee (Palgrave Macmillan); *Confessions of a Sociopath: A Life Spent Hiding in Plain Sight*, by M.E. Thomas (Crown); *Luck and Circumstance: A Coming of Age in New York* and *Hollywood* and *Points Beyond*, by Michael Lindsay-Hogg (Knopf).

HOW TO CONTACT E-query, with a synopsis and some sample pages. The agency will respond only if interested. Accepts simultaneous submissions.

EINSTEIN LITERARY MANAGEMENT

27 W. 20th St., No. 1003, New York NY 10011. (212)221-8797. **E-mail:** info@einsteinliterary.com. **Website:** http://einsteinliterary.com. **Contact:** Susanna Einstein.

MEMBER AGENTS Susanna Einstein, Susan Graham, Paloma Hernando.

HANDLES "As an agency we represent a broad range of literary and commercial fiction, including upmarket women's fiction, crime fiction, historical fiction, romance, and books for middle-grade children and young adults, including picture books and graphic novels. We also handle nonfiction including cookbooks, memoir and narrative, and blog-to-book projects. Please see agent bios on the website for specific information about what each of ELM's agents represents." Does not want poetry, textbooks, or screenplays.

HOW TO CONTACT Please submit a query letter and the first 10 double-spaced pages of your manuscript in the body of the e-mail (no attachments). Does not respond to mail queries or telephone queries or queries that are not specifically addressed to this agency. Accepts simultaneous submissions.

ETHAN ELLENBERG LITERARY AGENCY

155 Suffolk St., No. 2R, New York NY 10002. (212)431-4554. **E-mail:** agent@ethanellenberg.com. **Website:** http://ethanellenberg.com. **Contact:** Ethan Ellenberg. This agency specializes in commercial fiction and nonfiction.

MEMBER AGENTS Ethan Ellenberg, president; Evan Gregory, senior agent; Ezra Ellenberg; Bibi Lewis.

HANDLES "We specialize in commercial fiction and children's books. In commercial fiction we want to see science fiction, fantasy, romance, mystery, thriller, women's fiction; all genres welcome. In children's books, we want to see everything: picture books, early reader, middle grade and young adult.We do some nonfiction: history, biography, military, popular science, and cutting edge books about any subject." Does not want to receive poetry, short stories, or screenplays.

HOW TO CONTACT Query by e-mail. Paste all of the material in the order listed. Fiction: query letter, synopsis, first 50 pages. Nonfiction: query letter, book proposal. Picture books: query letter, complete ms, 4-5 sample illustrations. Illustrators: query letter, 4-5 sample illustrations, link to online portfolio. Will not respond unless interested. Accepts simultaneous submissions.

EMPIRE LITERARY

115 W. 29th St., 3rd Floor, New York NY 10001. (917)213-7082. **E-mail:** abarzvi@empireliterary.com. **Website:** www.empireliterary.com.

MEMBER AGENTS Andrea Barzvi.

HOW TO CONTACT Please only query one agent at a time. "If we are interested in reading more we will get in touch with you as soon as possible." Accepts simultaneous submissions.

FAIRBANK LITERARY REPRESENTATION

Post Office Box Six, Hudson NY 12534-0006. (617)576-0030. **Website:** www.fairbankliterary.com; www.publishersmarketplace.com/members/SorcheFairbank/. **Contact:** Sorche Elizabeth Fairbank. A small, selective agency and member of AAR, the Author's Guild, the Agents Round Table, PEN, and Grub Street's Literary Advisory Council, Fairbank Literary Representation is happily in its nineteenth year. Clients range from first-time authors to international best-sellers, prize winning-journalists to professionals at the top of their fields. They can be found with all the major publishers, as well as in the *New York Times, The Boston Globe, Harper's, The Atlantic, The New Yorker, Granta, Best American Short Stories, McSweeney's, Tin House, Glimmertrain*, and more. Our tastes tend toward literary and international fiction; voice-y novels with a strong sense of place; big memoir that goes beyond the me-moir; topical or narrative nonfiction with a strong interest in women's voices, global perspectives, and class and race issues; children's picture books & middle grade from illustrator/artists only; quality lifestyle books (food, wine, and design); pop culture; craft; and gift and humor books. We are most likely to pick up works that are of social or cultural significance, newsworthy, or that cause us to take great delight in the words, images, or ideas on the page. Lately, we have been doing extremely well in the humor/gift/pop culture category, literary-leaning fiction, and children's picture books by illustrator artists, and we'd love to take on more projects in those categories. Above all, we look for a fresh voice, approach, story, or idea.

MEMBER AGENTS Sorche Fairbank (narrative nonfiction, commercial and literary fiction, memoir, food and wine); Matthew Frederick, matt@fairbankliterary.com (scout for sports nonfiction, architecture, design).

HANDLES "I tend to gravitate toward literary fiction and narrative nonfiction, with a strong interest in women's issues and women's voices, international voices, class and race issues, and projects that simply teach me something new about the greater world and society around us. We work closely and developmentally with our authors, and love what we do." Actively seeking literary fiction, international and culturally diverse voices, narrative nonfiction, topical subjects (politics, current affairs), history, sports, humor, architecture/design, and humor/pop culture. Also looking for picture books by illustrator authors only and illustrated middle grade. Does not want to receive romance, screenplays, poetry, science fiction or fantasy, or children's works unless by an illustrator author.

RECENT SALES Literary fiction about the British Partition of India, by Shilpi Suneja to Milkweed Editions; photo-heavy, fun book about opossums by Ally Burguieres to Quirk Books; 2-book deal for children's picture books (biographies) by Katie Mazeika to Beach Lane Books (Simon & Schuster); 3-book deal for Lisa Currie's doodle journals to TarcherPerigee (Penguin Random House); A new issue of Angie Bailey's *Texts From Mittens* to Hanover Square (Harlequin/Harper Collins); 3-book deal for Terry Border for picture books to Philomel; scratch & sniff spin-off and an early reader adaptation of Terry Border's best-selling *Peanut Butter & Cupcake* to Grosset and Dunlap/Penguin; 10-book deal for Matthew Frederick for his bestselling *101 Things I Learned Series* to Crown (Penguin Random House).

TERMS Agent receives 15% commission on domestic sales; 20% commission on foreign sales. Offers written contract, binding for 12 months; 60-day notice must be given to terminate contract.

HOW TO CONTACT No phone queries please! By e-mail: queries@fairbankliterary.com. Please paste the first five pages of your work below your query. No attachments. Accepts simultaneous submissions. Obtains most new clients through recommendations from others, solicitations, conferences, ideas generated in-house.

TIPS "Show me that you know your audience—and your competition. Have the writing and/or proposal at the very, very best it can be before starting the querying process. Don't assume that if someone likes it enough they'll 'fix' it. The biggest mistake new writers make is starting the querying process before they—

and the work—are ready. Take your time and do it right."

LEIGH FELDMAN LITERARY

E-mail: assistant@lfliterary.com. **Website:** http://lfliterary.com. **Contact:** Leigh Feldman.

HANDLES Does not want mystery, thriller, romance, paranormal, sci-fi.

RECENT SALES List of recent sales and best known sales are available on the agency website.

HOW TO CONTACT E-query. "Please include 'query' in the subject line. Due to large volume of submissions, we regret that we can not respond to all queries individually. Please include the first chapter or the first 10 pages of your manuscript (or proposal) pasted after your query letter. I'd love to know what led you to query me in particular, and please let me know if you are querying other agents as well." Accepts simultaneous submissions.

FINEPRINT LITERARY MANAGEMENT

207 W. 106th St., Suite 1D, New York NY 10025. (212)279-1412. **Website:** www.fineprintlit.com. **Contact:** Peter Rubie. I like books, whether fiction or nonfiction, that try to tell us who we are, where we've been, and where we may be going. They won't all necessarily tackle all of those questions, but at least focusing on them helps us find material that is relevant to contemporary readers.

MEMBER AGENTS To submit to FinePrint agents send a query and sample material to submissions@fineprintlit.com, and address the email to the particular agent you are hoping to get you rmaterial to. Peter Rubie, CEO, (nonfiction interests include narrative nonfiction, popular science, spirituality, history, biography, pop culture, business, technology, parenting, health, self help, music, and food; fiction interests include literate thrillers, crime fiction, science fiction and fantasy, military fiction and literary fiction, middle grade and boy-oriented YA fiction); Laura Wood, (serious nonfiction, especially in the areas of science and nature, along with substantial titles in business, history, religion, and other areas by academics, experienced professionals, and journalists; select genre fiction only (no poetry, literary fiction or memoir) in the categories of science fiction & fantasy and mystery); Lauren Bieker, (Lauren is looking for commercial and upmarket women's fiction and some well-crafted and differentiated YA novels. She is also open to select science fiction, as well as high concept and literary fiction works. She appreciates great storytelling and is a "sucker" for outstanding writing and convincing characters. While primarily interested in fiction, she will consider nonfiction proposals. She is looking for #ownvoices stories, Feminist lit/#MeToo stories, and LGBTQIA+ authors in both fiction and nonfiction. Her goals is to "hold the mic" for authors to tell their stories and be a helpful support system.); Bobby O'Neil (Bobby is looking for middle grade and young adult fiction across the board ranging from the grounded to the fantastic. In adult fiction, he is primarily interested in fantasy and speculative fiction that push the conventions of the genre, and character-driven commercial fiction. For nonfiction, he loves a strong narrative and is especially partial to memoir and historical. He is drawn to powerful voices and unique points of view that tell the stories from under-represented communities, and LGBTQIA+ authors in both fiction and nonfiction).

TERMS Agent receives 15% commission on domestic sales; 20% commission on foreign sales.

HOW TO CONTACT E-query. For fiction, send a query, synopsis, bio, and 30 pages. For nonfiction, send a query only; proposal requested later if the agent is interested. Send to submissions@fineprintlit.com and address the email to the appropriate FP agent. Accepts simultaneous submissions. Obtains most new clients through recommendations from others, solicitations.

FLANNERY LITERARY

E-mail: jennifer@flanneryliterary.com. **Website:** flanneryliterary.com. **Contact:** Jennifer Flannery. "Flannery Literary is a Chicago-area literary agency representing writers of books for children and young adults because the most interesting, well-written, and time-honored books are written with young people in mind."

HANDLES This agency specializes in middle grade and young adult fiction and nonfiction, we also represent picturebook, text only. 100% juvenile books. Actively seeking middle grade and young adult novels. No rhyming picture books nor bodily function topics, please. Also I do not open attachments unless instructed.

TERMS Agent receives 15% commission on domestic sales; 20% commission on foreign sales. Offers written contract, binding for life of book in print.

HOW TO CONTACT Query by e-mail only. "Multiple queries are fine, but please inform us. Please no attachments. If you're sending a query about a novel, please embed in the e-mail the first 5-10 pages; if it's a picture book, please embed the entire text in the e-mail. We do not open attachments unless they have been requested." Accepts simultaneous submissions. Obtains new clients through referrals and queries.

TIPS "Write an engrossing, succinct query describing your work. We are always looking for a fresh new voice."

FLETCHER & COMPANY

78 Fifth Ave., 3rd Floor, New York NY 10011. **Website:** www.fletcherandco.com. **Contact:** Christy Fletcher. Today, Fletcher & Co. is a full-service literary management and production company dedicated to writers of upmarket nonfiction as well as commercial and literary fiction.

MEMBER AGENTS Christy Fletcher (referrals only); Melissa Chinchillo (select list of her own authors); Rebecca Gradinger (literary fiction, up-market commercial fiction, narrative nonfiction, self-help, memoir, Women's studies, humor, and pop culture); Gráinne Fox (literary fiction and quality commercial authors, award-winning journalists and food writers, American voices, international, literary crime, upmarket fiction, narrative nonfiction); Lisa Grubka (fiction—literary, upmarket women's, and young adult; and nonfiction—narrative, food, science, and more); Eric Lupfer; Sarah Fuentes; Veronica Goldstein; Eve MacSweeney; Peter Steinberg.

RECENT SALES *The Profiteers*, by Sally Denton; *The Longest Night*, by Andrea Williams; *Disrupted: My Misadventure in the Start-Up Bubble*, by Dan Lyons; *Free Re-Fills: A Doctor Confronts His Addiction*, by Peter Grinspoon, M.D.; *Black Man in a White Coat: A Doctor's Reflections on Race and Medicine*, by Damon Tweedy, M.D.

HOW TO CONTACT Send queries to info@fletcherandco.com. Please do not include e-mail attachments with your initial query, as they will be deleted. Address your query to a specific agent. No snail mail queries. Accepts simultaneous submissions.

FOLIO LITERARY MANAGEMENT, LLC

The Film Center Building, 630 Ninth Ave., Suite 1101, New York NY 10036. (212)400-1494. **Fax:** (212)967-0977. **Website:** www.foliolit.com.

This agency has many agents, and their specialties are listed on the website.

MEMBER AGENTS Claudia Cross (romance novels, commercial women's fiction, cooking and food writing, serious nonfiction on religious and spiritual topics); Jeff Kleinman (bookclub fiction (not genre commercial, like mysteries or romances), literary fiction, thrillers and suspense novels, narrative nonfiction, memoir); Dado Derviskadic (nonfiction: cultural history, biography, memoir, pop science, motivational self-help, health/nutrition, pop culture, cookbooks; fiction that's gritty, introspective, or serious); Frank Weimann (biography, business/investing/finance, history, religious, mind/body/spirit, health, lifestyle, cookbooks, sports, African-American, science, memoir, special forces/CIA/FBI/mafia, military, prescriptive nonfiction, humor, celebrity; adult and children's fiction); Michael Harriot (commercial nonfiction (both narrative and prescriptive) and fantasy/science fiction); Erin Harris (book club, historical fiction, literary, narrative nonfiction, psychological suspense, young adult); Katherine Latshaw (blogs-to-books, food/cooking, middle grade, narrative and prescriptive nonfiction); Erin Niumata (fiction: commercial women's fiction, romance, historical fiction, mysteries, psychological thrillers, suspense, humor; nonfiction: self-help, women's issues, pop culture and humor, pet care/pets, memoirs, and anything blogger); Marcy Posner (adult: commercial women's fiction, historical fiction, mystery, biography, history, health, and lifestyle, commercial novels, thrillers, narrative nonfiction; children's: contemporary YA and MG, mystery series for boys, select historical fiction and fantasy); Steve Troha; Emily van Beek (YA, MG, picture books), Melissa White (general nonfiction, literary and commercial fiction, MG, YA); John Cusick (middle grade, picture books, YA); Jamie Chambliss; Roger Freet; Jan Baumer; Sonali Chanchani; Will Murphy; Rachel Ekstrom; Karen Gormandy; Katherine Odom-Tomehin; Adriann Ranta Zurhellen; Margaret Sutherland Brown.

HANDLES No poetry, stage plays, or screenplays.

HOW TO CONTACT Query via e-mail only (no attachments). Read agent bios online for specific submission guidelines and e-mail addresses, and to check if someone is closed to queries. "All agents respond to queries as soon as possible, whether interested or not. If you haven't heard back from the individual agent within the time period that they specify on their bio page, it's possible that something has gone wrong, and your query has been lost—in that case, please e-mail a follow-up."

TIPS "Please do not submit simultaneously to more than one agent at Folio. If you're not sure which of us is exactly right for your book, don't worry. We work closely as a team, and if one of our agents gets a query that might be more appropriate for someone else, we'll always pass it along. It's important that you check each agent's bio page for clear directions as to how to submit, as well as when to expect feedback."

FOX LITERARY

110 W. 40th St., Suite 2305, New York NY 10018. **Website:** foxliterary.com. Fox Literary is a boutique agency which represents commercial fiction, along with select works of literary fiction and nonfiction that have broad commercial appeal.

HANDLES Fox Literary is actively seeking the following: young adult fiction (all genres), science fiction/fantasy, romance, historical fiction, literary fiction, thrillers, horror, and graphic novels. We're always interested in books that cross genres and reinvent popular concepts with an engaging new twist (especially when there's a historical and/or speculative element involved). On the nonfiction side, we're interested in memoirs, biography, and smart narrative nonfiction; Diana particularly enjoys memoirs and other nonfiction about sex work, addiction and recovery, popular science, and pop culture. Isabel is especially interested in narratives focused on travel, food, and the science of beauty, as well as microhistories of all things decadent and frivolous. screenplays, category Westerns, Christian/inspirational, or children's picture books

HOW TO CONTACT Please email query and first 5 pages in body of email, and include the name of the agent to whom the submission is directed in the salutation of the email. No email attachments or hard copy submissions. Authors may query more than one agent within the agency at the same time, but if doing so author must send separate queries to each agent rather than a single query addressed to multiple agents. With all submissions, agents may jointly review and determine which agent will be the best fit. Accepts simultaneous submissions.

SARAH JANE FREYMANN LITERARY AGENCY

(212)362-9277. **E-mail:** sarah@sarahjanefreymann.com. **Website:** www.sarahjanefreymann.com. **Contact:** Sarah Jane Freymann, Steve Schwartz.

MEMBER AGENTS Sarah Jane Freymann (nonfiction: spiritual, psychology, self-help, women/men's issues, books by health experts [conventional and alternative], cookbooks, narrative nonfiction, natural science, nature, memoirs, cutting-edge journalism, travel, multicultural issues, parenting, lifestyle, fiction: literary, mainstream YA); Steven Schwartz, steve@sarahjanefreymann.com (popular fiction [crime, thrillers, and historical novels], world and national affairs, business books, self-help, psychology, humor, sports and travel).

TERMS Charges clients for long distance, overseas postage, photocopying. 100% of business is derived from commissions on ms sales.

HOW TO CONTACT Query via e-mail. No attachments. Below the query, please paste the first 10 pages of your work. Accepts simultaneous submissions.

REBECCA FRIEDMAN LITERARY AGENCY

E-mail: queries@rfliterary.com. **Website:** www.rfliterary.com.

RECENT SALES A complete list of agency authors is available online.

HOW TO CONTACT Please submit your brief query letter and first chapter (no more than 15 pages, double-spaced). No attachments. Accepts simultaneous submissions.

THE FRIEDRICH AGENCY

(212)317-8810. **E-mail:** mfriedrich@friedrichagency.com; lcarson@friedrichagency.com; hcarr@friedrichagency.com; hbrattesani@friedrichagency.com. **Website:** www.friedrichagency.com. **Contact:** Molly Friedrich; Lucy Carson; Heather Carr; Hannah Brattesani.

MEMBER AGENTS Molly Friedrich, founder and agent (open to queries); Lucy Carson, TV/film rights director and agent (open to queries); Hannah Brattesani, foreign rights director and agent (open to queries); Heather Carr, contracts director and agent (open to queries).

RECENT SALES *W is For Wasted*, by Sue Grafton; *Olive Kitteridge*, by Elizabeth Strout. Other clients include Frank McCourt, Jane Smiley, Esmeralda Santiago, Terry McMillan, Cathy Schine, Ruth Ozeki, Karen Joy Fowler, and more.

HOW TO CONTACT Query by e-mail only. Please query only 1 agent at this agency. Accepts simultaneous submissions.

FULL CIRCLE LITERARY, LLC

Website: www.fullcircleliterary.com. **Contact:** Stefanie Von Borstel. "Full Circle Literary is a full-service literary agency, offering a full circle approach to literary representation. Our team has diverse experience in book publishing including editorial, marketing, publicity, legal and rights, which we use collectively to build careers book by book. We work with both award-winning veteran and debut writers and artists and our team has a knack for finding and developing new and diverse talent. Learn more about our agency and submission guidelines by visiting our website." This agency goes deeply into depth about what they are seeking and submission guidelines on their agency website.

MEMBER AGENTS Stefanie Sanchez Von Borstel; Adriana Dominguez; Taylor Martindale Kean; Lilly Ghahremani, Nicole Geiger.

HANDLES Actively seeking nonfiction and fiction projects that offer new and diverse viewpoints, and literature with a global or multicultural perspective. "We are particularly interested in books with a Latino or Middle Eastern angle."

TERMS Agent receives 15% commission on domestic sales; 25% commission on foreign sales. Offers written contract which outlines responsibilities of the author and the agent.

HOW TO CONTACT Online submissions only via Query Manager (links on website fullcircleliterary.com). Please note agency wishlists and areas of representation. Illustrators please include link to your online Portfolio or website. Accepts simultaneous submissions. Obtains most new clients through recommendations from others and conferences.

FUSE LITERARY

Foreword Literary, Inc. dba FUSE LITERARY, P.O. Box 258, La Honda CA 94020. **E-mail:** info@fuseliterary.com. **Website:** www.fuseliterary.com. **Contact:** info@fuseliterary.com. Fuse Literary is a full-service, hybrid literary agency based in San Francisco with offices in California, New York, Texas, Massachusetts and Canada. "We blend the tried-and-true methods of traditional publishing with the brash new opportunities engendered by digital publishing, emerging technologies, and an evolving author-agent relationship. Fuse manages a wide variety of clients, from bestsellers to debut authors, working with fiction and nonfiction for children and adults worldwide. We combine technical efficiency with outside-the-covers creative thinking so that each individual client's career is specifically fine-tuned for them. We are not an agency that sells a book and then washes our hands of the project. We realize that our ongoing success directly results from that of our clients, so we remain at their side to cultivate and strategize throughout the many lives of each book, both before and after the initial sale. Innovations include Fuse Club for client collaboration, and our Short Fuse client publishing program, which helps bridge the gaps between books, growing and maintaining the author's fan base without lag. The partners launched Fuse following tenures at established agencies, bringing with them experience in writing, teaching, professional editing, book marketing, blogging and social media, running high-tech companies, and marketing new technologies. A boutique, collaborative agency, Fuse provides each client with the expertise and forward vision of the group. We pride ourselves on our flexibility and passion for progression in an ever-changing publishing environment. We believe that the agency of the future will not just react to change but will actively create change, pushing markets and advancing formats to provide authors with the best possible outlets for their art."

MEMBER AGENTS Laurie McLean, genre fiction for adults, young adults and middle grade; Gordon Warnock, fiction: high-concept commercial fiction, literary fiction (adults through YA), graphic novels (adults through MG); nonfiction: memoir (adult, YA, NA, graphic), cookbooks/food narrative/food studies, illustrated/art/photography (especially graphic nonfiction), political and current events, pop science, pop culture (especially punk culture and geek culture), self-help, how-to, humor, pets, business and career); Connor Goldsmith, books by and about people from marginalized perspectives, such as LGBT people and/or racial minorities; nonfiction (from recognized experts with established platforms): history (particularly of the ancient world), theater, cinema, music, television, mass media, popular culture, feminism and gender studies, LGBT issues, race relations, and the sex industry; Michelle Richter, primarily seeking fiction, specifically book club reads, literary fiction, and mystery/suspense/thrillers; for nonfiction, seeking fashion, pop culture, science/medicine, sociology/social trends, and economics); Emily S. Keyes, picture books, middle grade and young adult children's books, plus select commercial fiction, including fantasy & science fiction, women's fiction, new adult fiction, pop culture and humor); Tricia Skinner, romance, science fiction, fantasy; Carlisle Webber, high-concept commercial fiction in middle grade, young adult, and adult; dark thrillers, mystery, horror, dark women's fiction, dark pop/mainstream fiction; especially interested in diverse authors and their stories; Veronica Park, specializes in nonfiction (the more creatively structured your narrative, the better,) women's fiction, and romance for all ages. Darker subject matter and wry humor are encouraged, even if they go hand in hand; Karly Dizon, represents picture books, middle grade and young adult fiction and nonfiction; Ernie Chiara, specializes in adult fantasy, science fiction, and magical realism, as well as young adult fantasy and graphic novels.

RECENT SALES Seven-figure and six-figure deals for NYT bestseller Julie Kagawa (YA); six-figure deal for debut Melissa D. Savage (MG); seven-figure and six-figure deals for Kerry Lonsdale (suspense); two six-figure audio deals for fantasy author Brian D. Anderson; *First Watch*, by Dale Lucas (fantasy); *This Is What a Librarian Looks Like*, by Kyle Cassidy (photo essay); *A Big Ship at the Edge of the Universe*, by Alex White (sci-fi); Runebinder Chronicles, by Alex Kahler (YA); *Perceptual Intelligence*, by Dr. Brian Boxler Wachler (science); *The Night Child*, by Anna Quinn (literary); *Hollywood Homicide*, by Kellye Garrett (mystery); Breakup Bash Series, by Nina Crespo (romance); *America's Next Reality Star*, by Laura Heffernan (women's fiction); *Losing the Girl*, by MariNaomi (graphic novel); *Maggie and Abby's Neverending Pillow Fort*, by Will Taylor (MG); *Idea Machine*, by Jorjeana Marie (how-to); six-figure deal for *Ebony Gate series* by Ken Bebelle & Julia Vee (fantasy); six-figure deal for *The Honeys* by Ryan LaSala (YA).

TERMS "We earn 15% on negotiated deals for books and with our co-agents earn 20-25% on foreign translation deals depending on the territory; 20% on TV/Movies/Plays; other multimedia deals are so new there is no established commission rate. The author has the last say, approving or not approving all deals." After the initial 90-day period, there is a 30-day termination of the agency agreement clause. No fees.

HOW TO CONTACT E-query an individual agent. Check the website to see if any individual agent has closed themselves to submissions, as well as for a description of each agent's individual submission preferences. (You can find these details by clicking on each agent's photo.) Accepts simultaneous submissions. Only accepts e-mailed queries that follow our online guidelines.

GALLT AND ZACKER LITERARY AGENCY

273 Charlton Ave., South Orange NJ 07079. **Website:** www.galltzacker.com. **Contact:** Nancy Gallt, Marietta Zacker. "At the Gallt and Zacker Literary Agency we represent people, not projects. We aim to bring to life stories and artwork that help readers throughout the world become life-long book enthusiasts and to inspire and entertain readers of all ages."

MEMBER AGENTS Nancy Gallt; Marietta Zacker; Linda Camacho; Beth Phelan; Ellan K. Greenberg; Erin Casey.

HANDLES Books for children and young adults. Actively seeking author, illustrators, author/illustrators who create books for young adults and younger readers.

RECENT SALES Rick Riordan's Books (Hyperion); *Trace*, by Pat Cummings (Harper); *I Got Next*, by Daria Peoples-Riley (Bloomsbury); *Gondra's Treasure*, illustrated by Jennifer Black Reinhardt (Clarion/HMH); *Caterpillar Summer*, by Gillian McDunn (Bloomsbury); *It Wasn't Me*, by Dana Alison Levy (Delacorte/Random House); *Five Midnights*, by Ann Dávila Cardinal (Tor/Macmillan); *Patron Saints of Nothing*, by Randy Ribay (Kokila/Penguin); *Rot*, by Ben Clanton (Simon & Schuster). *The Year They Fell*, by David Kreizman (Imprint/Macmillan); *Manhattan Maps*, by Jennifer Thermes (Abrams); *The Moon Within*, by Aida Salazar (Scholastic); *Artist in Space*, by Dean Robbins (Scholastic); *Where Are You From?*, by Mary Amato (Holiday House); *Where Are You From?*, by Yamile Saied Méndez (Harper); *The Girl King*, by Mimi Yu (Bloomsbury); *Narwhal and Jelly*, by Ben Clanton (Tundra/Penguin Random House Canada).

TERMS Agent receives 15% commission on domestic sales; 20% commission on foreign sales. Offers written contract; 30-day notice must be given to terminate contract.

HOW TO CONTACT Submission guidelines on our website: http://galltzacker.com/submissions.html. No e-mail queries, please. Accepts simultaneous submissions. Obtains new clients through submissions, conferences and recommendations from others.

TIPS "Writing and illustrations stand on their own, so submissions should tell the most compelling stories possible—whether visually, in narrative, or both."

GELFMAN SCHNEIDER/ICM PARTNERS

850 7th Ave., Suite 903, New York NY 10019. **Website:** www.gelfmanschneider.com. **Contact:** Jane Gelfman, Deborah Schneider.

MEMBER AGENTS Deborah Schneider (all categories of literary and commercial fiction and nonfiction); Jane Gelfman; Heather Mitchell (particularly interested in narrative nonfiction, historical fiction and young debut authors with strong voices); Penelope Burns, penelope.gsliterary@gmail.com (literary and commercial fiction and nonfiction, as well as a variety of young adult and middle grade).

HANDLES "Among our diverse list of clients are novelists, journalists, playwrights, scientists, activists & humorists writing narrative nonfiction, memoir, political & current affairs, popular science and popular culture nonfiction, as well as literary & commercial fiction, women's fiction, and historical fiction." Does not currently accept screenplays or scripts, poetry, or picture book queries.

TERMS Agent receives 15% commission on domestic sales; 20% commission on foreign sales; 15% commission on film sales. Offers written contract. Charges clients for photocopying and messengers/couriers.

HOW TO CONTACT Query. Check Submissions page of website to see which agents are open to queries and further instructions. Accepts simultaneous submissions.

THE GERNERT COMPANY

136 E. 57th St., New York NY 10022. (212)838-7777. **E-mail:** info@thegernertco.com. **Website:** www.thegernertco.com. "Our client list is as broad as the market; we represent equal parts fiction and nonfiction."

MEMBER AGENTS Sarah Burnes (literary fiction and nonfiction; children's fiction); Chris Parris-Lamb (nonfiction, literary fiction); Seth Fishman (looking for the new voice, the original idea, the entirely breathtaking creative angle in both fiction and nonfiction); Will Roberts (smart, original thrillers with distinctive voices, compelling backgrounds, and fast-paced narratives); Erika Storella (nonfiction projects that make an argument, narrate a history, and/or provide a new perspective); Sarah Bolling (literary fiction, smart genre fiction—particularly sci-fi—memoir, pop culture, and style); Anna Worrall (smart women's literary and commercial fiction, psychological thrillers, and narrative nonfiction); Ellen Coughtrey (women's literary and commercial fiction, historical fiction, narrative nonfiction and smart, original thrillers, plus well-written Southern Gothic anything); Jack Gernert (stories about heroes—both real and imagined); Joy Fowlkes; Nora Gonzalez; Sophie Pugh-Sellers; Nicole Tourtelot. At this time, Courtney Gatewood and Rebecca Gardner are closed to queries. See the website to find out the tastes of each agent.

RECENT SALES *Partners*, by John Grisham; *The River Why*, by David James Duncan; *The Thin Green Line*, by Paul Sullivan; *A Fireproof Home for the Bride*, by Amy Scheibe; *The Only Girl in School*, by Natalie Standiford.

HOW TO CONTACT Please send us a query letter by e-mail to info@thegernertco.com describing the work you'd like to submit, along with some information about yourself and a sample chapter if appropriate. Please indicate in your letter which agent you are querying. Please do not send e-mails directly to individual agents. It's our policy to respond to your query only if we are interested in seeing more material, usually within 4-6 weeks. See company website for more instructions. Accepts simultaneous submissions. Obtains most new clients through recommendations from others, solicitations.

BARRY GOLDBLATT LITERARY LLC

c/o Industrious - Brooklyn, 594 Dean St., 2nd Floor, Brooklyn NY 11238. **Website:** www.bgliterary.com. **Contact:** Barry Goldblatt.

HANDLES "Please see our website for specific submission guidelines and information on our particular tastes."

RECENT SALES *Trolled*, by Bruce Coville; *Grim Tidings*, by Caitlin Kittridge; *Max at Night*, by Ed Vere.

TERMS Agent receives 15% commission on domestic sales; 20% on foreign and dramatic sales. Offers written contract. 60 days notice must be given to terminate contract.

HOW TO CONTACT "E-mail queries can be sent to query@bgliterary.com and should include the word 'query' in the subject line. To query Jen Udden specifically, e-mail queries can be sent to query.judden@gmail.com. Please know that we will read and respond to every e-query that we receive, provided it is properly addressed and follows the submission guidelines below. We will not respond to e-queries that are addressed to no one, or to multiple recipients. Your e-mail query should include the following within the body of the e-mail: your query letter, a synopsis of the book, and the first 5 pages of your manuscript. We will not open or respond to any e-mails that have attachments. If we like the sound of your work, we will request more from you. Our response time is 4 weeks on queries, 6-8 weeks on full manuscripts. If you haven't heard from us within that time, feel free to check in via e-mail." Accepts simultaneous submissions. Obtains clients through referrals, queries, and conferences.

TIPS "We're a hands-on agency, focused on building an author's career, not just making an initial sale. We don't care about trends or what's hot; we just want to sign great writers."

IRENE GOODMAN LITERARY AGENCY

27 W. 24th St., Suite 804, New York NY 10010. **E-mail:** miriam.queries@irenegoodman.com, barbara.queries@irenegoodman.com, kim.queries@irenegoodman.com, victoria.queries@irenegoodman.com, irene.queries@irenegoodman.com, whitney.queries@irenegoodman.com, pam.queries@irenegoodman.com, maggie.queries@irenegoodman.com, margaret.queries@irenegoodman.com, lee.queries@irenegoodman.com. **Website:** www.irenegoodman.com. **Contact:** Maggie Kane.

MEMBER AGENTS Irene Goodman, Miriam Kriss, Barbara Poelle, Kim Perel, Victoria Marini, Whitney Ross, Pam Gruber, Maggie Kane, Margaret Danko, Lee O'Brien; Natalie Lakosil; Danny Baror; Heather Baror-Shapiro.

HANDLES Commercial and literary fiction and nonfiction. No screenplays, poetry, or inspirational fiction.

TERMS 15% commission.

HOW TO CONTACT Query. Submit synopsis, first 10 pages pasted into the body of the email. E-mail queries only! See the website submission page. No e-mail attachments. Query 1 agent only. Accepts simultaneous submissions.

TIPS "We are receiving an unprecedented amount of e-mail queries. If you find that the mailbox is full, please try again in two weeks. E-mail queries to our personal addresses will not be answered. E-mails to our personal inboxes will be deleted."

DOUG GRAD LITERARY AGENCY, INC.

156 Prospect Park West, #3L, Brooklyn NY 11215. **Website:** www.dgliterary.com. **Contact:** Doug Grad. Throughout Doug's editorial career, he was always an author's advocate—the kind of editor authors wanted to work with because of his keen eye, integrity, and talent for developing projects. He was also a skillful negotiator, sometimes to the chagrin of literary agents. For the last 10 years, he has been bringing those experiences to the other side of the table in offering publishers the kind of high-quality commercial fiction and nonfiction that he himself was proud to publish. He has sold award-winning and bestselling authors.

MEMBER AGENTS Doug Grad (narrative nonfiction, military, sports, celebrity memoir, thrillers, mysteries, cozies, historical fiction, music, style, business, home improvement, food, science and theater).

HANDLES Does not want fantasy, young adult, or children's picture books.

RECENT SALES *Net Force* series created by Tom Clancy and Steve Pieczenik, written by Jerome Preisler (Hanover Square); *A Serial Killer's Daughter* by Kerri Rawson (Thomas Nelson); *The Next Greatest Generation*, by Joseph L. Galloway and Marvin J. Wolf (Thomas Nelson); *All Available Boats* by L. Douglas Keeney (Lyons Press); *Here Comes the Body*, Book 1 in the Catering Hall mystery series, by Agatha Award-winner Ellen Byron writing as Maria DiRico (Kensington); *Please Don't Feed the Mayor* and *Alaskan Catch*, by Sue Pethick (Kensington).

HOW TO CONTACT Query by e-mail first. No sample material unless requested; no printed submissions by mail. Accepts simultaneous submissions.

SANFORD J. GREENBURGER ASSOCIATES, INC.

55 Fifth Ave., New York NY 10003. (212)206-5600. **Fax:** (212)463-8718. **Website:** www.greenburger.com. "Large enough to be a full service agency, including international rights, but small enough to manage and service clients personally, SJGA works closely with authors to edit and fine-tune proposals, refine concepts and ensure that the best work reaches editors. The agents freely share information and expertise, creating a collaborative partnership unique to the industry. The combined result is reflected in the numerous successes of the agency's authors (including Dan Brown, Patrick Rothfuss, and Robin Preiss Glasser)."

MEMBER AGENTS Matt Bialer, querymb@sjga.com (fantasy, science fiction, thrillers, and mysteries as well as a select group of literary writers, and also loves smart narrative nonfiction including books about current events, popular culture, biography, history, music, race, and sports); Faith Hamlin, fhamlin@sjga.com (receives submissions by referral); Heide Lange, queryhl@sjga.com (receives submissions by referral); Daniel Mandel, querydm@sjga.com (literary and commercial fiction, as well as memoirs and nonfiction about business, art, history, politics, sports, and popular culture); Rachael Dillon Fried, rfried@sjga.com (both fiction and nonfiction authors, with a keen interest in unique literary voices, women's fiction, narrative nonfiction, memoir, and comedy); Stephanie Delman, sdelman@sjga.com (literary/upmarket contemporary fiction, psychological thrillers/suspense, and atmospheric, near-historical fiction); Ed Maxwell, emaxwell@sjga.com (expert and narrative nonfiction authors, novelists and graphic novelists, as well as children's book authors and illustrators); Wendi Gu, wgu@sjga.com; Sarah Phair, sphair@sjga.com; Abigail Frank, afrank@sjga.com; Iwalani Kim, ikim@sjga.com; Bailey Tamayo, btamayo@sjga.com.

HANDLES No screenplays.

RECENT SALES *Origin*, by Dan Brown; *Sweet Pea and Friends: A Sheepover*, by John Churchman and Jennifer Churchman; *Code of Conduct*, by Brad Thor.

TERMS Agent receives 15% commission on domestic sales; 20% commission on foreign sales. Charges for photocopying and books for foreign and subsidiary rights submissions.

HOW TO CONTACT E-query. "Please look at each agent's profile page for current information about what each agent is looking for and for the correct email address to use for queries to that agent. Please be sure to use the correct query e-mail address for each agent." Obtains most new clients through recommendations from others.

THE GREENHOUSE LITERARY AGENCY

E-mail: submissions@greenhouseliterary.com. **Website:** www.greenhouseliterary.com. **Contact:** Sarah Davies.

"At Greenhouse we aim to establish strong, long-term relationships with clients and work hard to find our authors the very best publisher and deal for their writing. We often get very involved editorially, working creatively with authors where necessary. Our goal is to submit high-quality manuscripts to publishers while respecting the role of the editor who will have their own publishing vision."

MEMBER AGENTS Sarah Davies, vice president (fiction and nonfiction by North American authors, chapter books through to middle grade and young adult); Chelsea Eberly; Kristin Ostby.

HANDLES "We represent authors writing fiction and nonfiction for children and teens. The agency has offices in both the US and UK, and the agency's commission structure reflects this—taking 15% for sales to both US and UK, thus treating both as 'domestic' market." All genres of children's and YA fiction. Occasionally, a nonfiction proposal will be considered. Does not want to receive picture books texts (ie, written by writers who aren't also illustrators) or short stories, educational or religious/inspirational work, pre-school/novelty material, screenplays. Represents novels and some nonfiction.Considers these fiction areas: juvenile, chapter book series, middle grade, young adult. Does not want to receive poetry, picture book texts (unless by author/illustrators) or work aimed at adults; short stories, educational or religious/inspirational work, pre-school/novelty material, or screenplays.

RECENT SALES *Agents of the Wild*, by Jennifer Bell & Alice Lickens (Walker UK); *Bookshop Girl in Paris*, by Chloe Coles (Hot Key); *Votes for Women*, by Winifred Conkling (Algonquin); *The Monster Catchers*, by George Brewington (Holt); *City of the Plague God*, by Sarwat Chadda (Disney-Hyperion); *Whiteout*, by Gabriel Dylan (Stripes); *The Lying Woods*, by Ashley Elston (Disney-Hyperion); *When You Trap a Tiger*, by Tae Keller (Random House); *We Speak in Storms*, by Natalie Lund (Philomel); *When We Wake*, by Elle Cosimano (HarperCollins); *Carpa Fortuna*, by Lindsay Eagar (Candlewick); *Instructions Not Included*, by Tami Lewis Brown & Debbie Loren Dunn (Disney-Hyperion); *Fake*, by Donna Cooner (Scholastic); *Unicorn Academy*, by Julie Sykes (Nosy Crow); *The Girl Who Sailed the Stars*, by Matilda Woods (Scholastic UK/Philomel US).

TERMS Agent receives 15% commission on domestic sales; 25% commission on foreign sales. Offers written contract. This agency occasionally charges for submission copies to film agents or foreign publishers.

HOW TO CONTACT Query 1 agent only. Put the target agent's name in the subject line. Paste the first 5 pages of your story after the query. Please see our website for up-to-date information as occasionally we close to queries for short periods of time. Accepts simultaneous submissions.

TIPS "Before submitting material, authors should visit the Greenhouse Literary Agency website and carefully read all submission guidelines."

KATHRYN GREEN LITERARY AGENCY, LLC

157 Columbus Ave., Suite 508, New York NY 10023. (212)245-4225. **E-mail:** query@kgreenagency.com. **Website:** www.kathryngreenliteraryagency.com. **Contact:** Kathy Green.

HANDLES "Considers all types of fiction but particularly like historical fiction, cozy mysteries, young adult and middle grade. For nonfiction, I am interested in memoir, parenting, humor with a pop culture bent, and history. Quirky nonfiction is also a particular favorite." Does not want to receive science fiction, fantasy, children's picture books, screenplays, or poetry.

RECENT SALES *The Last Secret I Ever Told* by Laurie Stolarz, *The Thing I'm Most Afraid Of* by Kristin Levine, *Deliberate Evil* by Edward Renehan, *Where I Belong* by Marcia Arqueta Mickelson, *A Place to Hang the Moon* by Kate Albus, *The Franklin Avenue Rookery for Wayward Babies* by Laura Newman, *When We Die* by Kenneth Doka, PhD.

TERMS Agent receives 15% commission on domestic sales; 20% commission on foreign sales.

HOW TO CONTACT Query by e-mail. Send no attachments unless requested. Do not send queries via regular mail. Responds in 4 weeks. "Queries do not have to be exclusive; however if further material is requested, please be in touch before accepting other representation." Accepts simultaneous submissions. Obtains most new clients through recommendations from others, solicitations, conferences.

JILL GRINBERG LITERARY MANAGEMENT, LLC

392 Vanderbilt Avenue, Brooklyn NY 11238. (212)620-5883. **Website:** www.jillgrinbergliterary.com. Founded by industry veteran Jill Grinberg, the agency's tastes are wide ranging—born out of deep curiosity and a passion for great writing in all its forms and for all readerships. Our clients win major awards—including the National Book Award, the Pulitzer Prize, the Printz Award and Newbery Honor—and regularly appear on U.S. and international bestseller lists. Our select client list features 48 New York Times bestsellers and 28 IndieBound bestsellers. Our authors include novelists and memoirists; historians and scientists; illustrators and musicians; cultural critics and humanitarians; entrepreneurs and innovators- united by the high quality of their writing, original and authentic voices, passion for their work, and brilliant storytelling.

MEMBER AGENTS Jill Grinberg; Katelyn Detweiler; Sophia Seidner; Sam Farkas; Larissa Melo Pienkowski; Jessica Saint Jean.

HANDLES "We do not accept unsolicited queries for screenplays."

HOW TO CONTACT Please send your query to **info@jillgrinbergliterary.com**. Your e-mail subject line should follow this general format: QUERY: Title of Project by Your Name / Your Book's Age Category and Genre / ATTN: Name of Agent. Paste your query letter in the body of the e-mail, addressed to the agent of your choice, and attach your materials as a docx file. Do not attach zip folders, Pages files, links to Google Docs, or links to download materials from file sharing sites. You will receive an auto-response confirming your submission was received. For fiction submissions, please send a query letter and the first fifty (50) pages of your manuscript. If we are interested in reading more, we will reach out to request the full manuscript. For nonfiction submissions, please send a query letter and proposal. Your nonfiction proposal should include a project overview or outline, proposed chapter summaries, comparable titles, a sample chapter, your biography, and a bibliography of any additional works. Picture book submissions should include the full text, which can either be attached as a docx. file or pasted in the body of the email below your query. If you are an author-illustrator, please provide a sketch dummy (as a lo-res PDF). We no longer accept or consider mailed hard copy submissions, and any materials received will be discarded unread. Accepts simultaneous submissions.

TIPS Please refer to our website, www.jillgrinbergliterary.com, for the most up-to-date agency information and submission guidelines.

HARTLINE LITERARY AGENCY

123 Queenston Dr., Pittsburgh PA 15235-5429. (412)829-2483. **E-mail:** jim@hartlineliterary.com.

Website: www.hartlineliterary.com. **Contact:** James D. Hart. Many of the agents at this agency are generalists. This agency also handles inspirational and Christian works.

MEMBER AGENTS Jim Hart, principal agent (jim@hartlineliterary.com); Joyce Hart, founder (joyce@hartlineliterary.com); Linda Glaz (linda@hartlineliterary.com); Cyle Young (cyle@hartlineliterary.com).

HANDLES "This agency specializes in the Christian bookseller market." We also represent general market, but no graphic sex or language. Actively seeking adult fiction, all genres, self-help, social issues, Christian living, parenting, marriage, business, biographies, narrative nonfiction, creative nonfiction. Does not want to receive erotica, horror, graphic violence or graphic language.

RECENT SALES *The Beautiful Ashes of Gomez Gomez*, by Buck Storm (Kregel); *The Mr. Rogers Effect*, by Dr. Anita Knight (Baker Books); *People Can Change*, by Dr. Mark W. Baker (Fortress); *Obedience Over Hustle*, by Malinda Fuller (Barbour); *Keller's Heart*, by John Gray, Illustrations Shanna Oblenus (Paraclete); *Create Your Yes*, by Angela Marie Hutchinson (Source Books); *Simply Spirit Filled*, by Dr. Andrew K. Gabriel (Thomas Nelson).

TERMS Agent receives 15% commission on domestic sales. Offers written contract.

HOW TO CONTACT E-mail submissions are preferred. Target one agent only. Each agent has specific interests, please refer to our web page for that information. All e-mail submissions sent to Hartline Agents should be sent as a MS Word doc attached to an e-mail with 'submission: title, authors name and word count' in the subject line. A proposal is a single document, not a collection of files. Place the query letter in the email itself. Do not send the entire proposal in the body of the e-mail. Further guidelines online. Accepts simultaneous submissions. Obtains most new clients through recommendations from others, and at conferences.

TIPS Please follow the guidelines on our web site www.hartlineliterary for the fastest response to your proposal. E-mail proposals only.

ANTONY HARWOOD LIMITED

103 Walton St., Oxford OX2 6EB, United Kingdom. (44)(018)6555-9615. **Website:** www.antonyharwood.com. **Contact:** Antony Harwood; James Macdonald Lockhart; Jo Williamson.

MEMBER AGENTS Antony Harwood, James Macdonald Lockhart, Jo Williamson (children's); Jonathan Gregory.

TERMS Agent receives 15% commission on domestic sales; 20% commission on foreign sales.

HOW TO CONTACT "We are happy to consider submissions of fiction and nonfiction in every genre and category except for screenwriting and poetry. If you wish to submit your work to us for consideration, please send a covering letter, brief outline and the opening 50 pages by e-mail. If you want to post your material to us, please be sure to enclose an SAE or the cost of return postage." Replies if interested. Accepts simultaneous submissions.

HELEN HELLER AGENCY INC.

4-216 Heath St. W., Toronto ON M5P 1N7, Canada. (416)489-0396. **E-mail:** info@helenhelleragency.com. **Website:** www.helenhelleragency.com. **Contact:** Helen Heller.

MEMBER AGENTS Helen Heller, helen@helenhelleragency.com (thrillers and front-list general fiction); Sarah Heller, sarah@helenhelleragency.com (front list commercial YA and adult fiction, with a particular interest in high concept historical fiction); Barbara Berson, barbara@helenhelleragency.com (literary fiction, nonfiction, and YA).

HOW TO CONTACT E-mail info@helenhelleragency.com. Submit a brief synopsis, publishing history, author bio, and writing sample, pasted in the body of the e-mail. No attachments with e-queries. Accepts simultaneous submissions. Responds within 3 months if interested. Accepts simultaneous submissions. Obtains most new clients through recommendations from others, solicitations.

TIPS "Whether you are an author searching for an agent, or whether an agent has approached you, it is in your best interest to first find out who the agent represents, what publishing houses has that agent sold to recently and what foreign sales have been made. You should be able to go to the bookstore, or search online and find the books the agent refers to. Many authors acknowledge their agents in the front or back or their books."

HERMAN AGENCY

350 Central Park W., Apt. 41, New York NY 10025. (212)749-4907. **E-mail:** ronnie@hermanagencyinc.com. **Website:** www.hermanagencyinc.com. Literary and artistic agency. Member of SCBWI, Graphic Artists' Guild and Authors' Guild. Some of the illustrators represented: Michael Rex, Troy Cummings, Mike Lester, Geoffrey Hayes. Currently not accepting new clients unless they have been successfully published by major trade publishing houses. **Contact:** Ronnie Ann Herman. "We are a small boutique literary agency that represents authors and artists for the children's book market. We are not accepting any submission except picture books or graphic middle grade by author/artists/

We are accepting very few new clients. If you do to hear from us within 8 weeks, please understand that that means we are not able to represent your work.

MEMBER AGENTS Ronnie Ann Herman, Katia Herman.

HANDLES Specializes in childrens' books of all genres. We only want author/artist projects

TERMS Agent receives 15% commission. Exclusive contract.

HOW TO CONTACT E-mail only. Responds in 8-16 weeks. For first contact, artists or author/artists should e-mail a link to their website with bio and list of published books as well as new picture book manuscript or dummy to Ronnie. We will contact you only if your samples are right for us. For first contact, authors of middle-grade should e-mail bio, list of published books and first ten pages. Finds illustrators and authors through recommendations from others, conferences, queries/solicitations. Submit via e-mail only. Accepts simultaneous submissions. Obtains extremely few new clients.

TIPS "Check our website to see if you belong with our agency." Remember only author/artist works.

HG LITERARY

Website: www.hgliterary.com. **Contact:** Carrie Hannigan; Josh Getzler; Soumeya Roberts; Julia Kardon; Rhea Lyons; Victoria Wells Arms. HG Literary is a boutique literary agency, formed by Carrie Hannigan and Josh Getzler in 2011 (then called HSG). Our agents have over forty years combined experience in the publishing industry and represent a diverse list of best-selling and award-winning clients. HG is a full-service literary agency that through collaborative and client-focused representation manages all aspects of an author's career, from manuscript shaping, to sale and publication, subsidiary rights management, marketing and publicity strategy, and beyond. Our diverse and skilled team represents all types of fiction and nonfiction, for both adults and children, and has strong relationships with every major publisher as well as familiarity with independent and start-up publishers offering a different approach to publishing. Our clients have access to the resources and expertise of every member of our agency team, which includes contracts professionals, a film/TV rights director, foreign rights managers, and royalty and accounting specialists. Most importantly, our worth is measured by the success of our clients, and so you will find in each HG agent not only a staunch advocate but a career-long ally.

MEMBER AGENTS Carrie Hannigan, Josh Getzler, Soumeya Roberts, Julia Kardon, Rhea Lyons, Victoria Wells Arms.

HANDLES Please see individual agent pages at https://www.hgliterary.com/our-team. Please note that we do not represent screenplays, romance fiction, or religious fiction.

RECENT SALES Some recent sales are *Resident Aliens*, by K-Ming Chang (One World); the third book in the *Vera Kelly* series by Rosalie Knecht (Tin House); *When Carrot Met Cookie* by Erica Perl and Jonathan Fenske (Penguin Workshop); *Let Me Be Frank* by Tracy Dawson (Harper Design); and *The Necklace* by Matt Witten (Oceanview).

HOW TO CONTACT HG Literary only accepts electronic submissions. Unless another method is specified below, please send a query letter and the first five pages of your manuscript (within the email–no attachments please!) to the appropriate agent for your book. If it is a picture book, please include the entire manuscript. If you were referred to us, please mention it in the first line of your query. We generally respond to queries within 6-8 weeks, although we do get behind occasionally. You can check out our agent bios for more information on each agent's particular interests. Please note that we do not represent screenplays, romance fiction, or religious fiction. We're not able to respond to each query with detailed feedback, but we do appreciate all of your efforts and wish you the best of success with your writing career! **Carrie**

Hannigan: http://QueryMe.Online/Hannigan; **Josh Getzler:** http://QueryMe.Online/Getzler; **Victoria Well Arms:** submissions@wellsarms.com (Note: If no response in three months, please assume it is not for us); **Soumeya Bendimerad Roberts:** https://QueryManager.com/SBR (Note: Due to the volume of queries Soumeya receives, she will only respond to those in which she's interested); **Julia Kardon:** https://querymanager.com/query/JuliaKardon (Note: Due to the volume of queries Julia receives, she will only respond to those in which she's interested); **Rhea Lyons:** Rhea is currently closed to queries; **Jon Cobb:** http://QueryMe.Online/Cobb All agents except Rhea Lyons are open to new clients.

DAVID HIGHAM ASSOCIATES

Incorporating Gregory & Gregory, 6th Floor, Waverley House, 7-12 Noel St., London W1F 8GQ, UK. **Website:** www.davidhigham.co.uk. "David Higham Associates aspire to be at the forefront of a media and social landscape that is changing more rapidly and fundamentally than ever before. We have some of the most successful literary careers of the twentieth and twenty-first centuries in our care, and believe it is our ability to foresee the future while safekeeping the past that makes us one of the most successful agencies in the world."

MEMBER AGENTS Veronique Baxter; Nicola Chang; Elise Dillsworth; Jemima Forrester; Georgia Glover; Anthony Goff; Andrew Gordon; Jane Gregory; Lizzy Kremer; Harriet Moore; Caroline Walsh; Jessica Woollard; Laura West; Camille Burns; Maddalena Cavaciuti; David Evans; Sara Langham; Christabel McKinley; Stephanie Glencross.

HOW TO CONTACT Accepts simultaneous submissions.

HILL NADELL LITERARY AGENCY

6442 Santa Monica Blvd., Suite 200A, Los Angeles CA 90038. (310)860-9605. **Website:** www.hillnadell.com.

MEMBER AGENTS Bonnie Nadell (nonfiction books include works on current affairs and food as well as memoirs and other narrative nonfiction; in fiction, she represents thrillers along with upmarket women's and literary fiction); Dara Hyde (literary and genre fiction, narrative nonfiction, graphic novels, memoir and the occasional young adult novel).

TERMS Agent receives 15% commission on domestic and film sales; 20% commission on foreign sales. Charges clients for photocopying and foreign mailings.

HOW TO CONTACT Send a query by mail or online form. Accepts simultaneous submissions.

HOLLOWAY LITERARY

P.O. Box 771, Cary NC 27512. **E-mail:** submissions@hollowayliteraryagency.com. **Website:** hollowayliteraryagency.com. **Contact:** Nikki Terpilowski. A full-service boutique literary agency located in Raleigh, NC.

MEMBER AGENTS Nikki Terpilowski (romance, women's fiction, Southern fiction, historical fiction, cozy mysteries, lifestyle nonfiction (minimalism, homesteading, southern, etc.) commercial, upmarket/book club fiction, African-American fiction of all types, literary).

HANDLES "Note to self-published authors: While we are happy to receive submissions from authors who have previously self-published novels, we do not represent self-published works. Send us your unpublished manuscripts only." Nikki is open to submissions and is selectively reviewing queries for cozy mysteries with culinary, historical or book/publishing industry themes written in the vein of Jaclyn Brady, Laura Childs, Julie Hyzy and Lucy Arlington; women's fiction with strong magical realism similar to Meena van Praag's *The Dress Shop of Dreams*, Sarah Addison Allen's *Garden Spells, Season of the Dragonflies* by Sarah Creech and Mary Robinette Kowal's Glamourist Series. She would love to find a wine-themed mystery series similar to Nadia Gordon's Sunny McCoskey series or Ellen Crosby's Wine County Mysteries that combine culinary themes with lots of great Southern history. Nikki is also interested in seeing contemporary romance set in the southern US or any wine county or featuring a culinary theme, dark, edgy historical romance, gritty military romance or romantic suspense with sexy Alpha heroes and lots of technical detail. She is also interested in acquiring historical fiction written in the vein of Alice Hoffman, Lalita Tademy and Isabel Allende. Nikki is also interested in espionage, military, political and AI thrillers similar to Tom Clancy, Robert Ludlum, Steve Berry, Vince Flynn, Brad Thor and Daniel Silva. Nikki has a special interest in nonfiction subjects related to governance, politics, military strategy and foreign relations; food and beverage, mindfulness, southern living and lifestyle. Does not want horror, true crime or novellas.

RECENT SALES A list of recent sales are listed on the agency website's "news" page.

HOW TO CONTACT Send query and first 15 pages of ms pasted into the body of e-mail to submissions@hollowayliteraryagency.com. In the subject header write: (Insert Agent's Name)/Title/Genre. Holloway Literary does accept submissions via mail (query letter and first 50 pages). Expect a response time of at least 3 months. Include e-mail address, phone number, social media accounts, and mailing address on your query letter. Accepts simultaneous submissions.

ICM PARTNERS

65 E. 55th St., New York NY 10022. (212)556-5600. **E-mail:** careersny@icmpartners.com. **Website:** www.icmtalent.com. **Contact:** Literary Department. With the most prestigious literary publications department in the world, ICM Partners represents a wide range of writers, including the authors of best-selling fiction, self-help and nonfiction books, as well as journalists who write for prominent newspapers and magazines. In addition to handling the sale of publication rights, ICM Partners' literary agents in New York work closely with a team of agents in Los Angeles dedicated exclusively to seeking out opportunities for film and television adaptations. Its foreign rights department works in partnership with the Curtis Brown agency in England, which sells book and magazine projects in the UK and other English-speaking countries as well foreign language translations throughout the world.

HOW TO CONTACT Accepts simultaneous submissions.

INKWELL MANAGEMENT, LLC

521 Fifth Ave., Suite 2600, New York NY 10175. (212)922-3500. **Fax:** (212)922-0535. **E-mail:** info@inkwellmanagement.com. **Website:** www.inkwellmanagement.com.

MEMBER AGENTS Stephen Barbara (select adult fiction and nonfiction); William Callahan (nonfiction of all stripes, especially American history and memoir, pop culture and illustrated books, as well as voice-driven fiction that stands out from the crowd); Michael V. Carlisle; Catherine Drayton (bestselling authors of books for children, young adults and women readers); David Forrer (literary, commercial, historical and crime fiction to suspense/thriller, humorous nonfiction and popular history); Alexis Hurley (literary and commercial fiction, memoir, narrative nonfiction and more); Nathaniel Jacks (memoir, narrative nonfiction, social sciences, health, current affairs, business,religion, and popular history, as well as fiction—literary and commercial, women's, young adult, historical, short story, among others); Richard Pine; Eliza Rothstein (literary and commercial fiction, narrative nonfiction, memoir, popular science, and food writing); David Hale Smith; Kimberly Witherspoon; Jenny Witherell; Charlie Olson; George Lucas; Lyndsey Blessing; Claire Friedman; Michael Mungiello; Jessica Mileo; Maria Whelan; Namoi Eisenbeiss; Laura Hill; Hannah Lehmkuhl; Tizom Pope; Jessie Thorsted; Kristin van Ogtrop.

TERMS Agent receives 15% commission on domestic sales; 20% commission on foreign sales. Offers written contract.

HOW TO CONTACT "In the body of your e-mail, please include a query letter and a short writing sample (1-2 chapters). We currently accept submissions in all genres except screenplays. Due to the volume of queries we receive, our response time may take up to 2 months. Feel free to put 'Query for [Agent Name]: [Your Book Title]' in the e-mail subject line." Accepts simultaneous submissions. Obtains most new clients through recommendations from others.

TIPS "We will not read mss before receiving a letter of inquiry."

INTERNATIONAL TRANSACTIONS, INC.

P.O. Box 97, Gila NM 88038-0097. (845)373-9696. **Website:** www.intltrans.com. **Contact:** Peter Riva. Since 1975, the company has specialized in international idea and intellectual property brokerage catering to multi-national, multi-lingual, licensing and rights' representation of authors and publishers as well as producing award-winning TV and other media. They have been responsible for over 40 years of production, in both media and product, resulting in excess of $1.6 billion in retail sales and several international historic events (the memorabilia of which are on permanent display in national institutions in America, Germany, and France as well as touring internationally). In 2000 by JoAnn Collins BA, RN joined the company and acts as an Associate Editor specializing in women's voices and issues. In 2013 they created an imprint, published by Skyhorse Publishing, called Yucca Publishing which featured over 40 new and independent voices–exciting additions to the book world. In 2015 they created an imprint,

Horseshoe Books, to facilitate out-of-print backlist titles to re-enter the marketplace.

HANDLES "We specialize in large and small projects, helping qualified authors perfect material for publication." Seeking intelligent, well-written innovative material that breaks new ground. Authors of nonfiction must have an active and wide-reaching platform to help promote their work (since publishers rarely work at that any more). Does not want to receive material influenced by TV (too much dialogue); a rehash of previous successful novels' themes, or poorly prepared material. Does not want to be sent any material being reviewed by others.

RECENT SALES Averaging 20+ book placements per year.

TERMS Agent receives 15% (25%+ on illustrated books) commission on domestic sales; 20% commission on foreign sales and media rights. Offers written contract; 100-day notice must be given to terminate contract. No additional fees, ever.

HOW TO CONTACT Update 2021: In the changing publishing world, we will have to be increasingly and extremely selective of new projects. First, e-query with an outline or synopsis. E-queries only. Put "Query: [Title]" in the e-mail subject line. Submissions or emails received without these conditions being met are automatically discarded. Obtains most new clients through recommendations from others.

TIPS "'Book'—a published work of literature. That last word is the key. Not a string of words, not a book of (TV or film) 'scenes,' and never a stream of consciousness unfathomable by anyone outside of the writer's coterie. A writer should only begin to get 'interested in getting an agent' if the work is polished, literate and ready to be presented to a publishing house. Anything less is either asking for a quick rejection or is a thinly disguised plea for creative assistance—which is often given but never fiscally sound for the agents involved. Writers, even published authors, have difficulty in being objective about their own work. Friends and family are of no assistance in that process either. Writers should attempt to get their work read by the most unlikely and stern critic as part of the editing process, months before any agent is approached. In another matter: the economics of our job have changed as well. As the publishing world goes through the transition to e-books (much as the music industry went through the change to downloadable music)—a transition we expect to see at 95% within 10 years—everyone is nervous and wants 'assured bestsellers' from which to eke out a living until they know what the new e-world will continue to bring. This makes the sales rate and, especially, the advance royalty rates, plummet. Hence, our ability to take risks and take on new clients' work is increasingly perilous financially for us and all agents."

J DE S ASSOCIATES, INC.

9 Shagbark Rd., Norwalk CT 06854. (203)838-7571. **Fax:** (203)866-2713. **E-mail:** jdespoel@aol.com. **Website:** www.jdesassociates.com. **Contact:** Jacques de Spoelberch.

RECENT SALES Joshilyn Jackson's new novel *A Grown-Up Kind of Pretty* (Grand Central); Margaret George's final Tudor historical *Elizabeth I* (Penguin); the fifth in Leighton Gage's series of Brazilian thrillers *A Vine in the Blood* (Soho); Genevieve Graham's romance *Under the Same Sky* (Berkley Sensation); Hilary Holladay's biography of the early Beat Herbert Huncke, *American Hipster* (Magnus); Ron Rozelle's *My Boys and Girls Are In There: The 1937 New London School Explosion* (Texas A&M); the concluding novel in Dom Testa's YA science fiction series, *The Galahad Legacy* (Tor); and Bruce Coston's new collection of animal stories *The Gift of Pets* (St. Martin's Press).

TERMS Agent receives 15% commission on domestic sales; 20% commission on foreign sales. Charges clients for foreign postage and photocopying.

HOW TO CONTACT "Brief queries by regular mail and e-mail are welcomed for fiction and nonfiction, but kindly do not include sample proposals or other material unless specifically requested to do so." Accepts simultaneous submissions. Obtains most new clients through recommendations from authors and other clients.

JABBERWOCKY LITERARY AGENCY

49 W. 45th St., 12th Floor, New York NY 10036. **Website:** www.awfulagent.com. **Contact:** Joshua Bilmes. Each agent at this agency is different in terms of openness to submissions. Most of our agents remain open to queries but sometimes close their submissions temporarily. Our website will always be updated as to who is accepting queries at any given time. Each agent page also specifies what an agent looks for in submissions so please be sure to check our website before submitting.

As of the agency updating this listing, Joshua Bilmes and Eddie Schneider are open to queries. Please check the agency website for more info.

MEMBER AGENTS Joshua Bilmes, Eddie Schneider, Lisa Rodgers, Brady McReynolds, Bridget Smith.

HANDLES This agency represents quite a lot of genre fiction (science fiction & fantasy), romance, and mystery; and is actively seeking to increase the amount of nonfiction projects. Select agents represent young adult and middle-grade projects. Book-length material and novellas only—no poetry, articles, or short fiction.

RECENT SALES *Rhythm of War* by Brandon Sanderson; *Mexican Gothic* by Silvia Moreno-Garcia; *The Russian Cage* by Charlaine Harris; *The Kingdom of Liars* by Nick Martell; *The Desert Prince* by Peter V. Brett; *Ophie's Ghosts* by Justina Ireland; *The Southern Book Club's Guide to Slaying Vampires* by Grady Hendrix; *Son of the Storm* by Suyi Davies Okungbowa. Other clients include Lilliam Rivera, Tanya Huff, Simon Green, Jack Campbell, Marie Brennan, K. Eason, T. Frohock, Michael Mammay, Jim Hines, Mark Hodder, Toni Kelner, Ari Marmell, Emma Mills, C.M. Waggoner, Ellery Queen, Erin Lindsey, Mallory O'Meara, and Walter Jon Williams.

TERMS Agent receives 15% commission on domestic sales; 20% commission on foreign sales. Offers written contract, binding for 1 year. Charges clients for book purchases, photocopying, international book/ms mailing.

HOW TO CONTACT We are currently open to unsolicited queries. No phone or fax queries, please; we only accept queries to our query inboxes. Please check our website, as there may be times during the year when we are not accepting queries. Query letter only; no manuscript material unless requested. Accepts simultaneous submissions. Obtains most new clients through solicitations, recommendation by current clients.

TIPS "In approaching with a query, the most important things to us are your credits and your biographical background to the extent it's relevant to your work. I (and most agents) will ignore the adjectives you may choose to describe your own work."

JANKLOW & NESBIT ASSOCIATES

285 Madison Ave., 21st Floor, New York NY 10017. (212)421-1700. **Fax:** (212)355-1403. **E-mail:** info@janklow.com. **Website:** www.janklowandnesbit.com.

MEMBER AGENTS Morton L. Janklow; Anne Sibbald; Lynn Nesbit; Luke Janklow; PJ Mark (interests are eclectic, including short stories and literary novels. His nonfiction interests include journalism, popular culture, memoir/narrative, essays and cultural criticism); Paul Lucas (literary and commercial fiction, focusing on literary thrillers, science fiction and fantasy; also seeks narrative histories of ideas and objects, as well as biographies and popular science); Emma Parry (nonfiction by experts, but will consider outstanding literary fiction and upmarket commercial fiction); Kirby Kim (formerly of WME); Marya Spence; Allison Hunter; Melissa Flashman; Stefanie Lieberman.

HOW TO CONTACT Be sure to address your submission to a particular agent. For fiction submissions, send an informative cover letter, a brief synopsis and the first 10 pages. "If you are sending an e-mail submission, please include the sample pages in the body of the e-mail below your query. For nonfiction submissions, send an informative cover letter, a full outline, and the first 10 pages of the ms. If you are sending an e-mail submission, please include the sample pages in the body of the e-mail below your query. For picture book submissions, send an informative cover letter, full outline, and include a picture book dummy and at least one full-color sample. If you are sending an e-mail submission, please attach a picture book dummy as a PDF and the full-color samples as JPEGs or PDFs." Accepts simultaneous submissions. Obtains most new clients through recommendations from others.

TIPS "Please send a short query with first 10 pages or artwork."

HARVEY KLINGER, INC.

300 W. 55th St., Suite 11V, New York NY 10019. (212)581-7068. **Website:** www.harveyklinger.com. **Contact:** Harvey Klinger. Always interested in considering new clients, both published and unpublished.

MEMBER AGENTS Harvey Klinger, harvey@harveyklinger.com; David Dunton, david@harveyklinger.com (popular culture, music-related books, literary fiction, young adult, fiction, and memoirs); Andrea Somberg, andrea@harveyklinger.com (literary fiction, commercial fiction, romance, sci-fi/fantasy, mysteries/thrillers, young adult, middle grade, quality narrative nonfiction, popular culture, how-to, self-help, humor, interior design, cookbooks, health/fitness);

Wendy Silbert Levinson, wendy@harveyklinger.com (literary and commercial fiction, occasional children's YA or MG, wide variety of nonfiction); Rachel Ridout, rachel@harveyklinger.com (children's MG and YA), Cate Hart, cate@harveyklinger.com (women's fiction, historicals, MG and YA), Analieze Cervantes, analieze@harveyklinger.com (primarily MG and YA in all categories), Jennifer Herrington, jennifer@harveyklinger.com (MG and YA in all categories, adult women's fiction).

HANDLES This agency specializes in big, mainstream, contemporary fiction and nonfiction. Great debut or established novelists and in nonfiction, authors with great ideas and a national platform already in place to help promote one's book. No screenplays, poetry, textbooks or anything too technical.

RECENT SALES The Dearly Beloved by Cara Wall, Other People's Children by R.J. Hoffmann *I Me, Myself and Us*, by Brian Little; *The Secret of Magic*, by Deborah Johnson; *Children of the Mist*, by Paula Quinn. Other clients include George Taber, Terry Kay, Scott Mebus, Jacqueline Kolosov, Jonathan Skariton Tara Altebrando, Alex McAuley, Eva Nagorski, Greg Kot, Justine Musk, Ashley Kahn, Barbara De Angelis, Robert Patton, Augusta Trobaugh, Deborah Blum, Andy Aledort, Alan Paul.

TERMS Agent receives 15% commission on domestic sales; 25% commission on foreign sales. Offers written contract. Charges for photocopying mss and overseas postage for mss.

HOW TO CONTACT Use online e-mail submission form on the website, or query with SASE via snail mail. No phone or fax queries. Don't send unsolicited mss or e-mail attachments. Make submission letter to the point and as brief as possible. A bit of biographical information is always welcome, particularly with nonfiction submissions where one's national platform is vitally important. Accepts simultaneous submissions. Obtains most new clients through recommendations from others.

THE KNIGHT AGENCY

232 W. Washington St., Madison GA 30650. **E-mail:** deidre.knight@knightagency.net. **Website:** http://knightagency.net/. **Contact:** Deidre Knight. The Knight Agency is a full-service literary agency with a focus on genre-based adult fiction, YA, MG and select nonfiction projects. With 9 agents and a full-time support staff, our agency strives to give our clients individualized attention. "Our philosophy emphasizes building the author's entire career, from editorial, to marketing, to subrights and social media. TKA has earned a reputation for discovering vivid, original works, and our authors routinely land bestsellers on the New York Times, USA Today, Publishers Weekly, Los Angeles Times, Barnes & Noble Bestseller and Amazon.com Hot 100 lists. Awards received by clients include the RITA, the Hugo, the Newberry Medal, Goodreads Choice Award, the Lambda, the Christy, and Romantic Times' Reviewer Choice Awards, to name only a few."

MEMBER AGENTS Deidre Knight (romance, women's fiction, erotica, commercial fiction, inspirational, m/m fiction, memoir and nonfiction narrative, personal finance, true crime, business, popular culture, self-help, religion, and health); Pamela Harty (romance, women's fiction, young adult, business, motivational, diet and health, memoir, parenting, pop culture, and true crime); Elaine Spencer (romance (single title and category), women's fiction, commercial "book-club" fiction, cozy mysteries, young adult and middle grade material); Lucienne Diver (fantasy, science fiction, romance, suspense and young adult); Nephele Tempest (literary/commercial fiction, women's fiction, fantasy, science fiction, romantic suspense, paranormal romance, contemporary romance, historical fiction, young adult and middle grade fiction); Melissa Jeglinski (romance [contemporary, category, historical, inspirational], young adult, middle grade, women's fiction and mystery); Kristy Hunter (romance, women's fiction, commercial fiction, young adult and middle grade material), Travis Pennington (young adult, middle grade, mysteries, thrillers, commercial fiction, and romance [nothing paranormal/fantasy in any genre for now]); Janna Bonikowski (romance, women's fiction, young adult, cozy mystery, upmarket fiction); Jackie Williams.

HANDLES Actively seeking Romance in all subgenres, including romantic suspense, paranormal romance, historical romance (a particular love of mine), LGBT, contemporary, and also category romance. Occasionally I represent new adult. I'm also seeking women's fiction with vivid voices, and strong concepts (think me before you). Further seeking YA and MG, and select nonfiction in the categories of personal development, self-help, finance/business, memoir, parenting and health. Does not want to receive screenplays, short stories, poetry, essays, or children's picture books.

TERMS 15% Simple agency agreement with open-ended commitment. 15% commission on all domestic sales, 20% on foreign and film.

HOW TO CONTACT E-queries only. "Your submission should include a one page query letter and the first five pages of your manuscript. All text must be contained in the body of your e-mail. Attachments will not be opened nor included in the consideration of your work. Queries must be addressed to a specific agent. Please do not query multiple agents." Accepts simultaneous submissions.

KT LITERARY, LLC

9249 S. Broadway, #200-543, Highlands Ranch CO 80129. **E-mail:** contact@ktliterary.com. **Website:** www.ktliterary.com. **Contact:** Kate Schafer Testerman, Sara Megibow, Renee Nyen, Hannah Fergesen, Hilary Harwell. KT Literary is a full-service literary agency operating out of Highlands Ranch, in the suburbs of Denver, Colorado, where every major publishing house is merely an e-mail or phone call away. We believe in the power of new technology to connect writers to readers, and authors to editors. We bring over a decade of experience in the New York publishing scene, an extensive list of contacts, and a lifetime love of reading to the foothills of the Rocky Mountains.

MEMBER AGENTS Kate Testerman (middle grade and young adult); Renee Nyen (middle grade and young adult); Sara Megibow (middle grade, young adult, romance, science fiction and fantasy); Hannah Fergesen (middle grade, young adult and speculative fiction); and Hilary Harwell (middle grade and young adult); Kelly Van Sant; Jas Perry; Chelsea Hensley; Aida Z. Lilly; Kate Linnea Walsh. Always LGBTQ and diversity friendly!

HANDLES Kate is looking only at young adult and middle grade fiction, especially #OwnVoices, and selective nonfiction for teens and tweens. Sara seeks authors in middle grade, young adult, romance, science fiction, and fantasy. Renee is looking for young adult and middle grade fiction only. Hannah is interested in speculative fiction in young adult, middle grade, and adult. Hilary is looking for young adult and middle grade fiction only. "We're thrilled to be actively seeking new clients with great writing, unique stories, and complex characters, for middle grade, young adult, and adult fiction. We are especially interested in diverse voices." Does not want adult mystery, thrillers, or adult literary fiction.

RECENT SALES *Most Likely*, by Sarah Watson, *All of Us With Wings*, by Michelle Ruiz Keil, *Postcards for a Songbird*, by Rebekah Crane, *The Tourist Trap*, by Sarah Morgenthaler, *The Last Year of James and Kat*, by Amy Spalding, and many more. A full list of clients and most recent sales are available on the agency website and some recent sales are available on Publishers Marketplace.

TERMS Agent receives 15% commission on domestic sales; 20% commission on foreign sales. Offers written contract; 30-day notice must be given to terminate contract.

HOW TO CONTACT "To query us, please select one of the agents at kt literary at a time. If we pass, you can feel free to submit to another. Please e-mail your query letter and the first 3 pages of your manuscript in the body of the e-mail to either Kate at katequery@ktliterary.com, Sara at saraquery@ktliterary.com, Renee at reneequery@ktliterary.com, Hannah at hannahquery@ktliterary.com, or Hilary at hilaryquery@ktliterary.com. The subject line of your e-mail should include the word 'Query' along with the title of your manuscript. Queries should not contain attachments. Attachments will not be read, and queries containing attachments will be deleted unread. We aim to reply to all queries within 4 weeks of receipt. For examples of query letters, please feel free to browse the About My Query archives on the KT Literary website. In addition, if you're an author who is sending a new query, but who previously submitted a novel to us for which we requested chapters but ultimately declined, please do say so in your query letter. If we like your query, we'll ask for the first 5 chapters and a complete synopsis. For our purposes, the synopsis should include the full plot of the book including the conclusion. Don't tease us. Thanks! We are not accepting snail mail queries or queries by phone at this time. We also do not accept pitches on social media." Accepts simultaneous submissions. Obtains most new clients through query slush pile.

LAUNCHBOOKS LITERARY AGENCY

E-mail: david@launchbooks.com. **Website:** www.launchbooks.com. **Contact:** David Fugate.

HANDLES "We're looking for genre-breaking fiction. Do you have the next *The Martian*? Or maybe the next *Red Rising, Ready Player One*, or *Dark Matter*? We're on the lookout for fun, engaging, contemporary novels that appeal to a broad audience. In nonfiction, we're interested in a broad range of topics. Check www.launchbooks.com/submissions for a complete list."

RECENT SALES *Project Hail Mary,Artemis* and *The Martian*, by Andy Weir (Ballantine); *The Fold*, by Peter Clines (Crown); *Cues* and *Captivate*, by Vanessa Van Edwards (Portfolio); *Side Hustle* (Crown) and *The Money Tree* (Portfolio), by Chris Guillebeau; *The Art of Invisibility*, by Kevin Mitnick (Little, Brown); the *Hell Divers* series, by Nicholas Smith (Blackstone); *It's OK That You're Not OK*, by Megan Devine (Sounds True); *She Builds*, by Jadah Sellner (Harper Business); *The Children of Red Peak*, by Craig DiLouie (Orbit).

TERMS Agent receives 15% commission on domestic sales; 25% commission on foreign sales. Offers written contract; 30-day notice to terminate contract. Charges occur very seldom. This agency's agreement limits any charges to $50 unless the author gives a written consent.

HOW TO CONTACT Query via e-mail. Accepts simultaneous submissions. Obtains most new clients through recommendations from others, solicitations.

THE LESHNE AGENCY

New York NY. **Website:** www.leshneagency.com. **Contact:** Lisa Leshne, agent and owner. "We are a full-service literary and talent management agency committed to the success of our clients over the course of their careers. We represent a select and growing number of writers, artists, and entertainers interested in building their brands, audience platforms, and developing long-term relationships via all forms of traditional and social media. We take a deeply personal approach by working closely with our clients to develop their best ideas for maximum impact and reach across print, digital and other formats, providing hands-on guidance and networking for lasting success."

MEMBER AGENTS Lisa Leshne, agent and owner; Sandy Hodgman, director of foreign rights; Samantha Morrice; Yvette Greenwald; Christine J. Lee.

HANDLES An avid reader of blogs, newspapers and magazines in addition to books, Lisa is most interested in narrative and prescriptive nonfiction, especially on social justice, sports, health, wellness, business, political and parenting topics. She loves memoirs that transport the reader into another person's head and give a voyeuristic view of someone else's extraordinary experiences. Lisa also enjoys literary and commercial fiction and some young adult and middle-grade books that take the reader on a journey and are just plain fun to read. Wants "authors across all genres. We are interested in narrative, memoir, and prescriptive nonfiction, with a particular interest in sports, wellness, business, political and parenting topics. We will also look at truly terrific commercial fiction and young adult and middle grade books."

HOW TO CONTACT The Leshne Agency is seeking new and existing authors across all genres. "We are especially interested in narrative; memoir; prescriptive nonfiction, with a particular interest in sports, health, wellness, business, political and parenting topics; and truly terrific commercial fiction, young adult and middle-grade books. We are not interested in screenplays; scripts; poetry; and picture books. If your submission is in a genre not specifically listed here, we are still open to considering it, but if your submission is for a genre we've mentioned as not being interested in, please don't bother sending it to us. All submissions should be made through the Authors.me portal by clicking on this link: https://app.authors.me/#submit/the-leshne-agency." Accepts simultaneous submissions.

LEVINE GREENBERG ROSTAN LITERARY AGENCY, INC.

307 Seventh Ave., Suite 2407, New York NY 10001. (212)337-0934. **E-mail:** submit@lgrliterary.com. **Website:** www.lgrliterary.com.

MEMBER AGENTS Jim Levine (nonfiction, including business, science, narrative nonfiction, social and political issues, psychology, health, spirituality, parenting); Stephanie Rostan (adult and YA fiction; nonfiction, including parenting, health & wellness, sports, memoir); Daniel Greenberg (nonfiction: popular culture, narrative nonfiction, memoir, and humor; literary fiction); Victoria Skurnick; Danielle Svetcov (nonfiction); Lindsay Edgecombe (narrative nonfiction, memoir, lifestyle and health, illustrated books, as well as literary fiction); Monika Verma (nonfiction: humor, pop culture, memoir, narrative nonfiction and style and fashion titles; some young adult fiction (paranormal, historical, contemporary); Kerry Sparks (young adult and middle grade; select adult fiction and occasional nonfiction); Tim Wojcik (nonfiction, including food narratives, humor, pop culture, popular history and science; literary fiction); Arielle Eckstut (no queries); Sarah Bedingfield (literary and upmarket commercial fiction, Epic family dramas, literary novels with notes of magical realism, darkly gothic stories, psychological suspense); Courtney Pagenelli; Rebecca Rodd.

RECENT SALES **Notorious RBG**, by Irin Carmon and Shana Knizhnik; **Pogue's Basics: Life**, by David Pogue; **Invisible City**, by Julia Dahl; **Gumption**, by Nick Offerman; **All the Bright Places**, by Jennifer Niven.

TERMS Agent receives 15% commission on domestic sales; 20% commission on foreign sales. Offers written contract. Charges clients for out-of-pocket expenses—telephone, fax, postage, photocopying—directly connected to the project.

HOW TO CONTACT E-query to submit@lgrliterary.com, or online submission form. "If you would like to direct your query to one of our agents specifically, please feel free to name them in the online form or in the email you send." Cannot respond to submissions by mail. Do not attach more than 50 pages. "Due to the volume of submissions we receive, we are unable to respond to each individually. If we would like more information about your project, we'll contact you within 3 weeks (though we do get backed up on occasion!)." Accepts simultaneous submissions. Obtains most new clients through recommendations from others.

TIPS "We focus on editorial development, business representation, and publicity and marketing strategy."

PAUL S. LEVINE LITERARY AGENCY

1054 Superba Ave., Venice CA 90291. (310)450-6711. **Fax:** (310)450-0181. **E-mail:** paul@paulslevinelit.com. **Website:** www.paulslevinelit.com. **Contact:** Paul S. Levine. Paul S. Levine "wears two hats"—he is a lawyer (www.paulslevine.com) and a literary agent (www.paulslevinelit.com). Mr. Levine has practiced entertainment law for over 35 years, specializing in the representation of writers, producers, actors, directors, composers, musicians, artists, authors, photographers, galleries, publishers, developers, production companies and theatre companies in the fields of motion pictures, television, interactive multimedia, live stage, recorded music, concerts, the visual arts, publishing, and advertising. In 1998, Mr. Levine opened the Paul S. Levine Literary Agency, specializing in the representation of book authors and the sale of motion picture and television rights in and to books. Since starting his literary agency, Mr. Levine has sold over 100 adult, young adult, and children's fiction and nonfiction books to at least 50 different publishers and has had many books developed as movies-for-television, television series, and feature films.

MEMBER AGENTS Paul S. Levine (children's and young adult fiction and nonfiction, adult fiction and nonfiction except sci-fi, fantasy, and horror); Loren R. Grossman (archeology, art/photography, architecture, child guidance/parenting, coffee table books,gardening, education/academics, health/medicine/science/technology, law, religion, memoirs, sociology).

HANDLES Does not want to receive science fiction, fantasy, or horror.

TERMS Agent receives 15% commission on domestic sales. Offers written contract. Charges for postage and actual, out-of-pocket costs only.

HOW TO CONTACT E-mail preferred; "snail mail" with SASE is also acceptable. Send a 1-page, single-spaced query letter. In your query letter, note your target market, with a summary of specifics on how your work differs from other authors' previously published work. Accepts simultaneous submissions. Obtains most new clients through conferences, referrals, giving classes and seminars, and listings on various websites and in directories.

TIPS "Write good, sellable books."

LKG AGENCY

E-mail: query@lkgagency.com. **Website:** lkgagency.com. **Contact:** Lauren Galit. The LKG Agency was founded in 2005 and is based on the Upper West Side of Manhattan. "We are a boutique literary agency that specializes in middle grade and young adult fiction, as well as nonfiction, both practical and narrative, with a particular interest in women-focused how-to. We invest a great deal of care and personal attention in each of our authors with the aim of developing long-term relationships that last well beyond the sale of a single book."

MEMBER AGENTS Lauren Galit (nonfiction, middle grade, young adult); Caitlen Rubino-Bradway (middle grade and young adult, some nonfiction).

HANDLES "The LKG Agency specializes in nonfiction, both practical and narrative, as well as middle grade and young adult fiction." Actively seeking parenting, beauty, celebrity, dating & relationships, entertainment, fashion, health, diet & fitness, home & design, lifestyle, memoir, narrative, pets, psychology, women's focused, middle grade & young adult fiction. Does not want history, biography, true crime, religion, picture books, spirituality, screenplays, poetry any fiction other than middle grade or young adult.

HOW TO CONTACT For nonfiction submissions, please send a query letter to nonfiction@lkgagency.com, along with a TOC and 2 sample chapters. The TOC should be fairly detailed, with a paragraph or 2 overview of the content of each chapter. Please also make sure to mention any publicity you have at your disposal. For middle grade and young adult submissions, please send a query, synopsis, and the three (3) chapters, and address all submissions to mgya@lkgagency.com. Please note: due to the high volume of submissions, we are unable to reply to every one. If you do not receive a reply, please consider that a rejection. Accepts simultaneous submissions.

STERLING LORD LITERISTIC, INC.

115 Broadway, New York NY 10006. (212)780-6050. **Fax:** (212)780-6095. **E-mail:** info@sll.com. **Website:** www.sll.com.

MEMBER AGENTS Philippa Brophy (represents journalists, nonfiction writers and novelists, and is most interested in current events, memoir, science, politics, biography, and women's issues); Laurie Liss (represents authors of commercial and literary fiction and nonfiction whose perspectives are well developed and unique); Peter Matson (abiding interest in storytelling, whether in the service of history, fiction, the sciences); Douglas Stewart (primarily fiction for all ages, from the innovatively literary to the unabashedly commercial); Neeti Madan (memoir, journalism, popular culture, lifestyle, women's issues, multicultural books and virtually any intelligent writing on intriguing topics); Robert Guinsler (literary and commercial fiction (including YA), journalism, narrative nonfiction with an emphasis on pop culture, science and current events, memoirs and biographies); Jim Rutman; Mary Krienke (literary fiction, memoir, and narrative nonfiction, including psychology, popular science, and cultural commentary); Jenny Stephens (nonfiction: cookbooks, practical lifestyle projects, transportive travel and nature writing, and creative nonfiction; fiction: contemporary literary narratives strongly rooted in place); Elizabeth Bewley; Jessica Friedman; Sarah Landis; Danielle Bukowski; Chris Combemale; Nell Pierce.

TERMS Agent receives 15% commission on domestic sales; 20% commission on foreign sales. Offers written contract.

HOW TO CONTACT Query via snail mail. "Please submit a query letter, a synopsis of the work, a brief proposal or the first 3 chapters of the manuscript, a brief bio or resume, and SASE for reply. Original artwork is not accepted. Enclose sufficient postage if you wish to have your materials returned to you. We do not respond to unsolicited e-mail inquiries." Accepts simultaneous submissions.

LOWENSTEIN ASSOCIATES INC.

115 E. 23rd St., Floor 4, New York NY 10010. (212)206-1630. **Website:** www.lowensteinassociates.com. **Contact:** Barbara Lowenstein.

MEMBER AGENTS Barbara Lowenstein, president (nonfiction interests include narrative nonfiction, health, money, finance, travel, multicultural, popular culture, and memoir; fiction interests include literary fiction and women's fiction); Ronald Gerber, agent and rights manager (areas represented include contemporary and historical fiction, literary fiction, domestic and psychological thrillers, horror, grounded science-fiction, romance/romantic comedy, biography and memoir, narrative nonfiction, true crime, middle grade, and #OwnVoices stories across all genres).

HANDLES Does not want textbooks, religious fiction/nonfiction, erotica, high fantasy, new adult, picture books, or books in need of translation.

TERMS Agent receives 15% commission on domestic sales; 20% commission on foreign sales. Offers written contract. Charges for large photocopy batches, messenger service, international postage.

HOW TO CONTACT "Barbara Lowenstein is not currently open to queries. To query Ronald Gerber, please send a query letter in the body of the email, along with the first chapter attached, to assistant@bookhaven.com. Please put the word 'QUERY' and the title of your project in the subject field of your email. If you do not hear back within 6 weeks, please consider it a pass from the agency. Please do NOT mail us queries or manuscripts, all submission mail will be discarded unopened.' Accepts simultaneous submissions. Obtains most new clients through recommendations from others, solicitations, conferences.

TIPS "Know the genre you are working in and read!"

ANDREW LOWNIE LITERARY AGENCY, LTD.

36 Great Smith St., London SW1P 3BU, United Kingdom. (44)(207)222-7574. **Fax:** (44)(207)222-7576. **E-mail:** lownie@globalnet.co.uk. **Website:** www.andrewlownie.co.uk. **Contact:** Andrew Lownie, nonfiction. The Andrew Lownie Literary Agency Ltd is one of the UK's leading boutique literary agencies with some 200 nonfiction authors. Its authors regularly win awards and appear in the bestseller lists. It prides itself on its personal attention to its clients and specializes both in launching new writers and taking established writers to a new level of recognition. According to Publishers Marketplace, Andrew Lownie has been the top selling nonfiction agent in the world for the last few years. He has also been shortlisted for 'Agent of the Year' at the British Bookseller Awards many times.

HANDLES This agent has wide publishing experience, extensive journalistic contacts, and a specialty in showbiz/celebrity memoir. Actively seeking showbiz memoirs, narrative histories, and biographies. No fiction, poetry, short stories, children's, academic, or scripts.

RECENT SALES Sells about fifty books a year, with over a dozen top 10 bestsellers including many number ones, as well as the memoirs of Queen Elizabeth II's press officer Dickie Arbiter, Lance Armstrong's masseuse Emma O'Reilly, actor Warwick Davis, Multiple Personality Disorder sufferer Alice Jamieson, round-the-world yachtsman Mike Perham, poker player Dave 'Devilfish' Ulliott, David Hasselhoff, Sam Faiers and Kirk Norcross from TOWIE, Spencer Matthews from Made in Chelsea, singer Kerry Katona. Other clients: Juliet Barker, Guy Bellamy, Joyce Cary estate, Roger Crowley, Patrick Dillon, Duncan Falconer, Cathy Glass, Timothy Good, Robert Hutchinson, Lawrence James, Christopher Lloyd, Sian Rees, Desmond Seward, Daniel Tammet, Casey Watson.

TERMS Agent receives 15% commission on domestic sales; 20% commission on foreign sales. Offers written contract; 30-day notice must be given to terminate contract.

HOW TO CONTACT Query by e-mail only. For nonfiction, submit outline and one sample chapter. Accepts simultaneous submissions. Obtains most new clients through recommendations from others and unsolicited through website.

DONALD MAASS LITERARY AGENCY

1000 Dean St., Suite 252, Brooklyn NY 11238. (212)727-8383. **Website:** www.maassagency.com. Literary agency for professional novelists, all genres.

MEMBER AGENTS Donald Maass (mainstream, literary, mystery/suspense, science fiction, romance, women's fiction); Jennifer Jackson (science fiction, fantasy, and horror for both adult and YA markets, thrillers that mine popular and controversial issues, YA that challenges traditional thinking); Cameron McClure (fantasy and science-fiction, literary, mystery/suspense, projects with multicultural, international, and environmental themes, gay/lesbian); Michael Curry (literary science fiction, fantasy, near future thrillers). Paul Stevens (science fiction, fantasy, horror, mystery, suspense, and humorous fiction, LBGT a plus); Jennie Goloboy (fun, innovative, diverse, and progressive science fiction and fantasy for adults; history for a popular, adult audience (no memoir); Caitlin McDonald (fantasy, science fiction, and horror for Adult/YA/MG/GN, genre-bending/cross-genre fiction, diversity); Kiana Nguyen (women's fiction/book club, edgy/dark, realistic/contemporary YA, SF/F—Adult/YA, horror—Adult/YA, domestic suspense, thrillers Adult/YA, contemporary romance—Adult/YA); Kat Kerr; Anne Tibbets.

HANDLES This agency specializes in commercial fiction, especially science fiction, fantasy, thrillers, suspense, women's fiction—for both the adult and YA markets. All types of fiction, including YA and MG. Does not want poetry, screenplays, picture books.

RECENT SALES *Battle Ground* by Jim Butcher (Penguin Random House); *Foundryside* by Robert Jackson Bennett (Crown); *Gideon the Ninth* by Tamsyn Muir (Macmillan); *Treachery at Lancaster Gate* by Anne Perry (Random House); *Crowbones* by Anne Bishop (Penguin Random House); *We Are the Ants*, by Shaun David Hutchinson (Simon & Schuster); *Binti* by Nnedi Okorafor (DAW); *Star Eater* by Kerstin Hall (Macmillan); *The Tyrant Baru Cormorant* by Seth Dickinson (Tor); *Nothing But Blackened Teeth* by Cassandra Khaw (Nightfire); *The Space Between Worlds* by Micaiah Johnson (Del Rey); *Machinehood* by S.B. Divya (Saga); *Million Dollar Demon* by Kim Harrison (PRH/Ace); *The Grey Bastards* by Jonathan French (Crown); *A Snake Falls to Earth* by Darcie Little Badger (Levine

Querido); *The Conductors*, by Nicole Glover (John Joseph Adams/HMH); *When the Sparrow Falls* by Neil Sharpson (Tor and Rebellion); *The Ones We Burn* by Rebecca Mix (Simon & Schuster); *Hot Copy* by Ruby Barrett (Harlequin); *Fugitive Telemetry* by Martha Wells (Macmillan); *The Midnight Bargain* by C.L. Polk (Erewhon); *The Archive Undying* by Emma Mieko Candon (Macmillan).

TERMS Agency receives 15% commission on domestic sales; 20% commission on foreign sales.

HOW TO CONTACT Query via e-mail only. All the agents have different submission addresses and instructions. See the website and each agent's online profile for exact submission instructions. Accepts simultaneous submissions.

TIPS "We are fiction specialists, also noted for our innovative approach to career planning. We are always open to submissions from new writers." Works with subagents in all principle foreign countries and for film and television.

GINA MACCOBY LITERARY AGENCY

P.O. Box 60, Chappaqua NY 10514. (914)238-5630. **Website:** www.publishersmarketplace.com/members/ginamaccoby/. **Contact:** Gina Maccoby. Gina Maccoby is a New York literary agent representing authors of literary and upmarket fiction and narrative nonfiction for adults and children, including New York Times bestselling and award-winning titles. First and foremost she is captured by an engaging, compelling voice; across all forms she is looking for strong storytelling and fresh perspectives. Areas of interest in nonfiction include history, biography, current events, long-form journalism, and popular science. In fiction she is looking for upmarket novels, mysteries and thrillers, middle grade, and young adult. Gina served four terms on the Board of Directors of the Association of Authors' Representatives and is a member of both the Royalties and Contracts Committees. She belongs to SCBWI and is a long-time member of the Authors Guild. Prior to establishing her own agency in 1986, she was a literary agent at Russell & Volkening for 6 years where she handled her own clients as well as first serial, foreign and movie rights for the agency. Gina grew up mostly in Northern California and graduated with Honors from Harvard College.

TERMS Agent receives 15% commission on domestic sales; 20-25% commission on foreign sales, which includes subagents commissions. May recover certain costs, such as purchasing books, shipping books overseas by airmail, legal fees for vetting motion picture contracts, bank fees for electronic funds transfers, overnight delivery services.

HOW TO CONTACT Query by e-mail only. Accepts simultaneous submissions. Obtains most new clients through recommendations.

CAROL MANN AGENCY

55 Fifth Ave., 18th Floor, New York NY 10003. (212)206-5635. **Fax:** (212)675-4809. **Website:** www.carolmannagency.com. **Contact:** Agnes Carlowicz.

MEMBER AGENTS Carol Mann (health/medical, religion, spirituality, self-help, parenting, narrative nonfiction, current affairs); Laura Yorke; Gareth Esersky; Myrsini Stephanides (nonfiction areas of interest: pop culture and music, humor, narrative nonfiction and memoir, cookbooks; fiction areas of interest: offbeat literary fiction, graphic works, and edgy YA fiction); Joanne Wyckoff (nonfiction areas of interest: memoir, narrative nonfiction, personal narrative, psychology, women's issues, education, health and wellness, parenting, serious self-help, natural history; also accepts fiction); Iris Blasi; Maile Beal; Agnes Carlowicz.

HANDLES Does not want to receive genre fiction (romance, mystery, etc.).

TERMS Agent receives 15% commission on domestic sales; 20% commission on foreign sales. Offers written contract.

HOW TO CONTACT Please see website for submission guidelines. Accepts simultaneous submissions.

MANSION STREET LITERARY MANAGEMENT

Website: mansionstreet.com. **Contact:** Jean Sagendorph; Michelle Witte.

MEMBER AGENTS Jean Sagendorph, querymansionstreet@gmail.com (pop culture, gift books, cookbooks, general nonfiction, lifestyle, design, brand extensions), Michelle Witte (young adult, middle grade, early readers, picture books from author-illustrators), juvenile nonfiction).

HANDLES Jean is not interested in memoirs or medical/reference. Typically sports and self-help are not a good fit; also does not represent travel books. Michelle is not interested in fiction or nonfiction for adults.

RECENT SALES *Shake and Fetch*, by Carli Davidson; *Bleed, Blister, Puke and Purge*, by J. Marin Younker; *Spectrum*, by Ginger Johnson; *I Left You a Present* and *Movie Night Trivia*, by Robb Pearlman; *Open Sesame!*, by Ashley Evanson; *Fox Hunt*, by Nilah Magruder; *ABC Now You See Me*, by Kim Siebold.

HOW TO CONTACT Mansion Street Literary Management has changed how we accept queries, so we now use a submission form. To query Jean, go to http://QueryMe.Online/mansionstreet. To query Michelle, go to http://QueryMe.Online/michellewitte. Accepts simultaneous submissions.

MARJACQ SCRIPTS LTD

235 High Holborn, London WC1V 7LE, United Kingdom. (44)(207)935-9499. **Fax:** (44)(207)935-9115. **E-mail:** enquiries@marjacq.com. **Website:** www.marjacq.com. **Contact:** Submissions: individual agent whose area of interest may include your work. Business matters: Guy Herbert. Founded in 1974 by Jacqui Lyons and the late screenwriter and novelist George Markstein, Marjacq is a full-service literary agency with a diverse range of authors across both fiction and nonfiction for adults, young adults and children. We work closely with our authors at every stage of the process, from editorial guidance and negotiating deals, to long-term career management—including selling their work into as many languages as possible and seeking the best opportunities for adaptation to Film, TV and other media. We are a member of the Association of Authors' Agents (AAA).

MEMBER AGENTS Philip Patterson (thrillers, commercial fiction and nonfiction); Sandra Sawicka (commercial, genre, speculative and upmarket fiction); Diana Beaumont (commercial and accessible literary fiction and nonfiction); Imogen Pelham (literary and upmarket fiction and nonfiction); Catherine Pellegrino (children's, middle grade and young adult, romance); Leah Middleton (Film & TV, commercial fiction, investigative journalism, popular science).

HANDLES Actively seeking quality fiction, nonfiction, children's books, and young adult books. New and experienced working screenwriters. Does not want to receive stage plays or poetry.

RECENT SALES 3-book deal for Stuart MacBride (Transworld) (repeated *Sunday Times* #1 bestseller); Alex North, *The Whisper Man* and *The Shadow Friend*; Book and TV rights for *The Cry* by Helen Fitzgerald; *Insatiable* by Daisy Buchanan.

TERMS Agent receives 15% commission on direct book sales; 20% on foreign rights, film etc. Offers written contract. Services include in-house business affairs consultant. No service fees other than commission. Recharges bank fees for money transfers.

HOW TO CONTACT Email submissions direct to the individual agent who you feel is the best fit. Submit outline, synopsis, 3 sample chapters, bio, covering letter. "Do not bother with fancy bindings and folders. Keep synopses, bio, and covering letter short." Accepts simultaneous submissions. Obtains most new clients through recommendations from others, solicitations, conferences.

TIPS "Keep trying! If one agent rejects you, you can try someone else. Perseverance and self-belief are important, but do listen to constructive criticism, and 'no' does mean no. Be warned, few agents will give you advice as a non-client. We just don't have the time. Be aware of what is being published. If you show awareness of what other writers are doing in your field/genre, you might be able to see how your book fits in and why an editor/agent might be interested in taking it on. But make your book the best you can rather than trying to devise your own marketing—that's what publishers are for. Take care with your submissions. Research the agency and pay attention to presentation: Always follow the specific agency submission guidelines. Doing so helps the agent assess your work. Join writers groups. Sharing your work is a good way to get constructive criticism. If you know anyone in the industry, use your contacts. A personal recommendation will get more notice than cold calling."

MARSAL LYON LITERARY AGENCY, LLC

PMB 121, 665 San Rodolfo Dr. 124, Solana Beach CA 92075. **E-mail:** jill@marsallyonliteraryagency.com; kevan@marsallyonliteraryagency.com; patricia@marsallyonliteraryagency.com; deborah@marsallyonliteraryagency.com; shannon@marsallyonliteraryagency.com; jolene@marsallyonliteraryagency.com. **Website:** www.marsallyonliteraryagency.com.

Please see our web site and visit the pages for each agent to best match your submission to our agents' interests.

MEMBER AGENTS Jill Marsal (all types of women's fiction, book club fiction, stories of family, friendships, relationships, secrets, and stories with strong emotion; historical fiction, mystery, cozy, suspense, psychological suspense, thriller; romance—contemporary, romantic suspense, historical, and category;

nonfiction in the areas of current events, business, health, self-help, relationships, psychology, parenting, history, science, and narrative nonfiction); Kevan Lyon (women's fiction of all types, both historical and contemporary); Patricia Nelson (literary fiction and commercial fiction, all types of women's fiction, contemporary and historical romance, young adult and middle grade fiction, LGBTQ fiction for both YA and adult); Deborah Ritchken (lifestyle books, specifically in the areas of food, design and entertaining; pop culture; women's issues; biography; and current events; her niche interest is projects about France, including fiction); Shannon Hassan (upmarket/bookclub fiction, historical fiction, thrillers, young adult fiction, middle grade fiction); Jolene Haley (literary and commercial fiction, all types of women's fiction and all genres of romance, mysteries and thrillers, young adult and middle grade fiction, and select nonfiction).

RECENT SALES All sales are posted on Publishers' Marketplace.

HOW TO CONTACT Query by e-mail. Query only one agent at this agency at a time. "Please visit our website to determine who is best suited for your work. Write 'query' in the subject line of your e-mail. Please allow up to several weeks to hear back on your query." Accepts simultaneous submissions.

TIPS "Our agency's mission is to help writers achieve their publishing dreams. We want to work with authors not just for a book but for a career; we are dedicated to building long-term relationships with our authors and publishing partners. Our goal is to help find homes for books that engage, entertain, and make a difference."

MARTIN LITERARY AND MEDIA MANAGEMENT

E-mail: Sharlene@MartinLit.com. **Website:** www.MartinLit.com. **Contact:** Sharlene Martin. "Please see our website at www.martinlit.com for company overview, testimonials, bios of literary managers."

Sharlene only handles nonfiction. She specifically is seeking high profile stories that can be adapted for film/tv. Also interested in high profile true crime, but only from the victim's point of view.

MEMBER AGENTS Sharlene Martin (nonfiction); Clelia Gore (children's, middle grade, young adult); Adria Goetz (Christian books, lifestyle books, children and YA); Lindsay Guzzardo (adult fiction).

HANDLES This agency has strong ties to film/TV. See her bio at IMDB.com Actively seeking nonfiction that is highly commercial and that can be adapted to film/television. "We are being inundated with queries and submissions that are wrongfully being submitted to us, which only results in more frustration for the writers. Please review our Submission Page on our website and direct your query accordingly."

RECENT SALES The Next Everest *by Jim Davidson; Soles of a Survivor by Nhi Aronheim; Taken At Birth by Jane Blasio; Victim F,* by Denise Huskins and Aaron Quinn; *Taking My Life Back*, by Rebekah Gregory with Anthony Flacco; *Breakthrough*, by Jack Andraka; *In the Matter of Nikola Tesla: A Romance of the Mind*, by Anthony Flacco; *Honor Bound: My Journey to Hell and Back with Amanda Knox*, by Raffaele Sollecito; *Impossible Odds: The Kidnapping of Jessica Buchanan and Dramatic Rescue by SEAL Team Six*, by Jessica Buchanan, Erik Landemalm and Anthony Flacco; *Walking on Eggshells*, by Lisa Chapman; *Newtown: An American Tragedy*, by Matthew Lysiak; *Publish Your Nonfiction Book*, by Sharlene Martin and Anthony Flacco.

TERMS Agent receives 15% commission on domestic sales. We are exclusive for foreign sales to Taryn Fagerness Agency. Offers written contract, binding for 1 year; 1-month notice must be given to terminate contract. 99% of materials are sent electronically to minimize charges to author for postage and copying.

HOW TO CONTACT Query via e-mail with MS Word only. No attachments on queries; place letter in body of e-mail. Accepts simultaneous submissions. Obtains most new clients through recommendations from others.

TIPS "Have a strong platform for nonfiction. Please don't call. (I can't tell how well you write by the sound of your voice.) I welcome e-mail. I'm very responsive when I'm interested in a query and work hard to get my clients' materials in the best possible shape before submissions. Do your homework prior to submission and only submit your best efforts. Please review our website carefully to make sure we're a good match for your work. If you read my book, *Publish Your Nonfiction Book: Strategies For Learning the Industry, Selling Your Book and Building a Successful Career* (Writer's Digest Books) you'll know exactly how to charm me."

MASSIE & MCQUILKIN

27 W. 20th St., Suite 305, New York NY 10011. **E-mail:** info@lmqlit.com. **Website:** www.lmqlit.com.

MEMBER AGENTS Laney Katz Becker, laney@lmqlit.com (book club fiction, upmarket women's fiction, suspense, thrillers and memoir); Ethan Bassoff, ethan@lmqlit.com (literary fiction, crime fiction, and narrative nonfiction in the areas of history, sports writing, journalism, science writing, pop culture, humor, and food writing); Jason Anthony, jason@lmqlit.com (commercial fiction of all types, including young adult, and nonfiction in the areas of memoir, pop culture, true crime, and general psychology and sociology); Will Lippincott, will@lmqlit.com (narrative nonfiction and nonfiction in the areas of politics, history, biography, foreign affairs, and health); Rob McQuilkin, rob@lmqlit.com (literary fiction; narrative nonfiction and nonfiction in the areas of memoir, history, biography, art history, cultural criticism, and popular sociology and psychology; Rayhane Sanders, rayhane@lmqlit.com (literary fiction, historical fiction, upmarket commercial fiction [including select YA], narrative nonfiction [including essays], and select memoir); Stephanie Abou (literary and upmarket commercial fiction (including select young adult and middle grade), crime fiction, memoir, and narrative nonfiction); Julie Stevenson (literary and upmarket fiction, narrative nonfiction, YA and children's books).

HANDLES "Massie & McQuilkin is a full-service literary agency that focuses on bringing fiction and nonfiction of quality to the largest possible audience."

RECENT SALES Clients include Roxane Gay, Peter Ho Davies, Kim Addonizio, Natasha Trethewey, David Sirota, Katie Crouch, Uwen Akpan, Lydia Millet, Tom Perrotta, Jonathan Lopez, Chris Hayes, Caroline Weber.

TERMS Agent receives 15% commission on domestic sales; 20% commission on foreign sales. Offers written contract; 30-day notice must be given to terminate contract. Only charges for reasonable business expenses upon successful sale.

HOW TO CONTACT E-query preferred. Include the word "Query" in the subject line of your e-mail. Review the agency's online page of agent bios (lmqlit.com/contact.html), as some agents want sample pages with their submissions and some do not. If you have not heard back from the agency in 4 weeks, assume they are not interested in seeing more. Accepts simultaneous submissions. Obtains most new clients through recommendations from others, solicitations, conferences.

MB ARTISTS

775 Sixth Ave., #6, New York NY 10001. (212)689-7830. **E-mail:** mela@mbartists.com. **Website:** www.mbartists.com. **Contact:** Mela Bolinao. MB Artists represents illustrators whose work is primarily intended for the juvenile market in books, editorial publications, licensing merhandise, advertising, games, puzzles, and toys.

HANDLES Specializes in illustration for juvenile markets. Markets include: advertising agencies; editorial/magazines; publishing/books, board games, stationary, etc.

TERMS Rep receives 25% commission. No geographic restrictions. Advertising costs are split: 75% paid by talent; 25% paid by representative.

HOW TO CONTACT For first contact, send query letter, direct mail flier/brochure, website address, tearsheets, slides, photographs or color copies and SASE or send website link to mela@mbartists.com. Portfolio should include at least 12 images appropriate for the juvenile market. Accepts simultaneous submissions.

MARGRET MCBRIDE LITERARY AGENCY

P.O. Box 9128, La Jolla CA 92038. (858)454-1550. **Website:** www.mcbrideliterary.com. The Margret McBride Literary Agency has been in business for almost 40 years and has successfully placed over 300 books with mainstream publishers such as Hachette, Hyperion, HarperCollins, Penguin Random House, Simon & Schuster, Rodale, Macmillan, John Wiley & Sons, Houghton Mifflin Harcourt, Workman and Thomas Nelson. We are always looking for new and interesting projects to get excited about. For information about submitting your work for our consideration, please see our website: www.mcbrideliterary.com."

Only accepts e-mail queries. No snail mail please.

HANDLES This agency specializes in mainstream nonfiction and some commercial fiction. Actively seeking commercial nonfiction, business, health, self-help. Does not want screenplays, romance, poetry, or children's.

RECENT SALES *Millennial Money*, by Grant Sabatier (Atria/Penguin Random House); *Nimble*, by Baba Prasad (Perigee/Penguin Random House—US and

World rights excluding India); *Carefrontation*, by Dr. Arlene Drake (Regan Arts/Phaidon); *There Are No Overachievers*, by Brian Biro (Crown Business/Penguin Random House); *Cheech Is Not My Real Name*, by Richard Marin (Grand Central Books/Hachette); *Killing It!*, by Sheryl O'Loughlin (Harper Business/HarperCollins); *Scrappy*, by Terri Sjodin (Portfolio/Penguin Random House).

TERMS Agent receives 15% commission on domestic sales; 25% commission on translation rights sales (15% to agency, 10% to sub-agent). Charges for overnight delivery and photocopying.

HOW TO CONTACT Please check our website, as instructions are subject to change. Use Query Manager. Accepts simultaneous submissions.

TIPS "E-mail queries only. Please don't call to pitch your work by phone."

SEAN MCCARTHY LITERARY AGENCY

E-mail: submissions@mccarthylit.com. **Website:** www.mccarthylit.com. **Contact:** Sean McCarthy.

HANDLES Sean is drawn to flawed, multifaceted characters with devastatingly concise writing in YA, and character-driven work or smartly paced mysteries/adventures in MG. In picture books, he looks more for unforgettable characters, off-beat humor, and especially clever endings. He is not currently interested in issue-driven stories or query letters that pose too many questions.

HOW TO CONTACT E-query. "Please include a brief description of your book, your biography, and any literary or relevant professional credits in your query letter. If you are a novelist: Please submit the first 3 chapters of your manuscript (or roughly 25 pages) and a 1-page synopsis in the body of the e-mail or as a Word or PDF attachment. If you are a picture book author: Please submit the complete text of your manuscript. We are not currently accepting picture book manuscripts over 1,000 words. If you are an illustrator: Please attach up to 3 JPEGs or PDFs of your work, along with a link to your website." Accepts simultaneous submissions.

MCINTOSH & OTIS, INC.

207 E. 37 Street, New York NY 10016. (212)687-7400. **Fax:** (212)687-6894. **E-mail:** info@mcintoshandotis.com. **Website:** www.mcintoshandotis.com. **Contact:** Elizabeth Winick Rubinstein. McIntosh & Otis has a long history of representing authors of adult and children's books. The children's department is a separate division.

HANDLES Actively seeking "books with memorable characters, distinctive voices, and great plots."

TERMS Agent receives 15% commission on domestic sales; 20% on foreign sales.

HOW TO CONTACT E-mail submissions only. Each agent has their own e-mail address for subs. For fiction: Please send a query letter, synopsis, author bio, and the first 3 consecutive chapters (no more than 30 pages) of your novel. For nonfiction: Please send a query letter, proposal, outline, author bio, and 3 sample chapters (no more than 30 pages) of the ms. For children's & young adult: Please send a query letter, synopsis and the first 3 consecutive chapters (not to exceed 25 pages) of the ms. Accepts simultaneous submissions. Obtains clients through recommendations from others, editors, conferences and queries.

MENDEL MEDIA GROUP, LLC

P.O. Box 5032, East Hampton NY 11937. (646)239-9896. **Website:** www.mendelmedia.com. The Mendel Media Group LLC is an independent literary agency in New York. We represent nonfiction writers in most subject areas, from biography and serious history to health and relationships. Our nonfiction clientele includes individual authors and institutions whose works, collections, archives, researchers and/or policy experts contribute to important public discussions and debates. We also represent more light-hearted nonfiction projects, when they suit the market particularly well. The agency's fiction writers principally write historical and contemporary multicultural fiction, contemporary thrillers and mainstream women's fiction. We help our clients develop their projects, and we market those projects to U.S., U.K., Australian and foreign language publishing houses. We negotiate all contracts to our clients' works and keep track of monies due them, and we serve as their champions and career advisors. Both critical and commercial success are as important to us as they are to our clients. We want writing to be the source of a significant portion of our individual clients' incomes. We also want our institutional clients' works to support their missions financially as well as intellectually. In addition, wherever possible and preferable we reserve and represent the subsidiary rights to our clients' properties, including magazine and newspaper serialization, translation and other foreign rights, film and television development, audio book, large-print, book club, electronic and merchandising rights. We always aim to multiply our clients' incomes by making strategic decisions about licensing and sub-licensing as many of those rights as possible. In accordance with the Canon of Ethics of the Association of Authors Representatives, we charge our clients no reading fees. We do not represent screenwriters, unless they are creating works derived from a literary work we have already developed and marketed.

HANDLES "I am interested in major works of history, current affairs, biography, business, politics, economics, science, major memoirs, narrative nonfiction, and other sorts of general nonfiction." Actively seeking new, major or definitive work on a subject of broad interest, or a controversial, but authoritative, new book on a subject that affects many people's lives. "I also represent more light-hearted nonfiction projects, such as gift or novelty books, when they suit the market particularly well." Does not want "queries about projects written years ago that were unsuccessfully shopped to a long list of trade publishers by either the author or another agent. I am specifically not interested in considering original plays or original film scripts."

TERMS Agent receives 15% commission on domestic sales; 20% commission on foreign sales.

HOW TO CONTACT You should e-mail your work to query@mendelmedia.com. We no longer accept or read submissions sent by mail, so please do not send inquiries by any other method. If we want to read more or discuss your work, we will respond to you by e-mail or phone. Fiction queries: If you have a novel you would like to submit, please paste a synopsis and the first twenty pages into the body of your email, below a detailed letter about your publication history and the history of the project, if it has been submitted previously to publishers or other agents. Please do not use attachments, as we will not open them. Nonfiction queries: If you have a completed nonfiction book proposal and sample chapters, you should paste those into the body of an e-mail, below a detailed letter about your publication history and the history of the project, if it has been submitted previously to any publishers or other agents. Please do not use attachments, as we will not open them. If we want to read more or discuss your work, we will call or e-mail you directly. If you do not receive a personal response within a few weeks, we are not going to offer representation. In any case, however, please do not call or email to inquire about your query. Accepts simultaneous submissions. Obtains most new clients through referrals.

TIPS "While I am not interested in being flattered by a prospective client, it does matter to me that she knows why she is writing to me in the first place. Is one of my clients a colleague of hers? Has she read a book by one of my clients that led her to believe I might be interested in her work? Authors of descriptive nonfiction should have real credentials and expertise in their subject areas, either as academics, journalists, or policy experts, and authors of prescriptive nonfiction should have legitimate expertise and considerable experience communicating their ideas in seminars and workshops, in a successful business, through the media, etc."

HOWARD MORHAIM LITERARY AGENCY

30 Pierrepont St., Brooklyn NY 11201. (718)222-8400. **Fax:** (718)222-5056. **E-mail:** info@morhaimliterary.com. **Website:** www.morhaimliterary.com.

MEMBER AGENTS Howard Morhaim, howard@morhaimliterary.com; Kate McKean, kmckean@morhaimliterary.com; DongWon Song, dongwon@morhaimliterary.com; Kim-Mei Kirtland, kimmei@morhaimliterary.com; Laura Southern.

HANDLES Agent Kate McKean represents young adult and middle grade when she is open to submissions. Concerning books for children and teens, she seeks "middle grade and young adult full-length novels only in the areas of: mystery, thriller, horror, romance, LGBTQ issues, contemporary fiction, sports, magical realism, fantasy, and science fiction." Concerning what not to send her, avoid sending the following: "books that feature dragons, angels/demons/Grim Reaper, werewolves/vampires/zombies etc., zany middle grade stories about a character's wacky adventures, stories about bullying, stories that center around orphans or parents who die in car crashes, ghost-teens back to right wrongs. No novels in verse. No picture books or chapter books." Kate McKean is open to many subgenres and categories of YA and MG fiction. Check the website for the most details. Actively seeking fiction, nonfiction, and young adult novels.

HOW TO CONTACT Query via e-mail with cover letter and 3 sample chapters. See each agent's listing for specifics. Accepts simultaneous submissions.

MOVEABLE TYPE MANAGEMENT

244 Madison Ave., Suite 334, New York NY 10016. **E-mail:** achromy@movabletm.com. **Website:** www.movabletm.com. **Contact:** Adam Chromy.

HANDLES Mr. Chromy is a generalist, meaning that he accepts fiction submissions of virtually any kind (except juvenile books aimed for middle grade and younger) as well as nonfiction. He has sold books in the following categories: new adult, women's, romance, memoir, pop culture, young adult, lifestyle, horror, how-to, general fiction, and more.

HOW TO CONTACT E-queries only. Responds if interested. For nonfiction: Send a query letter in the body of an e-mail that precisely introduces your topic and approach, and includes a descriptive bio. For journalists and academics, please also feel free to include a CV. Fiction: Send your query letter and the first 10 pages of your novel in the body of an e-mail. Your subject line needs to contain the word "Query" or your message will not reach the agency. No attachments and no snail mail. Accepts simultaneous submissions.

ERIN MURPHY LITERARY AGENCY

824 Roosevelt Trail, #290, Windham ME 04062. **Website:** emliterary.com. **Contact:** Erin Murphy, president; Ammi-Joan Paquette, senior agent; Tricia Lawrence, senior agent; Kevin Lewis, agent; Tara Gonzalez, associate agent; Miranda Paul, associate agent.

This agency only represents children's books. "We do not accept unsolicited manuscripts or queries. We consider new clients by referral or personal contact only (such as meeting at writers conferences or requesting in online pitch contests)."

HANDLES Specializes in children's books only.

TERMS Agent receives 15% commission on domestic sales; 20-30% on foreign sales. Offers written contract. 30 days notice must be given to terminate contract.

HOW TO CONTACT Accepts simultaneous submissions.

TIPS "Please do not submit to more than one agent at EMLA at a time."

JEAN V. NAGGAR LITERARY AGENCY, INC.

JVNLA, Inc., 216 E. 75th St., Suite 1E, New York NY 10021. (212)794-1082. **Website:** www.jvnla.com. **Contact:** Jennifer Weltz.

MEMBER AGENTS Jennifer Weltz (well-researched and original historicals, thrillers with a unique voice, wry dark humor, and magical realism; enthralling narrative nonfiction; voice driven young adult, middle grade); Alice Tasman (literary, commercial, YA, middle grade, and nonfiction in the categories of narrative, biography, music or pop culture); Ariana Philips (nonfiction both prescriptive and narrative); Alicia Brooks (fiction, nonfiction and YA).

HANDLES This agency specializes in mainstream fiction and nonfiction and literary fiction with commercial potential as well as young adult, middle grade, and picture books. Does not want to receive screenplays.

RECENT SALES *Enola Holmes and the Black Barouche*, by Nancy Springer; *The City of Incurable Women(e)*, by Maud Casey; *Stuck*, by Jennifer Swender; *The Cage*, Bonnie Kistler; *Lucious / Tender / Juicy* , by Kathy Hunt; *A Matter of Live and Death*, by Phillip Margolin; *Doomed*, by John Florio and Ouisie Shapiro; *This Book is Made of Clouds*, by Misha Blaise; *Drop*, by Emily Kate Moon; *The Girl in his Shadow*, by Audrey Blake; *Skip to My Moo*, by Iza Trapani; *America Made Me a Black Man*, by Boyah Farah; *The 3-D Universe: How to Hold the Universe in Your Hand*, by Kimberly Arcand and Megan Watzke; *All the Children are home*, by Patry Francis; *Those Who Are Saved*, by Alexis Landau; *This Story Will Change*, by Elizabeth Crane.

TERMS Agent receives 15% commission on domestic sales; 20% commission on foreign and film sales. Offers written contract. Charges for overseas mailing, messenger services, book purchases, photocopying—all deductible from royalties received.

HOW TO CONTACT "Visit our website to send submissions and see what our individual agents are looking for. No snail mail submissions please!" Accepts simultaneous submissions.

TIPS "We recommend courage, fortitude, and patience: the courage to be true to your own vision, the fortitude to finish a novel and polish it again and again before sending it out, and the patience to accept rejection gracefully and wait for the stars to align themselves appropriately for success."

NELSON LITERARY AGENCY

1732 Wazee St., Suite 207, Denver CO 80202. (303)292-2805. **E-mail:** query@nelsonagency.com. **Website:** www.nelsonagency.com. **Contact:** Kristin Nelson, President. In business for nearly two decades, NLA is a full service literary and media representation agency with a proven track record and a reputation of advocating for authors above all else. Our mission is for every NLA author to make a living solely by writing. We build authors from debut to bestseller. We enjoy storytellers and love what we do. NLA clients have topped bestseller lists, become international bestselling stars, experienced blockbuster film success, earned major advances, and have sold millions of copies in the U.S. and around the world. We have a reputation for author advocacy, transparency, and we are one of the few agencies that actively audits publishing royalty statements—which has resulted in close to a million dollars recovered on behalf of our clients.

NLA is looking for fiction with strong, tight plots, complex characters faced with compelling plights, and upmarket voices. We love cerebral humor and charming poignancy as much as we love dark worlds and twisted villains. We are actively acquiring work from underrepresented and marginalized authors. We are most interested in women's fiction, mainstream fiction, book-club fiction, thrillers, magical realism, sci-fi, fantasy, horror, romantic comedies, humorous fiction, and anything that can be described as quirky or whimsical.

MEMBER AGENTS Danielle Burby, Joanna MacKenzie, Quressa Robinson.

HANDLES NLA specializes in representing commercial fiction as well as high-caliber literary fiction. Regardless of genre, we are actively seeking good stories well told. We do not represent scripts/screenplays, short-story collections, prescriptive nonfiction, abuse narratives, political works, or material for the Christian/inspirational market.

TERMS Agency charges industry standard commission.

HOW TO CONTACT Please visit our website to learn about what each agent is currently seeking. Please choose only one agent at NLA to query. We do share queries with each other here at NLA so a pass from one of us is a pass from all. Submit through QueryManager (find links on our website) with the following: a brief bio, including any writing credentials; the title, genre, and word count of your work; your query letter; the first ten pages of your manuscript. Accepts simultaneous submissions.

TIPS If you would like to learn how to write an awesome pitch paragraph for your query letter or would like any info on how publishing contracts work, please visit Pub Rants, Kristin's popular industry: https://nelsonagency.com/pub-rants/.

NEW LEAF LITERARY & MEDIA, INC.

110 W. 40th St., Suite 2201, New York NY 10018. (646)248-7989. **Fax:** (646)861-4654. **Website:** www.newleafliterary.com. "We are a passionate agency with a relentless focus on building our clients' careers. Our approach is big picture, offering a one-stop shop built without silos and access to a variety of services including international sales, film and television, and branding resources for all clients. Our aim is to challenge conformity and re-imagine the marketplace while equipping our clients with the tools necessary to navigate an evolving landscape and succeed."

MEMBER AGENTS Joanna Volpe (women's fiction, thriller, horror, speculative fiction, literary fiction and historical fiction, young adult, middle grade, art-focused picture books); Kathleen Ortiz, Director of Subsidiary Rights and literary agent (new voices in YA and animator/illustrator talent); Suzie Townsend (new adult, young adult, middle grade, romance [all subgenres], fantasy [urban fantasy, science fiction, steampunk, epic fantasy] and crime fiction [mysteries, thrillers]); Pouya Shahbazian, Director of Film and Television (no unsolicited queries); JL Stermer (nonfiction, smart pop culture, comedy/satire, fashion, health & wellness, self-help, and memoir); Jordan Hamessley; Stephanie Kim; Patrice Caldwell; Janna Morishima.

RECENT SALES *Carve the Mark*, by Veronica Roth (HarperCollins); *Red Queen*, by Victoria Aveyard (HarperCollins); *Lobster is the Best Medicine*, by Liz Climo (Running Press); *Ninth House*, by Leigh Bardugo (Henry Holt); *A Snicker of Magic*, by Natalie Lloyd (Scholastic).

HOW TO CONTACT Send query via e-mail. Please do not query via phone. The word "Query" must be in the subject line, plus the agent's name, e.g., Subject: Query, Suzie Townsend. You may include up to 5 double-spaced sample pages within the body of the e-mail. No attachments, unless specifically requested. Include all necessary contact information. You will receive an auto-response confirming receipt of your query. "We only respond if we are interested in seeing your work."

PARK & FINE

55 Broadway, Suite 1601, New York NY 10006. (212)691-3500. **E-mail:** info@parkliterary.com. **Website:** www.parkliterary.com.

MEMBER AGENTS Theresa Park (plot-driven fiction and serious nonfiction); Abigail Koons (popular science, history, politics, current affairs and art, and women's fiction); Peter Knapp (children's and YA); Celeste Fine; Susanna Alvarez; Ema Barnes; Jaidre Braddix; Charlotte Gillies; John Maas; Alison MacKeen; Sarah Passick; Anna Petkovich; Mia Vitale.

HANDLES The Park Literary Group represents fiction and nonfiction with a boutique approach: an emphasis on servicing a relatively small number of clients, with the highest professional standards and focused personal attention. Does not want to receive poetry or screenplays.

RECENT SALES This agency's client list is on their website. It includes bestsellers Nicholas Sparks, Soman Chainani, Emily Giffin, and Debbie Macomber.

HOW TO CONTACT Please specify the first and last name of the agent to whom you are submitting in the subject line of the e-mail. All materials must be in the body of the e-mail. Responds if interested. For fiction submissions, please include a query letter with short synopsis and the first 3 chapters of your work. Accepts simultaneous submissions.

L. PERKINS AGENCY

5800 Arlington Ave., Riverdale NY 10471. (718)543-5344. **E-mail:** submissions@lperkinsagency.com. **Website:** lperkinsagency.com. Full service New York literary agency comprised of 6 agents with sub agents in 11 foreign countries and film associates. Specializes in romance (all types), science fiction, fantasy, horror, pop culture, thrillers, women's fiction, YA and middle grade, as well as literary fiction.

Handles both fiction and nonfiction, most genres, but no plays, scripts, short stories, poetry or westerns. Very few children's books.

MEMBER AGENTS Lori Perkins (not currently taking new clients); Leon Husock (science fiction & fantasy, as well as young adult and middle-grade); Maximilian Ximinez (fiction: science fiction, fantasy, horror, thrillers; nonfiction: popular science, true crime, arts and trends in developing fields and cultures); Ben Grange.

HANDLES "Most of our clients write both fiction and nonfiction. This combination keeps our clients publishing for years. The founder of the agency is also a published author, so we know what it takes to write a good book." Actively seeking erotic romance, romance, young adult, middle grade, science fiction, fantasy, memoir, pop culture, thrillers. Does not want poetry, stand alone short stories or novellas, scripts, plays, westerns, textbooks.

RECENT SALES *Arena*, by Holly Jennings; *Taking the Lead*, by Cecilia Tan; *The Girl with Ghost Eyes*, by M. H. Boroson; *Silent Attraction*, by Lauren Brown.

TERMS Agent receives 15% commission on domestic sales; 20% commission on foreign sales. No written contract. Charges clients for photocopying.

HOW TO CONTACT E-queries only. Include your query, a 1-page synopsis, and the first 5 pages from your novel pasted into the e-mail, or your proposal. No attachments. Submit to only 1 agent at the agency. No snail mail queries. "If you are submitting to one of our agents, please be sure to check the submission status of the agent by visiting their social media accounts listed [on the agency website]." Accepts simultaneous submissions. Obtains most new clients through recommendations from others, solicitations, conferences.

TIPS "Research your field and contact professional writers' organizations to see who is looking for what. Finish your novel before querying agents. Read my book, *An Insider's Guide to Getting an Agent*, to get a sense of how agents operate. Read agent blogs-agentinthemiddle.blogspot.com and ravenousromance.blogspot.com."

RUBIN PFEFFER CONTENT

648 Hammond St., Chestnut Hill MA 02467. **E-mail:** info@rpcontent.com. **Website:** www.rpcontent.com. **Contact:** Rubin Pfeffer. Rubin Pfeffer Content is a literary agency exclusively representing children's and young adult literature, as well as content that will serve educational publishers and digital developers. Working closely with authors and illustrators, RPC is devoted to producing long-lasting children's literature: work that exemplifies outstanding writing, innovative creativity, and artistic excellence.

HANDLES High-quality children's fiction and nonfiction, including picture books, middle-grade, and young adult. No manuscripts intended for an adult audience.

HOW TO CONTACT Note: Rubin Pfeffer accepts submissions by referral only. Melissa Nasson is open to queries for picture books, middle-grade, and young adult fiction and nonfiction. To query Melissa, email her at melissa@rpcontent.com, include the query letter in the body of the email, and attach the first 50 pages as a Word doc or PDF. If you wish to query Rubin Pfeffer by referral only, specify the contact information of your reference when submitting. Authors/illustrators should send a query and a 1-3 chapter ms via e-mail (no postal submissions). The query, placed in the body of the e-mail, should include a synopsis of the piece, as well as any relevant information regarding previous publications, referrals, websites, and biographies. The ms may be attached as a .doc or a .pdf file. Specifically for illustrators, attach a PDF of the dummy or artwork to the e-mail. Accepts simultaneous submissions.

PIPPIN PROPERTIES, INC.

(212)338-9310. **E-mail:** info@pippinproperties.com. **Website:** www.pippinproperties.com. **Contact:** Holly McGhee. Pippin Properties, Inc. opened its doors in 1998, and for the past 17 years we have been privileged to help build careers for authors and artists whose work stands the test of time, many of whom have become household names in their own right such as Peter H. Reynolds, Kate DiCamillo, Sujean Rim, Doreen Cronin, Renata Liwska, Sarah Weeks, Harry Bliss, Kate & Jim McMullan, Katherine Applegate, David Small, and Kathi Appelt. We also love to launch new careers for amazing authors and artists such as Jason Reynolds, Anna Kang and Chris Weyant, and Jandy Nelson.

MEMBER AGENTS Holly McGhee; Elena Giovinazzo; Sara Crowe. Although each of the agents take children's books, you can find in-depth preferences for each agent on the Pippin website.

HANDLES "We are strictly a children's literary agency devoted to the management of authors and artists in all media. We are small and discerning in choosing our clientele."

TERMS Agent receives 15% commission on domestic sales; 25% commission on foreign sales. Offers written contract; 30-day notice must be given to terminate contract.

HOW TO CONTACT If you are a writer who is interested in submitting a ms, please query us via e-mail, and within the body of that e-mail please include: the first chapter of your novel with a short synopsis of the work or the entire picture book ms. For illustrators interested in submitting their work, please send a query letter detailing your background in illustration and include links to website with a dummy or other examples of your work. Direct all queries to the agent whom you wish to query and please do not query more than one. No attachments, please. Accepts simultaneous submissions. Obtains most new clients through recommendations from others.

TIPS "Please do not call after sending a submission."

PONTAS LITERARY & FILM AGENCY

Sèneca, 31, principal 08006, Barcelona, Spain. (34) (93)218-2212. **E-mail:** info@pontas-agency.com. **Website:** www.pontas-agency.com. Founded in 1992 by Anna Soler-Pont, Pontas is a literary and film agency representing internationally a wide range of authors from all over the world. "All together we can read and write in several languages and our aim is to provide the best service to our clients. Pontas attends more than ten events annually between book fairs, literary festivals and film markets. At some of them, such as the Frankfurt Book Fair, we have been present every year since 1992 with no exception."

MEMBER AGENTS Anna Soler-Pont; Richard Domingo; Marc de Gouvenain; Maria Cadona Serra; Carla Briner.

HANDLES "At this moment in time, we are only looking for works of adult fiction written in English and French." Please defer to send any materials that do not match this requirement. Does not want original film screenplays, theatre plays, poetry, sci-fi, fantasy, romance, children's, illustrated.

HOW TO CONTACT When submitting work, include a brief cover letter with your name and title of your mss in the e-mail subject, a detailed synopsis of your plot, your biography, and the full work in PDF or Word format. Accepts simultaneous submissions.

PRENTIS LITERARY

PMB 496 6830 NE Bothell Way, Kenmore WA 98028. **Website:** prentisliterary.com. **Contact:** Autumn Frisse, acquisitions; Terry Johnson, business manager. A boutique author focused agency with a devotion to words and the innovative voices that put those words to good use. The agency has always centered on finding books we are passionate about homes. When Linn Prentis was alive, this was her mission and long before she passed, it indeed has been ours as well. Many a time passion has lead us to love, champion and sell books that defy pat definition. While we obviously are seeking the commercially successful, we also demand good writing which we admire that sparks our passion.

HANDLES Special interest in sci-fi and fantasy, but fiction is what truly interests us. Nonfiction projects have to be something we just can't resist. Actively seeking science fiction/fantasy, POC/intersectional, women's fiction, LBGTQ+, literary fiction, children's fiction, YA, MG, mystery, horror, romance, nonfiction/memoir. Please visit website for comprehensive list. Does not want to "receive books for little kids."

RECENT SALES Sales include *The Relic Hunter: A Gina Miyoko Mystery* for *NYT* bestselling author Maya Bohnhoff; *Substrate Phantoms* for Jessica Reisman; *Vienna* for William Kirby; *Hunting Ground, Frost Burned* and *Night Broken* titles in two series for *NY Times* bestselling author Patricia Briggs (as well as a graphic novel *Homecoming*) and a story collection; a duology of novels for A. M. Dellamonica, whose first book, *Indigo Springs*, won Canada's annual award for best fantasy; as well as several books abroad for client Tachyon Publications.

TERMS Agent receives 15% commission on domestic sales; 20% commission on foreign sales. Offers written contract; 60-day notice must be given to terminate contract.

HOW TO CONTACT No phone or fax queries. No surface mail. For submission use our submission form posted on our submission page or e-mail acquisitions afrisse@prentisliterary.com. For other business business questions e-mail: tjohnson@prentisliterary.com. Accepts simultaneous submissions. Obtains most new clients through recommendations from others, solicitations.

AARON M. PRIEST LITERARY AGENCY

200 W. 41st St., 21st Floor, New York NY 10036. (212)818-0344. **Fax:** (212)573-9417. **E-mail:** info@aaronpriest.com. **Website:** www.aaronpriest.com.

MEMBER AGENTS Aaron Priest, querypriest@aaronpriest.com (thrillers, commercial fiction, biographies); Lisa Erbach Vance, queryvance@aaronpriest.com (contemporary fiction, thrillers/suspense, international fiction, narrative nonfiction); Lucy Childs, querychilds@aaronpriest.com (literary and commercial fiction, memoir, edgy women's fiction); Mitch Hoffman, queryhoffman@aaronpriest.com (thrillers, suspense, crime fiction, and literary fiction, as well as narrative nonfiction, politics, popular science, history, memoir, current events, and pop culture); Arleen Gradinger Priest; Francis Jalet-Miller; Kristen Pini.

HANDLES Does not want to receive poetry, screenplays, horror or sci-fi.

TERMS Agent receives 15% commission on domestic sales.

HOW TO CONTACT Query one of the agents using the appropriate e-mail listed on the website. "Please do not submit to more than 1 agent at this agency. We urge you to check our website and consider each agent's emphasis before submitting. Your query letter should be about one page long and describe your work as well as your background. You may also paste the first chapter of your work in the body of the e-mail. Do not send attachments." Accepts simultaneous submissions.

PROSPECT AGENCY

551 Valley Rd., PMB 377, Upper Montclair NJ 07043. (718)788-3217. **Fax:** (718)360-9582. **Website:** www.prospectagency.com. "Prospect Agency was founded in 2005 with the goal of offering clients top notch representation, creating a community-centered haven for authors and illustrators, and taking a leadership role in creating bold, innovative literature. The agency focuses on both the adult and children's markets, and is currently looking for the next generation of writers and illustrators to shape the literary landscape. We are a small, personal agency that helps each client reach success through hands-on editorial assistance and professional contract negotiations. We also strive to be on the cutting edge of technologically. The agents here spend a lot of time forming personal relationships with authors and their work. Every agent here has incredibly strong editorial skills, and works directly with clients to balance the goals of selling individual books and managing a career."

MEMBER AGENTS Emily Sylvan Kim focuses on romance, women's, commercial, young adult, new adult, nonfiction and memoir. She is currently looking for commercial and upmarket women's fiction; self-published authors looking to explore a hybrid career; established and strong debut romance writing mainstream romance; memoir and high interest nonfiction; literary and commercial YA fiction; and select middle grade and early reader fiction with strong commercial appeal. Rachel Orr focuses on picture books, illustrators, middle grade and young adult. She is currently looking for short, punchy picture books (either in prose or rhyme) that are humorous and have a strong marketing hook; nonfiction picture books (especially biographies or stories with a historical angle); illustrators for the trade market; and literary and commercial middle-grade and YA (all time periods and genres.) Ann Rose focuses on middle grade, young adult and commercial adult fiction. She is currently seeking YA of all genres; MG of all genres, especially ones that push the boundaries of middle grade; Swoony romances; Light sci-fi or fantasy; Commercial fiction; Heartwarming (or heart wrenching) contemporaries; any stories with unique voices, diverse perspectives, vivid settings; stories that explore tough topics; and dark and edgy stories with unlikeable characters. Emma Sector focuses on picture books, illustrators, middle grade and young adult. She is currently seeking quirky, character driven chapter books; literary and commercial middle-grade and YA Novels; picture book authors and illustrators; middle-grade graphic novels; and nonfiction middle-grade. Tin Shen; Charlotte Wenger. Please use the agency form to submit your query: https://www.prospectagency.com/submit.html.

HANDLES Handles nonfiction, fiction, picture books, middle grade, young adult. "We're looking for strong, unique voices and unforgettable stories and characters."

TERMS Agent receives 15% on domestic sales, 20% on foreign sales sold directly and 25% on sales using a subagent. Offers written contract.

HOW TO CONTACT All submissions are electronic and must be submitted through the portal at prospectagency.com/submit.html. We do not accept any submissions through snail mail. Accepts simultaneous submissions. Obtains new clients through conferences, recommendations, queries, and some scouting.

P.S. LITERARY AGENCY

2010 Winston Park Dr., 2nd Floor, Oakville ON L6H 5R7, Canada. **E-mail:** info@psliterary.com. **Website:** www.psliterary.com. **Contact:** Curtis Russell, principal agent; Carly Watters, senior agent; Maria Vicente, senior agent; Eric Smith, literary agent; Claire Harris, literary agent; Stephanie Winter, associate agent; Cecilia Lyra, associate agent. The P.S. Literary Agency (PSLA) represents both fiction and nonfiction works to leading publishers in North America, Europe and throughout the World. We maintain a small but select client list that receives our undivided attention and focused efforts. PSLA seeks to work with clients who are professional and committed to their goals. It is our desire to work with clients for the duration of their careers.

"The P.S. Literary Agency represents both fiction and nonfiction in a variety of categories. Seeking both new and established writers."

MEMBER AGENTS Curtis Russell (literary/commercial fiction, mystery, thriller, suspense, romance, young adult, middle grade, picture books, business, history, politics, current affairs, memoirs, health/wellness, sports, humor, pop culture, pop science, pop psychology); Carly Watters (upmarket/commercial fiction, women's fiction, book club fiction, domestic suspense, literary mystery/thrillers, historical fiction, contemporary romance, cookbooks, lifestyle, memoirs, business, pop science, psychology); Maria Vicente (young adult, middle grade, chapter books, illustrated picture books, graphic novels, pop culture, science, lifestyle, design, gift books); Eric Smith (young adult, middle grade, literary/commercial fiction, cookbooks, pop culture, humor, essay collections); Claire Harris (commercial psychological thrillers, mystery/suspense, contemporary fiction, adult rom-coms, lifestyle, pop culture, pop psychology, humor, true crime, illustrated books for adults); Stephanie Winter (adult, young adult, middle grade, graphic novels, adult rom-coms, thrillers, illustrated nonfiction); Cecilia Lyra (literary/commercial fiction, psychology, pop culture, science, business, lifestyles).

HANDLES Actively seeking both fiction and nonfiction. Seeking both new and established writers. Does not want to receive poetry or screenplays.

TERMS Agent receives 15% commission on domestic sales; 25% commission on foreign sales. "We offer a written contract, with 30-days notice to terminate."

HOW TO CONTACT Query letters should be directed to query@psliterary.com. PSLA does not accept or respond to phone, paper, or social media queries. Obtains most new clients through solicitations.

TIPS "Please review our website for the most up-to-date submission guidelines. We do not charge reading fees. We do not offer a critique service."

THE PURCELL AGENCY

E-mail: tpaqueries@gmail.com. **Website:** www.thepurcellagency.com. **Contact:** Tina P. Schwartz. This is an agency for authors of children's and teen literature.

MEMBER AGENTS Tina P. Schwartz, Catherine Hedrick, Bonnie Swanson.

HANDLES This agency also takes juvenile nonfiction for MG and YA markets. At this point, the agency is not considering fantasy, science fiction or picture book submissions.

RECENT SALES *Man Up, by Kim Oclon, Between Safe & Real, by Dannie Olguin, Cody Matthis & Me, by Sarah Kaminski, Duke & The Lonely Boy, by Lynn Langan, Seven Suspects*, by Renee James; *A Kind of Justice*, by Renee James; *Adventures at Hound Hotel*, by Shelley Swanson Sateren; *Adventures at Tabby Towers*, by Shelley Swanson Sateren; *Keys to Freedom*, by Karen Meade.

HOW TO CONTACT Check the website to see if agency is open to submissions and for submission guidelines. Accepts simultaneous submissions.

REES LITERARY AGENCY

One Westinghouse Plaza, Suite A203, Boston MA 02136. (617)227-9014. **E-mail:** lorin@reesagency.com. **Website:** reesagency.com.

MEMBER AGENTS Ann Collette, agent10702@aol.com (fiction: literary, upscale commercial women's, crime [including mystery, thriller and psychological suspense], upscale western, historical, military and war, and horror; nonfiction: narrative, military and war, books on race and class, works set in Southeast Asia, biography, pop culture, books on film and opera, humor, and memoir); Lorin Rees, lorin@reesagency.com (literary fiction, memoirs, business books, self-help, science, history, psychology, and narrative nonfiction); Rebecca Podos, rebecca@reesagency.com (young adult and middle grade fiction, particularly books about complex female relationships, beautifully written contemporary, genre novels with a strong focus on character, romance with more at stake than "will they/won't they," and LGBTQ books across all genres); Kelly Peterson; Ashley Herring Blake.

TERMS Agent receives 15% commission on domestic sales; 20% commission on foreign sales.

HOW TO CONTACT Consult website for each agent's submission guidelines and e-mail addresses, as they differ. Accepts simultaneous submissions. Obtains most new clients through recommendations from others, conferences, submissions.

REGAL HOFFMANN & ASSOCIATES LLC

143 West 29th St., Suite 901, New York NY 10001. (212)684-7900. **E-mail:** info@rhaliterary.com. **Website:** www.rhaliterary.com. Regal Hoffmann & Associates LLC, a full-service agency based in New York, was founded in 2002. We represent works in a wide range of categories, with an emphasis on literary fiction, outstanding thriller and crime fiction, and serious narrative nonfiction.

MEMBER AGENTS Claire Anderson-Wheeler (nonfiction: memoirs and biographies, narrative histories, popular science, popular psychology; adult fiction: primarily character-driven literary fiction, but open to genre fiction, high-concept fiction; all genres of young adult/middle grade fiction); Markus Hoffmann (international and literary fiction, crime, [pop] cultural studies, current affairs, economics, history, music, popular science, and travel literature); Stephanie Steiker (serious and narrative nonfiction, literary fiction, graphic novels, history, philosophy, current affairs, cultural studies, biography, music, international writing); Elianna Kan (Spanish-language fiction and nonfiction writers, literature in translation); Joseph Regal.

HANDLES We represent works in a wide range of categories, with an emphasis on literary fiction, outstanding thriller and crime fiction, and serious narrative nonfiction. Actively seeking literary fiction and narrative nonfiction. Does not want romance, science fiction, poetry, or screenplays.

RECENT SALES *Wily Snare*, by Adam Jay Epstein; *Perfectly Undone*, by Jamie Raintree; *A Sister in My House*, by Linda Olsson; *This Is How It Really Sounds*, by Stuart Archer Cohen; *Autofocus*, by Lauren Gibaldi; *We've Already Gone This Far*, by Patrick Dacey; *A Fierce and Subtle Poison*, by Samantha Mabry; *The Life of the World to Come*, by Dan Cluchey; *Willful Disregard*, by Lena Andersson; *The Sweetheart*, by Angelina Mirabella.

TERMS Agent receives 15% commission on domestic sales; 20% commission on foreign sales. We charge no reading fees.

HOW TO CONTACT Query with SASE or via Submittable (https://rhaliterary.submittable.com/submit). No phone calls. Submissions should consist of a 1-page query letter detailing the book in question, as well as the qualifications of the author. For fiction, submissions may also include the first 10 pages of the novel or one short story from a collection. Accepts simultaneous submissions.

TIPS "We are deeply committed to every aspect of our clients' careers, and are engaged in everything from the editorial work of developing a great book proposal or line editing a fiction manuscript to negotiating state-of-the-art book deals and working to promote and publicize the book when it's published. We are at the forefront of the effort to increase authors' rights in publishing contracts in a rapidly changing commercial environment. We deal directly with co-agents and publishers in every foreign territory and also work directly and with co-agents for feature film and television rights, with extraordinary success in both arenas. Many of our clients' works have sold in dozens of translation markets, and a high proportion of our books have been sold in Hollywood. We have strong relationships with speaking agents, who can assist in arranging author tours and other corporate and college speaking opportunities when appropriate."

THE LISA RICHARDS AGENCY

108 Upper Leeson St., Dublin D04 E3E7 , Ireland. (03) (531)637-5000. **E-mail:** info@lisarichards.ie. **Website:** www.lisarichards.ie.

HANDLES "For fiction, I am always looking for exciting new writing–distinctive voices, original, strong storylines, and intriguing characters." Doesn't handle horror, science fiction, screenplays, or children's picture books.

RECENT SALES Clients include Arlene Hunt, Roisin Ingle, Declan Lynch, Kevin Rafter.

HOW TO CONTACT Contact If sending fiction, please limit your submission to the first three or four chapters, and include a covering letter and an SASE if required. If sending nonfiction, please send a detailed proposal about your book, a sample chapter and a cover letter. Every effort will be made to respond to submissions within 3 months of receipt. Accepts simultaneous submissions.

THE RIGHTS FACTORY

P.O. Box 499, Station C, Toronto ON M6J 3P6, Canada. **Website:** www.therightsfactory.com. "The Rights Factory is an international literary agency."

MEMBER AGENTS Sam Hiyate (President: fiction, nonfiction (narrative business, wellness, lifestyle and memoir) and graphic novel); Stacey Kondla (Agent: YA and children's literature of all kinds); Natalie Kimber (Agent: literary and commercial fiction and creative nonfiction in categories such as memoir, cooking, pop-culture, spirituality, and sustainability); Haskell Nussbaum (Associate Agent: literature of all kinds); Lindsay Leggett (Associate Agent: SFF, horror, ownvoices, children's). Kathryn Willms Associate Agent (literary and commercial fiction and creative nonfiction), Karmen Wells Associate Agent, Film and TV (all genres, especially horror), Tasneem Motala Assistant Agent (character-driven MG and YA by BIPOC authors).

HANDLES Plays, screenplays, textbooks.

HOW TO CONTACT There is a submission form on this agency's website. Accepts simultaneous submissions.

RODEEN LITERARY MANAGEMENT

3501 N. Southport #497, Chicago IL 60657. **E-mail:** submissions@rodeenliterary.com. **Website:** www.rodeenliterary.com. **Contact:** Paul Rodeen.

HANDLES Actively seeking "writers and illustrators of all genres of children's literature including picture books, early readers, middle-grade fiction and nonfiction, graphic novels and comic books, as well as young adult fiction and nonfiction." This is primarily an agency devoted to children's books.

HOW TO CONTACT Unsolicited submissions are accepted by e-mail only. Cover letters with synopsis and contact information should be included in the body of your e-mail. An initial submission of 50 pages from a novel or a longer work of nonfiction will suffice and should be pasted into the body of your e-mail. Accepts simultaneous submissions.

ROGERS, COLERIDGE & WHITE

20 Powis Mews, London England W11 1JN, United Kingdom. (44)(207)221-3717. **Fax:** (44)(207)229-9084. **Website:** www.rcwlitagency.com. **Contact:** David Miller, agent.

MEMBER AGENTS Gill Coleridge; Georgia Garrett; Pat White (illustrated and children's books); Peter Straus; David Miller; Claire Wilson (children's and YA); Zoe Waldie (literary fiction and nonfiction); Emma Paterson; Laurence Laluyaux (foreign rights); Stephen Edwards (translation rights); Peter Robinson (fiction and nonfiction with particular interests in crime, thrillers and historical fiction, together with history and popular science); Sam Copeland (literary and commercial fiction, all genre fiction, children's, and a smattering of nonfiction); Jenny Hewson (strong literary voices and compelling storytelling, both fiction and nonfiction); Jo Unwin (literary fiction, commercial women's fiction, Young Adult fiction and fiction for children aged 9+; comic writing; narrative nonfiction); Rebecca Jones (foreign rights); Cara Jones (fiction: particularly crime and thrillers; narrative nonfiction).

HANDLES This agency takes virtually all subjects and genres. Does not want to receive scripts for theatre, film or television.

TERMS Agent receives 15% commission on domestic sales. Agent receives 20% commission on foreign sales. Offers written contract.

HOW TO CONTACT "Submissions should include a covering letter telling us about yourself and the background to the book. In the case of fiction, they should consist of the first 3 chapters or approximately the first 50 pages of the work to a natural break, and a brief synopsis. Nonfiction submissions should take the form of a proposal up to 20 pages in length explaining what the work is about and why you are best placed to write it. Material should be printed out in 12 point font, in double-spacing and on one side only of A4 paper. YA and YA and children's fiction should be submitted via email to clairewilson@rcwlitagency.com. We regret that this department cannot undertake to read submissions from the US due to the large volume received." Agents who are open to general e-mail submissions indicate so on their individual agent page on the website. Accepts simultaneous submissions. Obtains most new clients through recommendations from others, solicitations, conferences.

ANDY ROSS LITERARY AGENCY

767 Santa Ray Ave., Oakland CA 94610. (510)238-8965. **E-mail:** andyrossagency@hotmail.com. **Website:** www.andyrossagency.com. **Contact:** Andy Ross. "I opened my literary agency in 2008. Prior to that, I was the owner of the legendary Cody's Books in Berkeley for 30 years. My agency represents books in a wide range of nonfiction genres including: narrative nonfiction, science, journalism, history, popular culture, memoir, and current events. I also represent literary, commercial, historical, crime, upmarket women's fiction, and YA fiction. For nonfiction, I look for writing with a strong voice, robust story arc, and books that tell a big story about culture and society by authors with the authority to write about their subject. In fiction, I like stories about real people in the real world. No vampires and trolls, thank you very much. I don't represent poetry, science fiction, paranormal, and romance. Authors I represent include: Daniel Ellsberg, Jeffrey Moussaieff Masson, Anjanette Delgado, Fritjof Capra, Susan Griffin, Tawni Waters, Randall Platt, Mary Jo McConahay, Gerald Nachman, Michael Parenti, Paul Krassner, Milton Viorst, and Michele Anna Jordan. I am a member of the Association of Author Representatives (AAR). Check out my website and blog."

HANDLES "This agency specializes in general nonfiction, politics and current events, history, biography, journalism and contemporary culture as well as literary, commercial, and YA fiction." Does not want to receive poetry.

RECENT SALES See my website.

TERMS Agent receives 15% commission on domestic sales; 20% commission on foreign sales or other deals made through a sub-agent. Offers written contract.

HOW TO CONTACT Queries should be less than half page. Please put the word "query" in the title header of the e-mail. In the first sentence, state the category of the project. Give a short description of the book and your qualifications for writing. Accepts simultaneous submissions.

JANE ROTROSEN AGENCY LLC

318 E. 51st St., New York NY 10022. (212)593-4330. **Fax:** (212)935-6985. **Website:** www.janerotrosen.com.

MEMBER AGENTS Jane Rotrosen Berkey (not taking on clients); Andrea Cirillo, acirillo@janerotrosen.com (general fiction, suspense, and women's fiction); Annelise Robey, arobey@janerotrosen.com (women's fiction, suspense, mystery, literary fiction, and select nonfiction); Meg Ruley, mruley@janerotrosen.com (commercial fiction, including suspense, mysteries, romance, and general fiction); Christina Hogrebe, chogrebe@janerotrosen.com (young adult, new adult, book club fiction, romantic comedies, mystery, and suspense); Amy Tannenbaum, atannenbaum@janerotrosen.com (contemporary romance, psychological suspense, thrillers, and new adult, as well as women's fiction that falls into that sweet spot between literary and commercial, memoir, narrative and prescriptive nonfiction in the areas of health, business, pop culture, humor, and popular psychology); Rebecca Scherer, rscherer@janerotrosen.com (women's fiction, mystery, suspense, thriller, romance, upmarket/literary-leaning fiction); Jessica Errera (assistant to Christina and Rebecca); Kathy Scheider; Hannah Strouth; Logan Harper.

HANDLES Jane Rotrosen Agency is best known for representing writers of commercial fiction: thrillers, mystery, suspense, women's fiction, romance, historical novels, mainstream fiction, young adult, etc. We also work with authors of memoirs, narrative and prescriptive nonfiction.

TERMS Agent receives 15% commission on domestic sales; 20% commission on foreign sales. Offers written contract, binding for 3 years; 2-month notice must be given to terminate contract. Charges clients for photocopying, express mail, overseas postage, book purchase.

HOW TO CONTACT Check website for guidelines. Accepts simultaneous submissions. Obtains most new clients through recommendations from others.

VICTORIA SANDERS & ASSOCIATES

(212)633-8811. **E-mail:** queriesvsa@gmail.com. **Website:** www.victoriasanders.com. **Contact:** Victoria Sanders.

MEMBER AGENTS Victoria Sanders; Bernadette Baker-Baughman.

HANDLES Various agents at this agency handle juvenile books, such as young adult and picture books.

TERMS Agent receives 15% commission on domestic sales; 20% commission on foreign/film sales. Offers written contract.

HOW TO CONTACT Authors who wish to contact us regarding potential representation should send a query letter with the first 3 chapters (or about 25 pages) pasted into the body of the message to queriesvsa@gmail.com. We will only accept queries via e-mail. Query letters should describe the project and the author in the body of a single, 1-page e-mail that does not contain any attached files. Important note: Please paste the first 3 chapters of your manuscript (or about 25 pages, and feel free to round up to a chapter break) into the body of your e-mail. Accepts simultaneous submissions.

TIPS "Limit query to letter (no calls) and give it your best shot. A good query is going to get a good response."

WENDY SCHMALZ AGENCY

402 Union St., #831, Hudson NY 12534. (518)672-7697. **E-mail:** wendy@schmalzagency.com. **Website:** www.schmalzagency.com. **Contact:** Wendy Schmalz.

HANDLES Not looking for picture books, science fiction or fantasy.

TERMS Agent receives 15% commission on domestic sales; 20% on foreign sales; 25% for Asia.

HOW TO CONTACT Accepts only e-mail queries. Paste synopsis into the e-mail. Do not attach the ms or sample chapters or synopsis. Replies to queries only if they want to read the ms. If you do not hear from this agency within 2 weeks, consider that a no. Accepts simultaneous submissions. Obtains clients through recommendations from others.

SUSAN SCHULMAN LITERARY AGENCY LLC

454 W. 44th St., New York NY 10036. (212)713-1633. **E-mail:** susan@schulmanagency.com. **Website:** www.publishersmarketplace.com/members/Schulman/. **Contact:** Susan Schulman. "A literary agency specializes in representing foreign rights, motion picture, television and allied rights, live stage including commercial theater, opera and dance adaptations, new media rights including e-book and digital applications, and other subsidiary rights on behalf of North American publishers and independent literary agents. The agency also represents its own clients domestically and internationally in all markets. The agency has a particular interest in fiction and nonfiction books for, by and about women and women's issues and interests. The agency's areas of focus include: commercial and literary fiction and nonfiction, specifically narrative memoir, politics, economics, social issues, history, urban planning, finance, law, health, psychology, body/mind/spirit, and creativity and writing."

HANDLES "We specialize in books for, by and about women and women's issues including nonfiction self-help books, fiction, and theater projects. We also handle the film, television. and allied rights for several agencies as well as foreign rights for several publishing houses." Actively seeking new nonfiction. Considers plays. Does not want to receive poetry, television scripts or concepts for television.

RECENT SALES Sold 70 titles in the last year; hundreds of subsidiary rights deals.

TERMS Agent receives 15% commission on domestic sales; 20% commission on foreign sales. Offers written contract; 30-day notice must be given to terminate contract.

HOW TO CONTACT "For fiction: query letter with outline and three sample chapters, resume and SASE.

For nonfiction: query letter with complete description of subject, at least one chapter, resume and SASE. Queries may be sent via regular mail or e-mail. Please do not submit queries via UPS or Federal Express. Please do not send attachments with e-mail queries Please incorporate the chapters into the body of the e-mail." Accepts simultaneous submissions. Obtains most new clients through recommendations from others, solicitations, conferences.

TIPS "Keep writing!" Schulman describes her agency as "professional boutique, long-standing, eclectic."

SELECTIC ARTISTS

9 Union Square, #123, Southbury CT 06488. **E-mail:** christopher@selectricartists.com. **Website:** www.selectricartists.com. **Contact:** Christopher Schelling. "Selectric Artists is an agency for literary and creative management founded and run by Christopher Schelling. Selectric's client list includes best-selling and critically-acclaimed authors in many genres, as well as a few New York pop-rock musicians. Schelling has been an agent for over twenty years and previously held executive editor positions at Dutton and HarperCollins."

HOW TO CONTACT E-mail only. Consult agency website for status on open submissions. Accepts simultaneous submissions.

LYNN SELIGMAN, LITERARY AGENT

400 Highland Ave., Upper Montclair NJ 07043. (973)783-3631. **E-mail:** seliglit@aol.com. **Contact:** Lynn Seligman.

HANDLES "This agency specializes in general nonfiction and fiction. I also do illustrated and photography books and have represented several photographers for books."

RECENT SALES Sold 10 titles in 2018 including work by Dee Ernst, Dr. Myrna Shure and Roberta Israeloff.

TERMS Agent receives 15% commission on domestic sales; 25% commission on foreign sales. Charges clients for photocopying, unusual postage, express mail, telephone expenses (checks with author first).

HOW TO CONTACT Query with SASE or via e-mail with no attachments. Prefers to read materials exclusively but if not, please inform. Answers written and most email queries. Accepts simultaneous submissions. Obtains new clients through referrals from other writers and editors as well as unsolicited queries.

SERENDIPITY LITERARY AGENCY, LLC

305 Gates Ave., Brooklyn NY 11216. **E-mail:** rbrooks@serendipitylit.com; info@serendipitylit.com. **Website:** www.serendipitylit.com; facebook.com/serendipitylit. **Contact:** Regina Brooks.

"Authors who have a hook, platform, and incredible writing are ideal. Must be willing to put efforts into promotion."

MEMBER AGENTS Regina Brooks; Christina Morgan (literary fiction, crime fiction, and narrative nonfiction in the categories of pop culture, sports, current events and memoir); Charles Kim; Kelly Thomas; Ameerah Holliday; Emma Loy-Santelli; Jitan Sharmayne Davidson.

TERMS Agent receives 15% commission on domestic sales; 20% commission on foreign sales. Offers written contract; 2-month notice must be given to terminate contract. Charges clients for office fees, which are taken from any advance.

HOW TO CONTACT Check the website, as there are online submission forms for fiction, nonfiction and juvenile. Website will also state if we're temporarily closed to submissions to any areas. Accepts simultaneous submissions. Obtains most new clients through conferences, referrals and social media.

TIPS "See the books *Writing Great Books for Young Adults* and *You Should Really Write a Book: How to Write, Sell, and Market Your Memoir.* We are looking for high concept ideas with big hooks. If you get writer's block try possibiliteas.co, it's a muse in a cup."

THE SEYMOUR AGENCY

475 Miner St., Canton NY 13617. (239)398-8209. **E-mail:** nicole@theseymouragency.com; julie@theseymouragency.com. **Website:** www.theseymouragency.com. We work with both fiction and nonfiction authors across the spectrum of topics and genres.

MEMBER AGENTS Nicole Rescinti, nicole@theseymouragency.com; Julie Gwinn, julie@theseymouragency.com; Tina Wainscott, tina@theseymouragency.com; Jennifer Wills, jennifer@theseymouragency.com; Lesley Sabga, lesley@theseymouragency.com; Elizabeth "Lizzie" Poteet; Elisa Houot; Michael L. Joy; Joyce Sweeney; Marisa Cleveland, marisa@theseymouragency.com; Lynette Novack.

TERMS Agent receives 12-15% commission on domestic sales.

HOW TO CONTACT Accepts e-mail queries. Check online for guidelines. Accepts simultaneous submissions.

KEN SHERMAN & ASSOCIATES

1275 N. Hayworth Ave., Suite 103, Los Angeles CA 90046. (310)273-8840. **E-mail:** kenshermanassociates@gmail.com. **Website:** www.kenshermanassociates.com. **Contact:** Ken Sherman.

HANDLES Fine writers.

TERMS Agent receives 15% commission on domestic and foreign sales; 10-15%, film and tv scripts, anything WGA, 10% Offers written contract. Charges clients for reasonable office expenses (postage, photocopying, etc.).

HOW TO CONTACT Contact by referral only, please. Reports in approximately 1 month. Accepts simultaneous submissions. Obtains most new clients through recommendations from others.

SPEILBURG LITERARY AGENCY

Website: speilburgliterary.com. **Contact:** Alice Speilburg. Speilburg Literary Agency represents authors in fiction and nonfiction. Our client list includes award-winning and debut authors, to whom we offer hands-on editorial attention and business management throughout their publishing careers.

MEMBER AGENTS Alice Speilburg worked for John Wiley & Sons and Howard Morhaim Literary Agency, before launching Speilburg Literary. She is a member of Romance Writers of America, Mystery Writers of America, and Society of Children's Book Writers and Illustrators, and she is a board member of Louisville Literary Arts. She represents commercial fiction and narrative nonfiction. Eva Scalzo has a B.A. in the Humanities from the University of Puerto Rico and a M.A. in Publishing and Writing from Emerson College. She has spent her career in scholarly publishing, working for Houghton Mifflin, Blackwell Publishing, John Wiley & Sons, and Cornell University in a variety of roles. Eva is looking to represent all subgenres of Romance, with the exclusion of inspirational romance, as well as Young Adult fiction; Lindsey Smith.

HANDLES Does not want picture books; screenplays; poetry.

HOW TO CONTACT In the subject line of your query e-mail, please include "Query [AGENT'S FIRST NAME]" followed by the title of your project. For fiction, please send the query letter and the first three chapters. For nonfiction, please send the query letter and a proposal, which should include a detailed TOC and a sample chapter. Accepts simultaneous submissions.

SPENCERHILL ASSOCIATES

1767 Lakewood Ranch Blvd, #268, Bradenton FL 34211. (941)907-3700. **E-mail:** submission@spencerhillassociates.com. **Website:** www.spencerhillassociates.com. **Contact:** Karen Solem, Nalini Akolekar, Amanda Leuck, Sandy Harding, and Ali Herring. Karen Solem founded Spencerhill in 2001 to represent authors of commercial, general-interest fiction. Specializing in romance and women's fiction, we work with talented writers in every genre at any stage of their career-from the well-known, successfully published and established author to the debut writer with an exciting new voice. Based in Florida, our agents travel to industry conferences nationally and internationally. Our goal is to maximize the careers of our authors by placing them with the right editors and publishers so their readerships can expand. In a complex and dynamic industry our personal approach provides experienced guidance through every phase of the publishing process.

HANDLES "We handle mostly commercial women's fiction, historical novels, romance (historical, contemporary, paranormal, urban fantasy), thrillers, and mysteries, in addition to middle grade and young adult novels. We also represent Christian fiction only—no nonfiction." No nonfiction, poetry, children's picture books, or scripts.

RECENT SALES A full list of sales and clients is available on the agency website.

TERMS Agent receives 15% commission on domestic sales; 20% commission on foreign sales. Offers written contract; 3-month notice must be given to terminate contract.

HOW TO CONTACT "We accept electronic submissions only. Please send us a query letter in the body of an e-mail, pitch us your project and tell us about yourself: Do you have prior publishing credits? Attach the first three chapters and synopsis preferably in .doc, rtf or txt format to your email. Send all queries to submission@spencerhillassociates.com. Or submit through the QueryManager link on our website. We do not have a preference for exclusive submissions, but do appreciate knowing if the submission is simultaneous. We receive thousands of submissions a year and each query receives our attention. Unfortunately, we are unable to respond to each query individually. If we are interested in your work, we will contact you within 12 weeks." Accepts simultaneous submissions.

STIMOLA LITERARY STUDIO, INC

308 Livingston Ct., Edgewater NJ 07020. **E-mail:** info@stimolaliterarystudio.com. **Website:** www.stimolaliterarystudio.com. **Contact:** Rosemary B. Stimola. "A full service literary agency devoted to representing authors and author/illustrators of fiction and nonfiction, pre-school through young adult, who bring unique and substantive contributions to the industry. And now, expanding our own horizons, our client list has now grown to include graphic novels for both young and adult readers, and projects in parenting, lifestyle, food culture, cookbooks, health and wellness, and green and sustainable eating."

HANDLES Actively seeking remarkable middle grade, young adult fiction, and debut picture book author/illustrators. Also seeking fresh graphic novels for juvenile and adult readers. No institutional books.

RECENT SALES *Bear Island*, by Matthew Cordell; *The Bear and the Moon*, by Matthew Burgess and Catia Chen; *Blue Barry and Pancakes*, by Dan Abdo and Jason Patterson; *The Cat Man of Aleppo* by Irene Latham, Karim Shashi-Basha and Yuko Shimizu; *Lupe Wong Won't Dance*, by Donna Barba Higuera; *The Ballad of Songbirds and Snakes*, by Suzanne Collins; *Bear Mouth*, by Liz Hyder; *Bed Head Ted* by Scott San Giacomo; *The Cousins*, by Karen M. McManus; *Call Me Athena*, by Colby Cedar Smith; *Motherhood: Facing and Finding Yourself*, by Lisa Marchiano; *Mornings with Monet*, by Barb Rosenstock and Mary GrandPre; *I Am Courage*, by Susan Verde; *For the Table* by Anna Stockwell; *52 Weeks at Catbird Cottage* by Melina Hammer; *The People We Used to Be* by Kyle Scheele.

TERMS Agent receives 15% commission on domestic sales; 20% (if subagents are employed) commission on foreign sales. Offers written contract, binding for all children's projects. 60 days notice must be given to terminate contract.

HOW TO CONTACT Query via e-mail as per submission guidelines on website. Author/illustrators of picture books may attach text and sample art. with query. A PDF dummy is preferred. Accepts simultaneous submissions. While unsolicited queries are welcome, most clients come through editor, agent, client referrals.

TIPS Agents are hands-on, no-nonsense. May request revisions. Does not line edit but may offer suggestions for improvement before submission. Well-respected by clients and editors. "Firm but reasonable deal negotiators."

STONESONG

270 W. 39th St. #201, New York NY 10018. (212)929-4600. **E-mail:** editors@stonesong.com. **Website:** stonesong.com.

MEMBER AGENTS Alison Fargis; Ellen Scordato; Judy Linden; Emmanuelle Morgen; Leila Campoli (business, science, technology, and self improvement); Maria Ribas (cookbooks, self-help, health, diet, home, parenting, and humor, all from authors with demonstrable platforms; she's also interested in narrative nonfiction and select memoir); Melissa Edwards (children's fiction and adult commercial fiction, as well as select pop-culture nonfiction); Alyssa Jennette (children's and adult fiction and picture books, and has dabbled in humor and pop culture nonfiction); Madelyn Burt (adult and children's fiction, as well as select historical nonfiction); Adrienne Rosado; Kim Lindman.

HANDLES Does not represent plays, screenplays, picture books, or poetry.

RECENT SALES *Sweet Laurel*, by Laurel Gallucci and Claire Thomas; *Terrain: A Seasonal Guide to Nature at Home*, by Terrain; *The Prince's Bane*, by Alexandra Christo; *Deep Listening*, by Jillian Pransky; *Change Resilience*, by Lior Arussy; *A Thousand Words*, by Brigit Young.

HOW TO CONTACT Accepts electronic queries for fiction and nonfiction. Submit query addressed to a specific agent. Include first chapter or first 10 pages of ms. Accepts simultaneous submissions.

STRACHAN LITERARY AGENCY

Website: www.strachanlit.com. **Contact:** Laura Strachan. Strachan Literary Agency is a boutique agency focused on literary fiction and narrative nonfiction: *Compelling stories, well told.*

MEMBER AGENTS Laura Strachan; Marisa Zeppieri-Caruana.

HANDLES "This agency specializes in literary fiction and narrative nonfiction."

HOW TO CONTACT Please query with description of project and short biographical statement. Do not paste or attach sample pages. Accepts simultaneous submissions.

THE STRINGER LITERARY AGENCY LLC

P.O. Box 111255, Naples FL 34108. **E-mail:** mstringer@stringerlit.com. **Website:** www.stringerlit.com. **Contact:** Marlene Stringer. This agency focuses on commercial fiction for adults and teens.

MEMBER AGENTS Marlene Stringer; Shari Maurer.

HANDLES This agency specializes in fiction, and select nonfiction. "We are an editorial agency, and work with clients to make their manuscripts the best they can be in preparation for submission. We focus on career planning, and help our clients reach their publishing goals. We advise clients on marketing and promotional strategies to help them reach their target readership. Because we are so hands-on, we limit the size of our list; however, we are always looking for exceptional voices and stories that demand we read to the end. You never know where the next great story is coming from." This agency is seeking thrillers, crime fiction, mystery, women's fiction, single title and category romance, fantasy (all subgenera), grounded science fiction (no space opera, aliens, etc.), YA/teen, MG, and picture books. Does not want to receive plays, short stories, scripts, or poetry. This is not the agency for inspirational romance or erotica. No space opera. The agency is not seeking any nonfiction other than memoir, biography, or narrative nonfiction at this time.

RECENT SALES *After She Was Mine* by Brian Charles; *The Dead Season* by Tessa Wegert; *Don't Believe It* by Charlie Donlea; *What's Left Unsaid*, by Emily Bleeker; Spellbreaker Series, by Charlie N. Holmberg; *Belle Chasse*, by Suzanne Johnson; Wings of Fury Series by Emily R. King; *Wilds of the Bayou*, by Susannah Sandlin; *Death in the Family* by Tessa Wegert; *The Raven Sisters* by Luanne Smith; The Swooning Virgins Society Series, by Anna Bradley; *Fly By Night*, by Andrea Thalasinos; The Dragonsworn Series, by Caitlyn McFarland; *The Devious Dr. Jekyll*, by Viola Carr; *The Dragon's Price*, by Bethany Wiggins; The Hundredth Queen Series, by Emily R. King; film rights to *The Paper Magician*, by Charlie N. Holmberg.

TERMS Standard commission. "We do not charge fees."

HOW TO CONTACT Electronic submissions through website only. Please make sure your ms is as good as it can be before you submit. Agents are not first readers. For specific information on what we like to see in query letters, refer to the information at www.stringerlit.com. Accepts simultaneous submissions. Obtains new clients through referrals, submissions, conferences.

TIPS "Check our website for submission information and updates. If your ms falls between categories, or you are not sure of the category, query and we'll let you know if we'd like to take a look. We strive to respond as quickly as possible. If you have not received a response in the time period indicated on website, please re-query."

THE STROTHMAN AGENCY, LLC

63 E. 9th St., 10X, New York NY 10003. **E-mail:** info@strothmanagency.com. **Website:** www.strothmanagency.com. **Contact:** Wendy Strothman, Lauren MacLeod. The Strothman Agency, LLC is a highly selective literary agency operating out of New York and Nashville, TN dedicated to advocating for authors of significant books through the entire publishing cycle. Recent Strothman Agency authors have won the Pulitzer Prize for Biography, the National Book Critics Circle Award for Nonfiction, the Lincoln Prize, and many other awards. Clients have appeared on New York Times bestsellers lists, on National Book Award Long Lists, and two were Finalists for the Pulitzer Prize in History.

MEMBER AGENTS Wendy Strothman (history, narrative nonfiction, narrative journalism, science and nature, and current affairs); Lauren MacLeod (young adult fiction and nonfiction, middle grade novels, as well as adult narrative nonfiction, particularly food writing, science, pop culture and history).

HANDLES Specializes in history, science, biography, politics, narrative journalism, nature and the environment, current affairs, narrative nonfiction, business and economics, young adult fiction and nonfiction, and middle grade fiction and nonfiction. "The Strothman Agency seeks out scholars, journalists, and other acknowledged and emerging experts in their fields. We specialize in history, science, narrative journalism, nature and the environment, current affairs, narrative nonfiction, business and economics, young adult fiction and nonfiction, middle grade fiction and nonfiction. We are not signing up projects in romance, science fiction, picture books, or poetry."

TERMS Agent receives 15% commission on domestic sales; 20% commission on foreign sales. Offers written contract; 30-day notice must be given to terminate contract.

HOW TO CONTACT Accepts queries only via e-mail. See submission guidelines online. Accepts simultaneous submissions. "All e-mails received will be responded to with an auto-reply. If we have not replied to your query within 6 weeks, we do not feel that it is right for us." Accepts simultaneous submissions. Obtains most new clients through recommendations from others.

EMMA SWEENEY AGENCY, LLC

245 E 80th St., Suite 7E, New York NY 10075. **E-mail:** info@emmasweeneyagency.com. **Website:** www.emmasweeneyagency.com.

MEMBER AGENTS Emma Sweeney, president; Margaret Sutherland Brown (commercial and literary fiction, mysteries and thrillers, narrative nonfiction, lifestyle, and cookbook); Hannah Brattesani (poetry, and literary fiction).

HANDLES Does not want erotica.

HOW TO CONTACT "We accept only electronic queries, and ask that all queries be sent to queries@emmasweeneyagency.com rather than to any agent directly. Please begin your query with a succinct (and hopefully catchy) description of your plot or proposal. Always include a brief cover letter telling us how you heard about ESA, your previous writing credits, and a few lines about yourself. We cannot open any attachments unless specifically requested, and ask that you paste the first 10 pages of your proposal or novel into the text of your e-mail." Accepts simultaneous submissions.

TALCOTT NOTCH LITERARY SERVICES, LLC

31 Cherry St., Suite 100, Milford CT 06460. (203)876-4959. **Fax:** (203)876-9517. **E-mail:** editorial@talcottnotch.net. **Website:** www.talcottnotch.net. **Contact:** Gina Panettieri, founder. Talcott Notch Literary is a four-member full-service literary and sub-rights agency with offices covering the East Coast, representing award-winning and bestselling adult and juvenile fiction and nonfiction from the freshest upcoming writers from the U.S. and the abroad.

MEMBER AGENTS Gina Panettieri, gpanettieri@talcottnotch.net (history, business, self-help, science, gardening, cookbooks, crafts, parenting, memoir, true crime and travel, YA, MG and women's fiction, paranormal, urban fantasy, horror, science fiction, historical, mystery, thrillers and suspense); Paula Munier, pmunier@talcottnotch.net (mystery/thriller, SF/fantasy, romance, YA, memoir, humor, pop culture, health & wellness, cooking, self-help, pop psych, New Age, inspirational, technology, science, and writing); Saba Sulaiman, ssulaiman@talcottnotch.net (upmarket literary and commercial fiction, romance [all subgenres except paranormal], character-driven psychological thrillers, cozy mysteries, memoir, young adult [except paranormal and sci-fi], middle grade, and nonfiction humor); Tia Mele, tmele@talcottnotch.net (YA and MG, fiction and nonfiction, limited adult projects); Amy Collins (nonfiction, gift, reference, history, fantasy, science fiction, historical fiction); Dennis Schleicher (biographies, Christian living, children's books, church life, devotional, inspirational, LGBTQ, theology, bible study, reference, health, finance, fiction, self-help, psychology, grief, suffering, marriage, family, women's, men's, philosophy, history, social issues, parenting, clean romance, LDS, and Mormonism).

HANDLES "We are most actively seeking projects featuring diverse characters and stories which expand the reader's understanding of our society and the wider world we live in."

RECENT SALES Agency sold 65 titles in the last year, including *Lies She Told*, by Cate Holahan (Crooked Lane Books); *American Operator*, by Brian Andrews and Jeffrey Wilson (Thomas & Mercer); *Reset*, by Brian Andrews (Thomas & Mercer); *A Lover's Pinch*, by Peter Tupper (Rowman & Littlefield); *Everlasting Nora*, by Marie Cruz (Tor); *A Borrowing of Bones*, by Paula Munier (St. Martin's); *Muslim Girls Rise*, by Saira Mir (Salaam Reads), *Belabored*, by Lyz Lenz (Nation Books); *Tarnished Are The Stars*, by Rosiee Thor (Scholastic): *The Complicated Math of Two Plus One*, by Cathleen Barnhart (Harper Children's); and many others.

TERMS Agent receives 15% commission on domestic sales; 20% commission on foreign sales. Offers written contract, binding for 1 year.

TIPS "Know your market and how to reach them. A strong platform is essential in your book proposal.

Can you effectively use social media/Are you a strong networker: Are you familiar with the book bloggers in your genre? Are you involved with the interest-specific groups that can help you? What can you do to break through the 'noise' and help present your book to your readers? Check our website for more tips and information on this topic."

THOMPSON LITERARY AGENCY

48 Great Jones St. #5F, New York NY 10012. (716)257-8153. **E-mail:** info@thompsonliterary.com. **Website:** thompsonliterary.com. **Contact:** Meg Thompson, founder.

MEMBER AGENTS Kiele Raymond, senior agent; John Thorn, affiliate agent; Sandy Hodgman, director of foreign rights; Meg Thompson; Samantha Wekstein.

HANDLES The agency is always on the lookout for both commercial and literary fiction, as well as young adult and children's books. "Nonfiction, however, is our specialty, and our interests include biography, memoir, music, popular science, politics, blog-to-book projects, cookbooks, sports, health and wellness, fashion, art, and popular culture." "Please note that we do not accept submissions for poetry collections or screenplays, and we only consider picture books by established illustrators."

HOW TO CONTACT Query via Query Manager.

THREE SEAS LITERARY AGENCY

P.O. Box 444, Sun Prairie WI 53590. (608)834-9317. **E-mail:** threeseaslit@aol.com. **Website:** threeseasagency.com. **Contact:** Michelle Grajkowski, Cori Deyoe, Stacey Graham. 3 Seas is a full-service literary agency, and we're all about building our authors' careers! We represent more than 85 authors who write romance, women's fiction, science fiction/fantasy, thrillers, young adult and middle grade fiction as well as select nonfiction titles. In the twenty years since the agency doors were opened, our agents have successfully sold into all the major publishing houses. Our clients consistently appear on the New York Times, USA Today and Publishers Weekly Best Sellers lists. They have been nominated, and won, many prestigious industry awards, including, the RITA, the Golden Heart, the Holt Medallion, the RT Reviewer's Choice, the ALA Best Book for Young Adults, the School Library Journal Best Book, and the Bookseller's Best. Our agents are extremely active in the publishing industry. They take appointments and speak at numerous regional and national conferences each year, and frequently guest blog about their publishing experiences. We are so proud of the amazing, talented authors we currently represent. And, our lists are always open for fantastic writers with a voice of their own. 3 Seas is an RWA recognized agency, and we belong to the Association of American Literary Agents (AALA) where we strongly believe in, and adhere to, their Canon of Ethics.

MEMBER AGENTS Michelle Grajkowski (romance, women's fiction, young adult and middle grade fiction, select nonfiction projects); Cori Deyoe (all sub-genres of romance, women's fiction, young adult, middle grade, picture books, thrillers, mysteries and select nonfiction); Stacey Graham (women's fiction, thrillers, young adult, middle grade and romance).

HANDLES "We represent more than 85 authors who write romance, women's fiction, science fiction/fantasy, thrillers, young adult and middle grade fiction, as well as select nonfiction titles. Currently, we are looking for fantastic authors with a voice of their own." 3 Seas does not represent poetry or screenplays.

TERMS Agent receives 15% commission on domestic sales; 20% commission on foreign sales. Offers written contract.

HOW TO CONTACT Please click the links below to be redirected to the query submission form. Michelle: http://QueryManager.com/Michelle3Seas; Cori: https://QueryManager.com/Cori3Seas; Stacey: http://QueryManager.com/Stacey3Seas. Accepts simultaneous submissions. Obtains most new clients through recommendations from others, conferences.

✪ TRANSATLANTIC LITERARY AGENCY

2 Bloor St. E., Suite 3500, Toronto ON M4W 1A8, Canada. (416)488-9214. **E-mail:** info@transatlanticagency.com. **Website:** transatlanticagency.com. The Transatlantic Agency represents adult and children's authors of all genres, including illustrators. We do not handle stage plays, musicals or screenplays. Please review the agency website and guidelines carefully before making any inquiries, as each agent has their own particular submission guidelines.

MEMBER AGENTS Amy Tompkins (adult: literary fiction, historical fiction, women's fiction including smart romance, narrative nonfiction, and quirky or original how-to books; children's: early readers, middle grade, young adult, and new adult); Samantha Haywood (literary fiction and upmarket commercial fiction, specifically literary thrillers and upmarket mystery, historical fiction, smart contemporary fiction, upmarket women's fiction and cross-over novels; narrative nonfiction, including investigative journalism, politics, women's issues, memoirs, environmental issues, historical narratives, sexuality, true crime; graphic novels (fiction/nonfiction): preferably full length graphic novels, story collections considered, memoirs, biographies, travel narratives); Marie Campbell (middle grade fiction); Shaun Bradley (referrals only; adult literary fiction and narrative nonfiction, primarily science and investigative journalism); Sandra Bishop (fiction; nonfiction: biography, memoir, and positive or humorous how-to books on advice/relationships, mind/body/spirit, religion, healthy living, finances, life-hacks, traveling, living a better life); Fiona Kenshole (children's and young adult; only accepting submissions from referrals or conferences she attends as faculty); Elizabeth Bennett; Marilyn Biderman; Evan Brown; Cody Caetano; Laura Cameron; Andrea Cascardi; Brenna English-Loeb; Rob Firing; Carolyn Forde; Devon Halliday; Chelene Knight; Amanda Orozco; Timothy Travaglini; Leonicka Valcius.

HANDLES "In both children's and adult literature, we market directly into the US, the United Kingdom and Canada." Represents adult and children's authors of all genres, including illustrators. Does not want to receive picture books, musicals, screenplays or stage plays.

RECENT SALES Sold 250 titles in the last year.

TERMS Agent receives 15% commission on domestic sales; 20% commission on foreign sales. Offers written contract; 45-day notice must be given to terminate contract. This agency charges for photocopying and postage when it exceeds $100.

HOW TO CONTACT Always refer to the website, as guidelines will change, and only various agents are open to new clients at any given time. Obtains most new clients through recommendations from others.

S©OTT TREIMEL NY

Scotty T., Inc., 434 Lafayette St., New York NY 10003. (212)505-8353. **E-mail:** general@scotttreimelny.com. **Website:** www.scotttreimelny.com.

HANDLES This agency specializes in tightly focused segments of the trade and institutional markets, representing both authors and illustrators of books for children and teens, m-g novels, YA.

RECENT SALES *Misunderstood Shark*, by Ame Dyckman (Scholastic); Tiny Barbarian, by Ame Dyckman (HarperCollins); *The Purple Puffy Coat*, by Maribeth Boelts (Candlewick); *Other Word-ly*, by Yee-Lum Mak (Chronicle); *The Magician's Visit*, by Barbara Diamond Golden (Apples & Honey Press); *How Dinosaurs Went Extinct: A Safety Guide*, by Ame Dyckman (Little Brown); *The New Kid Has Fleas, by Ame Dyckman (Roaring Brook Press); Alaina*, by Eloise Greenfield (Alazar Press); *The Women Who Caught the Babies*, by Eloise Greenfield (Alazar Books).

TERMS Agent receives 15% commission on domestic sales; 20% commission on foreign sales. Offers verbal or written contract, standard terms. Only charges fees for books needed to sell subsidiary rights—foreign, film, etc.

HOW TO CONTACT No longer accepts unsolicited submissions. Wants—via e-mail only—queries from writers recommended by his clients and/or editor pals or that he has met at conferences. Accepts simultaneous submissions.

TIPS "We look for dedicated authors and illustrators able to sustain longtime careers in our increasingly competitive field. I want fresh, not derivative story concepts with overly familiar characters. We look for gripping stories, characters, pacing, and themes. We read for an authentic (to the age) point-of-view, and look for original voices. We spend significant time hunting for the best new work, and do launch debut talent each year. It is best not to send warm-up manuscripts or those already seen all over town."

TRIADA US

P.O. Box 561, Sewickley PA 15143. (412)401-3376. **E-mail:** uwe@triadaus.com; brent@triadaus.com; laura@triadaus.com; lauren@triadaus.com; amelia@triadaus.com; elle@triadaus.com. **Website:** www.triadaus.com. **Contact:** Dr. Uwe Stender, President. Triada US was founded by Dr. Uwe Stender over twelve years ago. Since then, the agency has built a high-quality list of fiction and nonfiction for kids, teens, and adults. Triada US titles are consistently critically acclaimed and translated into multiple languages.

MEMBER AGENTS Uwe Stender; Brent Taylor; Laura Crockett; Lauren Spieller; Amelia Appel; Elle Thompson.

HANDLES Actively seeking fiction and nonfiction across a broad range of categories of all age levels.

RECENT SALES *Always Young And Restless* by Melody Thomas Scott (Diversion Books), *Roman And Jewel* by Dana L. Davis (Harper Collins/Inkyard), *The Obsession* by Jesse Q. Sutanto (Sourcebooks), *Hani And Ishu's Guide To Fake Dating* by Adiba Jaigirdar (Page Street Kids), *Force of Fire* by Sayantani DasGupta (Scholastic), *Just Pretend* by Tori Sharp (Little, Brown), *Poultrygeist* by Eric Geron (Candlewick), *Red, White, and Whole* by Rajani LaRocca (Quill Tree), *Don't Date Rosa Santos* by Nina Moreno (Little Brown Young Readers), *These Violent Delights* by Chloe Gong (McElderry Books), *The Jasmine Throne* by Tasha Suri (Orbit), *Malice* by Heather Walter (Del Rey), *Within These Wicked Walls* by Lauren Blackwood (Wednesday Books), *Flower Crowns & Fearsome Things* by Amanda Lovelace (Andrews McMeel), *Barakah Beats* by Maleeha Siddiqui (Scholastic), *The Kill Club* by Wendy Heard (Mira), *The Devil Makes Three* by Tori Bovalino (Page Street Kids), *Throw Like a Girl, Cheer Like a Boy* by Robyn Ryle (Rowman & Littlefield Publishers), *The Unexpected Guest* by Michael Konik (Diversion Books).

TERMS Triada US retains 15% commission on domestic sales and 20% commission on foreign and translation sales. Offers written contract; 30-day notice must be given prior to termination.

HOW TO CONTACT E-mail queries preferred. Please paste your query letter and the first 10 pages of your ms into the body of a message e-mailed to the agent of your choice. Do not simultaneously query multiple Triada agents. Please query one and wait for their response before moving onto another agent within our agency. Obtains most new clients through submission inbox (query letters and requested mss), client referrals, and conferences.

TRIDENT MEDIA GROUP

355 Lexington Ave., Floor 12, New York NY 10017. (212)333-1511. **E-mail:** info@tridentmediagroup.com. **Website:** www.tridentmediagroup.com. **Contact:** Ellen Levine.

MEMBER AGENTS Scott Miller, smiller@tridentmediagroup.com (commercial fiction, including thrillers, crime fiction, women's, book club fiction, middle grade, young adult; nonfiction, including military, celebrity and pop culture, narrative, sports, prescriptive, and current events); Don Fehr, dfehr@tridentmediagroup.com (literary and commercial fiction, young adult fiction, narrative nonfiction, memoirs, travel, science, and health); Erica Spellman-Silverman; Ellen Levine, levine.assistant@tridentmediagroup.com (popular commercial fiction and compelling nonfiction, including memoir, popular culture, narrative nonfiction, history, politics, biography, science, and the odd quirky book); Mark Gottlieb (fiction: science fiction, fantasy, young adult, graphic novels, historical, middle grade, mystery, romance, suspense, thrillers; nonfiction: business, finance, history, religious, health, cookbooks, sports, African-American, biography, memoir, travel, mind/body/spirit, narrative nonfiction, science, technology); Alexander Slater, aslater@tridentmdiagroup.com (children's, middle grade, and young adult fiction); Alexa Stark, astark@tridentmediagroup.com (literary fiction, upmarket commercial fiction, young adult, memoir, narrative nonfiction, popular science, cultural criticism and women's issues); Amanda Annis; Martha Wydysh; Tess Weitzner.

HANDLES Actively seeking new or established authors in a variety of fiction and nonfiction genres.

HOW TO CONTACT Submit through the agency's online submission form on the agency website. Query only one agent at a time. If you e-query, include no attachments. Accepts simultaneous submissions.

TIPS "If you have any questions, please check FAQ page before e-mailing us."

THE UNTER AGENCY

23 W. 73rd St., Suite 100, New York NY 10023. (212)401-4068. **E-mail:** jennifer@theunteragency.com. **Website:** www.theunteragency.com. **Contact:** Jennifer Unter.

HANDLES This agency specializes in children's, nonfiction, and quality fiction.

RECENT SALES A full list of recent sales/titles is available on the agency website.

HOW TO CONTACT Send an e-query. There is also an online submission form. If you do not hear back from this agency within 3 months, consider that a no. Accepts simultaneous submissions.

UPSTART CROW LITERARY

594 Dean St., Office 47, Brooklyn NY 11238. **Website:** www.upstartcrowliterary.com. **Contact:** Danielle Chiotti, Alexandra Penfold.

MEMBER AGENTS Michael Stearns (not accepting submissions); Danielle Chiotti (all genres of young adult and middle grade fiction; adult upmarket commercial fiction [not considering romance, mystery/suspense/thriller, science fiction, horror, or erotica]; nonfiction in the areas of narrative/memoir, lifestyle, relationships, humor, current events, food, wine, and cooking); Ted Malawer (not accepting submissions); Alexandra Penfold (not accepting submissions); Susan Hawk (books for children and teens only); Kayla Cichello.

HOW TO CONTACT Submit a query and 20 pages pasted into an e-mail. Accepts simultaneous submissions.

VERITAS LITERARY AGENCY

601 Van Ness Ave., Opera Plaza, Suite E, San Francisco CA 94102. (415)647-6964. **Fax:** (415)647-6965. **Website:** www.veritasliterary.com. **Contact:** Katherine Boyle.

MEMBER AGENTS Katherine Boyle, katherine@veritasliterary.com (literary fiction, middle grade, young adult, narrative nonfiction/memoir, historical fiction, crime/suspense, history, pop culture, popular science, business/career); Michael Carr, michael@veritasliterary.com (historical fiction, women's fiction, science fiction and fantasy, nonfiction); Chiara Rosati, literary scout.

HOW TO CONTACT This agency accepts short queries or proposals via e-mail only. "Fiction: Please include a cover letter listing previously published work, a one-page summary and the first 5 pages in the body of the e-mail (not as an attachment). Nonfiction: If you are sending a proposal, please include an author biography, an overview, a chapter-by-chapter summary, and an analysis of competitive titles. We do our best to review all queries within 4-6 weeks; however, if you have not heard from us in 12 weeks, consider that a no." Accepts simultaneous submissions.

WATERSIDE PRODUCTIONS, INC.

2055 Oxford Ave., Cardiff CA 92007. (760)632-9190. **Fax:** (760)632-9295. **E-mail:** admin@waterside.com. **Website:** www.waterside.com.

MEMBER AGENTS Bill Gladstone (big nonfiction books); Margot Maley Hutchinson (computer, health, psychology, parenting, fitness, pop culture, and business); Carole Jelen, carole@jelenpub.com (innovation and thought leaders especially in business, technology, lifestyle and self-help); Jill Kramer, watersideagentjk@aol.com (quality fiction with empowering themes for adults and YA (including crossovers); nonfiction, including mind-body-spirit, self-help, celebrity memoirs, relationships, sociology, finance, psychology, health and fitness, diet/nutrition, inspiration, business, family/parenting issues); Natasha Gladstone, (picture books, books with film tie-ins, books with established animated characters, and educational titles); Johanna Maaghul, johanna@waterside.com (nonfiction and select fiction); Kimberly Brabec, rights@waterside.com (Director of International Rights); Kristen Moeller (self-improvement/women); Michael Gosney.

HANDLES Specializes in computer and technical titles, and also represent other nonfiction genres, including self-help, cooking, travel, and more. Note that most agents here are nonfiction only, so target your query to the appropriate agent.

HOW TO CONTACT "Please read each agent bio [on the website] to determine who you think would best represent your genre of work. When you have chosen your agent, please write his or her name in the subject line of your e-mail and send it to admin@waterside.com with your query letter in the body of the e-mail, and your proposal or sample material as an attached word document." Nonfiction submission guidelines are available on the website. Accepts simultaneous submissions. Obtains most new clients through referrals from established client and publisher list.

TIPS "For new writers, a quality proposal and a strong knowledge of the market you're writing for goes a long way toward helping us turn you into a published author. We like to see a strong author platform."

WAXMAN LITERARY AGENCY, INC.

Fax: (212)675-1381. **Website:** www.waxmanagency.com.

MEMBER AGENTS Scott Waxman (nonfiction: history, biography, health and science, adventure, business, inspirational sports); Susan Canavan (narrative nonfiction, history, adventure, sports, memoir, journalism, health, science, pop culture, parenting, nature, literary fiction, and historical fiction); Ashley Lopez (literary fiction, women's fiction (commercial and upmarket, memoir, narrative nonfiction, pop science/pop culture, cultural criticism).

HANDLES Agent Holly Root at this agency handles young adult and middle grade. Agent Taylor Haggerty handles young adult fiction.

TERMS Agent receives 15% commission on domestic sales; 10% commission on foreign sales. Offers written contract; 2-month notice must be given to terminate contract.

HOW TO CONTACT To submit a project, please send a query letter only via e-mail to one of the addresses included on the website. Do not send attachments, though for fiction you may include 10 pages of your manuscript in the body of your e-mail. "Due to the high volume of submissions, agents will reach out to you directly if interested. The typical time range for consideration is 6-8 weeks. Please do not query more than 1 agent at our agency simultaneously." (To see the types of projects each agent is looking for, refer to the Agent Biographies page on website.) Accepts simultaneous submissions.

WELLS ARMS LITERARY

Website: www.wellsarms.com. Wells Arms Literary represents children's book authors and illustrators to the trade children's book market.

HANDLES "We focus on books for young readers of all ages: board books, picture books, readers, chapter books, middle grade, and young adult fiction." Actively seeking middle grade, young adult, magical realism, contemporary, romance, fantasy. "We do not represent to the textbook, magazine, adult romance or fine art markets."

HOW TO CONTACT Wells Arms Literary is currently closed to queries or submissions "unless you've met me at a conference." Accepts simultaneous submissions.

WERNICK & PRATT AGENCY

Website: www.wernickpratt.com. **Contact:** Marcia Wernick; Linda Pratt; Emily Mitchell. "Wernick & Pratt Agency provides each client with personal attention and the highest quality of advice and service that has been the hallmark of our reputations in the industry. We have the resources and accumulated knowledge to assist clients in all aspects of their creative lives including editorial input, contract negotiations, and subsidiary rights management. Our goal is to represent and manage the careers of our clients so they may achieve industry wide and international recognition, as well as the highest level of financial potential."

Dedicated to children's books.

MEMBER AGENTS Marcia Wernick, Linda Pratt, Emily Mitchell; Shannon Gallagher.

HANDLES "Wernick & Pratt Agency specializes in children's books of all genres, from picture books through young adult literature and everything in between. We represent both authors and illustrators. We do not represent authors of adult books." Wants people who both write and illustrate in the picture book genre; humorous young chapter books with strong voice, and which are unique and compelling; middle grade/YA novels, both literary and commercial. No picture book mss of more than 750 words, or mood pieces; work specifically targeted to the educational market; fiction about the American Revolution, Civil War, or World War II unless it is told from a very unique perspective.

HOW TO CONTACT Submit via e-mail only to submissions@wernickpratt.com. "Please indicate to which agent you are submitting." Detailed submission guidelines available on website. "Submissions will only be responded to further if we are interested in them. If you do not hear from us within 6 weeks of your submission, it should be considered declined." Accepts simultaneous submissions.

WESTWOOD CREATIVE ARTISTS, LTD.

386 Huron St., Toronto ON M5S 2G6, Canada. (416)964-3302. **E-mail:** submissions@wcaltd.com. **Website:** www.wcaltd.com. Westwood Creative Artists is Canada's largest literary agency. It's also one of the oldest and most respected. "Situated in Toronto's Annex neighbourhood, our staff of 11 includes 6 full-time book agents who are supported by an in-house international rights agent and an outstanding network of twenty-four international co-agents. We take great pride in the enthusiastic response to our list from publishers around the world and in the wide praise our writers receive from Canadian and international critics. We are honored that many of the writers we represent have won and been shortlisted for such esteemed prizes as the Man Booker Prize, the Nobel Prize, and the Scotiabank Giller Prize."

MEMBER AGENTS Jackie Kaiser (President and COO); Michael A. Levine (Chairman); Hilary McMahon (Executive Vice President, fiction, nonfiction, children's); John Pearce (fiction and nonfiction); Bruce Westwood (Founder, Managing Director and CEO); Chris Casuccio; Emmy Nordstrom Higdon; Max Alexandre Tremblay; Meg Wheeler.

HANDLES "We take on children's and young adult writers very selectively. The agents bring their diverse interests to their client lists, but are generally looking for authors with a mastery of language, a passionate, expert or original perspective on their subject, and a gift for storytelling." "Please note that WCA does not represent screenwriters, and our agents are not currently seeking poetry or children's picture book submissions."

HOW TO CONTACT E-query only. Include credentials, synopsis, and no more than 10 pages. No attachments. Accepts simultaneous submissions.

TIPS "We will reject outright complete, unsolicited manuscripts, or projects that are presented poorly in the query letter. We prefer to receive exclusive submissions and request that you do not query more than one agent at the agency simultaneously. It's often best if you approach WCA after you have accumulated some publishing credits."

WHIMSY LITERARY AGENCY, LLC

49 N. 8th St., 6G, Brooklyn NY 11249. (212) 674-7162. **E-mail:** whimsynyc@aol.com. **Contact:** Jackie Meyer and Aria Gmitter, agents. Whimsy Literary Agency LLC, specializes in nonfiction books and authors that educate, entertain, and inspire people.

HANDLES "Whimsy looks for nonfiction projects that are concept- and platform-driven. We seek books that educate, inspire, and entertain." Actively seeking experts in their field with integrated and established platforms.

TERMS Agent receives 15% commission on domestic sales; 20% commission on foreign sales. Offers written contract.

HOW TO CONTACT Send your proposal via e-mail to whimsynyc@aol.com (include your media platform, table of contents with full description of each chapter). First-time authors: "We appreciate proposals that are professional and complete. Please consult the many fine books available on writing book proposals. We are not considering poetry, or screenplays. Please Note: Due to the volume of queries and submissions, we are unable to respond unless they are of interest to us." Accepts simultaneous submissions. Obtains most new clients through recommendations from others, solicitations.

WOLFSON LITERARY AGENCY

P.O. Box 266, New York NY 10276. **E-mail:** query@wolfsonliterary.com. **Website:** www.wolfsonliterary.com. **Contact:** Michelle Wolfson.

HANDLES Actively seeking commercial fiction: young adult, mainstream, women's fiction, romance. "I am not taking on new nonfiction clients at this time."

TERMS Agent receives 15% commission on domestic sales; 25% commission on foreign sales. Offers written contract; 30-day notice must be given to terminate contract.

HOW TO CONTACT E-queries only. Accepts simultaneous submissions. Obtains most new clients through queries or recommendations from others.

TIPS "Be persistent."

WORDSERVE LITERARY GROUP

7500 E. Arapahoe Rd., Suite 285, Centennial CO 80112. **E-mail:** admin@wordserveliterary.com. **Website:** www.wordserveliterary.com. **Contact:** Greg Johnson. WordServe Literary Group was founded in 2003 by veteran literary agent Greg Johnson. After more than a decade in serving authors, the agency has represented more than 900 books in every fiction category and nonfiction genre. "We specialize serving authors of faith in all of their creative endeavors, as well as select titles and genres in the general market." Greg Johnson represents a broad array of adult fiction, primarily in the Christian market. He works with pastors and speakers, male and female, who have important and compelling messages to author for their constituents. He has also carved a niche by representing military nonfiction/memoir for those who have served our country from WWII until today. Business books, history, health and humor rounds out what he is looking to acquire. Sarah Freese acquires Christian fiction, particularly in the areas of contemporary romance, historical romance, contemporary women's fiction, and suspense. She also considers memoir, narrative non-fiction, and marriage/family/parenting books from bloggers with a large platform. Nick Harrison represents character-driven historical fiction, contemporary literary fiction and some genre fiction (mystery, romance, Amish). For nonfiction, he elcomes well-written memoirs, books by high-profile speakers or entertainers, health-related books, issue-related books, and "deeper life" Christian living books. Keely is looking looking for smart, well-crafted contemporary and literary fiction; narrative nonfiction and memoir; and well-researched nonfiction books in the areas of health and wellness, business (especially books targeting women in the workplace), parenting and family life, social justice, and religious studies; as well as projects from diverse and under-represented voices. For the Christian market, she is seeking books in the areas of Christian Living, spiritual transformation, devotion and worship, and women's topics including motherhood, relationships and marriage, work-life balance, and calling. She is not looking for thrillers, sci-fi, fantasy, or romance.

MEMBER AGENTS Greg Johnson, Nick Harrison, Sarah Freese, and Keely Boeving.

HANDLES Materials with a faith-based angle, as well as the general market categories of business, health, history, military. No gift books, poetry, short stories, screenplays, graphic novels, children's picture books, science fiction or fantasy. Please do not send mss that are more than 120,000 words.

TERMS Agent receives 15% commission on domestic sales; 10-15% commission on foreign sales. Offers written contract; up to 60-day notice must be given to terminate contract.

HOW TO CONTACT E-query admin@wordserveliterary.com. In the subject line, include the word "query." All queries should include the following three elements: a pitch for the book, information about you and your platform (for nonfiction) or writing background (for fiction), and the first 5 (or so) pages of the manuscript pasted into the e-mail. Please view our website for full guidelines: http://www.wordserveliterary.com/submission-guidlines/. Accepts simultaneous submissions. Obtains most new clients through recommendations from others.

TIPS "We are looking for good proposals, great writing and authors willing to market their books. We specialize in projects with a faith element bent. See the website before submitting. Though we are not a member of AAR, we abide by all of the rules for agents."

WRITERS HOUSE

21 W. 26th St., New York NY 10010. (212)685-2400. **Fax:** (212)685-1781. **Website:** www.writershouse.com.

MEMBER AGENTS Amy Berkower; Stephen Barr; Susan Cohen; Dan Conaway; Lisa DiMona; Susan Ginsburg; Susan Golomb; Merrilee Heifetz; Brianne Johnson; Daniel Lazar; Simon Lipskar; Steven Malk; Jodi Reamer, Esq.; Robin Rue; Rebecca Sherman; Geri Thoma; Albert Zuckerman; Alec Shane; Stacy Testa; Victoria Doherty-Munro; Beth Miller; Andrea Morrison; Johanna V. Castillo; Lindsay Davis Auld; Alexandra Levick; Hannah Mann; Rebecca Eskildsen; Meredith Viguet.

HANDLES This agency specializes in all types of popular fiction and nonfiction, for both adult and juvenile books as well as illustrators. Does not want to receive scholarly, professional, poetry, plays, or screenplays.

TERMS Agent receives 15% commission on domestic sales. Agent receives 20% commission on foreign sales. Offers written contract, binding for 1 year. Agency charges fees for copying mss/proposals and overseas airmail of books.

HOW TO CONTACT Individual agent email addresses are available on the website. "Please e-mail us a query letter, which includes your credentials, an explanation of what makes your book unique and special, and a synopsis. Some agents within our agency have different requirements. Please consult their individual Publisher's Marketplace (PM) profile for details. We respond to all queries, generally within six to eight weeks." If you prefer to submit my mail, address it to an individual agent, and please include SASE for our reply. (If submitting to Steven Malk: Writers House, 7660 Fay Ave., #338H, La Jolla, CA 92037.) Accepts simultaneous submissions. Obtains most new clients through recommendations from authors and editors.

TIPS "Do not send mss. Write a compelling letter. If you do, we'll ask to see your work. Follow submission guidelines and please do not simultaneously submit your work to more than one Writers House agent."

JASON YARN LITERARY AGENCY

Website: www.jasonyarnliteraryagency.com.

HOW TO CONTACT Please e-mail your query to jason@jasonyarnliteraryagency.com with the word "Query" in the subject line, and please paste the first 10 pages of your manuscript or proposal into the text of your e-mail. Do not send any attachments. "Visit the About page for information on what we are interested in, and please note that JYLA does not accept queries for film, TV, or stage scripts." Accepts simultaneous submissions.

CLUBS & ORGANIZATIONS

Contacts made through organizations such as the ones listed in this section can be quite beneficial for children's writers and illustrators. Professional organizations provide numerous educational, business, and legal services in the form of newsletters, workshops, or seminars. Organizations can provide tips about how to be a more successful writer or artist, as well as what types of business cards to keep, health and life insurance coverage to carry, and competitions to consider.

An added benefit of belonging to an organization is the opportunity to network with those who have similar interests, creating a support system. As in any business, knowing the right people can often help your career, and important contacts can be made through your peers. Membership in a writer's or artist's organization also shows publishers you're serious about your craft. This provides no guarantee your work will be published, but it gives you an added dimension of credibility and professionalism.

Some of the organizations listed here welcome anyone with an interest, while others are only open to published writers and professional artists. Organizations such as the Society of Children's Book Writers and Illustrators (SCBWI, www.scbwi.org) have varying levels of membership. SCBWI offers associate membership to those with no publishing credits, and full membership to those who have had work for children published. International organizations such as SCBWI also have regional chapters throughout the US and the world. Write or call for more information regarding any group that interests you, or check the websites of the many organizations that list them. Be sure to get information about local chapters, membership qualifications, and services offered.

AMERICAN ALLIANCE FOR THEATRE & EDUCATION

718 7th St. NW, Washington DC 20001. (202)909-1194. **E-mail:** info@aate.com. **Website:** www.aate.com. Purpose of organization: to promote standards of excellence in theatre and drama education. "We achieve this by assimilating quality practices in theatre and theatre education, connecting artists, educators, researchers and scholars with each other, and by providing opportunities for our members to learn, exchange and diversify their work, their audiences and their perspectives." Membership cost: $115 annually for individual in U.S. and Canada, $220 annually for organization, $60 annually for students, and $70 annually for retired people, $310 annually for University Departmental memberships; add $30 outside Canada and U.S. Holds annual conference (July or August). Contests held for unpublished play reading project and annual awards in various categories. Awards plaque and stickers for published playbooks. Publishes list of unpublished plays deemed worthy of performance and stages readings at conference. Contact national office at number above or see website for contact information for Playwriting Network Chairpersons.

AMERICAN SOCIETY OF JOURNALISTS AND AUTHORS

355 Lexington Ave., 15th Floor, New York NY 10017. (212)997-0947. **Website:** www.asja.org. Qualifications for membership: "Need to be a professional freelance nonfiction writer. Refer to website for further qualifications." Membership cost: Application fee—$50; annual dues—$210. Group sponsors national conferences. Professional seminars online and in person around the country. Workshops/conferences open to nonmembers. Publishes a newsletter for members that provides confidential information for nonfiction writers. **Contact:** Holly Koenig, interim executive director.

ARIZONA AUTHORS' ASSOCIATION

6939 East Chaparral Rd., Paradise Valley AZ 85253. (602)510-8076. **E-mail:** azauthors@gmail.com. **Website:** www.arizonaauthors.com. Since 1978, Arizona Authors' Association has served to offer professional, educational and social opportunities to writers and authors and serves as an informational and referral network for the literary community. Members must be authors, writers working toward publication, agents, publishers, publicists, printers, illustrators, etc. Az Authors' publishes a bimonthly newsletter and the renown annual *Arizona Literary Magazine*. The Association sponsors the international Arizona Literary Contest including poetry, essays, short stories, new drama writing, novels, and published books with cash prizes and awards bestowed at a Fall ceremony. Winning entries are published or advertised in the *Arizona Literary Magazine*. First and second place winners in poetry, essay and short story categories are entered in the annual Pushcart Prize. Learn more online. **Contact:** Lisa Aquilina, President.

THE AUTHORS GUILD, INC.

31 E. 32nd St., 7th Floor, New York NY 10016. (212)563-5904. **Fax:** (212)564-5363. **E-mail:** staff@authorsguild.org. **Website:** www.authorsguild.org. Purpose of organization: to offer services and materials intended to help authors with the business and legal aspects of their work, including contract problems, copyright matters, freedom of expression and taxation. Guild has 8,000 members. Qualifications for membership: Must be book author published by an established American publisher within 7 years or any author who has had 3 works (fiction or nonfiction) published by a magazine or magazines of general circulation in the last 18 months. Associate membership also available. Different levels of membership include: associate membership with all rights except voting available to an author who has a firm contract offer or is currently negotiating a royalty contract from an established American publisher. "The Guild offers free contract reviews to its members. The Guild conducts several symposia each year at which experts provide information, offer advice and answer questions on subjects of interest and concern to authors. Typical subjects have been the rights of privacy and publicity, libel, wills and estates, taxation, copyright, editors and editing, the art of interviewing, standards of criticism and book reviewing. Transcripts of these symposia are published and circulated to members. The *Authors Guild Bulletin*, a quarterly journal, contains articles on matters of interest to writers, reports of Guild activities, contract surveys, advice on problem clauses in contracts, transcripts of Guild and League symposia and information on a variety of professional topics. Subscription included in the cost of the annual dues. **Contact:** Mary Rasenberger, executive director.

CANADIAN SOCIETY OF CHILDREN'S AUTHORS, ILLUSTRATORS AND PERFORMERS

720 Bathurst St., Suite 503, Toronto ON M5S 2R4, Canada. (416)515-1559. **E-mail:** office@canscaip.org. **Website:** www.canscaip.org. Purpose of organization: development of Canadian children's culture and support for authors, illustrators and performers working in this field. Qualifications for membership: Members—professionals who have been published (not self-published) or have paid public performances/records/tapes to their credit. Friends—share interest in field of children's culture. Sponsors workshops/conferences. Manuscript evaluation services; publishes newsletter: includes profiles of members; news roundup of members' activities countrywide; market news; news on awards, grants, etc; columns related to professional concerns. **Contact:** Helena Aalto, administrative director.

LEWIS CARROLL SOCIETY OF NORTH AMERICA

11935 Beltsville Dr., Beltsville MD 20705. **E-mail:** secretary@lewiscarroll.org. **Website:** www.lewiscarroll.org. "We are an organization of Carroll admirers of all ages and interests and a center for Carroll studies." Qualifications for membership: "An interest in Lewis Carroll and a simple love for Alice (or the Snark for that matter)." Membership cost: $35 (regular membership), $50 (foreign membership), $100 (sustaining membership). The Society meets twice a year—in spring and in fall; locations vary. Publishes a semi-annual journal, *Knight Letter*, and maintains an active publishing program. **Contact:** Sandra Lee Parker, secretary.

GRAPHIC ARTISTS GUILD

32 Broadway, Suite 1114, New York NY 10004. (212)791-3400. **Fax:** 212-791-0333. **E-mail:** admin@gag.org. **Website:** www.graphicartistsguild.org. Purpose of organization: "To promote and protect the economic interests of member artists. It is committed to improving conditions for all creators of graphic arts and raising standards for the entire industry." Qualification for full membership: 50% of income derived from the creation of graphic artwork. Associate members include those in allied fields and students. Initiation fee: $30. Full memberships: $200; student membership: $75/year. Associate membership: $170/year. Publishes *Graphic Artists Guild Handbook, Pricing and Ethical Guidelines* (members receive a copy as part of their membership). **Contact:** Patricia McKiernan, executive director.

HORROR WRITERS ASSOCIATION

P.O. Box 56687, Sherman Oaks CA 91413. (818)220-3965. **E-mail:** hwa@horror.org; membership@horror.org; admin@horror.org. **Website:** www.horror.org. Purpose of organization: To encourage public interest in horror and dark fantasy and to provide networking and career tools for members. Qualifications for membership: Complete membership rules online at www.horror.org/memrule.htm. At least one low-level sale is required to join as an affiliate. Nonwriting professionals who can show income from a horror-related field may join as an associate (booksellers, editors, agents, librarians, etc.). To qualify for full active membership, you must be a published, professional writer of horror. Membership cost: $69 annually. Holds annual Stoker Awards Weekend and HWA Business Meeting. Publishes monthly newsletter focusing on market news, industry news, HWA business for members. Sponsors awards. We give the Bram Stoker Awards for superior achievement in horror annually. Awards include a handmade Stoker trophy designed by sculptor Stephen Kirk. Awards open to nonmembers. **Contact:** Brad Hodson, Administrator.

INTERNATIONAL LITERACY ASSOCIATION

P.O. Box 8139, Newark DE 19714. (302)731-1600. **E-mail:** councils@reading.org. **Website:** www.literacyworldwide.org. The International Literacy Association seeks to promote high levels of literacy for all by improving the quality of reading instruction through studying the reading process and teaching techniques; serving as a clearinghouse for the dissemination of reading research through conferences, journals, and other publications; and actively encouraging the lifetime reading habit. Its goals include professional development, advocacy, partnerships, research, and global literacy development. Sponsors annual convention. Publishes a newsletter called "Reading Today." Sponsors a number of awards and fellowships. More information online.

INTERNATIONAL WOMEN'S WRITING GUILD

International Women's Writing Guild, 5 Penn Plaza, 19th Floor, PMB# 19059, New York NY 10001.

(917)720-6959. **E-mail:** iwwgquestions@gmail.com. **Website:** www.iwwg.wildapricot.org. IWWG is a network for the personal and professional empowerment of women through writing. Open to any woman connected to the written word regardless of professional portfolio. IWWG sponsors several annual conferences in all areas of the U.S. The major event, held in the summer, is a week-long conference attracting hundreds of women writers from around the globe. **Contact:** Marj Hahne, Interim Director of Operations.

THE NATIONAL LEAGUE OF AMERICAN PEN WOMEN

Pen Arts Building, 1300 17th St. N.W., Washington D.C. 20036-1973. (202)785-1997. **Fax:** (202)452-6868. **E-mail:** contact@nlapw.org. **Website:** www.americanpenwomen.org. Purpose of organization: to promote professional female work in art, letters, and music since 1897. Qualifications for membership: An applicant must show "proof of sale" in each chosen category—art, letters, and music. Levels of membership include: Active, Associate, International Affiliate, Members-at-Large, Honorary Members (in one or more of the following classifications: Art, Letters, and Music). Holds workshops/conferences. Publishes magazine 4 times/year titled *The Pen Woman*. Sponsors various contests in areas of Art, Letters, and Music. Awards made at Biennial Convention. Biannual scholarships awarded to non-Pen Women for mature women. Awards include cash prizes—up to $1,000. Specialized contests open to nonmembers. **Contact:** Nina Brooks, corresponding secretary.

NATIONAL WRITERS ASSOCIATION

10940 S. Parker Rd., #508, Parker CO 80138. **E-mail:** natlwritersassn@hotmail.com. **Website:** www.nationalwriters.com. Association for freelance writers. Qualifications for membership: associate membership—must be serious about writing; professional membership—must be published and paid writer (cite credentials). Sponsors workshops/conferences: TV/screenwriting workshops, NWAF Annual Conferences, Literary Clearinghouse, editing and critiquing services, local chapters, National Writer's School. Open to non-members. Publishes industry news of interest to freelance writers; how-to articles; market information; member news and networking opportunities. Sponsors poetry contest; short story contest; article contest; novel contest. Awards cash for top 3 winners; books and/or certificates for other winners; honorable mention certificate places 5-10. Contests open to nonmembers.

NATIONAL WRITERS UNION

256 W. 38th St., Suite 703, New York NY 10018. (212)254-0279. **Fax:** (212)254-0673. **E-mail:** nwu@nwu.org. **Website:** www.nwu.org. Advocacy for freelance writers. Qualifications for membership: "Membership in the NWU is open to all qualified writers, and no one shall be barred or in any manner prejudiced within the Union on account of race, age, sex, sexual orientation, disability, national origin, religion or ideology. You are eligible for membership if you have published a book, a play, three articles, five poems, one short story or an equivalent amount of newsletter, publicity, technical, commercial, government or institutional copy. You are also eligible for membership if you have written an equal amount of unpublished material and you are actively writing and attempting to publish your work." Holds workshops throughout the country. Members only section on website offers rich resources for freelance writers. Skilled contract advice and grievance help for members.

PEN AMERICAN CENTER

588 Broadway, Suite 303, New York NY 10012. (212)334-1660. **E-mail:** info@pen.org. **Website:** www.pen.org. An association of writers working to advance literature, to defend free expression, and to foster international literary fellowship. PEN welcomes to its membership all writers and those belonging to the larger literary community. We ask that writers have at least one book published or be writers with proven records as professional writers; playwrights and screenwriters should have at least one work produced in a professional setting. Others should have achieved recognition in the literary field. Editors, literary agents, literary scouts, publicists, journalists, bloggers, and other literary professionals are all invited to join as Professional Members. If you feel you do not meet these guidelines, please consider joining as an Advocate Member. Candidates for membership may be nominated by a PEN member or they may nominate themselves with the support of two references from the literary community or from a current PEN member. PEN members receive a subscription to the PEN journal, the PEN Annual Report, and have access to medical insurance at group rates. Members living in the New York metropolitan and tri-state area, or near

the Branches, are invited to PEN events throughout the year. Membership in PEN American Center includes reciprocal privileges in PEN American Center branches and in foreign PEN Centers for those traveling abroad. Application forms are available online. PEN American Center is the largest of the 141 centers of PEN International, the world's oldest human rights organization and the oldest international literary organization. PEN International was founded in 1921 to dispel national, ethnic, and racial hatreds and to promote understanding among all countries. PEN American Center, founded a year later, works to advance literature, to defend free expression, and to foster international literary fellowship. The Center has a membership of 3,400 distinguished writers, editors, and translators. In addition to defending writers in prison or in danger of imprisonment for their work, PEN American Center sponsors public literary programs and forums on current issues, sends prominent authors to inner-city schools to encourage reading and writing, administers literary prizes, promotes international literature that might otherwise go unread in the United States, and offers grants and loans to writers facing financial or medical emergencies.

PUPPETEERS OF AMERICA, INC.

Sabathani Community Center, 310 East 38th St., Suite 127, Minneapolis MN 55409. (888)568-6235. **E-mail:** membership@puppeteers.org; execdir@puppeteers.org. **Website:** www.puppeteers.org. Purpose of organization: to promote the art and appreciation of puppetry as a means of communications and as a performing art. The Puppeteers of America boasts an international membership. There are 9 different levels of membership, from family to youth to library to senior and more. See the website for all details. Costs are $35-90 per year.

SCIENCE-FICTION AND FANTASY WRITERS OF AMERICA, INC.

P.O. Box 3238, Enfield CT 06083. **Website:** www.sfwa.org. Purpose of organization: to encourage public interest in science fiction literature and provide organization format for writers/editors/artists within the genre. Qualifications for membership: at least 1 professional sale or other professional involvement within the field. Different levels of membership include: active—requires 3 professional short stories or 1 novel published; associate—requires 1 professional sale; or affiliate—which requires some other professional involvement such as artist, editor, librarian, bookseller, teacher, etc. Workshops/conferences: annual awards banquet, usually in April or May. Open to nonmembers. Publishes quarterly journal, the *SFWA Bulletin*. Sponsors Nebula Awards for best published science fiction or fantasy in the categories of novel, novella, novelette and short story. Awards trophy. Also presents the Damon Knight Memorial Grand Master Award for Lifetime Achievement, and the Andre Norton Award for Outstanding Young Adult Science Fiction or Fantasy Book of the Year.

SOCIETY OF CHILDREN'S BOOK WRITERS AND ILLUSTRATORS

4727 Wilshire Blvd #301, Los Angeles CA 90010. (323)782-1010. **Fax:** (323)782-1892. **E-mail:** scbwi@scbwi.org; membership@scbwi.org. **Website:** www.scbwi.org. Purpose of organization: to assist writers and illustrators working or interested in the field. Qualifications for membership: an interest in children's literature and illustration. Membership cost: $80/year. Plus one time $95 initiation fee. Different levels of membership include: P.A.L. membership—published by publisher listed in SCBWI Market Surveys; full membership—published authors/illustrators (includes self-published); associate membership—unpublished writers/illustrators. Holds 100 events (workshops/conferences) worldwide each year. National Conference open to nonmembers. Publishes bi-monthly magazine on writing and illustrating children's books. Sponsors annual awards and grants for writers and illustrators who are members. **Contact:** Stephen Mooser, president; Lin Oliver, executive director.

SOCIETY OF ILLUSTRATORS

128 E. 63rd St., New York NY 10065. (212)838-2560. **Fax:** (212)838-2561. **E-mail:** info@societyillustrators.org. **Website:** www.societyillustrators.org. "Our mission is to promote the art and appreciation of illustration, its history and evolving nature through exhibitions, lectures and education. Annual dues for nonresident illustrator members (those living more than 125 air miles from SI's headquarters): $300. Dues for resident illustrator members: $500 per year; resident associate members: $500. Artist members shall include those who make illustration their profession and earn at least 60% of their income from their illustration. Associate members are those who earn their living in the arts or who have made a substantial con-

tribution to the art of illustration. This includes art directors, art buyers, creative supervisors, instructors, publishers and like categories. The candidate must complete and sign the application form, which requires a brief biography, a listing of schools attended, other training and a résumé of his or her professional career. Candidates for illustrators membership, in addition to the above requirements, must submit examples of their work." **Contact:** Anelle Miller, executive director.

SOCIETY OF MIDLAND AUTHORS

P.O. Box 10419, Chicago IL 60610. **Website:** www.midlandauthors.com. Purpose of organization: create closer association among writers of the Middle West; stimulate creative literary effort; maintain collection of members' works; encourage interest in reading and literature by cooperating with other educational and cultural agencies. Qualifications for membership: membership by invitation only. Must be author or co-author of a book demonstrating literary style and published by a recognized publisher and be identified through residence with Illinois, Indiana, Iowa, Kansas, Michigan, Minnesota, Missouri, Nebraska, North Dakota, Ohio, South Dakota or Wisconsin. **Open to students** (if authors). Membership cost: $40/year dues. Different levels of membership include: regular—published book authors; associate, nonvoting—not published as above but having some connection with literature, such as librarians, teachers, publishers and editors. Program meetings held 5 times a year, featuring authors, publishers, editors or the like individually or on panels. Usually second Tuesday of October, November, February, March and April. Also holds annual awards dinner in May. Publishes a newsletter focusing on news of members and general items of interest to writers. Sponsors contests. "Annual awards in six categories, given at annual dinner in May. Monetary awards for books published that premiered professionally in previous calendar year. Send SASE to contact person for details." Categories include adult fiction, adult nonfiction, juvenile fiction, juvenile nonfiction, poetry, biography. No picture books. Contest open to nonmembers. **Contact:** Meg Tebo, president.

SOCIETY OF SOUTHWESTERN AUTHORS

Fax: (520)751-7877. **E-mail:** wporter202@aol.com. **Website:** www.ssa-az.org. Purpose of organization: to promote fellowship among professional and associate members of the writing profession, to recognize members' achievements, to stimulate further achievement, and to assist persons seeking to become professional writers. Qualifications for membership: Professional Membership: proof of publication of a book, articles, TV screenplay, etc. Associate Membership: proof of desire to write, and/or become a professional. Self-published authors may receive status of Professional Membership at the discretion of the board of directors. Membership cost: see website.

TEXT & ACADEMIC AUTHORS ASSOCIATION (TAA)

TAA, P.O. Box 367, Fountain City WI 54629. (727)563-0020. **E-mail:** info@taaonline.net. **Website:** www.taaonline.net. TAA's overall mission is "To support textbook and academic authors in the creation of top-quality educational and scholarly works that stimulate the love of learning and foster the pursuit of knowledge." Qualifications for membership: all authors and prospective authors are welcome. Membership cost: $20-$200. Workshops/conferences: June each year. Newsletter focuses on all areas of interest to textbook and academic authors.

THEATRE FOR YOUNG AUDIENCES/USA

c/o The Theatre School, 2350 N. Racine Ave., Chicago IL 60614. (773)325-7981. **Fax:** (773)325-7920. **E-mail:** info@tyausa.org. **Website:** tyausa.org. Purpose of organization: to promote theater for children and young people by linking professional theaters and artists together; sponsoring national, international and regional conferences and providing publications and information. Also serves as U.S. Center for International Association of the Theatre for Children and Young People. Different levels of memberships include: organizations, individuals, students, retirees, libraries. TYA Today includes original articles, reviews and works of criticism and theory, all of interest to theater practitioners (included with membership). Publishes *Marquee*, a directory that focuses on information on members in U.S.

VOLUNTEER LAWYERS FOR THE ARTS

1 E. 53rd St., 6th Floor, New York NY 10022. (212)319-2787, ext. 1. **Fax:** (212)752-6575. **E-mail:** vlany@vlany.org. **Website:** www.vlany.org. Purpose of organization: Volunteer Lawyers for the Arts is dedicated to providing free arts-related legal assistance to low-income artists and not-for-profit arts organizations in all creative fields. Over 1,000 attorneys in the New

York area donate their time through VLA to artists and arts organizations unable to afford legal counsel. Everyone is welcome to use VLA's Art Law Line, a legal hotline for any artist or arts organization needing quick answers to arts-related questions. VLA also provides clinics, seminars, and publications designed to educate artists on legal issues that affect their careers. Members receive discounts on publications and seminars as well as other benefits.

WRITERS' FEDERATION OF NEW BRUNSWICK

P.O. Box 4528, Rothesay NB E2E 5X2, Canada. (506)224-0364. **E-mail:** info@wfnb.ca. **Website:** www.wfnb.ca. Purpose of organization: "to promote New Brunswick writing and to help writers at all stages of their development." Qualifications for membership: interest in writing. Membership cost: $50 basic annual membership; $5, high school students; $50, institutional membership. Holds workshops/conferences. Publishes a newsletter with articles concerning the craft of writing, member news, contests, markets, workshops and conference listings. Sponsors annual literary competition, $20-$35 entry fee for members, $25-$40 for nonmembers. Categories: fiction, nonfiction, poetry, children's literature. **Contact:** Cathy Fynn, executive director.

WRITERS' FEDERATION OF NOVA SCOTIA

1113 Marginal Rd., Halifax NS B3H 4P7, Canada. (902)423-8116. **Fax:** (902)422-0881. **E-mail:** director@writers.ns.ca. **Website:** www.writers.ns.ca. Purpose of organization: "to foster creative writing and the profession of writing in Nova Scotia; to provide advice and assistance to writers at all stages of their careers; and to encourage greater public recognition of Nova Scotian writers and their achievements." Regional organization open to anybody who writes. Currently has 800+ members. Offerings include resource library with over 2,500 titles, promotional services, workshop series, annual festivals, mentorship program. Publishes *Eastword*, a bimonthly newsletter containing "a plethora of information on who's doing what; markets and contests; and current writing events and issues." Members and nationally known writers give readings that are open to the public. Additional information online. **Contact:** Marilyn Smulders, executive director.

WRITERS' GUILD OF ALBERTA

11759 Groat Rd. NW, Edmonton AB T5M 3K6, Canada. (780)422-8174. **E-mail:** mail@writersguild.ca. **Website:** writersguild.ca. Purpose of organization: to support, encourage and promote writers and writing, to safeguard the freedom to write and to read, and to advocate for the well-being of writers in Alberta. Currently has over 1,000 members. Offerings include retreats/conferences; monthly events; bimonthly magazine that includes articles on writing and a market section; weekly electronic bulletin with markets and event listings; and the Stephan G. Stephansson Award for Poetry (Alberta residents only). Holds workshops/conferences. Publishes a newsletter focusing on markets, competitions, contemporary issues related to the literary arts (writing, publishing, censorship, royalties etc.). Sponsors annual literary awards in 5 categories (novel, nonfiction, children's literature, poetry, drama). Awards include $1,500. Open to nonmembers. **Contact:** Carol Holmes.

CONFERENCES & WORKSHOPS

Writers and illustrators eager to expand their knowledge of the children's publishing industry should consider attending one of the many conferences and workshops held each year. Whether you're a novice or seasoned professional, conferences and workshops are great places to pick up information on a variety of topics and network with experts in the publishing industry, as well as with your peers.

Listings in this section provide details about what conference and workshop courses are offered, where and when they are held, and the costs. Some of the national writing and art organizations also offer regional workshops throughout the year. Write, call, or visit websites for information.

Members of the Society of Children's Book Writers and Illustrators (SCBWI) can find information on conferences in national and local SCBWI newsletters. Nonmembers may attend SCBWI events as well. (Some SCBWI regional events are listed in this section.) For information on SCBWI's annual national conferences and all of their regional events, check their website (scbwi.org) for a complete calendar of conferences and happenings.

AGENTS & EDITORS CONFERENCE

Writers' League of Texas, 611 S. Congress Ave., Suite 200 A-3, Austin TX 78704. (512)499-8914. **E-mail:** wlt@writersleague.org. **Website:** www.writersleague.org/38/conference. Annual conference held in summer. This standout conference gives each attendee the opportunity to become a publishing insider. Meet more than 25 top agents, editors, and industry professionals through one-on-one consultations and receptions. Get tips and strategies for revising and improving your manuscript from keynote speakers and presenters (including award-winning and best-selling writers). Discounted rates are available at the conference hotel.

COSTS Registration for the conference opens in November for WLT members and n December for everyone.

ALASKA CONFERENCE FOR WRITERS & ILLUSTRATORS

Alaska Writers Guild, SCBWI Alaska, & RWA Alaska, P.O. Box 670014, Chugiak AK 99567. **E-mail:** alaskawritersguild.awg@gmail.com. **Website:** alaskawritersguild.com. Join the Alaska Writers Guild, SCBWI Alaska, and Alaska RWA for this annual 2-day conference event! Optional Friday workshops and round tables, 1:1 Manuscript Reviews and pitches, and an all-day event of keynotes, panels, and breakout sessions. Topics range from writing 101 to advanced revisions, traditional to self published, and Kidlit to steamy romance. Plus everything in between!

ANNUAL SPRING POETRY FESTIVAL

City College, 160 Convent Ave., New York NY 10031. (212)650-6356. **Website:** www.ccny.cuny.edu/poetry/festival. Workshops geared to all levels. Open to students. Write for more information. Site: Theater B of Aaron Davis Hall.

ATLANTA WRITERS CONFERENCE

Atlanta Writers Club, Westin Atlanta Airport Hotel, 4736 Best Rd., Atlanta GA 30337. **E-mail:** awconference@gmail.com. **Website:** www.atlantawritersconference.com. **Contact:** George Weinstein. Annual conference held in spring and fall. Literary agents and editors are in attendance to take pitches and critique ms samples and query letters. Conference offers a writing craft workshop, instructional sessions with local authors, and separate question-and-answer panels with the agents and editors. Site: Westin Airport Atlanta Hotel. A block of rooms is reserved at the conference hotel. Booking instructions will be sent in the registration confirmation e-mail.

COSTS Manuscript critiques are $170 each (2 spots/waitlists maximum). Pitches are $70 each (2 spots/waitlists maximum). There's no charge for waitlists unless a spot opens. Query letter critiques are $70 (1 spot maximum). Other workshops and panels may also cost extra; see website. The "all activities" option is $620 and includes 2 manuscript critiques, 2 pitches, and 1 of each remaining activity.

ADDITIONAL INFORMATION A free shuttle runs between the airport and the hotel.

BIG SUR WRITING WORKSHOP

PO Box 256, Quincy MA 02171. (617)479-5774. **E-mail:** lisa@bigsurchildrenswriters.com. **Website:** https://www.bigsurchildrenswriters.com/. Annual workshop focusing on children's writing (picture books, middle-grade, and young adult). Held every spring in Cape Cod, MA and the first weekend in December at either the Big Sur Lodge in Pfeiffer State Park or the Hyatt. Cost for this workshop includes 4 mentoring sessions with agents, publishers and authors, panel discussions, meals and lodging. This event is helmed by the literary agents of the Andrea Brown Literary Agency. All attendees meet with at least 2 faculty members to have their work critiqued. Check website for conference dates. Due to the size of this workshop we want to be sure this is the right forum for you. Writers will need to submit material (1st three pages of MG or YA) or 1 PB, for consideration to attend the Workshop. When we are at the Lodge, shared cabins are reserved with a few single cabins available. At the Hyatt and Sea Crest Beach Hotel, you will be paired with another writer. Unless you prefer a single room. Single rooms do come with an additional cost

Full editorial schedule and much more available online.

COSTS Please check the website.

BOOKS-IN-PROGRESS CONFERENCE

Carnegie Center for Literacy and Learning, 251 W. Second St., Lexington KY 40507. (859)254-4175. **E-mail:** info@carnegiecenterlex.org. **Website:** carnegiecenterlex.org. This is an annual writing conference at the Carnegie Center for Literacy and Learning in Lexington, Kentucky. It typically happens in June. "Each conference will offer writing and publishing workshops and includes a keynote presentation." Literary agents are flown in to meet with writers and hear pitches. Website is updated several months prior to each annual event. See website for list of area hotels.

"Personal meetings with faculty (agents and editors) are only available to full conference participants. Limited slots available. Please choose only one agent; only one pitching session per participant."

CAPE COD WRITERS CENTER ANNUAL CONFERENCE

Cape Cod Writers Center, P.O. Box 408, Osterville MA 02655. (508)420-0200. **E-mail:** writers@capecodwriterscenter.org. **Website:** www.capecodwriterscenter.org. **Contact:** Nancy Rubin Stuart, executive director. Workshops in fiction, screenwriting, poetry, memoir, mystery, writing for children, writing for young adults, character, dialogue, setting and self-editing. Manuscript mentoring offered with editors and faculty. Resort and Conference Center of Hyannis, Massachusetts.

COSTS Costs vary, depending on the number of courses and membership. Registration also includes annual membership to the Cape Cod Writers Center's year-round programs.

CLARKSVILLE WRITERS CONFERENCE

(931)551-8870. **E-mail:** writers@artsandheritage.us. **Website:** www.artsandheritage.us/writers. **Contact:** Dr. Ellen Kanervo, Conference Chair. Valuable to writers and interesting to readers, our conference offers something for everyone. 16 writing workshops and presentations will be held on 2 days in August, on the campus of Austin Peay State University in Clarksville, Tennessee. Lunch and refreshments will be provided each day, and book signing will be available. A keynote banquet featuring Joshilyn Jackson, critically acclaimed novelist and recipient of the Sixth Annual "Patricia Winn Award for Southern Literature," will be held the evening of Thursday, August 12. In addition to Joshilyn Jackson, presenting authors for 2021 include Kelly J. Beard, Dana Chamblee Carpenter, Kiezha Smith Ferrell, Debra Coleman Jeter, Joy Jordan-Lake, Bobby Keel, Robert Mangeot, James Nihan, S.M. Williams and Renea Winchester.

COSTS We offer a complete package including all conference activities, as well as a la carte options. Discounted rates are available for early registration, which is postmarked on or before July 29. Late registration is postmarked between July 30 and August 5.

ADDITIONAL INFORMATION Professional editing consultations with Librum Artis Editorial Services editor Kiezha Smith Ferrell are available free of charge to anyone attending the conference presentations and workshops on Thursday, August 12, and/or Friday, August 13. Appointments may be made on a first-come, first-served basis at the time of registration.

COLORADO GOLD WRITERS CONFERENCE

Rocky Mountain Fiction Writers, P.O. Box 711, Monroe CO 81402. **E-mail:** conference@rmfw.org. **Website:** www.rmfw.org. **Contact:** Pamela Nowak and Susan Brooks. Annual conference held in September. Duration: 3 days. Average attendance: 400+. Themes include general fiction, genre fiction, contemporary romance, mystery, science fiction/fantasy, mainstream, young adult, screenwriting, short stories, and historical fiction, as well as marketing and career management. Past speakers have included Kate Moretti, James Scott Bell, Christopher Paolini, Diana Gabaldon, Sherry Thomas, Lori Rader-Day, Ann Hood, Robert J. Sawyer, Jeffery Deaver, William Kent Krueger, Margaret George, Jodi Thomas, Bernard Cornwell, Terry Brooks, Dorothy Cannell, Patricia Gardner Evans, Diane Mott Davidson, Constance O'Day, and Connie Willis. Approximately 16 acquiring editors and agents attend annually. Special rates will be available at conference hotel.

COSTS Available on website.

ADDITIONAL INFORMATION Pitch appointments available at no charge. Add-on options include agent and editor critiques, master classes, pitch coaching, query letter coaching, special critiques, and more.

CONFERENCE FOR WRITERS & ILLUSTRATORS OF CHILDREN'S BOOKS

Book Passage, 51 Tamal Vista Blvd., Corte Madera CA 94925. (415)927-0960, ext. 401. **E-mail:** plivingston@bookpassage.com. **Website:** www.bookpassage.com. Conference for writers and illustrators geared toward beginner and intermediate levels. Sessions cover such topics as the nuts and bolts of writing and illustrating, publisher's spotlight, market trends, developing characters, finding a voice, and the author–agent relationship.

COSTS Travel Writers and Photographers: New Attendee Price: $650; Alumni Price: $575; Mystery Writers: New Attendee Price: $575; Alumni Price: $500.

GOTHAM WRITERS WORKSHOP

writingclasses.com, 555 Eighth Ave., Suite 1402, New York NY 10018. (212)974-8377. **E-mail:** contact@gothamwriters.com. **Website:** www.writingclasses.com. Offers craft-oriented creative writing courses in general creative writing, fiction writing, screenwriting, nonfiction writing, article writing, stand-up comedy writing, humor writing, memoir writing, novel writing, children's book writing, playwriting, poetry, songwriting, mystery writing, science fiction writing, romance writing, television writing, article writing, travel writing, and business writing, as well as classes on freelancing, selling your screenplay, blogging, writing a nonfiction book proposal, and getting published. Also, the workshop offers a teen program, private instruction, and a mentoring program. Classes are held at various schools in New York as well as online. Online classes are held throughout the year. Agents and editors participate in some workshops.

ADDITIONAL INFORMATION See the website for courses, pricing, and instructors.

HAMPTON ROADS WRITERS CONFERENCE

Hampton Roads Writers, P.O. Box 56228, Virginia Beach VA 23456. (757)639-6146. **E-mail:** info@hamptonroadswriters.org. **Website:** hamptonroadswriters.org. Annual conference held in September. Virginia Beach-Norfolk Hotel & Conference Center. Workshops cover fiction, nonfiction, memoir, poetry, lyric writing, screenwriting, and the business of getting published. A bookshop, 3 free contests with cash prizes, free evening networking social, and many networking opportunities will be available. Multiple literary agents are in attendance each year to meet with writers and hear ten-minute pitches. Much more information available on the website.

COSTS Costs vary. There are discounts for members, for early bird registration, for students, and more.

HIGHLIGHTS FOUNDATION FOUNDERS WORKSHOPS

814 Court St., Honesdale PA 18431. (877)288-3410. **Fax:** (570)253-0179. **E-mail:** klbrown@highlightsfoundation.org. **Website:** highlightsfoundation.org. Workshops geared toward those interested in writing and illustrating for children, intermediate and advanced levels. Classes offered include: Writing Novels for Young Adults, Biography, Nonfiction Writing, Writing Historical Fiction, Wordplay: Writing Poetry for Children, Heart of the Novel, Nature Writing for Kids, Visual Art of the Picture Book, The Whole Novel Workshop, and more (see website for updated list). Workshops held near Honesdale, PA. Workshops limited to between 8 and 14 people. Cost of workshops range from $695 and up. Cost of workshop includes tuition, meals, conference supplies and private housing. Call for application and more information. **Contact:** Kent L. Brown, Jr. Offers more than 40 workshops per year. Duration: 3-7 days. Attendance: limited to 10-14. Genre-specific workshops and retreats on children's writing, including fiction, nonfiction, poetry, and promotions. "Our goal is to improve, over time, the quality of literature for children by educating future generations of children's authors." Retreat center location: Highlights Founders' home in Boyds Mills, Pennsylvania. Coordinates pickup at local airport. Offers overnight accommodations. Participants stay in guest cabins on the wooded grounds surrounding Highlights Founders' home adjacent to the house/conference center.

"Applications will be reviewed and accepted on a first-come, first-served basis. Applicants must demonstrate specific experience in the writing area of the workshop they are applying for—writing samples are required for many of the workshops."

COSTS Prices vary based on workshop. Check website for details.

ADDITIONAL INFORMATION Some workshops require pre-workshop assignment. Brochure available for SASE, by e-mail, on website, by phone, by fax. Accepts inquiries by phone, fax, e-mail, SASE. Editors attend conference.

HOUSTON WRITERS GUILD CONFERENCE

Writefest Houston, Houston Writers Guild, P.O. Box 42255, Houston TX 77242. (281)736-7168. **E-mail:** info@houstonwritersguild.org. **Website:** houstonwritersguild.org. This annual conference, organized by the Houston Writers Guild, happens in the spring and has concurrent sessions and tracks on the craft and business of writing. Each year, multiple agents are in attendance taking pitches from writers. The festival, Writefest, is now a weeklong event with various tracks of sessions during the weekday evenings as well as during the weekend of the festival. Literary journals as well as publishing companies and agents are featured.

COSTS Costs are different for members and non-members. Costs depend on how many days and events you sign up for.

ADDITIONAL INFORMATION Each year the conference takes place either the last weekend of April or the first weekend of May depending on venue availability. The Guild also hosts a conference the last weekend of September called Indiepalooza. This conference focuses on marketing and branding for all authors and specific presentations and sessions for authors who are self-publishing.

IOWA SUMMER WRITING FESTIVAL

The University of Iowa, 250 Continuing Education Facility, University of Iowa, Iowa City IA 52242. (319)335-4160. **Fax:** (319)335-4039. **E-mail:** iswfestival@uiowa.edu. **Website:** https://iowasummerwritingfestival.org/. Annual festival held in June and July. More than 100 workshops and more than 50 instructors. Workshops are 1 week or a weekend. Attendance is limited to 12 people per class, with more than 1,500 participants throughout the summer. Offers courses across the genres: novel, short story, poetry, essay, memoir, humor, travel, playwriting, screenwriting, writing for children, and women's writing. Held at the University of Iowa campus. Speakers have included Marvin Bell, Lan Samantha Chang, John Dalton, Hope Edelman, Katie Ford, Patricia Foster, Bret Anthony Johnston, and Barbara Robinette Moss. Accommodations available at area hotels. Information on overnight accommodations available by phone or on website.

COSTS See website for registration and conference fees.

ADDITIONAL INFORMATION Brochures are available in February. Inquire via e-mail or on website. "Register early. Classes fill quickly."

JAMES RIVER WRITERS CONFERENCE

2319 E. Broad St., Richmond VA 23223. (804)433-3790. **E-mail:** info@jamesriverwriters.org. **Website:** www.jamesriverwriters.org. **Contact:** Katharine Herndon. Nonprofit supporting writers in the Richmond, VA, area and beyond. Annual conference held in October. The event has master classes, agent pitching, critiques, panels, and more. Previous attending speakers include Ellen Oh, Margot Lee Shetterly, David Baldacci, Jeannette Walls, Adriana Trigiani, Jacqueline Woodson, and more.

The James River Writers conference is frequently recognized for its friendly atmosphere and southern hospitality.

COSTS Check website for updated pricing.

KENTUCKY WRITERS CONFERENCE

Southern Kentucky Book Fest, WKU South Campus, 2355 Nashville Rd., Bowling Green KY 42101. (270)745-4502. **E-mail:** sara.volpi@wku.edu. **Website:** www.sokybookfest.org. **Contact:** Sara Volpi. This event is entirely free to the public in April. Duration: 2 days. Part of the 2-day Southern Kentucky Book Fest. Authors who will be participating in the Book Fest on Saturday will give attendees at the conference the benefit of their wisdom on Friday (16 sessions available). For the first time, additional workshops will be offered on Saturday! Free workshops on a variety of writing topics will be presented. Sessions run for 75 minutes, and the day begins at 9 a.m. and ends at 3:30 p.m. The conference is open to anyone who would like to attend, including high school students, college students, teachers, and the general public. Registration will open online in February.

Since the event is free, interested attendees are asked to register in advance. Information on how to do so is on the website.

KINDLING WORDS EAST

Website: www.kindlingwords.org. Annual retreat held early in the year near Burlington, Vermont. 2020 dates: January 30-February 2. A retreat with 3 strands: writer, illustrator, and editor; professional level. Intensive workshops for each strand and an open schedule for conversations and networking. Registration limited to approximately 70. Hosted by the 4-star Inn at Essex (room and board extra). Participants must be published by a CCBC listed publisher, or if in publishing, occupy a professional position. Registration opens August 1 or as posted on the website and fills quickly. Check website to see if spaces are available, to sign up to be notified when registration opens each year, or for more information. Inquire via contact form on the website.

KINDLING WORDS WEST

Website: www.kindlingwords.org. Annual retreat specifically for children's book writers held in spring out west. Kindling Words West is an artist's colony-style week with workshops by gifted teachers followed by a working retreat. Participants gather just before dinner to have white-space discussions; evenings include fireside readings, star gazing, and songs. Participants must be published by CBC-recognized publisher.

LA JOLLA WRITERS CONFERENCE

P.O. Box 178122, San Diego CA 92177. **Website:** www.lajollawritersconference.com. Annual conference held in fall. Conference duration: 3 days. Attendance: 200 maximum. The LaJolla Writers Conference covers all genres in both fiction and nonfiction as well as the business of writing. "We take particular pride in educating our attendees on the business aspect of the book industry and have agents, editors, publishers, publicists, and distributors teach classes. There is unprecedented access to faculty. Our conference offers lecture sessions that run for 50 minutes and workshops that run for 110 minutes. Each block period is dedicated to either workshop or lecture-style classes with 6-8 classes on various topics available each block. For most workshop classes, you are encouraged to bring written work for review. Literary agents from prestigious agencies such as the Andrea Brown Literary Agency, the Dijkstra Agency, the McBride Agency, Full Circle Literary Group, the Zimmerman Literary Agency, the Van Haitsma Literary Agency, the Farris Literary Agency, and more have participated in the past, teaching workshops in which they are familiarized with attendee work. Late night and early bird sessions are also available. The conference creates a strong sense of community, and it has seen many of its attendees successfully published."

COSTS $395 for full conference registration (doesn't include lodging or breakfast).

LEAGUE OF UTAH WRITERS' ANNUAL WRITER'S CONFERENCES

Pre-Quill Conference and Quills Conference, 1042 East Fort Union Blvd. #443, Midvale UT 84047. **E-mail:** president@leagueofutahwriters.org. **Website:** https://www.leagueofutahwriters.com. **Contact:** John M. Olsen. The annual Pre-Quill Conference presented by League of Utah Writers in April includes a full day of workshops and presentations focused on improving your skills as a writer. Please join us! The Quills Conference is an Intermountain West professional writer's four-day event in August. Come learn from industry professionals what you need to be successful in writing and publishing. This event is packed with presentations on poetry, prose, and screenwriting and includes pitch sessions with both editors and agents. The conference is held at the beautiful University Marriott adjacent to the University of Utah campus. An awards banquet is held on Saturday. Exact dates vary year-to-year, so check www.leagueofutahwriters.com for schedules and guest announcements. We reserve a section of rooms at the Salt Lake City Marriott University Park for our Quills conference.

COSTS Spring Conference is $40 for members and $50 for general public. Quills Conference starts at $175 for members and $200 for general public. See website for details.

MIDWEST WRITERS WORKSHOP

Muncie IN 47306. (765)282-1055. **Website:** www.midwestwriters.org. **Contact:** Jama Kehoe Bigger, director. Writing conferences in east central Indiana, geared toward writers of all levels, including craft and business sessions. Topics include most genres. Faculty/speakers have included Angie Thomas, Becky Albertalli, Julie Murphy, Joyce Carol Oates, Marcus Sakey, William Kent Krueger, William Zinsser, John Gilstrap, Jane Friedman, and numerous best-selling mystery, literary fiction, young adult, and children's authors. Conferences with agent pitch sessions, ms evaluation, query letter critiques.

COSTS $155-425. Some meals included.

ADDITIONAL INFORMATION See website for more information. Keep in touch with the MWW at twitter.com/midwestwriters.

MISSOURI WRITERS' GUILD CONFERENCE

St. Louis MO **E-mail:** mwgconferenceinfo@gmail.com. **Website:** www.missouriwritersguild.org. **Contact:** Tricia Sanders, vice president/conference chair. Annual conference held in spring. Writer and illustrator workshops geared to all levels. Open to students. "Gives writers the opportunity to hear outstanding speakers and to receive information on marketing, research, and writing techniques." Agents, editors, and published authors in attendance.

ADDITIONAL INFORMATION The primary contact individual changes every year, because the conference chair changes every year. See the website for contact info.

MONTROSE CHRISTIAN WRITERS' CONFERENCE

Montrose Bible Conference, 218 Locust St., Montrose PA 18801. (570)278-1001 or (800)598-5030.

Fax: (570)278-3061. **E-mail:** mbc@montrosebible.org. **Website:** www.montrosebible.org. "Annual conference held in July. Offers workshops, editorial appointments, and professional critiques. We try to meet writing needs, for beginners and advanced, covering fiction, poetry, and writing for children. It is small enough to allow personal interaction between attendees and faculty. Speakers have included William Petersen, Mona Hodgson, Jim Watkins, and Bob Hostetler." Held in Montrose. Will meet planes in Binghamton, New York, and Scranton, Pennsylvania. On-site accommodations: room and board $360-490/conference, including food. RV court available.

COSTS Tuition is around $200.

ADDITIONAL INFORMATION "Writers can send work ahead of time and have it critiqued for a small fee." The attendees are usually church related. The writing has a Christian emphasis. Conference information available in April. For brochure, visit website, e-mail, or call. Accepts inquiries by phone or e-mail.

MOUNT HERMON CHRISTIAN WRITERS CONFERENCE

P.O. Box 413, Mount Hermon CA 95041. **E-mail:** info@mounthermon.org. **Website:** writers.mounthermon.org. **Contact:** Kathy Ide, director. Annual professional conference held over Palm Sunday weekend. Friday lunch through Tuesday breakfast. Preconference mentoring clinics run from Wednesday dinner till Friday lunch. Average attendance: 350-400. Sponsored by and held at the 440-acre Mount Hermon Christian Conference Center near San Jose, California, in the heart of the coastal redwoods. We are a broad-ranging conference for all areas of Christian writing, including fiction, nonfiction, sci-fi/fantasy, children's, teen, young adult, poetry, magazines, and devotional writing. This is a working, how-to conference, with Major Morning Tracks in several genres (including tracks for teen writers and professional authors), Morning Mentoring Clinics, and 40 or more afternoon workshops. Faculty-to-student ratio is about 1 to 6. Many of our more than 70 faculty members are literary agents, acquisitions editors, and representatives from major Christian publishing houses nationwide. Attendees can submit up to two manuscript samples to faculty members for review or critique for no additional charge. Ample opportunities for one-on-one appointments. Options include modern cabins (with full kitchens) or lodges (similar to hotel rooms), available in economy, standard, and deluxe. See website for pricing.

MUSE AND THE MARKETPLACE

Grub Street, P.O. Box 418, Boston MA 02476. (617)695-0075. **E-mail:** muse@grubstreet.org. **Website:** museandthemarketplace.com. GrubStreet's national conference for writers. Held in the spring, such as in early April. Conference duration: 3 days. Average attendance: 550. Dozens of agents are in attendance to meet writers and give direct one-on-one feedback on manuscript samples. The conference has sessions on all aspects of writing. Boston Park Plaza Hotel.

The Muse and the Marketplace is designed to give aspiring writers a better understanding of the craft of writing fiction and nonfiction, to prepare them for the changing world of publishing and promotion, and to create opportunities for meaningful networking. On all 3 days, prominent and nationally recognized, established and emerging authors lead sessions on the craft of writing—the "muse" side of things—while editors, literary agents, publicists, and other industry professionals lead sessions on the business side—the "marketplace."

NORTH CAROLINA WRITERS' NETWORK FALL CONFERENCE

P.O. Box 21591, Winston-Salem NC 27120. (336)293-8844. **E-mail:** mail@ncwriters.org. **Website:** www.ncwriters.org. Annual Fall Conference the first weekend of November rotates throughout the state each year. Average attendance: 225. This organization hosts 2 conferences: 1 in the spring and 1 in the fall. Each conference is a weekend full of workshops, panels, book signings, and readings (including open mic). There will be a keynote speaker, a variety of sessions on the craft and business of writing, and an opportunity to meet with agents and editors.

COSTS Approximately $260 (all days, with meals).

NORTHERN COLORADO WRITERS CONFERENCE

2770 Arapahoe Rd., Suite 132-1110, Lafayette CO 80026. (575)430-7543. **E-mail:** info@northerncoloradowriters.com. **Website:** www.northerncoloradowriters.com. Annual conference held in Fort Collins. Duration: 2-3 days. The conference features a variety of speakers, agents, and editors. There are workshops and presentations on fiction, nonfiction, screenwriting, children's books, marketing, magazine writing, staying inspired, and more. Previous agents who have attended and taken pitches from writers include Jessica Regel, Kristen Nelson, Jennifer March Soloway, Andrea Brown, Ken Sherman, Jessica Faust, Gordon Warnock, and Taylor Martindale. Each conference features more than 30 workshops from which to choose from. Previous keynotes include Chuck Wendig, Andrew McCarthy, and Stephen J. Cannell. Conference hotel offers rooms at a discounted rate.

COSTS Prices vary depending on a number of factors. See website for details.

ODYSSEY WRITING WORKSHOP

P.O. Box 75, Mont Vernon NH 03057. (603)673-6234. **Website:** www.odysseyworkshop.org. **Contact:** Jeanne Cavelos. Saint Anselm College, 100 Saint Anselm Dr., Manchester NH 03102. Annual workshop held in June (through July). Conference duration: 6 weeks. Average attendance: 15. A workshop for fantasy, science fiction, and horror writers that combines an intensive learning and writing experience with in-depth feedback on students' mss. Held on the campus of Saint Anselm College in Manchester, New Hampshire. Speakers have included George R.R. Martin, Elizabeth Hand, Jane Yolen, Catherynne M. Valente, Holly Black, and Dan Simmons. Most students stay in Saint Anselm College apartments to get the full Odyssey experience. Each apartment has 2 bedrooms and can house a total of 2 to 3 people (with each bedroom holding 1 or 2 students). The apartments are equipped with kitchens, so you may buy and prepare your own food, which is a money-saving option, or you may eat at the college's Coffee Shop or Dining Hall. Wireless internet access and use of laundry facilities are provided at no cost. Students with cars will receive a campus parking permit.

Since its founding in 1996, the Odyssey Writing Workshop has become one of the most highly respected workshops for writers of fantasy, science fiction, and horror in the world. Top authors, editors and agents have served as guests at Odyssey. Fifty-nine percent of graduates have gone on to be professionally published. Among Odyssey's graduates are *New York Times* bestsellers, Amazon bestsellers, and award winners.

COSTS $2,060 tuition, $195 textbook, $892 housing (double room), $1,784 housing (single room), $40 application fee, $600 food (approximate), $1,000 optional processing fee to receive college credit.

ADDITIONAL INFORMATION Students must apply and include a writing sample. Application deadline: April 1. Students' works are critiqued throughout the 6 weeks. Workshop information available in October. For brochure/guidelines, send SASE, e-mail, visit website, or call.

OKLAHOMA WRITERS' FEDERATION, INC. ANNUAL CONFERENCE

Website: www.owfi.org. Annual conference held first weekend in May, just outside Oklahoma City. Writer workshops geared toward all levels. "The goal of the conference is to create good stories with strong bones. We will be exploring cultural writing and cultural sensitivity in writing." Several literary agents are in attendance each year to meet with writers and hear pitches.

COSTS Costs vary depending on when registrants sign up. Cost includes awards banquet and famous author banquet. 3 extra sessions are available for an extra fee. Visit the event website for more information and a complete faculty list.

OUTDOOR WRITERS ASSOCIATION OF AMERICA ANNUAL CONFERENCE

2814 Brooks St., Box 442, Missoula MT 59801. (406)728-7434. **E-mail:** info@owaa.org. **Website:** owaa.org. **Contact:** Jessica Seitz, conference and membership coordinator. Outdoor communicator workshops geared toward all levels. Annual 3-day conference includes craft improvement seminars and newsmaker sessions. Site: Little Rock, Arkansas. Cost includes attendance at all workshops and meals.

COSTS Full 3 Days-$249; 2 Days-$200; One Day-$100.

OZARK CREATIVE WRITERS, INC. CONFERENCE

207 W. Van Buren St., Eureka Springs AR 72632. (336)407-9098. **E-mail:** ozarkcreativewriters@ozarkcreativewriters.com. **Website:** www.ozarkcreativewriters.com. The annual event is held in October at the Inn of the Ozarks, in the resort town of Eureka Springs, Arkansas. Approximately 200 writers attend each year; many also enter the creative writing competitions. Open to professional and amateur writers, workshops are geared toward all levels and all forms of the creative process and literary arts; sessions sometimes also include songwriting. Includes

presentations by best-selling authors, editors, and agents. Offering writing competitions in all genres.

A full list of sessions and speakers is online. The conference usually has agents and/or editors in attendance to meet with writers.

COSTS Full Conference Early Bird Registration: $185; after August 25: $248. Conference-Only Registration: $140; after August 25: $150.

PACIFIC COAST CHILDREN'S WRITERS WHOLE-NOVEL WORKSHOP: FOR ADULTS AND TEENS

P.O. Box 244, Aptos CA 95001. **Website:** www.childrenswritersworkshop.com. Annual seminar since 2003. **Dates:** Oct. weekends, see website. **Content:** Character-driven upper middle-grade and young adult novels. Team-taught master classes (open clinic manuscript critiques) explore topics such as "Story Architecture and Arcs." Collegial; interactive. Reading peer manuscripts before faculty-led discussions maximizes learning. Close contact with top-notch faculty. In a concurrent workshop, teen writers give adults target-reader feedback while honing their craft. **Enrollment:** 16 maximum. For best options, submit e-application by May (dates on website); registration is open until filled. Enrollees often land book deals with faculty.

COSTS Visit website for tiered fees (includes lodging, meals), schedule, and more. E-mail Director Nancy Sondel via the contact form.

PENNWRITERS CONFERENCE

P.O. Box 685, Dalton PA 18414. **E-mail:** info@pennwriters.org. **Website:** pennwriters.org. The mission of Pennwriters, Inc. is to help writers of all levels, from the novice to the award-winning and multi-published, improve and succeed in their craft. The annual Pennwriters conference is held every year in May in Pennsylvania, switching between locations—Lancaster in even numbered years and Pittsburgh in odd numbered years. Literary agents are in attendance to meet with writers. Costs vary. Pennwriters members in good standing get a slightly reduced rate.

As the official writing organization of Pennsylvania, Pennwriters has 8 different areas with smaller writing groups that meet. Each of these areas sometimes has their own, smaller event during the year in addition to the annual writing conference.

ADDITIONAL INFORMATION Sponsors contest. Published authors judge fiction in various categories. Agent/editor appointments are available on a first-come, first-served basis.

PHILADELPHIA WRITERS' CONFERENCE

Website: pwcwriters.org. Annual conference held in June. Duration: 3 days. Average attendance: 160-200. Conference covers many forms of writing: novel, short story, genre fiction, nonfiction book, magazine writing, blogging, juvenile, poetry. See website for details. Hotel may offer discount for early registration.

Offers 14 workshops, usually 4 seminars, several "manuscript rap" sessions, a Friday Roundtable Forum Buffet with speaker, and the Saturday Annual Awards Banquet with speaker. Attendees may submit mss in advance for criticism by the workshop leaders and are eligible to submit entries in more than 10 contest categories. Cash prizes and certificates are given to first and second place winners, plus full tuition for the following year's conference to first place winners.

ADDITIONAL INFORMATION Accepts inquiries by e-mail. Agents and editors attend the conference. Many questions are answered online.

PIKES PEAK WRITERS CONFERENCE

Pikes Peak Writers, P.O. Box 64273, Colorado Springs CO 80962. (719)244-6220. **E-mail:** registrar@pikespeakwriters.com. **Website:** www.pikespeakwriters.com/ppwc. Annual conference held in April. Conference duration: 3 days. Average attendance: 300. Workshops, presentations, and panels focus on writing and publishing mainstream and genre fiction (romance, science fiction/fantasy, suspense/thrillers, action/adventure, mysteries, children's, young adult). Agents and editors are available for meetings with attendees on Saturday. Speakers have included Jeff Lindsay, Rachel Caine, and Kevin J. Anderson. Marriott Colorado Springs holds a block of rooms at a special rate for attendees until late March.

COSTS $405-465 (includes all 7 meals).

ADDITIONAL INFORMATION Readings with critiques are available on Friday afternoon. Registration forms are online; brochures are available in January. Send inquiries via e-mail.

PNWA WRITERS CONFERENCE

Writers' Cottage, 317 NW Gilman Blvd. Suite 8, Issaquah WA 98027. (425)673-2665. **E-mail:** pnwa@pnwa.org. **Website:** www.pnwa.org. **Contact:** Pam Binder. Annual conference. Duration: 5 days. Average attendance: 400. Attendees have the chance to meet agents and editors, learn craft from authors, and uncover marketing secrets. Speakers have included J.A. Jance, Sheree Bykofsky, Kimberley Cameron, Jennie Dunham, Donald Maass, Jandy Nelson, Robert Dugoni, and Terry Brooks.

COSTS See website for costs.

SAN FRANCISCO WRITERS CONFERENCE

SFWC Main Office, P.O. Box 326, Oakley CA 94561. (925)420-6223. **E-mail:** barbara@sfwriters.org. **Website:** sfwriters.org. **Contact:** Barbara Santos, marketing director. Annual conference held President's Day weekend in February. Average attendance: 700. "More than 100 top authors, respected literary agents, and major publishing houses are at the event so attendees can make face-to-face contact with all the right people. Writers of nonfiction, fiction, poetry, and specialty writing (children's books, lifestyle books, etc.) will all benefit from the event. There are important sessions on marketing, self-publishing, technology, and trends in the publishing industry. Plus, there's an optional session called Speed Dating with Agents AND individual meetings where attendees can meet with literary agents, editors and book marketing professionals. Past speakers have included Walter Mosley, Jane Smiley, Debbie Macomber, Clive Cussler, Guy Kawasaki, Jennifer Crusie, R.L. Stine, Lisa See, Steve Berry, and Jacquelyn Mitchard. Bestselling authors, agents and several editors from traditional publishing houses participate each year, and many will be available for meetings with attendees. The Hyatt Regency San Francisco on the Embarcadero offers a discounted SFWC rate (based on availability. Use Code on the SFWC website or call directly: (415) 788-1234. Across from the Ferry Building in San Francisco, the hotel is located so that everyone arriving at the Oakland or San Francisco airport can take the BART to the Embarcadero exit, directly in front of the hotel.

Keynoters will be announced in late September. Attendees can take educational sessions and network with the 100+ presenters from the publishing world. Free editorial and PR consults, exhibitor hall, pitching and networking opportunities available throughout the four-day event. Also several free sessions offered to the public. See website for details or sign up for the SFWC Newsletter for updates.

COSTS Full registration is $895 with a $795 early bird registration rate until December 31.

ADDITIONAL INFORMATION "Present yourself in a professional manner, and the contacts you will make will be invaluable to your writing career. Fliers, details, and registration information are online."

SANTA BARBARA WRITERS CONFERENCE

27 W. Anapamu St., Suite 305, Santa Barbara CA 93101. (805)568-1516. **E-mail:** info@sbwriters.com. **Website:** www.sbwriters.com. Annual conference held in June. Average attendance: 200. 30+ writing workshops, panels, speakers, agents, and fellow word crafters. Covers fiction, nonfiction, journalism, memoir, poetry, playwriting, screenwriting, travel writing, young adult, children's literature, humor, and marketing. Speakers have included Ray Bradbury, William Styron, Eudora Welty, James Michener, Sue Grafton, Charles M. Schulz, Clive Cussler, Fannie Flagg, Elmore Leonard, and T.C. Boyle. Agents will appear on a panel; in addition, there will be an agents and editors day that allows writers to pitch their projects in one-on-one meetings. Hyatt Santa Barbara.

COSTS $150 for single-day; $699 for full conference.

ADDITIONAL INFORMATION Register online or contact for brochure and registration forms.

SCBWI—AUSTIN CONFERENCE

E-mail: austin@scbwi.org. **Website:** austin.scbwi.org. **Contact:** Samantha Clark, regional advisor. Annual conference features a faculty of published authors and illustrators. Our conference has expanded this year. The schedule includes two keynotes; a publishing panel; 16 breakout sessions on writing, illustrating and professional development; intensives on picture books, novels and illustration; along with critiques, pitches, portfolio showcase, cookies and more. Editors and agents are in attendance to meet with writers. The schedule consists of keynotes and breakout sessions with tracks for writing (picture book and novel), illustrating, and professional development.

COSTS Costs vary for members, students and nonmembers, and discounted early-bird pricing is available. Visit website for full pricing options.

SCBWI—CENTRAL-COASTAL CALIFORNIA; FALL CONFERENCE

E-mail: cencal@scbwi.org. **Website:** cencal.scbwi.org. Annual children's writing conference held in October. Geared to all levels. Speakers include editors, authors, illustrators, and agents. Fiction and nonfiction picture books, middle-grade, and young adult novels, and magazine submissions addressed. There is an annual writing contest in all genres plus illustration display. For fees and other information, e-mail or visit website.

SCBWI—COLORADO/WYOMING (ROCKY MOUNTAIN); EVENTS

E-mail: rmc@scbwi.org. **Website:** www.rmc.scbwi.org. SCBWI Rocky Mountain chapter (Colorado/Wyoming) offers special events, schmoozes, meetings, and conferences throughout the year. Major events: Fall Conference (annual, September); Summer Retreat, "Big Sur in the Rockies" (bi- and tri-annual). More info on website.

SCBWI—EASTERN NEW YORK; FALLING LEAVES MASTER CLASS RETREAT

Silver Bay NY. **E-mail:** easternny@scbwi.org. **Website:** easternny.scbwi.org. We'll return next year for a weekend focused on picture books! The dates will be announced soon. Annual master class retreat hosted by SCBWI Eastern New York and held in November in Silver Bay on Lake George. Holds ms and portfolio critiques, question-and-answer and speaker sessions, intensives, and more, with respected authors and editors. Theme varies each year between picture books, novels, and nonfiction. See website for more information.

SCBWI—MID-ATLANTIC; ANNUAL FALL CONFERENCE

P.O. Box 3215, Reston VA 20195-1215. **E-mail:** midatlantic@scbwi.org. **Website:** midatlantic.scbwi.org/. **Contact:** Valerie Patterson and Erin Teagan, co-regional advisors. For updates and details, visit website. Registration limited to 250. Conference fills quickly. Includes continental breakfast and boxed lunch. Optional craft-focused workshops and individual consultations with conference faculty are available for additional fees.

This conference takes place in October. Previous conferences have been held in Sterling, Virginia.

SCBWI—NEW ENGLAND; WHISPERING PINES WRITERS' RETREATS

E-mail: whisperingpinesretreat@yahoo.com. **Website:** newengland.scbwi.org; www.whisperingpines-retreat.org. Three-day retreat (with stays overnight). A working retreat. No frills. No faculty. Just focus. Come alone or bring your critique group. Write. Illustrate. Outline. Draft. Revise. Outstanding accommodations and delicious food. Let's get down to work! Registration details coming soon. Offers the opportunity to work intimately with professionals in an idyllic setting. Attendees will work with others who are committed to quality children's literature in small groups and will benefit from a 30-minute one-on-one critique with a mentor. Also includes mentors' presentations and an intimate question-and-answer session, Team Kid Lit Jeopardy with prizes, and more. Retreat limited to 32 full-time participants.

COSTS $175-615 depending on day/overnight attendee, participation level, member/non-member, etc. Please see website for details.

SCBWI—NEW JERSEY; ANNUAL SUMMER CONFERENCE

Website: newjersey.scbwi.org. This weekend conference is held in the summer. Highlights include multiple one-on-one critiques; "how to" workshops for every level; first page sessions; agent pitches; and interaction with the faculty of editors, agents, art director, and authors. On Friday, attendees can sign up for writing intensives or register for illustrators' day with the art directors. Published authors attending the conference can sign up to participate in the bookfair to sell and autograph their books; illustrators have the opportunity to display their artwork. Attendees have the option to participate in group critiques after dinner on Saturday evening and attend a mix-and-mingle with the faculty on Friday night. Meals are included with the cost of admission. Conference is known for its high ratio of faculty to attendees and interaction opportunities.

SCBWI WINTER CONFERENCE ON WRITING AND ILLUSTRATING FOR CHILDREN

4727 Wilshire Blvd #301, Los Angeles CA 90010. (323)782-1010. **E-mail:** info@scbwi.org. **Website:** www.scbwi.org. Average attendance: 1,000. Conference is to promote writing and illustrating for children (picture books, middle-grade, and young adult) and to give participants an opportunity to network with professionals. Covers financial planning for writers, marketing your book, art exhibitions, and more. The winter conference is held in Manhattan; the summer conference in Los Angeles.

COSTS See website for current cost and conference information; $525-675.

ADDITIONAL INFORMATION SCBWI also holds an annual summer conference in August in Los Angeles.

SOUTH CAROLINA WRITERS WORKSHOP

1219 Taylor St., Columbia SC 29201. **E-mail:** scwritersassociationpresident@gmail.com. **Website:** www.myscwa.org. Conference held in October at the Metropolitan Conference Center in Columbia. Held almost every year. Conference duration: 3 days. Features critique sessions, open mic readings, and presentations from agents and editors. More than 50 different workshops for writers to choose from, dealing with all subjects of writing craft, writing business, getting an agent, and more. Agents will be in attendance.

SPACE COAST WRITERS GUILD ANNUAL CONFERENCE

P.O. Box 262, Melbourne FL 32902. **E-mail:** stilley@scwg.org. **Website:** www.scwg.org. Conference held along the east coast of central Florida in the last weekend of January, though necessarily every year. Check website for up-to-date information. Conference duration: 2 days. Average attendance: 150+. This conference is hosted in Florida and features a variety of presenters on all topics. Critiques are available for a price, and agents in attendance will take pitches from writers. Previous presenters have included Debra Dixon, Davis Bunn (writer), Ellen Pepus (agent), Jennifer Crusie, Chuck Sambuchino, Madeline Smoot, Mike Resnick, Christina York, Ben Bova, and Elizabeth Sinclair. The conference is hosted in a beachside hotel, with special room rates available.

COSTS Check website for current pricing.

STEAMBOAT SPRINGS WRITERS CONFERENCE

A Day For Writers, Steamboat Springs Arts Council, Eleanor Bliss Center for the Arts at the Depot, P.O. Box 774284, Steamboat Springs CO 80477. (970)879-9008. **E-mail:** info@steamboatwriters.com. **Website:** www.steamboatwriters.com. **Contact:** Barbara Sparks. Other address: 1001 13th St., Steamboat Springs CO 80487.

"A Day for Writers" emphasizes instruction within the seminar format. Novices and polished professionals benefit from a unique feature that offers one workshop at a time. All participants engage together, adding to the informal and intimate community feeling. It's perfect for fiction and nonfiction writers seeking a combination of inspiration, craft techniques and camaraderie. Check www.Steamboatwriters.com for information about upcoming events.

SURREY INTERNATIONAL WRITERS' CONFERENCE

SiWC, 151-10090 152 St., Suite 544, Surrey BC V3R 8X8, Canada. **E-mail:** kathychung@siwc.ca. **Website:** www.siwc.ca. **Contact:** Kathy Chung, proposals contact and conference coordinator. Annual professional development writing conference outside Vancouver, Canada, held every October. Writing workshops geared toward beginner, intermediate, and advanced levels. When in person, SiWC offers more than 80 workshops and panels, on all topics and genres, plus pre-conference master classes. Blue Pencil and agent/editor pitch sessions included. Different conference price packages available. Check the conference website for more information. This event has many literary agents in attendance taking pitches. Annual fiction writing contest open to all with $1,000 prize for first place. Conference registration opens in early June every year. Register very early to avoid disappointment as the conference is likely to sell out quickly.

TEXAS WRITING RETREAT

Navasota TX. **E-mail:** paultcuclis@gmail.com. **Website:** www.texaswritingretreat.com. **Contact:** Paul Cuclis, coordinator. The Texas Writing Retreat is an intimate event with a limited number of attendees. Held on a private residence ranch an hour outside of Houston, the retreat has an agent and editor in attendance teaching. All attendees get to pitch the attending agent. Meals, excursions, and amenities are included. This is a unique event that combines craft sessions, business sessions, time for writing, relaxation, and more. The retreat is not held every year; it's best to check the website.

COSTS Costs vary per event. There are different pricing options for those staying on-site versus commuters.

UNICORN WRITERS CONFERENCE

PO Box 176, Redding CT 06876. (203)938-7405. **E-mail:** unicornwritersconference@gmail.com. **Website:** www.unicornwritersconference.com. **Contact:** Jan L. Kardys, chair. For all the information about our guest agents, editors, and speakers, manuscript review sessions, and workshops please take a look through our site. This writers conference draws upon its close proximity to New York and pulls in over 40 literary agents and 15 major New York editors to pitch each year. There are manuscript review sessions (40 pages equals 30 minutes with an agent/editor), query/manuscript review sessions, and 6 different workshops every hour. Cost: $325, includes all workshops and 3 meals. Held at Reid Castle, Purchase, New York. Directions available on event website.

"The forty pages for manuscript reviews are read in advance by your selected agents/editors, but follow the submission guidelines on the website. Check the genre chart for each agent and editor before you make your selection."

ADDITIONAL INFORMATION The first self-published authors will be featured on the website, and the bookstore will sell their books at the event.

WESLEYAN WRITERS CONFERENCE

Wesleyan University, 294 High St., Room 207, Middletown CT 06459. (860)685-3604. **Fax:** (860)685-2441. **E-mail:** agreene@wesleyan.edu. **Website:** www.wesleyan.edu/writing/conference. **Contact:** Anne Greene, director. Annual conference held in June. Average attendance: 100. Focuses on the novel, fiction techniques, short stories, poetry, screenwriting, nonfiction, literary journalism, memoir, mixed media work, and publishing. The conference is held on the campus of Wesleyan University, in the hills overlooking the Connecticut River. Features a faculty of award-winning writers, seminars, and readings of new fiction, poetry, nonfiction, and mixed media forms—as well as guest lectures on a range of topics including publishing. Both new and experienced writers are welcome. Participants may attend seminars in all genres. Speakers have included Esmond Harmsworth (Zachary Shuster Harmsworth), Daniel Mandel (Sanford J. Greenburger Associates), Amy Williams (ICM and Collins McCormick), and many others. Agents will be speaking and available for meetings with attendees. Participants are often successful in finding agents and publishers for their mss. Wesleyan participants are also frequently featured in the anthology *Best New American Voices*. Meals are provided on campus. Lodging is available on campus or in town.

ADDITIONAL INFORMATION Ms critiques are available but not required.

WILLAMETTE WRITERS CONFERENCE

5331 SW Macadam Ave., Suite 258, PMB 215, Portland OR 97239. (971) 200-5382. **E-mail:** conf.chair@willamettewriters.org. **Website:** willamettewriters.com/wwcon/. Over 700 attendees will gather for a weekend that's all about writers and writing. Meet industry professionals, learn from world-class faculty, and keynotes, and connect with a community of writers. 50th consecutive year Willamette Writers has hosted one of the largest and most-beloved writing conferences in North America. We have worked tirelessly to reach our golden anniversary, providing a wide array of opportunities for writers to build their craft, meet successful professionals, and become part of a dynamic group of writers from all walks of life.

COSTS Pricing schedule available online. Conference price includes breakfast, lunch, and an appetizer reception on Friday and Saturday. Workshops on Friday, Saturday, and Sunday are included—first come, first serve. No additional registration is required for workshops. You must sign up at an additional cost to participate in Master Classes and Sunday Intensives.

WINTER POETRY & PROSE GETAWAY

Murphy Writing of Stockton University, 30 Front Street, Hammonton NJ 08037. (609)626-3594. **E-mail:** info@wintergetaway.com. **Website:** www.stockton.edu/wintergetaway; stockton.edu/murphywriting. **Contact:** Amanda Murphy, Director. Annual January conference at the Jersey Shore. Join us at the historic Seaview Hotel near Atlantic City. Enjoy challenging and supportive workshops, insightful feedback and an encouraging community. Choose from workshops in poetry, fiction, nonfiction, memoir, and more. Room packages at the historic Stockton Seaview Hotel are available.

"At most conferences, writers listen to talks and panels and sit in sessions where previously written work is discussed. At the Getaway, they write. Most workshops are limited to 10 or fewer participants. By spending the entire weekend in one workshop, participants will venture deeper into their writing, making more progress than they thought possible."

COSTS See website or call for past fee information. Scholarships available.

ADDITIONAL INFORMATION Previous faculty has included Julianna Baggott, Christian Bauman, Laure-Anne Bosselaar, Kurt Brown, Mark Doty (National Book Award winner), Stephen Dunn (Pulitzer Prize winner), Dorianne Laux, Carol Plum-Ucci, James Richardson, Mimi Schwartz, Terese Svoboda, and more.

WOMEN WRITING THE WEST

PO Box 1886, Durango, CO 81302. **E-mail:** wwwconference2021@gmail.com. **Website:** www.womenwritingthewest.org. **Contact:** Conference Chair: Kathy Sechrist. Women Writing the West is a nonprofit association of writers, editors, publishers, agents, booksellers, and other professionals writing and promoting the "Women's West." As such, they elevate literature that authentically portrays women and girls in the North American West. In addition, the organization provides support, encouragement, and inspiration to anyone writing about any facet of women's western experiences. Membership is open to all interested persons worldwide, including students. WWW membership also allows the choice of participation in our marketing marvel, the annual WWW Catalog of Author's Books. An annual conference is held every fall. The event covers research, writing techniques, multiple genres, marketing/promotion, and more. Agents and editors share ideas in a panel format as well as meeting one-on-one for pitch sessions with attendees. Conference location changes each year. The blog and social media outlets publish current WWW activities, features market research, and shares articles of interest pertaining to North American West literature and member news. WWW annually sponsors The WILLA Literary Awards, which is given in several categories for outstanding literature featuring women's or girls' stories set in the West. The Winner of a WILLA literary Award receives a cash award and a trophy at the annual conference. This competition is open to non-members. Visit www.womenwritingthewest.org.

COSTS See website. Discounts available for members.

WRITEAWAYS

E-mail: writeawaysinfo@gmail.com. **Website:** https://www.writeaways.com. **Contact:** Mimi Herman. "We created Writeaways workshops to help you find the time you need to write. We provide writing instruction, fabulous food and company in beautiful places, and an inspiring place for you to take a writing vacation with your muse. We pamper you while providing rigorous, supportive assistance to help you become the best writer possible. We have week-long workshops in France, Italy, and New Mexico." France: Chateau du Pin, near Champtocé-sur Loire (18 miles west of Angers). Italy: Villas Cini and Casanova, near Bucine, between Siena and Arezzo. New Mexico: Abiquiu.

COSTS France and Italy: $2,450 single room, $2,100 shared rooms. The Grand Tour (France and Italy): $4,400 each single room, $4,000 each shared room.

WRITE-BY-THE-LAKE WRITER'S WORKSHOP & RETREAT

21 N. Park St., 7th Floor, Madison WI 53715. (608)262-3447. **E-mail:** christine.desmet@wisc.edu. **Website:** www.dcs.wisc.edu/lsa/writing. **Contact:** Christine DeSmet, director. Open to all writers and students; 12 or more workshops for all levels. Includes classes for full novel critique and one master class for 50 pages. Usually held the third week of June on the University of Wisconsin-Madison campus. Registration limited to 15 each section; fewer in master classes. Writing facilities available; computer labs, wifi in all buildings and on the outdoor lakeside terrace. E-mail for more information. "Registration opens every January for following June."

COSTS $425 before May 20; $475 after that. Additional cost for master classes and college credits. Cost includes instruction, welcome luncheon, pastry/coffee each day, open mic, guest speaker presentations, one-on-one meetings with the Writing Doctor.

WRITE IN THE HARBOR

Website: continuingedtacoma.com/writeintheharbor. 3993 Hunt St., Gig Harbor WA 98335. (253)460-2424. **Website:** continuingedtacoma.com/writeintheharbor. Annual conference held in fall. Offers workshops geared toward beginner, intermediate, advanced, and professional levels. Includes welcome reception, keynote speaker, and several presenters. Registration limited to 150. Early bird enrollment opens July 1. See website for more information. Annual conference held in fall.

COSTS See website.

WRITE ON THE SOUND

WOTS, City of Edmonds Arts Commission, Frances Anderson Center, 700 Main St., Edmonds WA 98020. (425)771-0228. **E-mail:** wots@edmondswa.gov. **Web-**

site: www.writeonthesound.com. Small, affordable annual conference focused on the craft of writing. Held the first weekend in October. Conference duration: 3 days. Average attendance: 275. Features over 30 presenters, keynote, writing contest, ms critique appts, round table discussions, book signing reception, onsite bookstore, and opportunity to network with faculty and attendees. Edmonds is located just north of Seattle on the Puget Sound. Best Western Plus/Edmonds Harbor Inn is a conference partner.

Past attendee says, "I came away from every session with ideas to incorporate into my own writer's toolbox. The energy was wonderful because everyone was there for a single purpose: to make the most of a weekend for writers, whatever the level of expertise. I can't thank all the organizers, presenters, and volunteers enough for a wonderful experience."

COSTS $90-300 (not including optional fees).

ADDITIONAL INFORMATION Schedule posted on website late spring/early summer. Registration opens mid-July. Attendees are required to select the sessions when they register. Wait lists for conference and manuscript appointments are available.

WRITE-TO-PUBLISH CONFERENCE

WordPro Communication Services, 9118 W. Elmwood Dr., Suite 1G, Niles IL 60714. (847)296-3964. **E-mail:** lin@writetopublish.com. **Website:** www.writetopublish.com. **Contact:** Lin Johnson, director. Annual conference. Average attendance: 175. Conference is focused on the Christian market and includes classes for writers at all levels and appointments with editors and agents. Open to high school students. Site: Wheaton College, Wheaton, Illinois (Chicago area). [This is not a function of Wheaton College.] Campus residence hall rooms available. See the website for current information and costs.

COSTS See the website for current costs.

ADDITIONAL INFORMATION Conference information available in late January or early February. For details, visit website, or e-mail brochure@writetopublish.com. Accepts inquiries by e-mail, phone.

WRITING AND ILLUSTRATING FOR YOUNG READERS CONFERENCE

WIFYR, 1480 E. 9400 S., Sandy UT 84093. **E-mail:** staff@wifyr.com. **Website:** www.wifyr.com. Annual workshop held in June. 5-day workshop designed for people who want to write for children or teenagers. Participants focus on a single market during daily 4-hour morning writing workshops: picture books, book-length fiction (novels), fantasy/science fiction, nonfiction, mystery, beginning writing or illustration. Afternoon workshop sessions feature a variety of topics of interest to writers for all youth ages. See website for workshop cost. Afternoon-only registration available; participants may attend these sessions all 5 days. See website for cost. Attendance at the Thursday evening banquet is included in addition to the afternoon mingle, plenary, and breakout sessions. **Contact:** Carol Lynch Williams. Annual workshop held in June. Duration: 5 days. Average attendance: more than 100. Learn how to write, illustrate, and publish in the children's and young adult markets. Beginning and advanced writers and illustrators are tutored in a small-group workshop setting by published authors and artists and receive instruction from and network with editors, major publishing house representatives, and literary agents. Afternoon attendees get to hear practical writing and publishing tips from published authors, literary agents, and editors. Site: Waterford School in Sandy, UT. Speakers have included John Cusick, Stephen Fraser, Alyson Heller, David Farland, and Ruth Katcher. A block of rooms is available at the Best Western Cotton Tree Inn in Sandy, UT, at a discounted rate. This rate is good as long as there are available rooms.

COSTS Varies from $99 - $1,200.

ADDITIONAL INFORMATION There is an online form to contact this event.

WYOMING WRITERS ANNUAL CONFERENCE

3615 Campstool Rd., Cheyenne WY 82007. **E-mail:** wyowriters@gmail.com. **Website:** wyowriters.org. This is a three-day conference for writers of all genres, with attendees generally coming from Wyoming and neighboring states. Each year multiple published authors, editors, and literary agents come to meet with attendees, hold educational sessions, and take pitches. Open reading sessions, peer critique, and keynote speakers highlight the event. Each year the conference location moves to different Wyoming locales, so that attendees can experience the true flavor of this smaller western conference.

CONTESTS, AWARDS & GRANTS

Publication is not the only way to get your work recognized. Contests and awards can also be great ways to gain recognition in the industry. Grants, offered by organizations like the Society of Children's Book Writers and Illustrators (SCBWI), offer monetary recognition to writers, giving them more financial freedom as they work on projects.

When considering contests or applying for grants, be sure to study guidelines and requirements. Regard entry deadlines as gospel and follow the rules to the letter.

Note that some contests require nominations. For published authors and illustrators, competitions provide an excellent way to promote your work. Your publisher may not be aware of local competitions such as state-sponsored awards—if your book is eligible, have the appropriate person at your publishing company nominate or enter your work for consideration.

To select potential contests and grants, read through the listings that interest you, then send for more information about the types of written or illustrated material considered and other important details. A number of contests offer information through websites given in their listings.

JANE ADDAMS CHILDREN'S BOOK AWARD

Jane Addams Peace Association, 777 United Nations Plaza, 6th Floor, New York NY 10017. (212)682-8830. **E-mail:** info@janeaddamspeace.org. **Website:** www.janeaddamspeace.org. **Contact:** Heather Palmer, Co-Chair. The Jane Addams Children's Book Award annually recognizes children's books, published the preceding year, that effectively promote the cause of peace, social justice, world community, and the equality of the sexes and all races, as well as meeting conventional standards for excellence. Books eligible for this award may be fiction, poetry, or nonfiction. Books may be any length. Entries should be suitable for ages 2-12. See website for specific details on guidelines and required book themes. Deadline: December 31. Judged by a national committee of WILPF members concerned with children's books and their social values is responsible for making the choices each year.

ALCUIN SOCIETY AWARDS FOR EXCELLENCE IN BOOK DESIGN IN CANADA

The Alcuin Society, P.O. Box 3216, Stn. Terminal, Vancouver BC V6B 3X8, Canada. **E-mail:** awards@alcuinsociety.com; info@alcuinsociety.com. **Website:** www.alcuinsociety.com. **Contact:** Leah Gordon. The Alcuin Society Awards for Excellence in Book Design in Canada is the only national competition for book design in Canada. Winners are selected from books designed and published in Canada. Awards are presented annually at appropriate ceremonies held each year. Winning books are exhibited nationally and internationally at the Tokyo, Frankfurt, and Leipzig Book Fairs, and are Canada's entries in the international competition in Leipzig, "Best Book Design from all over the World," in the following spring. Submit previously published material from the year before the award's call for entries. Submissions made by the publisher (Canadian), author (any), or designer (Canadian). Deadline: varies annually. Prizes: 1st, 2nd, 3rd, and Honourable Mention in each category (at the discretion of the judges). Judged by professionals and those experienced in the field of book design.

AMERICAS AWARD

Website: http://claspprograms.org/americasaward. **Contact:** Denise Woltering. The Américas Award encourages and commends authors, illustrators, and publishers who produce quality children's and young adult books that portray Latin America, the Caribbean, or Latinos in the United States. Up to 2 awards (for primary and secondary reading levels) are given in recognition of US published works of fiction, poetry, folklore, or selected nonfiction (from picture books to works for young adults). The award winners and commended titles are selected for their (1) distinctive literary quality; (2) cultural contextualization; (3) exceptional integration of text, illustration and design; and (4) potential for classroom use. To nominate a copyright title from the previous year, publishers are invited to submit review copies to the committee members listed on the website. Publishers should send 8 copies of the nominated book. Deadline: January 4. Prize: $500, plaque and a formal presentation at the Library of Congress, Washington DC.

HANS CHRISTIAN ANDERSEN AWARD

Nonnenweg 12, Postfach Basel CH-4009, Switzerland. **E-mail:** liz.page@ibby.org; ibby@ibby.org. **Website:** www.ibby.org. **Contact:** Liz Page, Director. The Hans Christian Andersen Award, awarded every two years by the International Board on Books for Young People (IBBY), is the highest international recognition given to an author and an illustrator of children's books. The Author's Award has been given since 1956, the Illustrator's Award since 1966. Her Majesty Queen Margrethe II of Denmark is the Patron of the Hans Christian Andersen Awards. The awards are presented at the biennial congresses of IBBY. Awarded to an author and to an illustrator, living at the time of the nomination, who by the outstanding value of their work are judged to have made a lasting contribution to literature for children and young people. The complete works of the author and of the illustrator will be taken into consideration in awarding the medal, which will be accompanied by a diploma. Candidates are nominated by National Sections of IBBY in good standing. Prize: Awards medals according to literary and artistic criteria. Judged by the Hans Christian Andersen International Jury.

MARILYN BAILLIE PICTURE BOOK AWARD

The Canadian Children's Book Centre, 40 Orchard View Blvd., Suite 217, Toronto ON M4R 1B9, Canada. (416)975-0010, ext. 222. **Fax:** (416)975-8970. **E-mail:** meghan@bookcentre.ca. **Website:** www.bookcentre.ca. **Contact:** Meghan Howe. The Marilyn Baillie Picture Book Award honors excellence in the illustrated picture book format. To be eligible, the book must be an original work in English, aimed at children ages 3-8, written and illustrated by Canadians. Books published in Canada or abroad are eligible. Eligible genres include fiction, nonfiction and poetry. Books must be published between Jan. 1 and Dec. 31 of the previous calendar year. New editions or re-issues of previously published books are not eligible for submission. Send 5 copies of title along with a completed submission form. Deadline: mid-December annually. Prize: $20,000.

MILDRED L. BATCHELDER AWARD

Association for Library Service to Children, Division of the American Library Association, 50 E. Huron St., Chicago IL 60611-2795. (800)545-2433. **Fax:** (312)280-5271. **Website:** www.ala.org/alsc/awardsgrants/bookmedia/batchelderaward. The Batchelder Award is given to the most outstanding children's book originally published in a language other than English in a country other than the United States, and subsequently translated into English for publication in the US. Visit website for terms and criteria of award. The purpose of the award, a citation to an American publisher, is to encourage international exchange of quality children's books by recognizing US publishers of such books in translation. Deadline: December 31.

JOHN AND PATRICIA BEATTY AWARD

E-mail: tbronzan@sonoma.lib.ca.us. **Website:** http://www.cla-net.org/?page=113. **Contact:** Tiffany Bronzan, award chair. The California Library Association's John and Patricia Beatty Award, sponsored by Baker & Taylor, honors the author of a distinguished book for children or young adults that best promotes an awareness of California and its people. Must be a children's or young adult books published in the previous year, set in California, and highlight California's cultural heritage or future. Send title suggestiosn to the committee members. Deadline: January 31. Prize: $500 and an engraved plaque. Judged by a committee of CLA members, who select the winning title from books published in the United States during the preceding year.

THE GEOFFREY BILSON AWARD FOR HISTORICAL FICTION FOR YOUNG PEOPLE

The Canadian Children's Book Centre, 40 Orchard View Blvd., Suite 217, Toronto ON M4R 1B9, Canada. (416)975-0010, ext. 222. **Fax:** (416)975-8970. **Website:** www.bookcentre.ca. **Contact:** Meghan Howe. Awarded annually to reward excellence in the writing of an outstanding work of historical fiction for young readers, by a Canadian author, published between Jan 1 and Dec 31 of the previous calendar year. Open to Canadian citizens and/or permanent residents of Canada. Books must be published between January 1 and December 31 of the previous year. Books must be first foreign or first Canadian editions. Autobiographies are not eligible. Jury members will consider the following: historical setting and accuracy; strong character and plot development; well-told, original story; and stability of book for its intended age group. Send 5 copies of the title along with a completed submission form. Deadline: January 15th, annually. Prize: $5,000.

THE IRMA S. AND JAMES H. BLACK AWARD

Bank Street College of Education, 610 W. 112th St., New York NY 10025-1898. (212)875-4458. **E-mail:** kfreda@bankstreet.edu. **Website:** http://bankstreet.edu/center-childrens-literature/irma-black-award/. **Contact:** Kristin Freda. Award give to an outstanding book for young children—a book in which text and illustrations are inseparable, each enhancing and enlarging on the other to produce a singular whole. Entries must have been published during the previous calendar year. Publishers submit books. Submit only 1 copy of each book. Does not accept unpublished mss. Deadline: December 6. A scroll with the recipient's name, and a gold seal designed by Maurice Sendak. Judged by a committee of older children and children's literature professionals. Final judges are first-, second-, and third-grade classes at a number of cooperating schools.

BOROONDARA LITERARY AWARDS

City of Boroondara, 340 Camberwell Rd., Camberwell VIC 3124, Australia. **E-mail:** bla@boroondara.vic.gov.au. **Website:** www.boroondara.vic.gov.au/literary-awards. Contest for unpublished work in 2 categories: Open Short Story from residents of Australia (1,500-3,000 words); and Young Writers who live, go to school or work in the City of Boroondara: 5th-6th grade (Junior), 7th-9th grade (Middle), and 10th-12th grade (Senior), prose and poetry on any theme. Deadline: 5pm on the last Friday of August. Prizes: Young Writers, Junior: 1st Place: $300; 2nd Place: $200; 3rd Place: $100. Young Writers, Middle: 1st Place: $450; 2nd Place: $300; 3rd Place: $150 and Senior: 1st Place: $600; 2nd Place: $400; 3rd Place:

$200. Open Short Story: 1st Place: $1,500; 2nd Place: $1000; 3rd Place $500.

BOSTON GLOBE-HORN BOOK AWARDS

The Boston Globe, Horn Book, Inc., 300 The Fenway, Palace Road Building, Suite P-311, Boston MA 02115. (617)278-0225. **Fax:** (617)278-6062. **E-mail:** bghb@hbook.com; info@hbook.com. **Website:** www.hbook.com/bghb/. Offered annually for excellence in literature for children and young adults (published June 1-May 31). Categories: picture book, fiction and poetry, nonfiction. Judges may also name up to 2 honor books in each category. Books must be published in the US, but may be written or illustrated by citizens of any country. The Horn Book Magazine publishes speeches given at awards ceremonies. Guidelines for submitting books online. Submit a book directly to each of the judges. See www.hbook.com/bghb-submissions for details on submitting, as well as contest guidelines. Deadline: May 15. Prize: $500 and an engraved silver bowl; honor-book recipients receive an engraved silver plate. Judged by a panel of 3 judges selected each year.

ANN CONNOR BRIMER BOOK AWARD

(902)490-2742. **Website:** www.atlanticbookawards.ca/. **Contact:** Laura Carter, Atlantic Book Awards Festival Coordinator. In 1990, the Nova Scotia Library Association established the Ann Connor Brimer Award for writers residing in Atlantic Canada who have made an outstanding contribution to writing for Atlantic Candian young people. Author must be alive and residing in Atlantic Canada at time of nomination. Book intended for youth up to the age of 15. Book in print and readily available. Fiction or nonfiction (except textbooks). Book must have been published within the previous year. November 1. Prize: $2,000. Two shortlisted titles: $250 each.

CALIFORNIA YOUNG PLAYWRIGHTS CONTEST

Playwrights Project, 3675 Ruffin Rd., Suite 330, San Diego CA 92123-1870. (858)384-2970. **Fax:** (858)384-2974. **E-mail:** write@playwrightsproject.org. **Website:** www.playwrightsproject.org/programs/contest/. **Contact:** Cecelia Kouma, Executive Director. The California Young Playwrights Contest is open to Californians under age 19. Every year, young playwrights submit original scripts to the contest. Every writer who requests feedback receives an individualized script critique. Selected writers win script readings or full professional productions in Plays by Young Writers festival. Distinguished artists from major theatres select festival scripts and write comments to the playwrights. Submissions are required to be unpublished and not produced professionally. Submissions made by the author. SASE for contest rules and entry form. Scripts must be a minimum of 10 standard typewritten pages. Scripts will *not* be returned. If requested, entrants receive detailed evaluation letter. Guidelines available online. Deadline: June 1. Prize: Scripts will be produced in spring at a professional theatre in San Diego. Writers submitting scripts of 10 or more pages receive a detailed script evaluation letter upon request. Judged by professionals in the theater community, a committee of 5-7; changes somewhat each year.

CASCADE WRITING CONTEST & AWARDS

Oregon Christian Writers, 1075 Willow Lake Road N., Keizer OR 97303. **E-mail:** cascade@oregonchristianwriters.org. **Website:** http://oregonchristianwriters.org/. **Contact:** Linda L. Kruschke. The Cascade Awards are presented at the annual Oregon Christian Writers Summer Conference (held at the Red Lion on the River in Portland, Oregon, each August) attended by national editors, agents, and professional authors. The contest is open for both published and unpublished works in the following categories: contemporary fiction book, historical fiction book, speculative fiction book, nonfiction book, memoir book, young adult/middle grade fiction book, young adult/middle grade nonfiction book, children's chapter book and picture book (fiction and nonfiction), poetry, devotional, article, column, story, or blog post. Two additional special Cascade Awards are presented each year: the Trailblazer Award to a writer who has distinguished him/herself in the field of Christian writing; and a Writer of Promise Award for a writer who demonstrates unusual promise in the field of Christian writing. For a full list of categories, entry rules, and scoring elements, visit website. Guidelines and rules available on the website. Entry forms will be available on the first day for entry. Annual multi-genre competition to encourage both published and emerging writers in the field of Christian writing. Deadline: March 15. Submissions period begins February 15. Prize: Award certificate and pin presented at the Cascade Awards ceremony during the Oregon Christian Writers Annual Summer Conference. Finalists are listed in the conference notebook and winners are listed online. Cascade Trophies are awarded to the recipients of the Trailblazer and Writer of Promise Awards. Judged by published authors, editors, librarians, and retail book store owners and employees. Final judging by editors, agents, and published authors from the Christian publishing industry.

CHILDREN'S AFRICANA BOOK AWARD

Outreach Council of the African Studies Association, c/o Rutgers University-Livingston campus, 54 Joyce Kilmer Ave., Piscataway NJ 08854. (703)549-8208; (301)585-9136. **E-mail:** africaaccess@aol.com; Harriet@AfricaAccessReview.org. **Website:** www.africaaccessreview.org. **Contact:** Brenda Randolph, Chairperson. The Children's Africana Book Awards are presented annually to the authors and illustrators of the best books on Africa for children and young people published or distributed in the U.S. The awards were created by the Outreach Council of the African Studies Association (ASA) to dispel stereotypes and encourage the publication and use of accurate, balanced children's materials about Africa. The awards are presented in 2 categories: Young Children and Older Readers. Entries must have been published in the calendar year previous to the award. Work submitted for awards must be suitable for children ages 4-18; a significant portion of book's content must be about Africa; must by copyrighted in the calendar year prior to award year; and must be published or distributed in the US. Books should be suitable for children and young adults, ages 4-18. A significant portion of the book's content should be about Africa. Deadline: December 31 of the year book is published. Judged by African Studies and Children's Literature scholars. Nominated titles are read by committee members and reviewed by external African Studies scholars with specialized academic training.

CHILDREN'S BOOK GUILD AWARD FOR NONFICTION

E-mail: theguild@childrensbookguild.org. **Website:** www.childrensbookguild.org. Annual award. "One doesn't enter. One is selected. Our jury annually selects one author for the award." Honors an author or illustrator whose total work has contributed significantly to the quality of nonfiction for children. Prize: Cash and an engraved crystal paperweight. Judged by a jury of Children's Book Guild specialists, authors, and illustrators.

CHILDREN'S LITERATURE LEGACY AWARD

50 E. Huron, Chicago IL 60611. (800)545-2433. **Fax:** (312)280-5271. **E-mail:** alscawards@ala.org. **Website:** http://www.ala.org/alsc/awardsgrants/bookmedia/clla. The Children's Literature Legacy Award honors an author or illustrator whose books, published in the United States, have made, over a period of years, a significant and lasting contribution to children's literature through books that demonstrate integrity and respect for all children's lives and experiences. The candidates must be nominated by ALSC members. Medal presented at Newbery/Caldecott/Legacy banquet during annual conference. Judging by Legacy Award Selection Committee.

CHRISTIAN BOOK AWARD® PROGRAM

ECPA/Christian Book Award®, 5801 S. McClintock Dr, Suite 104, Tempe AZ 85283. (480)966-3998. **Fax:** (480)966-1944. **E-mail:** info@ecpa.org. **Website:** www.ecpa.org. **Contact:** Cindy Carter. The Evangelical Christian Publishers Association (ECPA) recognizes quality and encourages excellence by presenting the ECPA Christian Book Awards® (formerly known as Gold Medallion) each year. Categories include Christian Living, Biography & Memoir, Faith & Culture, Children, Young People's Literature, Devotion & Gift, Bibles, Bible Reference Works, Bible Study, Ministry Resources, Audio and New Author. All entries must be evangelical in nature and submitted through an ECPA member publisher. Books must have been published in the calendar year prior to the award. Publishing companies submitting entries must be ECPA members in good standing. See website for details. The Christian Book Award® recognizes the highest quality in Christian books and is among the oldest and most prestigious awards program in Christian publishing. Submission period runs September 1-30. Judged by experts, authors, and retailers with years of experience in their field.

Book entries are submitted by ECPA member publishers according to criteria including date of publication and category.

THE CITY OF VANCOUVER BOOK AWARD

Cultural Services Dept., Woodward's Heritage Building, 111 W. Hastings St., Suite 501, Vancouver BC V6B 1H4, Canada. (604)871-6634. **Fax:** (604)871-6005. **E-mail:** marnie.rice@vancouver.ca; culture@vancouver.ca. **Website:** https://vancouver.ca/people-programs/

city-of-vancouver-book-award.aspx. The annual City of Vancouver Book Award recognizes authors of excellence of any genre that reflect Vancouver's unique character, rich diversity and culture, history and residents. The book must exhibit excellence in one or more of the following areas: content, illustration, design, format. The book must not be copyrighted prior to the previous year. Submit four copies of book. See website for details and guidelines. Deadline: May 22. Prize: $3,000. Judged by an independent jury.

COLORADO BOOK AWARDS

Colorado Humanities & Center for the Book, 7935 E. Prentice Ave., Suite 450, Greenwood Village CO 80111. (303)894-7951. **Fax:** (303)864-9361. **E-mail:** bess@coloradohumanities.org. **Website:** www.coloradohumanities.org. **Contact:** Bess Maher. An annual program that celebrates the accomplishments of Colorado's outstanding authors, editors, illustrators, and photographers. Awards are presented in at least ten categories including anthology/collection, biography, children's, creative nonfiction, fiction, history, nonfiction, pictorial, poetry, and young adult. To be eligible for a Colorado Book Award, a primary contributor to the book must be a Colorado writer, editor, illustrator, or photographer. Current Colorado residents are eligible, as are individuals engaged in ongoing literary work in the state and authors whose personal history, identity, or literary work reflect a strong Colorado influence. Authors not currently Colorado residents who feel their work is inspired by or connected to Colorado should submit a letter with his/her entry describing the connection. Deadline: January 9.

CWW ANNUAL WISCONSIN WRITERS AWARDS

Council for Wisconsin Writers, 4964 Gilkeson Rd, Waunakee WI 53597. **E-mail:** karlahuston@gmail.com. **Website:** www.wiswriters.org. **Contact:** Geoff Gilpin, president and annual awards co-chair; Karla Huston, secretary and annual awards co-chair; Sylvia Cavanaugh, annual awards co-chair; Edward Schultz, annual awards co-chair, Erik Richardson, annual awards co-chair. Offered annually for work published by Wisconsin writers during the previous calendar year. Nine awards: Major Achievement (presented in alternate years); short fiction; short nonfiction; nonfiction book; poetry book; fiction book; children's literature; Lorine Niedecker Poetry Award; Christopher Latham Sholes Award for Outstanding Service to Wisconsin Writers (presented in alternate years); Essay Award for Young Writers. Open to Wisconsin residents. Entries may be submitted via postal mail only. See website for guidelines and entry forms. Deadline: January 31. Submissions open on November 1. Prizes: First place prizes: $500. Honorable mentions: $50. List of judges available on website.

MARGARET A. EDWARDS AWARD

50 East Huron St., Chicago IL 60611-2795. (312)280-4390 or (800)545-2433. **Fax:** (312)280-5276. **E-mail:** yalsa@ala.org. **Website:** www.ala.org/yalsa/edwards. **Contact:** Nichole O'Connor. Annual award administered by the Young Adult Library Services Association (YALSA) of the American Library Association (ALA) and sponsored by *School Library Journal* magazine. Awarded to an author whose book or books, over a period of time, have been accepted by young adults as an authentic voice that continues to illuminate their experiences and emotions, giving insight into their lives. The book or books should enable them to understand themselves, the world in which they live, and their relationship with others and with society. The book or books must be in print at the time of the nomination. Submissions must be previously published no less than 5 years prior to the first meeting of the current Margaret A. Edwards Award Committee at Midwinter Meeting. Nomination form is available on the YALSA website. Deadline: December 1. Prize: $2,000. Judged by members of the Young Adult Library Services Association.

SHUBERT FENDRICH MEMORIAL PLAYWRITING CONTEST

Pioneer Drama Service, Inc., Pioneer Drama Service, Inc. - Att'n: Submissions Editor, P.O. Box 4267, Englewood CO 80155-4267. (303)779-4035. **Fax:** (303)779-4315. **E-mail:** editors@pioneerdrama.com; submissions@pioneerdrama.com. **Website:** www.pioneerdrama.com. **Contact:** Brian Taylor, Acquisitions Editor. Annual competition that encourages the development of quality theatrical material for educational, community, and children's theatre markets. Previously unpublished submissions only. Only considers mss with a running time between 20-120 minutes. Open to all writers not currently published by Pioneer Drama Service. Guidelines available online. No entry fee. Cover letter, SASE for return of ms, and proof of production or staged reading must accompany all submissions. Deadline: Ongoing contest; a winner is selected by June 1 each year from all submissions received the previous year. Prize: $1,000 royalty advance in addition to publication. Judged by editors.

THE NORMA FLECK AWARD FOR CANADIAN CHILDREN'S NONFICTION

The Canadian Children's Book Centre, Norma Fleck Award for Canadian Children's Non-Fiction, c/o The Canadian Children's Book Centre, Suite 217, 40 Orchard View Blvd., Toronto ON M4R 1B9, Canada. (416)975-0010 ext. 222. **Fax:** (416)975-8970. **E-mail:** meghan@bookcentre.ca. **Website:** www.bookcentre.ca. **Contact:** Meghan Howe. The Norma Fleck Award was established by the Fleck Family Foundation to recognize and raise the profile of exceptional nonfiction books for children. Offered annually for books published between January 1 and December 31 of the previous calendar year. Open to Canadian citizens and/or permanent residents. Books must be first foreign or first Canadian editions. Nonfiction books in the following categories are eligible: culture and the arts, science, biography, history, geography, reference, sports, activities, and pastimes. Deadline: January 15. Prize: $10,000. The award will go to the author unless 40% or more of the text area is composed of original illustrations, in which case the award will be divided equally between author and illustrator.

DON FREEMAN ILLUSTRATOR GRANTS

6363 Wilshire Blvd. Suite 425, Los Angeles CA 90048. (323)782-1010. **Fax:** (323)782-1010. **E-mail:** grants@scbwi.org; sarahbaker@scbwi.org. **Website:** www.scbwi.org. **Contact:** Sarah Baker. The grant-in-aid is available to both full and associate members of the SCBWI who, as artists, seriously intend to make picture books their chief contribution to the field of children's literature. Applications and prepared materials are available in October. Grant awarded and announced in August. SASE for award rules and entry forms. SASE for return of entries. Enables picture-book artists to further their understanding, training, and work in the picture-book genre. Deadline: March 31. Submission period begins March 1. Prize: Two grants of $1,000 each awarded annually. One grant to a published illustrator and one to a pre-published illustrator.

THEODOR SEUSS GEISEL AWARD

Association for Library Service to Children, Division of the American Library Association, 50 E. Huron, Chicago IL 60611. (800)545-2433. **Fax:** (312)280-5271. **E-mail:** alscawards@ala.org. **Website:** http://www.ala.org/alsc/awardsgrants/bookmedia/geiselaward. The Theodor Seuss Geisel Award is given annually to the author(s) and illustrator(s) of the most distinguished American book for beginning readers published in English in the United States during the preceding year. The award is to recognize the author(s) and illustrator(s) who demonstrate great creativity and imagination in his/her/their literary and artistic achievements to engage children in reading. Terms and criteria for the award are listed on the website. Entry will not be returned. Deadline: December 31. Prize: Medal, given at awards ceremony during the ALA Annual Conference.

GOLDEN KITE AWARDS

Society of Children's Book Writers and Illustrators (SCBWI), SCBWI Golden Kite Awards, 8271 Beverly Blvd., Los Angeles CA 90048-4515. (323)782-1010. **Fax:** (323)782-1892. **E-mail:** bonniebader@scbwi.org. **Website:** www.scbwi.org. **Contact:** Bonnie Bader, Golden Kite Coordinator. Given annually to recognize excellence in children's literature in 4 categories: fiction, nonfiction, picture-book text, and picture-book illustration. Books submitted must be published in the previous calendar year. Both individuals and publishers may submit. Submit 4 copies of book. Submit to one category only, except in the case of picture books. Must be a current member of the SCBWI. Prize: One Golden Kite Award Winner and at least one Honor Book will be chosen per category. Winners and Honorees will receive a commemorative poster, also sent to publishers, bookstores, libraries, and schools; a press release; and an announcement on the SCBWI website and on SCBWI Social Networks.

GOVERNOR GENERAL'S LITERARY AWARDS

Canada Council for the Arts, 150 Elgin St., P.O. Box 1047, Ottawa ON K1P 5V8, Canada. (800)263-5588, ext. 5573 or (613)566-4414, ext. 5573. **Website:** ggbooks.ca. The Canada Council for the Arts provides a wide range of grants and services to professional Canadian artists and art organizations in dance, media arts, music, theatre, writing, publishing, and the visual arts. Books must be first-edition literary trade books written, translated, or illustrated by Canadian citizens or permanent residents of Canada and published in Canada or abroad in the previous year. In the case of translation, the original work must also be a Canadian-authored title. For complete eligibility criteria, deadlines, and submission procedures, please visit the website at www.canadacouncil.ca. The Governor General's Literary Awards are given annually for the best English-language and French-language work in each of 7 categories, including fiction, nonfiction, poetry, drama, young people's literature (text), young people's literature (illustrated books), and translation. Deadline: Depends on the book's publication date. See website for details. Prize: Each GG winner receives $25,000. Non-winning finalists receive $1,000. Publishers of the winning titles receive a $3,000 grant for promotional purposes. Evaluated by fellow authors, translators, and illustrators. For each category, a jury makes the final selection.

GUGGENHEIM FELLOWSHIPS

John Simon Guggenheim Memorial Foundation, John Simon Guggenheim Memorial Foundation, 90 Park Ave., New York NY 10016. (212)687-4470. **E-mail:** fellowships@gf.org. **Website:** www.gf.org. Often characterized as "midcareer" awards, Guggenheim Fellowships are intended for men and women who have already demonstrated exceptional capacity for productive scholarship or exceptional creative ability in the arts. Fellowships are awarded through two annual competitions: one open to citizens and permanent residents of the United States and Canada, and the other open to citizens and permanent residents of Latin America and the Caribbean. Candidates must apply to the Guggenheim Foundation in order to be considered in either of these competitions. The Foundation receives between 3,500 and 4,000 applications each year. Although no one who applies is guaranteed success in the competition, there is no prescreening: all applications are reviewed. Approximately 200 Fellowships are awarded each year. Deadline: September 17.

HACKNEY LITERARY AWARDS

Hackney Literary Awards, 4650 Old Looney Mill Rd., Birmingham AL 35243. **E-mail:** info@hackneyliteraryawards.org. **Website:** www.hackneyliteraryawards.org. **Contact:** Myra Crawford, PhD, Executive Director. Offered annually for unpublished novels, short stories (maximum 5,000 words), and poetry (50 line limit). Guidelines on website. Deadline: September 30 (novels), November 30 (short stories and poetry). Prize: $5,000 in annual prizes for poetry and short fiction ($2,500 national and $2,500 state level). 1st Place: $600; 2nd Place: $400; 3rd Place: $250; plus $5,000 for an unpublished novel. Competition winners will be announced on the website each March.

AURAND HARRIS MEMORIAL PLAYWRITING AWARD

The New England Theatre Conference, Inc., 215 Knob Hill Dr., Hamden CT 06518. **Fax:** (203)288-5938. **E-mail:** mail@netconline.org. **Website:** www.netconline.org. Offered annually for an unpublished full-length play for young audiences. Guidelines available online or for SASE. Open to all. All scripts submitted by email *only*. Deadline: May 1.

ERIC HOFFER AWARD

Hopewell Publications, LLC, P.O. Box 11, Titusville NJ 08560-0011. **Fax:** (609)964-1718. **E-mail:** info@hopepubs.com. **Website:** www.hofferaward.com. **Contact:** Dawn Shows, EHA Coordinator. Annual contest for previously published books. Recognizes excellence in independent publishing in many unique categories that cover every genre in publishing: Art (titles capture the experience, execution, or demonstration of the arts); Poetry (all styles); Chapbook (40 pages or less, artistic assembly); Children (titles for young children); Middle Reader; Young Adult (titles aimed at the juvenile and teen markets); Commercial Fiction (genre-specific fiction); General Fiction (nongenre-specific fiction and literature); Historical Fiction; Mystery/Crime; Romance; Science Fiction/Fantasy; Short Story/Anthology; Spiritual Fiction; Business (titles with application to today's business environment and emerging trends); Culture (titles demonstrating the human or world experience); Home (titles with practical applications to home or home-related issues, including family); Health (titles promoting physical, mental, and emotional well-being); Memoir (titles relating to personal experience); Reference (titles from traditional and emerging reference areas); Self-help (titles involving new and emerging topics in self-help); Spiritual (titles involving the mind and spirit, including religion); Legacy Fiction and Nonfiction (titles over 2 years of age that hold particular relevance to any subject matter or form); E-book Fiction; E-book Nonfiction. Open to any writer of published work within the last 2 years, including categories for older books. This contest recognizes excellence in independent publishing in many unique categories. Also awards the Montaigne Medal for most thought-provoking book, the Da Vinci Eye for best cover, the Medal Provocateur from cutting-edge poetry, and the First Horizon Award for best new authors. Results published in the US Review of Books. Deadline: January 21. Grand Prize: $2,500; grand prize finalists; honors (winner, runner-up, honorable mentions) in each category; also the Montaigne Medal (most thought-provoking), da Vinci Art (cover art), Medal Provocateur (cutting-edge poetry), First Horizon (first book), Best in Press (small, academic, micro, self-published), and a coveted list of category finalist (books that scored highly but just missed category distinction). Publishing and business professionals, as well as carefully vetted readers. While judging for the Hoffer Award is a valued experience, about 25% of the judges are retired and replaced each year.

The Eric Hoffer Award, with permission from the Hoffer estate, was created by noted author Christopher Klim who wanted the type of award for which he'd register his own book. For more than a decade, he's kept the entrance fee at marginal levels to cover a small judges' honorarium and expensive book shipment. There are nearly 200 judges who read and evaluate every book twice or more. Unlike other awards, a single category entry qualifies your book for not only category and grand prize consideration, but also press type awards, the Montaigne Medal, the da Vinci Eye, the Medal Provocateur (for poetry), and (if it's a first book) the First Horizon Award. Yes, international books predominantly in English are accepted and honored. Both printed and digital submissions are allowed within their own categories. After visiting our robust FAQ under the NOMINATE link, contact us with questions.

MARILYN HOLLINSHEAD VISITING SCHOLARS FELLOWSHIP

University of Minnesota, Marilyn Hollinshead Visiting Scholars Fellowship, 113 Anderson Library, 222 21st Ave. South, Minneapolis MN 55455. **Website:** http://www.lib.umn.edu/clrc/awards-grants-and-fellowships. Marilyn Hollinshead Visiting Scholars Fund for Travel to the Kerlan Collection is available for research study. Applicants may request up to $1,500. Send a letter with the proposed purpose, plan to use specific research materials (manuscripts and art), dates, and budget (including airfare and per diem). Travel and a written report on the project must be completed and submitted in the previous year. Deadline: January 30.

THE JULIA WARD HOWE/BOSTON AUTHORS AWARD

The Boston Authors Club, The Boston Authors Club, Boston Authors Club, Attn. Mary Cronin, 2400 Beacon Street, Unit 208, Chestnut Hill MA 02467. **E-mail:** bostonauthors@aol.com. **Website:** www.bostonauthorsclub.org. **Contact:** Alan Lawson. This annual award honors Julia Ward Howe and her literary friends who founded the Boston Authors Club in 1900. It also honors the membership over 110 years; consisting of novelists, biographers, historians, governors, senators, philosophers, poets, playwrights, and other luminaries. Boston Authors Club has been awarding the Julia Ward Howe Prizes (named after the Club's first President) to outstanding adult and young-reader books for over 20 years. These awards recognize exceptional books by Boston-area authors in four separate categories: Fiction, Nonfiction, Poetry, and the Young Reader category. Authors must live or have lived (college counts) within a hundred 100-mile radius of Boston within the last 5 years. Subsidized books, cook books and picture books are not eligible. Deadline: January 31. Prize: $1,000. Judged by the members.

CAROL OTIS HURST CHILDREN'S BOOK PRIZE

Westfield Athenaeum, 6 Elm St., Westfield MA 01085. (413)562-6158, Ext. 5. **Website:** www.westath.org. **Contact:** Sarah Scott, Youth Services Librarian. The Carol Otis Hurst Children's Book Prize honors outstanding works of fiction and nonfiction, including biography and memoir, written for children and young adults through the age of 18, which exemplify the highest standards of research, analysis, and authorship in their portrayal of the New England Experience. The prize will be presented annually to an author whose book treats the region's history as broadly conceived to encompass one or more of the following elements: political experience, social development, fine and performing artistic expression, domestic life and arts, transportation and communication, changing technology, military experience at home and abroad, schooling, business and manufacturing, workers and the labor movement, agriculture and its transformation, racial and ethnic diversity, religious life and institutions, immigration and adjustment, sports at all levels, and the evolution of popular entertainment. The public presentation of the prize will be accompanied by a reading and/or talk by the recipient at a mutually agreed upon time during the spring immediately following the publication year. Books must have been copyrighted in their original format during the calendar year, January 1 to December 31, of the year preceding the year in which the prize is awarded. Any individual, publisher, or organization may nominate a book. See website for details and guidelines. Deadline: December 31. Prize: $500.

INTERNATIONAL LITERACY ASSOCIATION CHILDREN'S AND YOUNG ADULT'S BOOK AWARDS

P.O. Box 8139, 800 Barksdale Rd., Newark DE 19714-8139. (302)731-1600, ext. 221. **E-mail:** kbaughman@reading.org; committees@reading.org. **Website:** www.literacyworldwide.org. **Contact:** Kathy Baughman. The ILA Children's and Young Adults Book Awards are intended for newly published authors who show unusual promise in the children's and young adult's book field. Awards are given for fiction and nonfiction in each of 3categories: primary, intermediate, and young adult. Books from all countries and published in English for the first time during the previous calendar year will be considered. See website for eligibility and criteria information. Entry should be the author's first or second book. Deadline: March 15. Prize: $1,000.

JEFFERSON CUP AWARD

P.O. Box 56312, Virginia Beach VA 23456. (757)689-0594. **Website:** www.vla.org. **Contact:** Salena Sullivan, Jefferson Cup Award Chairperson. The Jefferson Cup honors a distinguished biography, historical fiction, or American history book for young people. The Jefferson Cup Committee's goal is to promote reading about America's past; to encourage the quality writing of United States history, biography, and historical fiction for young people; and to recognize authors in these disciplines. Deadline: January 31.

THE EZRA JACK KEATS BOOK AWARD FOR NEW WRITER AND NEW ILLUSTRATOR

University of Southern Mississippi, de Grummond Children's Literature Collection, 118 College Dr., #5148, Hattiesburg MS 39406-0001. **E-mail:** ellen.ruffin@usm.edu or claire.thompson@usm.edu. **Website:** https://www.degrummond.org/. **Contact:** Ellen Ruffin, Curator of the de Grummond Children's Literature Collection and Claire Thompson, Ezra Jack Keats Book Award Coordinator. Annual award to an outstanding new author and new illustrator of children's books that portray universal qualities of childhood in our multicultural world. Many past winners have gone on to distinguished careers, creating books beloved by parents, children, librarians, and teachers around the world. Writers and illustrators must have had no more than 3 books previously published. Prize: The winning author and illustrator will each receive a cash award of $3,000. Judged by a distinguished selection committee of early childhood education specialists, librarians, illustrators, and experts in children's literature.

EZRA JACK KEATS/KERLAN MEMORIAL FELLOWSHIP

University of Minnesota Libraries, 113 Elmer L. Andersen Library, 222 21st Ave. S, Minneapolis MN 55455. **E-mail:** asc-clrc@umn.edu. **Website:** https://www.lib.umn.edu/clrc/awards-grants-and-fellowships. This fellowship from the Ezra Jack Keats Foundation will provide $3,000 to a talented writer and/or illustrator of children's books who wishes to use the Kerlan Collection for the furtherance of his or her artistic development. Special consideration will be given to someone who would find it difficult to finance a visit to the Kerlan Collection. The Ezra Jack Keats Fellowship recipient will receive transportation costs and a per diem allotment. See website for application deadline and for digital application materials. Winner will be notified in February. Study and written report must be completed within the calendar year. Deadline: January 30. $3,000 to fund a trip to visit the Kerlan Collection.

KENTUCKY BLUEGRASS AWARD

Website: www.kasl.us. The Kentucky Bluegrass Award is a student-choice program. The KBA promotes and encourages Pre-K through 12th-grade students to read a variety of quality literature. Each year, a KBA committee for each grade category chooses the books for the 4 Master Lists (K-2, 3-5, 6-8, and 9-12). All Kentucky public and private schools, as well as public libraries, are welcome to participate in the program. To nominate a book, see the website for form and details. Deadline: March 1. Judged by students who read books and choose their favorite.

CORETTA SCOTT KING BOOK AWARDS

ALA American Library Association, 50 E. Huron St., Chicago IL 60611-2795. (800)545-2433. **E-mail:** olos@ala.org. **Website:** www.ala.org/csk. **Contact:** Office for Diversity, Literacy and Outreach Services.

The Coretta Scott King Book Awards are given annually to outstanding African American authors and illustrators of books for children and young adults that demonstrate an appreciation of African American culture and universal human values. The award commemorates the life and work of Dr. Martin Luther King, Jr., and honors his wife, Mrs. Coretta Scott King, for her courage and determination to continue the work for peace and world brotherhood. Must be written for a youth audience in 1 of 3 categories: preschool-4th grade; 5th-8th grade; or 9th-12th grade. Book must be published in the year preceding the year the award is given, evidenced by the copyright date in the book. See website for full details, criteria, and eligibility concerns. Purpose is to encourage the artistic expression of the African American experience via literature and the graphic arts; including biographical, historical, and social history treatments by African American authors and illustrators. Deadline: December 2nd at 4pm CST. Judged by the Coretta Scott King Book Awards Committee.

THE STEPHEN LEACOCK MEMORIAL MEDAL FOR HUMOUR

Bette Walker, 149 Peter St. N., Orillia ON L3V 4Z4, Canada. (705)326-9286. **E-mail:** awardschair@leacock.ca. **Website:** www.leacock.ca. **Contact:** Bette Walker, Award Committee, Stephen Leacock Associates. The Leacock Associates awards the prestigious Leacock Medal for the best book of literary humor written by a Canadian and published in the current year. The winning author also receives a cash prize of $15,000, thanks to the generous support of the TD Financial Group. 2 runners-up are each awarded a cash prize of $3,000. Deadline: Postmarked before December 31. Prize: $15,000.

LOUISE LOUIS/EMILY F. BOURNE STUDENT POETRY AWARD

Website: www.poetrysociety.org. Poetry Society of America, 15 Gramercy Park, New York, NY 10003. (212)254-9628. **Fax:** (212)673-2352. **Website:** www.poetrysociety.org. **Contact:** Program Director. **Open to students.** Annual award. Purpose of the award: award is for the best unpublished poem by a high or preparatory school student (grades 9-12) from the U.S. and its territories. Unpublished submissions only. Deadline for entries: October 1-December 22. SASE for award rules and entry forms. Entries not returned. "High schools can send an unlimited number of submissions with one entry per individual student for a flat fee of $20. (High school students may send a single entry for $5.)" Award: $250. Judging by a professional poet. Requirements for entrants: Award open to all high school and preparatory students from the U.S. and its territories. School attended, as well as name and address, should be noted. PSA submission guidelines must be followed. These are printed in our fall calendar on our website and are readily available if those interested send us a SASE. Line limit: none. "The award-winning poem will be included in a sheaf of poems that will be part of the program at the award ceremony and sent to all PSA members."

MCKNIGHT FELLOWSHIPS FOR WRITERS, LOFT AWARD(S) IN CHILDREN'S LITERATURE/CREATIVE PROSE/POETRY

The Loft Literary Center, 1011 Washington Ave. S., Suite 200, Open Book, Minneapolis MN 55415. (612)215-2575. **Fax:** (612)215-2576. **E-mail:** loft@loft.org. **Website:** www.loft.org. **Contact:** Bao Phi. The Loft administers the McKnight Artists Fellowships for Writers. Five $25,000 awards are presented annually to accomplished Minnesota writers and spoken word artists. Four awards alternate annually between creative prose (fiction and creative nonfiction) and poetry/spoken word. The fifth award is presented in children's literature and alternates annually for writing for ages 8 and under and writing for children older than 8. The awards provide the writers the opportunity to focus on their craft for the course of the fellowship year. Prize: $25,000, plus up to $3,000 in reimbursement for a writer's retreat or conference. The judge is announced after selections are made.

THE VICKY METCALF AWARD FOR LITERATURE FOR YOUNG PEOPLE

The Writers' Trust of Canada, 460 Richmond St. W., Suite 600, Toronto ON M5V 1Y1, Canada. (416)504-8222. **E-mail:** djackson@writerstrust.com. **Website:** www.writerstrust.com. **Contact:** Devon Jackson. The Vicky Metcalf Award is presented to a Canadian writer for a body of work in children's literature at The Writers' Trust Awards event held in Toronto each fall. Open to Canadian citizens and permanent residents only. Prize: $25,000.

MINNESOTA BOOK AWARDS

The Friends of the Saint Paul Public Library, 1080 Montreal Ave., Suite 2, St. Paul MN 55116. (651)222-3242. **Fax:** (651)222-1988. **E-mail:** mnbookawards@

thefriends.org. **Website:** www.mnbookawards.org. **Contact:** Bailey Veesenmeyer: bailey@thefriends.org. A year-round program celebrating and honoring Minnesota's best books, culminating in an annual awards ceremony. Recognizes and honors achievement by members of Minnesota's book and book arts community. All books must be the work of a Minnesota author or primary artistic creator (current Minnesota resident who maintains a year-round residence in Minnesota). All books must be published within the calendar year prior to the Awards presentation. Deadline: Books should be entered by 5 p.m. on the third Friday in November.

NATIONAL BOOK AWARDS

The National Book Foundation, 90 Broad St., Suite 604, New York NY 10004. (212)685-0261. **E-mail:** nationalbook@nationalbook.org. **Website:** www.nationalbook.org. The National Book Foundation and the National Book Awards celebrate the best of American literature, expand its audience, and enhance the cultural value of great writing in America. The contest offers prizes in 4 categories: fiction, nonfiction, poetry, and young people's literature. Books should be published between December 1 and November 30 of the previous year. Submissions must be previously published and must be entered by the publisher. General guidelines available on website. Interested publishes should phone or e-mail the Foundation. Deadline: Submit entry form, payment, and a copy of the book by May 15. Prize: $10,000 in each category. Finalists will each receive a prize of $1,000. Judged by a category specific panel of 5 judges for each category.

NATIONAL OUTDOOR BOOK AWARDS

National Outdoor Book Award Foundation, 921 S. 8th Ave., Stop 8128, Pocatello ID 83209, USA. (208)282-3912. **E-mail:** wattron@isu.edu. **Website:** www.noba-web.org. **Contact:** Ron Watters. Nine categories: History/biography, outdoor literature, instructional texts, outdoor adventure guides, nature guides, children's books, design/artistic merit, natural history literature, and nature and the environment. Additionally, a special award, the Outdoor Classic Award, is given annually to books which, over a period of time, have proven to be exceptionally valuable works in the outdoor field. Application forms and eligibility requirements are available online. Applications for the Awards program become available in early June. Recognize and encourage outstanding writing and publishing in the outdoor and natural history fields Deadline: August 19. Prize: Winning books are promoted nationally and are entitled to display the National Outdoor Book Award (NOBA) medallion. The winners are chosen by a panel of judges consisting of educators, academics, book reviewers, authors, editors, and outdoor columnists from throughout the country.

NATIONAL WRITERS ASSOCIATION SHORT STORY CONTEST

NWA Short Story Contest, 10940 S. Parker Rd., #508, Parker CO 80134. **E-mail:** natlwritersassn@hotmail.com. **Website:** www.nationalwriters.com. Any genre of short story manuscript may be entered. All entries must be postmarked by July 1. Contest opens April 1. Only unpublished works may be submitted. All manuscripts must be typed, double-spaced, in the English language. Maximum length is 5,000 words. Those unsure of proper manuscript format should request Research Report #35. The entry must be accompanied by an entry form (photocopies are acceptable) and return SASE if you wish the material and rating sheets returned. Submissions will be destroyed, otherwise. Receipt of entry will not be acknowledged without a return postcard. Author's name and address must appear on the first page. Entries remain the property of the author and may be submitted during the contest as long as they are not published before the final notification of winners. Final prizes will be awarded in June. The purpose of the National Writers Assn. Short Story Contest is to encourage the development of creative skills, recognize and reward outstanding ability in the area of short story writing. July 1 (postmarked). Prize: 1st Prize: $250; 2nd Prize: $100; 3rd Prize: $50; 4th-10th places will receive a book. 1st-3rd place winners may be asked to grant one-time rights for publication in *Authorship* magazine. Honorable Mentions receive a certificate. Judging will be based on originality, marketability, research, and reader interest. Copies of the judges' evaluation sheets will be sent to entrants furnishing an SASE with their entry.

NATIONAL YOUNGARTS FOUNDATION

National YoungArts Foundation, 2100 Biscayne Blvd., Miami FL 33137. (305)377-1140. **Fax:** (305)377-1149. **E-mail:** info@youngarts.org; apply@youngarts.org. **Website:** www.youngarts.org. The National YoungArts Foundation (formerly known as the National Foundation for Advancement in the Arts) was established in 1981 by Lin and Ted Arison to identify and support the next generation of artists and to contribute to the cultural vitality of the nation by investing in the artistic development of talented young artists in the visual, literary, design, and performing arts. Each year, there are approximately 11,000 applications submitted to YoungArts from 15-18 year old (grades 10-12) artists. From these, approximately 700 winners are selected who are eligible to participate in programs in Miami, New York, Los Angeles, and Washington D.C. (with Chicago and other regions in the works). YoungArts provides these emerging artists with life-changing experiences and validation by renowned mentors, access to significant scholarships, national recognition, and other opportunities throughout their careers to help ensure that the nation's most outstanding emerging artists are encouraged to pursue careers in the arts. See website for details about applying. Prize: Cash awards up to $10,000.

JOHN NEWBERY MEDAL

Association for Library Service to Children, Division of the American Library Association, 50 E. Huron, Chicago IL 60611. (800)545-2433. **Fax:** (312)280-5271. **E-mail:** alscawards@ala.org. **Website:** http://www.ala.org/alsc/awardsgrants/bookmedia/newberymedal/newberymedal. The Newbery Medal is awarded annually by the American Library Association for the most distinguished contribution to American literature for children. Previously published submissions only; must be published prior to year award is given. SASE for award rules. Entries not returned. Medal awarded at Caldecott/Newbery/Legacy banquet during ALA annual conference. Deadline: December 31. Judged by Newbery Award Selection Committee.

NEW ENGLAND BOOK AWARDS

NEIBA, 1955 Massachusetts Ave., #2, Cambridge MA 02140. (617)547-3642. **Fax:** (617)547-3759. **E-mail:** ali@neba.org. **Website:** www.newenglandbooks.org. **Contact:** Nan Sorensen, Administrative Coordinator. All books must be either written by a New-England-based author or be set in New England. Submissions made by New England booksellers and publishers. Submit written nominations only; actual books should not be sent. Award is given to a specific title: fiction, non-fiction, children's, or young adult. The titles must be either about New England, set in New England. or by an author residing in the New England. The titles must be hardcover, paperback original, or reissue that was published between September 1 and August 31. Entries must be still in print and available. Deadline: June 14. Prize: Winners will receive $250 for literacy to a charity of their choice. Judged by NEIBA membership.

NOVA WRITES COMPETITION FOR UNPUBLISHED MANUSCRIPTS

Writers' Federation of Nova Scotia, 1113 Marginal Rd., Halifax NS B3H 4P7. (902)423-8116. **Fax:** (902)422-0881. **E-mail:** programs@writers.ns.ca. **Website:** www.writers.ns.ca. **Contact:** Robin Spittal, Communications and Development Officer. Annual program designed to honor work by unpublished writers in all 4 Atlantic Provinces. Entry is open to writers unpublished in the category of writing they wish to enter. Prizes are presented in the fall of each year. Categories include: short form creative nonfiction, long form creative nonfiction, novel, poetry, short story, and writing for children/young adult novel. Judges return written comments when competition is concluded. Page lengths and rules vary based on categories. See website for details. Anyone resident in the Atlantic Provinces since September 1st immediately prior to the deadline date is eligible to enter. Only 1 entry per category is allowed. Each entry requires its own entry form and registration fee. Deadline: January 3. Prizes vary based on categories. See website for details.

OHIOANA BOOK AWARDS

Ohioana Library Association, 274 E. First Ave., Suite 300, Columbus OH 43201-3673. (614)466-3831. **Fax:** (614)728-6974. **E-mail:** ohioana@ohioana.org. **Website:** www.ohioana.org. **Contact:** David Weaver, executive director. Writers must have been born in Ohio or lived in Ohio for at least 5 years, but books about Ohio or an Ohioan need not be written by an Ohioan. Finalists announced in May and winners in July. Winners notified by mail in early summer. Offered annually to bring national attention to Ohio authors and their books, published in the last year. (Books can only be considered once.) Categories: Fiction, nonfiction, juvenile, poetry, and books about Ohio or an Ohioan. Deadline: December 31. Prize: $1,000 cash prize, certificate, and glass sculpture. Judged by a jury selected by librarians, book reviewers, writers and other knowledgeable people.

OKLAHOMA BOOK AWARDS

200 NE 18th St., Oklahoma City OK 73105. (405)521-2502. **Fax:** (405)525-7804. **E-mail:** connie.armstrong@libraries.ok.gov. **Website:** www.odl.state.

ok.us/ocb. **Contact:** Connie Armstrong, executive director. This award honors Oklahoma writers and books about Oklahoma. Awards are presented to best books in fiction, nonfiction, children's, design and illustration, and poetry books about Oklahoma or books written by an author who was born, is living or has lived in Oklahoma. SASE for award rules and entry forms. Winner will be announced at banquet in Oklahoma City. The Arrell Gibson Lifetime Achievement Award is also presented each year for a body of work. Previously published submissions only. Submissions made by the author, author's agent, or entered by a person or group of people, including the publisher. Must be published during the calendar year preceding the award. Deadline: January 10. Prize: Awards a medal. Judging by a panel of 5 people for each category, generally a librarian, a working writer in the genre, booksellers, editors, etc.

OREGON BOOK AWARDS

925 SW Washington St., Portland OR 97205. (503)227-2583. **Fax:** (503)241-4256. **E-mail:** la@literary-arts.org. **Website:** www.literary-arts.org. **Contact:** Susan Denning, director of programs and events. The annual Oregon Book Awards celebrate Oregon authors in the areas of poetry, fiction, nonfiction, drama and young readers' literature published between August 1 and July 31 of the previous calendar year. Awards are available for every category. See website for details. Entry fee determined by initial print run; see website for details. Entries must be previously published. Oregon residents only. Accepts inquiries by phone and e-mail. Finalists announced in January. Winners announced at an awards ceremony in November. List of winners available in April. Deadline: August 26. Prize: Grant of $2,500. (Grant money could vary.) Judged by writers who are selected from outside Oregon for their expertise in a genre. Past judges include Mark Doty, Colson Whitehead and Kim Barnes.

OREGON LITERARY FELLOWSHIPS

925 S.W. Washington, Portland OR 97205. (503)227-2583. **E-mail:** susan@literary-arts.org. **Website:** www.literary-arts.org. **Contact:** Susan Moore, Director of programs and events. Oregon Literary Fellowships are intended to help Oregon writers initiate, develop, or complete literary projects in poetry, fiction, literary nonfiction, drama, and young readers literature. Writers in the early stages of their career are encouraged to apply. The awards are merit-based. Guidelines available in February for SASE. Accepts inquiries by e-mail, phone. Oregon residents only. Recipients announced in January. Deadline: Last Friday in June. Prize: $3,000 minimum award, for approximately 8 writers and 2 publishers. Judged by out-of-state writers.

THE ORIGINAL ART

128 E. 63rd St., New York NY 10065. (212)838-2560. **Fax:** (212)838-2561. **E-mail:** kim@societyillustrators.org; info@societyillustrators.org. **Website:** www.societyillustrators.org. **Contact:** Kate Feirtag, exhibition director. The Original Art is an annual exhibit created to showcase illustrations from the year's best children's books published in the US. For editors and art directors, it's an inspiration and a treasure trove of talent to draw upon. Previously published submissions only. Request "call for entries" to receive contest rules and entry forms. Works will be displayed at the Society of Illustrators Museum of American Illustration in New York City October-November annually. Deadline: July 18. Judged by 7 professional artists and editors.

PATERSON PRIZE FOR BOOKS FOR YOUNG PEOPLE

The Poetry Center at Passaic County Community College, One College Blvd., Paterson NJ 07505. (973)684-6555. **Fax:** (973)523-6085. **E-mail:** mgillan@pccc.edu. **Website:** www.pccc.edu/poetry. **Contact:** Maria Mazziotti Gillan, executive director. Award for a book published in the previous year in each age category (Pre-K-Grade 3, Grades 4-6, Grades 7-12). Deadline: February 1. Prize: $500.

THE KATHERINE PATERSON PRIZE FOR YOUNG ADULT AND CHILDREN'S WRITING

Hunger Mountain, Vermont College of Fine Arts, 36 College St., Montpelier VT 05602. (802)828-8517. **E-mail:** hungermtn@vcfa.edu. **Website:** www.hungermtn.org. **Contact:** Cameron Finch, managing editor. The annual Katherine Paterson Prize for Young Adult and Children's Writing honors the best in young adult and children's literature. Submit young adult or middle grade mss, and writing for younger children, short stories, picture books, poetry, or novel excerpts, under 10,000 words. Guidelines available on website. Deadline: March 1. Prize: $1,000 and publication for the first place winner; $100 each and publication for the three category winners. Judged by a guest judge every year.

PENNSYLVANIA YOUNG READERS' CHOICE AWARDS PROGRAM

Pennsylvania School Librarians Association, 134 Bisbing Road, Henryville PA 18332. **E-mail:** pyrca.psla@gmail.com. **Website:** www.psla.org. **Contact:** Alice L. Cyphers, co-coordinator. Submissions nominated by a person or group. Must be published within 5 years of the award. Check the Program wiki at pyrca.wikispaces.com for submission information. View information at the Pennsylvania School Librarians' website or the Program wiki. Must be currently living in North America. The purpose of the Pennsylvania Young Reader's Choice Awards Program is to promote the reading of quality books by young people in the Commonwealth of Pennsylvania, to encourage teacher and librarian collaboration and involvement in children's literature, and to honor authors whose works have been recognized by the students of Pennsylvania. Deadline: September 15. Prize: Framed certificate to winning authors. Four awards are given, one for each of the following grade level divisions: K-3, 3-6, 6-8, YA. Judged by children of Pennsylvania (they vote).

PEN/PHYLLIS NAYLOR WORKING WRITER FELLOWSHIP

E-mail: awards@pen.org. **Website:** www.pen.org/awards. Offered annually to an author of children's or young-adult fiction. The Fellowship has been developed to help writers whose work is of high literary caliber but who have not yet attracted a broad readership. The Fellowship is designed to assist a writer at a crucial moment in his or her career to complete a book-length work-in-progress. Candidates have published at least one novel for children or young adults which have been received warmly by literary critics, but have not generated sufficient income to support the author. Writers must be nominated by an editor or fellow author. See website for eligibility and nomination guidelines. Deadline: Submissions open during the summer of each year. Visit PEN.org/awards for up-to-date information on deadlines. Prize: $5,000.

PNWA WRITING CONTEST

Pacifc Northwest Writers Association, PMB 2717, 1420 NW Gilman Blvd., Suite 2, Issaquah WA 98027. (452)673-2665. **E-mail:** pnwa@pnwa.org. **Website:** www.pnwa.org. Annual writing contest with 12 different categories. See website for details and specific guidelines. Each entry receives 2 critiques. Winners announced at the PNWA FallConference, held annually. Deadline: March 31st. Prize: 1st Place: $600; 2nd Place: $300; 3rd Place: $100. Finalists are judged by an agent or editor.

POCKETS FICTION-WRITING CONTEST

P.O. Box 340004, Nashville TN 37203-0004. (615)340-7333. **Fax:** (615)340-7267. **E-mail:** pockets@upperroom.org. **Website:** www.pockets.upperroom.org. **Contact:** Lynn W. Gilliam, senior editor. Designed for 6- to 12-year-olds, *Pockets* magazine offers wholesome devotional readings that teach about God's love and presence in life. The content includes fiction, scripture stories, puzzles and games, poems, recipes, colorful pictures, activities, and scripture readings. Freelance submissions of stories, poems, recipes, puzzles and games, and activities are welcome. Stories should be 750-1,000 words. Multiple submissions are permitted. Past winners are ineligible. The primary purpose of *Pockets* is to help children grow in their relationship with God and to claim the good news of the gospel of Jesus Christ by applying it to their daily lives. *Pockets* espouses respect for all human beings and for God's creation. It regards a child's faith journey as an integral part of all of life and sees prayer as undergirding that journey. Deadline: August 15. Submission period begins March 15. Prize: $500 and publication in magazine.

EDGAR ALLAN POE AWARD

1140 Broadway, Suite 1507, New York NY 10001. (212)888-8171. **E-mail:** mwa@mysterywriters.org. **Website:** www.mysterywriters.org. Mystery Writers of America is the leading association for professional crime writers in the United States. Members of MWA include most major writers of crime fiction and nonfiction, as well as screenwriters, dramatists, editors, publishers, and other professionals in the field. Categories include: Best Novel, Best First Novel by an American Author, Best Paperback/E-Book Original, Best Fact Crime, Best Critical/Biographical, Best Short Story, Best Juvenile Mystery, Best Young Adult Mystery, Best Television Series Episode Teleplay, and Mary Higgins Clark Award. Purpose of the award: Honor authors of distinguished works in the mystery field. Previously published submissions only. Submissions should be made by the publisher. Work must be published/produced the year of the contest. Deadline: November 30. Prize: Awards ceramic bust of "Edgar" for winner; certificates for all nominees.

Judged by active status members of Mystery Writers of America (writers).

MICHAEL L. PRINTZ AWARD

Young Adult Library Services Association, Division of the American Library Association, 50 E. Huron, Chicago IL 60611. (800)545-2433. **Fax:** (312)280-5276. **E-mail:** yalsa@ala.org. **Website:** www.ala.org/yalsa/printz. **Contact:** Nichole O'Connor, program officer for events and conferences. The Michael L. Printz Award annually honors the best book written for teens, based entirely on its literary merit, each year. In addition, the Printz Committee names up to 4 honor books, which also represent the best writing in young adult literature. The award-winning book can be fiction, nonfiction, poetry or an anthology, and can be a work of joint authorship or editorship. The books must be published between January 1 and December 31 of the preceding year and be designated by its publisher as being either a young adult book or one published for the age range that YALSA defines as young adult, e.g. ages 12 through 18. Deadline: December 1. Judged by an award committee.

PURPLE DRAGONFLY BOOK AWARDS

Story Monsters LLC, 4696 W Tyson St, Chandler AZ 85226-2903. (480)940-8182. **Fax:** (480)940-8787. **E-mail:** linda@storymonsters.com. **Website:** www.dragonflybookawards.com. **Contact:** Cristy Bertini, contest coordinator. The Purple Dragonfly Book Awards were conceived with children in mind. Not only do we want to recognize and honor accomplished authors in the field of children's literature, but we also want to highlight up-and-coming, newly published authors, and younger published writers. Divided into 55 distinct subject categories ranging from books on the environment and cooking to sports and family issues, and even marketing collateral that complements a book, the Purple Dragonfly Book Awards are geared toward stories that appeal to children of all ages. We are looking for books that are original, innovative and creative in both content and design. A Purple Dragonfly Book Awards seal on your book's cover, marketing materials, or website tells parents, grandparents, educators, and caregivers that they are giving children the very best in reading excellence. Our judges are industry experts with specific knowledge about the categories over which they preside. Being honored with a Purple Dragonfly Book Award confers credibility upon the winner and gives published authors the recognition they deserve and provide a helping hand to further their careers. The awards are open to books published in any calendar year and in any country that are available for purchase. Books entered must be printed in English. Traditionally published, partnership published and self-published books are permitted, as long as they fit the above criteria. Submit materials to: Cristy Bertini, Attn: Dragonfly Book Awards, 1271 Turkey St., Ware, MA 01082. Deadline: May 1. The grand prize winner will receive a $500 cash prize, a certificate commemorating their accomplishment, 100 Grand Prize seals, a one-hour marketing consulting session with Linda F. Radke, a news release announcing the winners sent to a comprehensive list of media outlets, and a listing on the Dragonfly Book Awards website. All first-place winners of categories will be put into a drawing for a $100 prize. In addition, each first-place winner in each category receives a certificate commemorating their accomplishment, 25 foil award seals, and mention on Dragonfly Book Awards website. All winners receive certificates and are listed in Story Monsters Ink magazine. Judged by industry experts with specific knowledge about the categories over which they preside.

QUILL AND SCROLL WRITING, PHOTO AND MULTIMEDIA CONTEST AND BLOGGING COMPETITION

School of Journalism, Univ. of Iowa, 100 Adler Journalism Bldg., Iowa City IA 52242-2004. (319)335-3457. **E-mail:** quill-scroll@uiowa.edu. **Website:** quilland-scroll.org. **Contact:** Jeffrey Browne, Contest Director. Entries must have been published in a high school or professional newspaper or website during the previous year, and be the work of a currently enrolled high school student when published. Open to students. Annual contest. Previously published submissions only. Submissions made by the author or school media adviser. Deadline: February 5. Prize: Winners will receive *Quill and Scroll*'s National Award Gold Key and, if seniors, are eligible to apply for one of the scholarships offered by *Quill and Scroll*. All winning entries are automatically eligible for the International Writing and Photo Sweepstakes Awards. Engraved plaque awarded to sweepstakes winners.

TOMÁS RIVERA MEXICAN AMERICAN CHILDREN'S BOOK AWARD

Dr. Jesse Gainer, Texas State University, 601 University Drive, San Marcos TX 78666-4613. (512)245-

2357. **E-mail:** riverabookaward@txstate.edu. **Website:** www.riverabookaward.org. **Contact:** Dr. Jesse Gainer, award director. Texas State University College of Education developed the Tomas Rivera Mexican American Children's Book Award to honor authors and illustrators who create literature that depicts the Mexican American experience. The award was established in 1995 and was named in honor of Dr. Tomas Rivera, a distinguished alumnus of Texas State University. The book will be written for younger children, ages pre-K to 5th grade (awarded in even years), or older children, ages 6th grade to 12 grade (awarded in odd years). The text and illustrations will be of highest quality. The portrayal/representations of Mexican Americans will be accurate and engaging, avoid stereotypes, and reflect rich characterization. The book may be fiction or non- fiction. See website for more details and directions. Deadline: November 1.

ROCKY MOUNTAIN BOOK AWARD: ALBERTA CHILDREN'S CHOICE BOOK AWARD

Box 42, Lethbridge AB T1J 3Y3, Canada. **E-mail:** rockymountainbookaward@shaw.ca. **Website:** www.rmba.info. **Contact:** Michelle Dimnik, contest director. Annual contest. No entry fee. Awards: Gold medal and author tour of selected Alberta schools. Judging by students. Canadian authors and/or illustrators only. Submit entries to Richard Chase. Previously unpublished submissions only. Submissions made by author's agent or nominated by a person or group. Must be published within the 3 years prior to that year's award. Register before January 20th to take part in the Rocky Mountain Book Award. SASE for contest rules and entry forms. Purpose of contest: "Reading motivation for students, promotion of Canadian authors, illustrators and publishers." Gold Medal and sponsored visit to several Alberta Schools or Public Libraries. Judged by students.

SASKATCHEWAN BOOK AWARDS

315-1102 8th Ave., Regina SK S4R 1C9, Canada. (306)569-1585. **E-mail:** director@bookawards.sk.ca. **Website:** www.bookawards.sk.ca. **Contact:** Courtney Bates-Hardy, executive director. Saskatchewan Book Awards celebrates, promotes, and rewards Saskatchewan authors and publishers worthy of recognition through 14 awards, granted on an annual or semiannual basis. Awards: Fiction, Nonfiction, Poetry, Scholarly, First Book, Prix du Livre Français, Regina, Saskatoon, Indigenous Peoples' Writing, Indigenous Peoples' Publishing, Publishing in Education, Publishing, Children's Literature/Young Adult Literature, Book of the Year. November 1. Prize: $2,000 (CAD) for all awards except Book of the Year, which is $3,000 (CAD). Juries are made up of writing and publishing professionals from outside of Saskatchewan.

Saskatchewan Book Awards is the only provincially focused book award program in Saskatchewan and a principal ambassador for Saskatchewan's literary community. Its solid reputation for celebrating artistic excellence in style is recognized nationally.

SCBWI MAGAZINE MERIT AWARDS

4727 Wilshire Blvd., Suite 301, Los Angeles CA 90010. (323)782-1010. **Fax:** (323)782-1892. **E-mail:** grants@scbwi.org. **Website:** www.scbwi.org. **Contact:** Stephanie Gordon, award coordinator. The SCBWI is a professional organization of writers and illustrators and others interested in children's literature. Membership is open to the general public at large. All magazine work for young people by an SCBWI member—writer, artist or photographer—is eligible during the year of original publication. In the case of co-authored work, both authors must be SCBWI members. Members must submit their own work. Requirements for entrants: 4 copies each of the published work and proof of publication (may be contents page) showing the name of the magazine and the date of issue. Previously published submissions only. For rules and procedures see website. Must be a SCBWI member. Recognizes outstanding original magazine work for young people published during that year, and having been written or illustrated by members of SCBWI. Deadline: December 15 of the year of publication. Submission period begins January 1. Prize: Awards plaques and honor certificates for each of 4 categories (fiction, nonfiction, illustration and poetry). Judged by a magazine editor and two "full" SCBWI members.

SKIPPING STONES BOOK AWARDS

Skipping Stones, P. O. Box 3939, Eugene OR 97403-0939. **E-mail:** editor@skippingstones.org. **Website:** www.skippingstones.org/wp. **Contact:** Arun N. Toke', Exec. Editor. Open to published books, publications/magazines, educational videos, and DVDs. Annual awards. Submissions made by the author or publishers and/or producers. Send request for contest rules and entry forms or visit website. Many educational publications announce the winners of our book awards. The winners are announced in the autumn issue of *Skipping Stones* and also on the website. In addition to announcements on social media pages, the reviews of winning titles are posted on website. For several years now, Multicultural Education, a quarterly journal has been republishing all the book award winners' reviews. *Skipping Stones* multicultural magazine has been published for over 32 years. Recognizes exceptional, literary and artistic contributions to juvenile/children's literature, as well as teaching resources and educational audio/video resources in the areas of multicultural awareness, nature and ecology, social issues, peace, and nonviolence. Deadline: February 28. Prize: Winners receive gold honor award seals, attractive honor certificates, and publicity via multiple outlets. Judged by a multicultural selection committee of editors, students, parents, teachers, and librarians.

SKIPPING STONES YOUTH AWARDS

P.O. Box 3939, Eugene OR 97403-0939. (541)342-4956. **Fax:** (541)342-4956. **E-mail:** editor@skippingstones.org. **Website:** www.skippingstones.org. **Contact:** Arun N. Toké. Annual awards to promote creativity as well as multicultural and nature awareness in youth. Cover letter should include name, address, phone, and e-mail. Entries must be unpublished. Length: 1,000 words maximum; 30 lines maximum for poems. Open to any writer between 7 and 17 years old. Guidelines available by SASE, e-mail, or on website. Accepts inquiries by e-mail or phone. Results announced in the October-December issue of *Skipping Stones*. Winners notified by mail. For contest results, visit website. Everyone who enters receives the issue which features the award winners. Deadline: June 25. Prize: Publication in the autumn issue of *Skipping Stones*, honor certificate, five back issues of the magazine, plus 5 multicultural and/or nature books. Judged by editors and reviewers at *Skipping Stones* magazine.

SKIPPING STONES YOUTH HONOR AWARDS

P. O. Box 3939, Eugene OR 97403-0939. (541)342-4956. **E-mail:** editor@skippingstones.org. **Website:** www.SkippingStones.org/wp. **Contact:** Arun N. Toké, editor. *Skipping Stones* is a winner of N.A.M.E., EDPRESS, Newsstand Resources, Writer and Parent's Choice Awards. Open to students ages 7 to 17. Annual awards. Submissions made by the author. The winners are published in the October-December issue of *Skipping Stones*. Everyone who enters the contest receives the Autumn issue featuring Youth Awards. SASE for contest rules or download from website. Entries must include certificate of originality by a parent and/or teacher and a cover letter that included cultural background information on the author. Submissions can either be mailed or e-mailed. Up to ten awards are given in three categories: (1) Compositions (essays, poems, short stories, songs, travelogues, etc.): Entries should be typed (double-spaced) or neatly handwritten. Fiction or nonfiction should be limited to 1,000 words; poems to 30 lines. Non-English writings are also welcome. (2) Artwork (drawings, cartoons, paintings or photo essays with captions): Entries should have the artist's name, age and address on the back of each page. Send the originals with SASE. Black & white photos are especially welcome. Limit: 8 pieces. (3) Youth Organizations: Describe how your club or group works to: (a) preserve the nature and ecology in your area, (b) enhance the quality of life for low-income, minority or disabled or (c) improve racial or cultural harmony in your school or community. Use the same format as for compositions. Recognizes youth, 7 to 17, for their contributions to multicultural awareness, nature and ecology, social issues, peace and nonviolence. Also promotes creativity, self-esteem and writing skills and to recognize important work being done by youth organizations. Deadline: June 25. Judged by *Skipping Stones* staff.

KAY SNOW WRITING CONTEST

Willamette Writers, Willamette Writers, 2108 Buck St., West Linn OR 97068. (503)305-6729. **Fax:** (503)344-6174. **E-mail:** reg@willamettewriters.com. **Website:** www.willamettewriters.org. Willamette Writers is the largest writers' organization in Oregon and one of the largest writers' organizations in the United States. It is a non-profit, tax-exempt Oregon corporation led by volunteers. Elected officials and directors administer an active program of monthly meetings, special seminars, workshops, and an annual writing conference. Continuing with established programs and starting new ones is only made possible by strong volunteer support. See website for specific details and rules. There are six different categories writers can enter: Adult Fiction, Adult Nonfiction, Poetry, Juvenile Short Story, Screenwriting, and Student Writer. The purpose of this annual writing contest, named in honor of Willamette Writer's founder, Kay

Snow, is to help writers reach professional goals in writing in a broad array of categories and to encourage student writers. Deadline: April 23. Submission deadline begins January 15. Prize: One first prize of $300, one second place prize of $150, and a third place prize of $50 per winning entry in each of the six categories. Student first prize is $50, $20 for second place, $10 for third.

SOCIETY OF MIDLAND AUTHORS AWARD

Society of Midland Authors, P.O. Box 10419, Chicago IL 60610-0419. **E-mail:** marlenetbrill@comcast.net. **Website:** www.midlandauthors.com. **Contact:** Marlene Targ Brill, awards chair. Since 1957, the Society has presented annual awards for the best books written by authors with a connection to one of twelve Midwest states: Illinois, Indiana, Iowa, Kansas, Michigan, Minnesota, Missouri, Nebraska, North Dakota, Ohio, South Dakota, and Wisconsin. The Society began in 1915. The contest is open to any title published within the year prior to the contest year. It is for adult and children's authors/poets who reside in, were born in, or have strong ties to a Midland state, which includes Illinois, Indiana, Iowa, Kansas, Michigan, Minnesota, Missouri, Nebraska, North Dakota, South Dakota, Ohio, and Wisconsin. Books and entry forms must be mailed to the 3 judges in each category. For a list of judges and entry and payment forms visit the SMA website. Do not mail books to the society's P.O. box. The fee can be sent to the SMA P.O. box or paid via Paypal at midlandauthors.com. The Society of Midland Authors (SMA) Award is presented to honor one title in each of 6 categories: adult nonfiction, adult fiction, adult biography and memoir, children's nonfiction, children's fiction, and poetry. There may be honor book winners in each category as well. Deadline: The first Saturday in January for books from the previous year. Prize: $500, a plaque, and award's book stickers that is awarded at the SMA banquet, usually in May in Chicago. Honorary winners receive a plaque. Check the SMA website for each year's judges at the end of October.

SOUTHWEST WRITERS ANNUAL WRITING CONTEST

3200 Carlisle Blvd., NE Suite #114, Albuquerque NM 87110. (505)830-6034. **E-mail:** swwriters@juno.com. **Website:** www.southwestwriters.com. The SouthWest Writers Writing Contest encourages and honors excellence in writing. In addition to competing for cash prizes, contest entrants may receive an optional written critique of their entry from a qualified contest critiquer. Non-profit organization dedicated to helping members of all levels in their writing. Members enjoy perks such as networking with professional and aspiring writers; substantial discounts on mini-conferences, workshops, writing classes, and annual and quarterly SWW writing contest; monthly newsletter; two writing programs per month; critique groups, critique service (also for nonmembers); discounts at bookstores and other businesses; and website linking. Deadline: May 1 (up to May 15 with a late fee). Submissions begin February 1. Prize: A 1st, 2nd, and 3rd place winner will be judged in each of the categories. 1st place: $300; 2nd place: $200; 3rd place: $150. Judged by a panel; the top 10 in each category will be sent to appropriate editors or literary agents to determine the final top 3 places.

STORY MONSTERS APPROVED BOOK AWARDS

Story Monsters LLC, 4696 W. Tyson St., Chandler AZ 85226. (480)940-8182. **Fax:** (480)940-8787. **E-mail:** linda@storymonsters.com; cristy@storymonsters.com. **Website:** www.dragonflybookawards.com. **Contact:** Cristy Bertini. The Story Monsters Approved! book designation program was developed to recognize and honor accomplished authors in the field of children's literature that inspire, inform, teach, or entertain. A Story Monsters seal of approval on your book tells teachers, librarians, and parents they are giving children the very best. Kids know when they see the Story Monsters Approved! seal, it means children their own age enjoyed the book and are recommending they read it, too. How do they know that? Because after books pass a first round of rigorous judging by industry experts, the books are then judged by a panel of youth judges who must also endorse the books before they can receive the official seal of approval. Guidelines available online. Send submissions to Cristy Bertini, Attn.: Dragonfly Book Awards, 1271 Turkey St., Ware, MA 01082. There is no deadline to enter. Books are sent for judging as they are received. The Book of the Year winner will receive $500, a certificate commemorating their accomplishment, and 200 Story Monsters Approved seals. Our judging panel includes industry experts in the fields of education and publishing, and student judges.

TD CANADIAN CHILDREN'S LITERATURE AWARD

The Canadian Children's Book Centre, 40 Orchard View Blvd., Suite 217, Toronto ON M4R 1B9, Canada. (416)975-0010, ext. 222. **Fax:** (416)975-8970. **E-mail:** meghan@bookcentre.ca. **Website:** www.bookcentre.ca. **Contact:** Meghan Howe. The TD Canadian Children's Literature Award is for the most distinguished book of the year. All books, in any genre, written and illustrated by Canadians and for children ages 1-12 are eligible. Only books published in Canada are eligible for submission. Books must be published between January 1 and December 31 of the previous calendar year. Open to Canadian citizens and/or permanent residents of Canada. Deadline: mid-December. Prizes: Two prizes of $50,000, 1 for English, 1 for French. $20,000 will be divided among the Honour Book English titles and Honour Book French titles, to a maximum of 4; $2,500 shall go to each of the publishers of the English and French grand-prize winning books for promotion and publicity.

TORONTO BOOK AWARDS

City of Toronto c/o Toronto Arts & Culture, Cultural Partnerships, City Hall, 9E, 100 Queen St. W., Toronto ON M5H 2N2, Canada. **E-mail:** shan@toronto.ca. **Website:** www.toronto.ca/book_awards. The Toronto Book Awards honor authors of books of literary or artistic merit that are evocative of Toronto. There are no separate categories; all books are judged together. Any fiction or nonfiction book published in English for adults and/or children that are evocative of Toronto are eligible. To be eligible, books must be published between January 1 and December 31 of previous year. Deadline: April 30. Prize: Each finalist receives $1,000 and the winning author receives $10,000 ($15,000 total in prize money available).

VEGETARIAN ESSAY CONTEST FOR CHILDREN

The Vegetarian Resource Group, P.O. Box 1463, Baltimore MD 21203. (410)366-8343. **Fax:** (410)366-8804. **E-mail:** vrg@vrg.org. **Website:** www.vrg.org. Write a 2-3 page essay on any aspect of veganism/vegetarianism. Entrants should base their paper on interviewing, research, and/or personal opinion. You need not be a vegetarian to enter. Three different entry categories: age 14-18; age 9-13; and age 8 and under. Prize: $50.

VFW VOICE OF DEMOCRACY

Veterans of Foreign Wars of the U.S., National Headquarters, 406 W. 34th St., Kansas City MO 64111. (816)968-1117. **E-mail:** kharmer@vfw.org. **Website:** https://www.vfw.org/VOD/. The Voice of Democracy Program is open to students in grades 9-12 (on the Nov. 1 deadline), who are enrolled in a public, private or parochial high school or home study program in the United States and its territories. Contact your local VFW Post to enter (entry must not be mailed to the VFW National Headquarters, only to a local, participating VFW Post). Purpose is to give high school students the opportunity to voice their opinions about their responsibility to our country and to convey those opinions via the broadcast media to all of America. Deadline: November 1. Prize: Winners receive awards ranging from $1,000-30,000.

WESTERN AUSTRALIAN PREMIER'S BOOK AWARDS

State Library of Western Australia, Perth Cultural Centre, 25 Francis St., Perth WA 6000, Australia. (61)(8)9427-3151. **E-mail:** premiersbookawards@slwa.wa.gov.au. **Website:** pba.slwa.wa.gov.au. **Contact:** Karen de San Miguel. Annual competition for Australian citizens or permanent residents of Australia, or writers whose work has Australia as its primary focus. Categories: children's books, digital narrative, fiction, nonfiction, poetry, scripts, writing for young adults, West Australian history, and Western Australian emerging writers. Submit 5 original copies of the work to be considered for the awards. All works must have been published between January 1 and December 31 of the prior year. See website for details and rules of entry. Deadline: January 31. Prize: Awards $25,000 for Premier's Prize; awards $15,000 each for the Children's Books, Digital Narrative, Fiction, and Nonfiction categories; awards $10,000 each for the Poetry, Scripts, Western Australian History, Western Australian Emerging Writers, and Writing for Young Adults; awards $5,000 for People's Choice Award.

WESTERN HERITAGE AWARDS

National Cowboy & Western Heritage Museum, 1700 NE 63rd St., Oklahoma City OK 73111-7997. (405)478-2250. **Fax:** (405)478-4714. **Website:** www.nationalcowboymuseum.org. **Contact:** Jessica Limestall. The National Cowboy & Western Heritage Museum Western Heritage Awards were established to honor and encourage the legacy of those whose works in literature, music, film, and television reflect the significant stories of the American West. Accepted categories for literary entries: western novel, nonfiction book, art book, photography book, juvenile book, magazine article, or poetry book. Previously published submissions only; must be published the calendar year before the awards are presented. Requirements for entrants: The material must pertain to the development or preservation of the West, either from a historical or contemporary viewpoint. Literary entries must have been published between December 1 and November 30 of calendar year. Five copies of each published work must be furnished for judging with each entry, along with the completed entry form. Works recognized during special awards ceremonies held annually at the museum. There is an autograph party preceding the awards. Awards ceremonies are sometimes broadcast. The WHA are presented annually to encourage the accurate and artistic telling of great stories of the West through 16 categories of western literature, television, film and music; including fiction, nonfiction, children's books and poetry. See website for details and category definitions. Deadline: November 30. Prize: Awards a Wrangler bronze sculpture designed by famed western artist, John Free. Judged by a panel of judges selected each year with distinction in various fields of western art and heritage.

WESTERN WRITERS OF AMERICA

271 CR 219, Encampment WY 82325. **E-mail:** wwa.moulton@gmail.com. **Website:** www.westernwriters.org. **Contact:** Candy Moulton, executive director. Eighteen Spur Award categories in various aspects of the American West. Send entry form with your published work. Accepts multiple submissions, each with its own entry form, available on our website. The nonprofit Western Writers of America has promoted and honored the best in Western literature with the annual Spur Awards, selected by panels of judges. Awards, for material published last year, are given for works whose inspirations, image and literary excellence best represent the reality and spirit of the American West. Deadline: January 10. Award: Plaque. Judged by independent judges.

JACKIE WHITE MEMORIAL NATIONAL CHILDREN'S PLAY WRITING CONTEST

1800 Nelwood Dr., Columbia MO 65202-1447. (573)874-5628. **E-mail:** jwmcontest@cectheatre.org. **Website:** www.cectheatre.org. **Contact:** Tom Phillips. Annual contest that encourages playwrights to write quality plays for family audiences. Previously unpublished submissions only. Submissions made by author. Play may be performed during the following season. All submissions will be read by at least 3 readers. Author will receive a written evaluation of the script. Guidelines available online. Deadline: June 1. Prize: $500 with production possible. Judging by current and past board members of CEC and by non-board members who direct plays at CEC.

WILLA LITERARY AWARD

Website: www.womenwritingthewest.org. **Contact:** Carmen Peone. The WILLA Literary Award honors the year's best in published literature featuring women's or girls' stories set in the West. Women Writing the West (WWW), a nonprofit association of writers and other professionals writing and promoting the Women's West, underwrites and presents the nationally recognized award annually (for work published between January 1 and December 31). The award is named in honor of Pulitzer Prize winner Willa Cather, one of the country's foremost novelists. The award is given in 8 categories: historical fiction, contemporary fiction, original softcover fiction, creative nonfiction, scholarly nonfiction, poetry, children's fiction and nonfiction and young adult fiction/nonfiction. Entry forms available on the website. Deadline: November 1–February 1. Prize: $150 and a trophy. Finalist receives a plaque. Both receive digital and sticker award emblems for book covers. Notice of Winning and Finalist titles mailed to more than 4,000 booksellers, libraries, and others. Award announcement is in early August, and awards are presented to the winners and finalists at the annual WWW Fall Conference. Also, the eight winners will participate in a drawing for 2 two week all expenses paid residencies donated by Playa at Summer Lake in Oregon. Judged by professional librarians not affiliated with WWW.

PAUL A. WITTY OUTSTANDING LITERATURE AWARD

P.O. Box 8139, Newark DE 19714-8139. (800)336-7323. **Fax:** (302)731-1057. **Website:** www.reading.org. **Contact:** Marcie Craig Post, executive director. This award recognizes excellence in original poetry or prose written by students. Elementary and secondary students whose work is selected will receive an award. Deadline: February 2. Prize: Not less than $25 and a citation of merit.

WORK-IN-PROGRESS GRANT

Society of Children's Book Writers and Illustrators (SCBWI), 8271 Beverly Blvd., Los Angeles CA 90048. (323)782-1010. **E-mail:** grants@scbwi.org; wipgrant@scbwi.org. **Website:** www.scbwi.org. Six grants—one designated specifically for picture book text, chapter book/early readers, middle grade, young adult fiction, nonfiction, and multicultural fiction or nonfiction—to assist SCBWI members in the completion of a specific project. Open to SCBWI members only. Deadline: March 31. Open to submissions on March 1.

WRITER'S DIGEST SELF-PUBLISHED BOOK AWARDS

Writer's Digest, 4665 Malsbary Rd., Blue Ash OH 45242. **E-mail:** writersdigestwritingcompetition@aimmedia.com. **Website:** www.writersdigest.com. **Contact:** Nicole Howard. Contest open to all English-language, self-published books for which the authors have paid the full cost of publication, or the cost of printing has been paid for by a grant or as part of a prize. Categories include: Mainstream/Literary Fiction, Genre Fiction, Nonfiction, Inspirational (spiritual/new age), Life Stories (biographies/autobiographies/family histories/memoirs), Children's Books, Reference Books (directories/encyclopedias/guide books), Poetry, and Middle-Grade/Young Adult Books. Judges reserve the right to re-categorize entries. Judges reserve the right to withhold prizes in any category. All winners will be notified in October. Entrants must send a printed and bound book. Entries will be evaluated on content, writing quality, and overall quality of production and appearance. No handwritten books are accepted. Books must have been published within the past 5 years from the competition deadline. Books which have previously won awards from *Writer's Digest* are not eligible. Early bird deadline: April 2. Prizes: Grand Prize: $8,000, a trip to the Writer's Digest Conference, promotion in *Writer's Digest*, and more; 1st Place (9 winners): $1,000 and promotion in *Writer's Digest*; and more prizes. All entrants will receive a brief commentary from one of the judges.

WRITER'S DIGEST SELF-PUBLISHED E-BOOK AWARDS

Writer's Digest, 4665 Malsbary Rd., Blue Ash OH 45242. **E-mail:** writersdigestwritingcompetition@aimmedia.com. **Website:** www.writersdigest.com. **Contact:** Nicole Howard. Contest open to all English-language, self-published e-books for which the authors have paid the full cost of publication, or the cost of publication has been paid for by a grant or as part of a prize. Categories include: Mainstream/Literary Fiction, Genre Fiction, Nonfiction (includes reference books), Inspirational (spiritual/new age), Life Stories (biographies/autobiographies/family histories/memoirs), Children's Books, Poetry, and Middle-Grade/Young Adult Books. Judges reserve the right to re-categorize entries. Judges reserve the right to withhold prizes in any category. All winners will be notified by December 31. Entrants must enter online. Entrants may provide a file of the book or submit entry by the Amazon gifting process. Acceptable file types include: .epub, .mobi, .ipa. Word processing documents will not be accepted. Entries will be evaluated on content, writing quality, and overall quality of production and appearance. Books must have been published within the past 5 years from the competition deadline. Books which have previously won awards from *Writer's Digest* are not eligible. Early bird deadline: August 1; Deadline: September 4. Prizes: Grand Prize: $5,000, promotion in *Writer's Digest*, and more; 1st Place (9 winners): $1,000 and promotion in *Writer's Digest*; and more prizes. All entrants will receive a brief commentary from one of the judges.

WRITERS' GUILD OF ALBERTA AWARDS

Writers' Guild of Alberta, Percy Page Centre, 11759 Groat Rd., Edmonton AB T5M 3K6, Canada. (780)422-8174. **E-mail:** mail@writersguild.ca. **Website:** writersguild.ca. **Contact:** Executive Director. Offers the following awards: Wilfrid Eggleston Award for Nonfiction; Georges Bugnet Award for Fiction; Howard O'Hagan Award for Short Story; Stephan G. Stephansson Award for Poetry; R. Ross Annett Award for Children's Literature; Gwen Pharis Ringwood Award for Drama; Jon Whyte Memorial Essay Award; James H. Gray Award for Short Nonfiction. Eligible entries will have been published anywhere in the world between January 1 and December 31 of the current year. The authors must have been residents of Alberta for at least 12 of the 18 months prior to December 31. Unpublished mss, except in the drama and essay categories, are not eligible. Anthologies are not eligible. Works may be submitted by authors, publishers, or any interested parties. Deadline: December 31. Prize: Winning authors receive $1,500; short piece prize winners receive $700.

WRITERS' LEAGUE OF TEXAS BOOK AWARDS

Writers' League of Texas, 611 S. Congress Ave., Suite 200A-3, Austin TX 78704. (512)499-8914. **Fax:** (512)499-0441. **E-mail:** sara@writersleague.org. **Website:** www.writersleague.org. **Contact:** Sara Kocek. Open to Texas authors of books published the previous year. To enter this contest, you must be a Texas author. "Texas author" is defined as anyone who (whether currently a resident or not) has lived in Texas for a period of 3 or more years. This contest is open to indie or self-published authors as well as traditionally-published authors. Deadline: February 28. Open to submissions October 7. Prize: $1,000 and a commemorative award.

YEARBOOK EXCELLENCE CONTEST

100 Adler Journalism Building, Iowa City IA 52242-2004. (319)335-3457. **Fax:** (319)335-3989. **E-mail:** quill-scroll@uiowa.edu. **Website:** www.quilland-scroll.org. **Contact:** Jeff Browne, executive director. High school students who are contributors to or staff members of a student yearbook at any public or private high school are invited to enter the competition. Awards will be made in each of the 18 divisions. There are two enrollment categories: Class A: more than 750 students; Class B: 749 or less. Winners will receive Quill and Scroll's National Award Gold Key and, if seniors, are eligible to apply for one of the Edward J. Nell Memorial or George and Ophelia Gallup scholarships. Open to students whose schools have Quill and Scroll charters. Previously published submissions only. Submissions made by the author or school yearbook adviser. Must be published in the 12-month span prior to contest deadline. Visit website for list of current and previous winners. Purpose is to recognize and reward student journalists for their work in yearbooks and to provide student winners an opportunity to apply for a scholarship to be used freshman year in college for students planning to major in journalism. Deadline: October 10.

THE YOUNG ADULT FICTION PRIZE

Victorian Premier's Literary Awards, State Government of Victoria, The Wheeler Centre, 176 Little Lonsdale Street, Melbourne VIC 3000, Australia. (61) (3)90947800. **E-mail:** vpla@wheelercentre.com. **Website:** http://www.wheelercentre.com/projects/victorian-premier-s-literary-awards-2016/about-the-awards. **Contact:** Project Officer. Visit website for guidelines and nomination forms. Prize: $25,000.

CAROL LYNN GRELLAS YOUNG ADULT PROSE PRIZE CATEGORY

Soul-Making Keats Literary Competition, The Webhallow House, 1544 Sweetwood Dr., Broadmoor Vlg. CA 94015-2029. (650)756-5279. **Fax:** (650)756-5279. **E-mail:** soulkeats@mail.com. **Website:** www.soul-makingcontest.us. **Contact:** Eileen Malone. For writers in grades 9-12 or equivalent age. Up to 3,000 words in prose form of choice. Complete rules and guidelines available online. Deadline: November 30 (postmarked). Prize: $100 for first place; $50 for second place; $25 for third place. Judged (and sponsored) by Rita Wiliams, an Emmy-award winning investigative reporter with KTVU-TV in Oakland, California.

YOUNG READER'S CHOICE AWARD

E-mail: hbray@missoula.lib.mt.us. **Website:** www.pnla.org. **Contact:** Honore Bray, president. The Pacific Northwest Library Association's Young Reader's Choice Award is the oldest children's choice award in the U.S. and Canada. Nominations are taken only from children, teachers, parents and librarians in the Pacific Northwest: Alaska, Alberta, British Columbia, Idaho, Montana and Washington. Nominations will not be accepted from publishers. Nominations may include fiction, nonfiction, graphic novels, anime, and manga. Nominated titles are those published 3 years prior to the award year. Deadline: February 1. Books will be judged on popularity with readers. Age appropriateness will be considered when choosing which of the three divisions a book is placed. Other considerations may include reading enjoyment; reading level; interest level; genre representation; gender representation; racial diversity; diversity of social, political, economic, or religions viewpoints; regional consideration; effectiveness of expression; and imagination. The Pacific Northwest Library Association is committed to intellectual freedom and diversity of ideas. No title will be excluded because of race, nationality, religion, gender, sexual orientation, political or social view of either the author or the material.

THE YOUTH HONOR AWARDS

Skipping Stones Youth Honor Awards, Skipping Stones Magazine, Skipping Stones Magazine, P. O. Box 3939, Eugene OR 97403. (541)342-4956. **E-mail:** info@skippingstones.org. **E-mail:** editor@skippingstones.org. **Website:** www.skippingstones.org/wp.

Contact: Arun N. Toke, Editor and Publisher. *Skipping Stones* is an international, literary, and multicultural, children's magazine that encourages cooperation, creativity, and celebration of cultural and linguistic diversity. It explores stewardship of the ecological and social webs that nurture us. It offers a forum for communication among children from different lands and backgrounds. *Skipping Stones* expands horizons in a playful, creative way. This is a non-commercial, non-profit magazine with no advertisements. In its 33rd year, it is now publishing new content on its website. You can read the whole content for *free*. Original writing and art from youth, ages 7 to 17, should be typed or neatly handwritten. The entries should be appropriate for ages 7 to 17. Prose under 1,000 words; poems under 30 lines. Word limit: 1,000. Poetry: 30 lines. Non-English and bilingual writings are welcome. To promote multicultural, international and nature awareness. Deadline: June 25. Prize: An Honor Award Certificate, issues of Skipping Stones magazine and five nature and/or multicultural books. They are also invited to join the Student Review Board. Everyone who enters the contest receives the autumn issue featuring the ten winners and other noteworthy entries. Editors and interns at the *Skipping Stones* magazine

Youth awards are for children only; you must be under 18 years of age to qualify.

PUBLISHERS & THEIR IMPRINTS

The publishing world is in constant transition. With all the buying, selling, reorganizing, consolidating, and dissolving, it's hard to keep the major publishers and their imprints straight. To help, here's a breakdown of major publishers (and their divisions), though this information changes frequently.

Most of these publishers (and their imprints) will require an agented submission, but it never hurts to check their individual websites for open submission periods or calls for submissions.

Hachette Book Group USA

www.hachettebookgroup.com

- Grand Central Publishing
    - Forever
    - Twelve
- Hachette Audio
- Hachette Nashville
    - Center Street
    - Faith Words
    - Worthy Publishing
- Little, Brown and Company
    - Back Bay Books
    - Little, Brown Spark
- Mulholland Books
    - Jimmy Patterson
    - Voracious Books
- Little, Brown Books for Young Readers
    - LB Kids

- Little, Brown Books for Young Readers
- Poppy

Orbit

Perseus Books

- Avalon Travel
- Basic Books
- Black Dog & Leventhal
- Hachette Books
- Hachette Go!
- Public Affairs
- Running Press
- Seal Press

HarperCollins Publishers

www.harpercollins.com

General Books

- Amistad
- Anthony Bourdain Books
- Avon
- Broadside Books
- Caedmon
- Custom House
- Dey Street Books
- Ecco
- Harper Books
- Harper Business
- Harper Design
- Harper Luxe
- Harper Perennial
- Harper Voyager
- Harper Wave
- HarperAudio
- HarperCollins 360
- HarperCollins Espanol
- HarperOne
- HarperVia
- William Morrow

- Children's
  - Amistad
  - Balzer + Bray
  - Greenwillow Books
  - HarperAlley
  - HarperChildren's Audio
  - HarperCollins Children's Books
  - HarperFestival
  - HarperTeen
  - Heartdrum
  - Katherine Tegen Books
  - Quill Tree Books
  - Walden Pond Press
- Christian Publishing
  - Bible Gateway
  - Editorial Vida
  - FaithGateway
  - Grupo Nelson
  - Nelson Books
  - Olive Tree
  - Thomas Nelson
  - Tommy Nelson
  - W Publishing Group
  - WestBow Press
  - Zonderkidz
  - Zondervan
  - Zondervan Academic
- Harlequin
  - Carina Press
  - Graydon House Books
  - Hanover Square Press
  - Harlequin Books
  - HQN Books
  - Inkyard Press
  - Love Inspired
  - MIRA Books
  - Park Row Books

Macmillan Publishers

https://us.macmillan.com

Adult Trade

- Celadon Books
- Tom Doherty Associates
  - Forge Books
  - Nightfire
  - Starscape
  - Tor Books
  - Tor Teen
- Farrar, Straus & Giroux
  - FSG Originals
  - MCD
  - Picador
- Flatiron Books
- Henry Holt & Co.
  - Holt Paperbacks
  - Metropolitan Books
- Macmillan Audio
  - Macmillan Young Listeners
- St. Martin's Publishing Group
  - Castle Point Books
  - Minotaur Books
  - St. Martin's Essentials
  - St. Martin's Griffin
  - St. Martin's Press
  - Wednesday Books

Children's

- Farrar, Straus & Giroux for Young Readers
- Feiwel & Friends
- First Second
- Henry Holt for Young Readers
  - Gowdin Books
- Neon Squid
- Odd Dot
- Priddy Books
- Roaring Brook Press
- Square Fish

Macmillan Learning

- Bedford/St. Martin's
- W. H. Freeman
- Hayden-McNeil
- Worth Publishers

Penguin Random House

www.penguinrandomhouse.com

DK

Penguin Publishing Group

- Avery
- Berkley
- DAW
- Dutton
- Family Tree Books
- Putnam
- Impact
- Interweave
- KP
- North Light Books
- Penguin Books
- Penguin Classics
- Penguin Press
- Plume
- Popular Woodworking Books
- Portfolio
- Riverhead
- Sentinel
- Tarcher Perigee
- Viking
- Writer's Digest Books

Penguin Random House Audio Publishing Group

- Books on Tape
- Listening Library
- Living Language
- Penguin Random House Audio Publishing
- Random House Large Print
- Random House Puzzles and Games

Random House Reference

Penguin Young Readers Group

Dial Books for Young Readers

Dutton Children's Books

Firebird

F. Warne & Co.

G. P. Putnam's Sons Books for Young Readers

Kathy Dawson Books

Kokila

Nancy Paulsen Books

Penguin Workshop

Philomel

Puffin

Razorbill

Speak

Viking Children's Books

Random House

Ballantine Books

Bantam

B\D\W\Y

Clarkson Potter

Convergent Books

Crown Archetype

Crown Forum

Crown Trade

Currency

Del Rey

Delacorte Press

Dell

The Dial Press

The Duggan Books

Harmony Books

Hogarth

Image

Lorena Jones Books

Loveswept

Lucas Books

Modern Library

One World
Random House
Rodale
Spiegel & Grau
Ten Speed Press
Three Rivers Press
Waterbrook Multnomah
Watson Guptill

Random House Children's Books

Alfred A. Knopf Books for Young Readers
Anne Schwartz Books
Crown Books for Young Readers
Delacorte Press
Doubleday
Dragonfly Books
Ember
Golden Books
Now I'm Reading!
Random House Books for Young Readers
Sylvan Learning
The Princeton Review
Wendy Lamb Books
Yearling Books

The Knopf Doubleday Publishing Group

Alfred A. Knopf
Anchor Books
Doubleday
Everyman's Library
Nan A. Talese
Pantheon Books
Schocken Books
Vintage Books
Vintage Espanol

Simon & Schuster

www.simonandschuster.com

Simon & Schuster Adult Publishing

Adams Media

- Atria
- Avid Reader Press
- Emily Bestler Books
- Enliven
- Folger Shakespeare Library
- Free Press
- Gallery
- Howard
- Jeter Publishing
- One Signal
- Scout Press
- Scribner
- Simon & Schuster
- Threshold
- Tiller Press
- Touchstone

Simon & Schuster Children's Publishing

- Aladdin
- Atheneum
- Beach Lane Books
- Little Simon
- Margaret K. McElderry
- Denene Millner Books
- Saga Press
- Salaam Reads
- Simon & Schuster Books for Young Readers
- Simon Spotlight
- Paula Wiseman Books

Simon & Schuster Audio Publishing

- Pimsleur
- Simon & Schuster Audio

Simon & Schuster International

- Simon & Schuster Australia
- Simon & Schuster Canada
- Simon & Schuster India
- Simon & Schuster UK

GLOSSARY OF INDUSTRY TERMS

Common terminology and lingo.

AAR. Association of Authors' Representatives.

ABA. American Booksellers Association.

ABC. Association of Booksellers for Children.

ADVANCE. A sum of money a publisher pays a writer or illustrator prior to the publication of a book. It is usually paid in installments, such as one half on signing the contract, one half on delivery of a complete and satisfactory manuscript. The advance is paid against the royalty money that will be earned by the book.

ALA. American Library Association.

ALL RIGHTS. The rights contracted to a publisher permitting the use of material anywhere and in any form, including movie and book club sales, without additional payment to the creator.

ANTHOLOGY. A collection of selected writings by various authors or gatherings of works by one author.

ANTHROPOMORPHIZATION. The act of attributing human form and personality to things not human (such as animals).

ASAP. As soon as possible.

ASSIGNMENT. An editor or art director asks a writer, illustrator, or photographer to produce a specific piece for an agreed-upon fee.

B&W. Black and white.

BACKLIST. A publisher's list of books not published during the current season but still in print.

BEA. BookExpo America.

BIENNIALLY. Occurring once every two years.

BIMONTHLY. Occurring once every two months.

BIWEEKLY. Occurring once every two weeks.

BOOK PACKAGER. A company that draws all elements of a book together, from the initial concept to writing and marketing strategies, then sells the book package to a book publisher and/or movie producer. Also known as book producer or book developer.

BOOK PROPOSAL. Package submitted to a publisher for consideration, usually consisting of a synopsis and outline as well as sample chapters.

BUSINESS-SIZE ENVELOPE. Also known as a #10 envelope. The standard size used in sending business correspondence.

CAMERA-READY. Refers to art that is completely prepared for copy camera platemaking.

CAPTION. A description of the subject matter of an illustration or photograph; photo captions include persons' names where appropriate. Also called cutline.

CBC. Children's Book Council.

CLEAN-COPY. A manuscript free of errors that needs no editing; it is ready for typesetting.

CLIPS. Samples, usually from newspapers or magazines, of a writer's published work.

CONCEPT BOOKS. Books that deal with ideas, concepts and large-scale problems, promoting an understanding of what's happening in a child's world. Most prevalent are alphabet and counting books, but also includes books dealing with specific concerns facing young people (such as divorce, birth of a sibling, friendship, or moving).

CONTRACT. A written agreement stating the rights to be purchased by an editor, art director, or producer and the amount of payment the writer, illustrator, or photographer will receive for that sale.

CONTRIBUTOR'S COPIES. The magazine issues sent to an author, illustrator, or photographer in which her work appears.

CO-OP PUBLISHER. A publisher that shares production costs with an author but, unlike subsidy publishers, handles all marketing and distribution. An author receives a high percentage of royalties until her initial investment is recouped, then standard royalties. (Children's Writer's & Illustrator's Market does not include co-op publishers.)

COPY. The actual written material of a manuscript.

COPYEDITING. Editing a manuscript for grammar usage, spelling, punctuation, and other general style.

COPYRIGHT. A means to legally protect an author's/illustrator's/photographer's work. This can be shown by writing the creator's name and the year of the work's creation.

COVER LETTER. A brief letter, accompanying a complete manuscript, especially useful if responding to an editor's request for a manuscript. May also accompany a book proposal.

CUTLINE. See caption.

DIVISION. An unincorporated branch of a company.

DUMMY. A loose mock-up of a book showing placement of text and artwork.

ELECTRONIC SUBMISSION. A submission of material by email or Web form.

FINAL DRAFT. The last version of a polished manuscript ready for submission to an editor.

FIRST NORTH AMERICAN SERIAL RIGHTS. The right to publish material in a periodical for the first time, in the U.S. or Canada.

F&GS. Folded and gathered sheets. An early, not-yet-bound copy of a picture book.

FLAT FEE. A one-time payment.

GALLEYS. The first typeset version of a manuscript that has not yet been divided into pages.

GENRE. A formulaic type of fiction, such as horror, mystery, romance, fantasy, suspense, thriller, science fiction, or western.

GLOSSY. A photograph with a shiny surface, as opposed to one with a matte finish.

GOUACHE. Opaque watercolor with an appreciable film thickness and an actual paint layer.

HALFTONE. Reproduction of a continuous tone illustration with the image formed by dots produced by a camera lens screen.

HARD COPY. The printed copy of a computer's output.

HARDWARE. Refers to all the mechanically integrated components of a computer that are not software—circuit boards, transistors, and the machines that are the actual computer.

HI-LO. High interest, low reading level.

HOME PAGE. The first page of a website.

IBBY. International Board on Books for Young People.

IMPRINT. Name applied to a publisher's specific line of books.

IRA. International Reading Association.

IRC. International Reply Coupon. Sold at the post office to enclose with text or artwork sent to a recipient outside your own country to cover postage costs when replying or returning work.

KEYLINE. Identification of the positions of illustrations and copy for the printer.

LAYOUT. Arrangement of illustrations, photographs, text and headlines for printed material.

LGBTQ. Lesbian/gay/bisexual/trans/queer.

LINE DRAWING. Illustration done with pencil or ink using no wash or other shading.

MASS MARKET BOOKS. Paperback books directed toward an extremely large audience sold in supermarkets, drugstores, airports, newsstands, online retailers, and bookstores.

MECHANICALS. Paste-up or preparation of work for printing.

MIDDLE-GRADE OR MID-GRADE. See middle reader.

MIDDLE READER. The general classification of books written for readers approximately ages nine to twelve. Often called middle-grade or mid-grade.

MS (MSS). Manuscript(s).

MULTIPLE SUBMISSIONS. See simultaneous submissions.

NCTE. National Council of Teachers of English.

NEW ADULT (NA). Novels with characters in their late teens or early twenties who are exploring what it means to be an adult.

ONE-TIME RIGHTS. Permission to publish a story in periodical or book form one time only.

PACKAGE SALE. The sale of a manuscript and illustrations/photos as a "package" paid for with one check.

PAYMENT ON ACCEPTANCE. The writer, artist, or photographer is paid for her work at the time the editor or art director decides to buy it.

PAYMENT ON PUBLICATION. The writer, artist, or photographer is paid for her work when it is published.

PICTURE BOOK. A type of book aimed at preschoolers to eight-year-olds that tells a story using a combination of text and artwork, or artwork only.

PRINT. An impression pulled from an original plate, stone, block, screen, or negative; also a positive made from a photographic negative.

PROOFREADING. Reading text to correct typographical errors.

QUERY. A letter to an editor or agent designed to capture interest in an article or book you have written or propose to write. (See the article "Before Your First Sale.")

READING FEE. Money charged by some agents and publishers to read a submitted manuscript. (Children's Writer's & Illustrator's Market does not include agencies that charge reading fees.)

REPRINT RIGHTS. Permission to print an already published work whose first rights have been sold to another magazine or book publisher.

RESPONSE TIME. The average length of time it takes an editor or art director to accept or reject a query or submission, and inform the creator of the decision.

RIGHTS. The bundle of permissions offered to an editor or art director in exchange for printing a manuscript, artwork, or photographs.

ROUGH DRAFT. A manuscript that has not been checked for errors in grammar, punctuation, spelling, or content.

ROUGHS. Preliminary sketches or drawings.

ROYALTY. An agreed percentage paid by a publisher to a writer, illustrator, or photographer for each copy of her work sold.

SAE. Self-addressed envelope.

SASE. Self-addressed, stamped envelope.

SCBWI. The Society of Children's Book Writers and Illustrators.

SECOND SERIAL RIGHTS. Permission for the reprinting of a work in another periodical after its first publication in book or magazine form.

SEMIANNUAL. Occurring every six months or twice a year.

SEMIMONTHLY. Occurring twice a month.

SEMIWEEKLY. Occurring twice a week.

SERIAL RIGHTS. The rights given by an author to a publisher to print a piece in one or more periodicals.

SIMULTANEOUS SUBMISSIONS. Queries or proposals sent to several publishers at the same time. Also called multiple submissions. (See the article "Before Your First Sale.")

SLANT. The approach to a story or piece of artwork that will appeal to readers of a particular publication.

SLUSH PILE. Editors' term for their collections of unsolicited manuscripts.

SOFTWARE. Programs and related documentation for use with a computer.

SOLICITED MANUSCRIPT. Material that an editor has asked for or agreed to consider before being sent by a writer.

SPAR. Society of Photographers and Artists Representatives.

SPECULATION (SPEC). Creating a piece with no assurance from an editor or art director that it will be purchased or any reimbursements for material or labor paid.

SUBSIDIARY RIGHTS. All rights other than book publishing rights included in a book contract, such as paperback, book club, and movie rights.

SUBSIDY PUBLISHER. A book publisher that charges the author for the cost of typesetting, printing and promoting a book. Also called a vanity publisher. (Note: Children's Writer's & Illustrator's Market does not include subsidy publishers.)

SYNOPSIS. A summary of a story or novel. Usually a page to a page and a half, single-spaced, if part of a book submission.

TABLOID. Publication printed on an ordinary newspaper page turned sideways and folded in half.

TEARSHEET. Page from a magazine or newspaper containing your printed art, story, article, poem, or photo.

THUMBNAIL. A rough layout in miniature.

TRADE BOOKS. Books sold in bookstores and through online retailers, aimed at a smaller audience than mass market books, and printed in smaller quantities by publishers.

TRANSPARENCIES. Positive color slides; not color prints.

UNSOLICITED MANUSCRIPT. Material sent without an editor's, art director's, or agent's request.

VANITY PUBLISHER. See subsidy publisher.

WORK-FOR-HIRE. An arrangement between a writer, illustrator, or photographer and a company under which the company retains complete control of the work's copyright.

YA. See young adult.

YOUNG ADULT. The general classification of books written for readers approximately ages twelve to sixteen. Often referred to as YA.

YOUNG READER. The general classification of books written for readers approximately ages five to eight.

GENERAL INDEX

SUBJECT INDEX

Animal

Animal NF

Anthology

Arts/Crafts

Biography

Careers

Cooking

Fantasy

Hobbies

How-to

Humor

Multicultural

Multicultural NF

Nature/Environment NF

Poetry

Sports NF

Suspense/Mystery

Textbooks

Travel

AGE-LEVEL INDEX

Middle Readers

Young Adult

Young Readers